⁓ BUDDHISM IN CHINESE SOCIETY ⁓

STUDIES IN ASIAN CULTURE

BUDDHISM IN CHINESE SOCIETY

AN ECONOMIC HISTORY
FROM THE FIFTH
TO THE TENTH CENTURIES

JACQUES GERNET

TRANSLATED BY FRANCISCUS VERELLEN

COLUMBIA UNIVERSITY PRESS   NEW YORK

The publisher gratefully acknowledges support toward publication given
by the Committee on Oriental Studies and the Institute for Advanced
Studies of World Religion at Columbia University.
*Les aspects économiques du bouddhisme dans la société chinoise du
V^e au Xe siècle.* Saigon: École Française d'Extrême-Orient, 1956

Columbia University Press
New York   Chichester, West Sussex
Copyright © 1995 Columbia University Press

Library of Congress Cataloging-in-Publication Data

Gernet, Jacques.
   [Aspects économiques du bouddhisme dans la société chinoise du Ve
au Xe siécle. English]
   Buddhism in Chinese society : an economic history from the fifth
to the tenth centuries / Jacques Gernet; translated by Franciscus
Verellen.
      p.   cm.
   Includes bibliographical references and index.
   ISBN 0–231–07380–1 — ISBN 0–231–11411–7 (pbk.)
   1. Buddhism—China—History—581–960. 2. Buddhism—Economic
aspects—China. I. Title.
BO638.G4713   1995
294.3'0951'09021—dc20   94–42484
                                                                  CIP

∞

Casebound editions of Columbia University Press books are printed on permanent
and durable acid-free paper.

Printed in the United States of America
c 10 9 8 7 6 5 4 3 2
p 10 9 8 7 6 5 4

CONTENTS

TRANSLATOR'S NOTE

The following translation is offered as a contribution to the Franco-American exchanges initiated by Wm. Theodore de Bary and Léon Vandermeersch and administered under the auspices of the Joint Committee for European-American Cooperation in East Asian Studies.

The translator is indebted to the Columbia Committee on Oriental Studies for enabling him, with the generous financial support of the French Foreign Ministry, to travel between Columbia University and the Collège de France for consultations with the author during the academic year 1989–1990.

Special thanks are due to Jacques Gernet for his patient review of numerous points of detail, to Denis Twitchett for his encouragement and expert advice, to Stephen Teiser for helpful comments on the draft, and to Jennifer Crewe, publisher for the humanities, Columbia University Press, for her unflagging support of this project.

PREFACE

This book, in its first form, was written between 1951 and 1955. Since then many works in Chinese, Japanese, and Western languages have appeared on the subject I treat here as well as on other topics bearing on the complicated history of Buddhism in China. The contributions made by these writers would have greatly enriched the present work and doubtless caused me to modify certain of my positions. If more time had been spent on this work, a richer crop of relevant Chinese sources could have been gathered: there are assuredly more such texts that remain to be discovered and exploited.

But in the admirable translation by Franciscus Verellen, this is no longer the same book that was published in Saigon in 1956. He has added to it new and valuable references, some useful additional data, a much richer, up-to-date bibliography, and an exhaustive index. Furthermore, and most important, he has worked with such care that he was able to clear up many inaccuracies and doubtful points that marred the original.

The translation of this book was planned following a symposium held at Columbia University on exchanges between Europe and the United States in the field of East Asian studies, an initiative launched by Wm. Theodore de Bary. The aim was to make selected works of European sinology more accessible to English-speaking researchers. *Les aspects économiques du bouddhisme dans la société chinoise du*

V^e au Xe siècle was deemed worthy of inclusion in the projected series.

Although the book does take up the technical question of the economic aspects of Buddhism in China—the subject of many significant publications in Japanese since as early as the 1930s—I thought it even more important to set these questions into the general framework of the vast phenomenon constituted by the Buddhist faith at the time of its highest development in China. This phenomenon, in all its diversity, seemed to me the real issue: economics are only one aspect of the whole social system. Account had to be taken of social and political organization, the types of cult associations inherited from the distant past, Chinese concepts of saintliness, aesthetic criteria, private and imperial cults, and even the legal system. The subject of this book, then, reaching beyond matters touching strictly on the economy, comprises the particular characteristics of Chinese society that emerged from an indigenous substratum and evolved under the influence of the spread of Buddhism. The project was clearly too ambitious to be realized in all its ramifications, but its primary aim was to open new perspectives rather than contribute to the always inexhaustible domain of pure scholarship.

My thanks go, once again, to Franciscus Verellen, along with my admiration for the precision and the excellence of his work, which has enriched and improved my own. I also thank Zhang Guangda, who provided various references, as well as Kuo Li-ying, who kindly revised the bibliography.

INTRODUCTION

At the beginning of the sixth century, a Parthian merchant was ply-
ing his trade along the Yangtze, between Szechwan and the East
China Sea. He had accumulated pearls and jewels, and the goods he
had acquired through commerce filled two junks. According to some,
the total value amounted to several thousand strings of cash. However, the more treasure he amassed, the greedier he became for riches,
and distressed not to possess more. In the course of his travels he
came to Mount Niu-t'ou in Hsin-ch'eng commandery where he
encountered the Dhyāna monk Ta, who preached Buddhism to him.
"The best thing to do," said the merchant to himself, "would be to
throw my treasures into the river and to enter into religion in order to
deliver myself from my attachments. To live simply and without a
care, is that not happiness?" And forthwith he sank one of his junks
into the river, where it was deepest. He was about to sink the other
when a troop of monks arrived on the scene and implored him to use
the remainder of his possessions for pious works.[1]

An authentic scene—and many like it can be found—which at the
outset will illustrate the concrete nature of this study, its particular
object and orientation. In truth, the incident is scandalous: it can be
explained neither by the pursuit of profit nor by material needs, the
motivations expected to drive every economy. Yet our Parthian
knows what he is doing, and the idea of spoiling a fortune accumu-

lated at great pains is not mere personal fantasy. Examples of analogous conduct can be found all around him. On the whole, the elements considered here are related to phenomena of collective psychology that can be historically situated. It is this relationship and the often intimate connections between economy, law, social structures, and customary practices and behavior that I have set out to analyze; and, finally, I have attempted to suggest the systematic nature of this complex.

The available evidence leaves no doubt as to the broad scope of the phenomenon. Nevertheless, its importance has not always been fully recognized. This is due to the usual choice of sources and, to an even greater extent, to the dispersal of the evidence. The official historians remained faithful to a narrow conception of their role, which consisted in noting events and deeds pertaining to the emperor and in tracing the careers of great courtiers. Religious movements were of no concern to them as such, nor were the details of daily life or technical matters. Moreover, their business was not so much to write as to orient history, to bring the authority of precedents to bear upon imperial decision making. Ill-disposed to Buddhism by education, they had no desire to concede it its rightful place, for that would have meant approving its future importance. And yet the silence is not as complete as these masters of China's history may have wished. The religious movement had such serious consequences for the finances of the empire that historians were compelled to give an account of the numerous criticisms and the various measures of control and rehabilitation and to provide, despite themselves, a certain amount of general information.

Invaluable details that are generally absent from the official record, information about the sanctuaries' wealth, the clergy's activities, and lay practices, are found, furthermore, in sources of Buddhist origin— histories of Buddhism in China and biographies of monks. I have given priority, however, to firsthand sources: stele inscriptions and manuscripts. The documents on paper recovered in Chinese Turkestan and, principally, in Tun-huang[2] constitute, by virtue of their precision and authenticity, a source of exceptional value that has hardly begun to be exploited as a whole. They comprise accountancy records, management reports, lists of offerings, loan and rental contracts, as well as various official documents: passports for monks, certificates, census fragments. Some of these texts have been studied by Japanese scholars, others have remained unpublished: they form an integral part of the present study.

Comparing the diverse sources with one another already brings a heterogeneous set of facts to light. From an early date, the movement was remarkable for the enormous material and human expenditures to which it gave rise over a period of three centuries. There was an overabundant monastic community, incessant construction work, a prodigious consumption of metals, wood, and cloth. This passion for spending manifested itself in the early fifth century, and reached its apogee during the sixth and seventh; it gave a new and lasting impulse to artistic activities, to the development of crafts and commerce. At the same time, phenomena of another order also made their appearance: the enrichment of the sanctuaries, the appropriation of lands, the formation of a class of monastic dependents, the engagement of Buddhist monks in commercial practices. Legal and technical notions entered into each of these developments. Some of the notions and techniques were of Indian provenance; their adaptation to the Chinese world calls for examination. Hence the need to employ another type of source material: the treatises on monastic discipline.

While all of the elements considered here are of an economic nature, it is understood that economic activity is manifold: gifts and offerings are not in the same category as usurious practices. In Buddhism, a religion that emphasizes the importance of giving, mercantile thinking paradoxically occupies a prominent place. This contradiction needs to be resolved, acknowledging the unity of the system as a whole.

I have deliberately adopted a particular point of view here by determining to consider the subject from an economic angle. In so doing, however, I recognize that the implications are multifarious.

Buddhism in medieval China was a religious movement. That was its essential characteristic. I allow that the better educated milieus attached some importance to Buddhist doctrine and cultivated doctrine for its own sake. At the same time, I reject the approach that virtually restricts its terms of reference to doctrinal aspects. The classic thesis runs like this: there were three great religions in China—Confucianism, Taoism, and Buddhism; the latter two are said to have confronted each other in a struggle that exhausted both.[3] What we mean by Confucianism is clear enough: the tradition of the literati and the ceremonies of an official cult of Chinese origin. Confucianism is to a much greater extent an attachment to a mode of thinking and traditional rites than a religion. As for the terrible conflicts in which Buddhism and Taoism allegedly engaged, I find no trace of them:[4] they were no more than squabbles between monks—spiteful, no doubt, but of little consequence. One finds as much within Buddhism itself between rival schools. At the end of the day, such disputes profit more than harm the vitality of doctrines and the health of religions. There were also quarrels over precedence, but that precedence pertained only to court ceremonies. How then did such conceptions about the relationship between Buddhism and Taoism, and that between Buddhism and Confucianism,[5] impose themselves on Western historians? If they are not founded on the Chinese evidence, then the memory of the religious struggles in the West, and the need to feel as if one stands on familiar ground, must have prevailed over the evidence. I can only suppose that that exclusive passion—the absolute belief in dogmatic truths peculiar to Western religion—was also ascribed to the Chinese, and that the attribution of such a disposition to them sprang from a desire to consider as "religious" only those narrowly defined, interior aspects that are not open to analysis.

In broad terms, it might be said that the religion found expression in a reorganization of the social sphere. Buddhism in China had its faithful, its debtors and its dependents; for the laity, the monasteries were at once granaries, treasuries, sanctuaries, and places from which religious power emanated. This linkage between the most heterogeneous aspects of Buddhism in China, between the religious and the commercial, was concretely realized within those urban and village communities that were the parishes of Buddhism.

Particular conditions for the formation of these groups of faithful and clients were rooted in indigenous tradition. The Buddhist monks maintained relations with various milieus of Chinese society, and each of these was characterized by its own needs, economic levels, and traditions. The movement was universal, but each social class was affected differently.

In the outskirts of towns, in the thriving commercial districts, in the villages, and in the mountains rose a multitude of small sanctuaries where ordinary people gathered on festival days. Primary sources permit us to form a fairly precise image of this local religious life. Communal meals and contributions constituted the fundamental practices of such groups: they readily evoke ancient peasant realities.

In a very different milieu, that of the upper-class laity, it seems that the passion for Buddhism was assimilated to a tradition of splendor and an inclination to extravagant spending, especially on behalf of ancestors. Political and economic interests, religious customs, and aesthetic tastes all converged in these prodigal displays. In the complex interplay of such dispositions we can glimpse the reasons for the laity's passionate adherence to Buddhism.

What emerges from the analysis is the essentially malleable nature of these customary modes of behavior and traditional relationships. On the level of offerings and peasant contributions to banquets as well as other types of expenditure—all of which defy the laws of a rational economy—the economic is inseparable from the religious.

In the end, we find a general disposition to spend and to hoard, and the appearance of new needs—aesthetic, social, economic—with implications beyond the religious domain. The ruling class, preoccupied by the ever precarious equilibrium between the production of primary goods and their consumption, had ulterior motives for lending their support to Buddhism, which were quite foreign to their true inclinations. Their efforts were consequently aimed at directing the movement toward their own ends. The ad hoc nature of their response is evident in the alternation of political favors granted Buddhism on the one hand with repressions designed to weaken it on the other.

The question of decadence must be addressed. During the centuries when religious fervor was most intense, the great festivals united disparate social classes. Great families and commoners alike joined in the lay associations. Undoubtedly it was this network of personal relationships that accounted for the universality of the Buddhist movement. Under the T'ang, however, a new mentality, which can be qualified as commercial, began to gain ground. It made its appearance precisely in those milieus that had shown greatest fervor: among monks and the families of wealthy lay followers. Avarice broke down the old systems of relationships, led to the isolation of the social classes, and hence undermined the very foundations of the religious movement.

For the realization of this study I am indebted to the teaching and advice of Paul Demiéville (1894–1979), one of the great masters of the history of Buddhism in China, who moreover generously gave me access to his rich library and had the excellent idea of engaging me for the compilation of the first volume of the *Catalogue* of Chinese manuscripts from Tun-huang held in the Bibliothèque Nationale.

BUDDHISM IN CHINESE SOCIETY

·⌣ PART ONE ⌣·

CHAPTER ONE

IMMEDIATE FACTS

Numbers of Sanctuaries and Monks

It is useful to visualize the imprint of Buddhism on Chinese soil in concrete terms. According to the texts, the skylines of certain great cities and rural landscapes start to crowd at an early stage—but especially from the end of the fifth century onward—with large and small monasteries, rising towers, sanctuaries, chapels, and hermitages. Buddhist constructions and monastic populations are denser in some places than in others. The capitals of the northern and southern dynasties, Lo-yang, Yeh,[1] Ch'ang-an, Chien-k'ang (modern Nanking), and their environs are completely invaded. Then there are the pilgrimage centers—sacred mountains of Buddhism in China—where temple constructions mushroom and throngs of monks and nuns reside. But places of worship are encountered everywhere, and some villages have their own chapels (fo-t'ang) or hermitages (lan-jo). One of the most obvious features of the imprint of religion on Chinese soil is the diversity: a salutary caution against the uniform and schematic view suggested by the official statistics concerning the numbers of monasteries and monks. The great monastery that permanently houses dozens of monks and the little village chapel or mountain hermitage inhabited by one or two have little in common. This sense of diversity only increases with any attempt to specify it. The monasticism of the great Buddhist centers differs in its way of life from that of the small sanctuaries: One would think that the former was more stable, more disciplined, and more orthodox than the latter, and the texts confirm this supposition. A further feature distinguishing different kinds of Buddhist establishments relates not to size but to status. Some monasteries are official places of worship and are recognized as such. They have received their name (0) by imperial bestowal as well as gifts of land, funds, servants, allotments of local families, and certain privileges. They are entitled to annual subventions from the court. Their monks have been selected and ordained by the emperor and are supervised by officially appointed clergy who are held accountable for their conduct. The other kind of establishments are merely tolerated and are always the first to fall victim to repressions. These are private places of worship, serving the great families as well as the people. Even if the term *private* does not appear in the texts, such was in fact their status.

Viewed from above, the situation seems clear enough. One could say, subject to qualifications, that there were three kinds of Chinese monks: the official monk, maintained at state expense and responsible for the performance of the ceremonies of the imperial cult, the private monk, fed and clothed by the great families, and, finally, the common monk who lived in the country side, either in isolation or as a member of a small group. It is evident that the influence of Buddhism extended not only across the empire but was also felt throughout society and at all levels of society. There were monks in the imperial palace, as there were monks in the forests and hamlets. Hence the profoundly distinct directions, tendencies, and characteristics exhibited by the religious phenomenon, depending on place and social group.

Fa-lin (572–640), whose *Pien-cheng lun* documents with figures the development of Buddhism under each dynasty, in two instances carefully distinguishes between three types of religious houses along the lines suggested above. This confirms the validity of the distinction and also gives an indication of the relative size of each category.

At the time of the Northern Wei (386–534) there were, according to Fa-lin,[2]
- 47 great state monasteries;
- 839 monasteries of princes, dukes, eminent families, nobles of the Five Degrees, and marquises;
- 30,000 or more monasteries built by commoners.

Under the Ch'en (557–589), there were
- 17 new state monasteries and

• 68 monasteries constructed by officials, out of a total of 1,232 monasteries.

[The remaining] 1,147 religious houses had been built by private individuals.[3]

The distinction between the two forms of Buddhism that could with some justification, if elliptically, be termed private and official, is significant, rich in implications, and very useful when it comes to disentangling the complex history of the relations between the imperial state and religion, a history that this distinction allows to appear in its true light.[4] The court, which was not hostile to Buddhism but was itself Buddhist after a fashion, with its own monks and sanctuaries, was obliged to resist two kinds of uncontrolled expansion of monasticism and religious constructions: the first, perpetrated by imperial relatives and high officials, was near at hand, highly visible, and thus would appear to have been liable to restraint, yet its patrons were often too influential to be effectively controlled. The second form of expansion was more diffuse and intangible. It operated through an anonymous and less known variety of Buddhism that developed at the popular level, though at times undoubtedly with the connivance of the upper classes and local administrations.

It had always been the ambition of great families favorably disposed toward Buddhism, and of eminent monks connected to the court, to secure the conversion of monasteries founded on their own initiative into official establishments. To this end they exercised all their influence. Thus a great number of Buddhist constructions that had not been undertaken at imperial behest came to enjoy the title and privileges of official monasteries.[5] Similarly, monks and nuns who had not been regularly ordained could from time to time benefit from a decree promulgating imperial ordinations.[6] This amounted to a steady and highly effective pressure exerted upon the religious policy of the court, tending to favor a development of Buddhism in China well beyond the bounds that governments might have reasonably wished to impose on it.

Here, then, are two important facts that may be helpful for the interpretation of the recorded and estimated numbers of religious and monasteries: large and medium-sized establishments were much less numerous than the small sanctuaries in the villages and towns and the total number of religious exceeded the regular census figures.

The following figures emerge from various sources:

Chin

Years	Clergy	Monasteries
307–312		42 in Lo-yang;[7]
316	3,700	182 [20][8]
		in the two capitals
317–320	24,000	1,768 [14]

Nan-pei Ch'ao: South

Years	Clergy	Monasteries
420–479	36,000	1,913 [19][10]
479–502	31,500	2,015 [16]
502–557	82,700	2,846 [29]
	*100,000[9]	
557–587	32,000	1,232 [26][11]

Nan-pei Ch'ao: North

Years	Clergy	Monasteries
476	2,000	100 [20][12] (Loyang)
512–515	77,258	6,478 [11.3][13]
534		13,727[14]
550–574	*2,000,000	30,886 [66][15]
	*3,000,000	40,000 [75][16]

Sui

Years	Clergy	Monasteries
590–604	230,000	3,792 [60.5][17]
590	*500,000	
590–617	236,000[19]	3,985 [59][20]

T'ang

Years	Clergy	Monasteries
624	50,000 (?)[21]	
	*200,000[22]	
648		3,716[23]
650–683	60,000	4,000 [15][24]
713–755	126,100	5,358 [23.5][25]
830	*700,000[26]	
842–845	360,000:	
	100,000	in 40,000
		small establishments and
	260,000	4,600 monasteries [56][27]

Wu-tai

Years	Clergy	Monasteries
955	61,000	6,030[28]

Sung

Years	Clergy	Monasteries
998–1022	458,855[29]	

Yüan

Years	Clergy	Monasteries
1291	213,148	42,318 [5][30]

Note: Average numbers of religious per establishment are indicated in brackets. Figures preceded by an asterisk are estimates.

This table would be of little use without an attempt at interpretation. Assuming that the figures in fact correspond to the numbers of religious and of monasteries under each period, the explanation for the considerable fluctuation in the size of the monastic community and the construction of religious houses must be political: the favors granted Buddhism by certain emperors are the only cause for the increase in monasteries and monks and persecutions the one and only reason for their decrease. Indeed, the general remarks made above concerning the density of the monastic community, and of religious buildings and the nature of Buddhist constructions, may be useful to explain the apparent variations and to suggest certain constants.

It is evident that up to the Sui dynasty all Buddhist establishments, regardless of their size and number of resident clergy, were designated as monasteries (ssu). This was a generic term applied, by long-standing convention, to any building inhabited by monks. "Today," reads an official text of the year 509,[31] "there is no place without a monastery .... Three to five shavelings constitute at times [the entire population of] a monastery (ssu)." The 30,000 to 40,000 monasteries mentioned for the middle of the sixth century, therefore, must have been for the most part small sanctuaries in which only a few religious resided. The censuses carried out during the years 842–845 yielded the figure of one hundred thousand religious in 40,000 hermitages (lan-jo). Thus there were two or three monks in each of these small places of worship, a number that approximately corresponds to the average indicated by the text of 509 for small Buddhist establishments in Lo-yang. This, then, yields two consistent indications, spanning a period of more than three centuries. Furthermore, the total number of great and minor Buddhist establishments remained almost constant across widely separated periods: between 30,000 and 40,000 in the middle of the sixth century, 44,600 in 845, and much later, in 1291, 42,318.[32]

From the Sui onward, however, censuses are representative of the great monasteries only. Their number remained roughly constant— around 4,000—for more than three centuries: 3,792 or 3,985 under the Sui, 3,716 in 648, 4,000 at the time of a census covering the years 650–683, 5,358 during 713–755,[33] and 4,600 in 845.[34] It is therefore impossible to draw any conclusions regarding the growth of the number of religious houses from the Chin to the end of the T'ang, unless the figures for the period before the Sui are considered separately from those available for the Sui and the T'ang. The total number of buildings, which stood at 1,768 at the beginning of the fifth century, increased to 8,391 (1,913 in the South and 6,478 in the North) around 476, to 15,000 or 16,000 at the beginning of the sixth century, and finally to close to 40,000 in the second half of that century. Thus, after a period of steady growth during the first three quarters of the fifth century, the number of Buddhist establishments rose suddenly at the end of that century. The greatest expansion of construction in North China fell under the first thirty years of the sixth century. In the South, too, the reign of Emperor Wu (502–549) was a period in which religious houses multiplied; the figures for the Sung, Ch'i, and Liang indicate a development that was analogous to that in the North, if on a lesser scale.[35]

The T'ang, it may be surmised, was another period of increased construction: there had been 3,716 official monasteries in 648, 4,000 in the second half of the seventh century, and 5,358 at the beginning of the reign of Hsüan-tsung.[36]

It should be remembered, however, that the number of official monasteries for which the historians provide figures corresponds to a contingent determined by the emperor, a situation that undoubtedly already obtained in Sui times. Thus it has to be recognized that the proportion of these establishments is to a certain extent independent of the total number of religious buildings.

"The number of monasteries was fixed," says the "Monograph on Officials" in the Chiu T'ang shu. "For each of the religious houses three supervisory members (san-kang)[37] were appointed [by the emperor]; monks of high moral standing were selected for these offices."

The full extent of religious construction and the ratio of small sanctuaries to large establishments appear to have remained approximately constant throughout history: it seems that a state of equilibrium or saturation had been attained when the number of great monasteries reached four to five thousand and that of the small, inhabited sanctuaries thirty to forty thousand. The extent of the destruction carried out by Emperor Wu of the Chou between 574 and 577 is unknown.[38] But however serious the effects of the repression may have been, the Buddhist patrimony in buildings had already been reconstituted by the beginning of the T'ang.[39]

The size of the clergy housed by chapels, sanctuaries, and hermitages is known. The censuses carried out in the middle of the ninth century assigned to these a population of 100,000. But what was the proportion of monks and nuns living in actual monasteries?

Some monasteries were well-populated. In the year 434, under the Liu Sung dynasty, 323 nuns lived at the Ying-fu ssu in Yang-tu.[40] Under the Sui, another monastery housed, more or less constantly, 300 monks.[41] In the second quarter of the ninth century, the Japanese pilgrim Ennin also reported communities numbering more than 300 religious, beside virtually uninhabited establishments. At the Kuo-ch'ing monastery of Mount T'ien-t'ai there were 150 monks permanently in residence, and during the summer retreat more than 300 came to stay there.[42]

These, however, were exceptions. The ordinary monastery had no more than twenty to fifty religious at most. Precise information concerning the numbers of monks, nuns, and novices in the monasteries of Tun-huang during the ninth and tenth centuries is available. The town had seventeen large Buddhist establishments in all. A Paris manuscript gives the following figures for five of them:[43]

Lung-hsing	40 monks[44]	20 novices	Total: 60
K'ai-yüan	24 "	14 "	" 38
Ch'ien-yüan	26 "	16 "	" 42
Yang-an	24 "	14 "	" 38
Chin-kuang	39 "	23 "	" 62[45]

Convents, on the other hand, housed larger communities—a fact that may be peculiar to Tun-huang:

Ta-ch'eng	60 nuns[46]
An-kuo	42 " [47]
P'u-kuang	127 " [48]
Other ssu	49 " [49]

The average ratio of clergy per establishment for the sample of monasteries mentioned here is 45. A meeting that seems to have comprised nearly the entire religious population of Tun-huang included 1,086 persons, among them 852 monks and nuns and 234 novices.[50] This produces an average of at most 50 clergy per monastery at Tun-huang.

Buddhist monasteries and hermitages never seem to have housed more than a limited number of religious; the average for Tun-huang—an important Buddhist center—was undoubtedly among the highest. Thus the figures for the middle of the sixth century, under the Sui, and for the year 845 (namely 66 in 534, 75 after 550, 60.5 and 59 under the Sui, and 56 in 845 for the great monasteries) probably do not correspond to overall averages.

Given the considerable variations of the averages of clergy per monastery, it may not in all cases be justifiable to place the census figures for religious side by side with those provided by the monasteries themselves. The available figures for the fourth and fifth centuries are very likely correct: 20 religious per establishment in 316 in the two capitals, counting the small sanctuaries, 14 under the Chin dynasty, in 317–320, 20 in 476 at Lo-yang, 11.3 in the same year under the Wei.[51] However, a number of religious who did not reside in monasteries must have been included in the census records under the Sui and in 845. It is known, in fact, that in the monasteries' nominal registers (ssu-chi) figured the names of monks who had no more than a purely formal affiliation with their institution. A monk named Fa-ch'ung who lived at the time of the Chou (557–580) had long refused to be enrolled in the official register (kuan-kuan). Yet after finally consenting to this formality, having almost reached the age of fifty (chih-ming), he preferred to live among the "springs and rocks" rather than at the Fa-chi monastery of Li-chou were he was officially registered as a resident monk.[52]

Name rolls of religious were moreover frequently falsified. The import of the following decree by Emperor Hsüan-tsung to this effect undoubtedly applies to other periods as well:

> It has come to Our attention that there are numerous monks and nuns, both Buddhist and Taoist, who are falsely enrolled on the nominal registers [for religious]. Either they have arranged to be attached to another monastery, or they maintain a private group of disciples (yang ssu-men) [the existence of which they dissemble].[53]

It is therefore necessary to take fraudulent registrations into account. The actual resident population of the monasteries may have been larger or smaller than the census figures indicate.[54] Furthermore, the sources account only for those religious who were officially registered and, in principle, regularly ordained.[55] Generally, official ordinations—which rarely benefited laymen—did not increase the actual numbers of monks and nuns; rather, they allowed certain religious to regularize their status. It was thus that the monk Fa-ch'ung received his belated ordination, availing himself of an imperial proclamation of ordinations to join the ranks. And his case is not unique. "During Chen-kuan (627–650), official ordinations were conferred.[56] Since the monk P'u-chi had not yet been registered,[57] he took the opportunity to enroll in the official registers of the monastic community."[58]

It could therefore be assumed that the number of regular monks and nuns was, generally speaking, inversely proportional to that of unregistered religious. Imperial policy had at any rate less of an effect on the real number of religious than one might think. It is possible that, underlying the variations emphasized by the censuses of different periods, much slower and less pronounced variations took place with respect to the overall number of religious.

When the official figures account only for regular monks residing in state monasteries, as was the case during the first half of the T'ang, it is necessary to add the itinerant monks and the entire population of the small sanctuaries to their numbers. As a result, the number of monks according to the census may at times have to be doubled to obtain the effective total. This was the view expressed by Su Kuei at the beginning of the eighth century: "In the whole empire," he memorialized the emperor, "fraudulent monks (wei-lan seng)[59] constitute approximately half the number of all the religious."[60] Thus the number of monks and nuns at that time would not have been 126,000 as indicated by the census, but rather 250,000 to 300,000. Already at the beginning of the T'ang dynasty, Fu I estimated the number of adult monks and nuns as 200,000, whereas the author of a refutation to that great official's projects, the monk Ming-kai, could justly rejoin: "Under the present dynasty, according to the monastic registers (ssu-chi), the two communities, Buddhist and Taoist, do not exceed 70,000. How could you have the impudence to deceive the emperor by claiming that there were 200,000 Buddhist monks and nuns?"[61]

Political conditions permitting, particularly around the middle of the sixth century and during the second half of the T'ang, a purely nominal growth of monasticism can be observed due to those for whom the tonsure or the acquisition of a religious title represented a means to escape taxation or corvée services owed to the state. This explains the two most extreme figures provided by the sources: 2 to 3 million religious between the years 534 and 574, and 700,000 in 830. The increase of the monastic community is in both cases only apparent: in the sixth century, this includes tonsured and frocked peasants, in 830, farmers who had purchased official ordination certificates. The laicizations undertaken by Emperor Wu of the Chou were therefore not as appalling as Buddhist sources were wont to make out, just as between 830 and 845 the number of monks and nuns did not melt away miraculously. For how else can the decline of their numbers from 700,000 to 360,000 between those two dates be explained?

If the two figures showing an extraordinary increase in the monastic community, which invite skepticism a priori, are not relied on, it is found on the contrary that the proportion of religious relative to the total population of China remained remarkably constant. At the very moment when the North witnessed such an unusual development of monasticism, the Liang dynasty had no more than 100,000 Buddhist monks and nuns, corresponding to .7 percent of a population of 13 million, despite the fact that Buddhism flourished in that kingdom, ruled by one of the most devout sovereigns in Chinese history: Similarly, under the T'ang, the Buddhist clergy amounted to .35 percent of the population of China in 624, and .58 percent at the beginning of the eighth century, if the very reasonable corrections by Fu I and Su Kuei are accepted. The highest percentage was reached around 845 with a little over 1 percent.[62]

A further consideration accords with our view that the real monastic community, i.e., the totality of those who actually lived on the trade of the religious, never constituted more than a small fraction of the Chinese population, remaining mostly, with slight variations, below 1 percent: that is, the feeble resources of the Chinese economy. Modern states dispose of means unknown to those whose economy remained essentially agricultural and where technical development was still rudimentary. It is a fact that the cultivation of the soil in "medieval" China scarcely assured the subsistence of the population as a whole, and that this precarious equilibrium was upset whenever a natural catastrophe occurred in a given region. However small the increase in the number of unproductive mouths that accompanied the development of Buddhism, it was enough to cause a serious problem. The monastic community was, by and large, of peasant origin and with it a part of the peasantry was withdrawn from agricultural labor.

Certain officials leveled their criticism against the general diminution of consumer goods due to Buddhism: "Monks eat without having to work the land and are clothed without having to weave." As far as the construction of religious buildings was concerned, they were useless to the well-being of men.

If Buddhism made China poorer, it is equally possible, given the rigidity of the Chinese economy, that it merely had the effect of absorbing a surplus of wealth: its introduction to China would hardly seem to have been possible without improvements in agricultural methods and the expansion of land under cultivation. It will be seen, first, that Buddhism itself contributed to bringing new land into cultivation in the Northwest, and, throughout the country, to developing land neglected by traditional agriculture. As for improvements in agricultural methods, they are by no means inconceivable.[63] Contrary to widespread opinion, the Chinese were not indifferent to technical progress, as the development of automatic mills from the Chin to the T'ang illustrates.[64] One thing is certain: the number of "idle eaters" (yu-shih) and, generally speaking, the size of the non-farming population increased greatly from the Six Dynasties to the T'ang. Indirectly, the development of commerce from the T'ang onward also suggests increased returns from agriculture. As Han Yü wrote in 819,[65]

In antiquity[66] there were four social classes [officials and nobles, peasants, craftsmen, and merchants]. Today there are six [with the addition of the clergy and the military]. In antiquity there was only one doctrine. Today there are three. For every farmer there are six consumers; for every craftsman, six persons who profit from his products; for every merchant, six persons to take advantage of his profits. Under such conditions, how could the people not become impoverished and turn to brigandage?

At about the same time, Li Chi-fu, for his part, estimated that three peasants fed seven idlers (sinecures, soldiers, and monks);[67] Tu Mu attributed the following words to Emperor Wen-tsung (r. 827–840):

In the past, three people lived on the labor of one farmer. Today, the soldier and the monk have been added to these so that one farmer supports five persons. Among these, it is the Buddhists who cause greatest harm to our people.[68]

It goes without saying that these different testimonies given by personalities well placed to evaluate the Chinese economy, one of whom, Li Chi-fu, surely had accurate data at his disposal, do not indicate that 70–80 percent of the population were not employed working the soil. For it is of course inconceivable that at the beginning of the ninth century only 20–30 percent of the Chinese population were farmers. What Han Yü, Li Chi-fu, and Emperor Wen-tsung intended to convey is that the nonagricultural proportion of the population had increased dangerously.[69]

The development of Buddhism in China, then, poses two distinct but related problems: one concerns the general effects of that religion on the Chinese economy, the other, the finances of the empire.[70]

General Effects on the Chinese Economy

If it is impossible to determine the global cost of Buddhism to China during the period of its greatest flourishing, that is, from the end of the fifth century to the second half of the T'ang, some questions at least can be identified.

One of the surest economic effects of the great Buddhist constructions was, frequently, an appalling misery for the peasant class. Taste for extravagant expenditure on the part of the wealthy faithful prevailed over their respect for Buddhist charity. The construction of a sumptuous monastery in Chien-k'ang (modern Nanking) under Emperor Ming of the Sung (r. 465–472), which had necessitated exhausting corvée services, reduced the common people to selling their wives and children.[71] Men and animals died in large numbers in the undertaking; allusions to peasant suffering made by authors not normally prone to pity deserve added credence. But not only were there constructions; other causes had the same effect. The frequent appropriation of goods by the religious and the usury practiced by the large monasteries were at the heart of many tragedies among the humble.[72]

The maintenance of an abundant monastic community and the construction of often sumptuous buildings could only have been assured by a sizeable levy imposed on the available wealth. However, the influence of Buddhism was not limited to this purely negative effect on the Chinese economy: its arrival also led to an increase in commercial and manufacturing activity at the expense of agriculture. The needs of the Buddhist communities and laity favored certain businesses—especially those related to construction, the timber trade, dyeing products, and others—and gave rise to or developed certain trades: builders, architects, sculptors, painters, goldsmiths, and copyists all benefited from the religious movement at the same time that agriculture suffered from the requisitioning or hiring of peasants for the great Buddhist construction works. One can go a step further: in a more general way, the success of Buddhism in China had the effect of developing consumption and distribution or, as some modern economists would say, of developing the "tertiary sector" at the expense of the production and other activities of the "primary sector" (agriculture and textiles). The monks themselves were a luxury. This change in the Chinese economy is so evident that one might be tempted to see in it not only one of the consequences of the religious movement but perhaps also one of its deepest psychological motivations. For an inclination to luxury, artistic pleasure in some,[73] prodigality, and religious needs as such accord with one another and respond to a general tendency that is, in a sense, economic in nature.

The examination of the census concerning the number of monks and of monasteries enables us to trace the overall development of Buddhism in China: the monastic community, maintained by the faithful and by the state, was no doubt a constant burden for the Chinese economy. But it does not appear, as has been seen, that the number of those who lived the trade of the religious[74] varied significantly after the end of the Northern Wei. The existence of this monastic community posed above all a fiscal problem for China, both with respect to the number of religious who were maintained at state expense and to the size of the fictitious monastic community consisting of laymen who profited illicitly from the fiscal privileges of the regular clergy. On the other hand, the passion that the Chinese invested into building, sculpting, and casting, which was to lend a new vigor and inspiration to Chinese art, was not continuous, or at least went through periods of particular intensity.

The first criticisms directed against the luxury and number of Buddhist constructions date from the beginning of the fifth century. In 435, under the Sung, Governor Hsiao Mu-chih of Tan-yang declared that Buddhist stūpa, monasteries, paintings, and statues numbered in the thousands and requested that all constructions and all castings of statues be subject to prior governmental authorization.[75] It was especially after 465, in North China, that unrestrained expenditure for the benefit of Buddhism began to assume proportions dangerous for the Chinese economy. Colossal proportions were in fashion. The famous statues carved into the rock at Yün-kang in the north of modern Shansi and those at Lung-men, to the south of Lo-yang, date from that period. From 500 to 523, the construction of an additional grotto at Yün-kang in honor of Emperor Shih-tsung cost 802,366 cash.[76]

In Lo-yang itself, there were only some one hundred Buddhist establishments in 476.[77] When Ts'ui Hsiao-fen was dispatched to that city by the controller of Buddhist clergy (*sha-men t'ung*) on a tour of inspection in 509, he counted more than five hundred.[78] At the end of the Northern Wei, around 534, the large and small monasteries of Lo-yang numbered 1,367.[79] The notes that Yang Hsüan-chih devoted to the monasteries of Lo-yang depict the extreme luxury of the most celebrated ones:

> Within [the precincts of the Yung-ning monastery] stood a nine-storied stūpa. Built with wooden framework, it rose to a height of ninety *chang*. With its pinnacle (*ch'a*, Skr. *chattra*) adding another ten *chang*, its total elevation amounted to one thousand feet (*sic:* nearly 300 m). [This tower] could be seen at a distance of a hundred *li* (50 km) from the capital. When its foundations were excavated, they reached the underworld. Thirty golden statues were discovered there. Because the empress regarded these as confirmation of her faith in Buddhism, the construction exceeded all measure. On top of the pinnacle was a precious golden jar with a capacity of twenty-five bushels. Beneath the precious vase were 30 golden plates for collecting dew. All around them hung small golden bells. . . . Golden bells were also attached to each corner of the reliquary tower, 120 of them in all. On each side of the four-sided stūpa, there were three doors and six windows. The doors were lacquered vermilion. On their leaves, each bore five rows of golden studs, in all 5,400. . . . To the north of the stūpa stood a Buddha Hall that was modeled on the T'ai-chi Hall [in the palace]. It contained an eighteen-foot golden statue, ten medium-sized statues—also in gold—three embroidered images studded with pearls, and five of woven materials. The artistry was extraordinary. . . . There was also a storied pavilion for the monks' cells measuring more than a thousand bays (*jian*). The perfection of the carved beams, painted walls and doors, and latticed windows was indescribable.[80]

If the richest monasteries and the biggest architectural complexes were constructed at state expense, members of the aristocracy and great officials were extensively patronizing constructions at the end of the Northern Wei period as well: according to Fa-lin, against 47 large state monasteries, 839 monasteries had been founded by great families at that time.[81] As Yang Hsüan-chih indicates, consortia were occasionally formed to defray the cost of construction. Thus the stele of the Cheng-shih monastery recorded that it had been built thanks to a common fund to which the president of the imperial chancellery Ts'ui Kuang contributed four hundred thousand cash, the marquis of Ch'en-liu, Li Ch'ung, two hundred thousand cash, and various other officials smaller amounts of not less than five thousand cash.[82] In the period approaching the end of the Northern Wei dynasty, an increasing number of restrictions against private construction were introduced. Already in 472, Emperor Kao-tsu warned the faithful against excesses of fervor detrimental to their patrimony and the common good.[83] A succession of prohibitions followed at the beginning of the sixth century, in 506, 509, 519, and in 538; the last pages of the "Monograph on Buddhism" in the *Wei shu* are almost entirely devoted to sumptuary edicts.[84]

The first great period of construction is thus situated at the end of the Northern Wei dynasty. Gigantic proportions in sculpture and architecture are indeed a characteristic feature of Buddhist art from this period to the T'ang. According to the decree of 472, the faithful vied with one another to build "higher and bigger,"[85] a revealing statement both with regard to the artistic tastes of the period and to the psychological motivations for prodigality.[86]

The material effects of this building passion may be imagined. They stem from the construction methods themselves: wood and brick were the two most common materials; the use of stone was rare. The construction during the Huang-hsing period (467–471) of a three-storied reliquary tower, apparently modeled on the wooden stūpa, yet built entirely of stone, is mentioned as a curiosity.[87] The production of bricks and tiles supplied a favorite argument to the partisans of sumptuary regulations, and one they borrowed from Buddhism itself: the earthwork and especially the firing caused the death of worms, ants, and subterranean insects. The construction of monasteries also had consequences other than of a moral order. One of these, the deforestation of certain regions, became perceptible only with time and did not give rise to undue concern. The demand for metals for ornaments and for the casting of bells and statues, on the other hand, quickly led to scarcities of gold, silver, and especially copper, posing serious difficulties for the imperial government.[88] Finally, since manpower for the earthworks and for transportation was drawn from the peasantry, agricultural production suffered whenever the works extended into the tilling season.

The most precise information available about the costs of construction concerns the T'ang period.

The erection of the Hsi-ming monastery in 657 and that of the Ching-ai ssu at Lo-yang each cost 210,000 strings of cash.[89] In the third year of Chin-lung (709), Wei Ssu-li memorialized Emperor Chung-tsung:

I observe that Buddhist and Taoist monastery constructions have
been very numerous in recent times. . . . The cost of the large ones
amounts to tens and hundreds of myriads of strings of cash, of the
smaller ones, from thirty to fifty thousand strings of cash. The total
amount for these constructions exceeds ten million strings of cash.[90]
When beams and blocks of stone are transported, there is no respite
for men and oxen. For the sake of these constructions, all [other] work
is suspended, to the grave detriment of agriculture.[91]

One of these extravagant expenditures was notorious: Under the reign
of Tai-tsung (763–779), the Chin-ko monastery at Mount Wu-t'ai was
tiled with gold-plated copper.[92]

In the collection of petitions and official acts concerning the monk
Pu-k'ung (Amoghavajra), figures an account of the expenditures
incurred in the construction of a pavilion dedicated to the bodhisattva
Mañjuśrī. It is dated fifth day, fourth month of Ta-li 10 (775). The
total expenditure amounted to 22,487 strings (of 1,000 cash each) and
950 cash.

Following are the details (in cash):

4,542,545 for the purchase of 610 and a half square beams;
974,810 for the purchase of 804 acacia columns;
1,491,170 for the purchase of 55,698 bricks;
214,500 for the purchase of 700 bundles of laths;
746,225 for the purchase of pine wood (doors and windows);
764,000 for the purchase and transport of quarry stones;
116,425 for the purchase of *ma-t'ao* (?);
339,591 for the purchase of nails;
80,000 to have *feng-cheng*[93] made for the two stories;
85,288 for the purchase of color products (lime, red soil,
   black wax);
2,478,946 for manufacture of gold and copper nails,
   and of animal figures for the doors;
694,550 hire for earthworks; masons for the foundations;
2,288,300 wages for carpenters;
800,000 for the purchase of fabrics, embroideries;
   wages for artisans;
1,051,296 wages for squarers (?);
350,000 wages for roofers;
1,518,900 wages for door and window makers;
330,000 wages for plasterers;

257,000 wages for draughtsmen and for the
  purchase of ornaments;
595,687 hire of coolies, carts, and boats for transportation;
357,700 wages for brickmakers;
162,548 for the purchase of bamboo objects, mats, paper, oil etc.;
100,982 wages for builders (?);
52,516 for the purchase of glue, hemp, ropes etc.;
312,790 hire of temporary laborers;
873,250 for the purchase of four carts and six oxen;
682,087 for fodder and cures for the oxen,
  and wages for cart-drivers.[94]

As will be noted from this list, the cost of unskilled labor—for earth-works and transportation—was relatively low, whereas specialists commanded high wages. The two principal items of expenditure, fur-thermore, were timber and metals.

Peasant labor was hired or, in the case of official constructions, req-uisitioned as for public works. A report by Wei Ts'ou[95] addresses the construction of two Taoist monasteries,[96] the Chin-hsien kuan and the Yü-chen kuan, at the expense of an imperial princess. Work began in the spring of the third year of Ching-lung (707). According to Wei Ts'ou, "Laborers were hired at inflated rates. Peasants from the three support-ing prefectures[97] rushed to take advantage of the offer, and abandoned their fields to seek employment as laborers. They relinquished the essential (pen, i.e., agriculture) to run after the accessory (mo)."

In fact, whenever earthworks were extensive or heavy timber was used, the building sites thronged with laborers. A story relates that when Hsüeh Huai-i, the Lo-yang drug merchant who became the lover of Empress Wu, was in charge of the construction of an immense palace, he organized his laborers into groups of one thousand persons, under the direction of a foreman, to haul the heaviest pieces.[98]

The second major period of construction, which began under the T'ang with the foundation of the Hsi-ming monastery in 657[99] and ended at the beginning of the reign of Emperor Hsüan-tsung, had indeed the effects on the Chinese economy already attributed to the construction of the great sanctuaries: increase of peasant corvées, depletion of metals, and deforestation. Early in the eighth century the taste for wasteful expenditure seems to have been most pronounced, particularly among members of the imperial family. In a memorial dated 707,[100] Hsin T'i-p'i complained that the defenders of the empire could no longer be recompensed for their pains and that supplies could no longer be sent to the armies. "Extensive constructions of monasteries are undertaken," he wrote,

> and large mansions are built. Even though for such works trees are felled to the point of stripping the mountains, it does not suffice to supply all the beams and all the columns required. Though earth is moved to the point of obstructing the roads, it does not suffice for the [production of bricks required for] walls and partitions. . . . Today there are countless Buddhist monasteries in the empire. The main hall of any of them is twice the size of the halls in the imperial palace; their extravagance is beyond measure. Indeed, out of the wealth of the whole empire, Buddhism possesses seven- or eight-tenths.

What is to be made of that last assertion? If not only the lands and commodities that were in the hands of monks and their communities but also the unproductive capital that the buildings of worship, the ornaments, and the statues represented are taken into account, Hsin T'i-p'i's estimate is perhaps less exaggerated than it at first appears. Of all the goods that were swallowed by Buddhist constructions, precious metals and copper constituted the core of this fixed and unproductive capital.

In addition to the produce and miscellaneous goods stored in their treasuries and granaries, the great Buddhist establishments owned monetary holdings that must often have been considerable, especially when they acted as pawnbrokers (chih-ch'ien), since for such loans the redemption of the pledge and the payment of interests were regularly transacted in cash.[101]

In one case, at least, the monetary holdings of a Buddhist monastery can be evaluated. Unfortunately, it appears to have been a small establishment. In the fragments of the accounts from the monastery of Mazār-tāgh dating around the year 720,[102] all expenditures are in cash. This was the usual method of payment wherever there was a sufficient supply of copper coins to cover current transactions. According to these accounts, the monastery spent:

- From the twenty-sixth day of the tenth month to the thirteenth day of the eleventh month: 16,055 cash;
- From the twenty-seventh day of the eleventh month to the fifteenth day of the twelfth month: 6,465 cash;

- From the thirtieth day of the twelfth month to the twenty-second day of the first month: 4,934 cash.

This amounts to an outlay of more than 27,454 cash in a period of sixty days, or an annual expenditure of 200,000 cash. The monetary reserves of such a small Buddhist establishment can be estimated on the basis of the ratio known for Tun-huang: the annual expenditures of large monasteries there amounted to only one-third or one-quarter of their liquid assets.[103]

By setting up shops in the markets, large monasteries were also able to turn to profit a significant part of the total volume of cash in circulation. More than 100,000 strings of cash annually left the pawn-broking shops and counters, which had been established by the monk Ch'ang-yen (d. 816) at the Fu-t'ien monastery.[104] The imperial government was thus induced to curtail the cash holdings of these banking establishments: a decree of the first month of the twelfth year of Yüan-ho (817) prohibited officials of all ranks—the nobility, commoners, merchants, and also Buddhist and Taoist monasteries and ward markets—from keeping more than 5,000 strings of cash.[105] The custom among the great Buddhist families of transporting cart loads of cash to the Inexhaustible Treasuries of the Hua-tu and Fu-hsien monasteries at the beginning of the year was no doubt one of the reasons for the confiscation of the goods of these treasuries in 713.[106]

It will further be noted that the circulation of cash was restricted to large urban centers and certain regions, notably the Yangtze valley, which seems to have become a major artery of commerce from the sixth century onward.[107] Elsewhere, transactions were carried out in cloth and in grain.

Overall, however, the cash reserves of large Buddhist monasteries constituted only a small part of their holdings in metals: the bulk were ritual objects and ornaments. The great repressions of Buddhism under the Chou emperor Wu between 574 and 577, under Wu-tsung in 842–845, and finally in 955, presented themselves primarily as measures of economic recovery: each of them provided an opportunity for the imperial government to procure the necessary copper for the minting of new coins. Though there is no proof of this, the monks themselves may have melted down devotional objects in copper to convert them into cash.[108] The reverse operation, however, the melting of cash for casting statues, seems to have been practiced frequently. A petition of the year 825 recommended treating the private

casting of Buddhist statues in the same category of offenses as counterfeiting: "In the tenth month of the first year of Pao-li, the governor
of Honan, Wang Ch'i, presented a memorial to the emperor in which
he proposed that those who melted down cash in order to make Buddhist statues be liable to the same punishment as counterfeiters."[109]

Wang Tse (502–549), governor of Lo-yang under the Eastern Wei in
538, had the Buddhist statues of that city destroyed in order to found
copper coins. They were called "Ho-yang cash."[110] Under Emperor
Ming of the Chou (r. 557–560), too, coins were founded from confiscated Buddhist statues.[111]

In 845 the Imperial Secretariat presented a memorial to the emperor
requesting that

> the statues, bells, and copper chimes of the destroyed monasteries
> should be made over to the Salt and Iron Commission (yen-t'ieh
> shih) for founding to coin money. Iron statues were to be transferred
> to the prefectures to be transformed into agricultural implements.
> Statues made of gold, silver, and brass would be melted down and
> made over to the Board of Finance. . . . As for statues of clay, wood,
> and stone, it was stipulated that they be left in the [remaining]
> monasteries.[112]

The following year (the eighth month of the sixth year of Hui-ch'ang),
it was decreed that only clay or wood could be used as materials for
Buddhist statues: this would be sufficient to demonstrate religious
veneration; the use of gold, silver, copper, iron, or precious metals and
rare stones of any kind was prohibited.[113]

The anti-Buddhist measures of 955 were also accompanied by collections of metals. According to the Fo-tsu t'ung-chi:

> In the ninth month of the second year of Hsien-te, it was decreed that,
> since no money had been coined in a long time, within fifty days all
> Buddhist utensils and statues made of copper in the possession of the
> population were to be made over to the government, which would
> reimburse their value. Exempted were objects of public utility and
> arms in the possession of the administration as well as bells, chimes,
> cymbals, and handbells in Buddhist and Taoist monasteries, which
> these were permitted to retain. Failure [by any household] to supply
> five pounds (!) of copper within the appointed period was punishable
> by death. . . . That same year, the impropriated monasteries numbered
> 3,336, and from the statues [of these sanctuaries] that had been
> destroyed, coins were minted.[114]

For a long time, until the scarcity of metals became acute around the middle of the T'ang dynasty, the court itself had been primarily responsible for the depletion of metal reserves and their transfer to places of worship. A memorial presented to the emperor of the Wei at the beginning of the sixth century read,

> Empress Ling had a passion for building. At the capital, she had the Yung-ning and the T'ai-shang kung monasteries erected at great expense, and in each of the outer prefectures, five-storied stūpa. Many were the great banquets for monks and laymen (i-ch'ieh chai-hui). The goods presented as offerings were reckoned in the millions. The common people were exhausted by corvée for the [transport of] earth and timber, and the price of metals [lit. of gold and silver, but undoubtedly including copper as well] had soared as a result of these constructions.[115]

The "Shih-Lao chih" reports that the construction of the statue in the T'ien-kung monastery in the year 467—which stood forty-three feet high—swallowed 100,000 pounds[116] of copper and 600 pounds of gold.[117] That same year, at the monastery Wu-chi t'ai ssu, Emperor Hsien-wen had five statues of Śākyamuni cast in honor of the five emperors who had succeeded T'ai-tsu (Wu-ti, Ming-ti, T'ai-wu ti, Wen-ti, and himself): 250,000 pounds of copper were said to have been consumed.[118]

In the South, at the time of Emperor Wu of the Liang, a reserve of copper had been established for the official founding of devotional objects, known as "copper for good works" (kung-te t'ung). The biography of an eminent monk in the Kao-seng chuan reveals the following incidentally:

> In the eighth year of T'ien-chien (509), a statue was cast at the small Chuang-yen ssu. The artisans had at first calculated that forty thousand pounds of copper would be required, but this sufficed merely to reach the Buddha's chest. The common people (po-hsing) then came to offer incalculable quantities of copper. It was still not enough. In addition, the government supplied more than three thousand pounds of "copper for good works."[119]

During the fifth and sixth centuries, in particular, very large statues were in fashion. If the castings required large amounts of metal, they cannot have been very numerous, and examples of private castings are rare. The Fa-hua chuan-chi[120] cites the case of a monk named Seng-hung who had made a statue six chang high (ca. 15 m). It was still in its mold when, in the twelfth year of I-hsi (416), a general prohibition of metal casting was decreed. Seng-hung was arrested and condemned to death.[121]

From the beginning of the T'ang dynasty, a new practice seems to have been followed by the faithful: they had statues cast that they purchased not for use in public places of worship but in their own dwellings. From this custom sprang a new trade in small devotional objects that seems to have flourished during the seventh and eighth centuries and continued in later times. This indicates an appreciable change in religious sentiments and artistic tastes: the fashion for colossal statues that had been one of the most remarkable features of the art of the Northern Wei abated; the empress Wu Tse-t'ien was virtually alone in remaining faithful to these megalomaniac tastes. The depletion of metals was not the only cause of this: even in rock and clay, fewer giant statues were created. The most significant factor, however, was that both the wealthy and ordinary people wanted to have their own statues at home.[122] A decree of Emperor T'ai-tsung (r. 626–649) reads,

> Families of skilled artisans frequently cast statues. Those wishing to do homage to the Buddha come vying with one another to buy these. They assess by touch the artistry or clumsiness of the work and try to estimate its weight. The buyers are scarcely concerned with accomplishing an act of merit,[123] but only seek to obtain the object at the lowest price. As for the sellers, who from the outset had no other aim but to enrich themselves, they think only of selling as dearly as possible. The accumulation of sins [resulting from this mercantile spirit applied to religious objects] is such that the merit acquired by these acts is reduced to nothing.[124] Since the teachings of the sacred texts are thereby violated, We have decided to prohibit such dealings. From now on, artisans are no longer permitted to fabricate Buddhist or Taoist statues for sale. However, those that have already been completed at the present time shall not be refounded: they are to be distributed to the Buddhist and Taoist monasteries, the communities of which shall pay their price. The administrators of each prefecture and county shall see to the implementation of this order, which is to be carried out within ten days.[125]

It is evident here how artistic and commercial activities may continue an independent existence even after their underlying religious sentiments have fallen away.

An apocryphal sutra dating from perhaps the eighth or ninth century recalls and condemns this commercial exploitation of Buddhist piety, assigning the following words to the Buddha:

> Sons of good family, in times to come evil persons will appear among the religious and the laymen, and they will make statues in my image and in that of the bodhisattva and will sell them for profit. . . . Buyers and sellers shall all atone for this sin: They themselves shall be endlessly resold by others [as slaves or animals] for a duration of five hundred existences.[126]

Undoubtedly, the connoisseurs to whom the decree of Emperor T'ai-tsung refers belonged to the upper classes of Chinese society: the humble manifested greater religious fervor. A decree of the seventh month, second year of K'ai-yüan (714) drew attention to the fact that commoners (po-hsing) would go to such extremes as to reduce themselves to suffering hunger and cold in their desire to obtain blessings. That decree aimed precisely at prohibiting the fabrication of and trade in devotional objects as well as the copying of Buddhist sutra:

> It has come to Our attention that shops are opened in the streets where sutra are copied and Buddhist statues are cast in broad daylight. Alcohol and meat are consumed in these places. . . . From now on, in the village[127] streets and markets, it shall be forbidden to do business casting statues and copying sacred texts.[128]

There is evidence that the practice of privately casting statuettes was still alive three centuries later. As the decree of 955 cited above (p. 22) indicated, laymen kept them in their dwellings. At the beginning of the Sung dynasty, on the day ting-yu, first month, fifth year of K'ai-pao (972), the emperor, "distressed because ignorant peasants destroyed their farming implements in order to obtain blessings, prohibited the casting of iron [representations of] stūpa, Buddha images, and other objects useless to men."[129]

PART TWO

CHAPTER TWO

SECONDARY FACTS:
THE FISCAL DEFICIT

I may note from the outset the imbalance between production and consumption caused by the Buddhist movement, the growth of subsidiary activities related to the construction of sanctuaries and the organization of festivals, as well as the diversion of commercial wealth toward the monasteries. The ruling class was aware of these general modifications of the economy. More than any other social group they were alert to the new evolution, and history records that they reacted vigorously against it. From the beginning of the fifth century they sought to slow the development of construction work; they repeatedly attempted laicizations with the principal aim of returning monks of peasant origin to their former occupations. But despite continuous and at times violent efforts to return to an earlier state of affairs, to a more exclusively agricultural economy, the new developments appear to have been irresistible.

Examination of the fiscal problems caused by Buddhism allows us to verify this general statement within a particular domain and to emphasize the progressive aggravation of the imbalance. The harm appears still more acute when to the diminution of the number of producers are added the effects of the de jure or de facto immunities enjoyed by the clergy and, to a lesser extent, by the assets of the Buddhist communities. Far from remedying this situation, the sale of ordination certificates from the middle of the eighth century onward—

a period that was evolving increasingly toward monetary taxation—
further aggravated the damage.

The Fiscal Status of the Monks

Of all the evils that Buddhism is accused of having brought to China,
none was felt more strongly by the ruling class than the diminution
of corvées and taxes. In principle, monks and nuns were exempted
from all taxes; in no case did they provide corvée services. There were
religious considerations behind this special status—it would have
been unworthy of a saint to perform corvée labor with the common
people—but there were also more immediate reasons. Producing
nothing and, theoretically, owning nothing, monks could not be
taxed. Having left their families (ch'u-chia), they were not entitled to
the allotments of land received by ordinary people. Taxation applied
to households and commercial transactions. The monk stood outside
of all the traditional categories of taxable persons. Furthermore, it
seems to have been accepted since the beginning of Buddhism in
China that the act of entering into religious life freed an individual
from his duties as a layman. When Tse Jung built a Buddhist temple
in the kingdom of Wu (220–280) and authorized the local peasants to
enter into religion (literally, to "receive the doctrine," shou-tao), he
exempted them from all impositions.[1] The principle of the monks'
immunity was rarely challenged in the course of history: it was the
validity of their religious state that was called into question. Normally, there was no suggestion that monks should pay taxes or, even
less, be required to perform corvées, which were considered ignomin-
ious. Rather, they were returned to lay life. Emperors apprehensive
about the expansion of Buddhism and the growing number of monks
and nuns had no other recourse than to radical measures: spoliation,
the weeding out of monks of bad conduct, qualifying examinations,
and massive laicizations.

For emperors, however, the justification for exemptions was by no
means an abstract or general rule. The granting of privileges constituted a means of recognizing the particular merit of a subject, just as
the bestowal of appanages and of lands and gifts of cloth or money. In
contrast to this policy, which aimed to favor only the best among the
religious—those who knew the scriptures and led a life in accordance
with the disciplinary rules—the exemptions decreed by Tse Jung
look like demagogic measures. As the absolute master of his

province, it was in the interest of Tse Jung to win the loyalty of the local peasantry, and Buddhism offered him the means and a pretext for doing so. If the principle of exemption could be turned to profit by private persons, it was in fact intended by the emperor to work only in the interest of the central government, and to apply only to those religious who were fully devoted to him. As a commentator of Huai-hai put it,

> The emperor has especially exempted our disciples from taxes and corvée duties so that in the tranquillity of their residences they may apply all their efforts to religious cultivation. Consequently, they should devote themselves to understanding the Buddha nature, observe the precepts, and morning and evening pronounce their good wishes for the well-being of the empire.[2]

I-jun lists ten great benefactions granted to Buddhism by emperors:

1. The great esteem in which were held the Three Jewels;
2. the official construction of monasteries;
3. the printing of the Buddhist canon [at state expense];[3]
4. the issuing of certificates of the [reception of the] precepts;
5. the bestowal of ordination certificates on monks which exempted them from all impositions;
6. gifts of imperial calligraphy (mo-pao);[4]
7. the conferral of titles of nobility and of appanages to members of the clergy;
8. the annual donations of incense and lamps;
9. the special institution of monastic officials, thanks to which religious could not be humiliated by laymen;[5]
10. exemption from corvée duties.[6]

The monks' immunity from taxation, however, was less absolute than it might be thought. There are indications that exemption from corvée duties in the sixth century was not universal, and that it entailed the payment of a compensatory tax.

According to a stele inscription,[7] the Wan-shou monastery in Ch'ang-an was enlarged by imperial order under the Chou (550–581). It then disposed of 197 bays (chien), woods in the vicinity of the courts to the right and left, more than 2 ch'ing and 60 mou (i.e., more than 14 ha) of "land for [buying] incense" (hsiang-ti). More than 120 monks were ordained by imperial order, and they received certificates exempting them from "detaching personnel" [to perform corvée duty] (mien ch'ai-jen).

From this text it can be concluded that under the Chou, at least, monks were obliged to supply lay substitutes, chosen perhaps among the dependents of their establishments, in compensation for the corvée duties from which their condition precluded them to submit in person. Possibly, as the memorial presented in 567 by Wei Yüan-sung to Emperor Wu of the Chou suggests, they even paid a tax:

> I request that the deserving poor may be exempted from the corvée duties imposed on adults (mien-ting)[8] against the payment of a tax (shu-k'o), and that this favor be no longer extended to rich monks. Granted to rich monks, it encourages avarice and self-interest among the clergy hoping to obtain an exemption from labor services [by accumulating the amount necessary for this tax]. If, on the other hand, the poor were exempted [for their merits], then all would devote themselves zealously to loyalty and obedience, in the hope of being freed from corvée duties.[9]

Tax exemptions were absolute for only certain monks who had been granted official certificates by the emperor. Since the state's need for corvée labor was immense, especially in times of trouble, monks were liable to a special tax as a result of the very immunity they enjoyed in principle.

The fiscal obligations of monks, however, were limited to that simple tax. All attempts to subject them to regular taxation or to actual corvée duty failed.

In the year 577, under the Ch'en, all monks were required by imperial order to perform military corvées because of the continuous fighting along the Huai and the Fei rivers (in modern Honan and Anhwei) at that time.[10] In a memorial to the throne, the Vinaya master Chih-wen enquired how the emperor, knowing the transgression committed by Emperor Wu of the Chou in proscribing Buddhism in his state (ca. 574–577), could accept to transform the glorious field of merit of the saṃgha into something as vile and vulgar as a pool of corvée labor. This was not, he concluded, a way to oppose the enemy effectively; it was to be feared, on the contrary, that such an act of impiety would bring great calamity upon the nation.[11]

Until the so-called militia system of enlisted peasants (fu-ping) was abolished under the T'ang dynasty in 722, its implementation having become increasingly difficult, the imperial government was short of soldiers for campaigns and for guarding the frontiers. The reluctance of the Chinese peasantry to submit to the rigors and dangers of military service undoubtedly explains in part the great number of entries into religious orders during the sixth century.

In the founding years of the T'ang, there had been a great demand for troops.[12] Thus Fu I ventured to propose the obligatory recruitment of monks, requesting, among other things,

> that the number of monasteries and stūpa be reduced. Then the people would be at peace and the government well regulated. With their superstitions and their twaddle, the monks persuade the people that [religious] constructions would procure blessings for them. The common people believe them and vie with one another in building monasteries and stūpa. Small monasteries comprise one hundred monks, large ones, two hundred.[13] By rounding up the monks, one could form a solid battalion[14] from the population of five monasteries. Counting all the monasteries in the empire, they would be more than sufficient to create six armies.[15]

Moreover, Fu I looked further, and evaluated the situation as a demographer. Monasticism not only deprived the state of part of the taxes it could levy on the peasantry, since "the Buddhists were for the most part of peasant origin,"[16] but also deprived it of future subjects liable to taxation and corvée duties:

> Under the great T'ang, the number of adult monks and nuns amounts to two hundred thousand. They unite their efforts to sow confusion in people's minds. Could this not be remedied? I request that they all be married. Within a year, they would give birth to one hundred thousand children.[17]

After 722, when on the initiative of Chang Yüeh a professional army was formed, the number of mercenaries grew rapidly. Less than sixty years later they numbered 768,000, and in 821–824, nearly 1,000,000.[18] The government's priority therefore shifted from recruiting men for an already abundant army to raising fiscal revenues.

At a council convened by Emperor Te-tsung at the end of the Ta-li era (766–780), the undersecretary of the Criminal Administration Bureau, P'eng Yen, declared,

> Vagrancy and idleness were prohibited by the sovereigns of antiquity. In their system, men of talent (yu-ts'ai) received titles and appanages,

while those who were good for nothing (pu-hsiao) produced taxes and corvées. This has been the constant principle since antiquity. . . . I respectfully request that Buddhist and Taoist monks less than fifty years of age supply four bolts of silk per annum, and nuns under fifty, two bolts; that with regard to the various corvée duties they be treated the same as commoners (po-hsing); that those with intellectual abilities be made officials; and that those who wish to return to private lay status be permitted to do so. If they were merely bound to perform their labor services and pay their taxes, why should this be harmful to the monks? In my estimation, their dues would yield no less than one-third of the current revenue from taxes.[19] Under such conditions, the empire would be well-off![20]

The emperor is said to have much commended these words, but in fact no measures of the kind proposed by P'eng Yen were implemented.

Twice under the Sung, between the beginnings of the Hsi-ning and the Yüan-yu periods (1068–1086) and again after the fifteenth year of Chao-hsing (1145), monks were obliged to pay an annual corvée exemption tax analogous to that attested in the third quarter of the sixth century for the Chou. This tax was variously called chu-i ch'ien,[21] mien-ting ch'ien, or ch'ing-hsien ch'ien. It amounted to a maximum of 15 strings of cash per annum.[22] Under this system, the clergy were grouped by the cloisters (yüan)[23] to which they were attached, and ranked in six classes according to their positions within the monastic hierarchy. Monks who were over sixty years of age or infirm were exempted from this tax. According to the Chien-yen i-lai ch'ao-yeh tsa-chi, the ch'ing-hsien ch'ien yielded a revenue of approximately 500,000 strings of cash annually for the state. But there were exemptions: one granted to the Buddhist and Taoist monks of the Ssu-ming region (in modern Chekiang) cost the state 10,116 strings and 600 cash in revenues.[24]

Based on indications in the Sung hui-yao, Tsukamoto Zenryū was able to compile the following table showing the amount of mien-ting ch'ien payable by the different classes of monks:[25]

	Monks of the cloisters of Vinaya, Preaching, and Recitation	Monks of the Dhyāna[26]	Taoist Monks
Ordinary Monks	5[27]	2	2

	Monks of the cloisters of Vinaya, Preaching, and Recitation	Monks of the Dhyāna[26]	Taoist Monks
Monks of the purple robe without honorary name; monks with religious name of two characters	6	3	3
Monks of the purple robe and religious name of four characters	8	5	4
Monks of the purple robe and religious name of six characters	9	6	5
Supervisiors (chien-ssu), bursars, and chih-sui[28]	8	5	5
Abbots and Reverends	15	10	8

Imperial patronage of the regular forms of Buddhism was not entirely passive in nature. For the state not only renounced some of its fiscal revenues in their favor—through frequent gifts and large donations, emperors and their kin also actively subsidized officially recognized monasteries, especially those that had been founded for the felicity of their dead.[29] It is difficult to give an accurate estimation of the burden that the mere existence of the monastic community represented for the economy as a whole. However, the evidence suggests that this burden grew incessantly until it became insupportable during the first half of the ninth century. It is precisely the excessive numbers of clergy at a time of widespread fiscal evasion following the An Lu-shan rebellion in 755–763 that explains the severity of the measures of lai-cization carried out in 843–845. Assuming, as is legitimate, that the census figures under the T'ang represent only the regular clergy,[30] their number can be estimated as close to 200,000 at the end of the

eighth century. They had increased steadily since the beginning of the
T'ang: nearly 50,000 in 624, 60,000 in 650–683, 126,100 under the
reign of Hsüan-tsung in the first half of the eighth century, and
260,000 before the laicizations of the years 843–845.

According to the monks themselves, the maintenance of the clergy
was not very costly. "Monks and nuns spend little," declared Ming-
kai in his refutation of the anti-Buddhist proposals by Fu I, ca. 624.[31]
The real culprits were those great officials who lived in luxury yet
complained of the detrimental effect the monastic community had on
the financial equilibrium of the state:

> What harm have the monks done the state by exchanging the plough
> for the bowl? . . . Do they [i.e., the enemies of Buddhism] not consider
> the embroidered garments of their wives? Do they not see their
> kitchen stoves? The amount their wives spend on "peach and plum
> tree powder" for a single day's makeup would suffice to feed a monk
> or a nun for ten days. As for the glittering, precious garments they
> wear, selling them would support a monk for a lifetime.[32]

Certain officials, however, were on the contrary deeply concerned
about the deficit caused by the tax and labor service exemptions
enjoyed by the monks. In 780, P'eng Yen wrote,

> Today the Buddhist and Taoist clergy throughout the empire eat but
> do not till, clothe themselves but do not weave. They disseminate
> dangerous talk and harmful theories with which to deceive the igno-
> rant. The annual cost of food and clothing for a single monk
> amounts to some thirty thousand cash. The taxes supplied by five
> adults do not equal that amount. On the basis of [the cost for] one
> monk, one can reckon the global expense [entailed by the whole
> monastic community].[33]

The estimate of Sun Ch'iao in 851 seems even more exaggerated. Sun
reckoned that the taxes of ten households scarcely sufficed to support
one monk!

> In the sixth month [of the fifth year of Ta-chung, the presented scholar
> (chin-shih) Sun Ch'iao of the capital submitted a letter to the emperor
> in which he said: "The common people (po-hsing), though their men
> till and their women weave, do not attain sufficiency in clothing and
> food. Meanwhile, throngs of monks sit and do nothing. They enjoy
> richly decorated dwellings and choice dishes in overabundance. As a
> general rule, ten lay households are unable to supply the goods nec-

essary for the maintenance of a single monk." Emperor Wu-tsung was angered by this situation and returned 270,000 Buddhist religious to lay life.[34] Henceforth 2,700,000 persons within the empire shall at last know some respite.

Next in his letter, Sun Ch'iao requested a prohibition of those religious who had already been defrocked from the resumption of monastic life and a stop to all reconstructions of monasteries. The emperor did not adopt his counsel.[35]

In the course of the T'ang dynasty, the fiscal deficit caused by the overgrown monastic community became increasingly acute. While the number of officially registered religious rose steadily between 624 and 845,[36] that of taxable peasants declined sharply in the course of the eighth century. The majority became either farmers or agricultural laborers, constituting a stable population that no longer depended on the state, but rather on its patrons, and an instable one that escaped controls because it was not sedentary. According to Lu Chih,[37] by the end of the eighth century, the households of free peasants constituted no more than 4–5 percent of the entire population. A report by Yang Yen dating from the year 780 gives the same figures.[38] But, undoubtedly, not all peasants who had been driven from their lands or had left them voluntarily were farmers: there were also monks and perhaps a fair number of small officials who had purchased their titles when the sale of public offices was instituted after the debacle of 756–757.[39] It was the sale of ordination certificates that permitted such an extraordinary increase in the number of regular monks after the An Lu-shan rebellion. At that time, the standard of the monks recruited by the large establishments had fallen lower than ever. However, besides the monks and nuns who had official diplomas and were in good standing with the imperial administration, a large number of persons had false ordination certificates. In 830, the latter were found to number three hundred thousand.[40] It is certain that the majority of these were not, properly speaking, religious, but laymen.

In the course of history, the imperial government had to struggle incessantly against the abusive extension of the clergy's privileges to the laity. Since the decrees ordering purges of the monastic community often aimed simultaneously at regular monks of ill conduct, irregular monks, and lay persons who had illegitimately assumed clerical status, it is difficult to distinguish between these different groups of religious or would-be religious. Yet it is useful to make the distinction here in order to clarify a rather confused story.

> As early as the tenth year of T'ai-huo (486), an official presented a memorial to the emperor: We previously received a decree stating that since the beginning of the institution of [monastic] registers, the common (lit. "ignorant") people (yü-min) had availed themselves of a crooked means of tax evasion by assuming the title "entered into religion" (ju-tao). Therefore, those monks and nuns who do not figure in the census registers shall be returned to lay life.[41]

It is undoubtedly to this form of lay monasticism that the controller of Buddhist clergy Hui-shen referred in his report of 509: "The laws instituted for monks and nuns may not be applied by the laity to their own advantage. Offenders shall be returned to the administration of their original [places of registration]."[42]

To a large extent, the official class seems to have relied upon the stringency of the monastic precepts and on the repugnance of their subjects for celibacy and the tonsure to discourage ordinations. That is why they attached such importance to adherence to the basic prescriptions of Buddhism and were so interested in the teachings of the Vinaya. However, the Greater Vehicle had introduced a much broader conception of religious life to China that accepted the possibility of seeking one's salvation in this world.[43] Thus the struggle of the lay authorities against fraudulent monks, which answered to a fiscal preoccupation, reflected at the same time the antagonism between two different conceptions of the religious life: that of the ruling class and the emperor's religious advisors and that of the people at large.

The same term ju-tao is found at the end of the "Monograph on Buddhism" by Wei Shou:

> After the Cheng-kuang era (520–525), the empire knew many hardships and corvée duties multiplied. Therefore registered subjects (pien-min) took to "entering into religion" (ju-tao) under the pretext of their affinity for the śramaṇa, but in reality to evade taxes and corvées. This abuse (wei-lan)[44] reached an extent never before attained in the history of Buddhism in China.[45]

It is significant that Wei Shou does not employ the usual expression ch'u-chia ("to leave the family") here, which one would expect in the case of authentic clergy. The only possible explanation for the extraordinary increase in monks and nuns during the fifth century is this:

if the number of bona fide monks did grow significantly, that of lay people "entered upon the path" was much greater still.

Subsequently, the term *ju-tao*, with the denotation suggested above, seems to have fallen into disuse. It may be noted, however, that in thirteenth-century Japan it precisely designated lay persons who profited from clerical status.[46] The *nyo dō* are the equivalent of the *po-hsing seng* (peasant-monks) at Tun-huang.[47] The confusion between monks and laity so prevalent in China leads to frequent uncertainty as to which kind of fraudulent monk one is dealing with: irregular monks engaged in lay activities or laymen having assumed the title of monk. For the lay authorities, the two groups merged and were the object of the same measures of repression. However, in contrast to irregular monks, who were itinerant or mixed with regular religious, the "peasant-monks" remained on their lands: "At the time of Chung-tsung (r. 705–710),[48] it was decreed that fraudulent monks (*seng wei-lan*) would be investigated. Those who had kept their hair and were engaged as farmers [were found to] number twelve thousand."[49]

Similarly, prior to the laicizations of 845, Li Te-yü discovered an entire village of peasant-monks in Szechwan:

> In Shu, beside the sanctuary of the first ruler of Shu,[50] there is the hamlet named Nao-ts'un. Its inhabitants were tonsured like Buddhists, [yet] they had kept their wives and children. [Li] Te-yü issued an order prohibiting this. How greatly morals have changed in Shu![51]

A decree of the Sung period[52] recalls that the tonsure was indispensable for claiming clerical status:

> Certain individuals seeking to evade corvée duties become Buddhists in name and pretend to be monks. It is decreed that the religious (*ch'u-chia che*) must be tonsured to be [recognized as] monks; only if this condition is met will they be granted tax exemption.

The spread of clerical status was checked only by the efficacy of the controls. In North China, from the end of the Wei to the laicizations around the year 574,[53] the limitations that the Northern Wei imposed on ordinations were no longer respected,[54] and the troubles of that period rendered all measures of correction impracticable. It may be assumed that 5–6 percent of the lay population evaded their obligations toward the imperial government in this way. Under the T'ang, finally, thanks to official and private sales of ordination certificates from the year 705 onward, it became a simple matter for reasonably well-to-do peasant families to shelter their adult members from all kinds of requisitioning.[55] During these two periods are witnessed an abnormal increase in the fictitious monastic community and, in the end, the two most terrible repressions of the history of Buddhism in China. Not even the communities of the great sanctuaries—already corrupt and permeated by a large proportion of irregular religious—escaped proscription.

However, registrations and controls were only feasible as applied to the resident monks in the great monasteries. In each of these establishments, monastic dignitaries (abbot, dean, and overseer, wei-na)[56] were responsible for the monks placed under their authority. By contrast, one cannot assume that a similar organization existed in small places of worship, hermitages and sanctuaries, where only a very restricted number of monks resided. By political necessity, governments were therefore induced, on the one hand, to regulate the monks and subject their movements to administrative formalities and, on the other, to select monks and resettle them in large monasteries as necessary.

"To found a new monastery," read a Northern Wei decree of 509, "it is necessary to assemble a minimum of fifty monks."[57] Not that there was a shortage of monks at that period or a surplus of buildings to receive them. On the contrary, the aim of the policy was to resettle a monastic community that was dispersed in many small sanctuaries. The purges always aimed at constituting larger communities in fewer official monasteries while at the same time eliminating undesirable monks. A decree, which was not put into effect, announced in 626:[58]

> Those who conduct themselves with zeal and in conformity with the disciplinary rules should be accommodated in large monasteries (Buddhist ssu and Taoist kuan). They shall be supplied with clothing and food and it is to be ensured that they lack nothing. But those who are unable to apply themselves to the observance of the precepts or who are rendered unworthy by misconduct shall be returned to their places of origin (sang-tzu). The officials concerned shall pass clear regulations to that effect, striving to conform to the teachings of the Two Religions, while [also] putting an end to all infringements of the [secular] law.

At the time of the laicizations of 845, the monks who were allowed to remain were resettled in large monasteries:

We have ascertained that the living quarters in the large monasteries are half empty. As for small monasteries within the [city] wards, they are either in severely reduced circumstances or their buildings are falling to ruin.[59] Since the number of [resident] monks and nuns is insufficient to ensure the functioning of these establishments, they should live together [in the large monasteries]. . . . Monks and nuns from the destroyed monasteries who are not of irreproachable conduct or are unfaithful to the precepts of their religion shall be returned to lay life. . . . The others shall be ordered to enter nearby large monasteries that have lodgings to receive them.[60]

Generally speaking, the monks seem to have loathed the sedentary life in the large establishments that the secular authorities wished to impose on them. Many were itinerant and had no fixed place of residence. Some were veritable vagrants. These wandering monks, in particular, were a source of concern to the imperial government. Moreover, the common people readily lodged and concealed them. A decree of the fourth month of the second year of Yen-hsing (472) states that:[61]

Certain bhikṣu do not live in monasteries but have for many years been wandering from village to village, committing all kinds of illegal and reprehensible acts. It is ordered that groups of five [households] shall be formed among the people, who shall be held mutually responsible (hsiang-pao) and are forbidden to lodge unregistered monks (wu-chi chih seng). Let efforts be redoubled to discover offenders. When discovered, they shall be handed over to the prefectural offices and garrisons or, in the capital territory, to the local administration. In the case of religious, however, who go among the people to convert them to the Three Jewels, those from outlying areas shall be issued with papers (wen-i) by the overseer of monks (wei-na) of their prefecture or garrison while those from the metropolitan territory shall bear the stamped certificate (yin-tieh) of the overseer of monks in the capital (tu wei-na) or other [ecclesiastical authorities]. They shall only be permitted to travel after having been issued with these authorizations. Offenders shall be punished.[62]

Apart from these itinerant monks whom the peasants willingly concealed, and from the irregular monks in the small sanctuaries, there existed a small number of religious who were patronized by rich laymen. In the fifth year of T'ai-p'ing chen-chün (444), on the wu-shen day of the first month, Emperor Shih-tsu of the Northern Wei decreed that "all from princes and dukes down to commoners who privately maintain śramaṇa or magicians must make these over to the imperial authorities. It is prohibited to conceal them."[63] At the end of the Northern Wei dynasty, the chief minister, Yü-wen T'ai, permanently kept more than a hundred masters of the law in his mansion.[64] Around the year 600, the prince of Chin and future emperor Yang-ti of the Sui founded the Hui-jih sanctuary at Chiang-tu and recruited eminent monks everywhere. The monk Hui-ch'eng was ordered to reside there and received the title of "family monk."[65]

On the day *wu-shen*, the seventh month of the second year of K'ai-yüan (714), Emperor Hsüan-tsung promulgated the following decree: "It has come to Our attention that many families of officials have Buddhist or Taoist monks and nuns as clients (*men-t'u*) who openly frequent their wives and children."[66]

Itinerant monks and those lodged by the laity thus constituted part of the irregular monastic community. But the monasteries themselves housed the largest number of fraudulent monks (*wei-lan seng*).[67] From the beginning of the fifth century, there were complaints at court that the monasteries served as subterfuges for peasants wanting to evade their corvée duties as well as for convicts and fugitive slaves:[68]

> Many are those who evade their corvée duties in the country [by becoming monks]. Buddhist monasteries and temples are filled with fugitives. This has reached the point where the thousands of good-for-nothings thus gathered within a county could form [whole] villages and where the assembled idlers (*yu-shih*) are as numerous as the population of an entire town.

Such was the criticism expressed by Huan Hsüan in a report of the twelfth month, first year of Yung-shih (404).[69] At the beginning of the sixth century, a sizeable proportion of the population in the monasteries of the South were tonsured laymen, and private ordinations of slaves were widespread in the North.[70] A decree of the second month, tenth year of K'ai-yüan (722), indicated that monks maintained private groups of disciples (*yang ssu-men*).[71] In 731, despite the fact that ordinations had been suspended since 712, the emperor was informed that outside the capital territory there were young monks and nuns less than thirty years of age.[72]

It is by means of "private ordinations" (*ssu-tu*), carried out on the monks' own initiative, that the irregular monastic community was for the most part recruited. The decree of 722 indicating the existence of private groups of disciples explains the formation of this unofficial monastic community.

The Chinese clergy seems to have been comprised of a multitude of small, independent groups headed by religious whose influence or teaching attracted a greater or lesser number of monks and laymen. Thus there could be several—sometimes several hundred—disciples in the following of one master. The monasteries, on the other hand, only constituted rather loose administrative units, which, if large, could be organized within their different cloisters (yüan) into schools specialized in specific disciplines (Vinaya, recitation, translation, Dhyāna, and others). It can be imagined how under these conditions the group formed by the master and his disciples, which constituted a unit analogous to that of the lay family, could assume the character of a private organization that more or less eluded the authority of the san-kang (dean, abbot, and overseer). What the texts designate as private ordinations alludes precisely to entries into religion within groups of disciples and outside the control of the administrative heads of the establishments and lay officials.

The Fiscal Status of the Communities' Assets

For the religious, the common possessions of the saṃgha constituted a sacred and inalienable property.[73] According to a widespread belief among the monks and the people at large, the appropriation of such goods caused torments in hell and, at the time of the next rebirth, a fall to the state of an animal or a slave.[74] Nevertheless, the assets of Buddhist communities were never entirely tax-exempt. The state levied taxes on Buddhist Church properties, as did certain officials on their own account. This undoubtedly confirms a rather marked propensity to unbelief among the ruling classes. By contrast, the anecdotes illustrating the fearsome consequences of the diversion of the "permanent assets" (ch'ang-chu wu or seng-wu) are clearly popular in origin.

Even if there seem to have been numerous exemptions, these always remained exceptional. The assets of each community and even their dependents had a variety of different statutes.[75] Underlying this diversity, however, was a basic division between officially recognized establishments and those whose existence was merely tolerated. It was of paramount importance for the monasteries to obtain imperial patronage, marked by the bestowal of an official name-panel (o). This was the safeguard against all future confiscations and even the destruction of the sanctuary. Since the Northern Wei period, a panel above the main entrance, bearing the name the monastery had been formally granted, displayed its status as an officially recognized sanctuary. Later, such panels formed part of the regular allocations bestowed on state monasteries.[76] When Emperor Wen of the Sui removed his capital, he had a hundred panels bearing the names of monasteries exhibited beneath the steps of the main hall of the palace. An edict proclaimed that those with the means to repair or construct a religious establishment could take the panels.[77] Several other cases are known in which emperors decreed the bestowal of official names. In 690, Empress Wu Tse-t'ien ordered the establishment of a monastery bearing the name Ta-yün ssu in every prefecture.[78] In 705, a monastery in each prefecture was named Lung-hsing ssu in commemoration of the founding of the T'ang.[79] On the first day of the sixth month in the twenty-sixth year of K'ai-yüan (738), each prefecture was authorized to have a K'ai-yüan ssu.[80]

The distinction between official Buddhism and irregular Buddhism became more sharply delineated under the Sui, when state control became more stringent. From that period onward, the distinction became normative of the court's religious policy. Previously, all sanctuaries were included in census registrations and indiscriminately entitled, it seems, to imperial patronage. Likewise, they suffered the effects of the anti-Buddhist measures decreed by Emperor Wu-ti of the Chou at the end of the sixth century indiscriminately. The T'ang, subsequently, applied a stricter differentiation: just as the religious who had been privately ordained (ssu-tu) were the first to fall victim to the laicizations—the examinations designed to purge the monastic community of its less educated members were especially instituted for these—so the sanctuaries that had not received official recognition were the first to be closed or destroyed under emperors who were less disposed to favor the growth of Buddhism. Most frequently, the small sanctuaries, chapels, and hermitages, which were numerous in the countryside and in the more popular city wards, were affected.

In the second year of Hsien-t'ien (713), Hsüan-tsung[81] ordered the civil inspecting commissioner (ts'ai-fang shih) Wang Chih-yin to destroy all Buddhist establishments in the prefectures that had not received deeds of official recognition from the emperor (wu-ch'ih ssu yüan).[82] This order does not appear to have been carried out, but fourteen years later an analogous measure was executed:

In the fifteenth year of K'ai-yüan (727), an imperial edict ordered the destruction of all small chapels in the villages and city wards (ts'un *fang fo-t'ang*). Their devotional objects (?)[83] were to be transferred to the nearest monasteries. As for large chapels, they were to have their doors barred. This caused a great stir everywhere, both in official and in private circles.

It is told that Li Hsü, the magistrate of Hsin-hsi in Yü-chou prefecture, was drunk when the imperial order reached him. In a fit of rage, he killed all those who ventured to demolish the chapels, with the result that most of them remained intact in the territory under his administration. According to the legend, this fine act of faith earned Li Hsü attenuation of the punishment in hell he had to undergo for his cruelty.[84]

At the end of the Ta-li era, in 778, Li Shu-ming proposed to destroy those hermitages (*lan-jo*) and sanctuaries (*tao-ch'ang*) that did not have official designations (*wu-ming*).[85]

During the great repressions of the years 843–845, mountain platforms (*shan-t'ai*), rustic establishments (*yeh-i*), and again, according to most of the sources, the hermitages (*lan-jo*), were the first to be destroyed.[86] The emperor determined to destroy the great monasteries last, and even then he preserved a small number of them for celebration of the official Buddhist cult.

Under the Later Chou, finally, in 955, at the time of the last of the most famous official reforms of Buddhism, a decree promulgated:

> The true teaching of Buddhism promotes the good in the world. But if one wishes to exalt this excellent doctrine, it is necessary to distinguish between good and evil elements. Henceforth the private ordination of monks and nuns is prohibited. Those whose parents have no support [from other family members] are not permitted to enter into religion. As for the monasteries that have not been recognized by the emperor (*wu-ch'ih ssu*), all shall be closed down.[87]

A fuller version of this decree elaborates that all monasteries and establishments in the villages and city wards of the various regions of the empire that had received official recognition through the bestowal of a name (*yu ch'ih-o*) were to be preserved, while all those that had not received a name from the emperor (*wu ch'ih-o*) were to be destroyed or closed down. Any devotional objects (*kung-te* ?)[88] and Buddhist statues housed by them were to be removed, along with their monks and nuns, to the remaining monasteries that were instructed to receive them.[89]

An anecdote recounted in the *Fo-tsu t'ung-chi*[90] illustrates how in practice the privilege of inscription in the list of official monasteries was acquired by certain establishments. Since some monks entertained contacts with well-placed personages in the offices of the central administration, gifts could be used to great effect.

The monk Fa-hsiang of Ling-yen monastery in Ch'i-chou had traveled to the capital to request the bestowal of an official name (o) for the monastery in which he resided. In his train, he had brought one hundred bolts of silk and two donkeys intended for the official who would be able to obtain this favor for him. Most fortunately, however, he encountered at the palace one of the titular benefactors (t'an-yüeh, Skr. dānapati) of his monastery who, as secretarial receptionist (t'ung-shih she-jen) responsible for introducing petitioners to imperial audiences enabled him to obtain the official name without spending a penny. Fa-hsiang took advantage of this windfall to buy himself silk, incense, and medicines on the market with thirty out of the one hundred bolts of silk entrusted to him.

A text of this kind informs us only incidentally about customs that were prevalent in the offices of the imperial government; the author's purpose was not to disclose a practice so common as to be scarcely worth mentioning but to prove that infernal torments awaited those who diverted Church property: Fa-hsiang died a violent death and was cast into hell.

Thus it cannot be said that there existed an absolute principle that accorded well-established privileges to Buddhist institutions. In general, the great monks who lived in the imperial entourage did much to increase the number of monasteries with official designations and tax exemptions. In a petition presented in the second year of Kuang-te (764), Pu-k'ung, the monk of Ceylonese origin who was so influential at the T'ang court under the reigns of Su-tsung and Tai-tsung, requested that forty-nine monks from different monasteries be appointed to the Ta hsing-shan ssu[91], and, citing the poverty of that establishment, he asked the emperor for the beneficence of exempting it from its various taxes and impositions (fang chu-tsa ch'ai-k'o).[92]

The fact alone that the texts mention particular exemptions applied to specific monastic assets proves that fiscal immunity was not the rule. Moreover, there is nothing surprising in the diversity of their fiscal status given the diverse modes of acquisition by which the Buddhist Church was able to assemble its rich patrimony. Some properties derived from imperial gifts, others were received as offerings from private individuals, others again were acquired by purchase, yet others were appropriated by the monks and communities through irregular means. In practice, the immunity to which the "permanent assets"[93] were entitled—as consecrated property—was only selectively applied to official establishments, to imperial gifts, and to assets having received tax-exempt status after their acquisition. The lands, various dependents, commercial real estate, and industrial installations belonging to the monasteries remained, for the most part, subject to taxation.

The A-yü wang monastery, founded in the first year of *I-hsi* under the Eastern Chin (405), received its official designation only in the third year of P'u-t'ung (522). On that occasion, no doubt, Emperor Wu of the Liang exempted the monastery from impositions in cereals (*fu*) and taxes paid in cloth (*tiao*).[94] Similarly, before Pu-k'ung's petition, cited above, had been approved by Tai-tsung, the Ta hsing-shan ssu was liable to diverse taxes that must have been identical to those levied on secular properties. Ownership of slaves and employment of agricultural laborers were taxable.[95] The Central Asian monastery, for which fragments of accounts were recovered at Mazār-tāgh,[96] paid heavy taxes on its staff of domestic servants (*chia-jen*): "1,730 strings of cash made over to a *hua-p'an*[97] named Ch'ih-yao-yao of Cheng-sheng ward in repayment of the tax collected for the domestic servant Hsi-mo-cheng and for the price of the straw and two straps [for making straw sandals] (?)."

The same formulae appear, under different names, in other account fragments of the same monastery—the tax amounts to, successively, 1,730, 200, 200, 550, and 800 strings of cash. It is probable that sums of that order were paid annually and, as indicated by the date of the payments, at the beginning or end of the year.[98]

In addition to dependents, the shops, loan agencies, and industrial installations seem to have formed a category of assets over which the government was reluctant to relinquish control.[99] The request made in 811 by the monks of the capital that the mills in their domains be tax-exempt had been categorically rejected.[100]

Finally, although the extant documents scarcely shed any light on the fact, it is probable that local officials frequently overstepped their rights and derived considerable benefits from taxation, which they imposed, on their own authority, on the assets of Buddhist communities. At times, the property of deceased monks was confiscated by the administration. An edict by Te-tsung recalled that, according to an old rule, the possessions of deceased monks were to be passed on to the community.[101] For some time, however, such properties had been confiscated by local officials, ostensibly because of legal disputes.[102]

An apocryphal sutra, probably of T'ang date, devotes several lines to this abuse of authority:[103]

> Sons of good families, in times to come secular officials, not believing in the retribution for good and evil deeds, will snatch away the possessions of the saṃgha by means of taxation. Either they will impose taxes, down to the last blade of grass [lit. "down to a hair"], on the animals and grain belonging to the saṃgha; or they will employ the slaves of the Three Jewels for their personal use—or again, they will ride in carts drawn by the oxen and horses of the Three Jewels. And yet, no secular official is permitted to benefit[104] from the slaves and animals of the Three Jewels; a slave of the Three Jewels is not even obliged to greet him. . . . Wherever there are strict prohibitions concerning the imposition of taxes,[105] I proclaim to secular officials that they take care not to tax the bhikṣu. For those who tax the clergy commit an immeasurable sin.

Government policy, which only granted favors to the official forms of Buddhism, was not initially bound by the Buddhist notion that the belongings of the saṃgha, its so-called permanent assets (ch'ang-chu), constituted an unalienable property that should ipso facto be exempted from all impositions by the secular authorities. The latters' differentiation of the fiscal status applied to Church property was in contradiction to a religious concept that, in principle, claimed universality.

Forms of Indirect Taxation

To mortgage away the future is a tempting solution for governments in times of financial difficulties. The sale of titles and offices that granted fiscal immunity to the holder was a procedure to which the imperial government took frequent recourse. The objects of this commerce were not only official ranks and titles of nobility, but also, with the introduction of Buddhism, high ecclesiastical offices. Though the immediate beneficiary was the imperial government, in the long term it was wealthy private individuals who benefited from this practice, which was periodically reinstated in China.

A passage in the "Monograph on the Economy" of the *Wei shu* reports the sale of offices and titles at the end of the Northern Wei.

The wars and budget deficit of the period sufficiently explain the adoption of this expedient at that time. The same text describes the recruitment of the great dignitaries of the Buddhist "clergy" of the period.[106] After the battle of Ho-yin (in modern Honan), and the disturbances brought about by Erh-chu Jung, Emperor Chuang (r. 528–529) put into effect a scheme for the sale of offices:

> For a payment of eight thousand *shih* of grain, one was made a nominal (*san*)[107] marquis; for six thousand, a nominal count; for four thousand, a nominal viscount; and for three thousand, a nominal baron. Officials who paid seven hundred *shih* were promoted one rank. . . . A śramaṇa who paid four thousand *shih* into the metropolitan granaries was awarded the controllership [of Buddhist clergy] (*[sha-men] t'ung*) in his prefecture. If there was no vacancy in that prefecture, he was given the post in a superior prefecture or in a commandery. If the millet was not entered into metropolitan granaries but into those of an outlying prefecture or commandery, for three thousand *shih* [the śramaṇa] was made controller general [of Buddhist clergy] (*[sha-men] tu-t'ung*) in the metropolitan commanderies, but in accordance with the regulations in force in the prefectures.[108] For five hundred *shih* paid into the metropolitan granaries, [a śramaṇa] was made a *karmadāna* overseer [of monks] (*wei-na*) in his own commandery or, if there was no vacancy, overseer in an outlying commandery. Those who paid seven hundred *shih* into the granaries of outlying prefectures or commanderies, or three hundred *shih* into a metropolitan granary, were made overseers of a county.[109]

It does not appear that simple ordinations were traded at the end of the Northern Wei. Corruption is primarily in evidence among the upper levels of the monastic community, the ecclesiastical dignitaries. The reason for the sale of the titles of *sha-men t'ung* and *tu wei-na* by the administration was that appointments to these posts depended exclusively on the emperor; this semisecular hierarchy was in fact a creation of the imperial government. Ordination remained initially a religious matter over which the political authorities exercised only limited control. But this was no longer the case under the T'ang, when every ordination and every transfer of clergy from one monastery to another were subject to prior authorizations by the emperor. The state's ascendancy had increased. These new conditions reflect the practice of preferential ordinations obtained through the intermediary of highly placed persons at court and members of the imperial family who at the beginning of the eighth century had established a monopoly on the sale of titles. In a memorial presented to the emperor in 707,[110] Hsin T'i-p'i wrote:

> Today those who can pay the price or have support in high places have all been ordained śramaṇa,[111] and likewise all those wishing to evade the corvée duties imposed by the state or to engage in dishonest dealings of various kinds. Only the poor and gentlemen have not yet been ordained. How is order to reign under such conditions? Where to raise taxes and impositions? Where to procure corvées? I thought that to enter religious orders was to abandon this world, to renounce partisanship, and to be free of all selfish attachments. But now these people are only concerned with enriching themselves and with trafficking for their own benefit. They form factions (tang) and have wives and children.

In this memorial, Hsin T'i-p'i specifically attacks the excessive favors bestowed by Emperor Chung-tsung upon the imperial princesses. The *Tzu-chih t'ung-chien*[112] records that under the reign of that emperor (705–710), the princesses An-lo and Ch'ang-ning and the empress Wei procured official ranks worth three hundred thousand strings of cash, and monastic ordinations for thirty thousand. The same source adds that even worthless folk and slaves were provided with such titles.[113]

It might thus be considered that at that time petitions presented to the emperor to undertake ordinations of religious were for the most part the result of a bargain struck with the postulant for ordination. The texts are sufficiently in agreement to establish a precise date for the beginning of this practice and to permit no uncertainty as to its mechanism. The practice persisted, apparently, until the accession of Hsüan-tsung. A memorial by Yao Ch'ung states that

> since the Shen-lung era (705–707), the princesses and other members of the imperial family[114] have all petitioned the emperor to undertake ordinations. They have even employed their own wealth to construct monasteries. Each time an imperial edict has been promulgated (ch'ih) [to sanction such constructions],[115] it was followed by irregularities and abuses.[116]

And a passage of the *Fo-tsu t'ung-chi*, dated first month, second year of K'ai-yüan (714):

> Since Chung-tsung (705), members of the nobility have presented memorials to the emperor requesting the ordination of monks. Able-

bodied male adults of wealthy commoner households (fu-hu) had themselves tonsured in large numbers to evade their corvée duties. [Therefore] the president of the Imperial Secretariat Yao Ch'ung presented a memorial in which he requested the prohibition of ordinations. Buddhism, he said, is not [a religion of the] exterior; it may be apprehended only through the mind. As for its manifestations, their aim is to obtain prosperity and peace for all beings. The emperor followed his counsel and ordered the responsible officials to carry out a purge (sha-t'ai) among the monks and nuns. Twelve thousand fraudulent clergy (wei-lan) were ordered to return to lay life.[117]

The indications supplied by another memorial, however, which was presented to the emperor in the first years of the eighth century, are more specific:[118]

People in religious orders today are so numerous that their dark habits fill the roads.[119] It has become the general rule to prefer those "without conduct"[120] to those with knowledge of the scriptures and morality (yu ching-yeh). Such individuals place themselves under the protection of powerful families, together with the fortunes they vainly bring [their future patrons].[121] Fixed prices have been established for the number of strings of cash required of those who wish to have their names cited before the emperor [to obtain an ordination]. In the past, when offices where purchased, the money at least entered the state coffers. But in today's sales of ordinations it benefits private families. Given such practices, entry into religion can no longer find inspiration in moral principles, and our customs sink into corruption. Such people become sham appointees (yu-shih, lit. "idle eaters"). Their example encourages misconduct among the [regular] clergy and fills the laity with disgust. They call themselves "ordained" (tu-jen): in reality they are but "cropped"!

In the first years of the reign of Hsüan-tsung, preferential ordinations came to a complete halt[122] and controls became more stringent. A decree dated 731[123] reads:

Long since having first perceived the nature of this evil, We have desired to stop it at the source. Now We have undertaken no ordinations for some twenty years. Yet inquiries have brought to Our attention the fact that outside the capital territory there are young monks and young nuns of less than thirty years of age. We therefore order the officials concerned and the prefectural administrations to make a clean sweep and take the appropriate steps.

No doubt the corruption of local officials in remote prefectures, where the central government exerted a lesser degree of control, accounts for the persistence of such irregular ordinations.

The difficulties engendered by the An Lu-shan rebellion—one of the most acute crises in Chinese history—prompted the official sale of ordination certificates (tu-tieh) by the imperial government. The implementation of the measures taken at that time was facilitated by the general requirement of such official diplomas decreed in 746.[124]

The economic chapters in the new and old histories of the T'ang contain the most precise information concerning the sale of certificates during the An Lu-shan rebellion:[125]

> When An Lu-shan revolted at Fen-yang (on December 16, 755),[126] the minister of works (ssu-k'ung), Yang Kuo-chung, considering it inappropriate to maintain the armies out of the regular resources of the Treasuries [of the two capitals], dispatched the serving censor (shih yü-shih) Ts'ui Chung to T'ai-yüan[127] to raise funds by selling ordination [certificates] to [prospective] Buddhist and Taoist monks and nuns. In ten days, he had collected one million strings of cash.[128] After the fall of the two capitals (Lo-yang was taken by the rebels on January 18, 756, Ch'ang-an on July 14), goods became scarce among the people, and the empire was stricken[129]. . . . The censor Cheng Shu-ch'ing and the chief minister P'ei Mien convened a council, as a result of which it was decided, because of the scarcity of public resources, to invite residents of all the provinces to obtain certificates of office (kao-shen) in which the name was left blank (k'ung-ming), honorary official titles, or nobiliary titles (i-hao) against sums of cash.[130] [On that occasion,] innumerable Taoist and Buddhist religious were [also] ordained; classics degrees (ming-ching) were conferred for one hundred thousand cash. Wealthy merchants who had supported the armies [through subsidies] were granted a tax exemption. At the time when the two capitals were pacified, further sums of cash were raised by ordaining ten thousand Taoist and Buddhist clergy in the region of the two capitals.[131]

There were thus, according to the economic chapters in the *Chiu T'ang shu* and the *Hsin T'ang shu*, three periods of sales of titles and ordinations between the beginning of the An Lu-shan rebellion and the period following the recovery of the capitals:

1. Between the beginning of the rebellion and the fall of Lo-yang, i.e., from the end of December 755 to January 756

2. Between the fall of the two capitals and their recovery, i.e., from July 756 (fall of Ch'ang-an) to November or December 757 (Ch'ang-an was recaptured in November, Lo-yang in December 757)
3. At the time of the pacification of the capital region, after the beginning of December 757

Regarding the first sales of ordinations, the information furnished by the "Monograph on the Economy" is sufficiently precise: the date (between December 22, 755 and January 18), the place (the modern region of Shansi), and the volume (one million strings of cash) of the sales are known. The comparatively vague indications provided by the two texts concerning the sale of ordination certificates during the subsequent periods, however, need to be supplemented.

The annals of the reign of Su-tsung in the *Chiu T'ang shu*[132] report that in the tenth month of the first year of Chih-te, "on the day *kuei-wei* (October 30, 756), because the resources for raising troops at P'eng-yüan[133] were insufficient, an exceptional sale of official ranks and ordination [certificates] for Buddhist monks and nuns was undertaken." It is no doubt to this measure that the *Fo-tsu t'ung-chi* is primarily alluding: "In the first year of Chih-te . . . when the emperor was at Ling-wu[134], the chief minister P'ei Mien requested a sale of ordination certificates (*tu-tieh*) for Buddhist and Taoist religious, because of the shortage of supplies for the armies. [These contributions] were called 'scented water money.' "[135] The future Su-tsung arrived at Ling-wu on August 9, 756, and was proclaimed emperor there on August 12: it is likely that the sales of certificates occurred a month and a half later, in October of the same year.

According to the same source, a new series of sales took place in the twelfth month or, more probably, at the beginning of the second year of Chih-te,[136] which corresponds to the last period of sales indicated by the "Monograph on the Economy":

> The emperor ordered the foundation of a monastery on each of the five sacred mountains.[137] Their abbots were to be monks especially selected for their high reputation. Lay persons capable of reciting five hundred pages[138] of sutra received the title of monk (*ch'u-shen wei-seng*) from the emperor. . . . Again, those who paid one hundred strings of cash were authorized to apply for certificates and receive the tonsure.[139]

This passage of the *Fo-tsu t'ung-chi* figures in a paragraph dated twelfth month of the first year of Chih-te, following the mention of a transfer of the relic of Fa-men monastery in Feng-hsiang to the imperial palace.[140] However, that elaborate ceremony usually took place at the beginning of a new year. It would therefore be more appropriate to date the foundation of the five monasteries at the beginning of the second year of Chih-te, as is also suggested by another source, the *Fo-tsu li-tai t'ung-tsai*:[141]

> In the second year of Chih-te, the emperor ordered the foundation of a monastery on each of the sacred mountains and the selection of śramaṇa of exceptional qualities as their abbots. He authorized lay persons capable of reciting five hundred pages of sutra to be ordained as monks. Optionally, they could pay one hundred strings of cash and apply for a certificate in order to receive the tonsure. The emperor also bestowed Classics degrees (*ming-ching*). When the two capitals had been recaptured, more than ten thousand additional persons in the capital territory (Kuan-fu) and the prefectures were ordained for a fee.

Evidently, this last work reproduces the information given in the "Monograph on the Economy," although relating events of different dates, with scant regard for chronology, to the second year of Chih-te. Nevertheless, it would seem that the date of the foundation of the five monasteries and the last sales of ordination certificates must be assigned to the beginning of that year.

There exists, moreover, further information concerning that last period: the *Sung kao-seng chuan*[142] refers to the selection of the monk Shen-hui to direct the ordinations on one of the platforms erected in each of the superior prefectures (*fu*). It seems likely that following the installation of ordination platforms (*chieh-t'an*) on the five sacred mountains, the institution was extended to the superior prefectures. At the end of 756 and the beginning of 757, Shen-hui was in exile at the K'ai-yüan ssu of Ching-chou (also known as Chiang-ling), which was in fact the seat of a superior prefecture.[143] The selection of Shen-hui as director of the ordination platforms came after the fall of Lo-yang and occurred most probably at the very moment of the recovery of the capital region by Kuo Tzu-i. The *Sung kao-seng chuan* alludes to monasteries and buildings destroyed by fire,[144] referring quite possibly to the town of Ching-chou, since the troops of An Lu-shan reached south as far as the territories of Teng and Hsü (i.e., the southern part of modern Honan).[145]

Two official documents found at Tun-huang attest to the fact that the exceptional measures taken at the time of the An Lu-shan rebellion continued to be applied after the pacification. It is indeed probable that the documents date to 758 or the following year. The two heavily mutilated texts are identical, except for the names of the religious who were presumably the owners of the documents. One of these reads:[146]

> The recently ordained Buddhist and Taoist monks and nuns in the territory of the Six Armies[147] and of the prefectures under our jurisdiction, who have not yet received official ordination titles (kao-tieh) from the Board of Sacrifices (ssu-pu) . . . number 666. The money obtained for writing the kao-tieh amounts to a total of 1,465 strings of cash.[148] There are [2]27 Buddhist monks and 169 nuns, and 137 Taoist monks and 33 nuns.

The document is made out to:

"Chang Chia-li fourteen years	Name in Religion: . . . Head of household: his elder brother	Prefecture of Sha-chou, Tun-huang county Shen-sha district Ling-. . . village"

The second document,[149] which is more complete, also mentions 169 Buddhist nuns and 137 Taoist monks. It is made out to the name of:

"Lo Fa-kuang, eighteen years	Name in religion: Ming-yen	Prefecture of Sha-chou, Tun-huang county Ts'ung-hua district, Mu-tao [village]."

The text following this name explains the circumstances under which the document was issued:

> In response to the memorial presented by Yang Hsiu-ming, chief administrator of Liang-chou prefecture and formerly serving censor (shih yü-shih), on the sixth day of the . . . month, first year of Ch'ien-yüan (758), we have received the following order: "The officials concerned shall see to the collection of the sums required for the ordination certificates (kao-tieh) of the Taoist and Buddhist clergy indicated above. . . . It is further stipulated that the ordained persons themselves

shall inscribe those whom they will entrust with effecting the payment to the officials. The administrations are authorized to set the deadline [for the inscriptions] themselves after due deliberation, and they shall inform us [of their decision]." In accordance with the memorial submitted on the first day of the first month of this year, we request that the date be set for the thirtieth day of the third month. . . . In accordance with the imperial instructions, we have had [each religious] complete the necessary information: village and district (hsiang li), name of the head of the family inscribed in the household registers (hu-kuan), personal name, religious name . . . and the Buddhist or Taoist monastery to which the postulant will be attached. . . . The senior officials (ch'ang-kuan) of the armies and prefectures have been ordered to carry out the collection of the fees.

Placed upon the names, written in large characters, of Chang Chia-li and Lo Fa-kuang, is the seal of the Bureau of Merit Titles, bearing the characters Shang-shu ssu-hsün kao-shen chih yin. The same seal is found on a Tun-huang manuscript preserved in the British Library, dated 755.[150] The two Paris documents, which still bear traces of needle holes, were perhaps sewn onto the habits of the religious. As the above text indicates,[151] these were not the definitive certificates—to be issued by the Board of Sacrifices (ssu-pu)—but merely provisional documents provided by the Bureau of Merit Titles (ssu-hsün), a department under the Board of Civil Office.[152] This may be regarded as evidence of the general interest taken by the Board of Civil Office as well as the Board of Finance[153] in matters pertaining to the ordination of the clergy.[154]

It is difficult to form an idea of the number of religious ordained or of the amount of fees collected by the imperial government in the course of the An Lu-shan rebellion. The exact price of the ordination certificates is unknown, and perhaps it varied. The only precise information provided by the economic chapters in the histories concerns the Classics degree (ming-ching), which cost one hundred thousand cash. No doubt a simple ordination cost less, even though the Buddhist sources concluded, on the basis of the text in the histories, that this was also the price of a tu-tieh: for the figure of one hundred strings of cash that they indicate clearly recalls the price for the Classics degree (ming-ching). The strings in question cannot be assumed to comprise less than the nominal one thousand cash.[155] On the other hand, it is known that the preferential ordinations bought from members of the imperial family at the beginning of the eighth century cost thirty thousand cash.[156] It is only natural that at the time of the An Lu-shan rebellion, which witnessed across-the-board price increases, the price for official ordinations was also markedly higher. Thus it can be reasonably supposed that the ordination certificates officially sold during the An Lu-shan rebellion cost between fifty and one hundred strings of cash. On that basis, perhaps twenty thousand clergy were ordained when Ts'ui Chung traveled to Shansi to sell certificates there. Adding to this figure the ten thousand new clergy mentioned for the year 757, the monastic community would have grown by thirty thousand members as a result of these two periods of sales. But it was between the fall of Ch'ang-an and the recovery of Lo-yang that ordinations were especially numerous: "An incalculable number of Taoist and Buddhist religious were ordained," state the economic chapters of the Histories.

Unfortunately, there are no census figures for monks and nuns for the years preceding the rebellion. The official figure for the K'ai-yüan era (713–742), which was no doubt valid at the beginning of that period, is 126,000. Despite the resumption of private ordinations (ssu-tu) around the year 730, and of official ordinations ca. 740,[157] the number of Buddhist monks must still have been far below the half million claimed at the end of the reign of Hsüan-tsung, on the eve of the An Lu-shan rebellion.

However, three-quarters of a century later, in 830, the number of Buddhist monks and nuns had risen to 700,000. Certainly, the sale of ordination certificates was the principal cause of this increase. As Yang Yen wrote in 780,[158]

> When there are many adults in a wealthy [peasant] household, they are usually made into officials or monks in order to evade the various corvée duties. But the poor do not have this means of escape, and their men stay on. Thus dues are avoided by those above, while the burden increases on those below. This is what brings the empire to ruin and causes it to be swamped by vagabonds (fu-jen). The resident population that has remained on its lands does not amount to 4 or 5 percent. This has gone on now for thirty years.

Already during the years 705–714, "among wealthy commoner households (fu-hu), able-bodied male adults had themselves tonsured in large numbers."[159] The sale of ordination certificates during the An Lu-shan rebellion and the centuries following it were to have the same effect on the recruitment of clergy—and to reinforce it: the majority of the monks under the T'ang came from the well-to-do peasantry.

Once such ordinations had become standard procedure, they were not to disappear again. The practice was further encouraged by political conditions in the wake of the great crisis in the middle of the eighth century. The end of the T'ang was characterized by the rule of military governments and an irreversible weakening of central power. This was the period of "government by toleration." Ordinations were carried out by virtually independent high officials, on their own authority and for their own profit. The *Ta Sung seng-shih lüeh* says that[160]

> from the end of the T'ang onward, the great personages of the empire[161] became independent. When the resources needed for their armies became insufficient, they invited [postulants] to seek ordination as Buddhist or Taoist monks. The postulants first paid a sum of money (this is what was known as "scented water money") and then they were issued certificates. On reflection, [I believe that] this detestable practice caused the ruin of our religion.

A famous example of these private sales were those carried out by Wang Chih-hsing in the region of modern Anhwei at the beginning of the ninth century. A memorial by Li Te-yü,[162] the administrator of the western part of modern Chekiang, reports,

> Since the Yüan-ho period (806–821), private ordinations (*ssu-tu*) of monks and nuns in the prefectures of the empire have repeatedly been prohibited by imperial orders. But Wang Chih-hsing, the military governor of Hsü-chou, amassed a huge fortune [by privately selling ordination certificates]. In the anniversary month of the birth of Emperor Ching-tsung, he proposed establishing an ordination platform at Ssu-chou[163] to obtain blessings [for the state] and derived considerable profits from it.[164] The peasants of the Yangtze-Huai region crossed the Huai in throngs [to go to Ssu-chou]. Li Te-yü thus memorialized the emperor: "Wang Chih-hsing has established an ordination platform for Buddhist monks and nuns in the prefecture of Ssu-chou, which he administers. Since last winter, he has had notices posted everywhere inviting people from south of the Yangtze and the Huai [to apply for ordination]. Since the second year of Yüan-ho (807), people no longer dared to seek private ordinations. Now I have learned that since there is an ordination platform in Ssu-chou, every household of three adult members [under my jurisdiction] is sure to have one who is ordained. Their aim is to evade taxes and shelter their property. Those who have been tonsured since the first month are innumerable. I have ordered

an inquiry into those who travel through the Mount Suan crossing. They numbered more than one hundred in a single day. When I had these questioned, [I learned that] fourteen were śramaṇa[165] [ordained] in recent days. The others were peasants from Ssu-chou and Ch'ang-chou. Neither group were in possession of official documents from their native prefectures. I therefore ordered them to return to their own administrations. My inquiries have yielded particulars concerning the ordination platform at Ssu-chou. Each [prospective] monk who comes to this ordination platform pays two strings of cash. Having received a certificate, they return immediately. There is no other religious ceremony. Unless a special ban is enforced, six hundred thousand adults (!) in the prime of life south of the Yangtze and the Huai shall have to be counted as lost to the state by the time of the emperor's next anniversary."[166]

The sale of certificates by Wang Chih-hsing was not an isolated occurrence in that period. The affair, however, caused a scandal because of the very advantageous price offered by the military governor of Hsü-chou (only two strings of cash per ordination certificate), which must indeed have attracted crowds of peasants. The annals of the reign of Ching-tsung consequently devoted several lines to this incident:[167]

Day *i-wei* [of the twelfth month, fourth year of Ch'ang-ch'ing] (January 825). Wang Chih-hsing of Hsü-Ssu requested permission to establish an ordination platform for Buddhist clergy. Li Te-yü, the civil governor of Che-hsi, presented a memorial to the emperor in which he exposed the misdeeds committed by Wang. At the time, [the erection of] platforms for the purpose of private ordinations had [already] been prohibited since the reign of Hsien-tsung (805–820). Wang Chih-hsing, in spite of the imperial order, presented a petition in which he made a case of the fact that ordination platforms had not been established for a long time. From then on, [prospective] monks rushed [to the ordination platform of Wang Chih-hsing] as if they feared they would not to reach it [in time]. Wang Chih-hsing derived an immense profit from the venture.

The same annals of the reign of Ching-tsung mention analogous examples of the private sale of certificates:

On the day *hsin-wei* [of the third month, second year of Pao-li] (826), the civil governor of Chiang-hsi, Yin Yu, presented a petition to install an ordination platform for Buddhist monks and nuns at the Pao-li monastery in Hung-chou.[168] An imperial order was promulgated to the effect that Yin Yu had on his own account, and in violation of imperial ordinances, installed an ordination platform.[169] As punishment, his emoluments for a full season were withheld.[170]

On a day chi-yu [in the tenth month in the third year of T'ai-ho, under the reign of Wen-tsung (829)], Shen Chuan-shih [who served at the time as civil governor of Chiang-hsi, having probably succeeded Yin Yu to that post] requested authorization to create an extended[171] ordination platform for monks and nuns on the anniversary month of the birth of the emperor. An imperial decree recalled [in response to this petition] that the ordination of clergy had already been prohibited by numerous imperial edicts.[172]

The official sale of ordination certificates at the time of the An Lu-shan rebellion and the private sales attested for the years 825–828 explain how the number of ordained clergy could have reached seven hundred thousand in 830. Some of these no doubt have to be considered simply as holders of certificates; it is not certain that they resided in monasteries nor even that they were engaged in any religious activities.

By the end of the T'ang, the purchase of an ordination certificate was not only a necessary but a sufficient condition for becoming a monk. In regions such as Tun-huang where coinage had disappeared, ordinations were purchased in kind. In a deed concerning the division of goods between two brothers,[173] one reads the following: "My elder brother had his daughter P'ing-niang ordained [a nun] by the governor-general An. To purchase the [certificate with the] seal of ordination (tu-yin), he required a donkey and a cow."

It is furthermore likely that the monk in charge of ordinations,[174] the local officials, and not least the state itself each derived profits from these sales.

The practice of buying and selling certificates, far from falling into disuse, developed to such a degree under the Sung that certificates became bills of exchange negotiated on the market. Nothing remained of their original significance. Travelers used them to pay for their traveling expenses, and merchants for their purchases: employed here was one of the earliest forms of paper money.

As under the T'ang, it was in order to meet the needs of the moment that the government proceeded to issue ordination certificates.[175] Honorary titles for religious, in particular the "purple robe" (tzu-i),[176] were also for sale:

On the day *wu-hsü* [of the seventh month, first year of Hsi-ning] (1068), the *chih-chien yüan* Ch'ien Fu stated: "To alleviate the distress due to the famine caused by a breach in the dikes of the [Yellow] River, the Bureau of Sacrifices has sold ordination certificates. . . . From now on the gratuitous distribution of ordination certificates on the anniversaries of our sage emperor[177] is prohibited. At the same time, bestowals of the 'purple robe' will be reduced by half [in order] to reduce the unnecessary multitude of the tonsured."[178]

In his study on the sale of *tu-tieh* in Sung times,[179] Tsukamoto Zenryū was able to establish the prices of the certificates from the beginning of the eleventh to the beginning of the thirteenth century. The available figures correspond for the most part to the official prices. Once they were offered for sale, the certificates became objects of bargaining and speculation; there existed a private rate sometimes above and sometimes below the official price. It will be noted, on the other hand, that the price of certificates rose steadily between the eleventh and the thirteenth century. This was probably due to a larger extent to currency depreciation rather than to an increase in the real value of the *tu-tieh* with which the market seems, on the contrary, to have been saturated:

Years	Official Price˙	Market Price˙
Northern Sung		
1068–1078	130	190
1080	170	
1101	220	
1107–1110	200	90 to 200
1117		⅓ of the official price
Southern Sung		
1131	200	
1136	120	30
1161	500	
1163–1164	250 to 300	
1174	500	
1185	700	
1194	800	
1207	800	
1208	1,200	
1212	800	

˙ in strings of cash

Some information is also available concerning the volume of the sales:

Years	Number of Tu-tieh p.a.
1068–1072	3,000–4,000
1073–1077	ca. 10,000
1078	8,360
1079	7,942
1080	ca. 5,000
1081	ca. 5,000
1082	9,897
1083	More than 8,000
1084 and following years	10,000 (hypothetical figure)
1110	30,000

The *Yen-i i-mou lu* reports that, in 1110, it was determined to suspend the issues for a period of three years.[180] After the announcement of this decision, peasants fought over the certificates, which reached a market value of twenty thousand cash. In the end, once speculators had joined the fray, the titles sold for one million cash.[181]

·᠆ PART THREE ᠆·

THE ACCUMULATION OF ASSETS

CHAPTER THREE

THE INDIAN HERITAGE

It is perhaps one of the principal innovations of Buddhism to have introduced into a world with scarcely a legal spirit—excepting the domain of penal law—a set of rules and institutions governing the preservation of religious patrimony and the rights of monks. These regulations imply the concept of a religious foundation and, consequently, of a legal entity. Ultimately, they presuppose the existence of a special status for persons having entered into religion. The interest and importance of the study of such a set of rules is evident. They not only served as guidelines for the functioning of the economy; in some cases they even originated new economic developments. Inasmuch as Buddhism made its appearance in China both as an organized religion and a great economic power, the first question that needs to be addressed concerns Indian monastic law.

Because India had a particular propensity for abstract speculation, and perhaps also because of its early development of maritime trade,[1] its legal conceptions and techniques were far in advance of Chinese laws and customs. One might therefore expect a Chinese interpretation, rather than strict imitation, of the institutions introduced from the cultural sphere of India.

An important fact that needs to be recalled from the outset is the late development of Buddhism in China. Sizeable Buddhist communities began to take form only under the Eastern Chin (317–420).[2] In the area of monastic institutions an analogous situation obtains. The great Indian treatises on discipline were translated into Chinese only during the first quarter of the fifth century. The creation of monastic institutions coincided with the growth of the monastic community. Evidence for the interest in Buddhist discipline at that period can be seen in the fact that the translations of the four great Vinaya, or treatises on discipline, which were to regulate the lives of Chinese monks,[3] were undertaken in the period between 404, at the earliest, and 424. The beginning of the fifth century thus deserves to be considered as a starting point. As the monk Tao-hsüan tells us in a note,[4] "In the North (Kuan-chung)[5], the Vinaya of the Mahāsāṃghika[6] was used at first; in the South,[7] that of the Sarvāstivāda."[8] The indication is valuable and invites close examination of these two treatises on discipline with a view to possible borrowings in China from Indian monastic regulations. The choice of the four Vinaya translated in the fifth century is probably explained by the fact that in many respects they were the most conciliatory and the least severe. Those of the Mahīśāsaka[9] and the Dharmaguptaka[10] seem to have been compiled by communities whose financial activities were less developed and where the original rules were applied with greater rigor. Despite this choice, however, a considerable discrepancy between theory and practice seems to have existed in China. The Vinaya corresponded to a relatively archaic stage in Buddhism and answered the needs of communities that were not highly developed or remained outside the Mahāyānist mainstream. Efforts to subject monks to the prescriptions of the Vinaya were made, in particular under the Northern Wei dynasty in the fifth century, but these efforts did not succeed in controlling their lack of discipline. While this failure is no doubt connected to certain fundamental traits of the Chinese mentality, it is also due to the fact that the Indian treatises on discipline reflected nothing of the great transformation of Buddhist ethics that occurred under the Greater Vehicle.[11] Nevertheless, the willingness of the Chinese to conform to the Vinaya, together with the direct influence of clergy from Serindia, were not without effect. Evidence of their repeated efforts to assimilate the principles of Buddhist discipline remains,[12] and it is this Indian heritage that will be examined first.

Consecrated Property

The legal concept of consecrated property proceeds from a religious notion. In Indian texts the term san-pao, Three Jewels (Skr. triratna), designates in a general manner the world of the Buddhist religion (the Buddha, the Law, and the Community). For the Chinese, however, it also referred to *this* world in a concrete sense: the statues, the halls that housed them, the reliquaries, the assets that provided for the expenditures of the cult and the maintenance of its sanctuaries; second, the scrolls of sacred texts, the preaching rostra, everything that served the propagation of the doctrine; finally, the monks' quarters, their lands, slaves, animals, etc. These properties were inalienable, and their assignation to the Three Jewels was "permanent" (*ch'ang-chu*): present, past, and future, as the Buddha himself, and his Law and Community. The term *ch'ang-chu*, "that which remains permanently," applied to all consecrated assets, and it appears regularly in Chinese texts to designate Church property. It is not known which Indian term it translates. Perhaps it referred to the goods that remained behind at the time of the annual displacement of the community. In fact, the "master of the monastery" or abbot (*ssu-chu*, Skr. *vihārasvāmin*) was originally a "permanently installed" monk (*ch'ang-chu pi-ch'iu*, Pāli *āvāsika-bhikkhu*) who acted as warden of the monastery and its property.[13] The expression *ch'ang-chu* is synonymous with *seng-wu*, "property of the saṃgha," or more precisely with *ssu-fang seng-wu*, "property of the saṃgha of the four directions (Skr. *caturdiśasaṃghasya*)." The term *seng-wu*, however, also had narrower denotations. The oldest excluded from the property of the saṃgha those goods that could be divided among the monks and were allotted to them individually. The *Mahīśāsakavinaya* states that

> there are five kinds of property of the saṃgha of the four directions. They may neither be owned, sold, or divided. What are they? They are the land upon which reside the saṃgha, the buildings, utensils, fruit trees, and the flowers and fruit.[14]

Infringement of this stipulation constituted a "grave transgression" (*thullaccaya*).

This distinction of five types of inalienable properties is again found in the *Sarvāsātivādavinaya*, which defines them in opposition to goods that may be divided among the bhikṣu:

> Goods that can be divided are those which are properly distributed among the bhikṣu present. What are they? They are, as opposed to all the "heavy goods" (*chung-wu*, Pāli *garubhaṇḍa*) of a deceased bhikṣu, all his "light goods" (*ch'ing-wu*, Pāli *lahubhaṇḍa*).[15] . . . Goods that

cannot be divided are those that must not be distributed among the bhikṣu present. What are they? They are, as opposed to all the articles of clothing (i-wu) of a deceased bhikṣu, all his heavy goods. These are the five things that may neither be distributed nor received. . . . What are these five things? They are the land of the saṃghārāma, the land of the dwellings, the saṃghārāma, the dwellings, and the furniture (beds and partition boards).[16]

The property of the saṃgha, however, could comprise all possessions that were effectively at the disposal of the community and, in particular, everything that was subject to being divided among the monks. It is thus that Tao-hsüan, in his commentary to the Vinaya of Dharmaguptaka, distinguished the following four types of property held by the saṃgha (seng wu):[17]

1. Estates
2. Victuals
3. Clothing, medicines, and utensils used in the cells
4. Light goods bequeathed by deceased monks

The first category of property held by the saṃgha, according to Tao-hsüan, constituted the most permanent of possessions,[18] namely the kitchens and stores, the monasteries and their buildings, miscellaneous objects, flowers and fruits, trees and woods, fields and gardens, as well as servants and domestic animals. Since these properties, by their very nature, extended to the "ten directions" (i.e., belonged to the universal saṃgha), they could neither be divided nor employed for personal use. Such goods could only be acquired and utilized; they could neither be divided nor sold.

The second type consisted of ch'ang-chu goods of the ten directions. These were, for example, the cooked food and drink offered to the monks in a monastery. By their nature, these goods belonged collectively to the saṃgha of the ten directions even though they were held by a particular monastery. The Samanta pāsādikā says: "Failure to strike the bell for the meals of the monks constitutes a sin." Today, explains a commentary, the bell and drum are sounded in the monasteries when the communal meal has been prepared. This is because the saṃgha of the ten directions partake of such goods.

The third category consisted of permanent assets of the saṃgha that were present (hsien-ch'ien ch'ang-chu). Two categories of goods came under this heading: the ch'ang-chu of goods that are present and the *ch'ang-chu* of persons that are present. Such goods could only be the object of donations.[19]

The fourth category were permanent assets of the saṃgha of the ten directions that were present. This term designates the gift of light goods (*lahubhaṇḍa*) left behind by deceased monks. By nature these goods belonged to the saṃgha of the ten directions, but they were located in a given monastery. It is because the saṃgha that are present are entitled to partake [in these goods that they are thus designated].[20]

The additional classification in Tao-hsüan's commentary on the *Ssu-fen lü* of clothing left by deceased monks and victuals as property of the saṃgha of the ten directions no doubt reflects particular practices: the great gatherings of monks belonging to the same religious territory (*sīmā*) for auctions of small possessions left by deceased monks,[21] the great communal banquets, and the free lodging of traveling monks.[22]

It is apparent, then, that the term *ch'ang-chu* could only have been applied by extension to the whole of the Buddhist Church's property, irrespective of whether it was subject to division among the monks. The Vinaya mention only lands and buildings as the property of the saṃgha of the four directions, and they specify that such properties were indivisible. Permanent estates, in the strict sense of the term, comprised only those assets that Tao-hsüan grouped under the first and fourth categories of *ch'ang-chu* goods. The lands and the buildings served the communal use of the saṃgha as a legal entity, and as such their ownership was inalienable. Meanwhile, as a result of the growth of the Buddhist cult a new development becomes discernible: the construction of sanctuaries and reliquaries and the making of statues modified the original conception of the property of the saṃgha as primarily communal. It was no longer their status as communal goods but rather their sanctity that qualified these new acquisitions as part of the religious patrimony, designated as property of the Buddha (*fo-wu*), whereas the property of the saṃgha (*seng-wu*) was restricted to the communal possessions of the bhikṣu.[23] The property of the Buddhist Church, then, was of a dual nature: it comprised communal as well as sacred goods, with the emphasis shifting between these two aspects of *ch'ang-chu* property.

If the assets constituting the property of the Three Jewels (triratna) are examined, they are found to be those that the bhikṣu as individuals were not permitted to own and that under no circumstances could be divided among them. According to the Vinaya, the religious were only allowed to possess "light goods," i.e., those that formed the indispensable baggage of the mendicant monk: clothing, bowls, and simple objects of daily use. Buddhist morality considered the possession by monks of valuables and of objects of a clearly profane nature as "impure" (pu-ching; Pāli akappiya). By contrast, the Vinaya allowed a certain latitude concerning such possessions as part of the communal property of the saṃgha, and increasingly so as the evolving needs of the cult brought about a relaxation of the early rules.[24] Items that monks could not keep for themselves without compromising their moral status and prestige as religious the saṃgha was authorized to use for the communal needs of its members or those of the cult.

The prohibition for bhikṣu to own heavy goods (garubhaṇḍa) was not justified on purely moral grounds alone. As the Chinese translation of the Pāli term akappiya already suggests, heavy goods, i.e., valuables and objects of a profane nature, were untouchable because they were impure (pu-ching).[25] This notion of the impurity of heavy goods also emerges clearly from the Vinaya of the Mahāsāṃghika, and the moral prohibition of their ownership was coupled with a specific taboo forbidding any contact with such objects. Without exception, the saṃgha managed its wealth, handled its precious metals, and had its lands cultivated by intermediaries. The reason why fully ordained monks did not work was undoubtedly that they may devote themselves entirely to pious activities. This also explains the role accorded to the lay servants of the Church by the Vinaya. For a community whose discipline recognized its right to own landed property, livestock, and precious metals, at least in the sense of communal and indivisible ownership, yet barred the direct contact with such possessions as taboo, needed to provide itself with intermediaries. Significantly, the latter were servants called "pure men" (ching-jen);[26] they were generally active in all those areas involving contact with impure objects: agriculture, animal rearing, commerce, and kitchen work.[27]

The Chinese, who in this respect, it seems, merely inherited an Indian tradition,[28] recognized eight categories of "impure things," and the list included actions as well as objects. They were, according to Kuan-ting's (561–632) commentary on the Mahāparinirvāṇa:[29] "Gold and silver, male and female slaves, cattle and sheep, granaries, commerce, agriculture, and kitchens." The Fo-tsu t'ung-chi[30] gives essentially the same list even if it diverges in detail: "Fields and gardens, agriculture, grains and cloth, keeping of slaves, rearing of animals, money and precious substances, blankets and saucepans and," the text adds, "all heavy goods."

The permanent property (*ch'ang-chu*) of the Buddhist Church was thus normally constituted of impure goods: only the saṃgha, as a legal entity endowed with special religious virtue, and "the Buddha," as an object of worship, could own profane goods without suffering the blemish of impurity as a result. Once having become the property of the saṃgha and the Buddha, impure goods were sanctified by their purpose and purified by association with the Three Jewels.[31] The religious were therefore barred from acquiring possession of permanent assets on two different grounds: as impure goods, they were a priori untouchable; and in addition, they were consecrated. It is true that Chinese monks did not strictly abide by the rules prescribed by the Indian treatises on discipline, that considerable concessions were made to the greater freedom of moral standards characteristic of the Greater Vehicle, and that monks always did own impure goods. And yet the separate, timeless (*ch'ang-chu*), and otherworldly nature of the property of the Three Jewels was actively resented both among the laity and the clergy in China. Some of the edifying stories recounted in the *Fo-tsu t'ung-chi* on this subject are worth citing:

In the first year of T'iao-lu (679), Abbot Hui-ch'eng of the Ch'i-fu monastery in Fen-chou was suffering from an infectious disease and died uttering a cry like the lowing of cattle. A monk of the same monastery, named Ch'ang-ning, had a vision of Hui-ch'eng during the night. He seemed unwell and weary. "I endure unspeakable sufferings," he said, "because I repeatedly used triratna goods [for myself]. Other sins are comparatively unimportant; none is more serious than using the goods of the *saṃghārāma* (i.e., the permanent assets). Kindly grant me your help." Ch'ang-ning then read sutra on [the abbot's] behalf and prayed for the remission of his sins. . . . Commentary: "If one is a śramaṇa but does not understand the doctrine of the retribution of deeds, and if he appropriates permanent assets (*ch'ang-chu*) for his personal use, he who utilizes such goods and he who receives them both undergo the evil consequences [of such abuse]. The lightest retribution is rebirth as an ox, a farmyard animal, or a slave; the most severe, to undergo [the torments of] the boiling cauldron or burning coals. If retribution is clearly explained, suffering can be avoided. As for the powerful and influential, they too fail to understand the meaning of retribution. That is why they will willingly accept the gift of a [simple] cake from an ignorant monk, unaware of the wrong thus committed; or encroach upon mountains [belonging to the saṃgha] to build tombs there, or sell ordination certificates and live in monasteries;[32] in each of these cases, both the host and the guest enter into the gate of sin. The likes of these are truly vile and shameful."[33]

In the second year [of I-feng (677)]. . . . When the monk Chih-kuei was serving as steward for the year (chih-sui) of the Kuo-ch'ing monastery, he gave ten pieces of cloth out of the permanent assets to Li I-chi,[34] the assistant magistrate of Shih-feng county (modern T'ien-t'ai in Chekiang). Time passed, but Li I-chi did not restitute [the goods]. When Chih-kuei died, he was reborn as a domestic slave in a monastery (ssu chia-nu), with the characters Chih-kuei imprinted on his back. When Li I-chi died in his turn, he too became a slave in a monastery with the characters Li I-chi on his back."[35]

In the paragraph under the fifth year of Hsien-ch'ing (660), the story of a monk of the Sheng-kuang ssu in Ch'ang-an is recorded, who on several occasions had offered fruit from the monastery to his parents as an act of filial devotion. He fell ill and spat blood. The commentary adds:

The Buddha instituted this precept: the money, grains, vegetables, fruits, implements, furniture, dwellings, fields, and mountains of a saṃghārāma (monastery) constitute property held in perpetuity by the saṃgha of the ten directions. They may not be taken or employed by anyone for his personal use.[36]

A passage in the Fo-ming ching contains numerous details concerning the various acts constituting thefts of permanent assets—embezzlement, exaction, dishonest management, etc., drawn presumably from the spectacle of Chinese mores. Thieves were punished by rebirth as animals (ox, horse, mule, ass, camel) or rebirth in hell or among the hungry ghosts (o-kuei, Skr. preta):

Thus one repays the debts of his previous existences with the strength of his body, with his flesh and his blood. If reborn as a human being, he becomes another man's slave. He does not have sufficient clothing to cover his body nor sufficient food to last his normal lifespan. Poverty and cold cause these wretches to endure such suffering that their humanity (jen-li) is virtually obliterated.[37]

Those who appropriate the property of the communities, who fail to repay debts owed to the Church, then become, in some cases, "oxen, farmyard animals, or slaves," and are reborn in the monasteries to become part of the saṃgha's permanent assets. This religious conception recalls the widespread legal practice of the civil imprisonment of insolvent debtors.[38] The alienation of the culprit's person is the consequence of his voluntary or involuntary contact with consecrated property. The consumption or possession of goods derived from the permanent estate of the Three Jewels created a most effective, and dangerous, religious bond, especially where such appropriation took place outside regular ceremonies (vegetarian feasts, chai) or without knowledge of the community (irregular loans and gifts). This corresponds to popular conceptions that were very widespread in China and, although they primarily concern the history of religious thought, also had a direct bearing on the economy.

It will be observed that the sacred nature of the permanent assets did not stand in the way of their investment in the lay world. Commercial operations were permitted, provided that the resulting profits returned to the saṃgha or the Buddha. The development of financial activities was probably linked to the growth of the religion, for it was the particularly sacred nature of the beneficiary, the triratna, that justified and at the same time enhanced a practice as profane as investment at interest.[39] The anecdotes cited in the *Fo-tsu t'ung-chi* date from the end of the seventh century. At that same time, the Inexhaustible Treasuries of the Buddhist Sect of the Three Stages were extending loans to lay followers, which, contrary to standard practice, were granted without contract.[40] They are said to have been repaid. Such a practice is conceivable only within a particular moral environment and presupposes an absolute *faith*: this faith is fundamentally religious but has implications for contractual law as well. Here it is the source of a legal innovation: a specific case that well illustrates the importance of psychological factors.

The Rights of Inheritance of Chinese Monks

The distinction between heavy goods and light goods appears in the Indian treatises on discipline with reference to the division of the property of deceased bhikṣu.[41] Light goods were divided among the bhikṣu, heavy goods were assigned to the common property of the saṃgha. Here it may be objected that if the possession of heavy goods was improper for religious they should not have figured among the legacy of Buddhist monks. The contradiction is only apparent. As M. Lingat has clearly shown, the question of the devolution of the prop erty of bhikṣu remained suspended after their entry into religion:[42] "The rules of the order required a monk to be separated from, not divested of, his property." Monks who remained owners of worldly goods but had become unfit to manage them, and were even forbidden to touch them, entrusted their possessions for the time of their religious life to a lay caretaker, who was normally a relative. After the owner's death, heavy goods of this kind devolved to the saṃgha,[43] unless he had left religious orders in the interim. Such was the practice in countries where Hīnayāna Buddhism prevailed. This usage is hardly conceivable except in a legal system that distinguishes between the notions of property and possession, and it presupposes a highly evolved legal tradition. One might expect a profoundly different situation in China, for two reasons: first, private law in China retained many archaic features, and its legal notions were not subject to systematic analysis; and second, the Greater Vehicle was much more lenient in matters of religious discipline.

However, the Vinaya themselves contain differences of interpretation revealing new departures in monastic law. The treatises on discipline devote a section to the misappropriation of goods intended for the saṃgha by certain donors.[44] In the Vinaya of the Mahīśāsaka,[45] the rule is simply stated without elaboration: Goods already dedicated to the community in advance may not be appropriated by an individual monk. Cited is the case of Upananda, who with deceptive arguments persuaded a donor to assign to himself the victuals and clothing that he had intended for the saṃgha.

In the corresponding passage of the Vinaya of the Mahāsāṃghika,[46] the scenario is different but the theme is the same: a monk has gone to śrāvastī to beg for food. From the mistress of a household he learns of her intention to make a gift of clothing to the saṃgha. "Make haste," he tells her, "for riches are transient and cause many a worry," and he hurries off to announce the good news to his companions. Six evil bhikṣu, having procured the address of the good woman's dwelling, make their way to the town by dawn and obtain the clothing intended for the saṃgha by promising the mistress to let it be known that it had come from her: "This will give you a fine reputation and you will be known in the community." Though skeptical, she gives in, for the six evil bhikṣu have "connections to the prince" and could undoubtedly cause trouble for her.

In the Vinaya of the Mūlasarvāstivāda,[47] the narrative has been divided into two. The title of the section is misleading, for the aim of these long elaborations is not to illustrate the prohibition against appropriating the property of the saṃgha but the principle that every donation, regardless of the beneficiary, was irrevocable. While the original basis of this principle (that monks were not permitted to possess saṃgha goods) no doubt remained valid, a new development is added here that removes the strictly religious character of its justification (consecrated property may not be appropriated by an individual) and transforms it into a general rule of law (donations are definitive). After having made a gift of a building to Rāhula for his personal use,[48] the master of a household disposes of it a second time in favor of the saṃgha, for the venerable monk had left it unoccupied and had departed for śrāvastī. The Buddha declares the donation illegitimate and that a donation given to one, two, or three persons could not be given subsequently to others, not even to the saṃgha. Not only was the donor at fault but also those who accepted a donation that had already been assigned to others.

Between the period of the latest Vinaya and the translation of treatises on discipline into Chinese, a development of monastic law had taken place in India and in the other countries to which Buddhism had spread at an early date. This can be ascertained from the notes taken by I-ching (635–713) during his travels in India. "Whenever the property of a deceased bhikṣu is divided," he reported,[49] "one first inquires whether he had debts, whether heirs had been designated, and who had nursed him during his final moments (the "sick-nurse," k'an-ping jen; Skr. glānopasthāna).[50] . . . In no case were fields, shops, beds, felt carpets, and copper or iron utensils to be divided." Among the objects that could be divided were bowls, dishes, locks, needles, knives, spoons, saucepans, stoves, and other sundry items. "As for wooden and bamboo vessels, bedding made of hides, tonsure instruments, slaves of both sexes, food and drink, cereals, leguminous plants, and lands and houses, all these devolved to the saṃgha of the four directions. Movable property was to be stored in the community's treasury so that the saṃgha of the four directions could use it communally. As for fields, gardens, houses, and other goods that could not be moved, they [too] were to be assigned to the saṃgha of the four directions." By contrast, all manner of clothing, hides, oil jars, and shoes were shared among the monks. Among quadrupeds, elephants, horses, camels, asses, and mules were offered to the prince's household. But oxen and sheep went to the saṃgha of the four directions and were not to be divided.

Special arrangements existed for specific goods: pearls, jades, and jewelry were divided into two equal parts, one allotted to the Law (in particular for the copying of sacred texts), the other to the saṃgha. Beds and partition boards made of (or decorated with?) precious metals were sold, and the proceeds of the sale divided among the monks present. Those made of wood were assigned to the saṃgha of the four directions for their use. Secular books were sold and the proceeds divided among the monks present. Goods made over by contract (ch'üan-ch'i chih wu) were divided among the bhikṣu present, if they could be recuperated in the short term. Otherwise, the contracts were deposited in the treasury; subsequently, when the collection of debts had taken place, the corresponding amount was set aside for use by the saṃgha of the four directions.

Gold and silver and objects made of gold or silver, cowrie money, ivory, and copper were divided into three parts: one for the Buddha, one for the Law, and the third for the saṃgha. A note explains that they were intended for (1) the repair and embellishment of chapels (fo-t'ang) and of reliquaries (stūpa) where hairs and fingernails were preserved, (2) the copying of sutra and provision of lion rostra for preaching, (3) division among the monks present.

This text provides rare evidence of later practices governing inheritance among Indian Buddhist communities—I-ching's travels in India and the South Sea took place in the years 671–695. It indicates that while the ancient rules prescribing the devolution of immovable property to the saṃgha were by and large still observed, the rights of the bhikṣu with respect to property and commerce had meanwhile been considerably extended. The prohibition of precious metals was disregarded, since one third of the gold and silver derived from the legacy of deceased monks was divided among the bhikṣu. Similarly, when the proceeds from the sale of valuable furniture and secular books were distributed to them, it was surely in the form of money. Moreover, the religious had at times not only incurred debts[51] but had granted loans as well. Finally, they could appoint heirs and dispose of their property as they wished before their death. The rules of the Vinaya only applied to monks who died without leaving a will and had no bearing on property already disposed of. It would appear, then, that the treatises only represent an ancient—and, at that, a rather theoretical—form of monastic discipline. During the period contemporaneous with the development of Buddhism in China, the wealthy communities in India, Central Asia, and Southeast Asia were no longer faithful to the letter of the interdictions pronounced by the Vinaya. It is understandable that despite the efforts of the official clergy, and despite the importance that was always attached to monastic discipline by the government, Chinese monks were little inclined to pay heed to their prescriptions: the example of the countries in which for them the tradition had originated is a sufficient explanation for their behavior.

It may be asked how such an increase in wealth—at odds with the comparative austerity of early monasticism—which was responsible for the evolution of monastic law as witnessed by the note of I-ching, could take place even in Buddhist communities outside the Chinese world. At the time when Buddhist communities were multiplying in China (toward the end of the fifth century), the religious in India and other early Buddhist countries lived not exclusively from food charity[52] but essentially on the revenue from lands given by the faithful and interest derived from the investment of assets that had been donated by the laity or set aside for that purpose out of the property of the saṃgha.

There is a particular moment in the history of the Buddhist communities marking the point of departure for the immense economic development that was to follow. It was perhaps not, as A. Foucher suggested,[53] the bestowal of the first parks on the saṃgha, but the institution of a new procedure for indirect donations: food charity, offerings of clothing, and even the donation of a resting place satisfied directly the needs of the bhikṣu; the donation of rent-earning property, however, and of interest-bearing assets to defray the cost of the monks' upkeep and the expenses of the cult constituted a crucial innovation in Buddhist almsgiving. It inevitably brought about a profound change in the relationship between the laity and the triratna, and its material consequences were considerable. Although the practice of begging for food and clothing persisted by virtue of its venerable tradition and religious significance, these forms of charity could not have preserved the same role and importance that they had in earlier times. To be sure, this still concerns a parasitic and unproductive economy, but one that has become singularly complex. The goods offered as donations—fields, cloth, precious metals, etc.—were not directly usable by the religious. As impure goods (akappiya), they first needed to be purified, and this transformation necessitates one or several commercial transactions involving a series of sales and purchases. Not even the produce from the fields could be consumed by the bhikṣu, but served only as a medium of exchange.[54] It was the introduction of *commerce* into the circuit of *giving* that turned a community of mendicant monks into a great economic power. This development accelerated in step with the growing needs of the cult, while the old communal rules, designed to protect the property of the saṃgha from appropriation by individuals, favored the formation of a Buddhist patrimony.

One item in particular must be borne in mind, even if it figures only in the background: the role played in this story by the faithful, the *upāsaka* or lay "assistants" of the religious.[55] Like the lay servants (*ching-jen*) in the monasteries, the *upāsaka* attended to all the profane tasks indispensable to the well-being of the monks and to the provisioning of the cult. Merchants and financiers,[56] converted to Buddhism, made the fortunes of the Indian communities by managing the consecrated properties in the monks' and monasteries' best interest. As a result, commercial practices that belonged properly to the lay world, and were condemned by Buddhist morality with respect to the religious, nevertheless progressively introduced themselves into the saṃgha.[57] In the end, the principle of the direct management of consecrated properties by the monks and communities themselves prevailed outright in China. This was undoubtedly true also of the Mahāyānist communities of Central Asia, but not of those in other parts of the Buddhist world, such as Ceylon and the countries of Southeast Asia, where monastic property remains entrusted to lay administrators to this day.

The worldly property of the monks and the "heavy goods" of the communities shared a common nature and a common fate. As impure goods, both needed to remain in impure hands, and together they eventually escaped lay management when such recourse to the faithful came to be viewed as an unnecessary complication, especially in places like China where the local tradition rendered the application of a highly evolved legal principle meaningless. The very notion of property was not familiar to the Chinese. Until the concept emerged with the development of commercial activities under the T'ang, an individual possessed only the land that he occupied and cultivated and owned only such goods as he held in his hands.[58]

The Vinaya did not prohibit monks and communities from owning worldly goods. They forbade them the contact with and the management and direct use of such goods. There was much subtlety in this rule, and of a kind that was lost on the Chinese. Without this defense against worldly temptation, the Chinese monks strove with little success for austerity.

First of all, a fact of a general order should be underlined: landed property, especially agricultural land, formed a separate category of property in China, as opposed to all kinds of movable goods.[59] In the event of a debtor's insolvency, the creditor was free to seize movables (chia-tzu) and animals (niu-ch'u); prohibited in principle, antichresis[60] and the sale of lands occurred only as a last resort, and under no circumstances were immovables subject to seizure.[61] Since the soil, even in the case of life holdings, belonged collectively to households (hu), and also because of the Chinese principle of granting land only to those who cultivated it, the Chinese monks, with their religious status of having "left the family" (ch'u-chia), theoretically had no right at all to own land.[62] It would appear that, on the contrary, they were destined to own property of a commercial nature, especially fungible goods (foodstuffs, cloth, and money), as a kind of compensation. Such at least was the general trend—one fraught with consequences—as attested by the evidence taken globally. This affirmation is subject to a minor qualification: apart from cultivated lands, which as "personal share lands" (k'ou-fen t'ien) were subject to life allotments, there existed a recognized right for anyone to clear uncultivated areas. Here was an opportunity for acquests, and as such these new lands could be bought and sold. Moreover, in spite of the legal prohibitions, and despite the reprobation that should have inhibited the trading of agricultural lands, a development at once moral and economic, accelerating under the T'ang, led to a conception of all lands as commercial assets. By the end of the eighth century, the system of allotting plots for cultivation was no longer applied, the number of free peasants had diminished, and the trading of land had become customary. Thus did some religious come to own landed property; and they probably gained increased access to landownership after the middle of the T'ang. This qualification, however, scarcely modifies our general statement that the property of Chinese monks consisted primarily of acquests and essentially of goods of a commercial nature.

There is little documentation concerning the rights of inheritance of the clergy in China. Testamentary provisions, however, seem to have been common among monks. They were coupled with the transmission of the doctrine. In fact, in the devolution of certain goods from master to disciple, their economic value was less important than their symbolic significance. These were the "appurtenances" of the deceased, i.e., objects of daily use with which he had been in contact over a long period of time, and they went by priority to his disciples. These minor objects were symbols of the master's character, imbued with his religious personality. According to legend, the first six patriarchs of the Chinese Dhyāna school are said to have transmitted, along with the secrets of their teaching, a religious cloak (kāṣāya) from master to disciple. Its possession constituted proof of orthodoxy. The Indian practice of attributing the "six principal objects" (liu-wu, Skr. parikkhāra) of the deceased to his sick-nurse (k'an-ping jen)—the person who had nursed him at the time of death—may have been inspired by analogous considerations. This was done prior to the general distribution of the legacy of light goods among the monks present. The six objects were tangible mementoes of the deceased bhikṣu: the saṃghāṭī (great cloak), the uttarāsaṅga (intermediate garment), the antarvāsa (undergarment), the iron bowl, the seat, and the gourd.[63] As for the sick-nurse, it may be assumed that he was the chief disciple.[64]

The disposition made by the great monk Pu-k'ung before his death in 774[65] bears out this general practice of attributing the closest personal belongings of the deceased to his disciples. To his religious disciples at the monasteries Pao-shou, Hua-tu, and Hsing-shan, Pu-k'ung left his personal seal,[66] "that they may transmit it." To his lay disciple, the commissioner of good works (kung-te shih) Li K'ai-fu, he bequeathed five copies of the Yü-ch'ieh[67], his religious utensils (tao-chü) in silver (five pieces), as well as three diamond pestles (chin-kang ch'u; Skr. vajra) and a bell. To the commissioner for overseeing Buddhist affairs (chien-shih), Li, he passed on some pestles and a wheel, to Chao Ch'ien, another layman, several scrolls of Buddhist texts.

The main part of Pu-k'ung's possessions, however, were assigned to the property held in perpetuity by the monasteries. It would seem that the purpose of the deed was to specify the modalities of a devolution that, in itself, was in any event obligatory:

Two oxen from his estate (chuang), valued at ten strings of cash or more each, were intended by Pu-k'ung for the permanent property [of the Hsing-shan monastery]. Carts, oxen, and landed estates were attributed to the chapel (tao-ch'ang) situated beneath the Mañjuśrī pavilion; they were to be used for the purchase of provisions for the officiants and of oil, incense, and firewood. Parasols, small statues, mats, straw mattresses, and copper objects were also assigned to the same chapel to provide for liturgical needs. Pu-k'ung's legacy further comprised 87 ounces of gold and 220.5 ounces of silver, which he bequeathed to two monasteries at Mount Wu-t'ai, together with mats, beds, and iron and earthenware objects. A diamond pestle with bells and rosaries, one of which was in rock crystal, with a box, were left to the Buddhist chaplaincy of the Imperial Palace.

As a stranger without family in China, however, Pu-k'ung's case was exceptional. Having come to East Asia at a very young age with his uncle, he would have lost even that relative by the time he composed his will. Furthermore, it was the administration of the monastery in which he resided that acted as guarantor for the execution of the will. The deed is signed by the bursar, the treasurer, the overseer of monks (tu wei-na), the abbot, and the dean of the Hsing-shan ssu.

Two testamentary deeds from Tun-huang show on the contrary that the lay family of the religious had a stake in the dispositions made by monks before their death, that it was eligible to inherit part of their possessions, and that their presence was required when the deed was drawn up. It also appears that it was not the nature of the possessions that was at issue—light goods or heavy goods in accordance with the Vinaya definitions—but their provenance. The family of the deceased was assuredly not entitled to claim property acquired by the monk in the course of his religious life, but it did retain the right to those of his possessions that derived from family patrimony.

Testament[68] of the nun Ling-hui.

On the twenty-third day of the tenth month in the sixth year of Hsien-t'ung (November 15, 865), having suddenly contracted a disease that has aggravated daily, the nun Ling-hui declares to her family (chu-ch'in) [then present] that none of her dispositions are made with an impaired mind but in full consciousness. Ling-hui possesses only one slave, born in her family and named Wei-niang, whom she bequeaths to her niece P'an-niang. She does not dispose of any other possessions in her cell.[69] Ling-hui requests P'an-niang to attend to the funeral arrangements after her death.

Having made these dispositions, her family will not be entitled to intervene. She had written this deed in the presence of her family to serve as subsequent proof of her dispositions. It is authenticated by the signatures.

Her younger brother Chin-kang;
The granddaughter of the So family;
Her niece, the nun Ling-kuei;

Her niece, the twelfth daughter (two fingerprints);
Her nephew, K'ang Mao (signature);
Her nephew Fu-sheng (signature);
Her nephew Shen-hsien (signature);
The water official So;
The governor-general of the left Ch'eng-chen;
Her nephew, So Chi-chi.[70]

There is no mention of the furniture, provisions, cloth, and miscellaneous possessions this nun must have owned. It is thus by virtue of their provenance that these goods could not be claimed by the lay family of Ling-hui.

Another document confirms the hypothesis that the destiny of the possessions of deceased religious depended on whether they were acquests or whether they derived from family property. This manuscript contains the testamentary dispositions made by a monk named Ch'ung-en who apparently descended from one the great families of Sha-chou.[71] This background presumably accounts for his considerable heritage:[72]

For each one hoe, one sickle, one saucepan, one . . . one cart . . . one millet silo, one copy of the *Jen-wang po-je ching*[73] are bequeathed in perpetuity to the Ching-t'u monastery. . . . Two estates along the Wu-ch'iung canal, two estates along the Yen-k'ang canal, draught oxen, saddle asses, and agricultural tools have been distributed according to the register deposited in the said monastery.

The following goods belonging to his monastic cell (*fang-tzu*) are left to the community of the entire town: seven pieces of silk cloth and of felt, one *kya*, one shirt, two suits of fine silk, stockings[74] . . . blankets, fur-lined cloaks, cloth and leather shoes, a belt set with fifteen ounces of gold and silver, silver dishes, three silk garments, a dragon beard belt, copper dishes, oil containers made of painted wood with lids and a spoon, etc., a she-ass of five years and an ass of four years.

With regard to the furniture, provisions, wagon, devotional objects (*kung-yang chü*), and Buddha vestments held by the Ching-t'u monastery, there is a separate deed. . . . The mare shall be used toward the purchase of the house to the south of the monastery, comprising a main building with outbuildings.

The goods [held by] Ch'ung-en as a result of his two terms as monastic administrator, i.e., either outstanding loans or . . . are made over to the treasurer of the monastery (*tu-ssu*).

A large bed, a partition board, and a tray in the form of a wheel made over to the Buddha Hall (*fo-tien*) for its use.

To his nephew, the monk Hui-lang, he leaves . . . and one cup worth five ounces of silver.

To his cousin, the general Yen Ying-ta, red embroidered stockings . . . to the nun Yen-ting. Aforementioned are five persons. . . .

After his impending death, an estate of twenty *mu* along the Chih-kua canal . . . a cow that he had given to his elder brother Master Fa-chu in his lifetime and that had four calves. . . .

A piece of fine, white silk, a square saucepan with handles, the body of a lamp worth seven ounces of silver, a small ivory dish . . . a four-year-old ox . . . also to the novice (*śrāmaṇerī*) I-niang.

To the monk Wen-hsin, who for many years has been his counselor in family matters inside and outside [the monastery] and who has exerted himself unstintingly, he leaves a plough ox and three *shih* of wheat as winter provision.

Little Wa-ch'ai, whom he had raised from infancy and who had grown up without ever disobeying or showing herself ungrateful, he now marries off. The little household servant, whom Ch'ung-en had bought some years ago to attend to him in his old age, he bequeaths to Wa-ch'ai to take into her service, and in order that she may not be demeaned.[75]

Clothing left behind by Ch'ung-en: [here follows a list of eleven items, including shoes, tunics, *kāṣāya*, etc.].

To the board president (*shang-shu*) . . . one mare . . . five . . . made of copper and one *hsi-lo* (?).

At the end of this deed figures an unfortunately incomplete list of legatees:

His nephew, the monk Hui-lang (signature);
His cousin, the general Yen (signed: Ying-ta);
His nephew, the governor-general (*tu-tu*) So (signature);
His nephew, the *yü-hou* So;
His nephew, the adjutant (*ping-ma [shih]*) So Ying-chih;
The husband of his niece, Ch'eng Chung-hsin;
The husband of his niece, Chang Chung-chün.

Two series of bequests were thus clearly distinguished: the first part of the deed concerns possessions bequeathed to monasteries. Some of these had already been the object of special dispositions of which the details, it is stated, had been recorded in the registers of the Ching-t'u monastery; there was also a separate deed (*pieh-wen*) concerning a set of goods that had been assigned to the same establishment. The second part is devoted to bequests made to individuals, both religious and lay. As the testament of Ling-hui already seemed to indicate, it may thus be assumed that lay relatives were entitled to part of the heritage of clergy, and that that part of the succession concerned goods that had originally been family property: the servant whom Ling-hui bequeathed to her niece had been "born in the family."[76] In the event that a religious died without leaving a will, lay relatives were perhaps legally entitled to the inheritance of possessions originally derived from family property.

This raises the question of the entitlement to the inheritance of household (hu) patrimony of those who entered religion. Normally, future monks were sent to the monasteries in their childhood or as young boys. Sometimes a small sum of money was kept in reserve for them. Entry into religion, however, could occasion the division of lands and personal estate among brothers, at least at Tun-huang. This practice was apparently peculiar to regions such as the Tun-huang area and Szechwan[77] where by T'ang times the cohesion of large households (hu) had weakened. The breaking up of the hu in Sha-chou found expression in an extreme parceling of the land into small, isolated plots of mostly less than half a hectare in size.[78]

In the Pelliot collection of manuscripts from Tun-huang is found a petition requesting the division of property between two brothers of whom the younger, named Ch'i Chou, had entered religion.[79] At the end of a detailed account of the use to which the two brothers had put their common property, and of their individual acquests, is found the following statement:

> The aforementioned Ch'i Chou had the misfortune to lose his father and mother at an early age. For some time Ch'i Chou had been living with his elder brother without having made any personal claims. Now, however, he has entered religion (ch'u-chia), and his elder brother has declared his intention of living separately.[80] These past days, Ch'i Chou and his brother have reasonably discussed the division of their [movable] property as well that of the real estate and animals. Not wishing to quibble, Ch'i Chou has preferred to offer the best of everything to his elder brother. The latter, however, giving credence to lies told by outsiders and to unfounded arguments, went about proclaiming that he had been wronged in the division. Now all this talk is untrue and should not merit the attention of a gentleman. To recapitulate: the family property required by Ch'i Chou for his ordination,[81] the possessions still held by him as well as those acquired externally, the cereals, diverse foodstuffs, the oxen and the animals at the disposal of his elder brother, seeds and quantities of

cereals that he had personally inherited from his uncle, have all been shared out and are accurately listed above. . . . Ch'i Chou requests that the cereals, diverse foodstuffs, carts, oxen, and household servants that he owned not long ago be returned to him (?). In wanting to discuss anew the division of numerous goods already settled between them, his brother seems to wish to infringe the law. Ch'i Chou hopes that you will kindly give the matter your consideration and decide upon the measures to be taken.

. . . day of the twelfth month of the year *ch'ou*, the monk Lung-tsang.

The customs no doubt varied according to regions and periods, for the division of family property between brothers can only have become current practice once land ceased to be allotted by the imperial administration and trading of landed property had become widespread.[82] The number of extant documents is not sufficient to determine conclusively how the inheritance of monks was regulated. Certain facts, however, can be ascertained: monks were able to own property that had come down to them from their families, and they were able to dispose of it at a profit.[83] The bulk of their heritage, however, devolved to the inalienable property of the monasteries.

Finally, it may be concluded that wherever the unity of the large rural family was maintained, those who entered religion had no claim on the real estate held by the *hu*. By necessity, Chinese monks were bound to own movables, while their exclusion from the *family* predisposed them toward commerce and usury.

Among all the rules regulating the inheritance of the bhikṣu in the Vinaya, one at least was upheld: that stipulating the division of the clothes of the deceased among the monastic community. It will be recalled that at the end of the dispositions made by Ch'ung-en before his death there was a list of "clothing left behind" (*wang-hou i-fu*). Since no legatee is designated for these items, it must be assumed that they were to be shared by the monks in accordance with the prescriptions of the treatises on discipline. If this practice had been preserved in China, however, it had also evolved. It had become a large-scale commercial operation and an important event in the life of the Buddhist communities. The documents from Tun-huang show how the clergy of the same parish (*chieh*, Skr. *sīmā*)[84] gathered for the auction of clothing and pieces of cloth. The proceeds were subsequently divided among the monks, nuns, and novices of both sexes.

The monk Tao-hsüan reported the custom of holding auctions as early as 626 in his commentary on the Vinaya of the Dharmaguptaka.[85] It may have been current much earlier, perhaps as early as the fifth century. In fact, the Vinaya's treatment of the subject was rather laconic, so much so that Tao-hsüan considered the practice to have been at variance with the rules of discipline:

> In the Vinaya, there is no mention of the division of [deceased monks'] property by sale; the division by sale practiced today [in China] is contrary to the law and contrary to the discipline. They are occasions for commotion and boisterous behavior. One does not think of the origin and end [of this practice] (?).[86] This custom has become the rule and would [now] be impossible to remedy.[87]

The Vinaya seem, in the end, to acknowledge a wide variety of procedures for the devolution of the light goods left by deceased monks, but distinguish above all between bequeathed possessions and possessions for which no heir had been designated, which had to be divided among the monks present. The Vinaya of the *Mahīśāsaka* recounts:

> Once a novice (śrāmaṇera) died; not knowing how to dispose of his possessions, the bhikṣu asked the Buddha. The Buddha said: "If in his lifetime he has made a gift [of his possessions] to someone, then they must be made over [to that person]. Otherwise, the monks present shall share them." One day, a bhikṣu who had few friends died, [leaving] his topgarment, his undergarment, and other objects. The bhikṣu, not knowing what [to do with them], asked the Buddha. "If he has not made a gift [of his possessions] to anyone during his lifetime," said the Buddha, "the monks present shall share them. But if in his lifetime he has made a gift [of his possessions] to someone, and if that person has not yet claimed them, then the monks must make them over to him with a double solemn declaration (jñaptidvitīyam karamavācā)."[88] A bhikṣu acting as herald shall say: "Reverend monks, listen. The bhikṣu so-and-so has died in this place. His possessions by way of clothing and other objects are now to be passed on to so-and-so by the monks present. When the saṃgha [has assembled], let the monks listen carefully. This is what we declare: . . . [the same formula again]. May all the elders who are in agreement keep their silence. If anyone is not in agreement, let him speak."[89]

Next comes the case of a deceased monk who had many friends and who had been the object of the munificence of princes, chief ministers, and private individuals. In this case, a distinction must be made between possessions that could be divided among the monks and those that were improper for the religious to own. The former were distributed in their entirety among the bhikṣu, the latter devolved to the collective property of the saṃgha.[90]

Attribution by public motion (jñaptikarma) seems to have applied especially to bequeathed property the devolution of which might otherwise have become the subject of litigation. The act of jñaptikarma was preliminary to the distribution of the goods among the monks. Tao-hsüan explains that

> once the ceremony is completed, one counts the number of monks and nuns [present] and measures out the shares accordingly. Then [the religious] cast tablets[91] to obtain their shares. According to the Vinaya of the Mahīśāsaka, if there is an insufficient number of garments, the community unanimously makes them over to one bhikṣu who has none.[92]

There is no mention in the Vinaya,[93] however, of the sale of the clothing of deceased monks. Not that the barter and purchase of petty objects were unknown among the saṃgha, but they occupied a minor role. The selling and buying of such clothing and small objects as monks were permitted to own were not prohibited within the communities, provided they did not give rise to shameful haggling ("unseemly language," pu-ching yü) and were not carried out with the intention of making a profit.

> "As of today," the Buddha declared,[94] "I authorize the sale of clothing within the community. The price [of the goods on sale] may be increased as long as it has not been called out three times." As the price increased, the bhikṣu felt regret and thought: "Shan't I take this garment?" The Buddha said: "As long as the three calls have not been completed, it is not sinful to raise the bidding."[95]

Sales by auction, however, did not appear in the treatises on discipline in connection with the division of the property of deceased monks. On the other hand, it is clear that the different Vinaya made certain allowances with regard to this practice. Only the Vinaya of the Mahāsāṃghika makes a discrete allusion to this method of sharing in distinguishing three procedures for the devolution of the light goods left by deceased monks:

1. by unanimous attribution [by public motion, *jñapti karma*] (*chieh-mo shou*);
2. by division into equal parts (*fen-fen shou*);
3. by division through sales (*mao-i fen shou*).[96]

The text, however, dwells only very briefly on this latter procedure. The Chinese were to point to different passages in the Vinaya, notably the *Sarvāstivādavinaya*, in support of the sale by auction of the minor possessions left by deceased monks:

[As for the division] of light goods within the saṃgha, a bhikṣu possessing the five dharma[97] is assigned to carry out the distribution among the monks present, for [otherwise] the shares would not be equitable. The Buddha permits that the saṃgha be assembled [for that occasion]. . . . The *Shih-sung lü* (the Vinaya of the Sarvāstivāda) says:[98] "During the sale of clothing, as long as one has not called out three times [putting the lots up for tender], the bhikṣu may raise the bidding . . ." The *Mātṛkā* (summary) [of the Mūlasarvāstivāda] says:[99] "According to the Buddha, when the dean (*shang-tso*, Skr. *sthavira*) determines the price of the garments for the first time [i.e., at the first call], it is appropriate that the price be moderate. It should be neither too high nor too low. Neither ought one to wait for the price to rise to attribute the articles. To take advantage of the absence of a taker to raise the price constitutes a sin (*duṣkṛta*)."[100]

Sales by auction (*ch'ang-i*) took place in China according to fairly precise ceremonial, as described in the *Po-chang ch'ing-kuei*:

After the funeral (*ch'a-p'i*, Skr. *śavya*), the hall master notifies the abbot and those in charge of the wings [of the monastery] that the sale will be held after the midday meal in front of the monks' hall. He informs the community according to custom by putting up a notice. . . . Inside the hall he installs a table on which he places a writing brush, an inkstone, a chimestone, scissors, cords, and the various objects required. . . . The overseer (*karmadāna*) unties the *kāṣāya* of the deceased monk, places it on the chimestone and changes the cordons. The hall master then takes each item in succession. He presents them, and they are passed from hand to hand. The *karmadāna* raises them up and says: "Such-and-such an article, number such-and-such, first call so-and-so much." If he evaluates the object at one string of [a thousand] cash, he initiates the bidding at one hundred cash. By successive calls, one thus arrives at one string of cash.[101]

We are fortunate to possess documents from Tun-huang that illustrate the importance of the great assemblies in the life of the Buddhist
monasteries in China, which were held for the sale of clothing, cloth,
and other minor articles received by the monasteries through gifts or
bequests. The custom provides a good example of the principle
according to which the possessions of the saṃgha were the common
property of the religious. Moreover, not only the small possessions of
deceased monks[102] were put on sale but also all the articles of clothing and pieces of cloth known by the special term of dakṣiṇā (Chin.
ch'en), offerings that were received by the monasteries in payment for
religious services.[103]

> The administrators of the donations (ch'en-ssu) made during the three
> past years (933–936) call a general meeting for a review of the
> accounts at the Ching-t'u monastery.
> For [an examination of] the receipts and expenditure for the past
> three years concerning all that has been received by official[104] and pri-
> vate donation, bequests made by deceased and sick monks and nuns,
> as well as . . . (?), gifts made on the occasion of vegetarian feasts (chai),
> and including the remaining balance [from the previous accounting
> period] (hui-ts'an) of gifts received previously in silk fabrics, flower
> fabrics, quilted materials, gauze, felt, cotton cloth as well as clothing
> articles, dishes and platters, items of furniture, etc., we request the
> clerical authorities (seng-shou) of the monasteries, the masters of
> Dhyāna and Vinaya, elders (su-lao), and other religious to attend the
> assembly of accounts (suan-hui) at the Ching-t'u monastery. Follow-
> ing is the complete list of names for each and all of the auction sales
> held by the monks and nuns within our religious district:
> Year ssu (933): articles of clothing received from officials yielded
> 2,320 ch'ih (ca. 696 m) of cotton cloth in the sale. The clothing arti-
> cles of the master and controller of monks (seng-t'ung) Yin yielded
> 9,032 ch'ih. Those of the master of Dharma and Vinaya (fa-lü)[105] Chia,
> 363 ch'ih. Those that Madame Yin gave before her death[106], 830 ch'ih.
> (Total for the year kuei-ssu: 12,545 ch'ih of cotton cloth).
> Year chia-wu (934): articles received by official donation yielded
> 2,320 ch'ih of cotton cloth in auction sales. One article of clothing,
> 4,810 ch'ih, another, 5,580 ch'ih. The vestments of the rector of
> monks (seng-cheng) Chang of the Lung-hsing monastery, 4,776 ch'ih.
> Those of Ching-chin of the P'u-kuang monastery, 2,918 ch'ih. (Total
> for this year: 20,404 ch'ih).
> Year i-wei (936): articles of clothing donated by the (p'u-yeh)[107]
> Ts'ao before his death yielded 3,540 ch'ih of cotton cloth. Those given
> by the grand prince (ta-wang) before his death, 8,320 ch'ih. Those of

the (ma-pu) Liang, before his death, 510 ch'ih. Those of the nun Wu-jan of the [monastery An-]kuo, 3,475. Those of the nun Hsiang-neng of the P'u-kuang monastery, 2,580. The silk tunic of Princess T'ien, 800 ch'ih. The clothes of the controller of monks (seng-t'ung) Wang, 6,382 ch'ih. Those of the master of Dharma and Vinaya Sun, 2,266. (Total for this year: 27,873 ch'ih of cotton cloth).

The above articles which were sold in auction yielded a total of 58,502 ch'ih of cotton cloth.[108]

During the past three years, a total (?) of 7 ch'ih of fine silk fabric, 5 ch'ih of raw silk material, 5 ch'ih of cotton, 128 ch'ih of raw silk, and 57 ch'ih of coarse wool material were received. Total: 1,452 ch'ih [of cotton cloth?]. [Also] received, 13 ch'ih of fine wool material, amounting to 325 ch'ih [of cotton cloth?], as well as 1,204 ch'ih of cotton cloth.

The articles of clothing sold previously and the woolen materials and cotton cloth [remaining at present] amount to a total of 61,456 ch'ih.

Expenditures: One piece of fine silk of the weaving loom (lou-chi ling) as a gift to the Empress of Khotan. Ditto for the purchase of a saddle to present to the officials. A piece of fine silk of large dimensions for the grand master of works (ssu-k'ung). A piece of fine silk woven at the loom for the location where the great assembly takes place. Two pieces of raw gauze to recompense the retainers of the Ta-yün and Yung-an monasteries.[109] Ditto for the ceremony held for the granddaughter of the lang-chün when she found her parents again . . .

The numbers of religious in our district having received shares from these donations are:

• 356 monks;
• 163 male novices (sha-mi, Skr. śrāmanera), equivalent of 81 and a half shares;[110]
• 379 fully ordained female probationers (śīkṣkanī);
• 71 female novices (ni sha-mi; Skr. śrāmanerī), equivalent of 35 and a half shares.

The total number of [shares received by the] religious amounted to 852. Monks and nuns received shares of 60 ch'ih (ca. 18 m) each; novices, both men and women, received 30 ch'ih each.

According to the preceding articles of this report, it can be seen that the remainder was more than half [of the total]. After distribution of the two kinds of shares [for the ordained religious and for novices], there remained a surplus of 4,686 ch'ih of cotton cloth.[111]

This piece is dated to the sixth month of the third year of Ch'ing-t'ai (i.e., first year of T'ien-fu, A.D. 936) and bears at the end the names of the three administrators of donations (ch'en-ssu). On the date is affixed the seal of the controller general of monks of Sha-chou (*Sha-chou tu seng-t'ung*).

Another Tun-huang manuscript, preserved in the Peking National Library, shows that, although shares were sometimes distributed to a much more limited number of religious, sales by auction remained a collective act in which all the monasteries of the region participated:

> The master of Dharma and Vinaya (*fa-lü*) Te-yung sold a pair of crimson silk shoes at auction for which he obtained 580 *ch'ih* (ca. 174 m) of cotton cloth. The distribution was as follows: for himself, 150 *ch'ih*; for Ting-chen, 150 *ch'ih*, for Teng-hui, 150; for Fu-ying of the [monastery Ling-] t'u, 150. Remainder, 20 *ch'ih*.[112]
>
> The gifts[113] formerly received by the master of Dharma and Vinaya Pao-hsüan [amounted to] 4,890 *ch'ih* (ca. 1,467 m) of cotton cloth.
>
> The rector of monks (*seng-cheng*) Yüan-ch'ing sold a quilted blanket of fine red silk at auction and obtained 1,520 *ch'ih* of cotton cloth for it. The gifts formerly received by him [amounted to] 1,000 *ch'ih*. He distributed this cloth as follows: for Hai-ming of the [monastery Ling-] t'u, 150 *ch'ih*; for Yüan-hu of the same monastery, 150 *ch'ih*; for Chih-ch'üan, 150 *ch'ih*; for Chih-yung, 150 *ch'ih*; for Fu-ying of the [monastery Ling-] t'u, 150 *ch'ih*; for Ying-ch'iu of the same monastery, 150 *ch'ih*; for Yüan-te of the same monastery, 150 *ch'ih*; for Fa-hsing of the same monastery, 150 *ch'ih*; for Ta-ying of the same monastery, 150 *ch'ih*; for Ying-hsiang of the same monastery, 150 *ch'ih*; for Ying-ch'ing of the same monastery, 150 *ch'ih*; for Ta-chin of the same monastery, 150 *ch'ih*; for Ta-yüan of the same monastery, 150 *ch'ih*; for T'ang-chi of the same monastery, 150 *ch'ih*; for Kuang-chin of the same monastery, 150 *ch'ih*. Remainder: 95 *ch'ih*.
>
> Chin-kang sold a fan at auction and obtained 55 *ch'ih* of cotton cloth for it. He attributed himself 150 *ch'ih*. Remainder: 95 *ch'ih*.
>
> Tao-ch'eng sold stockings of fine white silk at auction and obtained 170 *ch'ih* (ca. 48 m) of cotton cloth for them. The distribution was as follows: for himself, 150 *ch'ih*, as well as for the nun Lieh-fa of the [monastery P'u-] kuang. Remainder: 130 *ch'ih*.
>
> The gifts received formerly by Tao-ming [amounted to] 390 *ch'ih*.
>
> Master Tao-ying sold stockings of fine white silk at auction and obtained 300 *ch'ih* of cotton cloth for them. He also sold a blanket of yellow . . . for which he obtained 500 *ch'ih*. The distribution was as follows: for Tao-ming of the [monastery Ling-] t'u, 150 *ch'ih*; for himself, 150 *ch'ih*; for Hsiang-ting of the [monastery Ling-] t'u, 150 *ch'ih*; for T'an-hsüan of the same monastery, 150 *ch'ih*; for T'an-hui of the same monastery, 150 *ch'ih*; for Chieh-yün of the same monastery, 150 *ch'ih*; for Hsien-hui, 150 *ch'ih*; for Hsiang-t'ung of the [monastery Ta-] yün, 150 *ch'ih* . . . [the end of the document is missing].[114]

Clearly, articles of clothing and pieces of cloth were the main items sold at auction during the great assemblies of the clergy of a parish. All payments and the distributions among the monks were carried out in cotton cloth (pu). As a result, fabrics in general, whether they originated in bequests or fees paid for religious services (dakṣiṇā), became associated with a particular economic network. They remained in the hands of monks. In fact, the monasteries possessed only small reserves of fabrics in their own right. The Ching-t'u monastery at Tun-huang, for example, held in the year 930 only 681 ch'ih of cotton cloth and 97 ch'ih of fine silk fabric in store.[115] These amounts are small in comparison to the shares distributed to the individual monks and nuns (60 ch'ih, i.e., ca. 18 m, of cotton cloth in the first document cited above, and 150 ch'ih,[116] or ca. 45 m, in the second). These pieces of cotton cloth must have served the clergy as currency.

Behind the Chinese, and perhaps Serindian, custom—for the direct example of the Buddhist communities in Central Asia is surely at the origin of the Chinese phenomenon—the fusion of two practices,[117] which still appeared in isolation in the Vinaya, can be discerned: the distribution of the clothing of deceased monks, and their purchase, in case of need, within the saṃgha.

The legal rule, according to which the minor possessions of deceased monks were to be divided among the community, which can only have had secondary importance owing to the small value of the goods concerned, thus appears at the origin of the individual property owned by Chinese monks. And the same rule was instrumental in determining the type of goods that were in their possession: essentially fabrics and, more generally, fungible goods.

One of the most striking features of the life of the Buddhist communities in China is the great freedom left to the monks in the management of their property. Virtually all of them devoted themselves to activities of a profane nature, and principally to the practice of usury. The monasteries were assured of the profit from these operations for, whether by the regular process of devolution or through pious donations, the community was ultimately the beneficiary of the acquests of its members. Thus, within the monasteries themselves, the communal rules and motivations of a religious order favored the accumulation of consecrated and inalienable property (ch'ang-chu).

The conceptions pertaining to such property, however, also permitted the use of "permanent assets" for commercial operations.

They even favored such use by protecting the property invested in the lay world against any form of appropriation. Thus can be discerned the general orientation of the economy of the Buddhist communities in China. It was an economy more concerned with returns and acquisitions than with production. Its principal novelty consisted of being founded on the notion of property, a comparatively new concept in China, where with respect to the property par excellence, i.e., land under cultivation, only a right of user had been known for a very long time. The monasteries, however, enjoyed exclusive ownership of their lands, and Buddhism no doubt contributed very effectively to the extension of this right of ownership. The idea that lands could be donated, sold, and purchased appeared increasingly as the accepted norm. Hence the profound social and economic transformation that took place in T'ang times.[118] Furthermore, by introducing to China new loan instruments inherited from India, Buddhism was certainly not extraneous to the accelerating development of commerce under the T'ang.

It may concluded, then, that the profound changes in the Chinese economy between the fifth and the tenth century were due in part to the influence of Buddhism.

CHAPTER FOUR

LANDS AND DEPENDENTS

Introduction

The monastic accounts from Tun-huang in the ninth and tenth centuries all mention the same kind of revenues for the Buddhist establishments:

> [Management report of the] stewards for the year (chih-sui)[1] of the Ching-t'u monastery, Chieh-pien and Pao-ch'üan.
>
> The said Chieh-pien and Pao-ch'üan [having been in charge] since the first day of the first month of the year ting-mao (907)[2] until the first day of the first month of the year wu-ch'en (908), the monks were convened for the assembly of accounts (suan-hui) for the preceding year:
>
> Balance of the account for the preceding year (ch'ien-chang hui-ts'an), and new receipts from
> - income from lands (t'ien-shou);
> - interest on loans (li-jun);
> - levies on gardens (yüan-shui);
>
> [other management reports here include rent from oil presses (liang-k'o) and mills (wei-k'o)];
> - miscellaneous gifts (san-shih) [made on the occasion of festivals];
> - fees received for the recitation of sutra (nien-sung), spring and autumn Buddha food (ch'un-ch'iu fo-shih), alms given on the occasion of vegetarian feasts (chai-ch'en).[3]

The above enumeration follows approximately the order:

a. revenues from immovable property: rent from lands and industrial installations;
b. interest on loans;
c. various donations.

It corresponds to the descending order of magnitude of the three types of revenues that were prevalent at Tun-huang at the time of these documents. However, since in an essentially agricultural economy immovable property forms the basis of all enduring power, it is appropriate to first examine the nature and extent of the landed and immovable property of the great economic power that the Buddhist Church represented in China.

Chinese monks, who for the most part stemmed from the peasantry, did not cultivate the land. This change of lifestyle may even be considered the most tangible result of their entry into religion: in leaving the family, they also abandoned agricultural labor. The tradition introduced from the West, according to which the clergy was to be maintained by the laity, and the constant efforts of dynasties to confer official status at least on the more deserving monks, established the Chinese monastic community as a separate class that could expect to be maintained by the community at large and to evade the obligations of the ordinary laity. China did not have a monastic tradition;[4] the salaried official and privileged nobility served as models for the status of the clergy. The analogy went so far as to include the system of examinations for monks, which was instituted at an early stage by the secular powers. Chinese monks, who controlled a servile workforce and received part of the peasants' harvest, dealt with the cultivation of the land only in the capacity of administrators and managers. There was an additional rationale for this conduct: the prohibition in the Indian treatises on discipline against harming plants and animals. It was left to others to take this sin upon themselves. The Vinaya forbade the bhikṣu to dig into the soil,[5] to fell trees, and to cut grass.[6] They considered, moreover, the acts of sowing and planting to be impure and improper.[7] For the most part one finds only novices handling the hoe in the gardens and fields, for they had not yet received full ordination and were not bound to every detail of the disciplinary prescriptions:[8]

Tao-an (312–385) left family life at the age of twenty. . . . Because of his ugliness he was not highly regarded by his master who put him to work in the fields and buildings. [Tao-an] toiled for three years without respite and without ever showing the least sign of resentment.[9]

Once Fa-hsien (late fourth century) was cutting rice in the fields with several of his codisciples when some starving brigands appeared, wanting to seize their grain. The novices (sha-mi) all ran and fled, except Fa-hsien. "If you need grain," he told them, "take all you wish. But if you are famished and miserable today, sirs, it is because you have failed to give alms in the past."[10]

There were also, however, monks who worked in the fields. Judging by the accounts of the monasteries at Tun-huang, it does seem that monks participated in agricultural labor. The fact is that Buddhism in China was not the essentially monastic religion represented by the Vinaya. If, moreover, animals occupied an important place in Buddhist preaching in China, if conversion to Buddhism was primarily marked by the observance of a vegetarian diet, particularly during feasts that previously provided occasions for the consumption of *meats*, agriculture remained outside the preoccupations of Chinese Buddhists. It was not affected by the prohibition that in Indian Buddhism applied to the clergy as opposed to the laity.

The Indian treatises on discipline commended a system of land tenure and peasant serfdom:

It is not permitted to accept or keep gold, silver, or other precious substances; nor cereals, millet, rice, or peas; nor gardens in the villages, nor slaves, oxen, sheep, or carts. All such goods, gold, silver, precious substances, etc., are received by the saṃgha. As for fields and gardens, it is again the community (the saṃgha) that owns them. They are to be let to the lay servants ("pure men," ching-jen) and other laymen, and a share is to be determined that they shall provide to the saṃgha as rental (k'o). As for the cereals, vegetables, and fruit that the servants and laborers (yung-tso jen) employed as cultivators shall harvest, all such produce is impure (pu-ching) and may not be consumed by the bhikṣu.[11]

This tenure system was in fact applied in the communities that we know from the Vinaya:

A layman had repeatedly used the monks' fields without paying rent (shui) to the community. When this layman was about to sow again, an old bhikṣu went to him and said: "You have repeatedly used our fields without paying the rent. Therefore do not sow. Or, if you wish to sow, you must pay." After these words, the layman made ready to plow his furrows. The old bhikṣu then lay down on the soil to stop the plow. The layman, greatly annoyed, desisted.[12]

Between the Indian communities and the laity, however, there existed not only such purely commercial relationships, both with regard to simple slaves and to converted peasants who considered their services rendered to a holy community to be meritorious. Among the lay servants of the saṃgha (the *ching-jen*), there was a large number of farmers. In the treatises on discipline, they are designated as "garden folk" (*yüan-min* or *shou-yüan min* ["keepers of the gardens"])[13]:

At that time every year, when the cereals had just come to maturity, the peasants of the monks' gardens offered a share to the monks to eat. What is the meaning of "every year, at the time of maturation?" It means when the rice is mature, when the beans are ripe, when cheese, oil, and honey [are newly produced].[14] From each of these commodities [the peasants] deducted a small part to be left at the same place as an offering to the monks.[15]

Devout princes occasionally made a gift of this peasant labor force to the Buddhist communities, when it did not seek the patronage of the saṃgha of its own accord:

Once the venerable Piliṇgavasta, who lived in a village, was plastering his cell himself. Just then the king Bimbisāra arrived on the scene and, seeing this, said to [the monk]: "What are you doing there, teacher (*ācārya*)?" "I am plastering my cell, servant (*śūdraka*)." "Have you no attendants, then? I shall give you some garden peasants." "You mustn't, *śūdraka*." This went on three times, while the venerable steadfastly refused to accept the gift. When the villagers heard what had happened, they came to the monk and insisted: "*Ācārya*, we wish to be taken on by you as garden peasants. We shall provide for you." "If you are able to observe the [first] five precepts of Buddhism," he replied, "then I shall take you [as garden peasants]."[16]

In the early fifth century, at the time of the pilgrimage of Fa-hsien, there were still peasants in the service of Buddhist communities in India. Fa-hsien reports, concerning Madhyadeśa:

After the Buddha attained *parinirvāṇa*, princes, householders, and private individuals erected monasteries for the saṃgha. They provided the lands, residences, gardens, vegetable plots, families of the people, livestock, with charters inscribed in iron [attesting to these donations].[17] Subsequently, the successive princes of the kingdom remained faithful to this tradition and dared not abolish it. The cells and buildings where the monks resided never lacked beds, straw mattresses, food and drink, or clothing. Everywhere it is like this. The monks are solely occupied with pious works, reciting sacred texts, and sitting in meditation (dhyāna).[18]

By the time the development of Buddhism was truly under way in China, the living example of the communities in India, Central Asia, and Southeast Asia is likely to have had a greater influence on the establishment of the Buddhist Church in that country than the treatises on discipline. If the principle was well-established that, in the words of the Chinese literati, the religious be "fed for doing nothing," the status of the farmers in the service of the monasteries varied a great deal, and there were also different kinds of landed property. The same practices obtained in China as in India and in countries influenced by India: lands were given to religious institutions by the secular powers or by private individuals, and farmers were either placed under the supervision of the monasteries or spontaneously sought their patronage. Conditions peculiar to China, however, gave a special character and orientation to this religious phenomenon, which tended to create property held in perpetuity by the Church: the history, geography, legal customs, and agrarian policies of China all played a determining role here. Such analogies as existed between India and China were no more than occasional and of a general order.

Buddhist Colonization

The support Buddhism received from certain dynasties in China was so remarkable that the favors extended by the political powers could appear to the Chinese of the T'ang and later periods to be the very foundation of the religion's success. More likely, imperial patronage was only a secondary factor that is insufficient to explain the success of the religious movement in China. Official support nevertheless did have important economic consequences: it was with the support of emperors, and in accordance with conceptions peculiar to the ruling class, that the economic establishment of Buddhism took place at specific times in specific regions. It will be seen to what extent the experience examined here was abnormal and exceptional with respect to overall development of the landed property of monasteries. The different forms that the ascendancy of the monasteries over Chinese soil assumed did, however, have at least one point in common, namely that regions and lands forsaken by peasant agriculture were first exploited by the Buddhist establishments.

To expand the area of land under cultivation was an abiding concern of Chinese dynasties. In T'ang terminology,[19] the distinction between "broad localities" (k'uan-hsiang) and "restricted localities" (hsia-hsiang) was primarily fiscal; in fact, however, it has a much larger significance and is not confined to that period in history.[20] The imperial government did its utmost to encourage the resettlement of peasants from regions of high population density to arid lands where exploitation was still incipient. Under the T'ang, land allotments in the latter doubled those in the restricted localities. Peasants wishing to emigrate to arid lands were exceptionally entitled to sell not only the small gardens or orchards situated near their dwellings, which constituted lands held in perpetuity (shih-yung yeh), but also their personal share lands (k'ou-fen t'ien).[21] In arid areas, the granting of more extensive lands was the rule, for they were poorly irrigated, if at all, and required more frequent fallowing.[22] At the same time, however, the practice was intended to provide an incentive for prospective colonists to emigrate. These were in fact not restrictive shares, as in overpopulated countries, but basic allotments: "Since it is vital to clear uncultivated land and obtain the greatest possible benefit from the soil," says the T'ang-lü shu-i,[23] "no sanction is provided, however extensive the fields appropriated (chan, i.e., here, "reclaimed wasteland").

What this legislation was unable to achieve, however—because of the peasants' sentimental attachment to their land and because farmers naturally tend to settle in low-lying areas—the imperial administration put into effect by means of forced deportations of farmers. The arid regions constituted the lands of agricultural colonies (ying-t'ien) and military colonies (t'un-t'ien)[24] par excellence. At the end of the fifth century in Northern China, under the Wei, the Buddhist Church[25] too was to benefit from this forced colonization.

The essential features of the economy of the Buddhist communities already plainly appear in the fundamental fifth-century source, the "Monograph on Buddhism and Taoism," "Shih-Lao chih," of the

Wei shu.[26] This treatise informs us most precisely about an institution that was of considerable importance because it provided a solid basis for the establishment of Buddhism in northwestern China.

> The controller of Buddhist clergy T'an-yao[27] presented a memorial to the emperor in which he requested that the households of P'ing-ch'i[28] and those of the people able to supply sixty *hu* of grain each year to the Office of Buddhist clergy (*seng-ts'ao*)[29] be designated "saṃgha households" (*seng-ch'i hu*), and [the grain] "saṃgha millet" (*seng-ch'i su*). This grain was to be distributed to the starving in years of famine. He further requested that felons (*fan chung-tsui*)[30] and state slaves be classed as Buddha households and charged with the maintenance ("sprinkling and sweeping")[31] of the monasteries as well as working the fields and bringing in the harvests.[32] Emperor Kao-tsu (Wench'eng ti, r. 452–465) granted these two petitions, and the two institutions as well as that of the monastery households (*ssu-hu*) subsequently spread throughout the prefectures and garrisons.[33]

The *Fo-tsu t'ung-chi* assigns T'an-yao's memorial to the year 469, under the reign of Emperor Hsien-tsu (Hsien-wen ti, 466–471).[34] This date is very likely correct for, as Tsukamoto Zenryū noted in his excellent article on the saṃgha households,[35] the commandery of P'ing-ch'i was established in the fifth month of the third year of Huang-hsien (March/April 469).[36]

In the year 476, T'an-yao presented a further petition concerning the creation of saṃgha households. In a report to the throne dated to the Yung-p'ing reign (508–511), the president of the Department of State Affairs, Kao Chao, said:

> I respectfully submit that, in accordance with the memorial formerly presented by the then controller of Buddhist clergy, T'an-yao, in the first year of Ch'eng-ming (476), two hundred army households (*chünhu*) at Liang-chou (in the eastern part of modern Kansu), including [the family of] Chao Kou-tzu and others,[37] became saṃgha households subject to a tax in millet as a reserve for years of famine. The relief was to be granted to all, clergy or laity.[38]

In the two cases mentioned, the saṃgha households instituted at P'ing-ch'i in 469 and those of Liang-chou in 476, populations of colonists deported to open up barren lands were placed at the disposal of the Buddhist monasteries, to serve as their agricultural workforce. From the biography of Mu-jung Po-ao,[39] it is known that the commandery of P'ing-ch'i had been founded in order to receive part of the population of the two captured cities. "Their excess population was reduced to slavery and distributed among the officials."[40] In short, the saṃgha households were subjected to forced agricultural labor. The sixty *hu* of millet demanded of them annually represented a particularly heavy contribution—probably close to half of their harvest. During a military expedition in which the emperor took part in 473,[41] an annual tax of fifty *shih* (fifty *hu*) was imposed on ten percent of the population in the prefectures and garrisons, for the needs of the army. This constituted an exceptional measure. An institution analogous to, and approximately contemporaneous with that of the saṃgha households informs us indirectly about the nature of the colonies in question which as such were nothing to do with Buddhism. A decree of the twelfth year of T'ai-ho (488) ordered:

> Let a special Office of Agriculture (*nung-kuan*) be instituted in order to recruit one tenth of the population constituting the households of the prefectures and commanderies to form military colonies (*t'un-min*).
>
> It shall examine which soils are suitable with respect to humidity and determine the numbers of *ch'ing* and of *mu* [to be allotted]. Using [confiscated] ill-gotten goods they shall purchase various implements. They are to purchase oxen to provide to the peasants according to regulations, and to put those families to work to the full extent. Each farmer is required to pay an annual tax of sixty *hu*. These peasants, however, are exempted from all regular taxes as well as the various civil and military corvée duties.[42]

It is possible to catch a glimpse here of the organization of the saṃgha households. They were farming under supervision. Possibly, the *seng-ch'i hu* were divided into cultivation units with collective responsibility, as were the monastery households at Tun-huang under the T'ang.[43] And when it was decided to institute the saṃgha households, it was surely also envisaged that the monasteries would provide the implements and oxen necessary for the exploitation of the land, for the *seng-ch'i hu* clearly had to work poorly irrigated soils; the type of cereal cultivated is in itself revealing: millet, while more labor-intensive than wheat (283 days per annum as against 177),[44] is on the other hand content with a dry soil and comparatively drought-resistant.[45]

If the organization of the saṃgha households and the principle underlying its institution were not entirely Chinese, as will be seen, the same could not be said of its objective: the saṃgha millet was to supply the price-regulating granaries[46] and to bring relief against the virtually chronic famine at that time.[47] For what reason, however, was a public service, which should normally have come under the authority of secular officials, under these circumstances entrusted to the Church? There may have been several motives. The establishment of colonies and the clearing of new lands for cultivation required significant funds, and the Church, grown rich in this period of intense faith, disposed of the sums necessary for the purchase of plow animals, plowing implements, and other equipment. This consideration, however, does not constitute a sufficient explanation. Even if the institution was fundamentally Chinese, the Church at least retained the right to use the millet kept in reserve for its own benefit and for pious purposes, whether for the upkeep of the monks or for liturgical needs. The fact alone that the distributions of grain to the starving were assured by the monasteries changed their character from material relief to charitable donation. It was acknowledged that acts of charity belonged to the domain, and constituted a privilege, of the Buddhist Church. Moreover, as the secular authorities proved incapable of relieving famines,[48] it was hoped that a population perhaps already under the sway of Buddhism[49] would let itself more easily be guided by monks. In serving the Three Jewels, they would be conscious of gaining merit and show greater enthusiasm for work. Even if the monks proved scarcely more lenient in their administration than the secular officials, the religious merit of the institution would in any event do credit to the ruling dynasty. The court was devout, and T'an-yao enjoyed the emperor's confidence.

The great monks who held the office of controller of Buddhist clergy (tao-jen t'ung, renamed sha-men t'ung by T'an-yao), seem to have been influential counselors in all religious matters. Thanks to them, the Wei emperors were probably informed about the basic rules of Buddhist discipline.[50] Indeed, the institutions of the saṃgha households and the Buddha households do not appear to have been pure inventions on the part of T'an-yao. He was, on the contrary, very likely to have been inspired by the Indian treatises on discipline. A passage in the Vinaya of the Sarvāstivāda says in fact:[51]

The Buddha permitted staff to be employed for the dwellings of the monks and also for the [buildings of the] Buddha (fo-t'u)[52]. These servants belonged either to the Buddha or to the community [according to their assignment]. They constituted what is known as human resources (jen-wu). As for nonhuman resources (fei-jen wu), the Buddha allowed that elephants, horses, camels, oxen, sheep, mules, and donkeys be owned by the Buddha and the saṃgha. These were what is known as nonhuman assets.

T'an-yao's distinction between Buddha households and saṃgha households is already present in this brief passage. The institution thus appears as an original synthesis of elements borrowed from the Indian treatises on discipline and the political tradition of China. It was entirely an imperial creation, and a creation of court monks. Emperors appear moreover to have liberally disposed of the saṃgha millet for the celebration of the official cult. A decree of Emperor Kao-tsu stated in 497:

> It is appropriate to order the monks in the prefectures to institute public sermons (chiang-shuo) during the monastic retreat this summer for every three hundred persons in large prefectures, for two hundred in medium-sized, and one hundred in small ones; the saṃgha millet (seng-ch'i su) shall provide for all these ceremonies. If the millet is scarce, or if the number of religious falls below the determined figure, the Bureau of Sacrifices (chao-hsüan [ts'ao])[53] shall be ordered to reduce [the quantities of millet] and to report to us [the measures taken].[54]

Very likely, joint commissions of monks and secular officials laid down the special legislation regulating the operation of the seng-ch'i hu and referred to in a memorial cited in the "Shih-Lao chih."[55] The influence of the treatises on discipline on the creation of the saṃgha households is as evident as the intervention of the secular powers; at the very foundation of that institution lay the notion of a common property belonging to the universal saṃgha that could not be alienated, whether for the benefit of individual monks or monasteries.[56] The Buddhist Church as a legal entity could the better substitute for the state and its officials as religious discipline forbade its members to appropriate the goods of the community. This seemed to provide an assurance against misappropriations, though it did not prove to be effective. In his report dated to the Yung-p'ing reign (508–511), Kao Chao said:

> According to the Vinaya, the saṃgha households may not belong to particular monasteries. Yet in a petition submitted to the emperor, the general overseers (tu wei-na, Skr. karmadāna) Seng-hsien, Seng-

p'in, and others, having succumbed to their passion [for gain], and in violation of imperial orders as well as their own discipline, have sought to obtain the promulgation of an [iniquitous] decree and have caused [the peasants] to fill the streets with their grumblings, abandon their children, and take their own lives. More than fifty have strangled or drowned themselves. Is this a way to show respect for the generous intentions of the emperor? [These monastic functionaries] have gravely undermined the faith of the emperor. They have led the people to roam the streets shouting and groaning, with no one before whom they can lay their grievances.[57]

The terms of the decree to which Kao Chao referred are unknown. One can imagine that it sanctioned a rather predictable evolution: the transformation of the saṃgha households into monastery households (ssu-hu), and that in stressing the autonomy of the Offices of Buddhist Clergy (seng-ts'ao), it confirmed the failure of the institution. As Kao Chao indicated in his memorial, the saṃgha households came under monastic jurisdiction and could not have recourse to secular officials. This particular status went hand in hand with a complete economic dependence revealed in an imperial decree of 511:

The saṃgha millet was originally intended as relief in the form of loans (ch'u-tai) in years of scarcity and was to be stored up in years of abundance. The monks and nuns in mountainous and wooded regions were to be provided with grain according to their needs, and when the people were destitute, they too were to receive immediate aid. Out of cupidity, however, the directors [of the Offices of Buddhist Clergy] seek to derive large interests [from the millet advanced in periods of scarcity], and when the debts are due they do not take humidity or drought into account. At times, the interest exceeds the principal; at times, the contracts (ch'üan-ch'i) are altered. They press the poor without limit. The lamentations and sufferings of the people increase from year to year and from month to month. . . . From now onward, [the management of the saṃgha millet] is withdrawn from the karmadāna overseers (wei-na tu-wei). The prefects shall conduct inquiries and the Department of State Affairs will be responsible for administering the centers in which the grain of the saṃgha [is stored]. They shall prepare inventories of all that is held in storage in each of their prefectures as well as accounts of entries and outgoings, of interests and of relief in millet. They shall note the dates of the loans and repayments. . . . Whenever the interest exceeds the principal, and in the event that the terms of the original contracts have been altered, the debt shall be annulled in accordance with the code (i-lü), and it will not be permissible to demand repayment of the claim. . . . The rate [of interest] (k'o)

required on repayment of the debt shall be determined in complete
accordance with the ancient regulations (i-chun chiu-ko).[58]

The response of the state, on the eve of a long period of discord at the
beginning of the sixth century, against the abuse of the power that it
had voluntarily conferred upon the Church, far from marking a return
to normal management, only highlights the decadence of the institution. The total power of the monasteries over part of the peasantry, a
constant feature of the history of Buddhism in China, was especially
apparent in the former regions of colonization. The economic pressure of the religious establishments manifested itself above all in
regions where it had historically the greatest freedom to exert itself.
The saṃgha households were the model for a particular type of Buddhist colonization of which traces were still to be found at Tun-huang
(in modern Kansu) in the ninth and tenth centuries.

After citing the petition in which T'an-yao had first requested the creation of the saṃgha households, the "Shih-Lao chih," in the passage
quoted above, added that "the two institutions, as well as that of
monastery households (ssu-hu) subsequently spread throughout the
prefectures and garrisons." The Buddhist establishments in the Tun-
huang region three centuries later had "monastery households."
These serfs appear in different documents where they are designated
either as ssu-hu or by the expression "households held in perpetuity"
(ch'ang-chu po-hsing).

Naba Toshisada has drawn attention to the text of a Tun-huang
manuscript of great interest,[59] in which he saw a "proclamation for
the preservation of the privileges of the Buddhist monasteries." This
incomplete document follows a legend concerning the "avatars of the
four animals (ssu-shou yin-yüan)." The kapila bird, the hare, the
monkey, and the white goose, after having sworn an oath of brother-
hood, accumulate meritorious acts and are destined to be reborn in
heaven as Tathāgata, Śariputra, Maudgalyāyana, and Ananda. This
legend and the text that follows it were apparently intended to be read
in the popular sermons (su-chiang) so widely preached under the
T'ang. Following is a tentative translation—owing to its many
obscure expressions—of the fragment in question.[60]

Thanks to the tranquil prosperity of the territories under our administration (tzu kuan-nei), the inhabitants of faraway countries desire to
come to our halberd gates.[61] We excel at subduing these. . . . It is as

though they came without being called. In the past they were ferocious enemies; now they have become ordinary [settled] folk (po-hsing) and diligent workers.[62] Aware of the immense power of the Three Jewels (triratna) and of the Four Deva Kings, they show even more respect and obedience. Imbued with this thought from morning to evening, how can one be indolent? When today our great assembly comprising two bodies (monks and nuns?) presents petitions or has recourse to official tribunals, setting out the matter in every detail from the beginning, how could [the secular authorities] dare not accede to its wishes?[63] The numerous contracts and petitions are properly executed in every detail. . . . The religious buildings in our district were founded by imperial order[64] or were completed and embellished by sages (i.e., emperors). The dwellings, mansions, estates, and the fields within [the monasteries] and without, all derive from pious donations. Our peasant families (hu-k'ou) and domestic servants (chia-jen) were offered to us by great donors (t'an-yüeh; Skr. dānapati, "titular benefactors") and intended to fill our buildings in perpetuity, as a hereditary endowment. Those who live in the world congratulate and glorify us. We must not be robbed of our property, nor must it be appropriated; on the contrary, our prosperity must be increased and furthered and [our buildings] embellished. This prosperity neither declines nor is exhausted. It is known as permanent (ch'ang-chu). All this accords with the ancient rules [of discipline]. It is as a mountain and cannot be displaced. With the exception of individuals formerly enfranchised by the deceased grand guardian (t'ai-pao)[65] or other imperial commissioners who issued them with deeds [of enfranchisement?], all the others serve, exactly as in the past, in the estates (chuang), water mills (shui-wei), and oil presses [within the territory] administered by our monasteries (ssu so-kuan) and apply themselves to their tasks. From now onward, all these goods shall be property held in perpetuity,[66] above [i.e., among valuables] to a needle, below [i.e., among things of little value] to a blade of grass, including the families (jen-hu), from the old to the youngest. No one shall be permitted to cause the alienation of these goods by taking advantage of his power or influence. As for the administration of goods loaned at interest, if certain [debtors] do not comply with this rule [and attempt to keep the amount borrowed], it shall be permitted . . . to bring the matter before the officials by petition; such people shall be severely punished. The property held in perpetuity shall be restored to the monastery and the fine shall be determined by the owner [himself].

The kinship relations of the households held in perpetuity (ch'ang-chu po-hsing) [are governed by] the five ritual precepts (wu-li). They are permitted to contract marriages within their own class, but may not marry peasants subordinate to the secular administration (hsiang-ssu po-hsing). In the event, however, that this rule is violated, and that a man held in perpetuity (*ch'ang-chu chang-fu*) indulges himself after his own inclinations and has relations with a woman subordinate to the secular administration, the child that she will bear, whether a girl or a boy, shall be assigned to the property held in perpetuity and shall permanently remain with the families [of the monasteries]. From generation to generation, our people are to devote themselves fervently to their work. . . . Children and adults, every one of them, shall comply with the taxes and labor services (*k'o-i*) levied by the monastery.

The prohibition to marry externally applied to the households held in perpetuity, the fact that the monasteries claimed the offspring in the event of "illegitimate" births, and the hereditary nature of the families' dependence on the Buddhist establishments plainly indicate that this was a class of serfs. Despite their strict subjection, however, they were not slaves (*nu-pi*). With a plot of land to cultivate, a trade to exercise (milling, oil pressing), and impositions (*k'o*) to pay in exchange for fields allocated to them or for the use of mills and presses, they enjoyed relative economic freedom.[67] At the same time, they depended, at least in fact if not by right, entirely on the monasteries. For the secular administration maintained a right of inspection over these families. Always conciliatory and always prepared to favor the monks, it was nevertheless informed about the number of peasants of the monasteries. In the accounts from an establishment at Tun-huang[68] figures the following item of expenditure: "Seven *sheng* of flour for the monks to prepare a census of the families for the use of the officials." A fragment from such a census also survives:

List of members, young and old, sons and grandsons, of the households held in perpetuity by the Pao-en monastery, this eleventh day of the tenth month of the year *ping-shen* (876 or 936?):
Family Chang Pao-shan. Son I-ch'eng, spouse A-yang. Son Ch'ou-tzu, spouse A-shih. Granddaughters Ts'an-wo, Seng-wo, Mai-ch'ai, Hui-yu, Hui-nu [ten persons].
Family Chang Yüan-t'ung, spouse Ting-niu. Younger brother Ts'ai-ch'ang, spouse Sheng-tzu, sons Fu-hsing, Hui-hsing, Hui-yu, daughter Ts'un-tzu [eight persons].
Family Yen Hai-ch'üan. Yonger brothers Hai-jun, Hai-ting, Hai-ch'ang. Mother A-chang. Sons Yüan-ch'ang, Yüan-t'ai. Sons Yüan-ts'un, Ts'un-tzu, Ts'un-yu, Ts'un-sui, Ts'un-hsing, Ts'un-sheng. Spouses I-tzu, Sheng-jui, Chang-t'ai. Daughter Wu-niang [seventeen persons].
Family Yen Ts'un-sui. Mother A-fan. Daughter Chang-t'ai [three persons].

Family Chao Yüan-chang. Younger brothers Yüan-shan, Chang-tzu, Liu-lang. Spouses Lien-ssu, Chang-niu. Sons Ting-chang, Ts'un-ting, Ting-hsing. Former spouse (? *ch'ien-ch'i*) Yüan-wo [ten persons].
Family Li Ting-yu. Spouse Yüan-t'ai . . .
Family Shih Pao-ch'üan. Younger brother . . .[69]

These large families, which formed around the head of the household (the father or eldest brother), his wife and descendants, female ascendants, younger brothers, and their wives and descendants, varied considerably in size. The present sample includes one family of seventeen members and one of three. The type of kinship organization that survived on the lands of the monasteries was traditional, for it is known that elsewhere, among the free peasants in the Tun-huang region, the great peasant family had for the most part split into smaller units.

Another peculiarity of the families of the monastic serfs is that they were organized into cultivation groups (*t'uan*) with collective responsibility. For each of these, the head of one of the households acted as the head of the group (*t'uan-t'ou*).[70] That is what emerges from numerous petitions presented by families of monasteries to obtain advances in cereals or seed.

> Petition of the families (*jen-hu*) of Pao-en monastery requesting the steward of the granary (*tu-ssu ts'ang*) to supply them with twenty-five loads (*t'o*)[71] of wheat:
> Reason: the families of the said monastery are lacking grain for seed and for their provisions for the year. Requesting today the amount of grain indicated above, they determine the eighth month in autumn as the date for its restitution [to the granary]. They hope that the matter will receive due deliberation and ask kindly to be advised.
> Note of the head of the group (*t'uan-t'ou*) Liu Sha-sha, this . . . day of the second month of the year *ch'ou*.[72]

> Petition of the families of the Chin kuang-ming monastery, presented by the head of the group Shih T'ai-p'ing [and] the families An Hu-hu, An Chin-han, An Ta-tzu, and Seng-nu. The families indicated above are totally lacking in provisions and seed. In their state of destitution, it is difficult for them to act. They have sought to obtain [resources], but to no avail. They request to be supplied with twenty loads of wheat, which they shall return [to the granary] in accordance with the amount indicated. They hope that the master of instruction (*chiao-shou ho-shang*)[73] will be so kind as to deliberate [the matter] and ask to be advised.
> Respectful notification of the above petition.

Note of the monastery household (*ssu-hu*) Shih T'ai-p'ing and the other families [of the same group], this . . . day of the second month of the year *ch'ou*.[74]

.⌣ ⌣.

Petition of the families under the authority (*t'ou-hsia* of the head of the group Liu Chin-kuo of the nunnery Ling-hsiu, [comprising] the families Wang Chün-tzu, Ch'iu Hai-ch'ao, and Ho Tsai-sheng . . . [75]

According to the petitions edited by Hsü Kuo-lin in his *Tun-huang shih-shih hsieh-ching t'i-chi yü Tun-huang tsa-lu*, the average amount of wheat requested by each family was 5 loads (4.35 *shih*):

	Number of families	Number of loads
p. 119	8	40
p. 120	1 group (5–6 f. ?)	25
p. 121	5	20
p. 122	4	20
p. 123	4 groups	50 per group
p. 124	7	30

Apparently the cultivation groups varied in size: there were groups of four, five, seven, and eight families.

Loan requests[76] were presented in the second month (approximately March) and repayments took place after the harvest in the autumn, toward the end of September. These documents are not actual *contracts*; there were no witnesses and the advances were simply to be restored by the same amounts. The dependence of the monastery households on the establishments to which they belonged by hereditary succession meant that there was no justification for loans with interest. Furthermore, to use the expression from Roman Law, such advances fell within the domain of "natural obligations."

Usually, the sanction provided for failure to restore the borrowed commodities is not even mentioned. It is, however, in the following petition where the debtors commit themselves to repay double the amount of the commodities borrowed if they exceed the agreed time limit:

Petition to the K'ai-yüan Monastery.
The families (*jen-hu*) request to borrow forty loads of wheat from the steward [of the granary]. The family [Chang] Seng-nu and the others request the supply of the amount of cereals indicated above

because they are at present lacking in seed grains and in provisions for the year. They themselves determine that autumn shall be the time limit for the restitution, and they shall return this grain at the agreed date. In the event that they exceed this time limit, they ask that the amount of wheat be doubled (pei). They hope to be advised after due deliberation of their petition.

Respectful petition of the monastery household (ssu-hu) Chang Seng-nu and the other families [of the same cultivation group], this . . . day of the second month of the year ch'ou.[77]

Shih Nu-tzu,
Shih Sheng-nu,
Chang Sheng-nu,
Chang Ti-ti,
Shih I-fu,
Shih Ch'ü-lo.

[The family names (hsing) are written under the character hu ("household") so as to form a single character].[78]

A different case obtained when families of a monastery solicited loans from an establishment other than that to which they belonged. As in the case of loans contracted by free peasants, a simple petition (chuang) or notification (tieh) did not suffice in that case, but the drawing up of a contract (ch'i) became necessary. Sometimes the deposit of a pledge was required, or the presence of guarantors and witnesses. The deed also always indicated the sanction provided in the event of default, namely the seizure of movable effects and animals.[79] However, no interest was charged in this case either.

There are other documents in which monastery households appear organized in cultivation groups. One of them shows that in addition to the imposition in cereals, which must have been on the basis of half of the harvest, the ssu-hu had to pay a tax in fodder, which at that time was provided in all the establishments at Tun-huang:

The eleventh day of the tenth month of the second year Ching-fu (893), the deputy controller of monks (fu seng-t'ung), the rector general of monks (tu seng-cheng), the rector of monks (seng-cheng), the recorder of the clergy (seng-lu), the masters of the Law and of Vinaya,[80] and the [monks or secular officials acting as?] executive officers ([tu-ssu] p'an-kuan) gathered in the fodder compound (ts'ao-yüan) to verify (?) the levies in fodder. Each payment was inscribed as follows:

Yen Li-li and Wu Ch'eng-nu of
    the eastern group (tung-t'uan)   200 bales

Ts'ao P'ing-nu of the central group
　　(*chung-t'uan*) of the [Ta-] yün [monastery]　　　　　　50 bales
Shih Hsing-hsing of the
　　K'ai- [yüan monastery]　　　　　　　　　　　　　　30 bales
Tung Chin of the
　　[Ta-] ch'eng [monastery]　　　　　　　　　　　　　40 bales
Shih . . . of the Lien- [t'ai monastery]　　　　　　　　　70 bales
Li . . . of the [Pao-]en [monastery]　　　　　　　　　　34 bales
So . . . of the western group (*hsi-t'uan*)　　　　　　　50 bales
Chang . . . -yang of the
　　Yung-[an monastery]　　　　　　　　　　　　　　　50 bales
Shih Hsing-yüan of the
　　[Ling-]t'u [monastery]　　　　　　　　　　　　　　50 bales
An Pao-pao of
　　Chin [kuang-ming monastery]　　　　　　　　　　　50 bales
Shih Hsing-tzu of the
　　P'u-[kuang monastery]　　　　　　　　　　　　　　64 bales[81]

The contributions of six or seven Tun-huang monasteries are missing here, and the text is certainly incomplete.

It is highly unlikely that the monasteries all imposed a levy in fodder on their peasant families at the same time for their own needs; it seems, rather, that these bales of fodder represented a tax levied by the secular administration, and that they were intended for the armies in the district of Ho-hsi.[82]

The monastery households at Tun-huang represent a type of the servile population corresponding to that of the saṃgha households instituted by T'an-yao. Yet they differed in several respects: they belonged not to the universal saṃgha but to specific monasteries, and, even though the wealth of certain Buddhist establishments permitted them to extend numerous loans to farmers in need, the very principle of the price-regulating granary as a public service had disappeared. Finally, if in the early period the *ssu-hu* had been able to participate in the clearing of new land, that was no longer the case in ninth and tenth century Tun-huang, for that region, in particular the soil situated within the river valley, was well irrigated and intensively cultivated. Nevertheless, it is possible that memories of the *seng-ch'i hu* had not entirely vanished in these border lands.

That Buddhism played the role of a large-scale colonizer during the period from the Northern Wei to the T'ang is by all accounts certain. Regions with inferior or dry soils constituted lands of choice for the

Buddhist Church because of the investment facilities of which it disposed, because of its internal organization and administrative aptitude, and perhaps also because of the sympathies that it encountered in the regions of the Northwest, to a greater extent than elsewhere. Undoubtedly, Buddhism played a part in the appreciable population growth that occurred in the Kansu region between the Six Dynasties period and the T'ang.[83]

In examining the formation of the monasteries' landed property, two entirely different types of law must be distinguished: that pertaining to real estate, on the one hand, which had a bearing on the lands themselves,[84] and on the special category of lands constituted by hills, valleys, and mountains,[85] and, on the other hand, the law pertaining to personal property, which was applied to cultivators and the products of their labor. The latter was normally exercised by the political authorities over the peasantry, though it was on occasion delegated. For this ancient type of ownership in China must be reserved the term *appanage* (*feng*). The institution of the saṃgha households[86] provides an example of an endowment of that kind, which doubtless had a considerable historical import. Apart from this remarkable attempt to adapt the distinctive conceptions of the ruling class to the needs of the Church, however, it may be said that the system scarcely extended to the monasteries.[87] References to appanages granted to monasteries are rare:

In the year 479, the Ch'i-hsing monastery of Mount Ch'i-hou built by the monk Hsüan-ch'ang, received by imperial order one hundred commoner families who were assigned to its service and exempted from taxation (*chüan*).[88]

At the end of the sixth century, the Prince of Chin made an additional gift of seventy families to the monastery, drawn no doubt from his personal appanage.[89]

When irrigated fields were allotted to monasteries, it was understood that it was not the actual ownership of the fields that fell to the monastery, but the right to collect the taxes. According to a stele of the Miao-hsien monastery at Mount Chi-t'ing,[90] in Hsüan-chou county (modern Hsüan-ch'eng, Anhwei), that place of worship had received irrigated land as "lands held in perpetuity" (*yung-yeh*); in 592, Yang Jung, who had just been promoted prefect of Hsüan-chou with special duties as overseer of monastic constructions (*chien tsao-ssu*), proposed to confer the official title of Miao-hsien monastery on this sanctuary (ch'ieh-lan), which had been founded the previous year by the monk Chih-yen (516–601). The emperor himself wrote the characters for this name for the entrance tablet (t'i-o).[91] And he ordered that a gift of two ch'ing and fifty mu (i.e., more than 13 ha) of irrigated fields be made to the monastery as lands held in perpetuity (yung-yeh). The same stele, however, goes on to reveal that fifty households from the surroundings of the monastery were assigned to it as appanage (feng) to serve in perpetuity in the maintenance of the buildings ("sprinkling and sweeping"). All the evidence suggests that the lands in question were cultivated and occupied by peasants from the neighborhood: the question of the ownership of the land did not arise. The important fact remains that the produce of these lands was assigned, on a permanent basis, to the needs of the sanctuary. In fact, the land belonged to whomever cultivated it. This customary rule, which remained valid in China in later periods, and the memory of which persisted even into modern times, was neither founded upon nor implied the notion of property.[92]

On balance, this form of indirect possession seems to be the exception in the history of the monasteries' landed property. From the beginning, permanent foundations analogous to those of tombs and sanctuaries were the rule. These exclusive possessions formed the nucleus of the monasteries' property and served as models for all subsequent acquisitions.[93] The consecration of anything had to be definitive. Thus the families made over to Buddhist establishments remained attached to them in a hereditary manner. In time, the control and protection of the secular powers were no longer felt. The history of the saṃgha households illustrates this development well, and the Tun-huang manuscripts provide direct evidence of the state of servitude to which the peasant monastery households found themselves reduced in the end.[94]

Other spontaneous phenomena, however, were analogous and essentially equivalent to the political act constituted by the conferral of an appanage: peasants sought the patronage of Buddhist communities of their own accord, and agreed voluntarily to supply a part of their harvests for the needs of the sanctuaries. These were not simple offerings but involved pious permanent endowments—in other words, the enfeoffment of the Buddhist Church.

A Chinese work reports the following anecdote, which is significant in more than one respect:

Under the Eastern Chin, during the I-hsi reign (405–418), a ferocious tiger ravaged Hsin-yang county. In [a village of] that county, the inhabitants had installed a sanctuary beneath the great tree of the soil god. The population of the environs numbered in the hundreds, and every night one or two of them fell victim to the tiger. One day the monk Fa-an passed through this village on his travels. Since the inhabitants had closed the gates of the village and of their houses early for fear of the tiger, Fa-an went and sat the whole night in meditation (dhyāna) beneath the tree. Toward dawn, he heard the tiger lay down [the body of] a man to the north of the tree. At the sight of the monk, the animal appeared at once joyful and fearful, prancing and crouching before him. Fa-an then preached the Law and transmitted the precepts of Buddhism to [the animal]. After a while, having remained prostrate and motionless on the ground, the tiger disappeared. When day had come, the villagers who had set out to look for the tiger were amazed to find the monk beneath the tree. They considered him a supernatural being (shen-jen). The news spread throughout the county, and people came in throngs to pay him homage, and they transformed the village temple into a Buddhist chapel. The tiger's ravages ceased from then on. The local inhabitants transformed the temple of the soil god into a Buddhist monastery where they invited Fa-an to reside, making over the surrounding fields and gardens as permanent assets for his community.[95]

The villagers continued to cultivate the fields and gardens they had *donated* in perpetuity, but assigned the harvest from these lands to the upkeep of the monk and the requirements of the cult. Donation here does not correspond to the actual conveyance of a good, even though the result is identical to that of a transfer of ownership.

It would appear that in the course of history many incidents analogous to that recounted in this anecdote occurred. Around the places of worship new groups formed that maintained relations, both moral and economic, with the monks. The integration of these faithful into the Buddhist Church was more or less equivocal. There is evidence of the creation of networks of personal relationships: peasant-monks (ju-tao in the sixth century, po-hsing seng at Tun-huang),[96] villages of converted and tonsured peasants.[97] This touches on a phenomenon extending beyond the strictly economic sphere. Religious motivations and the desire for material protection[98] encouraged the tendency towards the enfeoffment of the Buddhist Church. During periods when the secular powers willingly relinquished their ascendancy, the Buddhist Church grew even more powerful. Such modifications of the social structure were possible in times of trouble. In normal times, however, the imperial administration exercised an efficient control over the free peasantry, which provided the greater part of its tax revenues and labor services.[99]

This size of this class of dependents, formed by peasants who escaped the control of the secular authorities because they had entered into the service and the patronage of the monks, thus depended on the prevailing political conditions. Always ready to adapt and expand, the development of this class depended, however, on conceptions that were already on the decline: ties of a personal nature tended to be replaced by purely economic relationships. The introduction of farmland into commercial circulation from the end of the sixth century onward[100] was to completely change the appearance of the Chinese world. China under the Sung was so profoundly different from the China of the Six Dynasties, the social transformation so perceptible between the sixth and the tenth century, that historians are naturally inclined to regard the intervening period as one of the great turning points in Chinese history. It is therefore not accidental that the sixth century is the period in which one finds the greatest number of voluntary dependents attached to monasteries and monks.[101] At that time, two to three million peasants were engaged in the service of the monks, and counted among the clergy,[102] in North China. This type of laity, however, was also not unknown in the South, and the following text provides information on this particular class of dependents:

> Kuo Tsu-shen (early sixth century) estimated the number of Buddhist establishments in the capital (modern Nanking) at more than five hundred, and their luxury was extreme. He estimated the number of monks and nuns at more than one hundred thousand. Their property and revenues were considerable. As for the commanderies and counties, [their numbers] exceeded all proportion. Moreover, the monks had lay followers (po-t'u) [at their service], and the nuns raised female [acolytes] (yang-nü). All these people were not registered by the census.[103] . . . May the [training of] lay [dependents] and the raising of female [acolytes] be prohibited [proposed Kuo Tsu-shen]. Let [instead] the possession of slaves be authorized. The slaves shall wear only black cotton cloth.[104] Let the monks and the nuns be obliged to follow a vegetarian diet exclusively. . . . If these steps are not taken, it is to be feared that monasteries will be founded everywhere and that lay families will one by one take the tonsure until in the end the empire will not be left with the least patch of land nor the last subject.[105]

Not only was a servile labor force thus absorbed by the monasteries but the peasantry in the environs also spontaneously supplied part of the harvest to them. This is undoubtedly what the concluding phrase of the report referred to: "in the end the empire will not be left with the least patch of land nor the last subject."

The Formation of the Landed Estates

The opposition between lowlands and highlands is probably the dominant feature of the rural history of China. The alluvial plains were the regions of traditional cultivation. This is where the population density was highest[106] and where most of the farmland was found. It is no accident that topography had such a tyrannical effect in China: it was due to agricultural techniques. Irrigation was indispensable to obtain high yields of wheat and millet in the dry climate of the North, and even more so for rice cultivation in the South, which was really profitable only on flooded paddies. The law accorded with this bipartite division of the land and with the nature itself of landed property. The large-scale farming lands, on alluvium soils, constituted properties that could be shared, divided, and exchanged at will: it sufficed, if necessary, to shift the dikes. These lowlands could be *used* but not owned, and this was certainly due to conceptions that were perennial and ran deep. It was not, as might be supposed, the result of an arbitrary decision on the part of the political authorities. The partition of the lowlands among the farmers corresponded to a peasant tradition to which the political powers yielded, and that they adapted to their own needs, by regulating the modalities, but that they would have been incapable of imposing. Furthermore, if it were necessary to adduce evidence of the persistence of these conceptions, it could be found in the law itself: by the eighth century, the trading of lands had already become customary, yet a century later the law was still loath to admit the idea of absolute land ownership and offered no more than feeble guaranties to buyers.[107]

It is significant that the law which at the beginning of the T'ang dynasty endeavored to protect farmland and to maintain the principle of lifetime allotments ("personal share lands") was, on the contrary, much more lenient with regard to fallow lands: these alone were susceptible to appropriation.[108] All lands outside large-scale cultivation could become transmissible goods. This was the case of the small peasant garden situated within a zone of habitation, at a distance from the irrigated fields; it was also the case of tomb lands and of the estates of the upper classes (*ming-t'ien* under the Han, *pieh-shu* and *chuang-yüan* at the beginning of the T'ang).[109] All of these private properties, the lands held in perpetuity (*yung-yeh*) by peasants and the estates of the great families, shared characteristic features and a particular appearance that distinguished them radically from irrigated lands: they were planted with trees, consisted of gardens and pastures, and were situated on hills, hillocks, or in valleys. If they included fields, then these had been reclaimed from the bush[110] and were used to grow drought-resistant crops. If low-lying lands had been annexed, it was merely the result of later developments that permitted wealthy landowners to snatch fields from the peasants who had the use of them.

It was within such untilled islets, which had emerged in the middle of irrigated fields, on uneven terrain, on mountains, in valleys, or on hillsides, that most of the monasteries were established. If a general indication can be derived from the documents that may serve as a common thread through the complex history of the landed estates of Buddhist establishments in China, it is this: in most cases, the original kernel of the monastic lands was constituted from mountainous or hilly terrains.

> At the beginning of his reign, Emperor Wu of the Ch'i (r. 483–493) dreamt that he was strolling on a mountain named Ch'i (as the dynasty). Not knowing in which prefecture it was situated, he dispatched messengers in all directions to search for it. At that moment an old man from Hui-chou (to the east of modern Ching-yüan county, Kansu) sent this report to the emperor: "The Minister's Mountain, seven *li* to the north of the ramparts of the town, was once called Ch'i-shan." Thereupon an imperial commissioner was sent to Ch'i-shan to found a hermitage on its summit. Monks were ordained and endowed with fields [in perpetuity].[111]

There is no doubt that the monasteries contributed in this way to increase the surface area of the lands under cultivation. There is clear evidence of this necessary Buddhist predilection for highlands: contrary to peasant properties that were all devoted to the cultivation of arable crops, the monastic estates—like those of the wealthy laity—were distinguished by the diversity of their farming: woods, copses, pastures, mountain gardens, and orchards there occupied a place of far greater importance than in the peasant economy.

However, even if newly founded monasteries were not given irrigated fields of which it would have been necessary to dispossess the peasantry, and if the most enterprising monks indeed proceeded on their own initiative to open up uncultivated lands, the estates of Buddhist monasteries nevertheless did incorporate peasant lands as they expanded into the neighboring plains. This process is well illustrated by the history of the landed property of the monastery of Mount A-yü-wang.[112]

Founded in the first year of I-hsi (405), the A-yü-wang monastery established permanent lands (ch'ang-chu t'ien)[113] at fifteen li to the east of its buildings, within the "stūpa estate" (t'a-shu).[114] It was exempted from taxes paid in cereals (fu) and cloth (tiao) by Emperor Wu of the Liang.[115] During the P'u-t'ung reign (520–526), a monk actively looked after the cultivation of the fields. Another religious, named Chi, pursued this effort of exploitation, marked out the embankments, and rectified the boundaries. But as troubles multiplied under the Ch'en (557–589) and the Sui (589–618), the country reverted to wilderness. At the beginning of the T'ang, the monastery was lacking in manpower, and young shepherds took advantage of the times when the fields were left without surveillance to steal the harvests. The monastery therefore decided to move the boundaries of its fields to the west of the lake, and to displace the embankments that served as boundary markers to introduce a strip of "protective land" (hsien-ti) between its fields and the neighboring pastures.[116]

It would appear that monastic lands remained confined to the highlands until the seventh century. The proximity of the herds and the return of the fields to wilderness at the end of the sixth century indicate that for centuries the monastery drew its resources from upland terrain. Under the T'ang, however, the lands of the A-yü-wang monastery expanded towards the plain; by Sung times (960–1279), its adjoining fields extended as far as the sea.

The exploitation of dry terrain by the Buddhist communities was not limited to the great expanses of Shansi and Kansu. The mountains and hills neglected by traditional agriculture, even at the heart of intensively cultivated regions, in the middle of the irrigated alluvial plains, were centers from which the monasteries proceeded to the conquest of the neighboring fields.

This then represents the general scheme; it remains to examine the historical modalities.

The vocation of Buddhism for upland and hillside areas was the result of a set of convergent causes. By virtue of a persistent tradition, antedating the introduction of Buddhism to China, places of worship were established on heights. Many Buddhist sanctuaries replaced native shrines.[117] Besides, both legal and political doctrine were opposed to the dispossession of free peasants; the protection of the irrigated fields of the peasantry constituted one of the principal duties of government. But that is not all. The exploitation of poor soils required capital, organized labor, oxen, and teams of laborers. Only the state, wealthy private individuals, and the monasteries could contemplate clearing new lands. This economic circumstance is evident in the history of the saṃgha households.

Numerous texts speak to the work of clearing undertaken by the Buddhist establishments and the religious. The landed estates of the monasteries included lands that had neither been given nor purchased, but that had been developed thanks to the funds of which the communities and their monks disposed. It is reported that Dharmamitra, upon arriving at Tun-huang (before 424), had planted one thousand fruit trees and cleared (k'ai) a garden of one hundred mu for cultivation.[118]

Monastic accounts found in Central Asia give an authentic impression of this exploitation, which necessitated irrigation works and the organization of an abundant labor force. The development was entrusted to estate bailiffs[119] who were chosen among the monks and resided permanently on the estates:

One hundred cash paid at the request of [the garden?] Hsien in the new estate which also asked that wine be bought to be offered to the peasants for the work of building the canal in the mountain.[120]

One hundred eighty cash paid at the request of the old western garden, asking that the district chiefs buy wine to be offered to the peasants for the work of building canals in the two sites.[121]

Three hundred seventy-five cash paid for the purchase of one shih of wine required for agricultural labor, at the request submitted by the western estate.[122]

In the biographies of eminent monks, it is not unusual to find references to the "institution" of lands or estates (chih-t'ien, chih-chuang), where the term chih clearly indicates that these lands were not purchased, but newly placed under cultivation.

In the ninth year of Ta-yeh (613), when the monk Tao-ying (d. 636) served as steward for the year (chih-sui) in his monastery, he was involved in endless disputes with the peasants over the land:

Later, he returned to the P'u-chi monastery in P'u-chou (Shansi). He established three estates comprising fields of hemp, wheat, and millet, which were all situated in the most sheltered part of Mount Tung-shan in Hsia-hsien. [Thereafter] there were no more disputes with the laity.[123]

The example is typical: the fields of the P'u-chi monastery were established on a mountain slope, at a distance from the lowlands, hence the removal of any grounds for dispute between the monks and the peasants.

Between the years 765 and 785, the monk Tao-piao installed six ordination platforms for those who wished to take the vows. Thanks to the strings of cash he accumulated in the course of twelve years [by selling the ordination certificates[124]], he was able to build up a property (t'ien-mu) for his monastery that yielded ten thousand *hu* annually.[125]

In the year 825, Nan-ts'ao, a monk of the Lung-hsing monastery of Hang-chou, raised a subscription among the religious of his community to establish one thousand *ch'ing* (!) of fields to defray the expenses for vegetarian feasts.[126]

During the T'ai-ho reign (827–836), the monk Ch'ing-yün created an estate of twelve *ch'ing* (more than 64 ha) for his monastery.[127]

Whenever an imperial bestowal or a donation by private individuals took place, or a sale in due form was accorded to a Buddhist establishment, it was a hilly or an uneven terrain that fell to the "permanent" assets held in perpetuity (ch'ang-chu) by the monasteries.

Invariably, they were separate from, if sometimes adjoining, large-scale farmlands. One of the characteristic features of these properties was that they comprised a large proportion of gardens and orchards.

One of the earliest references to the purchase of lands by Buddhist establishments is found in the "Shih-Lao chih." In 518–519, the prince Ch'eng of Jen-ch'eng proposed to reduce the number of monasteries and to restructure their clergy and property:

> Those of their lands that have been acquired by purchase, as evidenced by formal contracts (ch'üan-cheng), may be transferred (chuan) [to the remaining monasteries]. But if official lands (kuan-ti) have been brought under cultivation by means of theft, they shall be restored to the government.[128]

The lands in question here cannot have been farmlands: the author of the memorial would have made provisions for their return to their previous owners. Undoubtedly, they formed part of those official lands mentioned immediately afterward in the same memorial. In fact, we possess a sales deed for an official property from a later period. At the beginning of the Ta-chung reign (847–860), the An-kuo monastery, situated in the northeastern part of Ch'ang-an, purchased an official estate at some distance from its buildings:[129]

An-kuo Monastery.

The price of the Chin-ching [estate] in Ch'en village, Ch'an-ch'uan district, Wan-nien county (eastern Ch'ang-an), has been estimated at 138 strings and 5[10] cash. [It comprises] a residential building of 19 bays (chien); an orchard planted with 49 trees of various species; a plot of land of 1[oo] mu in 9 parcels. This estate (chuang) is situated on the East Road bordering against a vegetable garden. To the west, it is delimited by the land of Li Sheng-ho; to the south by Dragon Street; northward it extends as far as the road.

In accordance with an imperial decision and after examination of the dossier, including the rector [of monks]'s ([seng-]cheng) petition requesting the purchase, the aforementioned estate has been sold. Since [the rector] has paid the price to the full amount agreed, the transfer of the estate has been carried out. . . . In the event of a retraction upon any item whatsoever, the sellers[130] shall be entitled to submit the case to the commissioner [for estates] . . .

The deed is signed by:

The executive officer, assistant to the department of carriages of the inner palace, P'eng;

Deputy commissioner and president of the treasury in the inner palace . . . Liu Hsing-hsüan;

Imperial commissioner and commissioner of the Hung-lu and Li-pin courts, the specially promoted . . . T'ien Shao-tsung.[131]

If no obstacles stood in the way of a sale, neither were there any objections to the bestowal of official lands to monasteries. For the estates in question comprised at best only a small proportion of tilled fields, and these could in any event not have been cultivated by free peasants, but by serfs or official slaves. Under the Northern Wei, the great families demanded that these estates be made over to the monasteries. A report by the prince Ch'eng of Jen-ch'eng in 518–519 read:

With the recent growth in private constructions, the number of monasteries [at Lo-yang] has reached into the hundreds. At times, [the bestowal of] public land (kung-ti) has been requested for the attainment of an individual's private felicity.[132]

Emperors in fact gave only what actually *belonged* to them to the monasteries to hold in perpetuity, and that did not include farmlands. The same may be said of wealthy private individuals.

At the end of the seventh and the beginning of the eighth century, the transformation of private estates into monastic estates had taken on such proportions that on his accession Emperor Hsüan-tsung wanted to put an end to this practice. A decree of the fourteenth day, fifth month, second year of Hsien-t'ien (713) forbade princes, dukes, and personages of lower rank to present petitions on their own initiative requesting the transformation of their city mansions (*chai*) into monasteries and of their estates (*chuang*) into monastic lands.[133] Yet the practice survived under his reign and resumed, at the very latest, around the year 730, which marked a turning point in Hsüan-tsung's religious policy.[134] In a petition presented that year, the Chin-hsien princess, a sister of the emperor, requested the authorization to make a gift of one of her private estates to a Buddhist establishment:

> In the eighteenth year of K'ai-yüan (730), the Chin-hsien princess presented a memorial to the emperor to obtain permission to donate four thousand scrolls of ancient and recent translations of sacred books [to the Yün-chü monastery]. . . . In addition, she memorialized that [her property] located in the village of Shang-fa, fifty *li* to the southeast of Fan-yang county, comprising an estate (*chuang*) and a wheat field in the marsh of Chao Hsiang-tzu, as well as an orchard and the wooded slope of Mount Huan, and that borders to the east on Mount Fang-nan, extends southward to Mount T'o, westward to the Po-tai gorge, and is delimited to the north by the branch of the river of the great mountain, be made over in perpetuity to the monastery for its use . . .
>
> Wang Shou-t'ai, a native of Mo prefecture and a former regular appointee (*ch'ang-hsüan*) of the Board of Civil Office, inscribed [this text] behind the stone stūpa on the summit of the mountain, on the eighth day of the winter of the *keng-ch'en* year, twenty-eighth year of K'ai-yüan (740).[135]

In the manner of the imperial nobility, high officials also donated their private estates to Buddhist establishments. These pious foundations were intended to ensure the perpetuation of family cults.

At the end of the T'ien-pao reign (742–756), Li Ch'eng thus made a gift of his patrimony (*chia-yeh*) to the Hui-lin monastery north of Lo-yang. Previously he had transformed his country house into the seat of this new monastic foundation.[136] In the second year of Ch'ien-yüan (759), Wang Wei and his brother Wang Chin requested permission to establish a monastery on their estate in Wang-ch'uan, because their mother had died.[137]

> In the second year of Ta-li (767), the eunuch Yü Ch'ao-en offered his estate (chuang) outside the T'ung-hua gate (in the northeastern wall of Ch'ang-an, to the north of the Ch'un-ming men gate), which he had received from the emperor, for the foundation of a new monastery in order to further the felicity beyond the grave of the empress Chang-ching. And he requested that this monastery be named Chang-ching ssu.[138]

A stele mentions the gift of a piece of mountain terrain (shan-ti) to a monastery in Szechwan. The text explains that the land, donated in order to insure offerings to the niche statues and the Bodhisattva with a Thousand Arms and Eyes, had been made over to the monk Hui-feng. Should the donor's elder or younger brothers or other relatives attempt to take back this land, they should die prematurely and without descendants. The author further explains that he had given this land because it was situated on a steep slope, because it had long lain fallow, and because he could not muster the strength to resume its cultivation. The donor wishes that the family of anyone who in the future might "issue a ban" concerning this land [i.e., claim it] be "struck by incurable disease."[139] The inscription served as proof of the donation. It concludes with the words "Contract of Chou Nu, donor of the land, this first day of the third month, first year of Yung-t'ai (765)" and bears the names of eight witnesses.[140]

Documents containing precise descriptions of the private estates of the upper classes indicate that lands used for growing cereals comprised only a small fraction of their total acreage. To take a well-known example, the estate of the brothers Wang at Wang-ch'uan comprised essentially a pleasure park, groves, gardens, and orchards. The terms chuang, frequently encountered in T'ang texts, meaning "private estate," as well as shu, pieh-shu, and pieh-yeh ("country estate"), were not normally applied to lands under large-scale cultivation. The fact that they increasingly incorporated tilled land, especially under the T'ang, reflects a later development. Originally, private estates were not established on farmland. The diversity of their land use (gardens, orchards, bamboo plantations, woods) belonged to a landscape different from that of the lowlands. The landed properties of the monasteries were of the former type. In the biography of the monk Hui-chou (559–627) of the Ch'ing-ch'an monastery at the capital the following assets are mentioned: "bamboo plantations, woods, gardens, vegetable plots, estates comprising flooded paddies and dry fields, granaries, mills, and treasuries." All these riches were due to the indefatigable zeal of Hui-chou.[141]

Among the monasteries' landed property, fields and gardens undoubtedly constituted the most profitable types of land use.[142] Although the texts are less eloquent about the other sources of wealth, some of these were not negligible, in particular woods, bamboo plantations, and pastures. Herds, which were kept at a distance from the lowlands, were frequently encountered on monastic properties.

> Shih-te (early eighth century) was grazing the oxen on the estate of the Kuo-ch'ing monastery. His song rose up to heaven. At the time of the fast (uposadha) at the monastery, Shih-te took his oxen to pasture in front of the hall in which the monks were assembled. Leaning against the door, he began pounding it with the palms of his hands and shouting with guffaws: "Hey, fellows!" The master of Vinaya (vinayadhara) and the dean reproached him: "Are you mad? Why do you prevent us from reciting the precepts with your shouting?" "But," replied Shih-te, "these are not oxen that I take to pasture. Of this herd, most are people from this monastery, and they know the Buddhist ceremonies well." Then he began calling out the names of deceased monks. After each call, an ox passed in front of him. Everyone was amazed.[143]

References to stockbreeding are common in Chinese Buddhist literature; virtually all the monasteries must have had some animals that they grazed on wastelands: draught oxen for plowing and transportation and, in Kansu, sheep for the manufacture of felt.

In the eighth century, the state endowed the monasteries of Shensi and Kansu with a sizeable allotment of pasture lands. It may be surmised that some of these lands were used for cultivation but retained their former purpose. During the Pao-ying reign (762–763), "lands [horse pens (hsien) and stables (chiu)][144] were distributed to the poor, to soldiers, and to officials. Of these lands, several thousands of ch'ing (1 ch'ing = 5.4 ha) were given to Buddhist and Taoist monasteries."[145]

The northwestern regions and the Chinese protectorates in Central Asia were breeding country. Some of the monasteries in those regions owned horses, as a manuscript found in the region of Turfān attests:

Liu-chung county	Report
Monastery of the	
seven-storied [stūpa]: 16 horses.	
1 white mare, eighteen years	
[seal of Liu-chung county]	
. . .	
1 jade-faced brown mare, two years	1 . . .
1 black mare, two years	1 . . . bay
1 black mare, two years	1 . . .
Monastery of the western stūpa: 7 horses	
1 white mare, six years	1 . . .
1 black mare, nine years	1 . . .
1 . . . , . . . years	. . . [146]

If the monasteries at Tun-huang owned irrigated lands, they also had pastures and herds, at a distance further removed from their buildings. Beside the narrow strip of tilled fields that occupied the valley, there were wide stretches of semidesert where the herds of the armies and of the Buddhist establishments grazed. The Tun-huang monasteries kept mainly ovine flocks, which they entrusted to shepherds of mostly barbarian origin. Certain animals had been donated to them by the faithful.[147] In 944, the Ching-t'u monastery owned a flock of 121 sheep and goats:

On the twenty-fourth day of the third month of the year *chia-ch'en,* we went to the Teng family estate (*chuang*) on the I-ch'iu [canal] to see the shepherd assigned by the monastery there, named Ho Paoting. There were 37 gelded sheep, large and small, 6 gelded billy goats, 9 nanny goats, 4 young billy goats, 15 lambs, and 9 ewe lambs.
The shepherd Ho Pao-ting [signature in the form of a cross].[148]

In exchange for their maintenance, the shepherds brought the monasteries wool, cheese made from curds, and small quantities of koumiss or similar fermented liquors.[149] Following are some of the expenditures relative to sheep rearing from the accounts of the Ching-t'u monastery:

.3 *shih* of millet for sheep-shearing (twice within the year 930);
Flour given to the shepherds who had sent curd cheeses;
3 oilcakes for feeding to the sheep;[150]
.8 *shih* of soya beans for feeding to the sheep;
3 *shih* of millet flour, 2 *shih* of coarse flour, .6 *shih* of white flour

given to the shepherd Li A-chu-tzu for provisions in the
eleventh month of the year *wu-hsü* (938);

7 *shih* of soya beans as provisions for the shepherds;[151]

1 *shih* of millet flour delivered to the shepherd for provisions on
the twenty-second day of the fifth month.[152]

There existed a general correspondence between types of labor force
and land use. The virgin lands and hill estates, of which the monasteries had exclusive ownership, were frequently cultivated by slaves.
Irrigated fields, however, which had already been occupied for a long
period of time, were worked by dependents of a lesser degree of servitude to the communities. To be sure, peasants assigned to the service
of sanctuaries and monks lost a part of their liberty, for the ties that
united them to the religious communities were of a hereditary nature.
They were serfs. Slaves (*nu-pi*) and domestic servants (*chia-jen*)
formed an entirely separate class of dependents. The latter differed
even from the class of agricultural laborers who were contractually
protected against the arbitrariness of their masters. Slaves, on the
other hand, constituted commercial goods that could be used for any
purpose.

> Since the monastery was sufficiently provided with domestic ser-
> vants (*ching-jen*),[153] the monk Hui-chou selected among them twenty
> head[154] who were not to be employed for labor services but who were
> to beat the drums and dance. On every feast day, a musical perfor-
> mance was thus organized in front of the statues, and people came
> from afar and from all directions to listen to the music and enjoy the
> entertainment.[155]

The main function of the monastic slaves seems to have been the
"sprinkling and sweeping," i.e., any of the menial tasks inside the
buildings. Occasionally, however, and on special orders, they were also
used to work the fields and gardens. During spring plowing and
autumns harvests, when a large labor force was required, the slaves
were also sent to assist the peasants in the large-scale cultivation areas.
Thus, at the request of T'an-yao, the Buddha households (*fo-t'u hu*) consisting of official slaves and convicts provided labor services for the
maintenance of the buildings and at the same time "worked the fields
(*ying-t'ien*) and brought in the harvests (*shu-su*)."[156] The term *fo-t'u* in
the designation of these families of slaves surely refers to the buildings
in places of worship:[157] as a general rule, slaves were constantly at the

service of their masters within the dwelling, or were occupied in the immediate vicinity. Probably they cultivated the gardens adjoining the buildings, inside the precincts of Buddhist establishments.

In the accounts of the Ching-t'u monastery at Tun-huang, some dependents are designated as *yüan-tzu*, a term that must no doubt be translated as "gardener," and others by the more enigmatic term *en-tzu*.[158] Possibly, these represented two classes of slaves or domestic servants, for the monastery took it upon itself to provide their food:

1 *shih* of wheat paid for the gardeners . . .

2.5 *shih* of wheat given to the gardeners as provisions for the spring.[159]

1 load of millet given to the gardeners as provisions for the autumn, and 2 *shih* of millet given to the *en-tzu* as provisions for the autumn . . .

2 *shih* of wheat and 2 *shih* of millet given to the *en-tzu* in the spring.[160]

As the following document from Central Asia indicates, when the slaves were taken to work outside, they were not left without surveillance:[161]

From Ta-yen, the monk in charge of external surveillance (*wai-hsün seng*) . . . Hu-kuo monastery . . . Upon arrival of the present billet at Yang-ling, the domestic servants (*chia-jen*)[162] designated above shall cut the grass for three days. One person shall be left behind to water the fields; the others shall leave; they will not be permitted to follow their own whims. If they disobey, they are to be punished according to the rules. Notification of the twenty-seventh day of the eighth month.

The general overseer (*tu wei-na*) Hui-ta;
The dean (*shang-tso*) Hui . . . ;
The abbot (*ssu-chu*) Hui-yün.

How were monastic slaves recruited?

The Buddha households were drawn from convicts who had been sentenced to death or forced labor, and from the official slaves. Under the Wei, it was a current practice to pardon criminals in order to make a gift of them to the Buddhist Church, and this practice lay at the origin of the *fo-t'u hu*. The secular authorities thus lost a labor force otherwise useful for public works—except in the case of convicts sentenced to death—but in return gained the protection of the Buddhist powers. The currency of the same practice in India may have served as a model. One of the traditional stories preserved in the Vinaya relates how the king Bimbisāra made a gift to the Buddhist community, together with fields and buildings, of five hundred brigands who merited capital punishment.[163] It is also possible that analogous customs from Central Asia inspired the Wei sovereigns, always scrupulous to conform to Buddhist tradition. Yang Hsüan-chih reports that the king of Khotan assigned four hundred families to the service of a great Buddhist monastery for "sprinkling and sweeping."[164]

"In the tenth month of the winter of the first year of Ch'eng-ming (476), the imperial retinue made a stopover at the Chien-ming monastery. The emperor pardoned a large number of criminals."[165] In the sixth month of that same year, the previous emperor, Hsien-tsu, had died. Tsukamoto Zenryū surmised, with some plausibility, that Kao-tsu went to the Chien-ming monastery in order to have a requiem service celebrated for Hsien-tsu, and that the criminals were freed on that occasion. There are good reasons to believe that the latter were transformed into slaves for the monastery.[166]

Under the Liang, certain monasteries received gifts of personal retainers (pu-ch'ü)[167] who were employed to work the land:

[Chang Hsiao-hsiu (d. 522)] then left his duties and returned to the mountains. He dwelled in the Tung-lin monastery. This monastery owned several dozens of ch'ing of tilled land and several hundreds of pu-ch'ü. They were employed to work the land [the income of which was] entirely devoted to the maintenance of the mountain community. From far and near visitors gladly came to the monastery. They went there as if it were a market.[168]

Slaves, like the land, came either from donations or were purchased:

"The monks," wrote Tu Mu after the proscription of 854,[169] "accumulated fortunes and purchased great residences and sturdy slaves, just like the ducal families and great officials."

It was above all by rearing, however, that the monks seem to have procured an abundant servile labor force, especially during the sixth century. When young slaves had reached the required age, they were summarily ordained, a way of withholding them once and for all from claims of the imperial government or of private individuals. A decree of the empress Ling of the Northern Wei proclaimed in 517:[170]

From now on, male and female slaves shall no longer enter into religion, and the princes and nobility of our kin shall no longer be authorized to present petitions [requesting the ordination of slaves]. Those who contravene this decree shall be judged. Monks and nuns who ordain on their own authority male or female slaves belonging to others shall be banished five hundred *li* as [simple] religious. There have been many cases in which monks and nuns have raised members of their families or of acquaintances and children of slaves belonging to others. When these reach adulthood, [the religious] ordain them privately (*ssu-tu*) and make them their disciples. As of now, this practice is prohibited. Offenders shall be laicized and persons thus raised shall be returned to their original status.[171]

Encroachment on Farmlands

Under the T'ang, the great families and the monasteries expanded their landed properties simultaneously and by the same means: the progressive encroachment of private estates on the large-scale farmlands. This economic development involved a parallel transformation of moral and legal conceptions. From the beginning of the seventh century onward, a growing number of decrees prohibiting the sale of farmlands was issued: a sure sign that such sales did occur. These decrees must undoubtedly be interpreted as an indication of a profound change in social relationships, rather than the affirmation of a general rule that was always valid.

> Earlier, during the Yung-hui reign (650–656), the sale and purchase of lands held in perpetuity (*yung-yeh*) [by the peasantry] and of personal share lands (*k'ou-fen*) had been prohibited. Subsequently, powerful families seized the land and the poor lost what had been theirs. Therefore, a decree ordered that the buyers of such lands return them and be penalized.[172]

A decree of the ninth month, twenty-third year of K'ai-yüan (735) read:[173]

> Personal share lands and the lands held in perpetuity by private individuals (*po-hsing*) have repeatedly been the object of measures prohibiting their sale and mortgage. I understand that [these operations] have not yet been effectively prevented.

A new social class of wage-earning agricultural laborers emerged and developed rapidly. According to Lu Chih, by the end of the eighth century the families of free peasants who worked personal share lands amounted to no more than 4–5 percent of the population.[174] In a report dated 780, Yang Yen gave exactly the same figures.[175]

Cultivated land tended to develop from an asset, of which the holder enjoyed the use, into a possession, of which he had exclusive ownership. Without this legal evolution, the great economic revolution of the seventh and the eighth centuries could not have taken place. A clear indication of this change of legal concepts may be seen in the fact that the reform of Yang Yen in 780 caused the land tax to be applied no longer on a household basis (hu) but according to the extent of the land under cultivation (mu).[176]

Since Han times, members of the upper classes had owned land that they were able to sell, donate, or bequeath. The transformation of farmland into a commodity of commerce could thus be regarded as an extension of that earlier mode of possession. It is in fact that extension witnessed, in a concrete manner, during the T'ang. A decree of the eleventh year of T'ien-pao (752) reads:[177]

> We understand that the families of princes, dukes, and great officials, as well as families of wealth, have for some time been building landed estates (chuang-t'ien). Heedless of the provisions in force, they indulge themselves in rapacious appropriation. Those who pretend that [the terrains in question are] uncultivated all possess tilled fields and use this pretext to appropriate [further lands]. Those who establish pastures, declare (chih)[178] owning only [untilled] mountain terrains. They will not even stop at trading the personal share lands and hereditary parcels [of the peasants]. Now they falsify the [cadastral] registers, now they pretend that the lands [in their possession] had been pledged [by their cultivators]. They leave [the peasants] without a place where they may reside in peace. Then they install them on their properties as retainers and have them till their fields. By depriving sedentary [farmers] of their means of subsistence, they are the true cause of instability among the population. This situation has prevailed for a long time now throughout the empire.

Monasteries purchased farmlands. The following indication is found in the accounts of the Ching-t'u monastery at Tun-huang: "Twenty *shih* of wheat and twenty *shih* of millet for the price of the land of the Lo family."[179]

Certain fields were also received as pious donations. It is possible

that these gifts in fact concealed commercial operations. A decree of
Emperor Jui-tsung (r. 684–690 and 710–712) declared:

> Buddhist and Taoist monasteries appropriate large tracts of fields and
> terrain, and their mills wrong the peasants.[180] . . . Officials and farm-
> ers who donate their estates (chuang), city mansions (chai), fields
> (t'ien), and lodgings (she) shall have these properties confiscated by
> the Court of Agriculture (ssu-nung), if in the capital; in the outlying
> prefectures, they shall be redistributed among the poorest families
> liable to taxation.[181]

For peasants in debt, such gifts may have been a convenient means of
discharge; for members of the upper classes, a way to gain tax exemptions for their lands by transforming them into monastic property.

The following Sung text, a report of the Court of Agriculture dated
1075, shows that gifts and sales of land were practiced concurrently:

> Many are the private individuals (po-hsing) in the prefectures who
> make definitive donations (she-shih) of their fields and habitations, or
> who mortgage (tien) or sell (mai) these to Buddhist and Taoist monas-
> teries by using the names of officials.[182]

From the T'ang to the Sung, imperial policy consistently aimed to
protect the farmlands. An official report of the year 1111 stated:

> In accordance with the law concerning private uncultivated terrains
> (ssu huang-t'ien fa), it is permitted to loan these with interest to Bud-
> dhist and Taoist monasteries. Many, however, declare (chih) rich and
> fertile fields as uncultivated terrain. The administration does not
> inspect these in situ. Or again, after a flood or drought the farmers'
> fields remain unattended. Once the human labor is discontinued,
> [these fields] return to wilderness. The monasteries appropriate them,
> never to return them to the peasants. The farmers bear the burden of
> this process.[183]

It seems, however, that the monasteries were above all able to
increase their landed properties indirectly, through the intermediary
of the religious themselves.[184] The immovable property of the monks
always fell in the end to the communal property, whether by donation
or bequest.

At Tun-huang in the ninth and tenth centuries, for the documents of interest here generally date to that period, there was scarcely a monk or nun who did not possess a field, or more usually, as a result of the extreme parceling of the land, several isolated plots. One brief manuscript fragment[185] mentions these individually held lands, a source of revenue for the monk and those who lived with him, his disciples and perhaps even his wife and children, for some of them were married:[186]

> The monk Kuang-yün [traveling][two individuals][187]:
> * a plot of fifteen *mu* on the Tu-yü-yang canal;
> * four *mu* on the Chieh canal [also leased by himself] [in addition to his personal share land (*k'ou-fen*) on the Chieh canal ... estate (*chuang*) with garden (*yüan*)[188] ... in all six *mu*].[189]
> The monk Li Su [two individuals]:
> * a plot of seven *mu* north of the town, on the Tung-chih canal [at present] [leased by himself].
> The monk Chin-yen [traveling] [three individuals]:
> * a plot of four *mu* [at present leased by the nun Chen-chih] [fallen into the possession of Chih-ying].
> The monk Wei-ming [one individual]:
> * ten *mu* on the Ts'ai-t'ien canal [allocated to the property held in perpetuity by the (Ta-)yün (monastery)].
> The monk Chieh-? [one individual]:
> * a plot of fifteen *mu* on the Kuan-chin canal [leased by himself].

These individually held lands were worked by laymen. The monks hired agricultural laborers for the year:

> This twelfth day of the second month if the year *i-yu* (presumably 865 or 925), the monk Pao-hsing of the Ch'ien-yüan monastery, requiring the help of a young man, engages the commoner (*po-hsing*) Teng Wu-tzu for a period of eight months [i.e., for the period of agricultural labor, from March to October]. He has settled the monthly hire at one load of millet and wheat.[190] He has three *mu* of wheat fields ... and four *mu* of millet fields. ... For summer garments, Teng Wu-tzu shall [be provided with] a long-sleeved robe, a suit, and a pair of leather shoes. From the moment the engagement takes effect, Teng Wu-tzu must appear at work every day of each month; he will not be allowed to shirk his duty. If he is idle during one day in a busy month, he shall be charged [a reduction of his hire of] five *tou*; if it is not a busy month,

he shall be charged one *tou* [per day of idleness]. If he dallies on the way or if he naps in the fields . . . if . . . he shall have to make amends. In case of illness, he shall be permitted to return to the village for five days; but in excess of that period, the amount [of the penalty for idleness] shall be calculated in accordance with the [above] rule. There shall be no retraction. In the event that one of the parties retracts . . . the two parties present, etc.[191]

Such property, held by the religious individually, had moreover been officially recognized in imperial legislation since the eighth century: like the peasants, regular monks were entitled to receive life allotments of large-scale farmlands (personal share lands). Their allocation, however, was reduced. It was normal that the clergy, who had sources of income not available to the laity, should be less well appointed. It is not impossible that the document from Tun-huang constitutes evidence of the continuity of that official practice. In any event, certain fields still retained in the ninth and tenth centuries the designation of share lands.

The decree that granted regular monks the possession of personal share lands (*k'ou-fen t'ien*) limited simultaneously, and no doubt purely theoretically, the extent of the lands held in perpetuity (*ch'ang-chu*) by the communities:

On the twenty-third day of the first month, tenth year of K'ai-yüan (722), the emperor issued the [following] order to the Board of Sacrifices (*ssu-pu*): Land was to be granted to the Buddhist and Taoist establishments in conformity with the law and according to whether [the recipients were] Buddhist monks or nuns or Taoist monks or nuns. Anything in excess of the determined amount was to be recuperated by the administration and distributed among poor peasants and landless adults.[192] As for the fields belonging to the property held in perpetuity by Buddhist and Taoist monasteries, [the Board of Sacrifices] was equally authorized to retrieve any excess relative to the number of monks and nuns: for a community counting more than one hundred persons, the fields were not to exceed ten *ch'ing* (54 ha);[193] for a community of more than fifty persons, they were not to exceed seven *ch'ing* (38 ha); and for less than fifty persons, they were not to exceed five *ch'ing* (27 ha).[194]

The *T'ang liu-tien* specifies the size of the allotments granted to the religious:[195]

"Taoist monks (*tao-shih*) are provided with thirty *mu* and Taoist nuns with twenty *mu;* the allocation is identical for Buddhist monks and nuns." Other sources indicate that these allotments were only granted to those religious who possessed a minimum of instruction.[196]

Thus it emerges that the lands possessed by the communities were in theory less extensive than those of the clergy. For a monastery of medium size, with a community of forty monks, the lands belonging to the property held in perpetuity would have amounted to only 27 ha, whereas the individual monks would have held a total of 65 ha between them. The law presumably no more than sanctioned an existing state of affairs: by T'ang times, the individual property of the religious was at least as extensive as that which was consecrated to communal use and to the cult. The figures determined by the law, meanwhile, remained very modest. It should be recalled that when, as the result of purges, the clergy were returned to lay life (i.e., to the life of the peasantry), the extent of the fields that assured their subsistence largely exceeded the thirty or twenty *mu* allocated to them by the law.[197]

It is in any case certain that by permitting the clergy to install themselves in the midst of farmlands, this legislation opened the way for widespread abuse and eventually favored the appropriation of fields reserved for the peasantry, to the profit of the monasteries.

The economic pressure exerted by the monasteries upon the peasant population became more pronounced under the T'ang; it no doubt also played a greater role than previously in the growth of the monastic estates. The documents found at Tun-huang permit an immediate apprehension of a situation merely suggested by the Chinese historians. The bulk of the loan contracts and hire engagements, and the presence of antichresis pledges, convey an impression of the progressive and irreversible indebtedness of the peasant class.

Peasants who were unable to repay their debts[198] hired out members of their families as agricultural laborers or left part of their land in the hands of their creditor until he obtained full indemnification. Following is the text of a contract from Tun-huang:[199]

This twenty-eighth day of the tenth month of the year *kuei-mao* (823, 883?),[200] Wu Ch'ing-shun and his two younger brothers have decided after deliberation, given the poverty and the extent of indebtedness of their family, to hire out (*tien,* lit. "engage") the person of Ch'ing-shun to the rector of monks (*seng-cheng*) So of the Lung-hsing monastery [as part of his domestic service, *chia*]. They shall receive immediately ten *shih* of wheat, ten *shih* and six *tou* of hemp equivalent to three *shih* and two *tou* of wheat and, in addition, nine *shih* of millet. There shall be no additional [compensation]. Once these goods have been paid, there will be no [further] payment for the man's hire, nor will interest be claimed for the commodities. At that time, the So household shall be permitted to put [Ch'ing-shun] to work immediately. Once [the brothers of Ch'ing-shun] have received the commodities in exchange, it will not be permissible to revoke these decisions. If Ch'ing-shun is detained on his way to [his employer's] house by people of ill will toward him [creditors?], or if he steals oxen, sheep, vegetables, wheat, or millet belonging to others, then Ch'ing-shun shall make amends. Such affairs are not his master's concern. If the brothers quarrel, and incite Ch'ing-shun to abscond from his work, they shall provide to the employer three *tou* of foodstuffs [wheat or millet] for each day [of idleness]. In the event of his master's death, Ch'ing-shun shall be required to return the commodities corresponding to the period of work he was thus unable to carry out. If Ch'ing-shun dies of an infectious disease, the goods received shall be returned by his younger brothers. After deliberation, the two parties present have thus decided.

To guard against ill faith, this deed was drawn up to serve as later proof.

The elder brother, hired: Wu Ch'ing-shun.

[Note: "One *shih* of wheat and two *shih* of millet were added. To guard against ill faith, may this signature serve as proof. Signed: the uncle Wu Fo-pi."]

As co-recipient of the commodities, Wu Wan-sheng, the younger.

As co-recipient of the commodities, Wu Ch'ing-hsin, the younger.

As guarantor, the uncle Wu Fo-pi.

As witness, the abbot An.

This eleventh day of the third month, seventh year of T'ien-fu (907), the commoner Kao Chia-ying of the district of Hung-ch'e, having contracted a debt of two *shih* of wheat and one *shih* of millet towards the monk Yüan-chi, and finding himself without the means to repay, herewith makes over [to Yüan-chi] five *mu* (.27 ha) of land, situated on the lower Sung canal, to till and to sow for a period of two years, so that Yüan-chi may be compensated for the value of the commodities [loaned].[201] The land tax (*ti-tzu*),[202] firewood, fodder, etc. due to the administration (*kuan-fu*) [as taxes] for this land, it will be incumbent upon the master of the land [Kao Chia-ying] to provide. It shall not be the concern of [the party entitled to] sow. If in the course of the two years someone comes forward as the [true] master of the field, then Kao Chia-ying shall be obliged to find five *mu* of land of good quality as replacement. The two parties present . . .[203] [the following text is missing].

The history of Japan can serve here as corroboration. The development of landed estates in Japan approximately paralleled that in China. Asakawa Kenji[204] traces the origin of the *shō* (Chin. *chuang*) in Japan to the eighth century, i.e., within a century of the period when the word also appeared in China to designate private estates. Originally, the *shō* comprised lands of limited extent that had been regained from fallow, and probably uneven, terrains. Only in the tenth century, however, were the *shō* officially sanctioned as an institution, when the state awarded charters to some of them exempting them from all impositions. In time, these privileged estates annexed neighboring lands of a very different nature and status. Thus the legal situation of each parcel was far from uniform. It could be rented land or land sold definitively, and the various divisions and contracts that intervened in the course of time rendered the history of each estate extremely complex. As an example, Asakawa studied the history of the immovable property of the Buddhist monastery of Mount Kōya fifty miles to the south of Kyōto. Founded in 816 by the monk Kōbō, the Kōya-ji possessed at the time only a small estate (*shō*), which, sixty years later, still consisted of little more than four hectares. To this initial nucleus were to be joined additional lands, either by purchase or through donations by the imperial family, the nobility, and wealthy families. At the end of the twelfth century, all of these lands were exempted from miscellaneous taxes, and some even from the principal tax. Apart from this fiscal immunity with respect to the state, however, the tenure and internal taxation system within the different parcels, and the control exercised over them by the monastery, varied to a great extent. Two main types of land can nevertheless be distinguished: those that were received as gifts of the emperor or high-ranking officials and those that derived from private individuals. Of the former, the monastery could dispose at will, but not of the latter, which were subject to certain constraints and rights retained by their former owners. Over the centuries, the monastery's efforts were directed at converting the parcels that did not benefit from fiscal immunity, and that remained partly dependant on private individuals, into the type of land that was exclusively owned by the monastery and free of all impositions.

Among the procedures that permitted the monastery to lay its hands definitively on those lands that partially escaped their control, two are particularly worth mentioning:

From the second half of the thirteenth century, individual monks took to leasing or purchasing land from the laity "for peace in the present and felicity in the life to come," or, again, "for the extinction of sins past, present, and future."[205]

Second, monks who lived in the world and were known as *nyu dō* (Chin. *ju-tao*),[206] paid a contribution on the produce of their farmwork to the monastery with which they remained affiliated. In some cases, clergy affiliated with the Kōya-ji owned the fields they occupied and paid part of their harvest to the monastery. These individual properties were transmitted from master to disciple, or circulated from monk to monk, or were eventually purchased by one of these who donated them definitively to the monastery. The Kōya-ji encouraged its own monks to acquire land by granting them an advantageous regime of impositions, for the monastery was thus better assured of receiving its dues than if the lands were cultivated by laymen.

By and large, these indications accord with the evidence provided by the Tun-huang manuscripts for the ninth and tenth centuries. With a certain interval, the Japanese historical facts are identical with those in China. In any event the role played by the monks themselves should be noted: through their agency, the monasteries succeeded in extending their estates. The influence of religious considerations on transactions concerning land should also be noted. Sometimes donations were concealed sales, and those who disposed of their fields for the benefit of the Three Jewels could give themselves the illusion of performing a work of piety, even when they were acting under necessity. The moral authority of the communities and the clergy no doubt aided them in the appropriation of land. The Buddhist Church thus disposed of a trump that the great lay families were lacking.

The landed properties of the monasteries in China and those of the great families, members of the imperial nobility and high officials, were of the same type: gardens, orchards, woods, and pastures occupied a much more important place in them than in the peasant economy where the cultivation of cereals and leguminous plants predominated. This partition of the soil has its origin, as described,[207] in social history, and was a result of techniques and topography. The figures for a period later than that under consideration underline our conclusion: in the twelfth and early thirteenth century, the monasteries held 17 percent of cultivated lands and 33 percent of mountainous terrains in Fu-chou; in the region of modern Chekiang, only 3 percent of cultivated lands and 13 percent of mountainous terrains.[208]

All considered, however, it was the seizure of farmlands by the Buddhist establishments that had the greatest social and economic consequences. Is it possible to give figures? The only period where one might have expected to obtain comprehensive information is that of the great proscription in the middle of the ninth century, in the course of which the imperial government confiscated most of the Buddhist Church's property. The available indications, however, are rather vague: "Of fields of good quality (liang-t'ien)," the texts declare,[209] "there were several thousand myriads of ch'ing." Similarly, the T'ang hui-yao[210] gives a very large and implausible figure: several tens of millions of ch'ing. It is known that at the end of the reign of Hsüan-tsung, around the middle of the eighth century, the total surface area of cultivated lands did not exceed fourteen million ch'ing.[211]

There are a few scattered indications concerning the extent of the lands owned by monasteries: those provided by the texts examined here suggest that the extent of the fields of the Buddhist establishments was for the most part in the range between ten and forty ch'ing and only rarely reached the figure of fifty ch'ing. The regulation of 722, which undoubtedly went unheeded, had imposed limitations of ten, seven, or five ching, depending on the size of the community.[212] The implied minimum was in virtually all cases exceeded and can safely be doubled on the basis of the information found elsewhere.

For Tun-huang, only figures for farm rent are available, which probably amounted to one-half of the harvest.[213] One monastic account features a list of revenues from "kitchen plots" (ch'u-t'ien) situated in the vicinity of canals.[214] The list is unfortunately incomplete; the total amounts to rents of more than 60 shih, corresponding to a production of 120 shih. Assuming a production of .5 shih per mu,[215] the extent of the lands in question would have been at least 2.5 ch'ing. There must have been additional lands as well.

At the Ching-t'u monastery, the following impositions (k'o or shui) were paid by the peasant families (in shih):

Plot/Year	924	930	Between 938 and 944		
On Ts'ai-t'ien canal	10	7.3	22.4	22	22.4
South of the garden	8.4	?	8.4	8.4	8.4[216]
On Yen-k'ang canal	10	10	19.5	?	?
On Wu-ch'iung canal	16	17	23	23	23[217]
Total:	44.4	34.3	73.3	53.4	53.8

Here again, the size of the land cultivated appears to have been rather modest, hardly in excess of three *ch'ing*.[218] It follows that the manuscripts from Tun-huang do not provide all the relevant information concerning the monasteries' land holdings.

At the time of the proscription of 845, there were said to have been forty-six hundred monasteries (*ssu*) and more than forty thousand small sanctuaries. Even supposing that the large establishments possessed thirty *ch'ing* on average and assuming that not even the smallest chapel had not been deprived of land to provide for its single monk and cult, it is not credible that the so-called lands held in perpetuity (*ch'ang-chu t'ien*) of the Buddhist Church in China should have exceeded two hundred thousand *ch'ing*. However, the monks themselves owned land privately; the same regulation of 722 granted thirty *mu* of fields to all regular clergy. This again indicates a theoretical minimum, and it may be thought that the law was violated in this case as well. But to what extent is not known.

There are, however, other means of forming an estimate. In the text already cited, Tu Mu provides precise indications for the number of dependents of the Buddhist Church: there were 150,000 male and female slaves (*nu-pi*)[219] and the number of freemen who had been dependents[220] of monasteries and were returned to the imperial administration "equaled the number of those that were laicized." Thus, on the basis of Tu Mu's text, the clergy and the Buddhist establishments would have employed a labor force of some 250,000 persons, including slaves, serfs, and peasants attached to the monasteries. For 360,500 monks and nuns were returned to lay life at that time. But not all of the slaves worked the fields.[221] Given the total number of these dependents, it would appear that the fields and gardens of the Church did not exceed several hundred thousands of *ch'ing*. After the confiscation the government granted each slave one hundred *mu* of these lands.[222] Assuming that about half of their number were women who would have received a smaller part, and that approximately the same surface area of one hundred *mu* had been cultivated by all the dependents of monasteries, one would arrive at a maximum of three hundred thousand *ch'ing*.

This certainly does not amount to much. Around the year 750, the total area of the land under cultivation was fourteen million *ch'ing*. Assuming that it cannot have changed a great deal in one century, three hundred thousand *ch'ing* would represent some 2 percent of tilled lands. Why then did the seizure of peasant lands by religious establishments cause such agitation among the officials? First, it should be noted that the monastic community comprised only 1 percent at most of the total population of China;[223] its possession of 2 percent of the arable land would have already constituted grounds for indignation. Second, the distribution of the lands controlled by the monks was very uneven. In some regions, they are not likely to have been either numerous or extensive, but elsewhere, especially in the region of Ch'ang-an and Lo-yang, the monasteries owned a very large part of the soil under cultivation. At the beginning of the sixth century, when Ts'ui Hsiao-fen was commissioned by the controller of Buddhist clergy Hui-shen to make a record of the Buddhist sanctuaries at Lo-yang, he indicated that during the short period since the establishment of the Wei court at Lo-yang (in 494) the monasteries had seized one-third of the inhabited land from the people.[224] In 695, "the greater part of the land and of public and private real estate [in the capital territory] was in the hands of monks."[225]

The same situation obtained under the reign of the T'ang emperor Tai-tsung (762–779), when "all the lands of good quality and all the farms producing good yields within the imperial domain belonged to Buddhist and Taoist monasteries."[226] Thus from the end of the fifth century until the confiscation of the monastic lands in the middle of the ninth century, the economic installation of the Buddhist Church in the region of Ch'ang-an and Lo-yang remained a constant feature: its wealth was concentrated in certain privileged places and was consequently the source of a particular kind of power. The texts emphasize the fact that the monks' land was the best. Even if the Buddhist establishments owned only about 2 percent of the land, there is every reason to believe that the *yield* of these lands represented a considerably higher percentage. It may have exceeded 10 percent of all cereal and garden produce.

After the reign of Wu-tsung and the Draconian measures of 841–845, the center of gravity shifted and the monasteries no longer held the largest expanses of fields and gardens in the region of the two capitals, but in Anhwei and Fukien. The transfer of wealth and economic influence to the South beginning at the end of the T'ang remained one of the salient features of the Sung period. By settling increasingly in the South, Buddhist communities undoubtedly contributed to this development.

With the movement of wealth toward the Yangtze valley and the South, a redistribution of land simultaneously took place among very large sanctuaries under the Sung. The beginnings of Buddhism in China were characterized by a proliferation of small sanctuaries and an extreme dispersion of the monastic community. From the Northern Wei to the T'ang, governments endeavored to put some order into this anarchy by favoring large establishments. Purges were almost invariably accompanied by a consolidation of monks who had not been returned to lay life into larger communities.[227] The economic development was to accord with imperial policy, leading in the long term to the elimination of small communities in favor of large ones that were wealthier and better equipped to survive. Under the Sung and Yüan, large Buddhist communities and large landed estates became the rule.

In the year 1056, under the Liao dynasty, the Ch'ao-hua monastery owned 540 ha of land and 2,000 fruit trees.[228] In 1107, the Kan-hua ssu, a monastery of three hundred monks, had 540 ha of land and 1,000 walnut trees as property held in perpetuity (ch'ang-chu), and its monks individually possessed 162 ha of which 54 were sown with wheat.[229] According to a work of the Sung period,[230]

Everywhere there are vast expanses of "permanent" fields (ch'ang-chu) belonging to the monasteries of the Buddhist clergy. During the Shao-hsing reign (1131–1162), the emperor Kao-tsung had these lands confiscated for the benefit of the state, to be used as appanages. . . . In the spring of the twentieth year (1150), the emperor ordered the assistant of the Court of Agriculture Chung Shih-ming to proceed to Min province (modern Fukien) to sequester the [excess] lands of the Buddhist and Taoist monasteries. After having reserved an amount of land [deemed] sufficient for the "permanent" revenues, he obtained the considerable sum of 340,000 strings of cash, which he remitted to the Treasury of the Left. The following year, the imperial commissioner Chang Ju-ying, who had just been promoted to the rank of general, requested at court that a further 60 to 70 percent [of the monastic land holdings] be recuperated. "Today," he said, "many of the lands held in perpetuity by the monasteries of Mount Yü-wang, of Ling-an, of Mount Ching and other localities in the region [of Ming-chou] extend over several ten thousand mu (i.e., several times 540 ha). Thanks to special imperial charters (t'e-chih), a large number of these properties benefit from an exemption from land taxes.[231] This is the cause of a great misfortune suffered by our people."

CHAPTER FIVE

INDUSTRIAL INSTALLATIONS

Mills

A major part of the revenues of the great Buddhist monasteries at Tun-huang was derived from mill rents (wei-k'o). Milling installations, including machines driven by water, must have constituted valuable assets; they are found only on the lands of the wealthy laity and the great monasteries. The growth of large private properties under the T'ang favored the development of these installations. Automatic milling devices had, however, been known in China since at least the beginning of the third century. The "Wei shu" of the San-kuo chih reports that when Emperor T'ai-tsu of the Wei (190–219) [Ts'ao Ts'ao] deported settlers of the three commanderies of Lung-hsi, T'ien-shui, and Nan-an (in modern Kansu) to populate the region north of the Yellow River, Chang Chi assuaged the discontent of the deported by remitting their taxes, constructing lodgings for them, and installing water-driven pounding pestles (shui-tui).[1] These were undoubtedly no more than small hulling devices of the kind that figure in the Keng-chih t'u and were called ts'ao-tui ("trough pestles").[2] The small size of this kind of rudimentary apparatus explains how Shih Ch'ung, prefect of Ching-chou at the beginning of the Yüan-k'ang reign period (291–199), could have owned more than thirty of them on his land.[3] The governor of Ho-nan during the T'ai-shih reign period (265–274), Tu Yü, on the other hand, is said to have been the inventor of a new machine that was more complex and no doubt bulkier, which he had constructed on the banks of the river Lo. This was a "multiple installation driven by water power" (lien-chi shui-wei).[4] Another figure well known for his interest in mills was Ts'ui Liang, president of the Board of Finance at the beginning of the sixth century under the Northern Wei.[5] It seems that the development of large-scale milling installations dates from his period.

The terminology of milling in China is poorly understood—as are so many technical vocabularies, and the precise meaning of the terms nien and wei, generally used to designate all milling equipment under the T'ang (nien-wei), is not clear.[6] One of the devices used at Tunhuang was analogous to those still found in Tonkin:[7] a large paddle wheel[8] is immersed in a diversion canal. Cams mounted at the end of its axle cause the rise and fall of rocking arms to which the pestles are fixed. The apparatus used for grinding grain to flour, on the other hand, must have consisted essentially of a round millstone (nien) that rotated horizontally.[9] The accounts of An-kuo ssu mention the purchase of a "pounding timber" (tao-mu) in 884 and list repairs to the sluice gates and the mill wheel in 886. The latter year's accounts also include a charge for clearing out the millrace (hsieh-k'ou).

The use of these hydraulic machines depended on geographical conditions: the water-driven nien-wei were found uphill on the irrigation canals above the cultivated lands. Since the installation and maintenance of these devices appear to have been costly, they were mainly encountered on the estates of wealthy land owners. In the region of the two T'ang capitals, Lo-yang and Ch'ang-an, automatic flour mills were plentiful: it is there that great private estates had been established by members of the imperial family, high officials, and the monasteries. Moreover, the region disposed of an ancient irrigation system. Well-known canals, such as the Cheng and the Po, discharged their waters into this area.[10] By contrast, in poorly irrigated places, it is probable that pestles and millstones operated by hand or by oxen continued to be used.

In the territory of the two capitals, on the borders of Honan and Shensi, monasteries and wealthy lay landowners vied with one another for influence, and it is in that region that their economic antagonism was also most in evidence. The flour mills became objects of disputes between monks and laymen. The Hsü shih-shuo[11] relates that when Li Yüan-hung was director of the prefectural service of finance hu-ts'ao at Yung-chou (modern Hsi-an fu), the T'ai-p'ing princess was engaged in litigation against Buddhist monks over the ownership of certain mills. Li Yüan-hung's judgment had decided the case in favor of the monks and ordered the return of the mills in question to the monasteries. But for fear of the princess's influence, Tou Huai-chen, the prefect (chang-shih) of Yung-chou, gave in to her demands and quashed the original verdict.

The great monasteries and the rich laity owned the same kinds of assets and had the same sources of revenue. It is likely that major hydraulic milling installations appeared simultaneously, around the beginning of the sixth century, on the lands of the great Buddhist monasteries and on those of the nobility and high officials.

References to water-driven devices in the monasteries are encountered from the end of the Northern Wei dynasty onward. The precincts of the Ching-ming ssu at Lo-yang, founded in the Ching-ming reign period (500–503) at a distance of one li outside the Hsüan-yang gate, extended within a perimeter of five hundred paces. Yang Hsüan-chih indicates in his description of that establishment[12] that its flour mills (nien-wei), mortars (ch'ung and winnowing baskets (po) were all driven by water power.[13]

The Hsü kao-seng chuan mentions mills and automatic "pounders" at the Ch'ing-ch'an monastery at the end of the sixth century:

> The Prince of Chin, of the house of Sui, who held the great masters of Dhyāna in high esteem, was pleased to be titular benefactor (dānap-ati) to that establishment. In the course of time, he donated, all in all, more than seventy households as well as water-driven pestles and millstones (shui-wei chi nien), comprising six installations from upstream to downstream. These assets were intended to constitute a permanent endowment for that monastery, and they have not ceased to generate revenues to this day.[14]

At that same period, Yang Su, an aristocrat despised for his excessive greed for gain, is said to have owned numerous water pestles (shui-wei) in addition to "hundreds of thousands" of shops (ti-tien), fields, and houses.[15]

In Shansi, in the modern prefecture of P'u-chou, the P'u-chiu monastery owned gardens, vegetable fields, and automatic "pounders" throughout the region. Having started with little, it became, thanks to the perseverance of the monk Tao-chi (568–636), a wealthy and important monastery.[16]

A stele in the hamlet of Po-ku, where the Shao-lin monastery owned an estate (chuang), also mentions, after the imperial gift of forty ch'ing (ca. 216 ha) of land on the fifteenth day of the second month, eighth year of the Wu-te period (625), the donation of a water mill (shui-nien).[17]

In 840, during his pilgrimage in China, the Japanese monk Ennin saw hydraulic milling installations called san-chiao shui-nien on an estate of the Ting-chiao monastery in Hsin county, modern Shansi.[18]

These installations, which constituted an important source of income for the great lay families and major monasteries, multiplied in parallel with the development of large landed properties under the T'ang. The imperial government was obliged to counter this new abuse, for the paddle wheels reduced the current and entailed the loss of part of the irrigation water. Moreover, they increased the silting of the canals. A special law therefore restricted the use of mills during certain periods of the year. At Tun-huang, the diversion canals on which the machines were installed, were in principle only to be opened between the thirtieth day of the eighth month and the first day of the first month, i.e., after the end and before the beginning of farm work. For the rest of the year the water officials maintained gates that were kept under lock. The use of water for irrigation had first priority. When rainfall was sufficient to make irrigation unnecessary, the exceptional operation of pounding and grinding machines was authorized.[19]

The texts preserve traces of the imperial government's struggle against millowners:

> By the beginning of the K'ai-yüan reign period (713–742), the princes, princesses, and influential families had all established mills along the secondary canals (p'ang-ch'ü). . . . Li Yüan-hung[20] had them all destroyed in order that the fields below could be irrigated.[21]

A few decades later, some of these installations must have been reconstituted, for in 764 the secretaries of the Boards of Finance and Justice together with a magistrate of the capital city submitted a joint memorial to the emperor requesting the destruction of more than seventy mills belonging to princes, princesses, and to Buddhist and Taoist monasteries on the banks of the Po and Cheng canals.[22] "At the end of the Ta-li reign period (766–780). . . . The peasants belonging to the appanage of the princess Chao-i at Sheng-p'ing accused her of having deprived them of water for the irrigation of their fields by installing a mill on a canal." As a result of this incident, the emperor ordered the destruction of eighty mills.[23] The same situation is reported, with further suggestive details, in the biography of Kuo Tzu-i:[24] in the thirteenth year of Ta-li (778), an imperial edict ordered the destruction of the mills built along the embranchments of the Po canals because they hindered the irrigation of the fields belonging to the people. The princess of Sheng-p'ing had two flour mills there and Kuo Tzu-i also owned two mills. Yet the officials concerned did not dare to destroy these installations.[25] However, after an interview with the emperor, the princess agreed to relinquish her mills, and her example was followed by others. As a result, more than eighty mills belonging to influential families were destroyed.[26]

Although the imperial government was at times obliged to take the part of the peasants, milling operations also constituted a source of fiscal receipts for the state. The T'ang hui-yao confirms that a tax was levied on milling installations:[27] "In the first month of the sixth year of Yüan-ho (811), the monks at the capital submitted a petition requesting that the mills on their estates be exempted from taxes (shui)." Chief minister Li Chi-fu replied in a report to the throne: "The money and grain due in taxes are determined by a fixed rate. It would certainly not be admissible to grant liberality to the monks, who already enjoy excessive privileges, and thereby crush as many poor peasants lacking all support." The emperor adopted his advice.

This indication concerning the state tax on milling installations is further borne out by the manuscripts from Tun-huang. The Ching-t'u monastery paid an annual tax that seems to have been proportional to the revenues. It was apparently levied in the spring and the autumn:

In 930, mention is made of 4 shih of wheat and 2 shih of millet for the mill tax (wei-k'o). The term employed is the same as that used for the rents collected by the monastery, but here it stands for an outlay, not a receipt.[28] In 944, the Ching-t'u ssu paid nine shih of millet in taxes for its mills; in another year, 7 shih of wheat.[29] Another year again, it paid 4 shih of wheat in the spring and 2.5 shih in the autumn.[30]

Thus it would seem that the Ching-t'u monastery was liable to a tax of between 6 and 9 shih of cereals for the installations it owned.

On the other hand, the rent earned by the same monastery from its milling installations yielded more than 60 shih of flour annually, of which 40 were delivered in the spring and 20 in the autumn.[31] Apart from this flour, a good third of the milling residues also entered the granaries of the Ching-t'u ssu: bran, used as feed for the horses (12 *shih* at the time of the spring milling and 6 *shih* at the time of the autumn milling), and the coarse flour (*ts'u-mien*) that the gauze sieves had not allowed to pass and that served to feed the female workforce at the monastery.[32] The coarse flour varied in quantity from one year to another: from 2.2 to 10.8 *shih* in the spring and from 3.5 to 8.4 *shih* in the autumn. In addition to wheat, the monastery also milled smaller quantities of millet, for the most part in the autumn (the figures range from 3 to 5.5 *shih* of millet flour) and occasionally in the spring (between 2 and 2.5 *shih*).

The Ching-t'u monastery is known to have had a population of fifty to seventy religious. According to Naba Toshisada,[33] half of the flour and its by-products received as rent would have amply sufficed for the needs of the community. The flour, however, was used as currency and sold to the laity. A note dated 924[34] indicates that officials (*kuan-chia*) had given 5.6 *shih* of wheat in exchange for flour. At the same time, the diverse outlays of the monastery for the remuneration of its artisans, for banquets offered to officials, to the associations of the faithful, and to famous monks passing through Sha-chou, have to be taken into account. In a Chinese monastery, a great many regular and occasional holidays were observed throughout the year, and these feasts involved considerable expenses.

The maintenance of the mills was at the expense of the religious community. The millers to whom the installations were rented did not repair the machines; in the event of the failure of a part, the monastery called upon the services of professional millwrights (*wei po-shih*).[35] Every important event concerning the operation of the milling machinery was celebrated with a banquet to which the artisans were invited. There were banquets to mark the end of repair work and the opening of the sluice gates: after the repair of a mill wheel, the nuns of An-kuo monastery feasted with 1 *shih* of flour, 3 *sheng* of oil, and 1.2 *shih* of millet. For a banquet on the occasion of the opening of the sluice gates, the nuns of the same monastery spent .3 *shih* of millet, .1 *shih* of wheat, and .5 *sheng* of oil.[36]

There were also nocturnal feasts with illuminations ("lamp festivals," *jan-teng*) at the mills: "Expenditure of 2 *ko* of oil for the feast of lamps at the mill."[37]

The monasteries not only took charge of all repairs but also supplied the millers with the materials they required: ".8 *shih* of cereals paid out for the millers (*wei-chia*) to buy gauze." The gauze would be used for making sieves.[38] The Ching-t'u monastery also rented the animals that transported the flour to the monastery's store houses: "Expenditure of 2.5 *shih* of bran for an ox to bring back the flour," and elsewhere, "3 *shih* for the rental of draught oxen for [the transport of] the flour."[39]

A part of the cereals processed by the mills was supplied by the monasteries themselves. But, in view of the relatively insignificant amounts of self-supplied cereals in comparison to the quantities of flour and by-products that annually left the mills, it is likely that a good part of the wheat and millet was brought in by the peasants who worked on the lands of the monastery, and even by outsiders. That is surely the explanation for the large quantity of flour received by the Ching-t'u monastery as "mill rent." It is even possible that all the cereals produced in the Sha-chou region passed through mills owned by the monasteries.

The available indications regarding the quantities of cereals supplied by the Ching-t'u ssu are as follows:

- six *shih* of wheat to be dried for the autumn milling;
- forty *shih* to be washed for the spring milling;
- three *shih* to be dried;
- twenty-two *shih* to be washed;[40]
- fifty-three *shih* supplied to the mills;[41]
- ninety-eight *shih* supplied in 939.[42]

In an account ledger are listed the quantities of cereals processed by eight milling households that must each have been in charge of an installation. It will be noted that the amounts vary considerably from one household to another:

During the spring milling of the *chi-ch'ou* year, the expert artisan (*tu-liao*) Wang [processed] thirty *shih* of *lo* wheat, one cartload of millet, and one cartload of wheat. Yin Kou-tzu [processed] three cartloads of *lo* wheat, one cartload of millet, and one cartload of dry wheat. Chu Shan-chu [processed] thirty *shih* of *lo* wheat; Chang Yüan-pao, one cartload of *lo* wheat; Wang Man-ch'eng, seven *shih* of millet and three *shih* of wheat; Ho A-ying, three *shih* of millet and three *shih* of wheat; K'ang A-to, fifteen *shih* of *lo* wheat; Mu Chang-san, twenty-five *shih* of *lo* wheat and six *shih* of dry wheat.[43]

Among the collection of Tun-huang manuscripts in Paris is found the request of a shepherd named An Yü-lüeh for the milling of a certain quantity of wheat and millet in his possession. This request would have been addressed, according to Naba Toshisada,[44] to the abbot or another high-ranking monk in a monastery. Such a document proves not only that the monasteries supplied cereals to their mills (nien-wei) but also that the milling households were not authorized to hull and mill on their own initiative: anyone wanting to have his grain turned into flour needed to first obtain the agreement of the monastery to which the milling installation belonged.

It may be asked who these millers and milling households (wei-chia, wei-hu) mentioned in the accounts of the monasteries at Tun-huang were and what status was assigned to them. According to the important text concerning the privileges of the Buddhist Church discussed by Naba Toshisada,[45] the wei-hu were, like the peasants on the estates (chuang), serfs who remained hereditarily attached to the monastery and were known as "households held in perpetuity" (ch'ang-chu po-hsing), or, more vaguely, as "monastery households" (ssu-hu). At Tun-huang, monastery households were likewise assigned to the oil presses.[46] It does not appear that the rents charged to the milling households were of the same kind in all monasteries. The annual variations of the mill rent (wei-k'o) at the Ching-t'u monastery suggest that that establishment reserved for itself a fixed percentage of the quantity of flour produced by its mills, therefore referring in this case to a production rent. Elsewhere, as at the An-kuo nunnery, the rent was no longer paid in flour, but in raw commodities. Moreover, it did not vary over the years. Thus in 884, 885, and 886, wei-k'o receipts earned the An-kuo ssu exactly 62.6 shih of wheat, 32.6 shih of millet, and 2.8 shih of hemp. In the accounts of an unidentified monastery, the mill rent is given as 54.5 shih of wheat and 43.5 shih of millet:[47] the same figures are also found in another account fragment belonging presumably to the same monastery.[48]

Other establishments also collected their mill rent in cereals. The following entries may be cited: "24 shih of wheat and 3 shih of millet collected in mill rent (wei-k'o)";[49] elsewhere, the rent amounted to 72 shih of wheat,[50] but at the San-chieh monastery it was 52.4 shih of flour. It was 24 shih of flour over a period of three years at the Pao-en monastery, or 8 shih per year. Revenues derived from the wei-k'o were thus not equally significant for all monasteries, some of which may not have owned any hulling and milling machinery at all. Furthermore, some of the milling households were required to pay a fixed annual rent, whereas others remitted to the monastery a portion of the flour they produced.

In any event, the mill rent constituted a very significant source of income for certain establishments in Tun-huang. In the case of the Ching-t'u ssu, regarding which there is the most information, it may be assumed that the wei-k'o accounted for the equivalent of one-third of its receipts in cereals: Naba Toshisada considers the total amount of flour and secondary milling products each year to have reached close to 120 shih, whereas receipts in wheat and millet amounted to 366.9 shih in 924 and only 136.83 shih in 930.[51] Flour of course is a far more valuable commodity than the same volume of cereals. However, there are more significant cases: at the An-kuo monastery in 884, 885, and 886, mill rents provided 294 shih (62.6 shih of wheat, 32.6 shih of millet, and 2.8 shih of hemp each year) out of 308.9 shih of wheat, millet, and hemp, or nearly the totality of these three commodities.[52]

Presses

Given the isolated location of Tun-huang and the small size of the town, its major monasteries must have been virtually self-sufficient. Indeed, it is clear that they were frequently surplus producers. Like flour, the oil produced by the monasteries could be sold outside. This degree of autonomy may have been peculiar to establishments at Tun-huang; in China proper, it is likely that the monasteries bought their oil from lay producers. In Tun-huang, there were special lands whose revenues were designated to defray the expenses for incense and lamps.[53] In fact, there was a considerable demand for oil in Buddhist establishments, and oil was among the most precious commodities.[54] The lamps that burned permanently in the Buddha Hall, and above all the "illuminations" (jan-teng) that frequently took place inside and outside the monasteries, consumed a great deal. At Tun-huang, the same oil was used for the lamps and for cooking. In addition, oil served as currency.

Following are some figures concerning expenses for oil according to the monastery accounts:

- .3 shih (18 liters) for the lamps lit permanently (ch'ang-ming teng);
- .025 for the lamp festival of the fifteenth day of the first month;
- .065 for a lamp festival on the eighth day of the second month;

- .0303 for the cold food festival *han-shih* (105 days after the winter solstice).

For the preparation of cakes for the *chai* banquets the expenditure was less onerous:

- .005 for a one-day *chai* and .02 for a great *chai* of four days duration.[55]

Occasionally, the monastery would also pay its artisans or its bills for purchases in oil:

- .0015 for a quilted gown and a meal.[56]
- .05 *shih* of oil for the sculptor-artisan Ling-hu and the workers who coated the walls.

The oilcake (*cha-ping* or *tzu-ping*) was used as food for sheep: In 924, the Ching-t'u ssu supplied its shepherds with 2 oilcakes to fatten their sheep; in 930, 11 oilcakes.[57]

The Ching-t'u monastery rented its oil presses out to oilery households (*liang-hu*) in exchange for an annual rent of 3 *shih* (ca. 180 l) of oil and 27 oilcakes. According to all the extant accounts, the rent from oil presses (*liang-k'o*) was invariable.[58] There seem to have been sixteen or seventeen oilery households in the service of that monastery. The rent was undoubtedly fixed by contract; evidence for this is provided by a deed dated the first day of the second month of a *ting-yu* year (877 or 937?) in which an oilery and a milling household (*wei-hu*) undertook to pay the price of their rent: "Should they fail to pay their rent," the document states, "their movables (*chia-tzu*) shall be seized; if one or the other party defaults, it shall suffer a penalty."[59]

Like the *wei-hu*, the oilery households were not held liable for the maintenance of their installations. The monastery used professional artisans to see to their repair. The oil that was left to the families operating the presses after payment of the rent could be used by them as currency. Whenever the monastery needed extra provisions of oil, it purchased them from the *liang-hu*. In one of the years where the entries of oil exceeded the three *shih* of the rent from the oil presses, the monastery purchased .04 *shih* of oil from the head of an oilery household, Kuo Huai-i, in exchange for 24 feet of wool cloth.[60]

At the same time, the monastery collected a tax on the quantity of oil purchased by laymen from its households: in 930, the Ching-t'u ssu collected .04 *shih* of oil from two laymen who had had their hemp pressed by oileries belonging to the monastery.[61]

It would seem, however, that it was the monastery that supplied the oileries with the necessary hemp to produce the 3 *shih* of oil collected annually. Deliveries of hemp to the oileries are in fact mentioned frequently:

"4.3 *shih* of hemp supplied to the *liang-hu* to make oil."[62]

"In the sixth month, .7 and 2.8 *shih* of hemp supplied [to the oileries]."[63]

The expenditures in hemp amounted to 5.3 *shih* in 924, to 9 *shih* in 930,[64] and at different times to 7.7,[65] 7, or 8.8 *shih*.[66] The hemp was not cultivated on the lands of the Ching-t'u monastery and had to be entirely procured from interest payments or donations. Thus in certain years the monastery received 11.85 *shih* of hemp,[67] 4.645 *shih*, 3.13 *shih*,[68] and 3.16 *shih*.[69] In 924, the faithful gave .74 *shih* of hemp, on the occasion of a banquet, "for the Buddha and the saṃgha;" in 930, on the occasion of a sutra recitation in the town during the twelfth month, .65 *shih*, "for oil to serve the needs of the Buddha and the monks."[70]

Oil presses were also owned by other monasteries: one of them received 2.8 *shih* of oil as rent from oil presses (*liang-k'o*)[71] and in the same year also collected 8.15 *shih* of hemp. But other establishments that did not own oil presses had to make do with what offerings they received. This was the case of the Pao-en monastery, which in a period of three years received a gift of 4.5 *shih* of hemp but no oil whatever— at a time when its stocks were very low (.005 *shih*);[72] or again of the Lien-t'ai ssu for which certain accounts indicate that it received .29 *shih* of oil in one year and 3.7 *shih* of hemp.[73]

Nevertheless, thanks to the industrial installations on their estates, the great monasteries at Tun-huang played a very important economic role in the region. It may be surmised that they provided the entire supply of flour and oil to the population of Tun-huang. To be sure, the profits they gained from this privileged position were well above those derived from farming.[74] Here may be witnessed the beginnings of a capitalist economy, the advantages of which quickly became apparent to the wealthy laity and the monasteries alike: it was not so much land itself that paid as turning one's wealth to good use in the most profitable enterprises. And while the latter were still related to agriculture, the connection was already beginning to loosen.

CHAPTER SIX

COMMERCE AND USURY

Whereas the growth of landed estates remained linked to larger structural, agricultural, and social developments, commercial activity was less dependent on such factors. Borrowings from the outside world were thus more likely in this area. Hence the relevance of an inquiry into the Indian prescriptions regulating commercial activities, not as interdictions—these were scarcely respected in China—but as points of departure in a process of evolution. Under the influence of converts from the merchant milieu, certain sects of the Lesser Vehicle increasingly took recourse to profane practices. As a result, an originally austere attitude gradually softened, and in the end commerce became fully integrated into the devout activities of the saṃgha. This evolution appears to have reached its completion under the Buddhism of the Greater Vehicle. The Chinese communities of that movement modeled themselves on their Serindian counterparts, whose practices are little known. The considerable information supplied by Indian treatises on discipline, however, suggests both a continuity of concepts and techniques and their eventual transmission to the Chinese world.

Indian Antecedents

Three of the acts condemned by the Vinaya are related to commercial activities: handling gold and silver (*jātarūpa-rajata-spaśana*), dealing in precious metals (rūpika-vyahāra), and buying and selling (kraya-vikraya). In theory, dealing in precious metals should be doubly reprehensible since it combines two types of offense, one resulting from the contact with gold or silver, the other flowing from commercial operations as such. However, the boundaries between the three types of offense are not very clear. These rules were set out in empirical fashion and not carefully put in order. Such empiricism and lack of elaboration are generally characteristic of the treatises on Buddhist discipline.

Some Vinaya limit themselves to a brief statement of the three interdictions; allusions to commercial activities are rare in these texts. Others dwell at greater length on the regulations in question. The Sarvāstivāda, Mahāsāṃghika, and Mūlasarvāstivāda represent a much more conciliatory position with regard to commerce and dealing with precious objects. They not only accommodate such activities but even discuss the commercial and financial practices in which religious communities engaged. Following are synopses of the relevant passages pertaining to the three interdictions in each of the five Vinaya as translated into Chinese:[1]

CONTACT WITH PRECIOUS OBJECTS

1. Mahīśāsakavinaya
Brief enunciation of the interdiction.[2]

2. Dharmaguptavinaya
A great minister and friend of Upananda[3] gives him a quarter of a pig. It is a festival day at Rājagṛha. Like all the inhabitants of the town, the son of this minister has been out all night. He returns hungry, hoping to eat some of the pork that had meanwhile been offered to Upananda by his father. When his mother informs him of the donation he gives her five coins to go and buy the quarter back from Upananda. Upananda accepts the bargain and picks up the coins laid on the ground before him by the wife of the minister. The transaction causes a scandal. The Buddha reminds the community that monks may not touch precious metals or money. Goods of that kind need to be entrusted to the keepers of the gardens (shou-yüan jen)[4] or to lay believers (upāsaka).[5]

3. Sarvāstivādavinaya
Contact with and handling of gold and silver are forbidden. Contact with certain moneys, however, made of iron, lead, copper, tin, leather,

wood, etc., only constitutes a minor sin (duṣkṛta). Small quantities of precious metals are passed on to a lay servant (ching-jen); where there is no servant, such goods are used to have beds made for the saṃgha of the four directions.[6]

4. Mahāsāṃghikavinaya

It is prohibited to store gold, silver, or money, for their possession engenders the five desires (of vision, hearing, taste, smell, and touch). Udāyi has received some money from a donor. Knowing that he must not touch it, he has it sown into a corner of his habit and goes to market to buy himself some cake. This subterfuge is condemned by the Buddha. Precious metals and money are to be given up to the saṃgha; it is not permitted to share them out among the monks. If the amount is large, it is assigned to the special category of goods designated "inexhaustible property" (wu-chin wu); if these produce interest, they shall be used for the construction of dwellings or the purchase of clothing for the monks. It no case may such moneys serve for feeding the religious, for they are impure. To handle them, certain precautions are necessary. Monks may receive donations in the form of money, but they may not take them into their own hands; they shall take recourse to a ching-jen. If their office requires them to handle large quantities of gold, silver, or money on behalf of the Buddha or the saṃgha, they shall take care to store them hidden in the ground whence they shall have them extracted by a lay servant (ching-jen). In the event that they are obliged to do so themselves, they shall veil their eyes with triple blindfolds and wrap their hands in cloth.[7]

Cult objects plated with gold or silver must not be touched by the bhikṣu (312b).[8] Fallen to the ground, they are picked up by the parts not covered with precious metals. If they are entirely covered, the monk wraps his hands with clothing. Money is likewise untouchable, regardless of the material of which it is made, including iron and bamboo. To touch money that is wrought or marked constitutes a "misdemeanor requiring relinquishment (i.e., the surrender of the goods obtained) and public repentance" (shih-to or ch'i-to; Skr. naiḥsargika prāyaścittika). But if the money is neither wrought nor marked, or if it is made of bronze, no sin is committed.[9]

5. Mūlasarvāstivādavinaya

The prohibition against handling precious objects applies to gold, silver, moneys [used as local currency], precious pearls, jades, mother-ofpearl (*vaidūrya*), cowrie, and ivory. But it is not sinful to handle moneys that are not used in the country, red copper, brass, copper, lead, and tin.

If the bhikṣu wish to construct a house, they must ask for thatch, wood, and for carts and workers; they may not ask for gold, silver, or money. As a result of this prohibition, even bhikṣu whose clothes are in tatters do not dare to accept money from the masters of alms to buy new clothing. The Buddha declares that they should have recourse to either monastery domestics (*ssu chia-jen*) or lay believers (*upāsaka*).[10] These would ensure the storage of impure and untouchable goods for the monks, if necessary by burying them in hiding places in the ground.[11]

BARTER

1. Mahīśāsakavinaya
Upananda exchanges a garment in rags for the new garment of a heretic. The heretic's companions, seeing that he had been tricked, demand the annulment of the transaction. In violation of the rules of commerce that stipulate a period of seven days before an operation becomes irrevocable, Upananda refuses to relinquish the bargain. As a result of this affair, the Buddha rules that it is not permissible to seek profit in barter.[12]

2. Dharmaguptavinaya
It is improper to pay for one's food and lodging as did Upananda when he procured provisions in a village in exchange for ginger. The story about the barter of the old garment for the heretic's new one is taken up again here. Upananda is reproached on two accounts: first, failure to commission a lay servant (*ching-jen*) to carry out the operation and, second, disregard for the rule that entitles the buyer to withdraw from the transaction after the transfer of the goods has taken place. Barter is accepted within the communities provided that it does not give rise to the kind of haggling that goes on in the marketplace. [The rite of relinquishing the goods acquired is here described (621a): the guilty bhikṣu presents himself before the community, his right shoulder bared and having removed his leather sandals. He approaches the dean and performs a salutation by kneeling with his right knee on the ground and joining both hands in a gesture of contrition.][13]

3. Sarvāstivādavinaya

Again, the story of the barter of garments won by Upananda. The barter of like objects (bowl against bowl, etc.) is condemned, as well as the barter of dissimilar goods (bowl against garment, etc.).[14] As a result of this prohibition, the bhikṣu want to take back the goods they have already exchanged. Disputes take place, and the Buddha declares that if a bargain is revoked within seven days of its conclusion, the goods have to be returned; beyond that period, the exchange becomes irrevocable.

If a bhikṣu has purchased for gain but does not resell for gain, this constitutes a simple sin (duṣkṛta). The same holds true if he sells for gain but buys nothing in exchange. But if he buys and resells for gain (that is, the commercial cycle of buying and reselling has been completed), then he has committed a naiḥsargika prāyaścittika, i.e., a sin for which atonement requires both repentance and the relinquishing of the goods. [Here follows a section concerning the prohibition of contact with precious objects that assuredly is out of place in the present paragraph: the consumption of food bought with gold, silver, or money is a duṣkṛta; the wearing of clothes thus obtained, constitutes a prāyaścittika]. In bartering, the usual period of seven days must be observed. Auction sales within the communities are accepted.[15]

4. Mahāsāṃghikavinaya

The six evil bhikṣu (liu-ch'ün pi-ch'iu; Skr. ṣaḍvargīka-bhikṣu)[16] purchase various victuals in the market. The Buddha condemns their bargaining and, even more, their acquisitions resulting from this bargaining. However, barter and auction sales are by and large permitted: all depends on intention and circumstance. Casuistry was highly developed among the Mahāsāṃghika. There are allusions to sales within the community that are accepted.[17]

5. Mūlasarvāstivādavinaya

The paragraph concerning barter is very short here. The nineteenth and twentieth naiḥsargika prāyaścittika seem to have been subject to modifications: the nineteenth naiḥsargika prāyaścittika, entitled "Seeking gain through commerce" (ch'u-na ch'iu li, a title that only remotely evokes the original rūpika-vikraya), incorporates part of the early tradition concerning barter and seems highly developed.

The twentieth naiḥsargika prāyaścittika: the six evil bhikṣu indulge in all kinds of transactions, in "a commerce that consists of taking and giving." "Taking," explains a note, means to supply goods that are expensive here and cheap elsewhere. "Giving" means to take away goods that are cheap here and expensive elsewhere. Buying in times of plenty and selling in times of shortage, is a *naiḥsargika*. If one purchases for gain but does not resell for gain, it is a *duṣkṛta* at the time of the purchase, but no sin is committed at the time of reselling. If one does not purchase for gain but resells for gain, it is the reverse, but the sin committed in reselling is a *prāyaścittika*. A profit realized without intention does not constitute a sin. Here follows a section concerning the barter featured in the nineteenth *naiḥsargika prāyaścittika*:[18] a mendicant monk (*nirgrantha*) receives the gift of a fine garment from merchants having come to Śrāvastī from the North. Upananda persuades him to exchange it for an old rag. The mendicant monk's companions, realizing that he had been taken in, go to Upananda to recuperate their property. Upon their approach, Upanada locks himself in his cell. The mendicant monks demand from the Buddha that the culprit be handed over to them for a heavy thrashing, and that he pay with his life if he refused just restitution.[19]

COMMERCE

1. Mahīśāsakavinaya
Nanda and Upananda used gold and silver as well as gold and silver currency and other moneys to purchase goods. They also sold these goods in order to procure precious metals and money. The wealth thus acquired must be relinquished to the saṃgha and may not be attributed to one, two, or three person (i.e., to individuals). If the saṃgha determined to expel [these impure goods], they should be cast into a pit, a fire, into flowing water, the bush, a place that may not be discovered. If the goods are not rejected, they must be handed over to a lay servant (*ching-jen*) who shall exchange them for food and clothing[20] for the saṃgha.[21]

2. Dharmaguptavinaya
Upananda exchanges currencies on the market. All transactions of that kind are condemned: exchange of raw precious metals against wrought metals, wrought metals against raw metals, etc., as well as diverse operations involving currencies. The goods acquired must be relinquished and entrusted to keepers of the gardens (*shou-yüan jen*)

or to lay believers (upāsaka) who shall exchange them against cloth-ing, bowls, furniture, needles, and cases for the saṃgha. They shall be called to account should they appropriate any of the goods thus entrusted to them.[22]

3. Sarvāstivādavinaya

The six evil bhikṣu utilize, to all kinds of ends, precious metals that had been abandoned in accordance with the Buddha's injunction. They have buildings constructed, establish gold markets, markets for hired labor (k'o-tso ssu), markets for coppersmiths, and markets for processing pearls. They raise herds of elephants, horses, camels, cat-tle, mules, sheep, and they raise slaves of both sexes, disciples, and commoners. Under these conditions, lands belonging to the people were seized by force and sold to the bhikṣu. Those who thus lost their possessions vent their anger complaining [to the Buddha]: "These śramaṇa, son of Śākya, pretend to goodness and virtue, yet here they are using precious metals in every manner to install markets and engage in commerce. Their conduct is no different from that of the king or the great ministers."[23] The Buddha then condemns all the uti-lizations of precious metals: exchange of wrought metals for raw met-als, etc., of similar objects made of precious metals for, and of dissim-ilar objects (?), etc. Currency dealings are likewise condemned. Small quantities of precious metals are to be discarded. If the amount is large, it should be entrusted to a lay servant. Where there are no lay servants, the goods are used to procure beds for the saṃgha of the four directions.[24]

4. Mahāsāṃghikavinaya

Nanda and Upananda, who have connections with the royal palace, buy gold from the king's household and have jewellery made from it by the king's goldsmith. Then they assign śramaṇa to sell the jew-ellery to ladies of high standing. This business harms the trade of the gold merchants and goldsmiths of the town, who complain. The Bud-dha condemns all traffic in precious metals, whether as worked objects or as raw material.[25]

5. Mūlasarvāstivādavinaya

At that time, the group of six [evil] bhikṣu indulged in all kinds of profit making [financial operations] consisting of taking, giving, pro-ducing, and taking against a pledge (chih). They traded finished products for finished products or finished products for raw materials, etc. To *take* means to receive valuable and desirable goods from foreign lands. When one is about to transport them to distant places, one seeks guarantors (*fang-shou jen*) and draws up contracts (*ch'üan-ch'i*). That is what is meant by *taking*. To *give* means to pass goods on to others, on the basis of contracts and certificates (*ch'i cheng*), within eight or ten days [of the conclusion of the bargain?]. That is what is called *giving*. To *produce* means to generate interest. One gives a small quantity of goods to others and receives large quantities of cereals or barley. At times, one's principal is increased by a fifth or one half, or it may be doubled. To accumulate quantities of cereals on the basis of contracts, that is what is meant by *producing* [interest]. To *receive in pledge* is to receive valuables, pearls, etc., and drawing up a contract as above. One seeks a trustworthy guarantee (*pao-cheng*) and hands over one's wealth and one's goods. That is what is called *receiving in pledge*. In this manner the bhikṣu traded to enrich themselves. Seeing this, the heretics expressed repugnance and contempt: "Son of Śākya, how do these śramaṇa who traffic for profit differ from laymen?" The Buddha declares that all these practices constituted *naiḥsargika prāyaścittika*.

The same section, devoted to the nineteenth *naiḥsargika prāyaścittika*, comprises a third part, which shows that the prohibition against allowing one's capital to bear fruit was not categorical: if the benefit accrued to the saṃgha, it was legitimate.

Observing that the monastery of the saṃgha was falling to ruins, the great patrons (*dānapati*) asked themselves: "How will it be after our death? We must provide inexhaustible property (*wu-chin wu*) so that it may be rebuilt." And they gave alms to the bhikṣu, saying: "Reverends, this inexhaustible property we give you for the purpose of rebuilding the monastery. Thus you should accept it. The bhikṣu replied that according to the precepts of the Buddha it was improper for them to accept. But they put the matter to the Buddha. "If it is for the saṃgha, and there are repairs to be carried out, said he, accept such inexhaustible property. Thus the bhikṣu's residence (*vihāra*) shall be rebuilt in three stories, and that of the bhikṣuṇī in two." The bhikṣu therefore received the inexhaustible property and placed it into the treasury. The masters of alms then came to ask them why their *vihāra* had not yet been rebuilt. "The reason, sirs, is that we have no money." "But have we not given you inexhaustible property?" "How could we use it (literally, eat it)? We have placed it into the treasury of the saṃgha, and it is still there." "That is not the way to employ it," replied the masters of alms, "for then would it not have remained just as well in our safekeeping? Why not trade it and earn interest?" The bhikṣu laid out the matter in detail before the Buddha, who instructed them that if it was for the benefit of the saṃgha, they ought to earn the interest. When the Brahman and simple believers learned of the Buddha's instruction, they began to make donations of inexhaustible property to the Buddha, the Law, and the saṃgha.[26] Thereupon, the bhikṣu returned their goods to the masters of alms in order to earn interest from them. However, when the time came to collect the interest, numerous disputes arose. "How dare you make property belonging to us the subject of your disputes," said the masters of alms. Informed of this affair, the Bhagavat told the bhikṣu no longer to invest their [inexhaustible] property with such people. Instead, they placed it with the poor. However, on the redemption date they had nothing. "When you lend goods," said the Buddha, "the conditions must be clearly established. Let there be pledges worth twice the value of the loan and contracts drawn up. In addition, a guarantee (pao-cheng) shall be deposited and the year and month recorded. The name of the dean (shang-tso, Skr. sthavira) shall be inscribed as well as those of the monks in charge (shou-shih jen). Even if you are dealing with an upāsaka, one who has received the five instructions, he shall likewise be obliged to furnish pledges."[27]

It will be noted that the different treatises on discipline adopt diverging solutions with regard to precious metals: (1) rejection, (2) referral to lay followers for the purchase of items of necessity ("pure" goods) for the monks, (3) deposit in reserve for utilization as loans.

In the Pāli Vinaya, exclusive recourse is taken to the first solution. The Sarvāstivāda employ (1) and (2) side by side: small quantities of metals are discarded; large quantities are used for purchases on behalf of the saṃgha. By contrast, the Mahāsāṃghika and Mūlasarvāstivāda purchase items of necessity with part of their precious metals and use the remainder to build a treasury for gainful investment.

Moreover, among the reprehensible acts for which monks are criticized, different levels of commercial activity may be distinguished:

1. The purchase of food, clothing and even accommodation, whether by means of barter or the payment of money.
2. Trading no longer with a view to procure the necessities of life but for profit.

3. Investments in enterprises that employ manpower: metal crafts, goldsmiths and jewellers, animal rearing, slave labor, agriculture (Sarvāstivāda and Mahāsāṃghika).
4. Loans for interest on the security of pledges and by written contract (Mūlasarvāstivāda).

Thus it appears that commercial and financial activities were unevenly developed in the circles in which the Vinaya were compiled and that the various Buddhist sects adopted a more or less conciliatory attitude with regard to commerce. This is undoubtedly due to differences of period and place.

Moreover, it is difficult to ascertain the precise object of the prohibitions concerning precious metals and money as well as barter: moral reprobation, taboo, or desire to preserve a certain type of monastic life?[28] Generally speaking, it appears that the precepts aim at mercantile activities as a whole on account of their profane nature,[29] and that because gold, silver, and money are the preferred media of exchange employed by commerce, their handling was forbidden to bhikṣu by extension.

It was an economy based on the exchange of gifts, including the exchange of alms against predication, that operated between the faithful and the Three Jewels (triratna). That was the only proper form of exchange: it was seemly and had a moral rationale as well. Things given freely have a unique significance for, in addition to their material value, they possess a kind of religious power and, in the case of Buddhism, a karmic productivity. Sold objects are on the contrary worth no more than their commercial base value. Exchanges of gifts and commercial transactions constitute two domains that are, if not of a different kind—for they share analogous features—at least antithetical. And their opposition becomes more pronounced as commerce develops and evolves its own set of rules, while the act of giving acquires, as in the case of Buddhism, a moral and religious value. Thus the question posed by the economic, commercial, and financial development of the Buddhist communities becomes clear: how, by what detour, were mercantile activities able to introduce themselves into the saṃgha? In fact it is not a question of the degree of relaxation of the early austerity, but of a veritable rupture, a leap from the religious domain to the utterly profane and quasi-immoral domain of sales and loans at interest. The question concerns above all the Buddhist religion, which made giving one of its cardinal virtues; it is also pertinent in the context of China's tradition of deep hostility toward mercantile activities: while the literati class were not insensitive to the moralizing tendencies of Buddhism, the economic activities of the church and the monks aroused strong reactions and severe criticism on their part.

In the beginning, the need for the saṃgha to transform the impure goods it inherited or received as gifts was clearly the point of departure for commercial activity within the Buddhist communities.[30] Impure possessions thus posed a problem that could only be resolved by recourse to bartering, and here lies the origin of one of the contradictions of Buddhism: commerce is at the same time repudiated and practiced, prohibited to the monks but recommended to the saṃgha. Moreover, donation and usury—two conflicting practices—became the two principal sources of the Buddhists communities' wealth. Curtailed by monastic discipline, the stocking of goods, bartering, and selling and buying were still confined to the framework of a rather rudimentary economy. There remained a further step to be taken, namely the placement of interest-bearing investments. Not all of the Indian sects had taken this step; those who did, meanwhile, were actively encouraged by the laity,[31] and especially, it seems, by those belonging to the milieu of merchants converted to Buddhism.[32] In this regard, a passage from the *Sarvāstivādavinaya* devoted to the permanent nature of the property attached to reliquaries (stūpa) is instructive:

> The merchants of Vaiśālī sold stūpa property for profit in order to pay homage to the stūpa. These merchants, about to depart to distant countries in order to enrich themselves, had goods belonging to the stūpa in their possession. They said to the bhikṣu: "Reverends, this stūpa property you ought to use to earn interest to pay homage to the stūpa." The bhikṣu replied: "The Buddha has not authorized us to place the property of the stūpa at interest in order to pay homage to it." They put the matter before the Buddha, and the Buddha declared: "I authorize the 'pure men' (*ching-jen*, i.e., lay servants) of the monasteries as well as lay believers (*upāsaka*) to draw interest from the property of the stūpa in order to pay homage to them."[33]

The sudden departure of the merchants here provides the impulse to transfer the lending activities to the religious community. According to time-honored procedure, however, the religious community appeals to the services of domestics and sedentary lay followers for the management of these impure goods. The *Sarvāstivādavinaya* seems to acknowledge the practice of earning interest from assets to provide offerings as routine, and there is also direct evidence of its implementation. An inscription pointed out by Sylvain Lévi shows that the earnings were not only intended for the needs of the cult but also for those of the monks:

> Other inscriptions at Nasik, at Karle (ca. fifty km south of Nasik)[34] further commemorate the pious foundations of Uṣavadāta, the Saka, and of the princess Dakṣamitrā, his wife. One of these is worth citing because of the light it throws on the modalities of these foundations. "Success! in the year 42, in the month of Vesākka (Vaiśākha), Uṣavadāta, son of Dūrika, son-in-law of the satrap Nahapāna the Kṣaharāta, gave this grotto to the universal community; he also donated, as a gift in perpetuity, three thousand *kāhāpaṇa*, which shall serve to clothe and maintain the members of the universal community residing in that grotto. These *kāhāpaṇa* have been deposited in accounts held by corporations with their seat at Govardhana, namely, two thousand at the corporation of weavers, at 1 *paḍika* percent [per month]; one thousand at another association of weavers, at ¾ of a *paḍika* percent. These *kāhāpaṇa* are not repayable; only the interest is to be claimed.[35] Of these amounts, two thousand placed at 1 *paḍika* percent are intended to defray the cost of clothing. Each of the twenty monks who will be lodged in my grotto during the rainy season shall receive twelve [*kāhāpaṇa*] for clothing. The one thousand placed at ¾ of a *paḍika* percent are intended for the cost of maintenance (? *kuśassa*)."[36]

At an early stage, this procedure, of lay provenance, which assured the continuity of offerings, was presumably practiced outside the community. The novelty occurred when one day the monks themselves took recourse to it.

That was the case among the Sarvāstivāda, with, however, the restriction that the goods in question not be managed by the monks themselves. The Mahāsāṃghika and Mūlasarvāstivāda were not constrained by that last obstacle or, rather, by that last vestige of the prohibitions governing the handling of impure goods. It may be assumed that by the time Buddhism was introduced to China the principle of direct management had already been accepted. In the course of his travels in India at the end of the seventh century, I-ching observed that the system of inexhaustible property was still in force in the monasteries of the West. He noted in particular that the monks' clothing was for the most part provided out of [earnings from] the permanent assets of the saṃgha. Or else, he adds, their habits were bought with the surplus of the harvest from the fields and gardens, or, again, from the *interest produced by the fruit of the orchards* that was annually allocated to the purchase of clothing. Moreover, he states, there were even landed estates (*chuang*) especially established for that purpose, and in China places of worship had specified lands ("places") for the provision of clothing.[37] These foundations made it possible to feed both monks and lay followers for, although the donors made their gifts to the monks, their beneficence extended without distinction to all and sundry.[38]

Three of the treatises on discipline give an account of practices pertaining to inexhaustible property or wealth (*wu-chin wu* or *wu-chin ts'ai*).[39] This has already been noted above with respect to the Mūlasarvāstivāda. The Mahāsāṃghika likewise took recourse to precious metals for interest-bearing investments, the type of goods best suited to such operations:

> Such gold and silver, whether in the form of coins, finished or raw, in large or small quantities, pure or alloyed, whether in the form of utensils, finished or unfinished, once made over to the saṃgha, they may not be taken back [by the bhikṣu]. If the quantity is large, they shall be assigned to the inexhaustible property. If as inexhaustible property they produce interest, this can be used to construct cells or lodgings for monks, but not to procure food [owing to its impurity].[40]

The produce of lands belonging to pious foundations, however, could be used to constitute inexhaustible property (as was the case among the Sarvāstivāda),[41] and it would seem that in that case the development of cult activities encouraged the development of this practice.

The Vinaya of the Mahāsāṃghika refers to the trees in the garden that surrounded the stūpa of the Buddha Kāśyapa. These trees, of five different species, were always in flower. The flowers served to pay homage to the Buddha and the fruit was given to the monks. When the flowers were plentiful, a portion was supplied to the garland makers who made garlands out of them and purchased the surplus. The amount earned by the monks was used for the maintenance of the lamps and the purchase of incense. If the amount was large, however, it was permitted to pay it into the inexhaustible property of the Buddha, and the same obtained for the flowers from the pond surrounding the stūpa on all four sides.

Surpluses of impure goods[42] were thus put to two different uses: a first portion was attributed to the current expenses of the cult and the needs of the religious; the remainder was held in reserve and placed to earn interest. An analogous practice is found in China.[43]

Introduced into the saṃgha through the example provided by the lay world, the custom of placing assets at interest did not fully penetrate there. As noted, the Sarvāstivāda remained suspicious of practices so blatantly profane: for them the management of loans had to be entrusted to monastery servants or to lay followers. The Mahāsāṃghika, by contrast, accepted that the monks deal with such operations themselves on the grounds that their pious intention justified their administration by the religious. The *Mahāsāṃghika-vinaya* mentions bhikṣu whose task it was to handle large amounts of gold and silver on "Buddha business" (*fo-shih*) or on "saṃgha business" (*seng-shih*).[44] The expansion of financial operations was undoubtedly encouraged by that of cult activities, for if the requirements of the monks needed to remain modest, those of the cult were not subjected to the same constraints. This may well be the reason for both the development of such practices and for the solution that in the end prevailed: the direct management by the religious.

Inexhaustible property was fundamentally of a dual nature: it consisted on the one hand of impure goods that, by Buddhist moral standards, were moreover the object of profane and reprehensible operations; yet at the same time their religious character, due to their provenance as gifts of faith and to their use in offerings, was sufficiently evident to be retained as justification.

All things considered, the institution does not occupy an important place in the treatises on discipline, and that is not surprising: inexhaustible property was sustained by little else than the sale of flowers or the produce from stūpa lands or by precious metals relinquished by monks at fault.[45] This was merely the beginning of a future development that appears to have taken place in the countries where the Greater Vehicle prevailed. In China, loans at interest, with or without pledges, were to become one of the principal activities of Buddhist monasteries and monks. But the institution also engendered new, entirely Mahāyānist notions: it no longer aimed solely to provide the triratna with offerings but also to relieve the suffering and miseries of all beings.

Commercial Activities of the Chinese Communities

There is a historical link between the spread of Buddhism in China and the development of commercial exchanges between East Asia and the Buddhist countries of Central Asia and India. The pious commerce in relics and sacred texts followed the same routes as mercantile commerce, and those that introduced Buddhism to China came from regions with a genius for trade.[46] With the monks, came the merchants from the West, such as the Parthian who in the sixth century plied his trade along the Yangtze.[47]

Moreover, Buddhism originated a new development of economic activity within China itself. The needs of the faithful and their places of worship prompted the appearance of crafts and commerce for the supply of devotional objects in the vicinity of the monasteries. In villages and townships, shops opened where sacred texts were copied and statuettes cast, and which occasionally appear to have been taverns as well.[48] The construction and decoration of buildings, the ornamentation of the streets at festival times, the maintenance of the mills and presses on the monastic estates required the services of craftsmen, technicians, and artists. A considerable number of trades are named in the manuscripts from Tun-huang: nail casters, tinsmiths, pot makers, furnace makers, cauldron repairmen, sculptors, locksmiths, glassworkers, roughcasters, hemp washers, felters, etc.[49] The registers of Mazār-tāgh show the importance of such crafts in the Chinese monasteries of Central Asia as well:

"Paid 120 cash to buy 3 *tou* of alcohol to give to Ssu-chin and the other laborers who worked hard on the Ch'ien-chung hall."[50]

"Paid 80 cash to the artisan Yeh-fan as remuneration for his services engaged to paint dragons and phoenixes on the banderoles and canopies of the procession in town."[51]

"Paid 100 cash to buy two rolls of paper, at 50 cash each, for pasting thirty-eight lanterns with streamers attached [for the festival of lamps on the fifteenth day of the first month]."[52]

"Paid 760 cash as remuneration for the artisan Kuei-ts'ai who helped make a felt carpet. He had previously been hired on the occasion of a ceremony for praying for good fortune."[53]

Buddhism, in other words, was good for business, and invigorated a whole sector of the Chinese economy. However, the development of crafts and trade in the neighborhood of the great places of worship was only a secondary phenomenon. The main element was the diversion of market traffic for the profit of the monasteries. Religious festivals and fairs are not without analogies: both were held in the same place,[54] and monasteries were frequently established near markets and in the busiest commercial streets.[55] When the wealthy laity, members of the aristocracy, high officials, and the great monasteries wished their assets to yield profits, they sought first of all access to the vantage points that were the markets. There they owned shops, which they rented out and on whose transactions they no doubt reserved themselves a percentage. And there they also operated loan stalls. The biography of Ts'ai Hsing-tsung (416–472) reports that "because princes, dukes, consorts, and princesses were establishing market shops (ti-she) in great numbers, and because they drew substantial profits from these and their demands were unlimited, [Ts'ai Hsing-tsung] proposed that this be curtailed."[56]

The great monasteries too had shops in the marketplaces: ti-she, ti-tien, or p'u-tien. These served, it seems, at once as inns for travelers, as shops, and as pawnshops.[57]

The rental of buildings of this kind seems to have been less common under the Six Dynasties than in following centuries, and references to ti-tien are found with increasing frequency in mid and late T'ang times: a further indication confirming the pronounced development of commercial activity under the T'ang. No longer do the wealthy laity and Buddhist establishments merely own shops, but also hotels (k'o-she)[58], carriage parks (chü-fang),[59] as well as mills (nien-wei).[60] It appears that by T'ang times the monasteries, together with the nobility and high-ranking officials, had gained control at least over the most important transactions.

> The master of the Law Ch'ang-yen (d. 816) had established commercial outlets (p'u-tien) on behalf of his monastery as well as shops providing loans against security (shou chih-ch'ien she-wu). The value of their annual business exceeded one hundred thousand cash.[61]

Near the Eastern Market, in Shan-ho ward, the Ta-hsiang monastery owned—in addition to major landed properties amounting to 56 ch'ing—"six and a half bays of shop space."[62]

Profits derived from the letting of shops (ti-tien) were also placed at interest. As we know from the act of grace dated fifth year of Hui-ch'ang (845):

According to the investigation entrusted to the commissioners of good works, We understand that rich monasteries own shops in many places. After having deducted the amount required for the "permanent assets" from the income of these houses, the remainder is used to carry out a busy commerce. It is not permissible for the monasteries to appropriate wealth in this way and to snatch away the property of people who are defenseless.[63]

The term *inexhaustible wealth* (*wu-chin ts'ai*),[64] borrowed from the treatises on discipline, was used in China to designate that part of the permanent assets (*ch'ang-chu wu*) dedicated to the provision of loans at interest. Lands, commodities, and money were sometimes donated by lay followers or by the monks themselves for that purpose. The texts emphasize the inalienable character of such property: the notion of permanent assets, originally confined to the community's immovables,[65] was in time extended in China to fungible goods as well and, in the end, came to denote in particular the various commodities and moneys that were stored in monastic treasuries.[66] It was precisely these fungible goods that served as loans; to dedicate their assets as "inexhaustible wealth" was a current means of ensuring the continuity of religious foundations.

The *Sung kao-seng chuan* reports that the monk Shen-ts'ou (744–817) was content with little and lived like an ascetic. Such remarkable comportment, for a Chinese monk, earned him quantities of alms. But Shen-ts'ou at once paid these into the inexhaustible wealth of the permanent assets (*ch'ang-chu wu-chin ts'ai*).[67]

Another monk, named Tao-piao (740–823), of Mount Ling-yin, had built up a substantial capital in cash for his community through the sale of ordination certificates (*tu-tieh*).[68] He was thus able to put a piece of land under cultivation that produced an annual revenue of ten thousand *hu* of cereals,[69] and he created—no doubt out of the revenue from these lands—a fund of inexhaustible wealth, which he made over to his community as property held in common.[70]

At the end of the T'ien-pao period (756), Li Ch'eng,[71] a high-ranking official and a Buddhist, donated his country estate (*pieh-shu*) to the Hui-lin monastery "as inexhaustible wealth to serve the needs of the community."[72]

Other references to "inexhaustible wealth" can no doubt be found in the biographies of famous monks and elsewhere. The above suffice to prove that the term and the practice were current in T'ang times.

But does this concern financial operations of the same type in each instance? Where they always simple loans at interest?

It is possible that India—especially through the intermediary of the Buddhist countries in Central Asia—introduced a new form of loan to China: the loans against pledges that were to appear first in Buddhist monasteries.[73] Thus the religious communities were more advanced in financial techniques than the laity.

The Vinaya of the Mūlasarvāstivāda, in an explanation concerning the necessary guarantees for the placement of "inexhaustible property" among the laity, mention pledges (chih).[74] Even though this ancient term was not unknown in commercial contexts, where it designated a certain type of contract, it appears that in the translations of Buddhist texts it was employed to denote an entirely new concept. The word pledge can in fact refer to two completely different institutions: the pledge named chih in the Vinaya plainly corresponds to the value of the loan; according to the Vinaya of the Mūlasarvāstivāda, it was even required to have twice the value of the loan.[75] This kind of pledge is recognized for its economic function; the system would be scarcely conceivable in an economy where money is not the normal means of exchange. The situation is less certain with regard to the pawn called tien in certain contracts of the T'ang period: the object pledged, far from representing a value that would enable the creditor to obtain compensation in the event of the debtor's default, seems to play the role of an exhibit. The pledge, in this case, is not an indifferent thing, but a strictly personal object that engages the debtor morally. At least that is what may be deduced from the contract cited below (p. 176), in which one of the parties deposits an iron cauldron as pledge: "If he exceeds the deadline without reimbursing his loan . . . the creditor shall be entitled to seize [the debtor's] movables and other effects (chia-tzu teng wu) to obtain compensation for the value of the wheat and millet [loaned]." If the pawn (tien) here played the same role as the pledge (chih), then the definitive appropriation and sale of the object alone would constitute the creditor's compensation and the only necessary sanction against defaulting on the agreement. In this case, however, not just the pawn remains in the possession of the creditor, but the latter can fully compensate his loss only by confiscating a part of the debtor's property. The single purpose of the redemption of the pledge that normally takes place on the expiration date is to fully release the debtor. Redemption does not enable him to avoid damages in the event that the pledge does not cover the combined value of loan and interest. The terms *chih* and *tien* therefore denote two different types of pledges.[76] To be sure, the system of granting loans against pledges operating in countries under Indian influence constituted an innovation that contrasted with the archaic institution of the *tien* pawn, which was very likely of Chinese origin.

According to Yang Lien-sheng, "The Buddhist origin of pawn-broking has been noted by several Chinese and Japanese scholars. The celebrated Sung poet Lu Yu (1127–1210) in his *Lao-hsüeh an pi-chi* mentions pawnshops known as *ch'ang-sheng k'u,* 'long-life trea-suries,' in Buddhist monasteries of his time and traces the practice back to the end of the fifth century."[77]

> The grandson of Chen Fa-ch'ung,[78] named Chen Pin, was esteemed in his village for his moral conduct. Once he took a bundle of ramie to the treasury of the Ch'ang-sha monastery at the prefecture as a pledge for [a loan of] money. When he later redeemed the ramie, he found five taels of gold inside the bundle. Pin wrapped these into a handkerchief and returned them to the treasury of the monastery. The monks were startled and said: "Recently someone pledged this gold for [a loan of] money. Circumstances prevented him at the time from retrieving it and it was left abandoned.". . . The monks offered Chen Pin half of the sum but he steadfastly refused.[79]

A second account, the events of which date to the years 482–483, fig-ures in the biography of Ch'u Ch'eng in the *Nan Ch'i shu*:

> After the death of [his father] Yüan, Ch'eng went to the Chao-t'i monastery with eleven thousand cash to redeem a seat cover in white marten skin, a fur coat in poor condition, and some tassels that had been bestowed upon Yüan by T'ai-tsu. He also redeemed Yüan's ear cap and hair ornament of rhinoceros horn as well as a yellow ox that Yüan had ridden.[80]

The monastic treasuries thus functioned as pawnshops. The objects deposited as security were undoubtedly evaluated below their market value and the loans granted for an undetermined period. In the first case the pledge is redeemed "later," and in the second Ch'u Ch'eng goes to the monastery only following the death of his father. The agreement thus applied to the bearer of the deed, which was trans-missible from father to son. Possibly it was even transferable to a third party. This assuredly constituted a great progress over the clas-sical Chinese practice of granting agricultural loans[81] at high interest rates and short expiration periods, an inconvenient arrangement that offered little scope for development. The T'ang imperial government had regulated the interest rates. In the case of loans against pledges (chih-chü), the interest was not to exceed one-fifth of the value of the principal:

"The interest on loans against pledges may not exceed one-fifth [per annum]. The government does not permit the interest to exceed the principal, nor to accumulate."[82]

In the case of an ordinary loan, by contrast, the interest rate could legally be a quarter; in reality, it seems almost always to have been one-half.[83]

The two accounts cited above reveal one of the characteristics of loans against pledges: they were loans of money. The pledges were likewise redeemed with money. The expression chih-ch'ien, "to borrow cash against the deposit of a pledge," is common, as is the synonymous expression chih-chü; in fact, the term chü seems to apply specifically to money loans.[84] Only the great monasteries and certain wealthy laymen had sufficient monetary reserves at their disposal to advance cash to those short of liquid assets. It also appears that these cash loans were directed to a particular clientele: not peasants who sought to procure the seed needed for the year or essential provisions to subsist until the next harvest, but the section of Chinese society that was already relatively well-off. In Central Asia, it was the local bourgeoisie that borrowed cash from the monasteries or from the clergy: a contract mentions the loan of fifteen hundred cash made to a woman, Madam A-sun, from the permanent assets of a monastery.[85] Only a woman belonging to the upper classes is likely to have possessed the means to contract a liability; Madam A-sun was probably a member of one of the great families of the locality.

The same observation holds for another contract of the same type:

In the . . . year of the Ta-li period (766–780) . . . the lady Hsü Ssu-she, being in urgent need of money and not knowing where to procure it . . . [pledges] a comb . . . for a loan of five hundred cash. Every month [the interest amounts to . . .] cash. The lady Hsü may . . . use the principal and interest to redeem [her pledge]. Should she exceed the period [determined] without redeeming it, [the pledge] shall be entirely confiscated and may be sold. Lest there be a breach of faith, a private contract has been drawn up. The two parties present, having found its dispositions just and clear . . .
     The owner of the money

The lady Hsü, twenty-six years of age
The co-borrower, her son Chin-chin, eight years of age
The witness.[86]

The monk Dharmarakṣa was born of a Yüeh-chih family that had set-tled at Tun-huang.[87] The leading clans (chia-tsu) of the town, know-ing that he was very rich, wanted to put him to the test by borrowing two hundred thousand cash from him.[88] Failing cash, high- and mid-dle-ranking officials borrowed cloth from the monasteries.

Li I-chi, assistant magistrate of Shih-feng county (modern T'ien-t'ai hsien in Chekiang), borrowed ten bolts of cloth from the perma-nent assets of a monastery and failed to restitute them.[89] A more senior official, Feng Ssu, president of the Censorate (yü-shih ta-fu), died a violent death in the second year of the Ching-lung period (708) for having failed to honor a debt of money, oil, and flour that he owed the T'ai-p'ing monastery.[90]

The loans were evidently not always repaid. Perhaps the monas-teries placed greater trust in debtors who were important personages or officials either known for their devotion or whose influence might prove useful to the religious community. Some loans did not even require a contract.[91] In any case, it is certain that the question of *credit* played a role in these operations, and one can imagine that large loans were only accorded clients known to be solvent and with whom close relations were maintained. The monasteries, consequently, extended their loans of cash, or its common substitute, cloth, to a rather restricted clientele consisting of officials and members of the aristocracy, and of donors and benefactors.

Loans against pledges continued to be granted by Buddhist com-munities long after the practice had spread to the lay world.[92] In the twelfth century, Lu Yu mentions that there existed pawn treasuries in the monasteries and that they bore a special name: "Today treasuries are frequently instituted [in the monasteries] for the purpose of grant-ing loans of cash against pledges (chih-ch'ien). They are called Long Life Treasuries (ch'ang-sheng k'u)."[93]

Two texts concerning Long Life Treasuries under the Sung seem to indicate that the funds of these treasuries were constituted from indi-vidual contributions made by the religious:

Even though the halls of that establishment had hall masters (tien-chu) to look after everything, there was still a lack of lamps lit permanently (ch'ang-ming teng). Thus a subscription was organized among the community that raised thirty-three strings of cash. These were paid into the Long Life Treasury. An Office of Lamps and Oil (teng yu ssu was instituted with the task of supervising the conservation of this capital from year to year. This office purchased oil with the interest earned from successive placements. The hall masters were even able to install permanent lamps made of enamel (liu-li ming teng) in their halls in addition to the ordinary lamps. It was determined that the treasurer (k'u-tzu) would present his accounts every month to the abbot (fang-chang) and managers (chih-shih) for their inspection and signatures.[94]

Hung Mai's *I-chien chih* reports that

> at the Lo-han cloister of the Yung-ning monastery, a pawn treasury (chih-k'u) was established by collecting the personal money belonging to the novices. The interests were accumulated in order to purchase their ordination certificates (tu-tieh).[95] This bank was called a Long Life Treasury. In all the towns of Lake P'o-yang, all the Dhyāna and Vinaya communities practiced this system alike. The monk in charge of the administration (hsing-cheng) of the Lo-han yüan had appointed a fellow monk, named Chih-hsi, to supervise the accounts. On the twenty-ninth day of the fourth month in the third year of the Ch'ing-yüan period (1197), as they were balancing the accounts and reviewing the objects placed on the shelves, they realized that a pin with a golden head was missing.[96]

One of the most remarkable features of the Long Life Treasuries might well be the subscription by their members to a mutual fund, a practice still found in certain village associations in modern times.[97] The Long Life Treasuries thus evoke one of the most interesting institutions of Chinese Buddhism: that of the associations of the laity and the clergy.[98]

It has been suggested that the great Buddhist establishments satisfied the needs of two different groups of clients: those belonging to the upper strata of society on the one hand and the peasantry on the other. This was done by means of two different types of loans based on entirely different principles. The first were, generally speaking, loans of money or cloth. They might involve the deposit of a pledge (chih), the value of which exceeded that of the loan. The transaction does not necessarily form the object of a written deed but may be based on trust in the good faith of that special clientele. The second type of loan are loans in kind, usually in cereals, wheat, or millet. They are short-term loans, granted for the duration of one agricultural year (seven to eight months), and the interest rate is high (50 percent). These loans are directed at the peasantry. The volume of money in circulation always remained significantly below the requirements of an entirely monetary economy. In areas with a sufficiency of money, purely commercial activities were most highly developed: the great cities of the North, the Yangtze basin, and the port of Canton. The peasants were not primarily interested in procuring cash but the seed and provisions needed until the next harvest.

The wealth in cereals possessed by certain Buddhist establishments permitted them to hold not only their own serfs but also the free peasantry in the monastery's surroundings in a state of permanent subjection. Admittedly, the texts hardly mention this important role played by the richest religious establishments in China as great agricultural banks: it was self-evident and did not hold the attention of contemporaries. But the manuscripts found at Tun-huang abound in loan contracts and requests for advances in cereals that reveal the powerful economic and social influence exercised in certain regions by the great Buddhist monasteries.

It has been seen that the monasteries in Shansi at the time of the saṃgha households toward the end of the fifth century—and after the institution had degenerated in the sixth century—extended advances of millet to farmers at rates that were most advantageous for the Buddhist communities and high monastic officers who abused the system to their profit.[99] The methods of grain conservation, economic considerations, as well as certain social habits had the effect that China had only large granaries: public granaries, collective granaries, and those belonging to wealthy landowners. At Tun-huang, the granaries of the Ching-t'u monastery must have contained more than seven hundred *shih* of cereals (four hundred hectoliters). One can assume that the seventeen Buddhist establishments of the Sha-chou region disposed of a reserve of close to five thousand hectoliters of cereals.[100] A peasant, after having spent his meager provisions at the time of the New Year festival, normally found himself completely destitute at the beginning of spring. This improvidence, encouraged by a permanently precarious existence, was part of his lifestyle. Moreover, there was no shortage of lenders. At Tun-huang, the peasants borrowed for the most part from the neighboring monastery. If they were serfs and worked the land of the establishment, they presented a simple request in which they engaged themselves to return twice the amount borrowed should they be unable to restitute the advance at the time of the harvest.[101] In the case of a serf belonging to another monastery, however, the operation was sealed by a contract:

> On the fifteenth day of the forth month of the year . . . Yen-chün, head of a monastery household (ssu-hu) at Sha-chou, requiring a certain quantity of grain and having sought [unsuccessfully to procure it], came to borrow three shih of wheat, measured in Chinese sheng, from the Buddhist accounts (fo-chang so) of the Ling-t'u monastery. He requested that the [date for the] restitution of the wheat be fixed as the eighth month in the autumn. With respect to this wheat, he also asked that, should he exceed the agreed date without having returned this advance . . . under appeal to the present contract . . .[102] his movables and other effects be seized in compensation for the value of the wheat. In the event that he should be absent ("to the east or the west") or deceased, the guarantors shall be required to undertake the restitution in his place. Lest there be a breach of faith, this contract was drawn up and this paper inscribed to serve as proof:
>   The borrower of the wheat, Yen-chün, thirty years of age
>   The guarantor Liu Kuei-tzu, twenty years of age
>   The guarantor
>   The witness, the monk Fa-ying
>   The witness, the abbot T'ang
>   The witness, [the monk] Chih-yüan.[103]

Sometimes the borrower deposited a pledge, which did not, however, prevent the seizure of his property in default of payment (cf. p. 170 above):

> On the sixth day of the second month of the year ssu, the head of a monastery household of the P'u-kuang monastery, Li Ssu-ssu, being in need a seed grain and a supply of cereals, requested the provision of four Chinese shih of wheat and eight Chinese shih of millet from the permanent assets of the Ling-t'u monastery. As a pledge (tien) he deposited an iron cauldron of the volume of two sheng. This wheat and millet shall be fully restituted in the course of the eighth month in autumn. Should he exceed that date without making the restitution . . . [the creditor] will be authorized to seize his movables and other effects in compensation for the value of the wheat and the millet. Should he himself be deceased, the guarantors shall undertake the restitution in his place. Lest there be a breach of faith, this contract was drawn up to serve as proof later:

The borrower of the wheat and the millet, Li Ssu-ssu (impression
of a round seal, two centimeters in diameter, in red)[104]
The guarantor, his son T'un-t'un (fingerprint)[105]

These loans did not bear interest. They were simple advances, as the
term employed by the contracts, *pien*, "to place at some one's disposal," clearly indicates. A loan at interest is designated by the term
tai or *tai-pien*.[106] Thus it can be seen that the monastery serfs, the
"households held in perpetuity" (*ch'ang-chu po-hsing*),[107] enjoyed
favored treatment, even when they addressed themselves to another
establishment. This kind of protectionism was no doubt based upon
a mutual understanding that linked all the monasteries at Tun-huang.

The majority of loans, however—those extended to free peasants—
constituted usurious operations. The interest rate was always set at
50 percent due at the time of the harvest. The quantities loaned were
relatively small: the entries in wheat for loans (*li-jun ju*) at the Ching-
t'u monastery amounted to a total of 128 *shih*[108] for the year 924,[109]
and these represent a multitude of small loans. In most cases they
comprise a few *tou* (ca. 6 l each) and it is rare that they amount to several *shih*. In addition to wheat and millet, hemp and soya were also
loaned.

Curiously, there is no trace of contracts concerning loans at interest from the monasteries' granaries among the Tun-huang manuscripts. At least it appears that not every transaction necessitated the
drawing up of a separate deed. For reasons of convenience, the loans
were recorded in certain registers of the monasteries' expenditures,
and presumably these records in themselves constituted a proof.[110]

The managers of granaries thus took care to note the borrower's
place of residence or family relationship with other persons. To this
the interested party added the signature, frequently reduced to a cross
or a simple sign, cf either the borrower or a guarantor (*k'ou-ch'eng jen*)
in his place:

"Li Hsing-tuan borrowed (*tai*) 1 *shih* of soya [which yielded] 1.5
shih in the autumn."

"Chang Ho-tzu borrowed 1 *shih* of soya [which yielded] 1.5 *shih* in
the autumn."

A note here adds: "He is the younger brother of the Chang Ch'u-tzu
of the oilery household (*liang-hu*)."

Elsewhere it is the borrower's place of residence that is specified:

"Resides east of the main road in front of the monastery."

"Resides in the ward of the Ch'ü family."

"Resides south of the house of the *tu-t'ou* Yang."[111]

The volume of loan operations at the Ching-t'u monastery was considerable. In 930, out of a total of 136 *shih* of wheat and millet entered into its granaries, more than 60 *shih* (ca. 36 hl) were due to interest on loans. Adding to that the interest earned from loans of hemp and soya, it may be surmised that the Ching-t'u monastery derived more than a third of its revenues from usury.[112] It emerges that the Buddhist establishments, whose revenues were essentially assured by placements at interest, by the offerings of the faithful, and by the operation of real estate (shops and mills), made no contribution to production. Theirs was a parasitical economy that nevertheless had its place in this country of agricultural civilization. When they were not assured by the imperial government, loans to farmers were provided by wealthy private individuals and, from the fifth century on, by the monasteries as well.

Loans Granted to Monks

Beside the privileged classes and the peasantry, the clergy constituted a third category of borrowers. Their situation was similar to that of the first group of debtors, and when they borrowed it was under identical conditions: the loans were long-term, and one relied more on their trustworthiness and piety to obtain the reimbursement of their debts than on methods of coercion. Moreover, the judicial execution of debts was not applied to officials or members of the nobility, and monks were not subject to secular jurisdiction for minor offenses.[113]

The *Fo-tsu t'ung-chi* reports a number of anecdotes concerning loans taken by religious from the permanent assets:

The monk Hsüan-hsü encountered in hell his cell companion the śramana Tao-ming of Hsiang-chou who was expiating his sin of having failed to return, with interest, a loan of firewood contracted from the permanent assets of his monastery. To put an end to his agonies, Tao-ming implored Hsüan-hsü to purchase a hundred faggots to repay in his name to the permanent assets in the place of the single faggot he had borrowed.[114]

The theme of an unpaid debt to the Three Jewels leading to rebirth as an animal, a slave, or an infernal being is common in Chinese Buddhist folklore. In all cases, the debtors featured are either officials or monks. It may therefore be supposed that, for these categories of borrowers, no recourse was taken to the seizure of property, that one relied on their trustworthiness, and, finally, that such long-term loans were reserved for the religious and members of the upper classes.

Among the Tun-huang manuscripts, there is a document that concerns loans made by monks to the permanent assets. It is entitled *Liang fa t'uan ju-chai wen-shu*[115] and is dated the twenty-ninth day of the first month of a *hsin-hai* year.[116]

"Shan-yin paid seventy-eight *ch'ih* of cloth [into the permanent assets], the equivalent (*chun*) of seventy-eight *tou* of wheat or millet, to reimburse thirty-nine *tou* of yellow hemp."[117]

"Yüan-t'ung paid seventy-five *chih* of woolens (*ho-pu*), the equivalent of eight *shih* of wheat or millet, to repay . . . *shih* of yellow hemp."

"Yüan-wei paid two elm roots, the equivalent of six *shih* of wheat or millet and forty *chih* of woolens to be sold in auction (? *ch'ang-ho*), worth four *shih* of wheat or millet. The price of the wood and the woolens is for reimbursing five *shih* of yellow hemp."

The monks Pao-jui and Pao-tuan paid diverse articles into the permanent assets, including a copper cauldron such as people use for pledges (? *jen shang tien-wu t'ung kuo-tzu*). All these articles were paid into the treasury in the presence of the community. The signatures of the five monks having borrowed hemp from the permanent assets were taken.

Following this, the same document contains a list of reimbursements made by five other monks, on the ninth day of the sixth month, for loans of wheat and millet. These loans amounted to forty *tou*, thirty-eight *tou*, forty *tou*, fifteen *tou*, and twenty-four *tou*. [118]

It is not said that these loans carried interest; it is on the contrary likely that the monks borrowed goods from the permanent assets in order to be able to lend them to the laity.[119]

According to the least rigorous of the treatises on discipline, the essential precept regarding commercial activities is to avoid defiling contacts. It is necessary to act through intermediaries. Likewise, it is not property and worldly goods as such that are prohibited to bhikṣu, but their direct use and possession. Thus the solution adopted by Upananda, according to a Vinaya work, to enrich himself with impunity is well within the logic of the treatises on discipline.

There was a layman who had received a commission from Upananda for a transaction of clothing. The two were on good terms and visited one another frequently. Now Upananda was a shrewd man, lucky and very rich, and it was his custom to place his valuables with this layman to make them yield a profit.[120]

Besides, the morality of the Vinaya is a morality of intention:

> If a bhikṣu has purchased for profit, but does not sell for profit, he commits a minor sin (duṣkṛta) [at the moment of the purchase]. If he does not purchase for profit but sells for profit, he commits a sin [at the time of the sale].[121]

To make a gain without seeking it does not constitute a sin.[122]

The Mūlasarvāstivāda monks themselves placed the "inexhaustible property" of the saṃgha at interest among the laity,[123] and it seems that the same practice was also current in Chinese monasteries. The following indication is found in a monastic account from Tun-huang:

> [Commodities] currently placed at the disposal of the monks in order that they may earn interest (hsien-tsai fu-seng shang ch'u-li):
> - Wheat: 58.5 shih
> - Millet: 50 shih
> - Soya: 50.4 shih
> - Hemp: 50.4 shih
>
> [Commodities] borrowed from the monks (seng shang tai-pien):
> - Hemp: 17.6 shih
> - Soya: 8.6 shih
> - Millet: 7.7 shih.[124]

The role of intermediary played by monks on behalf of their communities, as well as the ease afforded by a morality of intention, was to engender among them a vocation for usury. From the beginning of the development of Buddhist communities in China, practices that contravened the teachings of the Vinaya were accepted. These were no doubt encouraged by the example of the religious of Central Asia whose monasteries served as staging posts for caravans and as important banking centers. At the end of the third century, at Tun-huang, the monk Dharmarakṣa was believed to have possessed an immense fortune (cf. p. 173 above).

In principle, investments were made in the name of the Three Jewels. This offered a twofold advantage to the borrower: to obtain a loan and accomplish a pious work at the same time. Having recalled that, in accordance with the Vinaya, monks were not permitted to own "impure goods," the controller of Buddhist clergy (sha-men t'ung) Hui-shen added in his report of the year 509: "For some time, monks and nuns have also loaned their private possessions in the name of the Three Jewels."[125]

A point that Hui-shen does not raise in his report is nevertheless clearly borne out by examples in the course of history: not all of the Buddhist clergy practiced usury, only the wealthiest among them and those who occupied important positions within the monastic hierarchy—it amounts to the same thing, since power gave access to riches: under the Northern Wei, the controllers of Buddhist clergy and the karmadāna overseers (wei-na) of the offices of Buddhist clergy (seng-ts'ao) in the prefectures and garrisons; at all times, the abbots and other dignitaries within the monasteries; and monks whose temporary functions (in particular those in charge of the accounts) placed them in a position to enrich themselves.

The exactions committed by the karmadāna Seng-hsien and Seng-p'in are a case in point (see p. 103 above). The contracts were doctored, the interest sometimes exceeded the principal, and "the peasants filled the streets with their grumbling of hatred." It was a tradition among the dignitaries of the saṃgha to enrich themselves through usury. Around the middle of the sixth century, under the Northern Ch'i, we find a character of this type:

> The monk Tao-yen was controller of Buddhist clergy at Chi-chou. His wealth was immense and yielded a great deal of interest within the commandery. He frequently called upon the commandery and county administrations to collect his debts. Each time he came to see [the prefect Su Ch'iung] hoping to collect, Ch'iung perceived his intention and fell to conversing and questioning him about abstruse points of doctrine, [treating him with utmost deference].[126] Tao-yan, who had come to talk about debts and figures, could not get a word in edgewise. When his disciples asked him the reason, Tao-yen replied: "Whenever I pay the prefect a visit, he leads me directly into the blue clouds—how can I discuss down-to-earth matters?"[127]

The importance of circulation is borne out here, since the placements were made throughout the large territory of a commandery. The freedom of movement enjoyed by the Chinese monks helped them in these operations. But this text invites an observation of a more general order. The execution of debts in default was the responsibility of the secular authorities.[128] The officials concerned, however, could pursue these matters more or less energetically. For Tao-yen, it seems that on the whole—despite the trick played on him by Su Ch'iung—the authorities cooperated: rich and influential monks were personages to be treated with consideration.[129]

Numerous loan contracts survive, from the region of Khotan and Tun-huang, constituting invaluable source materials for the economic and legal history of China. Frequently, in more than half of the cases, the loans are granted by the clergy.[130] These religious usually hold posts and titles that distinguish them from ordinary monks: abbots (ssu-chu), deans (shang-tso), masters of Dharma and Vinaya (fa-lü). I have already pointed out that the number of monks with sufficient means to grant loans at interest was rather small. As for the borrowers, they belonged to all classes of society: soldiers, peasants, members of the local bourgeoisie.

In the eighth century, in the region of Khotan, cash had not yet disappeared as was the case in Tun-huang in the ninth and tenth. In two contracts found at Dandān-Uiliq,[131] the lender is a monk of the Hu-kuo monastery[132] and the amounts loaned are significant: in one of these deeds, the monk, a certain Ch'ien-ying, advances 1,000 cash and in the other, 17 shih of millet. According to the monastic accounts found at Mazār-tāgh, dating from the first half of the eighth century, a shih of millet was worth 150 cash. Thus the value of the second loan amounted to more than 2,500 cash.

> On the twelfth day of the seventh month of the third year in the Chien-chung reign period (782), the soldier Ma Ling-chih, being in urgent need of money and having no other means of procuring it, addressed himself to Ch'ien-ying, a monk of the Hu-kuo monastery, and borrowed (chü) one thousand coins of money from him. This amount shall yield a monthly interest of one hundred cash. Should Ch'ien-ying himself need the money urgently, he will request Ma Ling-chih to reimburse the full amount of the principal and the interest. If Ma Ling-chih is unable to do so [at that time], Ch'ien-ying will be authorized to seize Ling-chih's movables, oxen, and animals in compensation for the value of the money. He shall not claim anything beyond that value. This private contract was drawn up lest there be a breach [of faith]. The two parties, having found its dispositions just and clear, affix their fingerprints to serve as marks.
> The owner of the money;
> The borrower (chü-ch'ien jen), Ma Ling-chih, twenty years of age;

The co-borrower (*t'ung-ch'ü jen*), his mother, the second daughter of the Fan family, fifty years of age;

The co-borrower, his younger sister, the daughter of the Ma family, twelve years of age.[133]

In the second deed featuring the same monk, the borrower is a local official:

In the seventeenth year of the Ta-li period (782)[134] . . . Ho Hsin-yüeh was in urgent need of grain and, not knowing [where to procure it], addressed himself to Ch'ien-ying, a monk of the Hu-kuo monastery, to borrow (*pien*) seventeen [*shih*] of millet from him. For [the restitution of] this grain, Ho Hsin-yüeh himself determined the ninth month.[135] If he exceeds that date without having returned the grain, his movables and oxen shall be seized by the monk Ch'ien-ying in compensation for the value of the grain. Nothing beyond that value shall be claimed. This contract was drawn up lest there be a breach of faith. The two parties present, having found it just and clear, have affixed their fingerprints to serve as marks.

The owner of the grain;

The borrower of the millet (*pien-su jen*), Ho Hsin-yüeh, thirty-seven years of age;

The co-borrower (*t'ung-pien jen*), his wife, the third daughter of the Ma family, thirty-five years of age;

The co-borrower (*t'ung-ch'ü jen*),[136] the eldest daughter Ho, aged fifteen.[137]

It will be noted that the second of these deeds only concerned a simple advance that did not bear interest. The payment of interest is not even tacitly assumed: the term employed, *pien*—the use of which is illustrated in the requests presented by monastery households (pp. 108–110 above)—is characteristic. This contract thus confirms an observation already made (p. 175–176): to some clients with whom close relations were maintained—serfs and lay followers—monks and monasteries granted loans at no interest.

To lend or advance cereals was unusual for monks. They were not great landowners; their possessions were of a more commercial nature, more convenient to handle and also easier to preserve: cash, that is, or were there was a shortage of cash, cloth. When they loaned cereals, these probably belonged to their monastery.[138] It is unlikely that the monk Ch'ien-ying personally had seventeen *shih* (ca. 1,020 l) of millet in store. Loans or advances of millet, wheat, soya, and hemp were the business of the monasteries, and it is remarkable that, conversely, the monasteries did not lend cloth. Their cloth reserves were limited, and apparently represented a type of possession that was reserved to the clergy: the auction sales at Tun-huang were occasions where a distribution of cloth to each monk, nun, and novice took place.[139] Thus they owned a small capital, which they did not neglect to turn to profit. It is therefore no coincidence that the contracts for loans of cloth are relatively numerous among the collections of Tun-huang manuscripts.

On the eighteenth day of the eighth month of the year *chia-wu* (874, 934?), Teng Shan-tzu, [requiring] a quantity of cloth, went to the monastery dean (*shang-tso*) Teng[140] and borrowed from him a roll of satin measuring 3.85 *chang* (ca. 11.5 m) and .19 *chang* (60 cm) wide. He further borrowed a roll of 3.9 *chang* of satin of the same width. The date of reimbursement was fixed as the eleventh month. Should that date be exceeded without reimbursement, interest will be charged on the full amount [due at that time].[141] Lest there be a breach of faith, this contract was drawn up to serve as proof later:
    The borrower of the satin, Teng Shan-tzu (signature);
    The witness, Guard Administrator (*ya-ya*) Chang Tsung-chin;
    The witness, Dean Tsung-fu.[142]

Occasionally the interest was paid in cloth:

On the twenty-fifth day of the tenth month of the year *hsin-ch'ou* (881, 941?), Chia Yen-ch'ang, having been conscripted (*ch'ung-shih*) to go to Hsi-chou (in the region of Turfān), sought out the dean Hsin-shan of the Lung-hsing monastery and borrowed from him a piece of raw silk (*sheng-chüan*) 37 *ch'ih* 2 *ts'un* in length and 1 *ch'ih* 8 *ts'un* wide. He further borrowed a piece of fine silk (? *po-shih mien-ling*) 23 *ch'ih* 6 *ts'un* long and 1 *ch'ih* 9 *ts'un* and a half wide. The loan having been concluded, [it was agreed that] he shall pay two pieces of machine-made (*li-chi*)[143] cloth in interest, each of 2.5 *chang* in length, on the day of his return from Hsi-chou. Should anything untoward happen to him on the road, appeal will be made to the guarantor, his younger brother Yen-yu, to reimburse the principal in satin and fine silk according to the amounts indicated, and that shall be all (*pien hsiu*, i.e., the debt will be extinguished). If all goes well, however, the interest shall be paid on the very day [of his return]. As for the principal, he shall have a period of one month to reimburse it. This contract was drawn up to serve as proof later:
    The borrower of the goods (*tai-wu jen*), Chia Yen-ch'ang;[144]
    The guarantor, his younger brother Yen-yu;
    The witness, Chao Fu-chu.[145]

But the interest may also be paid in cereals, presumably depending on the requirements of the creditor and the preference of the debtor:

> Contract established on the first day of the third month of the year *chia-tzu*. The elder brother Fan Huai-t'ung and his younger brothers, residents of our ward, being short of cloth, came before the master of Dharma and Vinaya (*fa-lü*) Li to borrow a piece of satin 3.8 *chang* in length and .205 *chang* wide. The loan having been concluded, [it was agreed that] they shall pay the interest amounting to 4 *shih* of wheat and millet in the autumn. In the second month of coming year, they shall reimburse the full amount of the principal. In default of payment by the dates determined, a monthly interest will be charged in accordance with the local practice.[146] The two parties present having decided [the terms of] this loan, it shall not be permitted to retract (?).
>
> The borrowers, Wen-ta (signature);
> Huai-ta;
> Huai-chu;
> Huai-t'ung, the elder brother.[147]

A contract from Tun-huang merits special mention here. It concerns a loan of cloth made by a merchant to a monk. This merchant intended to journey to Nan-shan (south of Tun-huang) to trade. The interest and the principal were to be reimbursed upon his return. The interest amounted to half the value of the principal, payable in the same type of cloth.[148]

The above suggests the spread of a new type of loan contract in the course of the T'ang. The deeds found in Dandān-Uiliq, dating from the eighth century, provide for the immediate seizure of personal estate in the event of insolvency. In the contracts from Tun-huang, dating from the ninth and tenth centuries, the same disposition is still occasionally found; more frequently, however, interests are allowed to cumulate according to the local practice. No doubt that is the meaning of the formula *yü hsiang-yüan sheng-li*. The debt is not extinguished by the seizure of property but, on the contrary, begins to swell after the expiration date, and it is likely that the debtor would eventually be forced to sell his land. The latter had been expressly protected by the clause that specified the seizure of movables and animals. Because of these indirect consequences for the agrarian system of China under the T'ang, the history of usurious loans merits special attention.[149] The rich monastic clergy carried part of the responsibility for the large-scale social transformation that took place in the T'ang period.

It is further apparent that antichresis of farmland was practiced at Tun-huang. An example was mentioned above: the peasant Kao Chia-ying, who owed the monk Yüan-chi two *shih* of cereals, relinquished the usufruct of a field of five *mou* to his creditor for a period of two years.[150]

It also happens that land functions as security for a loan. The land, valued below its actual price, is made over to the creditor for a fixed period of time. A good example of this type of contract is provided by a draft of a deed for a "peasant-monk"[151] in 904:

> Contract established on the seventeenth day of the eighth month of the *chia-tzu* year, fourth year of the T'ien-fu reign period (September 28, 904). The monk Ling-hu Fa-hsing, a commoner in the district of Shen-sha, owns 8 *mou* (.43 ha) [in the margin: "two beds"] of personal share land (*k'ou-fen ti*) in the lower part of the Meng-shou canal area. Being in need of provisions for his expenses, he took the land designated above and negotiated with his neighbor of the same district, the commoner Chia Yüan-tzu. He borrowed (*ch'ü*) one piece of raw silk (*sheng-chüan*) of the first quality 8 *tsung* [152] in length, and a piece of cotton 2 *chang* 5 *ch'ih* in length. He rents (*tsu*) the aforementioned land to Chia Yüan-tzu to work and sow for twenty-two years.[153] At the end of the period from the present *i-ch'ou* year to the following *ping-hsü* year (905–926), it shall revert to the original owner. All the taxes and impositions levied on this land with the exception of the land tax (*ti-tzu*)[154] shall be collected from the owner. The *ti-tzu* shall be paid annually by Yüan-tzu (the occupier). The labor dues for work on the canals and waterways shall be halved between the two households. If an imperial act of grace is promulgated it shall not be taken into account.[155] Likewise, if a relative or other person lays claim to this land, the guarantor shall be required to find and provide another piece of land of good quality in the neighborhood as compensation.
>
> The dispositions having been made by the two parties and found just and clear, there shall be no revocation. Should one of the parties retract, the matter will be placed before the administration. This contract was drawn up to serve as evidence and shall be binding:
>
> The owner of the land, the monk Ling-hu Fa-hsing;
>
> The witness Wu Hsien-hsin;
>
> The witness Pien Yüan-chu;
>
> The witness, the executive treasurer of the monastery (*tu-ssu p'an-kuan*) Fan Heng;
>
> The witness . . . Yin Tsai-yü;
>
> The witness, guard administrator (*ya-ya*) Chang;
>
> The legal representative of the provincial governor (*tu-yü hou*), Lu.[156]

ANNEX

The management reports of the monasteries at Tun-huang permit a precise evaluation of the revenues, reserves, and outlays of the Buddhist establishments of that town. Following is the management report of the monk Pao-hu, steward for the year (*chih-sui*) in 924 of the Ching-t'u monastery:[157]

> The community having gathered in the North Cloister for the assembly of accounts (*suan-hui*),[158] [the assets] entered by Pao-hu comprise the balance of the preceding account and, for the past year, the revenues from farmland (*t'ien-shou*), the levies on gardens (*yüan-shui*),[159] the rent from oil presses, the interest on loans, miscellaneous donations, and gifts of food for the Buddha in the form of wheat, millet, oil, little milk (koumiss?), rice, flour, yellow hemp, bran, oilcake, soya, as well as cotton cloth, felt, and paper.
>
> The total amounting to 1,388 *shih*, 33 *sheng* and half a *ch'ao*, namely,
>
> | | |
> |---|---|
> | 378.66 | *shih* of wheat |
> | 390.5 | *shih* of millet |
> | 5.06025 | *shih* of oil |
> | .0401 | *shih* of koumiss |
> | .14 | *shih* of rice |
> | 65.03 | *shih* of flour |
> | 11.03 | *shih* of coarse flour |
> | .15 | *shih* of millet flour |
> | 86.105 | *shih* of hemp |
> | 30 | *shih* of bran (?) |
> | 101 | oilcakes |
> | 208.8 | *shih* of soya |
>
> Plus:
> 849 *ch'ih* of cotton cloth
> 148 *ch'ih* of felt roll
> 200 sheets of paper.[160]

The goods measurable in *shih* amount to ca. 1,176.5 *shih*. The discrepancy of ca. 211.8 *shih* with the figure for the total in the report presumably represents the converted value in cereals (wheat or millet) of the 101 oilcakes, the cloth, and the paper.

> Management report of the monk Fa-sung, administrator of *saṃgha* property at the San-chieh monastery. Accounts for the full year from the first day of the first month of the year *i-ssu*[161] to the first day of the first month of the year *ping-wu*. The members of the community have gathered in the North Cloister for the assembly of accounts supervised

by Fa-sung and comprising the revenues for the permanent assets, that is, rents from oil presses and mills and miscellaneous donations made by the various families. Included are the balance of the account for the preceding year (ch'ien-chang hui-ts'an) and receipts in the course of the year in wheat, millet, oil, flour, hemp, bran, oilcake, soya, cotton cloth, and felt. The total amounts to 416.139 shih, namely,

    112.2 shih of wheat
    117.8 shih of millet
    4.45 shih of lamp oil
    52.4 shih of white flour
    32.53 shih of hemp
    29.25 shih of soya
    10 shih of coarse flour
    9.2 shih of millet flour
    18.9 shih of bran
Plus:
    200 ch'ih of cotton cloth and 110 ch'ih of felt.[162]

The figures provided by the different management reports show that the receipts and expenditures vary a great deal from one monastery to the next. There were extremely wealthy monasteries like the Ching-t'u ssu that granted numerous loans in wheat, millet, soya, and hemp and had several sources of revenues: lands, mills, and oil presses. Other monasteries apparently had to make do with the donations they received and a little income from lands. Following are some figures that plainly show the inequality of the resources of the monasteries at Tun-huang (in units of shih as provided by the management reports):

CHING-T'U

Receipts	Year	Outlays	Year	Reserves	Year
541.94	924	168.685	924	1,050.955	end 924
253.24	930	324.71	930	1,153.58	end 930[163]
542.34	?	439.59	?	?	
575.95	?	705.12	?	?	
433.95	?	557.081	?	?[164]	
		1,195.15	?[165]		

AN-KUO

Receipts from rent for mills, presses, and lands, spanning a period of two years, plus the existing reserves at the time of the steward's appointment: 348.93 (accounts dated January 12, 887).[166]

PAO-EN

Annual receipts: 55.31 (?).[167] Receipts for three years plus reserves at the time of [the steward's] appointment: 662.115.

SAN-CHIEH

Receipts for one year plus reserves at the time of [the steward's] appointment: 416.139.[168]

The proportions between the different sources of revenues, where they can be established, are of interest. Calculation is at least possible in the case of the Ching-t'u monastery's revenues in cereals.

In 930 the Ching-t'u ssu entered into its granaries:

73.83 *shih* of wheat and
63 *shih* of millet,[169]

that is, a total of 136.83 *shih* of the two cereals that served as current substitutes for cash at Tun-huang at the end of the T'ang and during the Five Dynasties. A *shih* of wheat or of millet had the same value in the region. Of this total,

32.8 *shih* were derived from land holdings;
60.43 *shih* from loans at interest;
41.6 *shih* from alms and religious services;
2 *shih* from a sale of soya.

Thus may be attributed approximately

23 percent to revenues from landed property;
45 percent to interest on loans;
32 percent to offerings.

The proportions between these three categories of revenues were different in 924. Of a total of 366.9 *shih* of wheat and millet, only 44.4 *shih* consisted of revenues from monastic lands. This was a source of income that could scarcely vary from one year to another. But more than 200 *shih* was earned from interest-bearing investments. The remainder (ca. 120 *shih*) was constituted by offerings and gains from various commercial operations (exchanges of commodities).[170] One may assume that lands procured only a small fraction of a monastery's revenues in cereals and that the bulk of its income was derived from loans. Soya and hemp were also used as loans to laymen.

Once, however, the significant revenues provided by the rent for the mills and presses[171] of the Ching-t'u monastery and the high prices of oil and flour are taken into account, a major position must be assigned to these sources of fixed income. Generally speaking, it may be considered that the three heads of receipts of the Ching-t'u monastery were, in decreasing order:

  a. revenues from industrial installations and lands;
  b. interests from loans of wheat, millet, soya, and hemp;
  c. donations received on the occasion of festivals and in
     remuneration for religious services.

Other management reports bear out the relatively insignificant positions occupied by offerings and rent from lands among the revenues of monasteries at Tun-huang:

Management report of the monk Ch'ing-kuo,[172] dated first month of the fourth year of the Ch'ien-ning era (897), for the preceding year:
    New receipts plus reserves at the time of [the steward's] appointment:
    Wheat: 77.6 shih
    Millet: 150.35 shih
    Soya: 15.2 shih
    Hemp: 50.4 shih
    Oil: 4.5051 shih
    Koumiss: .36 shih.
Report of Shen-wei, dated first month of the fifth year of Ch'ien-ning (898):
    Reserves at the time of [the steward's] appointment:
    Wheat: 14.3 shih
    Millet: 88.95 shih
    Hemp: 45 shih
    Soya: 9.7 shih
    Oil: 1.3051 shih
    Koumiss: .36 shih.
Receipts:
    Wheat: 64.5 shih
    Millet: 61.1 shih
    Hemp: 5.4 shih
    Soya: 5.5 shih

Oil: 3.2 *shih*.

In 896, rent from mills yielded 58.4 *shih* of wheat, 45.6 *shih* of millet, 5.2 *shih* of soya, and 2.8 *shih* of hemp;

Rent from presses yielded 3.2 *shih* of oil and 10 oilcakes;

The income from lands that year amounted to 2.3 *shih* of wheat, 5.6 *shih* of millet, and 2.6 *shih* of hemp;

7.5 *shih* of millet were received in payment for a purchase of oil made by officials;

2.8 *shih* of wheat and 1.4 *shih* of millet were given as an offering by officials to serve for vegetarian feasts;

.8 *shih* of wheat, 1.3 *shih* of millet, and .3 *shih* of soya received in the form of various gifts.[173]

PART FOUR

CHAPTER SEVEN

THE CIRCUIT OF GIVING

Introduction

The clergy and sanctuaries owed the bulk of their revenues to a set of commercial practices of diverse origin. Some had originated in the Chinese world: loans of cereals to peasants, rents on shops and mills, and levies imposed on the produce of the land on the basis of either a right over persons or, more usually, a right to the land. The others were of Indian origin: loans against pledges and auction sales of clothing and fabrics. All the revenues generated in these different ways were of a broadly commercial nature, and the mechanisms brought into play were those that operated in the lay world. Gifts and offerings, by contrast, stand out by the act of free consent they imply and the psychological and religious motivations that underlie them. Between such economic activities on the one hand and purely gratuitous acts on the other, resorting neither to constraint nor to particular techniques, there seems to exist an irreducible opposition. Indian Buddhism, as we know it from the treatises on discipline, only gradually made room for commercial practices, and with much reluctance. In the beginning, these had been the work of lay converts who sought to ensure the perpetuity of their offerings either by the donation of real estate, of which the earnings were to support the cult and the clergy, or of an interest-bearing capital. Among the sects of the Lesser Vehicle, these practices remained for the most part on the periphery of their religious activities. The requirements of a cult that underwent a remarkable development and was inclined to expenditure, however, as well as the closer association between lay followers and the saṃgha, seem to be at the origin of a different evolution within the communities of the Greater Vehicle: farming and usury were integrated into the circulation of pious gifts. By a series of mutations, gifts were transformed into commercial goods and worldly gain into offerings.

The juxtaposition of these different types of revenues—gifts and profane profits—can thus be explained historically. But one can also perceive what it was that united the economic and religious aspects of the Buddhist movement. It defined itself with reference to the activities of production—agriculture and weaving—and in opposition to the traditional lifestyle of the peasantry. If agriculture constituted in reality—and for the ruling classes as a matter of principle—the fundamental activity, then all other activities had to appear as secondary and, by that token, as mutually analogous. It will be recalled that the Buddhist movement translated into an extraordinary development of minor trades, including painters, sculptors, architects, manufacturers, and merchants. Buddhism channeled their activities to its advantage. Buddhist art stopped at no expenditure. Whether bells, statues, or chimes, ritual objects needed to be not only beautiful and elaborate but sumptuous. The materials incorporated into this art had a monetary value, and a constant transformation that took place should be recalled here: the casting of statues from coins and the minting of coins from statues. Religious activity appears as a luxury: the construction and ornamentation of sanctuaries, the considerable expense lavished on ceremonies, the emergence of a new social class supported at the expense of the community, all these facts fall within the province of an entirely gratuitous activity. The monks themselves were a luxury. The services they provided to the laity (ritual, medical, divinatory, etc.) were on the same level as those provided by the artisans and the merchants.

The complex of circumstances where Buddhism appears only in the form of an economic movement, in which religious factors no longer play any role whatever, merits special attention here. Many among the peasantry turned themselves into monks with the object of enriching themselves or, more generally, of gaining access to means of existence other than those imposed by the agricultural tradition of China. We would be at liberty to affirm that these facts are peripheral to the religious phenomenon, of which they merely constitute a particular consequence, had we determined to make a distinction, according to preestablished criteria, between "regular" practices in Chinese Buddhism—that is, forms of communal religious life subject to monastic discipline and to control by the secular powers—and those to be considered as "irregular." But we are not free here to make that distinction: the facts that matter are all of an economic order, as regards the religious phenomenon, and it is the sum of the particular elements that we seek to "comprehend." The constraints imposed upon a lay individual by his family, his village community, and— either through their intermediary or directly—by the imperial government, vanished almost entirely when he left that family life (ch'u-chia). Entry into religion (ch'u-chia) meant for the individual moral and material emancipation. To become a monk was to change one's way of life, to abandon the plow for other means of existence that were not necessarily of a religious character. It is significant that in times of danger or persecution, monks sought to subsist by exercising various trades sooner than resuming a peasant existence. When, after the rebellion of Ko Wu and the scandal of the monks of Ch'ang-an, Buddhist monks were hunted down in the kingdom of Wei, the controller of Buddhist clergy Shih-hsien transformed himself into a lay physician, a status that enabled him to evade his pursuers.[1] During the period 734–745, the monk Shen-hui, fearing recognition by enemies bent on his destruction, turned himself into an itinerant merchant.[2] Chinese monks willingly pursued different callings: among them were found painters, sculptors, and architects.[3] When, in 830, Li Te-yü despatched men to Nan-chao to retrieve artisans who had been captured, they obtained more than four thousand skilled Buddhist and Taoist artisans whom they brought back to Ch'eng-tu.[4]

A reproach commonly leveled at Chinese monks was that they gave themselves up to lucrative pursuits. These were not only unworthy of their calling and contrary to monastic discipline but also ill-regarded by the ruling classes as aiming at the satisfaction of private needs rather than contributing to primary production. On two different levels, secular morality and Indian discipline accorded with one another in condemning the economically superfluous. From the beginning of the fifth century, the monk Tao-heng, in his Shih po lun,[5] criticized the moral standards of the clergy in his day: they occupied themselves with all sorts of trades, cleared lands for cultivation, engaged in commerce, practiced medicine and divination, accumulated riches, and owned far more than was needed for their livelihood. As a decree of the fifth month, ninth year of the Wu-te era (626) put it,

> Good-for-nothings seeking but their own interest, idlers, and vagabonds fraudulently have themselves tonsured as a means of evading corvée services. Under the protection of their clerical status they abandon themselves without restraint to their passion for gain. They freely come and go in the villages, tour the markets, press their farm laborers, and amass fortunes. Tilling and weaving are their livelihood,[6] commerce is their trade. Their occupations are those of the people, their actions those of commoners. They violate the rules of monastic discipline and disregard the teachings of secular morality to the point where they band together as brigands or thieve individually. They invent fables. They are violent and treacherous.[7]

The following decree was promulgated on the day *chi-wei* of the sixth month in the nineteenth year of the K'ai-yüan era (731):

> The true goal of Buddhism is quietude. It is to that end that the clergy was instituted, with the task of serving the religion. But the monks bustle about secondary activities and forget the essential. . . . They benefit from the privileges of their class and thus shielded enrich themselves. It is to no avail that they are exempted from taxes and corvée services. They pile up deception. They are roaming laymen that go about the business of magicians, straining their discourse and thinking.[8]

An apocryphal sutra of the T'ang asks:

> Why is it that all laymen shall scorn the Three Jewels [at the time of the Counterfeit Law (*pratirūpakadharma*)]? It is precisely because the bhikṣu and the bhikṣunī will not conform to the Law. They will clothe themselves in religious habits but their conduct will be unscrupulous like that of laymen. Some will engage in commerce in the marketplace in order to enrich themselves. Others will traffic by the roadside for a living. Others again will ply the trades of painters and artisans. Others will devote themselves to the arts of divination and physiognomy and predict good and evil fortune. They will inebriate themselves, disturb the peace, sing and dance, and make music. Some will play chess and the boardgame *liu-po*. There will be bhikṣu who will preach false teachings to please the people. There will be those who shall pretend to be devotees of Dhyāna even though they be incapable of concentrating their minds. They will prophesy the future on the basis of texts that falsely claim to be canonical. Some

will practice acupuncture and apply moxa. They will proffer all kinds of potions and cures in exchange for food and clothing. Under these conditions, laymen will have no respect for the Law.[9]

The biographies of monks introduce a certain number of these wandering religious who lived among the people, some of whom acquired sufficient celebrity to figure in Buddhist hagiographies:

> Pei-tu, who lived at the beginning of the fifth century, was a monk-magician known for crossing rivers in a wooden cup.[10] He went from family to family and was lodged by them. The vice-president of the imperial Secretariat K'ung Ning-tzu, who was suffering from dysentery, summoned him. Pei-tu pronounced a magic formula (mantra), and [K'ung] was healed. He did the same for the wife of a certain Ch'i Hsieh and organized, in addition, a vegetarian feast to ask that she be healed.[11]

A certain Seng-hui (d. ca. 500) visited families where there were invalids. If he went into a rage, the patient would die; if he appeared good-humored, it meant that the patient would be healed.[12]

And then there was a whole class of wandering monks who lived solely on alms:[13]

> A monk named Fu-shang, who lived at the time of the Chou (557–581), took up residence at a place on the road where he had buried a relic.[14] He remained squatting there and chanting sutras all day long. People passed in front of him, yet he never asked for alms. If someone threw him a coin, he pronounced no good wishes (chou-yüan) to thank his benefactor. A believer once told him: "To the east of the city walls, to the north of the city walls, there are crowds and alms are plentiful. Why do you remain here?" "One or two cash [per day] are sufficient to keep me alive," replied Fu-shang. "What should I do with more?"[15]

Other monks retired to their hermitages in the mountains after having begged in the villages: Tao-hsiu, holding his bowl and staff of pewter, left his solitude to beg for food. Once his bowl was filled, he ate wherever he happened to be and then returned to his hut.[16]

The Buddhist monks met one another in the markets, at fairs, in taverns. They made their living in all kinds of trades. Underlying all this is one objective fact: a general disaffection for the peasant life that must certainly be connected to the phenomenon of religion.

To understand what is analogous among the different activities to which Buddhist religious devoted themselves in China, it is necessary to consider them in their concrete context. Communities or individuals seek to attain sanctity by means of a particular way of life and practices. But they are also—and that is for us the essential fact—specialists.[17] It is certainly in that capacity that they were integrated into Chinese society. The Buddhist biographies classify the monks by discipline: translation, recitation, Vinaya, magic, Dhyāna, etc. They exercised specific crafts, and we may legitimately emphasize the professional character of their activities. The transmission that took place from master to disciple is analogous to that which assured the handing down of particular techniques from master artisan to apprentice. In short, Chinese monks cultivated arts that tended to satisfy various needs in the lay world.

The matter is simple with respect to single monks who were in regular contact with the laity. Even those who lived in religious communities, however, had fairly frequent dealings with the lay followers. They were called upon by the outside world to practice their specialist skills for the benefit of private individuals: sutra recitations for the dead, divination, healing, knowledge of magic formulae. The services they provided were worth a price, as were those of professional physicians or artisans. They received offerings for a vegetarian feast, or cash, or lengths of cloth. These constituted a remuneration, but at the same time they were also pious donations, freely given in the expectation of the salutary effects that were associated with faith offerings. The transaction was thus situated halfway between a gift and a commercial payment.

This type of offering was in fact more widespread than might a priori be expected: it also took place within the sanctuary, on the occasion of official and private ceremonies of all kinds. The faithful offered gifts as an act of devotion—in a spirit that must be qualified as religious—and at the same time in exchange for specific services.

Variety of the Offerings

The monastery accounts found at Tun-huang mention among the diverse offerings made in the course of the year:

"Various gifts on the occasion of the aspersion of the statues (yü-hsiang san-shih)," i.e., all the offerings made for the great annual ceremonies;

"Offerings for the spring and autumn food of the Buddha (ch'un-ch'iu fo-shih);"

"Gifts offered to the monks on the occasion of vegetarian feasts [held for the benefit of the dead] (chai-ch'en).[18]

Since the majority of the offerings were made at the time of the great annual festivals, there is every interest in following the chronological order of the major festivities that punctuated the life of the religious communities and of the faithful in the present account. Following are the indications that may be gathered from two management reports from the Ching-t'u monastery at Tun-huang:[19]

On the fifteenth day of the first month a lamp festival (jan-teng) takes place in the grottoes belonging to the monastery. The officials and the associations of the faithful (she)[20] are invited. In 930, the associations offered for this festival .3 shih of wheat and the same quantity of millet. The monastery spent .25 shih of flour to feed the monks in the grottoes, .2 shih of millet and .1 shih of wheat for the banquet offered to the lay followers and religious, and 1.5 shih for feeding the camels and horses of the officials, not counting the oil used for the illuminations. The festival comprised, among other ceremonies, rites of thanksgiving to the Divine Kings (devarāja).[21]

On the sixth and seventh day of the second month, the procession of the statues (hsing-hsiang) in town took place under the sponsorship of the associations of the faithful. In 930, the monks received from these and other lay associations .7 shih of soya, 3 shih of wheat, and 6.8 shih of millet. But they spent .6 shih of millet to "provide drink for the bearers of the statues," who were invited, on that occasion, to the northern gate of the monastery. On the seventh day, the monks offered a banquet that cost 1.2 shih of millet. A further 2.1 shih of millet were spent for a larger banquet on the eighth day in which both the monastic community and lay associations took part, as well as those who had handled the statues. This major feast of the second month began on the sixth day and ended on the ninth. It comprised, on the seventh day, a lamp festival and, on the ninth day, a ceremony named "the reception of the Buddha's clothing (shou fo-i)."

In 924, on the seventh day, a reception was offered to the associations that cost the monastery .4 shih of millet. That same year, on the seventh day, the monks brought back .4 shih of millet from their collection in town, and, on the eighth day, .3 shih of wheat and .5 shih of millet.[22]

In the spring of 924, on an unspecified date, a great vegetarian feast (chai) was held to which the officials were invited. The latter made a gift, in the form of a fee for religious services (dakṣiṇā),[23] of 1.1 shih of millet, .1 shih of hemp, and one length of cloth. Another great banquet of the same type took place in the autumn. It seems to have been less important and is only mentioned for the year 924. On that occasion, the officials made a gift of one length of cloth. The official offerings made by local administrators in the spring and autumn are designated as "food of the Buddha" (fo-shih) in the management reports.[24]

On the fourteenth and fifteenth days of the seventh month, the great festival of the dead (yü-lan p'en; Skr. avalambana) took place. The principal episode was the "breaking of the bowls (p'o-p'en)." In fact, as the entries on expenditure show, these bowls were gourds (kua) that had been emptied and dried: In 930, the monastery purchased gourds for the "breaking of the bowls" worth .2 shih of soya.[25] The same year it spent 4.55 shih of flour[26] to make "Buddha bowls" (fo-p'en) and invited the officials to a banquet in the grottoes. In addition, a nocturnal celebration took place in the course of which the "the hillock was burned" (shao-p'ei) by igniting a pile of five oilcakes.

In the twelfth month the monks went to recite the sutras in town.[27] They begged for "food for the gods and the Buddha and for provisions for the monks (shen fo shih chi seng-liao)." A rostrum was constructed (chieh-t'an) from which the most eloquent of the monks would preach. Around that time, a vegetarian banquet of purification (chieh-chai) took place on the winter solstice. This banquet and the food offerings for the Buddha cost .9 shih of flour in 924. But the monastery collected 1.15 shih of wheat and .64 shih of hemp in donations. In 930, at the time of the same festival, the monastery had received 1 shih of wheat and .6 shih of hemp.

In addition to these four great annual festivals in the first, second, seventh, and twelfth months, there were other ceremonies of less importance. We find a reference to a banquet organized on the occasion of "two days of prayer for [a good harvest of] hemp." At that time, the monastery received 1.1 shih of millet. In 930, it spent 1.4 shih of millet and .05 shih of oil for a ceremony initiated by the monk Yinhui to "send off the locusts" (song huang-ch'ung)[28] and for a banquet to obtain "deliverance from fire" (chieh-huo) that may have taken place at the end of the Cold Food (han-shih) period, 105 days after the winter solstice.

For a certain number of offerings the monastery accounts do not specify the occasion or date:

In 924, the monks had received 13 *shih* plus 15.4 *shih* of wheat and 7.5 *shih* of millet "for the price of the vegetables (*ts'ai-chia*)," that is, for food for the monks; in 930, the quantities under this heading were 7.5 and 9.7 *shih* of wheat and 6 *shih* of millet; in another year,[29] the monastery Ching-t'u received for the price of the vegetables 1.7 *shih* of wheat and 11.7 *shih* of millet.

Thus a variety of offerings were made on a regular basis, nearly always at the time of the great communal or official ceremonies, by the associations of the faithful, by simple laymen, and by local officials. These great feasts, which involved hundreds of monks and lay followers, cost a great deal for decorations and food, and the monasteries spent approximately as much on them as they received.

If historical sources inform us almost exclusively about the rich donations offered by emperors and great personages, the Tun-huang manuscripts provide on the contrary an insight into contributions made by the common people as well as more current practices. In most cases, the offerings are presented to the monastery for the recitation of Buddhist texts. At the same time, they may serve specific devotional purposes: a religious feast, a Buddhist construction project, the casting of a bell, etc. And the donor expects an equally specific benefit as a result of the gift: the healing of diseases, a safe journey, repose of deceased relatives, etc.

A few lists of donations received by Buddhist establishments survive among the collections of Tun-huang manuscripts. It will be noted that the offerings were made by both clergy and laity:

One *shih* of millet offered for the construction—
The intention of the believer is to act on behalf of his diseased mother for whom no cure has as yet been found. Today he comes to the sanctuary (*tao-ch'ang*) to request the recitation of sutra for her—
Note by the believer Chih Kang-kang, the thirtieth day of the first month, year *ch'en*.
One gown of white silk offered for the construction—
(same intention, same date).
One length of cloth given by a believer of the Wang family . . .
Half an ounce of glue and a mirror offered by a believer for the festival of the procession of the statues, on the eighth day of the second month . . .
Five haircuts offered for the construction by an anonymous believer, for the benefit of her younger brother having departed on a western journey. She hopes that nothing untoward will happen to him and that he may soon be able to return.

Five fans, one *shih* of wheat, and one *shih* of millet offered by Chang I-tzu for the construction, so that his deceased mother may be reborn in the Pure Land, and for the benefit of his father, suffering from eye disease. The eighth day of the second month.

All of these donors request the monks to recite sutra for them.[30]

Another list of offerings, dating from the period of the Tibetan occupation of Sha-chou (787–848),[31] mentions gifts of cloth, brocade, oxen, gold, and embossed silver dishes, presented by two Tibetan generals on the fifteenth day of the first month and the ninth day of the tenth month of the year *shen* (828?).[32]

A gift of fourteen *kaṣāya* (religious habits) and several pieces of cloth and clothing was made by the bhikṣunī Hsiu-te, on the fifteenth day of the twelfth month. These gifts were intended for the community at large of the town.[33] Hsiu-te further made a gift of a length of yellow cord for pulling the statues in the procession of the Buddha of Ling-t'u monastery, and of eight feet of fine cloth for the performance of rituals (*fa-shih*). All these donations were intended to obtain healing for herself, and she requested the monks to pray for her sins.

Gifts of the nun Tz'u-hsin: fabrics for the permanent assets of the Pao-en monastery, embossed kitchen utensils for the permanent assets of the Ling-hsiu monastery. She requests sutra recitations on her behalf, for she is ill and, as a woman, acknowledges all her sins.

One believer gave a blanket for the benefit of the community at large in the town: He was ill and none of the cures he had taken in the course of the past month had been able to heal him. He now came to the monastery to ask the monks to recite sutra for him.[34]

Another document mentions offerings, made on the first day of the first month, that were intended for the casting of a bell:

Seven feet of cloth and a quantity of copper for the casting of the bell;
   A lump of *a-li-lo* (note: *hsiu[?]-ju* cure);
   These offerings are made in the first place on behalf of my deceased father and mother: I do not know what fate has befallen them since their death; second, on my own behalf, to save me from death (?) and ensure my good health. On this day, I present myself at the monastery to request the recitation of sutra. The believer Li Chi-tzu, on the first day of the first month.
   Three rams for the casting of the bell.
   This offering is made for the benefit of my eldest son who has journeyed to the south, to the kingdom of the Tibetans, may his journey

encounter no obstacles or troubles; second, on behalf of my younger son and one of my daughters who have departed to the east, that no mishaps or annoyances may befall them. Hoping that they may have a favorable journey and reach their destination, and to see them again soon, I present myself on this day. . . . The believer T'ang Hsi-chen, on the first day of the first month.

One ram for the casting of the bell.

This offering is made so that the entire family, young and old, may be in good health. I present myself . . . an anonymous believer, on the first day of the first month.

The list mentions further offerings: 1 pound of red flowers, 1 pound of iron, 2 *shih* of millet, and 1 length of cloth; 1 *shih* of millet and 1 pound of copper; 1 ream of paper. The document bears, on the joints between sheets, the name of the monk Hui-chao who must have been the administrator of donations (*ch'en-ssu*).[35]

In the accounts of the Ching-t'u monastery, in the first half of the tenth century, the recitation of sutra (*nien-sung*) costs about .4 *shih* of cereals, wheat or millet:[36]

The monk Fu-en gave .45 *shih* of wheat to have sutra recited;
Kuo Ku-erh, whose wife has died, gave .7 *shih*;
Kao K'ung-erh, whose mother has died, gave .35 *shih* and, another time, .4 *shih*;
The master of Dharma and Vinaya (*fa-lü*) Cheng of the An-kuo monastery gave 1.5 *shih* of millet, and two other persons, also to have sutra recited, .3 and .4 *shih* of millet.[37]

Certain great ceremonies took place simultaneously in the monasteries of Tun-huang:

Fees paid at the time of the vegetarian feast held on the one hundredth day after the death of the rector of monks (*seng-[cheng]*) K'ung: 6 *shih* of millet;
Expenditure for the monks' vegetarian feast that took place on the last day of the sutra recitations in all the monasteries following the death of the young lady Chang: 8 *shih* of flour and .02 *shih* of oil.[38]

Some sutra recitations were patronized by officials. One manuscript features a list of the overseers (*wei-na*) in each establishment that were in charge of supervising the recitation of a part of the great *Prajñāpāramitā* by their monks. These recitations, commissioned by the Tsan-p'u of Tibet, were to place on the thirtieth day of a ninth month. Another service of the same kind was to be celebrated on behalf of a high Tibetan official on the twenty-second day of a twelfth month.[39]

There were also major rituals that were not performed in the monastery but in the homes of private individuals. To be able to invite famous monks to a private residence and offer them a vegetarian feast (chai) was a sign of great wealth. Several letters of invitation to services of that kind are found among the Tun-huang manuscripts.

> To the San-chieh monastery:
> I request Rector (seng-cheng ho-shang) Chang, Headmaster (shou ta-shih) Pan, Grand Masters (ta-shih) Li and two others, Rectors Tung, Chou, and Ch'en, and the (?) managing instructors (p'an-kuan she-li; Skr. ācārya) Liu and Chang to be so good as to come to my residence in order to conduct recitations and to perform a memorial service (hsiao-hsiang)[40] for my deceased son, the guard administrator (ya-ya). I hope that you will do me the kindness (tz'u-pei) to come to my home on the date indicated.
> The believer Sung Tz'u-shun, administrator of the governor's guard (tu ya-ya), on the twentieth day of the eighth month in the year chi-ssu.[41]

On the basis of the various letters of invitation found at Tun-huang, it may be concluded that it was mostly officials of low or middle rank who had monks celebrate mortuary services in their residences. Among the patrons are:

an administrator of the governor's guard (tu ya-ya),[42]
an administrator of the military governor's guard (chieh-tu ya-ya),[43]
an area commander (tsung tu-t'ou),[44]
the magistrate of Shou-ch'ang,[45]
the monk Shan-hui.[46]

The number of monks invited varies from one letter to another: eleven, eight, four, three, and one, and they belong to different monasteries: the San-chieh ssu,[47] the Ching-t'u ssu,[48] the Ch'ien-yüan ssu,[49] and the Lung-hsing ssu.[50]

Appeal to the services of monks on behalf of deceased relatives, however, was a widespread practice among the upper classes of T'ang society, as attested by historical sources. It was in fact so well established that Yao Ch'ung, a high official hostile to Buddhism, who died in 721, felt unable to prevent his sons and nephews from conforming to that deplorable custom. In a letter to which Yao consigned his last wishes, he instructed them:

> If after my death you are incapable of conforming yourselves entirely to the good principles and must follow the customs of our times, you could order a Buddhist service (chai) celebrated by seven monks every seven days after my death.[51] But when you have to make the alms offering for these services, give my clothes and personal objects and nothing else. That would be unnecessary and unreasonable. And neither must you give of your own belongings in compliance with empty talk about the "beatitude of the dead" (chui-fu).[52]

The Tun-huang manuscripts constitute the only source of precise information available; they enable us to determine that a particular monastery in a given region in the first half of the tenth century acquired about a quarter of its revenues in the form of petty objects.[53] The manuscripts also reveal which specific functions of religious establishments and the clergy were recognized: the organization of official ceremonies, of the major festivals, and the celebration of religious services for private families, in particular for the benefit of the dead. In terms of patronage, three levels of religious services may be distinguished: those on behalf of the empire and the dynasty, of the local community in its entirety, and those performed for private individuals.

Among the multitude of offerings provided by the court, local officials, groups of faithful, and private families, it is difficult to extricate data that would be useful for economic history. It is at least clear that the number and size of the offerings varied greatly according to time and place.

A consistent principle of successive governments was to provide officially ordained monks, who had been selected because of their scriptural knowledge and particular merit, with everything they needed. The regular communities, who were in charge of celebrating the imperial cult, were not to concern themselves with their own upkeep. Consequently, the mendicant monk who begged for his food among the people was an irregular phenomenon and a suspect figure in China.

Such a life of roaming and independence was not the normal condition of the monks belonging to large communities. When they begged, they did so as a group, and not for their own subsistence, which was already assured. There must have been considerable truth in the portraits of these monks drawn by anticlerical literati that represent them sitting in idleness, richly clothed, and fed on choice dishes. The clergy of the great cult centers, in the towns or on the sacred mountains, could rest assured that offerings would come flooding in, whether from official quarters or from private individuals. In Lo-yang, at the beginning of the sixth century, the residents of certain city wards volunteered to provide for the upkeep of the monks. In the Chien-yang ward alone, there were ten monasteries and "in that ward more than two thousand families, nobles and commoners, faithfully honored the Three Jewels (triratna). They furnished the monks with all they needed."[54] Later, under the T'ang, high officials would sacrifice some of their considerable wealth in support of the Buddhist communities. In the second half of the eighth century, Wang Chin, Yüan Tsai, and Tu Hung-chien among others, whose Buddhist faith was coupled with a pronounced taste for splendor and extravagance, were cases in point.[55]

What mattered most, however, was the renown of the cult site and its monks, and the sanctity that was ascribed to them.

Emperors summoned the great monks to court and heaped favors upon them. As for the recognized establishments, they received offerings in the form of special privileges, buildings, and fungible goods together with their official monastic titles:

At the beginning of the K'ai-huang era (581–600), the emperor ordered that a donation be made [to the Ch'ing-ch'an monastery][56] consisting of fourteen thousand pieces of satin, five thousand bolts of cloth, one thousand bales of silk wadding, two hundred bolts of fine silk fabric, twenty bolts of silk with a flower pattern, and one thousand shih of the five kinds of cereals of the first quality. The empress for her part ordered gifts of five thousand strings of cash, fifty pieces of felt, and fifty razors to be made over to the same establishment.[57]

According to the stele of the Miao-hsien monastery at Mount Chi-t'ing in Hsüan-chou county, this sanctuary had been founded under the Sui by the monk Chih-yen (516–601), in the year 591. Various gifts were bestowed by the emperor on the occasion of the founding: 5,000 strings of cash and two thousand bolts of silk for pharmacy expenses, two hundred hu of lo-chih rice, a collection of canonical texts, fifteen jade and stone statues, and forty-nine incense burners. All of this was intended to serve the cult in perpetuity.[58]

In the first year of the Ta-yeh reign (605), the emperor visited Chiang-tu (in modern Anhwei). . . . He had a Buddhist banquet organized for a thousand monks and ordained forty-nine religious. He also made a gift to the monastery [of that community ?] of two thousand bolts of cloth, three thousand *shih* of rice, of incense, little milk (koumiss?), and other provisions.[59]

But, once their reputation had attracted the attention of the court, the monks themselves were as much recipients of imperial donations as communities and monasteries. Such officially bestowed goods became the monks' sole property[60] which they used, in addition to contributions to the common and inalienable property (*ch'ang-chu*) of their monastery, for pious works and gifts to the poor or religious foundations.

Already prior to his accession, the future emperor T'ai-tsung of the Sung held the monk Tao-meng (411–475) in great esteem. When he ascended the throne in 465, he made the monk a gift of 300,000 cash for his personal needs, and a few years later decreed monthly provisions of 30,000 cash.[61] At the same time, the emperor bestowed on Tao-meng twenty-four scribes and guards, a carriage, and a sedan chair. But Tao-meng donated all of these for the benefit of the poor and for temple constructions.[62]

A widely attested practice was to have well-known monks, sometimes representing different doctrines (Buddhism and Taoism in the period of the Northern and Southern Dynasties), hold forth and to richly reward the winner of the contest:

In the second month of the first year of the T'ai-ho era (477), the emperor [Hsiao-wen of the Northern Wei] visited the Yung-ning monastery to hold a vegetarian banquet (*chai*) there. . . . In the third month, he went there again for a great assembly with further ceremonies and sermons. He ordered his private secretary and members of the imperial Secretariat to engage the monks in discussions of the principles of Buddhism and to reward the monks with clothing and precious utensils according to their ability.[63]

Toward the end of the sixth century, the monk Fa-tsang was awarded 210 strings of cash because he had been able to reply to Emperor Wu of the Chou in his own language (the *hsien-pei*).[64]

From the multitude of offerings made by emperors to sanctuaries and to monks may be inferred the universality of the practice to *reward* the deserving for their sanctity, their talents, or simply their reputation. An element to be emphasized here is the inequality of the treatment enjoyed by monasteries and monks. Some remained poor while others became very wealthy. Moreover, the success of certain doctrines created fortunes for particular sects.

The Inexhaustible Treasuries

The present discussion will be limited to typical cases. The history of the prodigious enrichment of the Sect of the Three Stages (San-chieh chiao) in the second half of the seventh century and up to the accession of Emperor Hsüan-tsung in the early eighth century is one such typical example. It is instructive on several accounts. The enrichment enjoyed by that sect seems to have been due only to offerings in the form of movables: cloth, money, precious objects, gold and silver. This fact is remarkable considering that for the majority of Chinese communities usury and tenure constituted the classical sources of wealth. Through the institutions of the sect, however, a mode of asset accumulation becomes perceptible that is peculiar to the whole of Chinese Buddhism: its foundations are of a psychological nature. It should be noted in this context that the period in question (ca. 640 to 713) was one of particularly intense religious fervor.[65] There are a number of indications for this. The *Liang-ching hsin-chi* reports that

> at the Hua-tu monastery [in Ch'ang-an][66] there was a Cloister of the Inexhaustible Treasury (Wu-chin tsang yüan). It had been instituted by the monk Hsin-hsing.[67] As a result of the donations that he received at the capital, this treasury flourished steadily. After the Chen-kuan reign (627–650), it held incalculable quantities of money, cloth, gold, and gold embroideries. Monks of repute were permanently assigned to oversee this treasury. Its assets were used for the restoration of monasteries (*saṃghārāma*) throughout the empire. Those intending to carry out such renovations came to the Inexhaustible Treasury from Yen (Hsü-chou, Szechwan), Liang (Wu-wei, Kansu), Shu (Ch'eng-tu, Szechwan), and Chao (Chao-chou, Hopeh) for supplies (*ch'ü-chi*). The volume of daily loans was beyond measure. Those who went there seeking loans, regardless of interest, came away without even having drawn up a deed in writing; they simply repaid their debts when they were due.[68]

The *T'ai-p'ing kuang-chi*, citing the *Pien-i chih* of Lu Ch'ang-yüan (d. 799), confirms the information provided by the *Liang-ching hsin-chi*, while adding some valuable details:

In the Wu-te reign period (618–627), there was a śramaṇa named Hsin-i who practiced Dhyāna and was engaged in the cause of the Three Stages. He established an Inexhaustible Treasury (Wu-chin tsang) at the Hua-tu monastery. After the Chen-kuan period, the accumulated donations of money, silks, gold, and jades became incalculable. Monks were permanently commissioned as supervisors [of the funds], which were divided into three parts: one part was to provide for the restorations of saṃghārāma throughout the realm; one part was to provide alms to relieve the suffering of all those in the realm who went hungry and for the field of compassion (pei-t'ien);[69] and the third part was assigned to religious services, which were thus amply provided for. Men and women of good society[70] came to present their offerings to the treasury, repenting and groaning. As the donors vainly disputed each other's place,[71] cartloads of money and silk were abandoned one after the other, without the [donors'] names being known.[72]

A decree dated 713 provides further details concerning these excessive offerings and shows that they took place especially at the beginning of the year:

Imperial decree of the fourth month, first year of the K'ai-yüan period (713) prohibiting men and women of good society (shih-nü) to make donations of money to Buddhist monasteries: at the Hua-tu monastery [in Ch'ang-an] and the Fu-hsien monastery [in Lo-yang],[73] the monks of the Sect of the Three Stages have instituted Inexhaustible Treasuries. Each year, on the fourth day of the first month,[74] members of the gentry throughout the empire present them with gifts of cash. The practice is known as "protecting the Law" (hu-fa). It is claimed that the purpose of this generosity is to relieve the poor and the orphans. But in fact there is nothing to it but excess and fraudulence. This business is not legitimate. Therefore We have decided to prohibit the practice. The money held in reserve by the Inexhaustible Treasuries shall be made over to the Censorate[75] and to the superior prefectures of the capital territory and of Honan so that these administrations may take control of management and inspect the accounts of these treasuries. They shall prepare a report to clarify the facts until such time that they will be informed of the dispositions to be taken.[76]

It is clear that the wealth of the Inexhaustible Treasuries at Ch'ang-an and Lo-yang derived from the offerings of the faithful. Their assets consisted for the most part of movables: money, cloth of various kinds, gold and silver, and jades. The decree ordering the confiscation of property held by the Inexhaustible Treasuries,[77] on the other hand, also mentions real estate.

> We have determined to distribute the entire holdings of the Inexhaustible Treasury of the Hua-tu monastery among the Buddhist and Taoist monasteries in the capital: valuables and commodities, lands and houses, and domestic animals. These goods shall be employed, first, for the repair of statues, halls, and bridges; the remainder shall be allocated to the permanent assets (ch'ang-chu) [of the monasteries] and may not be divided among the private cells (ssu-fang [i.e., the monks]. The distribution shall benefit the poorest monasteries first.

It is known that Wu Tse-t'ien had intended to endow the Inexhaustible Treasuries, perhaps especially that created by herself for the Fu-hsien monastery in Lo-yang, with real estate. In her preface to the Buddhist canon of 685, she declared:

> Take the property accumulated by my father and mother, use the old appanages of the two capitals, all that does not serve the construction of monasteries (chao-t'i chih yü: dwellings of the saṃgha of the Four Directions), and let all this be paid into the Inexhaustible Treasury (Treasuries?).[78]

These lands and buildings, however, played only an accessory role among the possessions of the Wu-chin tsang, a system characterized by the dynamic circulation of wealth. As the *Liang-ching hsin-chi* had put it, "The volume of daily loans was beyond measure."

On a fixed date, the fourth day of the first month, members of the upper classes throughout the empire sent offerings of cash to the Inexhaustible Treasuries. Those seeking subsidies for the construction or restoration of sanctuaries likewise came to the treasuries from all regions. This was another original feature of the institution: it extended throughout all China. It was particularly well represented in the regions of modern Szechwan, Kansu, and Hopeh. Clearly, the Inexhaustible Treasuries had local branches and stores in many regions, for the confiscation decree cited above stipulated that senior officials in the prefectures would liquidate the cash and commodities seized in their jurisdiction.

The Inexhaustible Treasuries received not only rich offerings from members of the gentry—those cartloads of money and silk; the common people were also invited to make donations. A text of the School of the Three Stages found at Tun-huang distinguishes between two kinds of donors: those who could offer 16 *fen*[79] of cash per day, and those able to give 30 *fen*.[80] Another text alludes to regular offerings of the same kind, but on the order of one *fen* per day, or 36 cash in a year, or of one *ko* of cereals (3.6 *tou* per annum).[81] These sort of offerings were plainly recommended to the poorest of the faithful.

The Tun-huang texts further confirm the existence of subsidiary banks of the Inexhaustible Treasury of Hua-tu monastery in the provinces. These repositories for offerings, named "merit offices" (*kung-te ch'u*), were temporarily opened on the date of the Avalambana festival:

> On the fifteenth day of the seventh month, the Avalambana festival, merit offices were established in the prefectures and counties everywhere so that everyone could make a contribution. . . . [Thus] it was unnecessary to send one's offerings to the Hua-tu monastery.[82]

The biography of one of the disciples of Hsin-hsing, the founder of the Sect of the Three Stages, a certain Te-mei (585–648), refers to these offerings of the feast of the seventh month: "Toward the end of the summer the monasteries received the bowls (*shou-p'en*) [of the Avalambana festival]. Wherever the bowls were, people would send their offerings. These were commonly called 'universal bowl money' (*p'u-p'en ch'ien*)."[83]

Thanks therefore to the treasuries in Ch'ang-an—the most important—and in Lo-yang, as well as the branches set up throughout China at the time of the Avalambana festival, the Sect of the Three Stages was able to tap a quantity of offerings in money, cloth, and cereals that must have been quite considerable. Two facts stand out: the donors belonged to all social classes, including great personages, nobles, and high court officials as well as commoners; and second, the offerings were mostly made at specific times of the year, the New Year festival and the feast of the dead.

The sect stood apart from the Buddhist community as a whole—its monks resided in buildings that did not communicate with the main courts of the monasteries.[84] Its independence and the level of organization suggested by the existence of these great repositories of offerings and their provincial branches no doubt favored its prodigious enrichment. But it is above all doctrine, based on the virtue of liberality, that accounts for the phenomenon. In this context, a point of view must be refuted that subsequently gained currency: the Inexhaustible Treasury, despite its name, evoking the practice of granting loans out of the inexhaustible wealth (wu-chin ts'ai),[85] did not essentially owe its wealth to placements at interest. This erroneous assumption was introduced by the author of the Shih-shih yao-lan under the Sung, citing the passage concerning the Inexhaustible Treasuries in the Liang-ching hsin-chi in his section devoted to the financial activities of the monasteries.[86] The Wu-chin tsang provided loans, to be sure, but of a quite particular kind: they were granted without contract and no doubt only to followers belonging to the upper classes.[87] It is manifestly not from these secondary activities that the treasuries derived the main part of their profits.

"There are two inexhaustibles," says a text of the School of the Three Stages:[88]

> The inexhaustible nature of the field of compassion (karuṇāpuṇyakṣetra) [that is due to] the ceaseless offerings [of the Inexhaustible Treasury] to the Buddha, the Law, the saṃgha, and all beings; and the inexhaustible nature of the seed (bīja) [as a result of the fact that] the donors never cease giving for a single day.[89]

The term inexhaustible, far from signifying an endless accumulation of interests, refers to the psychological mechanism that motivates the gifts. A gift invites a gift in return, and giving is contagious. The texts of the sect show clearly that this is both the core of the doctrine of the Three Stages and the foundation of the institution of the Inexhaustible Treasury:

> The Lesser Vehicle has no other aim than personal interest. The pursuit of that personal interest is the bane of families, monasteries, kingdoms, and the life in religion, for it ruins enlightenment (bodhi) in the practitioner. The Greater Vehicle, by contrast, aims simultaneously at personal interest and the interest of all others. That is why the bodhisattva, in their spirit of great compassion, instituted the method of the inexhaustible receptacle (wu-chin tsang). Of the ten virtues, charity is the first; of the four means of solicitation, liberality is the principal.[90]

The author cites two passages from the sutra that bring out the dual function of the Inexhaustible Treasuries whose resources were destined, first, to the Three Jewels (the field of reverence, ching-t'ien; Skr. satkārapunyakṣetra), and second, to the poor and the sick (the field of compassion (pei-t'ien; Skr. karuṇāpunyakṣetra). According to the Garland Sutra:

> The bodhisattva emit a radiance named "revealer of jewels" that enables the poor and destitute to discover treasures. It is by their gifts to the Three Jewels and thanks to their Inexhaustible Treasury (Wu-chin tsang) that they acquire this radiance capable of revealing jewels.[91]

And according to the Teaching of Vimalakīrti: "For all those who are poor and destitute, the bodhisattva instituted Inexhaustible Trea-suries. In this manner, they encourage them to do good and engender in them a spirit of bodhi."[92] A work of the School of the Three Stages[93] indicates that donations made to the Inexhaustible Treasury had the effect of permanently assuring the following sixteen cate-gories of expenditure and of inciting the faithful to give with these sixteen purposes in mind:

1. Offerings to the Buddha
2. Offerings to the Law
3. Offerings to the saṃgha[94]
4. Offerings to all beings
5. Works that strive to ward off evil
6. Works that strive to do good
7. Offerings of incense
8. Offerings of lamps
9. Offerings for the baths [of the monks]
10. Offerings for bells and chants
11. Offerings of clothing
12. Offerings of dwellings
13. Offerings of beds and seats
14. Offerings of receptacles for food
15. Offerings of coal and fire
16. Offerings of food and drink[95]

In this list, charitable donations and pious donations, those that ben-efit the laity and those intended for religious establishments, are treated alike. They were considered to be of the same kind and insep-arable from one another. The function of the Inexhaustible Treasury, where the small offerings of individual followers merged together and their religious efficacy seemed to multiply, was to redistribute the goods received by channeling them into liturgical services and charitable works.

This institution—accommodating religious doctrine to the practice of giving based on both the psychology of the gift and a formidable organization—was an original creation of China. The theoretical borrowings of the School of the Three Stages from India regarding the Inexhaustible Treasury in fact did not support such a concrete application. The inexhaustible treasuries, or rather receptacles (*tsang*), constituted a rubric of the Greater Vehicle that applied to the moral qualities of the bodhisattva. The bodhisattva possessed ten inexhaustible receptacles: faith (*śraddhā*), observance of the precepts (*śīla*), dignity (*hrī*), sense of honor (*apatrāpya*), teaching (*śruta*), liberality (*dāna*),[96] wisdom (*prajñā*), steadfastness (*dhāraṇī*), and eloquence (*pratibhāna*).[97] In China, the notion of the inexhaustible receptacles was borrowed from the two scriptures cited above, the Garland Sutra (*Avataṃsaka-sūtra*) and the Teaching of Vimalakīrti (*Vimalakīrtinirdeśa*).

The facts concerning the Inexhaustible Treasuries cannot be isolated from their doctrinal and historical contexts. The seventh century was a period of intense fervor, and it was that particular moral atmosphere that permitted the rapid enrichment of the treasuries of the School of the Three Stages. A doctrinal current placing a special emphasis on liberality and charity, however, was already forming at the end of the sixth century. The term *wu-chin tsang* appears prior to the foundation of the Inexhaustible Treasury of the Hua-tu monastery, in the biography of the monk Chi-tsang (549–623).[98] In Ch'ang-an, under the reign of Emperor Wen of the Sui (581–604), there was a master of Dhyāna named T'an-hsien whose sermons were immensely popular.

Members of the great families and noble houses (*hao-tsu kuei-yu*)[99] exhausted all their wealth in offerings. The faithful and religious were pleased to be subject to their influence. Chi-tsang's work of conversion (*fa-hua*) was boundless, while donations of material goods (*ts'ai-shih*)[100] accumulated. Chi-tsang distributed all these offerings as soon as they arrived to institute fields of merit (*fu-t'ien*; Skr. *puṇyakṣetra*).[101] The remainder he placed into the tenfold inexhaustible receptacle (*shih wu-chin tsang*)[102] for T'an-hsien to use for the benefit of [the fields of] reverence and compassion (*ching pei*).[103]

By various means, the Inexhaustible Treasuries ensured the collection of offerings from all parts of Chinese society—offerings received in quantity at particular times of the year and regular offerings collected in the form of a daily levy. At the same time, they oversaw the redistribution of these offerings to a variety of ends, the main beneficiaries of the Wu-chin tsang being religious establishments and, to a lesser extent, the laity.

Pious and charitable offerings together formed a coherent system that did not aim at an accumulation of goods but at their redistribution and circulation; not at growing profits but at expenditure. The charitable donations were an essential element in this system: they constituted a form of investment that was highly advantageous because it incited new offerings in turn. According to a work of the School of the Three Stages, the method of the inexhaustible receptacle had two effects:

> Since it consists of giving—thanks to the many offerings received—to beings that are prone to greed, it is conducive to thoughts of goodness, and that is easily done. Second, it teaches the poor to share their meager resources by joining them to the gifts made to the inexhaustible receptacle by other bodhisattva. As a result, they may gradually attain a spirit of *bodhi*.[104]

To receive the gifts of the Three Jewels engendered pious thoughts as well as feelings of gratitude and respect: one was bound by such gratuitous generosity. But the effect of giving to the triratna was more profound yet, for it led to the gradual transformation of the donor into a bodhisattva. The notion of communion is crucial here: it is made concrete by the receptacle at once unique and inexhaustible—thanks to the multitude of the offerings—that is the Inexhaustible Treasury.[105]

Charitable Activities

Buddhism of the Lesser Vehicle was faithful to the Indian conception of the word as a source of particularly efficacious power—an exalted good—a conception that regarded the "gift of the Law" (*dharmatyāga*) as the noble counterpart to the "gift of material goods" (*āmiṣatyāga*). The role of the monks was to preach the good doctrine; that of the laity, to procure the clergy's livelihood in exchange. If that opposition survived in Mahāyāna Buddhism it was less apparent because the faithful and the beings (*sattva*) to be converted had acquired their own place within the community and were more highly regarded. The alms no longer went exclusively to the clergy but were also addressed, as charitable donations, to the poor and the sick among the laity.[106] Moreover, the growing importance of acts of devotion tended to reduce the gulf between the monks and the faithful. What really mattered was pious works (kung-te), and these works necessitated a collaboration between clergy and laity.

Like the faithful, the Chinese monks devoted a part of their possessions to pious works. The biographies of famous monks frequently depict them as founders of hermitages, chapels, and monasteries or engaged in purchasing lands and buildings on behalf of their communities. They bequeathed their property to the monasteries and, like laymen, had sutra recited for themselves. In short, their attitude toward the sacred is identical to that of the faithful. In the inscriptions at Lung-men, the clergy frequently figure among the donors: "In the second year of Yung-p'ing (509) the nuns Fa-wen, Fa-lung and others . . . exhausted their personal possessions (ssu-ts'ai) to have a statue of Maitreya made.[107] . . . The nun Seng-hsien . . . to have a statue of Maitreya made."[108]

The Tun-huang manuscripts confirm this attitude of the Chinese clergy towards pious works: they were donors like the others, and the right to own property that they enjoyed permitted them to comport themselves in the same manner as lay followers. One of these documents from Tun-huang contains the text of a contract between a monk and an artisan with the object of constructing a chapel in the open country:

On the seventh day of the eighth month of the year yin, the monk Tz'u-teng, in order to construct a chapel (fo-t'ang) on the property of the East Canal but not [knowing where to find] an expert artisan (po-shih), addressed himself to the commoner (po-hsing) Fan Ying-chen of the Hsi-tung-sa tribe (pu-lo). . . . The price of 8[0] shih of wheat was settled prior to the construction. The outer facade of the chapel shall measure 1 chang and 4 ch'ih (4.2 m). Fan Ying-chen is to build the walls and to apply a thin coat of plaster. Construction shall begin on the fifteenth day of the eighth month. The [price in] wheat having been judged equitable (?), one bolt of cloth worth 4 shih and 2 tou will [in addition] be paid for each day of work.[109] . . . These arrangements having been made, it shall not be permissible to retract. If one of the parties withdraws, it shall pay a penalty of three loads of wheat to the other. Lest there be a breach of faith, this contract was drawn up. The two parties [present], having found its dispositions just and clear, wrote out this deed to serve as proof.[110]

The faithful gave to the monks and the monasteries in order that they might use the offerings received for further pious works. This general observation is well illustrated by the example of the Inexhaustible Treasuries. The share of the goods required for the upkeep of the communities, which formed the main part of all offerings under the Lesser Vehicle, became minute in the economy of Chinese Mahāyāna where the biggest expenditures went into the construction of sanctuaries, the casting of bells and statues, festivals, and, finally, charitable activities.

Charity was not a subsidiary religious activity: it was a means of propaganda and conversion, and hence one of the most effective procedures of enrichment.

Alms to the poor and care for the sick were always accompanied by preaching to draw the recipient's attention to Buddhism. As one Chinese Mahāyānist work recommended:[111]

> When you encounter the poor, ask of them first: "Are you capable of taking refuge in the Three Jewels and receiving the precepts?" If they say yes, let them first take the triple refuge and the vows, then give them alms. If they reply that they are incapable, continue as follows: "If you are not capable of doing so, can you follow us at least when we preach the impermanence and nonbeing of all things and the extinction in nirvana?" If the answer is yes, then they are to be instructed in these truths, and once they are instructed they should be given alms . . .
>
> Those who are poor and without resources shall recite the formulae for healing and the various incantations. Those who ask for money, broth, and medicines shall receive them. Their illnesses are to be diagnosed with the greatest care and the appropriate cure shall be seen to. . . . It will be explained to the sick person that his pains are due to an evil contracted in a previous existence and that since he now suffers painful retribution, it is time to repent. Upon these words the invalid may become angry and utter coarse insults. [The person treating him] will keep his silence and refrain from replying, yet will not abandon [the invalid].[112]

Many monks practiced charity on their own initiative, providing care for the sick, making gifts of cures, distributing food to the hungry. And the main recipients of offerings were precisely the monks who were distinguished by their generosity, their detachment from worldly possessions, and their asceticism.

The monk Tan Tao-k'ai had a storied turret built near his cell. It was twenty meters high, and on top of it he installed a wicker basket that served him as a meditation chamber. He remained permanently squatting in it. The third sovereign of the Later Chao, Shih-hu (d. 349), made him sumptuous gifts, but Tan Tao-k'ai distributed them all to the needy.[113]

Another monk, named Fa-hsiang, is supposed to have encountered a spirit that invited him to lift a stone slab weighing several tons. Having removed it effortlessly, he discovered a treasure that he used entirely for alms to the poor.[114]

Some distributed gruel to the hungry in times of shortage or famine. In 618, at the end of the Sui, T'an-hsien attracted in this manner the favors of Emperor Yang who founded the Tz'u-pei monastery in his honor.[115] In 756, at the time of the exile of Hsüan-tsung in Szechwan, the eunuch Kao Li-shih presented a memorial reporting that in the market south of the ramparts there was a monk named Ying-kan who distributed gruel in the thoroughfares to save the poor and the hungry of Ch'eng-tu. In response, the emperor wrote in his own hand the characters "Ta-sheng tz'u ssu" for the name panel [of the monastery] and bestowed on it one thousand *mu* of land.[116] And during a period of dearth, in the Ta-chung era (847–860), Ch'ing-kuan distributed food to the starving peasants.[117]

At the end of the sixth century, under the Ch'en (557–589), probably more than half of the population of that kingdom died in epidemics. The monk Hui-ta installed a large dispensary (*ta yao-tsang*) in the great market at Yang-tu, which supplied cures to all those in need of them.[118]

The general terms designating devout activities on the one hand—the field of reverence (*ching-t'ien*)—and charitable activities on the other—the field of compassion (*pei-t'ien*)—came into current usage only toward the end of the sixth century. That is not to say that before that date the Buddhist communities did not devote a part of their wealth in aid of the poor and the sick: there are many examples of charitable monks who cared for the sick or distributed help to the victims of famines. And the institution of the saṃgha households, at the end of the fifth century, served in principle a charitable purpose. But it seems that the development of the doctrinal concept of charity and of charitable works in practice was particularly appreciable in the sixth century, the period in which an authentically Chinese form of Buddhism was constituted.

One of the earliest mentions of the terms *ching-t'ien* and *pei-t'ien* occurs in the biography of the monk Te-mei (585–648), one of the disciples of the founder of the School of the Three Stages. A few days before his death, the master of Dhyāna Mo transmitted to Te-mei his "heritage of the universal field of merit (*fu-t'ien*)." Each year, Te-mei used all of its revenues for the two fields of reverence and compassion, either in the form of gifts of clothing or of aid in cereals. The offices of pious works (*ts'ao-fu ch'u*) [119] in the region, whose coffers were mostly empty, came to him to be helped out with subsidies.[120] As I-ching wrote, "Pious foundations thus make it possible to feed the clergy and the laity at the same time, for even though the donors present their offerings to the monks, their kindness in fact extends to all without distinction (*p'u-t'ung i-ch'ieh*)."[121]

This then was the principle of the charitable institutions: like cult foundations, whose aim was either the upkeep of the clergy or the provision of goods necessary for worship and ceremonies, they were founded on real estate, the special use of which was fixed once and for all.

Beginnings of the different charitable activities of the Mahāyāna movement in China can be found in the texts of the Lesser Vehicle. But these are only concerned with offerings to the clergy, and more precisely to those who traveled and to those who were ill. In a series of seven particularly recommended donations (*ch'i-shih*; Skr. *aupadhika puṇyakriyāvastu*)[122] are mentioned gifts to the sick (*glāna*), the sick-nurses (*glānopasthāna*), and to arriving travelers (*āgantuka*) and departing travelers (*gamika*). Charity, however, which was limited to the relatively restricted circle of the religious under the Lesser Vehicle, was extended to the whole universe of sentient beings in Mahāyāna Buddhism: pilgrims, the faithful visiting monasteries, participants in the great Buddhist assemblies, the poor, the hungry, the sick, and animals.

In fact, little is known about the charitable institutions of Buddhist monasteries in China. An imperial decree provides incidental information about the subject: In the course of the Ch'ang-an reign period (701–705), the empress Wu Tse-t'ien instituted lay commissioners to oversee all the activities of the Buddhist Church pertaining to the field of compassion: support for orphans, the destitute, the elderly, and the sick.[123] Japan in the eighth century, when Chinese institutions were faithfully copied, also provides indirect testimony:

> At Nara, there were four charitable organizations, of which the foundation in support of the clergy, the Keiden-in (Chin. *ching-t'ien yüan*),[124] and the society for the distribution of alms to the poor, Hiden-in (Chin. *pei-t'ien yüan*) were the most important. . . . In addition, there was a hospital, Seryyō (Chin. *shih-liao yüan*), and a dispensary, Seyaku-in (Chin. *shih-yao yüan*), where the sick received free cures.[125]

In the years around 750–753, the monk Chien-chen (Jap. Kanshin, 688–763) instituted a field of compassion at Yang-chou, on the lower Yangtze, the produce of which was used to alleviate the misery of the poor, as well as a field of reverence to provide for offerings to the Three Jewels.[126]

In the twenty-second year of the K'ai-yüan period, Emperor Hsüan-tsung forbade begging within the walls of the capital and created hospitals (*ping-fang*) where the beggers where to be fed.[127] The commentary of Hu San-hsing adds that "the establishment at that time of hospitals within the monasteries where the sick were supported thanks to the 'field of compassion' is of Buddhist origin."

A Buddhist hospital is already mentioned at the beginning of the seventh century: "The monk Chih-yen (d. 654) then went to Shih-t'ou (in modern Nanking) where he stayed at the leper house (*li-jen fang*). He preached Buddhism to the lepers and attended to their every need: sucked their abscesses, washed them, etc."[128]

Given the period of the available evidence, and given also the use of the terms *ching-t'ien* and *pei-t'ien*, which were late to appear, it may be assumed that these charitable foundations only began to develop under the Sui dynasty. The funds needed for the care of the sick and the poor were provided from the revenues of designated lands. The expression *pei-t'ien*, like *ching-t'ien*, in effect, referred to fields under cultivation in China, whereas in Indian Buddhism the word *kṣetra* was a pure metaphor.[129] According to a widespread practice among the Buddhist communities, greater resources still were no doubt derived from the placement at interest of the produce of these lands: when in the years 843–845 the monastic hospitals were laicized, Li Te-yü memorialized the throne requesting that 10 ch'ing (ca. 54 ha) of land belonging to the monasteries that had been closed down be attributed to the hospitals in the capital, 7 ch'ing to those in superior prefectures, and 5 *ch'ing* to those in ordinary prefectures. At the same time he also recommended the placement of excess funds at interest, a practice that he considered both convenient and particularly advantageous.[130] It is likely that, to defray the costs of their hospital services, the monasteries also took recourse to this method, which was, moreover, consecrated by Buddhist tradition. The *Mahīśāsakavinaya* relates the following story.[131] A householder, before all of his possessions were depleted by the monks he supported, expressly set up a loan shop to provide for the care of sick bhikṣu out of the interests earned.[132] In China, however, the monks administered the charitable foundations themselves, whereas in the countries of the Lesser Vehicle the laymen retained the ownership of the goods consecrated to the foundation, leaving merely their usufruct to the clergy.[133]

Monasteries in China are public places. Outside the numerous festivals that draw clergy and laity to their precincts, they are also popular places for excursions. Some sanctuaries have gardens where all the features of nature are united: woods, ponds, rocks, and brooks. At Lo-yang, in the first half of the sixth century, monasteries known for their sumptuous buildings and parks served members of good society as places of recreation.[134] Some even used them as meeting places. Visits to mountain hermitages constitute a well-known theme in T'ang poetry:

"On each excursion to the mountain monastery," wrote Po Chü-i, "I spend a good many nights there. Having left the city for a moment, I suddenly find that weeks have passed."[135]

There were laymen who resided in Buddhist establishments. One of the sons of Li Ch'eng, named Yüan, had made a vow of celibacy and abstinence from meat and alcohol. He went to live in a cell of Hui-lin monastery, north of Lo-yang, and abided by the monastic rules.[136] Lay administrators were also to be found there, such as that seemingly devout individual who one day made off with the gold reserves of the Inexhaustible Treasury from Hua-tu monastery in Ch'ang-an.[137]

Buddhist establishments, especially those in the lonely mountain settings celebrated in Chinese painting and poetry, served as places of sojourn and refuge not only for important personages with whom the monks had an interest to maintain good relations. Buddhist sanctuaries were not only frequented by individuals of such good repute; remote chapels and monasteries situated far from the great routes of communication and major population centers also gave shelter to vagabonds. When certain officials denounced these establishments as brigands' lairs and hideouts for convicts and draft evaders (cf. p. 42 above), we have no reason to deny them all credence. To welcome those whom society rejected was at once to perform an act of charity and to secure a fully devoted lay clientele. Setting aside this political aspect, however, the spread of small and large sanctuaries may have had a positive economic effect by facilitating communications for traveling officials, soldiers,[138] and merchants, as it evidently did for the clergy themselves.

The monasteries of Central Asia were the obvious staging posts for both pilgrims and merchants. It has been maintained that the Wei found it in their interest to favor Buddhism and lend it official support in order to preserve their influence in Central Asia and to keep open the great trade routes to the west.[139] Here is one ground for the connection between Buddhism and trade already pointed out. Through the proliferation of its sanctuaries, Buddhism furthered exchanges in China.

Under the heading of charitable works, a Mahāyāna text mentions the construction of shelters for travelers.[140] Similarly, all works of public utility were recommended to the saṃgha and lay followers: roads, tree plantations, wells, bridges, fords, ferries, etc.[141] The disciplinary code established for the Dhyāna communities by the master Huai-hai devotes a paragraph to the reception of guests:

Whenever an official, a great patron (dānapati), an honorable elder or an important personality in the region passes by the monastery, the visitors' attendant (chih-k'o) receives him by burning incense and offering him tea. He then sends the abbot's attendant (hsing-che) to announce the visitor to the abbot, to whom he is led for the introductions. The abbot sees to it that the visitor is well installed and lacks nothing, and then leaves him. If the visitor is not a guest of the first rank he is simply received by the officers in charge of visitors (k'o-ssu). If he wishes to see the abbot, treasurer, or other [monastic] officers, then the abbot's attendant leads him before these. If [the visitor] stays overnight, the attendant shall prepare a monk's bed for him and furnish him with all that is needed: curtains, lamp, oil, and firewood. If he visits [the monastery] for the first time, he shall be treated with special consideration. If the karmadāna overseer is on leave, he shall be replaced in his functions.[142]

While all Buddhist establishments were required to receive lay visitors and if necessary accommodate them, certain sanctuaries, situated in important pilgrimage sites, operated veritable hostelries. The shelters that were strung out along the road from Ch'ang-an to Mount Wu-t'ai[143] are among the best known, thanks to the account of the Japanese monk Ennin who traveled in China from 837 to 847. These buildings were named common cloisters (p'u-t'ung yüan), i.e., were open to all who came. Installed at intervals corresponding to half a day's walking distance, they offered shelter and sometimes food to all passing lay and religious pilgrims to Mt. Wu-t'ai. Ennin's diary entry for the twenty-third day [of the fourth month, 840] records that "every person who came to rest there was provided with a monk's lodging. As for food, it was only supplied as available.[144] Since no one, monk or layman, was denied hospitality there, these places were known as common cloisters."[145] Thus Ennin himself was able to lodge in several such shelters (Liang-ling, Ching-shui, Chang-hua, Chüeh-shih) and was sometimes offered a free meal.[146] These hermitages could house more than a hundred people, and were administered by an abbot (yüan-chu: the master of a cloister, counterpart of the ssu-chu, master of a monastery). The yüan-chu were not always very welcoming, as Ennin remarked, referring to that of the county and of Ch'ing-liang (Wu-t'ai): "He did not know the rites of hospitality." These public shelters were not only found in mountainous and inaccessible areas, but also in the plains, villages, or beneath the ramparts of walled cities. Thus Ennin lodged in a village shelter in Fen prefecture at Chin-chou, "in the Common Cloister east of the market."[147]

Elsewhere (second day, seventh month, 840), Ennin reports that the Ta-hua yen monastery at Mt. Wu-t'ai had a dining hall that was open to clergy and laity, and to men, women, and children alike.[148]

And the hotels for pilgrims at Mt. Wu-t'ai were not the only ones in China: at the Yün-chü monastery of Mount Fang (in P'ing-shan county in modern Hopeh) there was an "equitable refectory" (i-fan t'ing).[149] Some chapels were even constructed for the specific purpose of providing a shelter to travelers.

> The road south of the county seat [of Chin-hua, modern Chekiang] connects Ch'ü and Wu [prefectures]. Along this stretch of more than one hundred li (ca. fifty kilometers) there is not a single sanctuary (ch'ieh-lan), and the Buddhist clergy that come and go have nowhere to rest. [The monk Shen-]yung (officially ordained in 738) "extended a Dharma bridge" (fa-ch'iao) to provide a resting place for voyagers, and considered that a Brahmā ground (fan-ch'ang)[150] could be con-

structed on Mount Ch'iao.[151] He secured the agreement of local people (*i-jen*) [of Chin-hua?], of the commandant of cavalry (*chi tu-wei*)
Ch'en Shao-ch'in, and others to engage the faithful for the construction of a hermitage (*ching-ch'a*).[152]

The monasteries' function as hostelries was quickly perceived by the
imperial government as a semipublic service. Under the T'ang the
great monasteries, especially those of Ch'ang-an and Lo-yang,
depended so closely on the secular authorities that it is hardly surprising to find that they were formally designated as the officials'
lodgings. An imperial order of the third year of the Yüan-ho period
(808) decreed that candidates in the official examinations who had
been retained too late into the night to return home were to be lodged
in the Kuang-chai monastery, and their attendants in the Pao-shou
monastery.[153]

If the institution could be used for the benefit of the state, it was
also a source of income for the monks. As a result of an evolution for
which other examples could be cited,[154] charitable activity transformed itself into a profitable enterprise. Under the T'ang, the monasteries let rooms to laymen for a fee. A decree of Emperor Tai-tsung,
dated eighth month of the first year of Pao-ying (762), reads: "It has
come to Our attention that in Buddhist and Taoist monasteries in the
prefectures and counties lodgings are frequently rented out, officially
or privately. Lest [the sanctuaries] be sullied, We strictly prohibit [this
practice]."[155]

Another decree of a slightly later date remarks upon the deteriora-
tion of the monasteries' living quarters due to lay occupants under the
reign of Te-tsung (779–805).[156] And an imperial order of the second
year of the Ta-chung era (848) reads:

It has come to Our attention that the Buddhist and Taoist monasteries
in the empire are frequently inhabited by civil and military officials
and other guests. Such promiscuity sullies the holy places . . . and damages their halls and living quarters. . . . Kitchens have been installed
under the covered galleries. . . . All this is forthwith prohibited.[157]

Ennin mentions that all the living quarters in the K'ai-yüan ssu at
Teng-chou (in modern Shantung) were occupied by traveling officials.
There was not one room left where one could be in peace, and monks
coming to the monastery could not be accommodated.[158]

Apart from secular officials and the military—possibly also merchants—there was another category of laymen that frequently resided or lived temporarily in monasteries: students and apprentice scribes. They found there the lamps, paper, and ink necessary for their work. And, as the collections of manuscripts found at Tun-huang show, monastic libraries did not contain exclusively Buddhist works. Some of the books of profane or Taoist content bear the seals of the K'ai-yüan, San-chieh, or Ching-t'u monasteries.

When Wang Chih, a magistrate in I-chou (in modern Szechwan), lodged temporarily in a monastery in the prefecture on his return to his native place in 658, he met a student who had rented a room there.[159] Li Ch'o of the T'ang cites the case of a certain Cheng Kuan-wen in his *Shang-shu ku-shih*[160] who for the purpose of studying calligraphy rented a cell in the Ta tz'u-en monastery at Ch'ang-an where he had the paper at his disposal needed for his exercises.

It has been demonstrated that the monastic Buddhism of the Lesser Vehicle commended a system of offering gifts to arriving monks (*āgantuka*) and departing monks (*gamika*),[161] and that the communal organization and property of the saṃgha made its application possible. Against this background, the magnitude of the evolution that the different forms of alms given to travelers underwent in the Greater Vehicle movement in China stands out. It concerned both the economy of the religious communities and that of the lay world. As places of passage and centers of communication, the monasteries did not form islands closed to the lay world: some laymen permanently resided there. The separation between the worlds of the sacred and the profane that the imperial authorities endeavored to impose was never effectively observed, an indication of the conflation of the religious and the profane that was one of the most characteristic features of Mahāyāna Buddhism in China.

Is it now possible to consider the historical evidence as a whole? The interpenetration of commerce and religion has been recognized: the recourse to guaranties of a supernatural order for loans without contract, for pious donations, and to safeguard the consecrated property of the Buddhist communities. But there is more. On two different levels, one and the same concept is concerned: that of productive capital. Before the introduction of Buddhism, China had scarcely been aware of this notion, nor of the mechanism of an automatic accumulation of interests. The activity of merchants consisted primarily in buying and reselling according to the going rate of the merchandise. If they became rich, it was due to luck and shrewdness. As for loans, they retained the nature of a risky gamble.[162] Loans against pledges, on the Indian model, offered security. Moreover, the possession of a fixed and inalienable capital—that of the "permanent assets"—lent a basis to commercial dealings that did not exist in pre-Buddhist China. Finally, and this seems to have been the most important innovation, Buddhist communities introduced a form of modern capitalism into China: consecrated property, constituted by an accumulation of offerings and commercial revenues, formed communal wealth, the communal management of which was more profitable than individual operations. But what is most remarkable about this conception is its religious origin. The Buddhist theory of giving already proceeded from a notion of productive capital; in concrete terms, we are dealing with a capitalization of offerings. The Inexhaustible Treasuries are a most revealing illustration of this system. The gift of an individual follower may be modest or significant, but the sum of the offerings form a fund whose productivity is incommensurate with that of the individual contributions. The donors to the Inexhaustible Treasuries are shareholders, not in the economic domain but in that of religion. The increase of the assets and that of their religious effect go hand in hand, and charitable gifts, again a form of investment in the lay world, appear as one of the essential elements in this system.

The institution of the Inexhaustible Treasuries was the result of a systematization, indicating that the circles who promoted the treasuries had taken note of these mechanisms. The particular case, meanwhile, may serve to raise a question of a more general order: if systematization took place, religious practice must have supplied the constituent elements. It is the deeper motivations of the economic movement that remain to be analyzed.

PART FIVE

THE HISTORICAL SUBSTRATA

CHAPTER EIGHT

ECONOMICS AND RELIGION

Introduction

The faithful presented sanctuaries and monks with small offerings in payment for specific services. At the same time, they instituted pious foundations that were protected by sanctions of a religious nature: both inside the saṃgha, since the monks could not appropriate consecrated goods without the risk of infernal punishment, and outside, because gifts of immovable property were accompanied by imprecations against possible despoilers.[1] The dread of the consequences of committing a sacrilege was sufficiently prevalent among the laity to act as an effective deterrent. It was rare that a donor simply parted with his property; normally, he would wish to reap the benefits of his pious deed (kung-te) by ensuring the perpetuity of a cult. New foundations were a means for arranging the provision of funds for the payment of regular and, in principle, perpetual ceremonies in the future. Meanwhile, the pious intention that justified the offerings and donations is an element that cannot be disregarded: economics and religion are inseparable here. From the outset, the Buddhist phenomenon was brought about by motivations of a psychological order, which gave it its momentum and ensured the maintenance of its religious patrimony through several centuries.

Is it possible to give, as a point of departure, an objective outline of the long-term development of the religious movement? If faith is judged by its effects, and by the magnitude of wealth sacrificed, it can be determined that Buddhist fervor enjoyed periods of particular intensity in China and that the Buddhist phenomenon itself described a characteristic curve. It is not impossible to date its beginning, apogee, and decline. The great period of Buddhist sculpture—during which immense assemblies of religious personages were carved into the rock, when the greatest and most splendid monasteries were built—extended from the last years of the fifth century to the end of the seventh. The finest Tun-huang manuscripts date from the sixth and seventh centuries. The Yun-kang caves, in the vicinity of the Northern Wei capital at Ta-t'ung, were for the most part sculptured during the years 489–523, before and after the transfer of the court to Lo-yang in 493. As for the famous Lung-men caves, Chavannes offers the following valuable observation in his study of the inscriptions at that great Buddhist site:

> Buddhist fervor at Lung-men had two periods of particular intensity, one during the time when the Northern Wei Dynasty had its capital at Lo-yang (495–534),[2] the other under the T'ang, during the second half of the reign of T'ai-tsung and the reigns of Kao-tsu and the empress Wu.[3]

The suspension or slowing down of the works at Lung-men between the sack of Lo-yang and circa 638 could be explained by the troubles that followed the end of the Northern Wei, by the Northern Chou's rather unfavorable policy toward Buddhism, and by the wars that followed the end of the Sui. But the indications already provided by the census figures on the number of monasteries seem to confirm Chavannes's remark: the two periods of greatest and most sumptuous construction activity fall at the beginning of the sixth century and at the end of the seventh. The evidence of Yang Hsüan-chih, in his memoir on the monasteries of Lo-yang at the end of the Northern Wei, accords well with that of the inscriptions at Lung-men: "Princes and dukes, the entire nobility, made offerings of their horses[4] . . . as easily as they would remove their shoes. Commoners and wealthy families gave up their possessions and their wealth as a person leaves behind his footsteps on the road."[5] The period when that rich bank of offerings, the Inexhaustible Treasury of the Hua-tu monastery, was in operation at Ch'ang-an coincides closely with the second phase of Buddhist fervor indicated by Chavannes. "After the Chen-kuan (627–650) period, the accumulated donations [received by the treasury] of money, silks, gold, and precious stones became incalculable."[6] The faithful were bringing their cash and silk to the treasury by the cartload. The decree of 713 ordering the confiscation of the goods of the Inexhaustible Treasuries and referring to the irregularities and abuses to which these excessive offerings had given rise marks the end of that period of intense faith.[7]

As strange as that passion for sacrifice with its outward signs of a collective frenzy may seem, with these two bursts it made its appearance in Chinese history only as short-lived crises. That is not to say that before and after these crises China did not know movements of a similar fervor—a fervor that always expressed itself with the same violence and the same excess, features peculiar to the Buddhist faith in China—but it is at that time, during the sixth and seventh centuries, that the religious phenomenon reached its maturity in China. This is borne out by the magnitude of the offerings, the number of inscriptions, the sumptuousness of the sanctuaries, down to the creation of Chinese Buddhist doctrines and the formation of the schools. This, then, stands out as an important fact inviting the scholar to renounce the view of the long history of Buddhism in China since the first century of our era down to modern times as a single whole comprised of elements of a similar nature. The fifth century—the period in which the true development of Chinese Buddhism took place, where an organized monastic community made its appearance and the number of sanctuaries multiplied—and the eighth and ninth centuries—during which is witnessed a degradation of the religious phenomenon: these frame the era of great fervor; they are the periods of the rise and decline of Buddhism in China.

Original Characteristics of Buddhist Faith in China

The forerunners of Buddhist enthusiasm in China are well-known. They go back, it seems, to the years around 435. In the North, the transfer of a population already exposed to Buddhism from Liang-chou to Shansi in the years 435–440 was, according to Wei Shou,[8] followed by a sudden development of the new religion. Some texts, however, suggest a motive behind this enthusiasm: not only did the faithful spend money for the construction of stūpa and monasteries, but they ruined themselves in the process, and vied with one another in ruining themselves.

When in the twelfth year of the Yüan-chia period (435), under the

Sung dynasty in Southern China, Hsiao Mo-chih was appointed governor of Tan-yang, he presented the following memorial to the emperor:

> It is said that Buddhism has spread its influence in China for four dynasties. The stūpa, monasteries, images, and statues are everywhere and number in the thousands. If this continues, that doctrine will have too great an ascendancy over the people's minds. If, however, it is curbed, then there will [still] be enough [witnesses to that religion] to attract and encourage people [to do good]. Recently the faithful, misled by ulterior interests, no longer consider the sincerity of their zeal as essential; what matters to them is to vie with one another in prodigality. They exceed the golden middle and violate the standard. It is thus appropriate to place them under surveillance. Otherwise it will be impossible to prevent this abuse.[9]

Nearly forty years later, in 472, a decree promulgated in the North reported the same rivalry in giving and formulated a similar criticism of the practice:

> The inhabitants of the capital territory and those of the provinces devote themselves to pious works (lit. "the establishment of felicity") and erect towering and magnificent stūpa and monasteries, worthy of glorifying the supreme doctrine of the Buddha. However, people mindlessly assert their pride in surpassing one another. Poor and rich compete with each other in exhausting their resources, bent on [building ever] higher and bigger.[10]

The subtle distinction made by some Chinese between the manifestations of a zeal that is both sincere and moderate in expenditure and of a pride that leads to ruin is of some interest, as it says much about the attitudes of the literati class. I will return to this distinction, one that is encountered in all periods. Although individual vanity and family pride seem to have played an important role in Buddhist devotion, it was nevertheless a universal phenomenon. If its content is examined objectively, nothing would justify separating these different elements.

The Buddhist faithful competed in spending, and ruined themselves in the process. It cannot be said that this claim represents simply a literary formula, for it recurs too frequently, in official memorials, decrees, and even in stele inscriptions. It must therefore be assumed that these competitions in wastefulness reveal a trait that is peculiar to the religious phenomenon itself.

Buddhism is known as a learned religion in which abstract speculation occupies an important place. At least one thinks of it primarily
as a doctrine, and it is presumably in that form that it was first introduced into China. Thus the manifestations of Buddhist fervor are
perceived as an effect of the new religion's adoption by the Chinese.
I will approach the problem from the opposite angle by examining
the indications that emerge from the material facts. One area for
study that is particularly rich in useful information about the relationship between religion and economics concerns festivals. The
Buddhist life of the Chinese is marked by a succession of feasts, festivities, and ceremonies, collective acts of contrition, and scenes of
mutilation that frequently bring together crowds of the faithful and
the clergy. The Buddhist faith expresses itself most authentically in
the processions of the statues through the towns, the nocturnal illuminations in the streets and the countryside. It is on such occasions
that communion between the religious and the laity takes place—
that conjunction of the world of the profane with the world of the
sacred without which the religion could be no more than an exercise
of recluse monks.

A fact of far-reaching implications may be noted in this connection: these great festivities joined all classes of Chinese society. The
emperor himself, whom ordinary subjects rarely saw in other circumstances, participated in them at the capital or, on his tours of inspection, in the prefectures. Members of the upper classes rubbed shoul-
ders with commoners. Buddhism, more than any other cult, brought
the empire, the aristocracy, and the common people into contact.
This was undoubtedly due to its teachings, which reserved an important place for compassion and, at the same time, aimed at obtaining
the salvation of all beings. But it was also due to particular circumstances. The traditional rites of the court concerned only a select circle. As for peasant festivals and Taoist practices, they were too popular in character to engender a ceremonial adapted to the manners of
the court.[11] Only Buddhism, from the moment of its introduction into
China, responded simultaneously to the diverse needs of Chinese
society. And it is in its great festivals that it realized that complete
social communion in a concrete manner.

Certain Buddhist festivals provided the occasion for an extraordinary display of sumptuousness. They created an atmosphere of exu-
berance and of collective excitement that is palpable in the descriptions of the historians. At such times, fervor reached its paroxysm and

acts of self-sacrifice and the renunciation of wealth became common-place. These great reunions, where entire fortunes were squandered gratuitously for entertainments and as offerings and where self-mutilations and self-immolations by fire took place, therefore provide an opportunity for apprehending the scope and underlying aims of the religious phenomenon.

[During the Cheng-kuang era (520–525)], on the seventh day of the fourth month, all the statues in the capital were transported to the Ching-ming monastery. The Board of Sacrifices under the Department of State Affairs made an inventory: there were in all more than a thousand [statues]. At the time of the festival of the eighth day,[12] they were taken in procession under the Hsüan-yang gate in the direction of the entry to the imperial palace. The emperor scattered flowers over them [from above the gate]. Golden flowers glittered in the sun and [ornate] parasols of precious materials drifted as numerous as the clouds. There were forests of streamers and banners. The smoke of the incense billowed like fog. The music and the Indian chants deafened Heaven and shook the Earth. The games (hsi) [13] were in full swing. Everywhere the crowds were thick. Virtuous hosts of famous monks came, carrying their staves; there were crowds of the Buddhist faithful, holding flowers; horsemen and carriages were packed beside each other in an endless mass.[14]

This text, which underlines the richness and beauty of the Buddhist ceremony, indicates at the same time that the festival was not confined to the solemn procession of the statues to the accompaniment of chants and music. There were also games and festivities of all kinds: one part ceremonial and one part popular amusement.

On the night of the full moon of the second year of the Hsien-t'ien period (713), the westerner P'o-t'o requested that hundreds and thousands of torches be lit and that, on this occasion, the curfew be lifted. . . . The emperor proceeded to the Yen-hsi gate to view the scene. The entertainments were allowed to continue day and night for a full month.[15]

The Fo-tsu t'ung-chi mentions another festival of the same kind in the first year of Hsien-t'ien (712). It had been organized, in homage of the Buddha, by an Indian monk named P'o-lo (no doubt the same individual mentioned in the text above). The account adds that there was an enormous wheel, some twenty chang (sixty meters) in height, on which five hundred golden and silver lamps had been lit. From a distance it looked like a tree in flower.[16]

The relaxation of the habitual rules, the opening of the city gates, the authorization granted the people to amuse themselves and to revel, these elements all bear a religious significance. Every religious festival, including Buddhist festivals, is something of a fair. We know nothing about the comportment of the participants, but we can imagine the excitement and agitation of the crowds.

The description of the great festival that took place in the first month of the fourteenth year of the Yüan-ho period (819) shows to what degree the frenzy of the faithful could rise in the course of Buddhist festivities:

> At the Fa-men monastery at Feng-hsiang (to the west of Ch'ang-an), there was the stūpa named Veritable Body, Protector of the State (Hu-kuo chen-shen) in which was preserved a joint of a finger of the Buddha Śākyamuni. According to a written tradition, this stūpa was opened once every thirty years.[17] When it was opened, the year was abundant and the people prospered. In the first month of the fourteenth year of Yüan-ho, the emperor ordered the imperial commissioner Tu Ying-ch'i to proceed to the staging post of Lin-kao with thirty palace guards bearing incense and flowers in order to welcome the bone of the Buddha, then to return by the Kuang-shun gate to deposit it for three days in the palace before sending it on to the monasteries [of the capital]. Princes, dukes, members of the nobility, and commoners all rushed in throngs to present their offerings, each fearing only to arrive late.[18]

As a result of witnessing such a public consecration of Buddhism by the emperor, says Han Yü, the common people

> burn the crowns of their heads and roast their fingers in groups of tens or hundreds. They untie their clothing and scatter coins from morning till evening. They do so in mutual emulation, fearing only to fall behind. Young or old, they ceaselessly rush to sacrifice their patrimony. If an end is not called to these manifestations forthwith and further transfers of the relic from monastery to monastery take place, then there will certainly be some who shall consider severing their arms or pieces of their bodies a form of veneration.[19]

The faithful performed acts of contrition, sacrificed their possessions, and burned themselves in a sort of collective delirium recalling the scenes that took place at the Inexhaustible Treasuries at the end of the seventh century and in the first years of the eighth. Those men and women of good society who were transporting cartloads of cash to the Hua-tu and Fu-hsien monasteries on the fourth day of the first month[20] wailed and disputed each other's turn to present offerings.

Like all festivals, the transfer of the relic offered an occasion for games and entertainments. As Han Yü memorialized Emperor Hsien-tsung,

> Benighted though I am, I fully realize that it is not because Your Majesty is in the least way influenced by Buddhism that you have instituted this ceremony, nor with the idea that it might bring down blessings (fu-hsiang), but that it is only[21] to conform yourself to the natural inclinations of your subjects, by virtue [of the tradition that associates] abundant harvests with human joyfulness, that you have wished to provide gentlemen and commoners with an extraordinary spectacle that is nothing more than a theatrical amusement (hsi-wan). For how is it possible that with your great intelligence you could lend credence to such things? The common people,[22] however, are stupid, easily misled and hard to enlighten. Seeing the emperor acting in such a manner, they will imagine that he is a sincere Buddhist, and they will tell themselves: "Our sage emperor displays single-minded faith and respect. Let us, then, who are so vile and contemptible before the Buddha, make a sacrifice of our lives![23]

The aim of Han Yü's criticism is clear. Those elements of the festival that derived from popular tradition seemed scarcely reprehensible to him. It was customary to revel and to give free reins to one's inclinations on certain exceptional occasions, especially at the beginning of a New Year. The principle of such festivities itself was not in question, but the abuses to which they gave rise: the squandering of fortunes, the mutilations, all that bore witness to an extravagant exaltation and seemed to attach itself to the Buddhist faith both as object and as pretext. This, to Han Yü the rationalist, was unacceptable.[24]

The essential elements that may be culled from the festival of the transfer of the relic from the Fa-men monastery in the first month of the year—unusual spectacle, games, carelessness, abnormal behavior of the participants, and even that which one would readily put down to Buddhist fervor alone, namely the sacrifices of fortunes—all this can be found, in a more popular form of plainly indigenous extraction, in a description of Chinese celebrations of the New Year at the end of the sixth century by Liu Yü. These celebrations simultaneously evoke the Buddhist lamp festival, which took place on precisely the same date:

> On every night of the first month's full moon (fifteenth day), I have seen crowded streets and alleys, both at the capital and in the outer prefectures, where the rolling of the drums deafen the heavens and the torches illumine the earth. People wear animal masks and men dress as women; singers and buffoons disguise themselves in strange costumes. Men and women go to see the spectacle together and find themselves reunited without avoiding one another. They squander their possessions, destroy their heritage, and in these revelries exhaust their domestic wealth in an instant.[25] Noble and lowly are treated the same, men and women mix in disorder, nor is there distinction between clergy and laity. And with these running wild, opportunities arise for thieves and brigands.[26]

There is nothing Buddhist about these New Year celebrations except the presence of religious mixed with the crowd, but there is also nothing that Buddhism was unable to make its own.

It is to state the obvious to say that festivals temporarily break down the prohibitions and usages of ordinary life. They represent a time of relaxation where one willingly behaves, in reaction against everyday constraints, in an irrational manner. In particular, one spends heedlessly and, if necessary, borrows in order to be able to spend. If certain festivals spell financial ruin, especially those at New Year, it is because the very excess is perceived as a way of "expelling the old and inviting the new." It is a means of moral and religious purification. In that sense, it could be said that the destructive fury directed against possessions, and even that competitive spirit in spending and in giving with which Chinese literati reproached the faithful, are not peculiar to Buddhism. The participants in the festival described by Liu Yü also contend with each other in ruining themselves, and it is a game that becomes increasingly stirring and fascinating as it becomes more dangerous.

The collective excitement that one observes in Buddhist festivals is not only a result of the gathering, the crowds, and the abnormal mixing of social classes but is sought for its own sake. The ceremonies, with their prosternations and acts of contrition, with the music and smoking incense that accompany them, are precisely intended to provoke those sentiments of exaltation and, in the end, the collective delirium in the faithful that incite them to vie with each other in making offerings and personal sacrifices. In this deliberate encouragement of enthusiasm, in the proper sense of the word, may be seen an extension of practices that were current among the Taoists[27] and probably even, broadly speaking, in popular religion. All this serves to emphasize how much, down to the competitions in expenditure, was *traditional* in the comportment of the Buddhist faithful. And yet the Buddhist influence is undeniable in this Chinese context. By lending an orientation to practices the emotional contents of which were so rich, and by endowing traits that lacked any specific significance in festivals with a new and particular meaning, this influence appears to have been decisive: it made its mark essentially in the luxuriousness of ornamentations and in the importance attached to the offerings and the sacrifices. These two aspects of Buddhism—ornamentation and giving—which define its originality in China with respect to the other religious movements, stand in close relationship to the subject under examination.

It may be said that to a large extent the aims of Buddhism are of an aesthetic order. Every religious festival is in some ways a spectacle. That this is true of Buddhist celebrations is borne out by their gorgeous trappings, the pomp of the ceremonies, the large numbers of participating monks and laymen who simultaneously fill the roles of actors and supernumeraries. This aspect, however, which is so pronounced in festivals, is equally present in all the manifestations of Buddhism in China. The implications here are various and not only limited to the strictly religious. It is also possible to regard Chinese Buddhism at its apogee as an artistic movement. Its schools of sculptors and painters are numerous. There too expenditure takes place, but it is of a human order and has a specific quality: the patience and the ingenuity of the artisan and the artist are manifest in the stūpa, the monasteries, the statues, and the decoration of the sanctuaries. Most revealing, however, are from our perspective the predilection of that art for precious metals and rare materials, the display of extravagant riches, a general tendency to the excessive and the colossal—for the statues and constructions frequently stand out by their gigantic dimensions—which accord with the equally excessive comportment of the faithful. This art came from the Indianized regions endowed with its own characteristics: transposed to and adopted in China, its tendency toward the sumptuous and the colossal provides, by contrast with a dominant Chinese tradition, a valuable indication of the moral and economic orientation of the religious movement itself. The marked contrast between the style of Mahāyāna texts, abounding in elaborations and rich descriptions, and the vigorous concision of the classical style reappears in architecture. Mahāyāna is avid for the incommensurable, whereas the classical tradition of China has all the characteristics of a humanism. Buddhism in China appears, not only in its effects but in its very nature, as an "antieconomic" movement. It reacts against the Chinese tradition that allowed only restricted space for the expression of aesthetic sentiment and whose precepts of daily life demanded moderation in expenditure, austerity, control of the emotions, and bearing. It could in fact be argued that the movement was not merely religious but was equally concerned with ways of feeling and of thinking.

It is not certain that among members of the upper classes pious works always corresponded to a sincere faith. But in those works, their taste for splendor found a pretext to express itself freely.[28] It is possible, without denigrating the importance of religious sentiments, of moral and aesthetic inclinations, and of family vanity, to regard the *spectacular* aspect of Buddhism in China as one of the reasons for its success. It happens that the passion for spectacles, the induction of emotion for its own sake, and the display and squandering of wealth correspond at the same time to religious objectives, to a desire to act upon the beyond.

The burns that the participants in the festival of the transfer of the Buddha relic voluntarily inflicted upon themselves can be put to the account of collective excitement. Han Yü even suggests that these possessed would go so far as to cut off parts of their bodies if allowed to go unchecked. Such acts nevertheless had to have a meaning; such comportment could not be wholly arbitrary. In these scenes of mutilation there is undoubtedly an element of horror, which was actively sought by the spectators and functioned as a catharsis. Beauty and horror are equally capable of inducing those exceptional emotions for which the faithful felt a need. Above all, those mutilations reveal the fact that the excessive offerings represented merely the economic aspect of an act of total self-sacrifice, in which the believer pledged not only his possessions but his person. In great festivals, one spends and one spends oneself.

In the collections of biographies of eminent monks, a special category is reserved for religious who owed their fame to acts of self-sacrifice or suicide.[29] It is clear that these suicides, so contrary to traditional morality, aimed to redeem the sins of all beings, to compel the gods and men at one and the same time. And they were staged: usually, in the fifth century, a pyre was erected on a mountain. The suicide took place in the presence of a large crowd uttering lamentations and bringing forward rich offerings. People of all social ranks attended the spectacle together. After the fire had burned out, the ashes of the monk were collected and a stūpa, a new place of worship, was erected to house them.[30]

When Hui-shao burned himself in 451, he instituted a great religious assembly. The multitudes of carts, horses, men, and [faithful] bearing offerings of precious goods were incalculable.[31]

In 463, the monk Hui-i burned himself to death in a cauldron filled with oil. Princes, palace ladies and empresses were present as well as crowds of religious, lay followers and persons of every rank that filled the mountain and its valleys. The clothes and jewels that were sacrificed were innumerable.[32]

At the beginning of the sixth century, when Seng-yai committed suicide on his pyre, the offerings formed enormous heaps. There was a lamenting crowd of more than a hundred thousand clergy and laity.[33]

Cases where monks allowed themselves to be devoured by wild animals,[34] gave of their flesh to the starving,[35] or of their blood to insects[36] are relatively numerous. In a general manner, mutilations were common among Chinese Buddhists, who frequently burned their fingers or arms. These practices, which appeared fairly early in the history of Buddhism in China, and are well attested from the beginning of the fifth century onward, thus represent an established tradition. They should not, however, be separated from their wider context: the related crises of collective exaltation that religious celebrations sought to induce, whose secrets were already known to the Taoists, as well as ecstatic techniques that allowed individual adepts to attain a state of total insensitivity.[37] Already the Indian theme of the bodhisattva who gives his flesh and his body in homage to the Buddha, or for the salvation of the beings, can be explained by the same techniques—even the complete indifference that he must demonstrate when he practices the virtue of giving: "It is when the bodhisattva gives everything to all, down to his eyes and the marrow in his bones, out of compassion and without wishing for blessings, that he fulfills the virtue of giving."[38]

The monks who vowed to ascend the pyre claimed to follow the example of the bodhissattva Bhaiṣajyarāja, whose "tale of exploits" (avadāna) is recounted in the Saddharmapuṇḍarīka.[39] The practice has its extension in religious thought. The acts of contrition, which were not unknown in China and corresponded to indigenous traditions, were taken to an extreme by the Mahāyāna movement, which made the sacrifice of an individual's person the highest gift, while at the same time giving it a doctrinal justification. However, these practices, and the religious thought that served as their foundation in Buddhism, engendered an economic movement of a vast scale.

Emperor Wu of the Liang dynasty is famous for having repeatedly given himself and his family to the Three Jewels. Each time, his ministers redeemed him with immense sums of cash. In 527,

> the emperor went to the T'ung-t'ai monastery to make a sacrifice of his person there. His ministers redeemed him with one hundred thousand myriads of cash. The emperor returned to the palace. . . . In the first year of Chung-ta-t'ung (529), because there was a great epidemic, the emperor held a Buddhist vegetarian feast (chai) at the Ch'ung-yün palace to supplicate for the end of the scourge. In his prayers, he offered up his own person. Again he went to the T'ung-t'ai monastery where he held a great assembly for monks and laymen (wu-che ta-hui). . . . Taking simple bedding and earthenware dishes, he mounted onto a small cart. . . . His ministers redeemed him with one hundred thousand myriads of cash. He held a great Buddhist vegetarian feast for fifty thousand monks and laymen.[40]

Literati later noted ironically the illogicality of these simulated sacrifices:

> It is not clear how the deed of Emperor Wu amounted to giving up his person. By renouncing his treasury, his wives, and his children he ceded his possessions, not his person. Had he truly given himself, then the Buddha should have taken him, of which there is no indication. To call his act a cession of his person therefore amounts to mental illusion and a misuse of words.[41]

The personal sacrifices of Emperor Wu of the Liang followed by his redemption are not isolated examples; they even correspond to a rather widespread practice among the faithful. Thus they give an insight into the true meaning of a whole complex of donations that stand out by their excessive and radical nature: in order for the gift to be efficacious, it must take the form of a self-sacrifice. It is accompanied by mortifications and its staging recalls a funerary ritual.[42] An equally famous example of self-sacrifice is that of the mother of P'ei Chih.

> When P'ei Chih was [prefect] of Ying-chou (modern Ho-chien, Hopeh), his mother, who was more than seventy years of age, gave herself as a slave to the Three Jewels. Clad in hemp cloth, she handled a broom and dustbin in the monastery. The younger brothers of P'ei Chih, Yü, Ts'an, and Yen, all followed her, wearing slave garments and wailing until the monks and laymen were moved. These three brothers redeemed their mother by offering several hundreds of lengths of cloth and silk. Thereupon, she entered into religion and became a nun.[43]

The brothers of P'ei Chih go to the monastery to redeem their mother, but their attitude, the clothes they wear, their lamentations signify that they are prepared to sacrifice themselves to take her place: the offerings are equivalent to the sacrifice of their persons; hence it is to be understood that they must be extreme.

We could add to these texts the interesting colophon to a copy of the *Prajñāpāramitā* that Lionel Giles translated in his study of the dated Tun-huang manuscripts in the British Museum:[44]

> On the fifteenth of the fourth moon of the second year of Chien-ming of the Great Tai [i.e., Wei] dynasty [May 16, 531], the Buddhist lay disciple Yüan Jung, since he lives in Mo-chieh in danger of his life, has long been parted from his home and has a constant longing to return, therefore in his own person and that of his wife and children, his male and female servants, and his domestic animals, makes on behalf of the Celestial King Vaiśravaṇa a donation to the triratna of the sum of a thousand silver cash; and as ransom money, a thousand cash to ransom himself and his wife and children, a thousand cash to ransom his servants, and a thousand cash to ransom his animals. The money thus paid to the Church is to be used for copying sutras, with the prayer that the Celestial King may become a Buddha, and that the disciple's family, servants, and livestock may be richly endowed with the blessing of long life, may attain enlightenment, and may all be permitted to return to the capital. This is his prayer.[45]

The gift of one's person could be symbolized by offering cuttings of hair,[46] or again by a gift of *belongings*: in the eighth year of the T'ien-chien period (509), Emperor Wu of the Liang made an offering of 117 pieces of personal goods and clothing (*shen tzu-fu*) to the Three Jewels.[47] Under the Southern Ch'i (479–502), the prince of Nan-chün simulated the sacrifice of his person by offering 118 objects "outside the skin" (chi-fu chih wai).[48]

It can be seen here to what extent economics proceed from the religious: the sacrifice of material goods symbolizes the offering of an individual's person while also representing the redemption of both the individual's person and of his sins. There is no difference in nature or meaning between the mutilations and suicides, on the one hand, and the sacrifice of patrimonies, on the other. It is clear, meanwhile, that with respect to the pious donations of the faithful in China we are dealing with an original psychological mechanism whose study is pertinent to the subject in hand.

The donation may be at one and the same time, and even while it takes place, an offering and the redemption of an individual's person. This simultaneity of two acts that should logically follow in sequence is a characteristic of pious gifts and reveals their ambivalence. A member of the literati tradition like Tu Mu was well aware of this: "One purchases felicity and sells one's sins just as in commercial operations 'right contracts' are remitted in exchange."[49]

In order for goods to be able to serve as substitute for a person or his sins, there must be continuity between the religious and the economic: the donation must be founded on conceptions of a more general order. The pronounced commercial character of pious giving invites us to consider several apparently unrelated transactions that are, however, in some ways analogous. Insolvent debts—those that cannot be paid in commercial values—are reimbursed in labor services performed for the creditor, i.e., paid in the debtor's own person. A person has an economic value. This observation makes a detail in the story of P'ei Chih's mother appear in a new light. It is as a slave, clad in hemp cloth, handling broom and dustbin in a monastery, that she gave herself to the Three Jewels. This expresses her desire, not only to humble herself but also to attach a price to her person. Conversely, it appears that debts had a religious character, as illustrated by popular beliefs regarding debts left unacquitted by the deceased:

"A debt of one cash is restituted through an entire lifetime of servitude, paid in [the debtor's] own strength," according to a saying recorded in a work of the School of the Three Stages.[50]

"With the strength of one's body, with one's flesh and blood, one repays the debts incurred in former existences."[51]

Notions of debt and sin appear conflated in the texts of the School of the Three Stages; another work of that sect sets forth the retribution for an insolvent debtor: he is reborn as an animal or a slave. The sole effect of human activities is to engender new causes of miserable existence. It is a spiral without hope. To acquit oneself of one's debts, it is necessary to acquire possessions. As an official, one extorts from the people their wealth through the abuse of power. As a plowman, one sets fire to the moors and the mountains, irrigates the dry fields, opens furrows, hoes, [smooths the ground] with a roller, and thereby destroys the nests and burrows of the animals. As keeper of oxen and mules, one pastures them in the neighbor's fields where they damage the crops. Or again, one scalds cocoons to make silk, smokes out bees to take their honey, or kills deer to obtain their musk. As master artisan, copyist of sacred texts, or caster of statues, one whittles away the Buddha's gold and steals the ink and paper used for the copy. One works little, but derives a great profit. On feast days, one goes to visit the Buddhist masters and is fed by the monks' kitchen, pillaging the property of the Three Jewels. The accumulation of such debts is inevitable.[52]

Thus the first cause of human misery and of the succession of sins (theft and murder) is of an economic order. Outstanding debt is sin, and a further cause of sin. Sins are debts and cause new debts. It is certain that the conditions of life of the poor classes in China, their permanent and frequently desperate state of indebtedness, had something to do with this conception. However, there was also unexpected relief, in this world as well as in the next: imperial amnesties that acquitted debtors, the goodwill of creditors, and pious donations. Offerings to the Three Jewels permitted the donor simultaneously to acquit himself of his debts and his sins.[53] In the work of the School of the Three Stages already cited, a speaker raises the following objection:

If each day one gave up one-tenth of one cash (fen) or one ko (ca. six centiliters) of millet [to the Inexhaustible Treasuries, as recommended to poor lay followers], in one year's time the total would not exceed thirty-six cash or thirty-six sheng of millet. How can one thus reimburse debts that have no beginning and obtain deliverance from all suffering? It is [goes the reply] as if a poor man owed one thousand strings of cash. Each time his creditor is about to proceed to the confiscation [of his personal estate], he is frightened and seeks out this great personage. "I have exceeded the redemption date," says he, "but I beg you to forgive my fault." Being poor, he will not be granted his request (?) and before long he will become a land laborer. Now, [supposing that] having earned one cash, he gives it to his creditor. His creditor will rejoice in this news and forgive him. He will no longer think of confiscation, and will pardon him from wearing the cangue. Is that not avoiding a great misfortune by means of a small offering? And giving to the Inexhaustible Treasuries is no different. If one does not take recourse to the Inexhaustible Treasuries, debts without beginning accumulate, debts that are passed down from a hundred existences, a thousand existences, a hundred kalpas of existences, ten thousand kalpas of existences. . . . But if one takes recourse to it, then all the old debts without beginning are extinguished at a stroke. One no longer has one's creditors to fear, and all obstacles to enlightenment (and deliverance) are suddenly obliterated.[54]

And the colophon of a copy of a sutra found at Tun-huang reads:

The faithful Li Heng respectfully had one copy made of this *Chin kuang-ming tsui-sheng wang ching* in ten *chüan*. He desires that his enemies and his *creditors*, for all the debts he has contracted since the year *i-ch'ou* and all the misdeeds for which he is liable, may profit from the merit of this sutra and rapidly experience enlightenment (*bodhi*). He wishes that they may cease harboring hatred for him, that they release him from his bonds, and that at the same time the officials of the prefecture be subject to the happy and salutary influence of this sutra.[55]

This assimilation of the notion of sin and the notion of debt is certainly not unique to the School of the Three Stages. It is founded upon archaic conceptions that fully come to life in religion.

Laymen maintained two kinds of relationships with the monasteries and the monks, one economic, the other religious. Neither monks nor lay followers appear to have conceived these relationships as being of a radically different nature. The loans given by Buddhist establishments, from consecrated property—the permanent assets of the saṃgha—had without any doubt a religious significance: those who neglected to restitute such debts died a violent death, were reborn in hell or as slaves or oxen in the monasteries. It is one's person that was given up in return for the goods of the saṃgha, received as gift or as loan. It is the person that is freed from an evil destiny and infernal tortures through restitution of the goods with usury. The act of giving extinguished debts as well as sins. And on that dual basis, it ensured a happy rebirth.

CHAPTER NINE

THE POPULAR SOCIAL ENVIRONMENT

The Formation of Cult Groups

Despite the sources' virtually complete silence concerning the most popular aspects of Buddhism in China, evidence is not entirely lacking on this subject. From at least the fifth century on, it is possible to form an idea of how the new "religion" may have developed in the countryside. Moreover, its influence was undeniably profound. This is borne out by two essential facts: first, the peasant origin of the majority of the monastic community and, second, the large number of small, rustic sanctuaries, hermitages, and votive towers. At the beginning of the sixth century, the streets of Lo-yang were lined with small shrines "in the vicinity of butcheries and taverns."[1] Biographies of monks frequently refer to villagers constructing some Buddhist tower dedicated to a holy monk. A certain category of monks was pursued by the imperial authorities on account of their loose morals, ignorance of monastic discipline, illiteracy, and their tendency to mix with the populace of the towns and in the country. It is this category that deserves our main attention here, for these wandering monks spread a vast popular religious movement. In reality, it was little to do with Buddhism, yet it embedded itself within the Buddhist movement, which cannot be understood as a whole without taking this particular current into account.

Buddhist doctrine was known and cultivated only by a small elite of monks whom emperors and highly placed individuals sometimes attached to their retinues. The majority of monks, even those entrusted with celebrating official ceremonies in the great sanctuaries, were illiterate. Their professional functions were for the most part limited to the recitation, from memory, of a few pages of sutra and the performance of ritual acts. As the monk T'an-chi stated in a memorial to the emperor T'ai-tsu of the Chou (r. 557–560):

> The monks were obliged to sit examinations. Now there are monks and nuns who have spent their lives in the monastery and who have proven to be modest and thrifty. They have taken vows to devote themselves to meditation upon their own minds and to observe the precepts. They burn incense, circumambulate the stūpa as gestures of reverence, prostrate themselves, heads to the ground with great zeal and application, join their hands, bow their heads, and well-nigh forget to eat and sleep over it. Only, they are endowed with imbecile and obtuse dispositions, unsuited for reading and recitation. Agonize as they may over their studies, they do not succeed in retaining a single character of writing.[2]

Moreover, Chinese monks did not regard the Buddhist rules of discipline as categorical prescriptions. Holiness, for them, was a matter of degree and faithfulness to the precepts depended on an individual's capacity. Superior men, declared the monk Ming-kai in his Decisive Replies to the Memorial of Fu I,[3] are able to content themselves with one meal per day; those of inferior capacity, however, should be allowed two meals and silk clothes. How could a single rule conceivably be applied to everyone? In any event, he hastened to add, the needs of monks and nuns were modest. This inclination to easeful devotion is so widespread that it is more surprising to find the precepts observed than ignored. The author of the *Sung kao-seng chuan* reports, as a noteworthy fact, that the monk Chih-hsüan was so strict in his observance of the rules of discipline and so modest in his desires that "he ate neither fruit nor vegetables after midday."[4]

Such moral indulgence was even more pronounced in the countryside than in the great sanctuaries where the control of the monastic authorities and secular powers was more easily enforced. The monk of the people, vagrant, indifferent to moral prescriptions, given over to all lucrative occupations, was far removed from the conception of the Buddhist religious held by the ruling class: the sedentary monk, dedicated to the empire, who did not associate with commoners except to instruct them in principles that accorded with traditional morality. Two functions in particular were expected of these monk-officials: to exercise a moralizing influence and to perform charitable deeds. The aims and conduct of the monks of the people were selfish and opposed to the intentions of imperial policy.

Beyond this opposition, which found expression primarily in the economic and behavioral spheres, it may be asked whether the antagonism was not more profound. The idea underlying the general attitude of Chinese monks toward the rules of discipline was that holiness could be dissimulated in the most unexpected of places, assuming the appearance of greatest profanity and disregard for ordinary religious propriety.[5] Behind the most popular aspects of Buddhism in China an indigenous concept of sanctity may be recognized. The life of the saint is synonymous with liberty. It is a life of roaming, untrammeled by all social and physical constraints. The Taoist hermit corresponds to this model of the saint, and the Buddhist monk frequently approaches it. Legend attributes supernatural powers and the gift of ubiquity to some of them.[6] It was such extraordinary faculties that tended to reveal holiness in men, rather than scrupulous obedience to disciplinary rules.

T'ung-chin was a monk who did not burden himself with rites and rules. He was fond of alcohol and declared to anyone prepared to listen that his drink was just as good as lustral water. He became famous by ingesting a deadly poison, without the least effect. When he died under the Sui, at ninety years of age, those who made the inventory of his clothes and bedding were astonished to find that they exuded the fragrance of incense and not a trace of the smell of alcohol.[7]

Thus it is tempting to see in the peasant or, more generally, popular forms of Buddhism in China by and large a complex of magical practices applied to private, individual, or family ends. On the whole, they represented a degradation of the authentic Buddhism practiced in the great sanctuaries. There was an entire class of itinerant monks, tricksters, wonder-workers, soothsayers, magicians, exorcists, and healers who lived on the performance of magical arts among the people. These religious benefited from the fiscal advantages granted to regular monks and enriched themselves by displaying their magical talents among the laity, at festivals, or in the marketplace. It would seem, then, that the origin and development of this class of irregular religious were essentially fostered by economic motives. In 636 Emperor T'ai-tsung decreed:

It has come to Our attention that numerous monks live immersed in the world. Some serve as mediums for demons and spirits and peddle miracle stories. Some falsely lay claim to magical healing powers and seek to enrich themselves by means of sorcery. Others burn their skin or pierce their bodies, frightening the vulgar and dumbfounding the simpleminded. Others again find their way to the offices of the administration where they seek to corrupt the officials. All of these sorts of people have a most harmful effect on the holy doctrine. Having no other aim but to uphold and protect the latter, We shall allow no indulgence.[8]

In the monasteries of Ch'ang-an there were many monk-magicians who had grown rich. In 842 more than three thousand of them were returned to lay life:

On the ninth day of the tenth month in the second year of Hui-ch'ang (842), the following decree was promulgated: "All monks and nuns in the empire who practice alchemy, sorcery, or incantations; draft evaders; those who bear the marks of flagellation, tattoos (niao-wen), or forced labor [as a result of previous offenses]; who indulge in debauchery, maintain wives, and disregard the Buddhist precepts; all these shall be defrocked. All money, provisions, grains, lands, estates, and gardens owned by these monks and nuns shall be confiscated by the government. Those who are loath to part with the money and riches they possessed and who wish to return to lay life, shall be ordered to do so and to acquit themselves of the two taxes and perform the labor services.[9] . . . Let the commissioners of good works (kung-te shih) of the streets to the right and left in the capital[10] post notices in all the monasteries prohibiting the monks and nuns to leave, and let them keep the gates closed."[11]

A later decree, dated second year of the Hsien-te reign period (955), shows the persistence of that class of religious:

In the past, monks, nuns, and lay folk performed self-sacrifices in great numbers, burned their arms, roasted their fingers, drove nails into their hands and feet, or severed these, attached bells to their belts, hung lamps from their bodies, and subjected themselves to all manner of mutilations. They toyed with their religious accouterments, practiced sorcery by means of charms and exorcisms, pretended to cause apparitions, recall souls, or undergo transformations, and conjured illusions with lustral water and holy lamps.[12]

In some cases they were taking advantage of popular credulity:

In the second year of the Pao-li period (826), it was reported that a miraculous spring had welled up in Po-chou (Anhwei) and that those who drank of its water were healed of their diseases. Li Te-yü presented a memorial to the throne: "I have learned that this spring was from the beginning the object of fables and lies invented by magician-monks (yao-seng)[13] to whom it represented a fine occasion to enrich themselves by asking money [of those who would be healed]. For some months now, crowds of inhabitants from Chiang-nan [i.e., the region south of the Yangtze] have been rushing up to Po-chou, obstructing the roads. Each group of twenty or thirty families hires a man to fetch of that water for them. The sick who wish to partake of it must first abstain from eating pungent vegetables (hun) and meat, and after they have drunk the water, they may only eat vegetables and rice gruel for two weeks: even the severely ill are healed by the end of that period. One bushel of this water costs three strings of cash, and those charged with fetching it further add in ordinary water. Along the roads it is passed on from tradesman to tradesman. The old and the sick drink of it. Those who are in critical condition pour themselves a few drops. Between thirty and fifty inhabitants of the two Che [i.e., the two parts of modern Chekiang] cross the river each day [in search of it].[14]

Here we have, then, a number of factors that primarily concern the economy. Is it possible to draw more far-reaching conclusions from these few texts, beyond the rather trivial observation of a commercial exploitation of the magical arts? We should underline here the important function of the mutilations.[15] The itinerant monks encountered in the marketplaces and in fairs and festivals were familiar with physical techniques that enabled them to attain a state of complete insensitivity. In fact, these were the same techniques as those used in religious asceticism. It was thanks to their possession of such techniques that the religious, in general, were thought of, by ordinary people, as men endowed with extraordinary powers.

The monk Tao-ying, who was steward for the year (chih-sui) at the Sheng-kuang monastery in the ninth year of the Ta-yeh period (613) had a dispute with laymen concerning the boundaries of certain fields. The quarrel was never resolved until one day he exclaimed: "Ah, I shall die!" and fell over backward, just as though he were dead. The laymen took counsel together: "Monks are very good at deceiving people. Lets prick him with a needle!" However, though they pierced him deeply, Tao-ying did not move. Furthermore, his breathing stopped, he grew pale, and his body appeared to begin swelling.

Now there was one peasant who was more shrewd than the others and found a way to bring him back to life: he swore that they would no longer dispute the boundaries and wished to see him revive. These words were hardly pronounced when Tao-ying sat up and began laughing and talking as if nothing had happened.[16]

The profitable methods employed by a whole class of itinerant monks sometimes served other ends as well: to persuade or convert the people. Whatever influence the Buddhist monks enjoyed in the countryside was certainly not due to the doctrines they preached but first of all to the admiration and amazement incited by their powers. In fact, it is conceivable that the success of Buddhism in China, usually envisaged as the triumph of a new doctrine and new moral conceptions, was originally due to motivations of a different order: not religious but technical. The methods of mental concentration and the breathing techniques introduced from India may have appeared to be, or actually have been, superior to those previously known in China.[17] The Buddhist monk, such as he appeared in the eyes of ordinary people—a person endowed with supernatural powers that defined him as a saint—corresponded undoubtedly to a traditional human type that had existed in China before the penetration of Buddhism. But Buddhism may have introduced methods of sanctity that were novel and more efficacious.

That the powers the biographies attribute to Buddhist monks have a certain basis in reality cannot be denied: they are able to approach ferocious animals, to mutilate themselves without suffering pain, to maintain absolute stillness, to die at a preappointed time, etc. Perhaps certain specialists of sorcery were able to do all of these things previously, but they did them less well or succeeded more rarely. Meanwhile, however important the role of such techniques in the introduction of Buddhism into China, the fact remains that it was a religion as well, i.e., both a moral doctrine and a cult. It may appear that there exists a fundamental difference between these religious aspects of Buddhism and its magical practices. Yet the opposition is only apparent.

We have seen that the preliminary treatment prescribed to the sick wishing to drink of the water of Po-chou consisted in the observance of certain Buddhist precepts: abstinence from meat and onions. What seems to be the province of doctrine was not necessarily conceived of or felt as such by the faithful. In the present case, it would not have been an issue of morality but a means of purification. No doubt this entailed an error of interpretation regarding the very foundations of Buddhism. But it was by that path, through the pursuit of holiness for its own sake, that certain rudiments of Buddhist doctrine were able to spread, imperceptibly, among the people. Indeed, it is difficult to image how they could have done so otherwise.

If cultural borrowing took place, however, it can only have had an effect on techniques and, whether directly or indirectly, on doctrines, but not on the forms of religious life themselves. The highlights of life in the country are the festivals and the fairs. Now there was scarcely a gathering of that kind where some monk did not slip in on the lookout for alms, ready to display his supernatural talents or even to preach a few rudiments of Buddhist doctrine. It emerges fairly clearly from the sources available that if the new doctrines were propagated in the villages, it was on the occasion of manifestations of the collective life that were purely indigenous. Hence the persistence of the same religious preoccupations and essential practices, despite the introduction of new notions and new forms of worship.

As for the evidence of the presence of Buddhist monks in Chinese festivals, only a few examples will be cited.[18] They are sufficiently persuasive and, moreover, of special interest for the first-hand accounts they provide of the process of conversion.

At the beginning of the Liang dynasty (502–557), the Buddhist master Hsiang went to live at the Fei-fu monastery on Mount Ch'ing-ch'eng (near Ch'eng-tu, in modern Szechwan). The custom was to visit that mountain on the third day of the third month for feasting. The local population brought alcohol and victuals and inebriated and amused themselves together. Hsiang reprimanded them, but in vain. The following year he took recourse, in order to convince them, to the following ruse: he had himself invited and quickly ate and drank everything his hosts set before him. It was like trying to fill a deep ditch. When evening fell, Master Hsiang vomited everything he had devoured. The chickens and sheep left his mouth alive. The fishes swam in the pool of wine that he brought up. The peasants, filled with wonder, swore never again to kill a living being.[19]

Another monk, named P'u-an (530–609), devoted himself to redeeming the animals being prepared by peasants as sacrifices to the God of the Soil (she). One day, P'u-an learned that peasants in a neighboring village were about to sacrifice three pigs. The animals were already tied up. Knowing the monk's obsession, the peasants feared to be prevented from killing the pigs when they saw him approach. Thus they exacted a high price, asking for as much as ten thousand cash. "Ah!" said P'u-an, "I have only three thousand cash on me. You have already raised your original price tenfold. Let me then have these pigs [for three thousand cash]." The villagers were unable to agree among themselves and fell to quarreling. In the end,[20] however, P'u-an obtained his pigs for nothing. He took his knife and sliced off pieces of his thighs. "This flesh here or that of the pigs," he said, "both are meat. Pigs feed on refuse and yet you eat their flesh. You should all the more eat human flesh, for humans eat grains and grains are better than refuse!" Hearing these words, the villagers took to their heels, leaving the victims behind.[21]

The presence of monks at religious festivals in China may have modified their content, but their framework remained unchanged. It may even be surmised that the place where the festivals were celebrated—in the vicinity of the villages or in the mountains—remained the same and that frequently the village sanctuary was transformed into a Buddhist cult site.[22] An example of this can be seen in an anecdote already cited above.

The monk Fa-an passes in his travels through a village where a tiger has been wreaking havoc. At nightfall, the peasants have already barricaded their doors. Fa-an, unable to find shelter, installs himself under the tree of the temple dedicated to the local spirits. According to the legend, he converts the tiger to Buddhism. The peasants declare Fa-an, who has delivered them from the beast, a supernatural being (shen-jen). They pay homage to him and transform their temple into a Buddhist chapel.[23]

But it also happened that the peasants' religious awe of the exploits of Buddhist monks led to the creation of new temples and, in consequence, new cults:

At the beginning of the Sung dynasty (420–479), a ferocious tiger was ramping about at the foot of Mount Chia in the district of the town of P'eng-ch'eng (modern T'ung-shan, Kiangsu). Every day, one or two villagers suffered his attacks. "If the tiger ate me," said the monk T'an-ch'eng to the villagers, "this scourge would certainly disappear." . . . At the third watch they heard the tiger seize the monk. The villagers followed the beast as far as the south mountain. There they saw that it had devoured the monk's entire body, except his head, which they buried. On that place, they erected a tower (stūpa), and from then on the ravages of the tiger ceased completely.[24]

The monks themselves frequently became the object of a cult and seem to have played, after their death, the role of protective spirits of villages.[25]

Buddhist life in the country, as well as in the popular wards of the great cities, centered on a multitude of small shrines, votive towers, and hermitages that were strewn through the villages, along the edges of roads and markets, and in the busiest streets. Since the sixth century, the number of these small sanctuaries amounted to more than thirty thousand, and it does not seem to have diminished in later periods.[26] In the winter of the the first year of Shen-kuei (518–519), Prince Ch'eng of the Northern Wei deplored the excessive increase in the number of the sanctuaries in a memorial to the throne:

> Today there is no place that does not have a Buddhist sanctuary.[27] Adjoining one another, they fill the cities. They encroach upon the meat markets and wine stores. . . . Indian chants and the shouts of butchers mingle under neighboring awnings. The statues and stūpa are impregnated with the smell of meat.[28]

An apocryphal sutra, probably composed toward the end of the sixth century,[29] already ascribes to the Buddha the following image of Buddhism in China:

> At that time, the clergy and the laity shall vie with each other in constructing the stūpa and monasteries that will fill the world. Everywhere towers and sanctuaries will be erected with their statues. Some will be in mountain forests, some in the open country, some along the roads, some in city streets, in filthy and reeking places.[30]

In the year 700, Ti Jen-chieh noted that "at the gates of the villages there are shops of copyists of sutra (ching-fang), at the gates of the markets, lodgings of monks (ching-she).[31] According to a decree dated 731,

> Buddhism and Taoism have their [great] monasteries where it is appropriate for them to uphold their own principles. However, certain monks shelter in obscure and withdrawn places or hide in the villages through which they pass. They abandon themselves to reprehensible activities. All this is harmful and deplorable. We understand that they disappear into the mountain forests to construct isolated hermitages, yet great assemblies gather there. They openly come and go. Certain monks, falsely adducing [the theory concerning] the conditions for

rebirth, allow themselves to keep lay families and live with these. All
this must be severely prohibited.[32]

The large numbers of these places of worship, stūpa, chapels, and hermitages[33] already attest the existence of a widespread Buddhist cult in
the country and in the popular wards of large towns.

But what was the content of this collective cult life? For Chinese
converts, the concept of *kung-te*, acts of piety for the purpose of conferring blessings, applied to all kinds of activity: the construction of
chapels, monasteries, reliquary towers, the casting of bells and statues, sutra recitations, the organization of Buddhist festivals, etc. All
of these devotional activities centered upon the Buddhist sanctuaries the construction or ornamentation of which was their principal
objective. If however there was one fundamental act of piety that
served as a model for all the others, it was the vegetarian feast *chai*.
The term translates the Sanskrit word *uposadha* in its original sense
of "purificatory fast." The subsequent evolution of the meaning of
the term is significant. It is well known that people never eat more
than at fasting times, that is, before and after the actual period of
fasting. Above all, the communal meal constituted in China the
essential act of religious life in the country,[34] and, generally speaking, there was no social life in the villages without a banquet; Chinese traditional practices contributed to the change in the meaning
of the word, and their persistence within Chinese Buddhism confirms this interpretation. Moreover, *chai* were vegetarian meals.
This was an innovation, introduced by Buddhist banquets, that justified the use of the word from an early stage: the banquets involved,
if not fasting, at any rate, abstinence from the consumption of meat.
The novelty of this must have been all the more striking because traditional Chinese festivals were characterized by an abundant consumption of mutton, pork, chicken, and fish—rich food that was
reserved for great occasions. It is significant that the first effort of
the Buddhist monks in the countryside was directed toward abol-
ishing the traditional slaughter of animals and consumption of meat
at festivals.[35]

To fully appreciate the importance of banquets as special moments
in the social life of a community, an effort of the imagination may be
necessary: food, where it is rare and shortages occur easily, acquires
a unique value. It represents wealth in more than the purely material sense, because moral and religious considerations are intimately

connected with its consumption. One does not eat alone. Furthermore, abundant and rich food is only consumed on specified occasions in the family or village life. The central role that the communal meal played in Chinese Buddhism can be surmised. The *chai* represented the first step of conversion to Buddhism, for essential points of doctrine were linked to the abstinence from meat: retribution and reincarnation. The *chai* also necessitated a collaboration between the clergy and the laity, an intimate participation of the monks in profane life and, in the end, that confusion of the categories "lay" and "religious" which characterized the Buddhism of the Greater Vehicle in China. Finally, the *chai* was not only a nutritional communion; according to a Chinese practice, which appears to be ancient, the banquet required the contribution of each participant toward the communal outlay. That contribution has closely associated religious, economic, and paralegal aspects and implications that deserve to be examined here.

The *chai*, then, appearing at the outset of the implantation of Buddhism in China, served as a model for all the different types of pious acts. Collaboration between monks and lay followers, contribution to and competition in expenditure are among the general and permanent features of Buddhist life in China. The groups involved are always situated at the local level, in city neighborhoods or village districts. The communal meals tighten periodically the bonds of friendship between families and the communion between the clergy and lay followers. This foundation of communal and local life must be borne in mind even when the texts do not refer to it:

Under the Northern Wei, more than three thousand families in the Yü-li ward of Lo-yang founded a monastery. Because of its proximity to the fish market, it was popularly known as the Fish and Turtle monastery.[36]

Monks and laymen vied with each other in offering contributions for the pious deed of casting a bell at the Yü-ch'üan monastery at Ching-chou (in southern Honan).[37]

A further element that may be present in this general scheme is rivalry between villages or neighboring districts. Local pride constituted an important psychological factor when it came to the organization of festivals and the construction or ornamentation of religious buildings. As Lu Yüan wrote in a memorial addressed to Emperor Kao-tsu (477–500) of the Northern Wei:[38]

The following rumor has come to my attention: For several years the population west of the passes have been competing in organizing Buddhist banquets. These people assume the names of great families in order to incite each other to sedition in openly held assemblies where they criticize the government. The sovereign could not be held in greater contempt. I submit that they should be punished swiftly, their activities brought to an end, and their leaders eliminated to set an example. Otherwise it is to be feared that this will lead to the horrors of the Yellow Turbans and the Red Eyebrows.[39]

This text reveals incidentally the political implications of autonomous cult activities that escaped the control of the secular authorities. It also provides evidence of their spontaneous nature as well as a new element of interpretation: the subversive aspects of popular Buddhism offer a partial explanation for the hostility of the imperial authorities toward religious movements that eluded their supervision.[40]

Organized Associations

Some forms of social life are accessible to all and sundry, while others constitute more or less closed circles. Their members are usually, though not necessarily, initiated, and their association thus takes on the character of a secret society. Buddhism in China did engender secret societies, but it also formed cult associations that joined together variable numbers of religious and lay followers.

The religious life creates bonds between those whom it brings together, but the de facto associations that unite the faithful of a given locality and the monks around whom they group themselves can take particular forms: there is a transition from a statutory state to a contractual state. The participants can acknowledge among themselves, in an explicit and precise manner, a set of mutual rights and duties that becomes permanent and no longer occasional.[41] Associations of the contractual type seem to have been very widespread in Chinese Buddhism.

A great number of acts of piety that were based on private initiative (as opposed to those that were undertaken at state expense) were undoubtedly attributable to religious societies. The stele inscriptions collected in Northern China and the manuscripts found at Tun-huang give precise information about two types of associations that were organized, or even possessed their own statutes. The type of association that is known from the inscriptions seems to have been current from the end of the fifth century to the first century of the T'ang period.[42] The Tun-huang manuscripts, on the other hand, reveal in documents dating by and large from the ninth and tenth centuries, associations of a different type and appellation. For the study of an institution of such great interest for the history of Buddhism in China, and even for the social history of Chinese generally, there remain, therefore, only two points of reference, separated by an interval of three centuries. Historical sources, however, supplement the archaeological documents and provide at the same time indications of the spread of these associations of clergy and faithful in Chinese Buddhism.

Despite their differences in organization, the two types of associations pursued the same aim: the "creation of blessings" (chien-fu) through the practice of pious deeds. Without denying the distinctive traits that contrast the two, their fundamental analogy nevertheless permits us to view their formation as a single phenomenon. Their very names are significant: the earliest were known as i, i-i, or i-hui; the most recent, as she, she-i, or i-she. The term i designates the inhabitants of the same locality or small town, and she evokes the ancient village assemblies around the altar of the God of the Soil. This indigenous Chinese cult of the God of the Soil was still being perpetuated in China, in both private and official forms, at the time when Buddhism reached its apogee. Thus it may be asked why the term she, denoting the altar of the God of the Soil and the assemblies of peasants before that altar, also came to designate associations of Buddhist monks and lay followers at Tun-huang as well as other regions of the Chinese world. Does this not concern two radically different institutions?

In a passage of the Shih-shih yao-lan, written in 1019, Tao-ch'eng does establish a connection between the later Lotus and Pure Land associations, on the one hand, and the Chinese institution of the she on the other.

> The she is the meeting that takes place after the days marking the beginning of spring (li-ch'un) and the beginning of autumn (li-ch'iu).[43] The day wu-wu is called the day of the she. At that time, all the peasants, having formed an association, make sacrifices to ask the god for a good harvest. The Po-hu t'ung says: "Why does the sovereign have a God of the Soil? Because all the world prays for blessings [in spring] and gives thanks to the Earth [in autumn]. Without the earth, men would be unable to feed themselves. But the earth, being vast, cannot

be worshipped everywhere. That is why a mound is made to fix the God of the Soil there." Today, the Buddhists create bonds of fellowship in the same manner, and clergy and laity thus consolidate the Law [together], pray for blessings, and seek rebirth in the Pure Land. But the Pure Lands are numerous, and if one sought them everywhere, the mind would become disorientated. That is why a specific place is designated for the Pure Land so that [worshippers] may pay homage to it in all tranquillity. That is where the god makes his dwelling. Hence the names *she* of the Lotus and *she* of the Pure [Land].[44]

The connection, based on the identity of the terms, would seem artificial and, in any event, the text is of a late date. It does, however, show that the Buddhist associations, or at least some of them, had private altars in certain monastery chapels and remote sanctuaries where their particular divinity resided.[45]

Better sources are, moreover, available: a passage in the biography of the monk P'u-an (503–609) shows the process of the transformation of indigenous cult groups into Buddhist associations. In addition, it indicates clearly that for Buddhists in the sixth century the term *i* was the equivalent of the term *she*, which at that time still denoted village groups formed for the purpose of offering sacrifices to the God of the Soil:

> Though he frequently lived in obscurity in the places where he happened to dwell, P'u-an practiced Buddhist charity at every opportunity. Many were the associations of the God of the Soil (*she*) that regularly, twice every year, performed bloody sacrifices. [P'u-an] made their rounds to save the animals being prepared as victims by redeeming them, and exhorted people to cultivate the principles of Buddhism. As a result, associations that eschewed the killing of living beings multiplied.[46]

This short passage has not only the merit of showing that the terms *she* and *i* could be used to refer to the same institution; it further reveals how certain religious groups of purely Chinese origin had become Buddhist associations: not by an abrupt or radical transformation, a sudden conversion, but rather by an evolution that never clashed head-on with local habits and concepts.[47] Conversion to Buddhism meant, in the first instance, merely respect for one of the tenets of Buddhism. Conversely, the same text suggests that indigenous customs and traditions were able to preserve a certain vigor within Chinese Buddhism; perhaps the renewed religious enthusiasm inspired by the arrival of Buddhism even revived religious practices that had already been in decline.

In the long study that Naba Toshisada devoted to the Buddhist associations at Tun-huang, the author recalls the principal characteristics of the Chinese institution of the altars to the God of the Soil:[48] in preparation for the propitiatory ceremonies in spring and the rites of thanksgiving after the harvest, *she* (the term designates the altar, the god, and the assembly of the family heads at the time of the sacrifice) were formed through the association of a fixed number of families (theoretical figures of ten, twenty, and twenty-five are indicated, later also one hundred). Each paid their share of the communal outlay for the days of the festival, for the feasting, drinking, singing, dancing, and the games. After the thanksgiving ceremony, all together drank the alcohol of the God of the Soil. The full amount of the means placed at the common disposal was spent, and on the occasion of the banquet a convention[49] of friendship and mutual aid among the villagers was proclaimed.

There were remarkable parallels between the Chinese institution of the God of the Soil and that of the Buddhist *she* at Tun-huang; the payment of dues by the members, principal meetings in the spring and the autumn, communal consumption of alcohol, banquets, and conventions were also characteristic features of the Buddhist associations at Tun-huang.

What is the date of the earliest associations of the faithful? According to a well-established, but untrustworthy, tradition, the first Buddhist *she* were due to the initiative of the great Hui-yüan of Lu-shan (334–416). The *Fo-tsu t'ung-chi* reports that in 416 Hui-yüan created an association (*she*) comprising 123 religious and lay members for the recitation of the Buddha's name (*nien-fo*).[50] It called itself White Lotus Association (*po-lien she*). There is nothing improbable about the creation as such of a religious society, even though the first societies known with certainty date to the late fifth century. Much later, under the Southern Sung (1127–1279), a Pure Land association of the White Lotus that claimed the patronage of Hui-yüan was founded by a monk of Su-chou named Mao Tzu-yüan.

According to the stele inscriptions studied by Chavannes,[51] and according to those collected in the *T'ao-chai ts'ang-shih chi*, Buddhist associations of the *i-hui* type seem to have been particularly numerous in the sixth century:

Year	Source	Number of Members
483	*Mission*, f. 1605	200
502	Ibid., f. 1606	32
502	Ibid., f. 1605	140
504 or 506	Ibid., f. 1614	?
519	Ibid., f. 1645	?
520	Ibid., f. 1648	32
525	Ibid., f. 1498	18
526–534	*T'ao-chai* 7.24a	40 or more
533	*Mission*, f. 1507	20 or more
534	*T'ao-chai* 7.21a	200
537	Ibid. 8.3a	40
538	Ibid. 8.6b	60
543	*Six monuments* III	?
543	*T'ao-chai* 9.1a	86
544	Ibid. 9.2a	300
554	*Six monuments* IV	?
556	*T'ao-chai* 10.7b	80
559	Ibid. 10.14a–b	71
570	*Mission*, f. 1692	58
575	Ibid., f. 1509	22

The monk Pao-ch'iung (d. 634) created a multitude of Buddhist associations in I-chou (modern Ch'eng-tu, Szechwan) that bore the name *i*. In his view,

> For leading on the population of the city wards and suburbs [of I-chou], there was nothing like the bond of fellowship [engendered] by the associations (*i-hui*). Thirty members were required to form an *i*. Every association had to recite the complete text of the *Ta-p'in ching*,[52] and each member recited a chapter. Every month they organized vegetarian feasts of purification, and each association in turn recited the sutra. There were as many as a thousand such associations (*i-i*).[53]

The extant information (steles of 483 and 653, mention of the *i-i* created by the monk Pao-ch'iung) indicates that this type of association was especially in vogue during the sixth century, but continued until about the middle of the seventh. It is precisely at that time that the first Buddhist associations named *she* made their appearance. The biographies of eminent monks provide enough information to fill in the lacuna left between the associations mentioned in the stele inscriptions and those found in Tun-huang in the ninth century.

According to the *Hsü kao-seng chuan*, the monk Chih-ts'ung (550–648) founded a "rice association" (*mi-she*) in the area of modern Yang-chou (Kiangsu):

> Since his mountain retreat was remote, provisions did not reach him easily. Thus he got three hundred lay followers from Yang-chou to form a rice association. Each of them was to supply one *shih* [of rice] per year. As a result, provisions were abundant in the mountain. Everyone, including monks and laymen, and even the animals, was given relief.[54]

About a hundred years later, the monk Shen-hao (717–791) instituted a "religious association of the Western [Paradise]" (*hsi-fang fa-she*). Its members recited more than nine thousand sections of the Lotus Sutra [every year].[55]

The epitaph of Shen-ts'ou (744–817), a monk from Chiang-chou (in modern Kiangsi), attributes to him the creation of an association for the incense and lamps of enlightenment (*p'u-t'i hsiang-huo she*).[56]

Finally, the biography of Chih-hsüan mentions the foundation of a Lotus association (*lien-she*) in the first half of the ninth century under his inspiration. Its members included a number of high officials.[57]

A text in the *T'ai-p'ing kuang-chi* mentions the creation of Buddhist associations in Shensi at the beginning of the eighth century.

> At the beginning of the K'ai-yüan era (713–742), several hundreds of families in the territory of T'ung prefecture (modern T'ung-chou fu) formed Samantabhadra associations (*p'u-hsien i-she*), one to the east and one to the west. Each month[58] they held a vegetarian feast (*chai*). The families belonging to the eastern association dressed in green. A son was born among them on the day of a banquet, at the time of the assembly. They named him Samantabhadra. When he reached the age of seventeen, he became a lowly servant, performing every menial task. Later, on the day of one of the association's ceremonies, this domestic suddenly pushed aside the statue [of Samantabhadra] and seated himself in its place. At this sight, the elders of the society were outraged and, not content to abuse [the servant], flogged him severely. Whereupon this Samantabhadra merely laughed and said to them: It is by your wish that I was born here. Now that you see a true Samantabhadra before you, you are incapable of showing him your respect. What then do you hope to gain from praying to this statue of clay?" Then he suddenly transformed his appearance into that of the

bodhisattva Samantabhadra. His body was the color of gold and he was seated upon an elephant of the Six Precepts. He rose into the air amidst a great radiance of light. Bright celestial flowers of the five colors gathered [above him] like clouds, then disappeared. Then the elders understood that they were in the presence of a saint. They were filled with fear and shame.

As for the western association, its members were giving a banquet in honor of Samantabhadra, and the monks had just assembled, when suddenly a pregnant woman appeared who was about to give birth and said: "I shall give birth." Then she entered the Bodhisattva Hall. Those present were indignant but unable to stop her. Thus she brought a boy into the world in front of the bodhisattva's throne. Since this was the first time she gave birth, the place was greatly soiled, but no one was willing to clean it. They were in the midst of heaping abuse upon [the woman] when they suddenly lost sight of her. The boy transformed himself into a brightly luminous bodhisattva Samantabhadra, his appearance proper and elegant. The soil changed into fragrant flowers. Thereupon, he mounted an elephant, rose into the air, and by and by disappeared. The elders reproached themselves for their foolish failure to realize that it was Samantabhadra [who had appeared to them], and there were several tens of people who blinded themselves. Since that time, there has been the saying "How should an ordinary person recognize the supernatural transformations of the bodhisattva?"[59]

The collection of documents related to the Buddhist court master Amoghavajra contains an imperial order bestowing, at the request of the great monk, an official monastery name (ssu-o) on a Buddhist chapel (fo-t'ang) in Hsi-yüan fang, Hsi-ho county (modern Fen-yang, Shansi): private individuals of that locality had founded an association (she-i) and undertaken the construction of this chapel in the Chih-te reign period (756–758). The works, immediately interrupted by the An Lu-shan rebellion, were only resumed after the pacification. The chapel was completed in the seventh year of Ta-li (772). The emperor conferred upon it the official monastery name Fa-chin. The imperial order was signed by Yüan Tsai, Wang Chin,[60] and two other officials.[61]

At Tun-huang, the majority of the documents related to associations are only dated by means of cyclical signs. However, there are some that bear exact dates:

858 (P. 3192 v°)
888 (P. 3666 v°)

894 (P. 3989)
896 (P. 3070 v°)
988 (P. 3145) [fifth intercalary month of the *wu-tzu* year]

The body of evidence that can be gathered from historical sources, stele inscriptions, and the collections of Tun-huang manuscripts shows the continuity of this institution from the fifth century until Sung times.[62] The activities of these associations were extremely varied. There was scarcely an act of piety (*kung-te*) that they did not perform: sculpture or casting of statues, arrangement of caves, construction of sanctuaries, organization of festivals, copying[63] and recitation of sutra.

A monk named Chih-yen composed formulas of contrition and vows that he was to pronounce in the course of a great assembly for monks and laymen (*wu-che ta-hui, i-ch'ieh hui*) for the benefit of Emperor Wu of the Liang (r. 502–549). An incomplete copy of this text survives among the Tun-huang manuscripts[64] and deserves mention here for the valuable information it provides:

The emperor, who refers to himself by his personal name Hsiao Yen, prays for his deceased father and mother, brothers, and other departed members of his family. He offers to take the place of those unable to endure their sufferings in hell and expresses his wish that wars, famines, inundations, droughts, epidemics, poisonings caused by plants, mishaps caused by fog, wind, fire, etc., may all cease. And he further invites those sufficiently courageous to follow him in his vows of sacrifice: they would be bound together by fellowship and "make no distinction between their possessions, which would form one property. They would together constitute one group, one association, one mind, one thought."

Thus the well-being of the deceased relatives depended upon a self-sacrifice, and that of mankind on the sacrifice of their lord. But an individual sacrifice was not enough. Hsiao Yen needed to take others with him whose destiny and whose persons were tied to his. This text offers a very suggestive insight into the associations of the faithful; it implies that at the origin of these societies there was a solemn engagement and an oath sworn in the presence of the Three Jewels, for these were effectively present at the great assemblies for monks and laymen.

The association proposed by Hsiao Yen involved more than the pooling of wealth for religious ends: it aimed at an identification of its members. In the mentality of the period, and still more in the particular circumstances in which this solemn engagement was formulated, one's possessions were a part of one's self.

It is clear that an engagement of such totality was dangerous and that its effects exceeded to a remarkable extent the mutual obligations of fellowship in modern societies.

The members of religious associations were lay followers united by a bond of friendship (chieh-yu) [65] or, better still, a kind of family relationship. On a stele studied by Chavannes[66] is found a list of members (i-tzu) of a Buddhist association who had all received personal names, like brothers, that shared an identical first character. It was the character hui, Wisdom (prajña).[67] However, these associations included different families. In the sixth century, members of associations frequently designated themselves as "brothers in the Law" (fa-i hsiung-ti). At Tun-huang, certain she were called "society of brothers" or "family society."[68] Whether or not they treated each others as brothers, the members of the she at Tun-huang acted in accordance with the rules of that chosen affinity: when joining an association, the new member engaged himself to make contributions on all the happy and unhappy occasions that would befall his associates.

"Whenever associations (i i-she) are created," reads a document from Tun-huang,[69] "it is first of all necessary to expel the evil and pursue blessings (chui-hsiung chu-chi)." By this is meant in particular, as the following text explains, that if one of the members died, each would provide his share toward the rental of the hearse and the expenditures for the Buddhist vegetarian feasts (chai).

In fact, the entire family of the association member could benefit from the religious and material advantages offered by the society. In a manuscript cited by Naba Toshisada,[70] a she of fourteen members decides to append a new article to its statues. No provisions had been made in the event that a close relative (brother, sister, or other immediate kin) of an association member should undertake a long journey. The new article stipulated that upon the return of a close relative from a journey or in the event of the death of an immediate kinsman of an associate, each member would supply a bolt of cloth. On the day of a departure on a journey of more than one thousand li, a jar of alcohol would be provided at joint expense. On the day of return, two jars of alcohol would be made over for the reception in honor of the voyager. No journey undertaken for private reasons would be considered.

For manifestations of filial devotion (ch'u-hsiao) [after the death of a relative], two jars of alcohol would be provided.

An essential objective of every association was to ensure the celebration and the continuity of the family cults. This intention appears very clearly in certain cases. It seems that being orphaned or without a male descendant were considered favorable qualifications for being admitted as a new member in a *she*:

> Petition of the candidate Ho Ts'ing-ts'ing.
> The above-named Ts'ing-ts'ing, having suffered ill fortune in life, having lost both his father and his mother, and having no longer any close kin or a wife to maintain [the offerings for] his deceased father and mother, found himself unable to repay their goodness. Yet suddenly he dares to behold upon their somber path, finally recompensed for their kindness. . . . He appeals to you, reverent Buddhist masters . . . . He hopes that the three directors and the secretary will be good enough to grant him a name (tz'u shou-ming) (?) [and to inscribe him in their registers] and requests them to take a favorable decision.[71]

The *she*, furthermore, were hereditary institutions. Members not only engaged their own persons and their families into the ties of fellowship within the association but also their lineage and all their male descendants. The heads of the family succeeded one another in the direct line of descent in the *she*:

"When an association (*she*) is founded," reads a document from Tun-huang,[72] "it should be made to last for a long period of time. When [a member] dies, his sons and grandsons shall take the succession." And "if this succession comes to an end for lack of descendants, it shall not be permitted to detach a member of a collateral branch [to assume the succession]."

We know from the cave inscriptions at Tun-huang that certain founding families, grouped in associations, hereditarily looked after the maintenance of the caves and their decoration.[73]

The strictly religious ties that united the members of *i* and of *she* associations were paralleled by conventions governing mutual aid and the exchange of goods and services. The members' rights and their duties toward one another were founded upon their fictive kinship.[74]

In his study of the associations at Tun-huang, Naba Toshisada maintained a distinction between two types of societies: one of Chinese origin, the other Buddhist. The *she* of the first kind were, in his view, only mutual aid associations formed for the purpose of celebrating the family rites at shared expense. The second pursued exclusively Buddhist activities. However, the quasi-familial ties that united association members were as important for the constitution of Buddhist *she* as for the other types of association. We are evidently dealing with a single institution the forms of which were more or less profoundly influenced by Buddhism.[75] Every association had a dual objective: to ensure, on the one hand, the performance of religious acts that were expected to benefit the association as a whole, or even a village community, and, on the other, to maintain the continuity of family cults.

At Tun-huang, the individual contribution of each member of a *she* permitted the celebration of communal banquets. This practice, however, such as it functioned within the associations, was more original than it might seem, and it left considerable room for the expression of that familial individualism the importance of which has been emphasized. A figure who appeared periodically in the *she* associations, on the occasion of the great festivals, was the *chai-chu*, the "master of the banquet," or *chu-jen*, "host." The following text mentions this figure and is also worth citing because of the intimate glimpse it offers of the life of the Buddhist associations at Tun-huang:

> The streets and alleys are swept and watered. The banners of the saṃgha are suspended in formation. The city gates are decorated. The Buddhas are placed on their precious thrones. Monks of renown are invited. Rich incense burners of a hundred fragrances are set out. In the preparation of such acts of piety, one's first concern should indeed be the ornamentation. From the administrator and secretary of our association down to the remainder of our honorable members, we all form the intention that our sins and the innumerable obstacles [to enlightenment] be obliterated this very day and that incommensurable blessings amass at this moment. May the riches of the Law accumulate and the lives of the good be prolonged. May disasters and misfortune be prevented from crossing the thresholds of our gates and trouble from entering our wards and our alleys.[76] Gaiety and joy in each family! Contentment in each dwelling! Let all partake of the bliss when the master of the banquet (*chai-chu*) cheers them on to the feast (?). Afterward, may there be no more wars, may wind and rain conform to the seasons, and may all beings of the present world (*dharma dhātu*) benefit together from these blessings.[77]

The circular letters of the associations (*she-ssu chuan-t'ieh*), large numbers of which were found at Tun-huang, show that the contributions were mostly deposited at the house of the master of the banquet or host: ".01 *shih* of millet, one pound of flour, and .05 *shih* of oil are to be delivered to the host Ts'ao Pu-nu for the spring banquet (*ch'un-tso chü-hsi*)."[78]

In another circular, identical quantities of the same foodstuffs were to be taken to the host (*chu-jen*). Elsewhere, the host Chang Ch'ou-tzu was to receive the contributions.[79]

If, as seems likely, the host or the master of the banquet was responsible for organizing the celebration and the banquet, it may be assumed that he paid nothing. He invited his fellow members, gave the feast in his name, and played the principal part, though he too would contribute his share when his turn came to be invited. As a result, the celebrations were not provided anonymously by the *she*, but by each of its members. The host would gain prestige and social dignity from this practice, which in turn obliged him to his guests: each gave little individually, but received much—and this flowed directly from the religious nature of the institution.

The Buddhist associations at Tun-huang celebrated six minor banquets each month (on the first, eighth, fifteenth, eighteenth, twenty-fourth, and twenty-eighth days) and three great banquets annually, in the first, fifth, and ninth month. The two most important feasts, the spring banquet and the autumn banquet (*ch'iu-tso chü-hsi*) followed the rhythm of the agricultural year: they marked the beginning of farm work, in the first month, and its closure after the harvest, in the ninth month. Buddhist cults superimposed themselves on these ancient practices, which continued through them. The communal meal, however, also constituted an essential act in the context of the family cult and, in particular, of the mortuary rites.[80]

The subsequent development of the institution can be sketched briefly: it is at the origin of the mutual benefit societies and the financial associations in China. We have seen that the Long Life Treasuries of the Sung period were constituted thanks to the contributions of associated monks.[81] This practice derived plainly from the model of the associations of monks and lay followers attested by the stele inscriptions and the Tun-huang manuscripts. One long tradition links the ancient village groups constituted in view of the sacrifices to the God of the Soil to the associations of peasant shareholders in modern China.[82]

By the manner in which they functioned, the religious associations, whether purely Chinese or influenced by Buddhism, permitted
everyone to occupy his appropriate place and to conduct himself in
the most important circumstances of public and family life in accordance with the requirements of tradition, and morality, as well as religion.[83] The Buddhist banquet was accompanied by prayers and acts of
repentance with the aim of obtaining blessings or good luck (chien-fu)
for the participants and their families (of "merit," puṇya, as the Indi-
ans would say), or again to invite such blessings on behalf of deceased
relatives (chui-fu). The reason for contributing to a banquet was no
doubt because the family was unable to assume the cost on its own.
But at the same time it was also because both the act of contributing
and the communal meal had a meaning and an effect that extended
well beyond that purely economic consideration.

By penetrating existing cult organizations, or by creating new ones
after their model, Buddhism spread through village and urban communities in China. Frequently these would use the gate of a monastery
or chapel as their meeting place. The influence of Buddhism was more
or less profound, but appears to have been dominant at the time of
great religious fervor in the sixth and seventh centuries. When it
comes to the associations (i-hui) as we know them from the stele
inscriptions, one can even speak of original creation.[84]

The size of the contributions within these groups of laymen and
monks depended on the faith and the resources of each. A stele
inscription mentions the twenty-odd members of a group of associates who had exhausted their family means.[85] The steles studied by
Chavannes show that beside a large number of ordinary members (i-
tzu or i-jen), whose contributions must have been modest, there also
figured certain donors wealthy enough to have commissioned the
sculpting of whole statues at their sole expense.

On the base of a Buddhist sculpture, the inscription of which is
dated 543,[86] is found a list of seventy-eight names. The first fifty are
described as i-tzu, except for the last three of this register who bear the
titles of "elders of the i" (i-lao). On the upper register appear the names
of members with more varied titles. There is an i-shih (Buddhist master of the i), the monk Fa-ch'ien; thirteen donors of the main statue;
the master of the banquet (chai-chu); and finally, a list of individual
donors: "the donor of the statue of Prabhūtaratna," "the donor of the
statue of Maitreya," "the donor of the incense and the lamps," etc.

Thus the wealthiest members of the *i-hui* contributed to the common good by taking in charge a specific portion of the whole. This makes the *i-hui* a freer form of association than the *she* of Tun-huang. A further indication supports this conclusion: the number of the members of *i-hui* in the sixth century varied widely—between twenty, two hundred, five hundred, and even one thousand—and were generally higher than those of the *she* of Tun-huang. Recruitment was thus presumably more broadly based and more liberal.

The distinguishing feature of the *she* at Tun-huang, on the other hand, was that their pooling of wealth corresponded to a more tamed and more regular form of giving. The contributions were regulated by statute. Individual members were no longer motivated to fulfill their duty by a sense of honor, the fear of being disregarded for giving less than their share, and the desire to outdo the others: giving was no longer entirely spontaneous, and defaults of statutory obligations were punished by fines (*fa*). Failure to appear at the appointed times and to provide one's share were liable to punishment. On the basis of their legal aspects, the *she* of Tun-huang represent a more highly developed form of religious association than the *i*. One might even consider, given the centuries that separate the stele inscriptions from the Tun-huang manuscripts concerning the *she*, that the perceptible evolution between the first and the second of these groupings corresponds to a parallel evolution of the faith that had become less of a piece and more reasoned toward the end of the T'ang period. An association circular from Tun-huang states:

> In accordance with our statutes, for the day of the "establishment of blessings" (*chien-fu*), each member shall bring two *hou* cakes and one *sheng* of millet. We request our honorable associates to assemble, after receipt of this circular, on the fourth day of the present month, at the hour *mao*, in front of the gate of the Ta-pei monastery. The second person to arrive late at the rendezvous shall be seized and condemned to pay a fine of one *chiao* of alcohol. Those who fail to come altogether shall be fined a demijar of alcohol. The present notice must circulate rapidly, and no one is permitted to stop its circulation. Anyone who stops it will be punished in accordance with our statutes. This notice, having been returned to us after completion of the round of the society members, shall serve as proof for imposing the fines.[87]
>
> The secretary (*lu-shih* Tung, on the third day of the first month of the *keng-yin* year (930 or 990).[88]

Here follows a list of the members of this *she*, which comprised twelve monastic dignitaries (*seng-cheng* and *fa-lü*) and eight lay men, all but one of whom were minor local officials (*ya-ya*).

Another text details the fines that were imposed by the bureau of the association:

> Note from the bureau of the association.
> The persons who failed to appear at the banquet (*chai*) of Li Tzu-tung in the fifth month are our president, Ho, and Liu Yüan-chen. Neither did the latter send the wheat intended for the banquet. Also failed to supply the wheat: Ch'eng Ch'ien-yung. Failed to appear for the offering of incense (*hsing-hsiang*): Lo Kuang-chin.
> The above members who did not come, either to the banquet or to the offering of incense, must be penalized according to the statutes.
> Note by Chao T'ing-lin, fifth month of the year *shen* . . . twenty-first day.[89]

The statute of an association of women in Tun-huang, founded on February 13, 959, stipulated that on the feast days as well as on the day of the first month consecrated to the "establishment of blessings" (*chien-fu*),[90] each member would bring specific quantities of oil, alcohol, and flour. The text of the statute continues:

> If any member of our association disregards precedence, in matters large or small, arouses shouting or disputes during meetings, or refuses to obey the orders of the president, then all the members shall assemble at the gate [of the monastery] and oblige her, as punishment, to supply a quantity of alcohol sufficient for an entire feast and that shall be shared among all the other members of the association.

Any member, finally, wishing to withdraw from the association was liable to three blows of the bamboo as punishment.[91]

Another document related to the foundation of *she* is signed by thirteen members, including the president (*she-chang*), the administrator (*she-kuan*), and the secretary (*lu-shih*).[92] It is dated tenth day, fifth month of the year *chia-yin*, third year of Ch'ing-fu (894, i.e., the first year of the Ch'ien-hsing period). The aims of the association are to create bonds of fellowship between its members and to ensure the observance of the rites, that is, mortuary ceremonies and all manifestations of filial piety. Each member, while paying out little, was assured a proper funeral for the members of his close family and could in addition count on the aid of his fellow members in all difficult circumstances. The statutes laid down the size of each contribution, the rules of discipline to be observed within the association (interdiction of drunkenness, of coming to blows), and the fines imposed on negligent members.[93]

Through the intermediary of religious groups, an intimate participation of the lay world in the life of the saṃgha was instituted. It was a fundamental principle of Mahāyāna Buddhism that the profane and the religious should attain their salvation together, and this principle found concrete and living expression in the lay-religious associations. Not only were the Buddhist *i* and *she* generally founded on the clergy's initiative, but there was also scarcely an association that did not have its Buddhist master. The associations of the sixth century all had clerical instructors with the title of *i-shih*, [94] and at Tun-huang monks and nuns are found among the members of the *she*.[95] The role of these religious was not limited to the instruction of their lay associates: they contributed their own sanctity, and, thanks to their presence, the efficacy of every act of piety undertaken by the community accrued.

From the beginning, when the faithful associated themselves with personages endowed with sanctity, it was no doubt in the hope that they would benefit from their aid in transmigrations to come.[96] Vegetarian feasts, town processions of the statues (*hsing-hsiang*), recitations of sutra (*chuan-ching*), nocturnal illuminations (*jan-teng*), all these acts of Buddhist life were the result of a collaboration between lay followers and monks. In most cases, the banquets were celebrated at the monastery, at the site of the particular cult practiced by the association. In the course of these celebrations, within the sanctuaries, new groups were formed and their statutes drawn up. A monastic account from Tun-huang mentions the following expenditure: ".65 *shih* of flour, 6 *ko* of oil, 2.1 *shih* of millet for fortifying wine (*wo-chiu*). Expenditure made in the ninth month, when His Excellency K'ung Mu was invited and when the members of the new association were received and the statutes drawn up."[97]

At Tun-huang, several *she* were apparently connected to the same monastery, and would all meet within its precincts at the time of the three great annual banquets.[98] The recorded expenditure of the Ching-t'u monastery for a major *chai* amounted to 1.2 *she* of flour and 41 *ko* of oil for the preparation of *pu-t'ou* cakes to be offered to the monks and lay associations.[99] Naba Toshisada[100] remarked that, counting 1 *ko* (.01 *shih*) of flour per cake and assuming that each guest consumed five of these, the assembly must have numbered between 200 and 250 persons.[101] The monks of the Ching-t'u monastery numbered between 60 and 70. On the basis of this reckoning, several associations of 20 to 40 members seem to have participated in these feasts.

The cohesion of the associations of lay followers and monks was periodically reaffirmed by the banquets, the acts of piety performed jointly, and the mutual services that the members rendered one another. Their continuity was ensured by the swearing of oaths, convention, and a system of sanctions to which all had freely consented to submit. I descry the preponderant influence that this institution of manifold forms and implications had on the history of Buddhism in China. The small places of worship scattered throughout the empire, whose number was estimated as forty thousand by some censuses, were the private sanctuaries of a multitude of popular associations: "We understand that they disappear into the mountain forests to construct isolated hermitages, yet great assemblies gather there. They openly come and go."[102] It is not without reason that in the eyes of the rulers monks were held to be creators of "parties" of factions (*p'eng-tang*).

Thanks to the means procured by the general contributions, perhaps also to the occasionally secret character of the societies, the manner in which Buddhist communities were able to support themselves in remote forest areas where access was difficult and little could be gained from working the land can be explained. Such contributions, from a lay association, enabled Che-ts'ung and his companions to remain in the mountains near Yang-chou.[103]

The institution accounts for the spread of Buddhism in the popular milieus. At the same time, it appears to have been a factor of social cohesion in the sixth and seventh centuries. The associations evoked by the stele inscriptions seem to have united commoners with members of the local great families. Associates of very different backgrounds could collaborate in the same acts of piety, even though practices were related to means: the system of contributions was mainly a phenomenon of the poorer classes, the competition in expenditure of the rich.[104]

An echo of the conceptions peculiar to the lay associations may, moreover, be found in the religious thought and institutions of the Buddhist Church in China:

Now let us assume that a man of great wealth practices giving, by himself, from his birth until his old age. His merit (fu, puṇya) would be slight and could not compare with that of a multitude of people who, without distinction between rich and poor, noble or lowly, clergy or laity, exhort one another [to do good]. They each give small amounts of wealth, but then, assembled (chü-chi) [105] in one place, decide to make a gift of these goods to the poor, the destitute, the orphans, the elderly, victims of sudden disasters, the gravely ill, those threatened by imminent danger. Their merits would be immense.[106]

The originality of the theory of the Inexhaustible Treasuries[107] consisted in extending conceptions and practices that originated in the lay associations to the world of the lay faithful at large. The Inexhaustible Treasuries played, like the she, a double role, both economic and religious. It was a mutual society based on the contributions of each donor. The idea of a religious communion among the faithful served as a foundation of the institution.

The religious phenomenon found expression in a proliferation of new groupings which, however, essentially borrowed their forms from existing indigenous associations. Moreover, their formation was not limited to religious societies: around the cult sites sprang up rural or urban communities that had links to the clergy and were more or less integrated with the saṃgha.

The monks of the monasteries at Tun-huang offered banquets to the artisans when these had completed their work. To be sure, this was a way to recompense them for their labor, but were these banquets, in which the monks participated themselves, not also acts of piety intended to mark the happy completion of the works and their inauguration?

It could be said that in Chinese society before the T'ang, and under the first half of the T'ang period, purely commercial transactions were unknown. A dependent was not paid for his work but recompensed, because his relationship to the employer—one of guest and host— exceeded the narrow economic framework. Individuals and unrelated families were united by personal, sometimes quasi-familial ties. Those whom one nourished (yang) were members of an artificial family whose extension could be indefinite. The power of the monasteries and the Buddhist monks in China was not specifically religious, economic, or political: it had all of these characteristics simultaneously and to varying degrees.

The Mahāyānist theories that acknowledged the possibility of seeking salvation in this world, that recognized the existence of bodhisattva within the world (*tsai-chia*), as well as those that had left the world (*ch'u-chia*), were immensely successful in China: their foundations were tangible, in the associations of laymen and monks, in the organization of the monastic dependents, in lay and religious clienteles. The Bodhisattva Vows (*p'u-sa chieh*) sufficed to tie the profane to the saṃgha. It was enough for laymen to establish ties with the clergy to become part of the Buddhist community. Thus the first fact to emerge from the history of the economic movement concerns these phenomena, of a very general order, of enfeoffment; they appear in the background, but possess by themselves, all considered, explanatory value.

CHAPTER TEN

THE WEALTHY LAITY

Traditional Comportments

In the China of the period under consideration, the fundamental social distinctions, in the final analysis, were made on the basis of wealth. The difference in economic standing between the impoverished masses, on the one hand, and the highly restricted group of rich families, on the other, was so marked that it is justified to contrast them in terms of classes. This is not to deny that some peasants who owned a few slaves and farm animals were more well-to-do than others, nor that the group that may be designated, for convenience, as the upper classes was far from homogeneous: it was constituted of the great families in the capitals and the prefectures, members of the imperial family, high officials, the retainers of the great and powerful, and finally rich merchants. It was an urban milieu that revolved round the central government. It comprised those who had direct access to or exercised an indirect influence on the conduct of government, as well as those who lived in contact with or under the patronage of the powerful. To wealth, then, must be added the factor of political influence. It was essentially, then, the milieu of the imperial court. In such a heterogeneous world divergent tendencies would naturally manifest themselves. With all due caution against systematization, however, one is obliged to recognize certain contrasts of a general order, in both the moral and the political spheres.

There existed a class of guardians of the orthodoxy, the literati. The classical tradition shows that they were bent on maintaining a world of thought, which, though not original, had the merit of forming a coherent whole. It had been proven, and remained, in terms of the practical management of everyday affairs, the only efficient instrument of government. The cohesion of families and village groups derived from respect for moral principles and the hierarchy, while social peace depended on economic prosperity: the literati's preoccupations were all oriented toward these concrete goals. Hence the fundamental materialism of the classical tradition, its reprobation of unnecessary expenditure, and its constant praise of the austere moral standards attributed to the rulers of antiquity. The moral doctrine of the literati stood in direct relationship with their economic and administrative program.

Against this literati class can be positioned all those who were not trained to such discipline or who felt no particular compulsion to conform to its worthy principles: members of the imperial aristocracy, women especially, and those who stood in the aristocrats' favor. Their comportment, too, had been molded by traditions extending back to antiquity: traditions of splendor and prestige, and policies of patronage, in which women played a special role because they were instrumental in forming alliances and, at the same time, interested in the acquisition of commercial power.[1]

If literati doctrines were entirely aimed at the maintenance and consolidation of legitimate power, subversive intentions can, on the contrary, be detected in the aristocratic current: the passion for luxury and gain, the attachment to kinship relations, and even the religious preoccupations of certain highly placed milieus always had implicitly and to varying degrees a political significance.

These are, to be sure, no more than general oppositions and tendencies. Individual psychology, adapting itself to contradictions, is always more complex. Yet it is relevant to our subject to have recognized these antithetical traditions, for the problem under investigation cannot be defined in terms of religious convictions alone, which never furnish more than a rather slim basis for analysis. The economic and political extensions of Buddhism suffice to indicate that its foundations were broader and perhaps also deeper. Certainly the Buddhist faith affected those who had been raised in the traditions of the literati now and then, but suffice it to say, this was merely the effect of contagion. It is not among these that Buddhism found a favorable soil for its development, but among the imperial family and their following. Thus a sketch emerges that will be filled in by further examination: that of a clan of pro-Buddhists united by shared tastes and interests. It is constituted of women of high social standing, rich and influential families, as well as self-made men, upstarts, merchants, slaves, eunuchs, monks who lived in the shadow of the great and entertained close relations with them.

Among the aristocratic milieu can be found traditional forms of comportment and collective traits of psychology that make the role of individual temperament appear secondary. The taste for extravagant expenditure and prodigality and the passion for grandeur are among these general features. And they are allied to others: remarkably, Buddhist fervor in this milieu accommodated itself to cruelty. The zeal they displayed in their pious works was contrary to the Buddhist principle of compassion. The most fervent adepts of Buddhism could be veritable monsters:

> Feng Hsi [the brother of Empress Wen-ch'eng wen-ming [d. 495]] was scarcely humane in his administration, but he was a Buddhist. He used his personal wealth to erect votive towers and sanctuaries in every region. There were seventy-two of them in all. He had sixteen copies of the Buddhist canon made. He invited śramaṇa of renown to reside with him whom he engaged with indefatigable zeal in daily discussions. His expenditures [for their upkeep] were enormous. Since the stūpa and the monasteries he had constructed were situated on high mountains or in steep places, numerous men and oxen perished in the undertaking. Certain monks implored him to discontinue the constructions, but Feng Hsi replied: "Once the work is completed, only the sanctuaries shall be seen, and none will suspect the loss in lives of men and animals it entailed."[2]

There was a type of Buddhist emperor that accorded with the traditional image projected by the literati of the evil ruler who was heedless of the well-being of his subjects, ostentatious, prone to superstitions, cruel: a stereotype that some nevertheless contrived to resemble. Emperor Kao Wei [r. 565–576] of the Northern Ch'i is a typical example. His court was filled with upstarts whom he showered with favors: slaves, eunuchs, merchants, musicians, fortune-tellers. He is reported to have

> hollowed out the West Mountain at Chin-yang to have a giant statue of the Buddha sculptured there. One night, ten thousand bowls of oil

were lit to illuminate the interior of the [grotto-] palace. He also commissioned the construction of the Monastery of Great Compassion (Ta-tz'u ssu) for [his concubine of the second rank][3] Hu Chao-i. . . . Great ingenuity and the most subtle artistry were expended; stones were transported there and sources filled in. The cost in human labor amounted to millions. Countless men and oxen perished.[4]

The usurper Wu Tse-t'ien is remembered in history for her cruelty, her lack of scruples, her megalomaniac tastes, and the favors she heaped on Buddhism. It is known that she planned the erection of an enormous statue, three hundred meters high (?), in the suburb of Loyang.[5] The Heavenly Palace (t'ien-t'ang), which she commissioned Hsüeh Huai-i to construct—her lover, a former merchant whom she ordained a Buddhist monk and granted a title of nobility—had five stories and contained a huge dry lacquer statue. The figure of Empress Wu represents an excessiveness that is fully in the tradition of the tyrants, that is also closely akin to the aesthetic tendencies of Buddhism, and that manifests itself on all occasions. The seat of the official cult, the Hall of Light (ming-t'ang), the construction of which she also entrusted to Hsüeh Huai-i, was likewise a gigantic and sumptuous building: it was crowned by a canopy topped with a phoenix in gold and precious stones.[6]

It should be noted that the same passion for spending applied to secular constructions and to Buddhist buildings. "Extensive constructions of monasteries are undertaken and large mansions are built," stated a memorial of 707.[7] The building projects involved the destruction of entire forests and gigantic terracing works. Taoism benefited from a comparable fervor: at the end of the seventh and the beginning of the eighth centuries, the same imperial princesses had both luxurious Buddhist and Taoist monasteries built.

Behind the name of Buddhism frequently hides a revival of old indigenous practices. While literati moral doctrine generally disapproved of these, they were at least Chinese. Mortuary cults often took extreme forms: funerals provided occasions for displays of wealth that served to express the faith of the survivors and the munificence of the family at the same time. The quantity and value of condolence gifts were a measure of the renown of the deceased. This profusion and display of wealth were not in themselves specifically Buddhist, but they were practiced in those social milieus that were also most receptive to the new religion. There were close connections between the Buddhist movement and the ancient practice of sumptuous burials. The renewal of that ruinous fashion coincided, under the T'ang, with the period of the greatest flourishing of Buddhism (the second half of the sixth and the beginning of the seventh centuries).

In the second year of Lung-shuo (662), Li I-fu, later chief minister under the Empress Wu, requested permission to transfer the remains of his forbears to a new tomb built into the mound Yung-k'ang: "At the time of the burial, the procession of chariots, horses, offerings to the ancestors, and funeral banners stretched uninterrupted over a distance of seventy li (ca. thirty-five kilometers) from the bridge over the Pa river to San-yüan."[8]

Under the reign of Hsüan-tsung (712–756), the eunuch Kao Li-shih celebrated an equally sumptuous funeral for his deceased wife. Crowds lined the streets and a steady convoy of horses and chariots reached from his residence to the tomb.[9] It is no coincidence that Kao Li-shih also spent a good part of his vast fortune on the constructions of monasteries.

At the beginning of his reign, Hsüan-tsung endeavored to suppress these practices, which were so contrary to the literati's principle of frugality. In a decree promulgated on a *chia-yin* day of the ninth month, second year of K'ai-yüan (714), he declared:

Sovereigns since high antiquity have always warned against practicing extravagant funerals (*hou-tsang*) for these are useless to the dead and disastrous for the patrimony of the living. Yet recent generations[10] have widely adopted such habits of prodigality. They have imitated and vied with each other [in ostentation] until gradually this became the established norm. The people not only squander their patrimony; many even reach total destitution. . . . Today lands and gardens (*t'ien-yüan*) are set aside [for the maintenance of the tombs and for mortuary rites] and such foundations are called *hsia-chang*. [11] As for the funerary objects [for burial in the tombs?], they engender rivalries in sumptuousness and excess.[12]

In the same period, Yao Ch'ung criticized such waste as follows:

Those who indulge in extravagant funerals are generally lacking in good sense. Some are influenced by reigning fashions and are scarcely preoccupied by the beyond, and all confound prodigality with filial piety, frugality with miserliness. . . . Even the most intelligent and perspicacious have been drawn into the current fashion.

Yao Ch'ung then abruptly turns on the Buddhists and requests for his own funeral a *chai* (meal and Buddhist ceremony) of the simplest kind.[13]

Buddhists were called upon to perform mortuary services from a very early date.[14] There were intimate links between Buddhism and the cult of the dead. Virtually all monasteries and chapels founded by members of the upper classes were erected for the benefit of a deceased personage of high standing: emperors, members of the imperial clan or of the great private families. Buddhist places of worship always functioned to some extent as funerary edifices[15] or as family sanctuaries.[16] For members of the upper classes, acts of piety (*kung-te*) were frequently motivated by family pride.

Future generations will accumulate merit in vain, says the *Hsiang-fa chüeh-i ching*, for their reward shall be slight. This is because their good deeds will only stem from a desire for glory or for material advantages, and from vanity. They will strive to surpass one another. They will neglect restoring old monasteries, preferring to build new ones. They will say: "This monastery was not erected by my ancestors, so why should I restore it?" And then there will be those who, seeing others join in acts of piety, shall think of nothing but their personal glory and exhaust all their wealth and patrimony in offerings. Yet that will not prevent them from driving away the poor and the orphaned with curses, without even granting them a mouthful for their subsistence.[17]

The criticism leveled by the literati against the lavishness of pious works and foundations leaves no doubt as to the essential function of these sumptuous practices. They conferred a prestige of an altogether this-worldly kind. But this prestige also had to accrue to the deceased, for the ancestors continued as part of the family and remained associated with its fortunes.

A particular problem raised by these resplendent practices is that of the relationship between the monks and the families of wealthy followers and of the orientation itself of these family cults. To the extent that such cults were strictly private, they seem to have been oriented toward magic. "On the *jen-tzu* day of the ninth month, ninth year of Wu-te (626), the emperor T'ai-tsung decreed that private families were prohibited to 'establish demonic spirits' (*li yao-shen*)." Performances of ceremonies of a magical nature and heterodox sacrifices were strictly forbidden. All forms of divination, with the exception of the classical methods by tortoiseshell and milfoil, were prohibited.[18] The great families retained their own alchemists and magicians. And from the fifth century at the latest, Buddhist monks began to appear side by side with these traditional figures.

On a *wu-shen* day in the fifth year of the T'ai-p'ing chen-chün era (444), the emperor Shih-tsu of the Wei ordered that all, from princes and dukes down to commoners who privately maintained śramaṇa or magicians, were to make these over to the imperial authorities. It was prohibited to conceal them.[19] These śramaṇa, who practiced divination according to "methods adopted from the western barbarians," were to be put to death; any family concealing them was to be exterminated.

A decree of the second year of K'ai-yüan (714) forbade officials to retain Buddhist or Taoist monks and nuns in their residences for the purpose of practicing divination. The decree added that if a family was under an obligation to hold a vegetarian feast (*chai*), the clergy [invited for the occasion] had to produce their certificates and declare their monasteries of residence to the government authorities. Only under these conditions were they allowed to proceed to the family concerned, and in numbers determined by prior authorization. The Censorate's police were under orders to seek out and punish violators.[20]

The higher the social status, the more pervasive the practice of private worship. It was accepted that empresses and princesses and the highest ranking members of the imperial family should have dependent monks and nuns and their own monasteries and chapels. Emperor Wu of the Liang had his "family monks"[21] and the T'ang had their palace chapel (*nei tao-ch'ang*). It seems that certain monasteries played a particular and important role. When Liang Wu-ti decided to "make a sacrifice of his person" to the Three Jewels in order to save the empire from various calamities, he always gave himself up to the T'ung-t'ai monastery. The empresses of the Northern Wei went to the Yao-kuang monastery to take the vows at the end of their lives. In 496, Empress Feng left the court for this retreat; in 515, Empress Kao did likewise, and so did Empress Hu in 528, shortly before her tragic death.[22]

There was a close intimacy between the members of the imperial family and certain Buddhist communities; nuns, in particular, played a remarkable role as educators. At times they supplied the women's apartment with concubines; those who were educated by the nuns were often destined to brilliant careers.[23] There are two well-known examples: that of the concubine of Emperor Hsüan-wu of the Wei (r. 500–516), the future Empress Hu, who exerted much—pro-Buddhist—political influence in the first years of the sixth century, and that of the empress Wu Tse-t'ien. Like Hu, with whom she shared a number of character traits, the usurper Wu, the first empress in title in Chinese history, had been raised by nuns. She had left the monastery only to enter the women's apartment of Emperor T'ai-tsung. Yang Chien himself, the future Emperor Wen of the Sui, was born and had spent his childhood (from 541 to 552) in a nunnery. In opposition to the classical learning of the literati, there existed a parallel system of Buddhist education that catered especially to the women in the imperial harem and undoubtedly exercised an indirect influence on imperial policies.

In the second year of the Ta-ming era (458), following a conspiracy led by the monk T'an-piao, Emperor Hsiao-wu of the Sung ordered a purge of the monastic community: "Those who do not abide by the precepts of Buddhism and do not led an ascetic life shall return to lay life." But certain nuns in the monasteries "who had access to the women's apartment" entered into contact with the empress and the emperor's favorites, as a result of which the order was not carried out.[24]

In one of his memorials against the Buddhist clergy, Fu I reports (ca. 624) that under the Ch'i dynasty Chang-ch'iu Tzu-t'o had presented a report to the throne in which he put forward the view that the excessive number of monasteries and stūpa entailed an unnecessary expenditure of cloth and precious metals. But the integrity of this official was slandered after interviews had taken place between the monks and the chief ministers. The nuns, for their part, who enjoyed the support of princesses and the emperor's favorites, spread treacherous insinuations about him. As a result, Chang-ch'iu Tzu-t'o was thrown into prison and eventually executed in the marketplace.[25]

The sad fate of Han Yü in the unhealthy lands of southern China is well-known. The reason for Han's misfortunes was his memorial against the transfer of the relic of the Fa-men monastery.[26] Intercessions on Han Yü's behalf by two literati, P'ei Tu and Ts'ui Ch'ün, failed to appease Emperor Hsien-tsung's anger. Opinion at court turned against the author of the memorial, and nobles and kinsmen of the emperor found further damning grievances against him. Han Yü was demoted to the post of prefect of Ch'ao-chou in Kwangtung province.[27]

The complicity of the women at court and the emperor's kin in general with the Buddhist clergy explains why so many measures that would have been necessary to deal with the plethora of monks and nuns, with exorbitant expenditures under the pretext of Buddhist piety, were revoked and why so many reform decrees that are preserved in the official histories were never implemented. It should be noted, moreover, that it was the most reprehensible aspects of Buddhism that the women and high personalities at court defended with the greatest passion. For their interests were best served by the religious retainers with whom they were closely involved: monk-magicians, fortune-tellers, and traffickers.

Political Effects

The esteem in which high-ranking court personalities held the clergy corresponds to tastes and a religious faith the sincerity of which there is no reason to doubt. But their attitudes in this respect could have political implications. Those with subversive designs had to rely on the monks: their situation on the margin of society and the connections some of them enjoyed at court predestined them for the role of the spies and interlopers that were indispensable to any well-mounted plot. The nuns were privy to the secrets of the imperial family and knew the underside of politics. The Buddhist communities represented a considerable economic power, but the monks also possessed powers of another kind: their knowledge of the magical arts and their gifts of prophecy. It was they who spread dangerous predictions for the stability of the dynasty among the people. For the high nobility these people of lowly extraction could serve as perfect allies.

In the beginning of the eighth century, the T'ai-p'ing Princess had taken a barbarian monk named Hui-fan as lover. This monk was very wealthy and served the interests of the powerful and noble with great skill. The princess presented a petition to the emperor in which she requested that Hui-fan be appointed abbot of the Sheng-shan monastery, promoted to the third official grade and a title of nobility, conferring him the rank of duke. They hatched a plot together. In 713, Emperor Hsüan-tsung considered the affair to have become dangerous—five ministers were involved—and decided to destroy the members of the faction among whom figured Tou Huai-chen,[28] Hsiao Chih-chung,[29] and Ts'en Hsi. The T'ai-p'ing Princess fled to a mountain monastery. When she left it again a few days later, she was accorded the imperial authorization to take her own life.[30]

When in the middle of the seventh century, the Kao-yang Princess instigated a plot against her brother, Emperor Kao-tsung, she called upon the Buddhist monks Chih-hsü, a fortune-teller, and Hui-hung, who was "able to see demons," as well as the Taoist monk Li Huang, an eminent physician. Also among her retainers and accomplices was the eunuch Ch'en Hsüan-yün. In 652, the plot was discovered and the conspirators executed.[31]

Some remained attached to Buddhism by family tradition. This was the case of the Hsiao, descendants of a branch that ruled southern China in the Liang period and produced the most Buddhist of all rulers of Chinese origin, Emperor Wu. It was likewise the case of the descendants of the Yang family, the founders of the Sui dynasty. These deposed dynastic branches maintained hopes of returning to power and entertained relations with monks that were not without subversive ends.[32]

In the course of the T'ien-pao reign period (742–756), Yang Shench'in teamed up with a defrocked monk named Shih Ching-chung. This Yang was reputed to be interested in works on divination, and Shih Ching-chung presumably advised him in his choices. The serving censor (shih yü-shih) Wang Hung one day said to chief minister Li Lin-fu: "Yang Shen-ch'in is a descendant of the house of Sui and is [surely] contemplating the restoration of that dynasty. Witness the fact that he is collecting books on magic, associates with unsavory characters, and holds forth about omens auspicious or inauspicious for the empire." A search of Yang's residence produced a hiding place full of books about divination.[33]

The fears of the central government were well justified: many a conspiracy and rebellion, led by members of the aristocracy, separatist officials, and monk-magicians had been founded upon the diffusion of omens and messianic theories.

In 481, Chang Ch'iu, director of the imperial library, together with some one hundred prominent individuals, recruited a troop of slaves. A monk named Fa-hsiu, who agitated the people by means of his prophecies, was their accomplice.[34]

In Chi-chou (in the southern part of modern Hopeh), a monk of reprehensible conduct named Fa-ch'ing was expelled by his companions. As he went his way, he took to making prophecies and discussing magic. Now Li Kui-po of Pu-hai had led the peasants of his region into rebellion. His band chose Fa-ch'ing as their chief. Fa-ch'ing assumed the title "Buddha of the Greater Vehicle" and bestowed on Li Kui-po that of "Bodhisattva of the Tenth Stage, Vanquisher of the Demon Māra and King of the Han." They destroyed monasteries, slit the throats of monks and nuns, burned the holy scriptures, and proclaimed that a new Buddha had come into the world and was about to expel all demons.[35]

The role of prophecies in the accession of Wu Tse-t'ien is amply known. This form of propaganda, practiced by Buddhist monks, was plainly very effective.[36]

Tsukamoto Zenryū drew up the following list of rebellions of Buddhist inspiration during the fifth and sixth centuries:

Date	Leader	Province
401	Chang Ch'iao	Hopeh
473	Hui-yin	Shansi
481	Fa-hsiu	Shansi
490	Ssu-ma Hui-yü	Shantung
509	Liu Hui-wang	Kansu
510	Kuang-hsiu	Kansu
514	Seng-shao	Hopeh
515–516	Fa-ch'ing and Li Kui-po	Hopeh
516–517	Liu Ching-hui	Hopeh[37]

The presence of economic factors in this semireligious and semipolitical context is not surprising. The great families borrowed readily from the monks and the monasteries.[38] At times Buddhist establishments also provided the local aristocracy with propitious places for sheltering their possessions. During rebellions they served as warehouses.

At the time of the rebellion of Ko Wu[39] at Hsing-ch'eng, the emperor of the Wei set out at the head of his troops and camped at Ch'ang-an.

Since the monks had sowed wheat within their monastery, the imperial grooms put their horses to pasture there. The emperor went inside to admire the animals, and the monks dispensed alcohol to his retinue. Upon entering into a storeroom, the latter discovered a quantity of bows, arrows, spears, and shields. When this was reported to the emperor, he was enraged: "These objects are scarcely suitable for the religious. They must have conspired with Ko Wu; their intentions are

assuredly criminal!" Thus he ordered his officials to judge and con-
demn all the residents of the monastery. Searches produced quantities
of instruments for fermenting spirits and myriads of articles the
administrators of the prefectures and commanderies as well as the
rich had stored and hidden in this monastery. There were also rooms
below ground where [the monks] gave themselves up to debauchery
with women of high society.[40]

Beyond such occasional complicities, there existed a community of
interest between rich families and the clergy. They owned the same
kinds of property, estates with gardens and orchards, mills, shops,
agencies for loans against pledges, etc. Hence their broadly shared
attitudes, notwithstanding occasional clashes.[41] Economic rivalry
does not exclude mutual support and tacit understanding.

The taste for grandeur was traditional among members of the Chinese aristocracy. Among their clients—upstarts who had come by
riches and owed their social elevation to the support of the great—it
corresponded to a mentality of nouveaux riches. Both went together
with a pronounced penchant for hoarding. A passion for commercial
traffic, corruption, venality are characteristic features of the pro-Buddhist milieus.

Throughout the history of Buddhism in China, there existed a
small class of corrupt and influential monks, often very wealthy, who
had close relations with members of the imperial family, the great
families, and officials. Some of them exercised wide influence in the
prefectures, and local governments were obliged to come to terms
with them. The Buddhist clerical dignitaries under the Wei, the controllers of Buddhist clergy (sha-men t'ung) and overseers (wei-na) of
the Office of Buddhist Clergy (seng-ts'ao) at the turn of the fifth and
sixth centuries, enriched by usury and the fraudulent management of
the millet of the saṃgha households (seng-ch'i hu),[42] are a case in
point. Tao-yen, controller of Buddhist clergy in Chi-chou around the
middle of the sixth century, is a typical example of that class of rich
and powerful clergy.[43] The Hsü shih-shuo reports the story of a monk
named Chien-hsü who in the Chen-yüan reign period (785–805) began
to seek influence and favors by means corruption. Since the officials
of the garrison were handsomely paid by his gifts and totally devoted
to the monk, no one dared to bring him to justice. Under the reign of
Hsien-tsung (r. 805–920), however, the vice-president of the Censorate, Hsüeh Ts'un-ch'eng, succeeded in having him condemned to
death and his property confiscated.[44]

Kung-tsung, prince regent from 428 to 451, is known in the history of the Northern Wei for having interceded with Emperor Shih-tsu to obtain a softening of the anti-Buddhist measures taken in 466 after the rebellion of Ko Wu (see above). Toward the middle of the fifth century, close kinsmen of the emperor and followers of Kung-tsung with known sympathies for Buddhism had taken to commercial dealings. Kao Yün thus criticized the bad example given by the imperial family: "They establish private properties, raise chickens and dogs and even traffic in the marketplace, disputing the common people their livelihood."[45]

In 713, after the conspiracy and suicide of the T'ai-p'ing Princess, daughter of Wu Tse-t'ien and likewise a fervent Buddhist, an inventory of her estate was drawn up:

> Her wealth was immense. The rare items were as numerous as those in the imperial treasury. To inventory all her possessions in livestock, horses and sheep, in fields, in gardens, and in pawn treasuries (chih-k'u)[46] was the work of several years. As for the wealth of her lover Hui-fan, it too amounted to hundreds of thousands of strings of cash.[47]

The eunuch Kao Li-shih, famous for his grandeur, was also immensely wealthy. In the northwest of the capital, he had the course of the River Feng adjusted to accommodate a great mill with five wheels that all functioned simultaneously. The mill had a capacity of three hundred hu of cereals per day.[48] The construction of a large monastery named Pao-shou in the Lai-t'ing ward (east of the imperial city) and that of a Taoist temple, the Hua-feng kuan in the Hsing-ning ward (north of the Hsing-ch'ing Palace), were due to the munificence of the same Kao Li-shih. When the great bell of the Pao-shou monastery was cast, Kao organized a Buddhist ceremony in the sanctuary to which all the high officers of the court were invited. He conceived of the idea of charging each person who would strike the bell the sum of one hundred strings of cash for every blow. Some struck the bell as many as twenty times [and paid two thousand strings to Kao Li-shih] and no one struck less than ten blows.[49]

The passion for trafficking was especially pronounced among the women of the imperial aristocracy, the empresses, princesses, and high-ranking concubines. Their power was above all founded on commercial wealth. Once again, a tradition can be discerned here.[50] In the luxurious and avaricious milieus of Chinese high society, it was they who set the tone. In addition, they possessed a hidden but decisive influence on imperial policy, an influence they also peddled.

> Empress Wei was able to obtain anything she wanted from the emperor Chung-tsung (r. 705–710). It was through her that all promotions and demotions of officials were decided. The dimensions of the mansions she had constructed and the Buddhist monastery An-lo that she erected rivaled those of the wings of the imperial palace. As for the art that was displayed there, it was even superior.[51]

The sway that court ladies held over emperors permitted them to gratify their personal sympathies and animosities but also to enrich themselves by selling imperial favors. Promotions and titles of nobility were purchased from them; their profitable trade in imperial authorizations for ordinations has been examined. The reign of Empress Wu and the period between the restoration and the accession of Hsüan-tsung (705–712), during which the princesses were all-powerful, were marked by a corruption of political ethics. At the same time, it was one of the periods of Buddhism's greatest flourishing, as evidenced by the splendor and number of constructions and the growth of the monastic community.

The economic and political interests of the distaff branches, and those of the women, who incarnate these particular interests, were served by the Buddhist movement. It is significant that the prophecies spread by the Buddhist monks at the time of Wu Tse-t'ien's accessions tended to justify this usurpation of supreme power by a woman.[52]

In the second half of the eighth century, under the reigns of Su-tsung and Tai-tsung, the great pro-Buddhist officials were placed where they could be of greatest use to the monastic community. Three of them are well-known: Wang Chin, who belonged to a family that was Buddhist by tradition,[53] the eunuch Tu Hung-chien, and Yüan Tsai. The official decrees promulgated in response to the petitions of the great master of Tantra (esoteric and magical school) at that time, Amoghavajra, were always countersigned by these three personalities.[54] The career of Yüan Tsai is of some interest here. He was a self-made man. The former steward of the estates of Lady Yüan, the wife of the Prince of Ts'ao, he adopted her family name and, no doubt propelled by his connections with the aristocracy, entered into an administrative career under Su-tsung. He was on terms of friendship with the eunuch Li Fu-kuo, another fervent Buddhist who "consumed neither garlic nor onion." In 777 Yüan Tsai was arrested together with Wang Chin on charges, quite likely well-founded, of favoritism and misappropriation. The latter's biography reports that

> the brothers of Wang Chin venerated the Buddha and abstained from eating garlic, onion, and meat. Wang Chin, late in life, was even more [sanctimonious]. With Tu Hung-chien he made donations for the construction of numerous monasteries. After the death of his wife, Lady Li, he made a gift of his mansion in the Tao-cheng ward (in the north of Lo-yang, near the Hui-an gate) to be made into a monastery in order to bring blessings upon her. At the entrance he had the name [of the reign period] Pao-ying (762–763) inscribed. Thirty monks were ordained to ensure permanent services at this monastery. Whenever civil or military governors of a region came to court, Wang Chin would retain them to take them to the Pao-ying ssu and give them to understand that they should offer some money for its embellishment.
>
> At the beginning [of his reign], Emperor Tai-tsung (762–779) was attached to the sacrifices according to the Chinese rites and paid scarce attention to Buddhism. However, Yüan Tsai, Tu Hing-chien, and Wang Chin were fond of maintaining communities of monks. One day, Tai-tsung questioned them on the subject of retribution for pious works. Yüan Tsai and his acolytes seized the opportunity to instruct him. From that time on, Tai-tsung paid the highest homage to the Buddha. Once he ordered more than a hundred monks into the palace to display statues and sacred texts and to psalmody their recitation. This institution was called the "palace chapel." The food and drink of these monks was abundant and refined. They came and went using the horses of the imperial stables. All their expenses were paid out of the public granaries. Whenever the western tribes of the Tibetans made an incursion, the emperor had eminent monks recite the *Jen-wang ching*[55] in order to repel and capture the pirates. If through good fortune they turned back, then the gifts and favors were multiplied. The barbarian monk Pu-k'ung rose in officialdom to the rank of chief minister and director (ch'ing-chien), was enfeoffed as duke of a principality, and enjoyed free access to the palace. By his influence at court he could move dukes and ministers. He disputed their power and claimed their authority, becoming daily more insolent and rapacious. . . . The officials were unable to remedy this situation. Even though the monks indulged in fraudulent and immoral operations and fomented trouble, and despite the murders that succeeded one another, Tai-tsung did not withdraw his confidence in them. He even decreed that no official in the empire was permitted to strike a monk or a nun. And if someone ventured a reproach, having seen Wang Chin and the others make donations and found monasteries of a splendor and sumptuousness beyond all measure, then they always found justification in [the doctrine of the] retribution [for

pious works], claiming that their meritorious deeds would ensure lasting blessings for the empire.[56]

By juxtaposing successive strokes, a moral portrait of the social milieus that were most favorable to Buddhism can be drawn. For it is clear that these psychological traits, attitudes, and traditional inclinations form a complementary whole. The ladies of the imperial family and their allies, representing a tradition that was opposed to that of the literati, and political interests that were in conflict with those of the legitimate authorities, appear in the final analysis as the promoters of the religious movement. Around them revolved the pro-Buddhist circles at court.

One is dealing with a world whose great influence can hardly be explained by its equally powerful motives alone. Buddhist faith enjoyed its greatest vitality in the upper strata of Chinese society. Its content and orientation in these milieus can be clearly defined: it was not a question of simple adhesion to a religious doctrine. Acts of piety had a context, and this context informs about their functions.

Many ruined themselves on pious works, but—and the texts themselves underline this—their extravagant expenditures were motivated by rivalry and vainglory. Above all, pious works generated prestige. The primary aim was to increase the family's private "fortune" while simultaneously ensuring the present well-being of the living and of the dead. They corresponded to customary practices that were peculiar to certain milieus and whose origins can be traced to remote antiquity. The sumptuousness of the religious art introduced from the west would have appealed to these milieus who perpetuated their own traditions of splendor. The fate of emperors, the imperial clan, and the empire itself were assuredly linked to their family cult and were thought to benefit from its propitious affects: Buddhism was an imperial cult as well as a universal religion. But in what sense? It was the religion of the imperial nobility rather than the legitimate government. It found special support among women and members of the distaff branches of the imperial family as well as their allies. Consequently, its influence was weak on those emperors who understood that it was in their interest to rely on the literati in order to resist the influence of their collaterals and their wives. The instruments and retainers of legitimate power, the literati themselves, accorded Buddhism no more interest than was due a reigning fashion. For the most part, their involvement was pure conformism.

Thus there was a rather clear cleavage among the milieus surrounding the emperor. To schematize, one could say that Buddhism was the religion of the women and the cognate branches and that the traditional rites of Confucianism represented the cult of the agnates. A variety of not strictly religious factors support this distinction. A political tradition emphasizing parsimony and the distribution of wealth clashes here with an aristocratic current whose grandeur, hording, commercial power, and patronage appear as signs of subversive tendencies or as means to further private political interests.

Leaving the narrow circle of the imperial court, let us consider the involvement of this Buddhism of the upper levels of society with popular Buddhism. While the court was in principle the locus from which all political power emanated, the center where rivalries of influence are best discernible, it is also true that those who resided there retained attachments to their native regions. They had their own fiefdoms, and certain families, owing to wealth, name, or prestige, did not relinquish their more or less extensive local powers. It happens that hardly any influential family did not have a territorial power base, whether in the environs of the capital or even in remote prefectures. These great families founded sanctuaries. They ruined themselves on pious works. What is the link between the religious activities of these families and the actual power they exercised? One suspects that their influence and the cults are not unrelated.

This is the place to return to the semiprivate and familial nature of the cult foundations. Certain small places of worship—village sanctuaries and isolated chapels—owed their existence to the generosity of wealthy local families. At Tun-huang, hermitages (lan-jo) bore the names of private families: hermitage of the Chou family, that of the Lo family; hermitage of An Chin-tzu. Some great families also maintained private places of worship or altars inside other sanctuaries. A decree of 727 ordering the destruction of the small monasteries and chapels in the prefectures mentions kung-te (lit. "merit" or "acts of piety")[57] that some of them contained: they were to be "transferred to neighboring large monasteries." The term kung-te remains enigmatic here unless it designated, in a concrete manner, the devotional objects, the statues, that were contained in the niches belonging to private families.[58] This might explain the violent resistance of the magistrate of Hsin-hsi, a certain Li Hsü, to the execution of the imperial order.[59]

After the massive laicizations and destructions of monasteries decreed by the T'ang emperor Wu-tsung, nobles and commoners were permitted in 851 to reconstruct the Buddhist sanctuaries.[60] A memorialist to the throne remarked: "This must not serve as a pretext for the faithful to conceal riff-raff among the clergy. I submit that officials be instructed to exercise a vigilant control over these village chapels."[61]

This scattered evidence suggests two distinct modes for the creation of cult centers in the countryside and small towns: one, already outlined above, was popular and entirely autonomous; the other proceeded, among the great, from a desire to ensure the perpetuity of a family cult. Now it might be thought that these cult foundations also fulfilled two different functions. For the founding families, they were private places of worship; for the peasantry, centers of a communal religious life. Hence a liturgical structure that united social classes at the opposite ends of the scale and that appears as the principle underlying the formation of new ties. And this is not a late phenomenon: from the beginnings of Buddhism in China, the introduction of the new religion into rural areas was partly due to the intervention of the great families. At the end of the second century, Tse Jung (d. 195), who governed the ancient land of Ch'u (in modern Shantung and Kiangsu) in virtual independence from the central government, erected a vast Buddhist temple where on feast days he offered free banquets to the peasants of the region:

> Tse Jung erected an immense Buddha temple and had a figure cast in copper and covered in gilt. He clothed it in embroidered silks. [From the summit of the building] he had nine series of copper plates suspended. Below, he built a pavilion with two stories and covered paths. This building could contain more than three thousand people who recited Buddhist texts in unison. He issued an edict granting permission to those who were followers of Buddhism, whether from the region or from neighboring commanderies, to come and receive the doctrine (shou-tao). These he exempted from all corvée duties in order to attract them. As a result of this measure, the households of commoners who gradually arrived at the temple from far and near numbered more than five thousand. At each festival of the Bathing of the Buddha, Tse Jung organized banquets of wine and food. The roads were covered with mats over a distance of several tens of li. Some ten thousand people would partake in the spectacle and the food. The expenditure amounted to fabulous sums.[62]

There is no doubt that the great families associated the local peasantry with their private cults. The historical record suggests that this constituted a form of political action, which was quite different from its modern, laicized counterparts. Moreover, peasant rebellions have even in modern times provided conclusive evidence of this connection between religion and politics. That the great founding families of monasteries, chapels, and hermitages availed themselves of such forces of social cohesion and political agitation is an important fact that needs to be taken into account in a general interpretation of the Buddhist movement in China.

The demagogic nature, furthermore, of the great religious assemblies is manifest: the Buddhist principle of charity served there as a pretext for an interested liberality. The feasts instituted by Tse Jung are an early example of this.

Hsüeh Huai-i, the drug merchant of Lo-yang who became the lover of the empress Wu Tse-t'ien and was ordained a monk to facilitate his comings and goings in the palace, was equally aware of the use of largess:

> Whenever he organized a great assembly for monks and laymen (wu-che ta-hui), he spent tens of thousands of strings of cash. As he emptied ten chariots full of cash onto the ground, crowds of men and women converged and fought over it. Some were trampled underfoot, and there were casualties.[63]

In addition, there is the direct evidence for such associations of commoners and great families in cult activities in the context of the Buddhist groups that, in the sixth century, were known as i-i or i-hui. [64] There, social class distinctions seem to have fallen away: beside a small number of donors rich enough to have large statues sculpted and to provide the major offerings, there were multitudes of ordinary members, with no other title than "member of the i" (i-tzu), who appear to have been commoners. The wealthy families played the leading role within the associations and derived prestige from competitive spending, the display of wealth, and practicing largesse. The poorest, meanwhile, provided petty contributions or perhaps, like members of the popular associations at Tun-huang, fixed dues on a modest scale.

The tastes of the lower classes in fact accorded well with the policies of the great squanderers, princesses greedy for power, nobles and separatist officials, usurpers like the Empress Wu. These policies were of a demagogic order. They relied on riff-raff, slaves, eunuchs, disreputable monks, and merchants. Elevated to the highest ranks, heaped with wealth and honors, these individuals knew how to prove their attachment to their benefactors and served their interests as best they could. Buddhism found its place in this context: from the splendor of the sanctuaries and festivals, the high nobility and their creatures derived part of their prestige among the humble. The peasantry, finally, in its state of misery, had a predilection for the magical arts, for prophecies and messianic theories: tastes that were shared by the great and that some pandered to for their own ends.

It is not easy to determine the importance of such interests and inclinations within the overall attitudes of members of the upper reaches of Chinese society converted to Buddhism. At the outset, they manifested an unquestionable fervor, but also a certain objectivity with respect to the religious phenomenon, a detachment that became more marked in the course of the centuries. It is certain that Buddhism gained nothing from this collusion with the great. The most faithful supporters of Buddhism were at the same time its principal corrupters. It was they who first saw in the religious movement a source of influence and profit.

CHAPTER ELEVEN

THE RULING CLASS

The Position of the Rationalists

The concurrence of the popular and aristocratic strands of Chinese Buddhism explains the success of its development as a whole. The religious movement appeared as the expression of diverse aspirations that were not all of a religious order but that jointly found satisfaction in Buddhism. A third current remains to be taken into account, that of the literati. We may call them the ruling class, for the needs of a constituted state whose power was already consolidated were fairly constant—flowing from a general desire for political stability—and the literati were best able to answer these needs. They understood the proven procedures whose prestige derived from the antiquity attributed to them. It will be useful to enquire into the specific motives of these pillars of legitimate power for either opposing or furthering the Buddhist movement, since their action curbed its development and even appears to have compromised it definitively from the middle of the ninth century on. On the other hand, when their reaction was favorable, it had the effect of orienting Buddhism in a particular direction.

Let me begin by briefly recalling the main repressions of Buddhism: those following the discovery of weapons in the possession of the monks of Ch'ang-an in 446[1] and again in 574 and the following years,[2] both of which were limited to northern China; finally, the most famous and effective, under the Hui-ch'ang reign period (841–847),[3] and the latest in date, in 955.[4] Although the immediate causes of the repressions varied, they were nevertheless all represented as measures of economic and political rehabilitation. They appear as brutal efforts on the part of the established government to regain control of a situation that was out of hand. It is true that they involved persecutions. The vigor with which the monks were pursued and the sacrilegious gusto with which their sanctuaries were destroyed would seem to justify de Groot's thesis that the literati persecuted Buddhism for sectarian and doctrinal reasons.[5] However, the brutality was a function of Chinese political traditions and governmental practice. Rebels were treated no differently; and it appears that religious and doctrinal considerations, far from running counter to Buddhism, played in its favor.

It is self-evident that those raised in the classical tradition could not be fervent Buddhists. Their rationalism restrained them from adopting common beliefs and superstitions. Noblewomen, by contrast, female members of the great families, self-made men, and commoners had no such protection against religious faith. These were more receptive to Buddhism. The literati, moreover, had an austerity of principle, an inclination to temperance and thrift, that disapproved of extravagant expenditures.

"The *yü-shih wei* Li Piao and Ch'ang Ching, prefect of Yu-chou," says Yang Hüan-chih in his description of Lo-yang in the sixth century, "issued from Confucian families, and their residences were simple and modest. Chang Lun, the director of agriculture, by contrast, was extremely lavish and prodigal." His garden and park were famous for the artistry of their imitations of the contours of nature, of rocks, mountains, and streams.[6]

The classical tradition maintained in certain families of high rank thus necessarily ran counter to a religious movement whose most manifest tendencies inclined it toward splendor and expenditure. As Fu I wrote on 624, "Let the monks and nuns clothe themselves in cotton cloth [rather than silk] and cut back the expenditure for their banquets (*chai*). Then the cultivation of silkworms shall cease to be ravaged and the poor shall no longer suffer hunger."[7] Fu I, whom certain Buddhist monks have wanted to make out as a Taoist bent on their destruction, did not refer to his religious convictions in his memorials against Buddhism. His position was that of any good member of the literati class, devoted to the dynasty and solely concerned with tax returns and the public welfare. This attitude, in which economic preoccupations came first, explains the literati's hostility toward the religious practices of the faithful and toward the extravagant expenditures and sumptuousness of the Buddhist Church. At the same time, the literati were concerned about the subversive tendencies of the religious movement. It is significant that the great proscription of the Hui-ch'ang era, in the middle of the ninth century, was preceded by a reaction of the upholders of the legitimate government against the factions of the eunuchs and the great pro-Buddhist officials: in the eleventh month of the fourteenth year of Ta-li (779), shortly after the accession of Te-tsung, Yüan Tsai received the order to commit suicide, and Wang Chin was banished the same year. In 780, the offices of the "commissioners of good works within and without" (nei wai kung-te shih), posts that had been occupied by eunuchs and military officers since their creation,[8] were abolished in accordance with the proposal of Liu Ch'ung-hsün. At court, the spectacle provided by the monks of the imperial palace, the arrogance of the eunuchs, the unbridled prodigality of the great devotees, all provoked the literati's hostility toward Buddhism. But behind the scenes one also detects a struggle for political influence.

There was no doubt a tactical element in the literati's constant reference to the moral principles of Buddhism, for it was not advisable to clash head-on with such passionately held convictions. They also knew the potential consequences of any attack directed against court monks and harem ladies,[9] and reversals of imperial policy were always to be feared. A further aspect was their desire to conform themselves with the reigning mores. However, even the most courageous opponents of Buddhism seem to have adhered in principle to the moral doctrines of the new religion in which they may have recognized echoes of the moral precepts with which they themselves had been inculcated. From these premises proceeded a Confucian interpretation of Buddhism, which in the spheres of the economy, morality, and religion found itself in agreement with the official tradition.

Buddhist charity was but another form of the sovereign's politically inspired humanitarianism (hui). In a text said to have been recited before a great Buddhist assembly by the emperor Wu-ti of the Ch'en (r. 557–560) figures the following revealing phrase with regard to the synthesis of Chinese and Buddhist notions: "To conquer oneself in the interest of others is the constant [distinctive] virtue of the superior man (chün-tzu), yet it is also the primordial precept of the bodhisattva."[10]

Empress Wu Tse-t'ien's project to construct a colossal statue in the suburb of Lo-yang aroused sharp reactions in literati circles. Chang T'ing-kuei recalled,

> The bodhisattva's rule of conduct is to ensure the happiness of all beings. . . . In contingent and political terms, this means first of all that the public treasuries in the empire and the border regions be well-stocked, so that human strength can be maintained; in terms of Buddhist doctrine, one must relieve the sufferings of the beings, save them from danger, annihilate the phenomenal (*hsiang*, Skr. *nimitta*), and exalt the unconditioned (*wu-wei*, Skr. *asaṃskṛta*).[11]

According to Yao Ch'ung,

> To fully put the principles of Buddhism into practice, it suffices to be just, tolerant, and charitable; to do good and avoid evil. Why indulge in fictions (*hsiao-shuo*) and be misled by monks? Why take pure allegories at their face value and have sutra copied, statues cast, ruin oneself, squander one's patrimony, even go so far as to sacrifice one's life without regrets? This is the height of folly![12]

To judge by the writings of the literati, if Buddhism in China effectively engendered unnecessary and ruinous expenditures that were contrary to the ideal of charity and harmful to the public welfare, then this was the result of widespread misconceptions as to its true principles. As Hsin T'i-p'i wrote in a memorial dated 707,[13]

> I submit that Buddhism considers purity as fundamental and charity as essential. Its teachings should therefore find expression in acts designed to save others and must not sacrifice men for the sake of profit. It should aim at self-denial in order to maintain what is natural in mankind and not attach itself to external ornamentations that are the ruin of its principles. Yet during the three seasons [of farmwork], mountains are tunneled and the earth excavated—this is harmful to life[14]. . . . Treasuries are exhausted and storehouses emptied—this is harmful to mankind. . . . I consider that if expenditures on jewellery were curtailed to help the poor and the destitute, that would be to act in accordance with the very spirit of Buddhism. If one put an end to exhausting terracing works in order to preserve the insects, that would conform with the principle of Buddhist generosity. If one stopped the outlay on constructions to supply the [soldiers on the] frontiers, that would conform with the efficacious policies of T'ang and Wu-wang (the founders of the Shang and Chou dynasties).[15]

The occasional free distributions of aid in times of scarcity by monks met with the authorities' approval: they helped to restrain the instability of the peasant population that represented one of the greatest threats to dynasties.

The moralizing influence of the monks in the countryside was also considered with approbation. Traditional peasant festivals were occasions for drinking bouts, excessive feasting, and a licentiousness that shocked those who had been raised in the observance of the rites. The Buddhist monks, at least those among them who had any notion of their religion, made an effort to introduce some moderation into these extravagant manifestations. Their first concern was to bring the peasants to renounce blood sacrifices and heavy drinking at these village fairs.[16] The Buddhist interdiction of the slaughter of animals was in agreement with the traditional moral doctrine of the literati. Indeed, as a result of the diffusion of Buddhist teachings, the imperial authorities condemned the sacrifice of animals during the peasant gatherings on the altar of the God of the Soil. And they instituted months during which slaughtering was prohibited.

> On the ten days of *chai* [Buddhist fasts and vegetarian feasts] of each month, the slaughter of animals is forbidden. In the villages, however, private soil god associations frequently kill animals for their banquets. This is intolerable to well-thinking people. The practice must be permanently discontinued.[17]

Emperor T'ai-tsung of the Northern Wei (409–424) decreed that the śramaṇa guide and instruct the laity and the common people.[18] In 452, the emperor Wen-ch'eng fixed by decree the number of monks to be ordained each year and added: "These religious shall be sufficient in number to exercise a good moral influence and to spread the Buddhist doctrine.[19] A decree of 472 granted passes to monks permitting them to go among the people "to convert them," that is, to inculcate them with the basic principles of Buddhist moral teaching.[20] In 731 Emperor Hsüan-tsung declared:

> We are concerned about practices that, having spread throughout China, undermine the supreme order. Everything is sacrificed for the sake of obtaining a favorable rebirth; all possessions are spent in order to procure blessings. Before the future effects of these pious works become discernible, present patrimonies are squandered: a deplorable fashion, and yet [its adherents] show no regret for their deeds. Fools

and the simpleminded thereby become liable to imperial punish-
ments. Thanks to our monks today, this folly has only increased.
With their public sermons about karmic causality (yin-yüan chiang-
shuo) they confuse the minds of the villagers. Their cupidity is boundless; their only preoccupation is to amass riches. While fords and
bridges are deteriorating, their religion, which is of no use to humanity, prospers undisturbed. They [the monks] agonize the laity. Some
are influential enough to wander from prefecture to county [unhin-
dered], others tour villages and districts engaging in unrestrained
indoctrination. They gather crowds [of listeners]. At times they are
even accommodated [by lay followers]. As of now, all this, excepting
the predicants on discipline, shall be prohibited.[21]

That last exception is significant. The ruling class was not opposed to
Buddhism as doctrine or opposed to the precepts that underlay its
moral teaching: not to kill, not to steal, not to commit adultery, not
to lie, not to inebriate oneself. Indeed, none of the positive aspects of
that moral doctrine—charity and compassion—contradicted the traditional precepts. The literati's condemnation was directed against
the improper application of the theory of the return on pious deeds,
the personal and material sacrifices, and the heterodox practices and
doctrines that spread among the people as a result of the Buddhist
movement. For these were harmful to the morale and the tranquillity
of rural populations.

Religious Pragmatism

The literati thus manifested a clear tendency to use Buddhism for
their own ends. Charitable works, moral propaganda, the reformist
sects' effort to encourage austerity, all this accorded with the traditional views of the literati. To the extent that it was orthodox and regulated, Buddhism provided a support for the official authorities. At
the same time, members of the ruling class expected assistance of a
religious nature from the monks and the supernatural powers that the
Buddhist cult brought into play. Buddhism had its place in the religious ceremonies of the court,[22] which explains why it was never radically and entirely proscribed. The Buddhist cult served the protection
of the dynasty in the same way as Chinese indigenous rites. The official communities were responsible for celebrating the imperial birth-
days and ceremonies on behalf of the empire. The aim of the literati
was not to proscribe Buddhism entirely but to reduce the number of

its monasteries and monks to the strict minimum that was indispensable for ensuring the celebrations of the official cult.

After having decided "to abolish Buddhism and Taoism everywhere," Emperor Wu of the Chou declared in the sixth month of the third year of Chien-te (574) that 120 eminent monks, who appear to have been spared the measures of repression, would be transformed into literati-officials. Wu-ti's ambition was plainly to fully integrate Buddhism and Taoism into the political organization of the state. A monk named Tao-an died as a result of a hunger strike protesting his "bureaucratization."[23] He is the only case where an official sacrilege was allowed to go to such extremes.

> At the end of the Ta-li era (766–780), P'eng Yen was appointed undersecretary of the Criminal Administration Bureau. At that time, the civil governor of Tung-ch'uan, in the region of Chien-nan (government seat in modern Ch'eng-tu, Szechwan), Li Shu-ming, memorialized the emperor about the uselessness of Buddhism under the present circumstances and requested permission to purge (ch'eng-t'ai) the Buddhist and Taoist monasteries in Tung-ch'uan. He asked at the same time that two categories [of monasteries] be established. The Buddhist establishments of the first category would house twenty religious; their Taoist counterparts, fourteen. Establishment of the second category would have their clergy reduced to seven. Care would be taken to select those of exemplary conduct; the others would be returned to lay life. The hermitages (lan-jo) and small sanctuaries (tao-ch'ang) that lacked official names would all be destroyed. Te-tsung declared that this project merited being implemented as a general rule throughout the empire, and not only in Chien-nan. He ordered the Department of State Affairs to convene a council [to discuss the matter].[24]

At the time of the great proscription of 845, the emperor decided to preserve four Buddhist monasteries at Ch'ang-an, with ten clergy per establishment, and two monasteries at Lo-yang. In each of the 34 regions under the administration of military or civil governors (chieh-tu shih and kuan-ch'a shih), and in the prefectures of T'ung-chou (Shansi), Hua-chou (Shansi), and Ju-chou (Honan), one monastery was to be preserved. As for the other prefectures under the administration of prefects (tz'u-shih), they are not permitted to have temples.[25]

The government always shied away from drastic steps that had the appearance of sacrilege. The following text, even though it comes from a Buddhist source, is indicative of the attitude of the emperors and their counselors:

In the fourth month of the ninth year of T'ai-ho (835), the academician Li Hsün presented a petition to abolish the palace chapel (*nei tao-ch'ang*) of the Ch'ang-sheng palace and to carry out a purge of irregular monks and nuns. Inauspicious omens prevented the implementation of these measures. In the seventh month, the same Li Hsün again requested that all the clergy be subjected to examinations in the sutra. However, accused to having plotted the demise of the eunuchs, [Li] was decapitated and the emperor ordered the clergy's exemption from all examinations. Meanwhile, the following year, the same emperor Wen-tsung declared to his ministers: "There are Buddhist monks who are of no benefit to the religion and who live as parasites on our country. Oh ministers, you may speak about them fully." One of them replied: "Since the time of your ancestors, Buddhism has flourished. Those in the dark habit [the clergy] have only increased in numbers. They are nothing but gnawing insects." The order was given to prohibit public recitations of the sutra. Thereupon, while boiling eggs for the imperial table, the cook heard small cries coming from the cauldron. Listening, he realized that the eggs were imploring the bodhisattva Avalokiteśvara. The emperor, having verified the matter, forbade the use of chicken eggs.[26]

The same reasons that justify the institution of an official Buddhist cult prevented its abolition. In the course of history, clear attempts were even made to deify emperors as buddha or bodhisattva. The monk Fa-kuo (d. 419), who under Emperor T'ai-tsu of the Wei was the first to hold the office of controller of Buddhist clergy,[27] was pleased to pronounce this point of view: "Our Emperor, who is intelligent and full of wisdom, holds Buddhism dear. Thus he is Tathāgata [the Buddha] manifest. The śramaṇa should honor him in the highest." He constantly saluted the emperor with his hands pressed together, saying to anyone prepared to listen: "The person best able to spread the holy doctrine is the master of mankind. It is not the Son of Heaven I salute: I am paying homage to the Buddha."[28] The practice of casting statues of the emperor in the image of the bodhisattva constitutes further evidence to the same effect, as does the idea, suggested by the monks to Wu Tse-t'ien, that the empress was a reincarnation of Maitreya.[29]

The government appears to have reacted to the religious movement only after the event, by imposing choices among sanctuaries that already existed. Similarly, they proceeded to carry out screenings among the monks. Religious powers with reputations of efficacy were annexed by the political authorities. Sanctuaries and monks exerted an attraction upon the lay world: for the rulers, it was a question, at the same time, of heightening a prestige that by rights exceeded any other and winning religious and moral powers over to their side by means of officials promotions and donations. These powers—this mana, one might say—could not be permitted to be used for private ends.

Thus in the memorials of the literati and the decrees of emperors a general attitude can be made out which is not fundamentally hostile to Buddhism, whether as cult or as doctrine. The idea that the new religion could serve the same ends as China's own classical moral doctrine and rites, and that it could be a useful ally of the imperial government, is in evidence here. The opposition of the literati was more qualified than it might appear at first sight. A priori, they were devoid of religious passion. However, whenever the Buddhist movement appeared as a spontaneous reaction against the traditional way of life and moral doctrine, the reaction was violent.

The hostility of the literati toward the religious movement was accentuated by the power struggles of rival factions at court. An ambivalence in the attitude of the emperors themselves should be underlined in this context: they combined within themselves the divergent aspirations of the nobility and the literati. Susceptible to the influence of their kin, and especially of the women of their harem, they were at the same time bound by the necessities of government to assimilate the views of a class that, by virtue of its traditional education, supplied the state with its administrators. They were obliged to prevent the distaff branches from exercising too much influence, for the latters' ambitions presented a constant threat to the stability of the empire. The fluctuations of Buddhist influence in China were thus to a lesser extent a consequence of sovereign and autonomous imperial policies than a function of corresponding fluctuations in political power between the great legitimist officials on the one hand and the emperor's kinsmen on the other. The political conflict was thus a reflection of a social conflict whose close connection with the history of Buddhism is beyond doubt.

CHAPTER TWELVE

INTERNAL CONTRADICTIONS IN THE
BUDDHIST MOVEMENT IN CHINA

Despite the repressive measures and the large-scale laicizations and destructions of sanctuaries, the Buddhist movement vigorously developed over a period of more than three centuries. Persecutions tend to have an energizing effect on religions. The Buddhist clergy did not fail to represent the attacks that were directed against the excesses of the church and the degradation of the monastic community as acts inspired by religious passion. The number of monks and sanctuaries scarcely varied in any event, and Buddhism usually recovered quickly after reform measures were imposed by emperors and their literati advisors.

The effects of one of the later repressions, however, in the years 843–845, seem to have been disastrous. Even though the orders to proceed with the destruction of the monasteries and the laicization of the clergy were not uniformly carried out in all parts of the empire, this virtually complete proscription was more efficient than its predecessors. Yet it seems to have merely contributed to a decline whose signs were already apparent for more than a century. An impending reaction on the part of the imperial authorities announced itself as early as the reign of Te-tsung (779–805).[1] Thus the repression of 845 can be said to have taken place within a larger historical context. Since the reign of Hsüan-tsung, religious fervor had become less absolute: the total self-sacrifices, excessive offerings, and building passion that characterized the late Northern Wei period in the first half of the sixth century, as well as the period of Empress Wu at the turn of the seventh and eighth centuries, had ceased. Doctrinal and artistic activities were in decline. There was in short less gratuitousness—with the religious and aesthetic implications that gratuitousness entails—and perhaps also more calculation. An important factor was that the growing unbelief among the upper classes, the milieus that actively promoted the religious movement—imperial kinsmen, eunuchs, and harem ladies—was related to their desire for enrichment. Since the beginning of the seventh century, imperial princesses had been selling preferential ordinations at high prices. The sale of ordination certificates, introduced in a moment of panic in 756 during the An Lu-shan rebellion, had been perpetuated during subsequent periods to the almost exclusive benefit of high provincial officials. From then on, entry into religion had for well-to-do peasants become nothing more than a means of evading their fiscal obligations. The management of Buddhist affairs was entrusted to the eunuchs and provided these, too, with opportunities for enrichment.

The importance of economic factors, linked to the decline of collective fervor, became more marked following the reconstruction of the monasteries and chapels and the renewal of ordinations after the repression of 845. The institution of private chapels, a privilege that emperors in time extended to all members of the upper classes, stood at the origin of an increasing appropriation of church property by the great families. It provided wealthy laymen with a pretext to interfere with the affairs of the saṃgha. Certain imperial decrees illustrate the practice, probably current under the Sung, of declaring official monasteries as family chapels:

> In the third year of Ta-kuan (1109), the emperor ordered that his meritorious subjects and kinsmen of the imperial family by marriage were to construct their private chapels (kung-te fen-ssu) and establish the fields set aside for the needs of their cult themselves. The emperor would restrict himself to granting them official names and tax exemptions. The monks who would perform the services were to be chosen by the families themselves, and it would not be permitted to improperly declare [already existing] monasteries in possession of a name bestowed by the emperor as private chapels.[2]

And a decree of 1137 states that "only small Buddhist buildings without official names may be transformed into private chapels."[3]

It would seem that the following note by Chih-p'an in the *Fo-tsu t'ung-chi* alludes to the improper spread of these "tomb-monasteries" (*fen-ssu*) and "sites of *bodhi*" (*p'u-t'i so*) in the middle of the thirteenth century:

> Today influential families, under the pretext of generosity, frequently seize monasteries [and their wealth]. Their sons, younger brothers, and stewards all take advantage of this to appropriate our property. They establish tombs ["sites of *bodhi*," presumably] attached to monasteries in the mountain, [even though] this means letting their [deceased] fathers and mothers suffer iniquity.[4] Throughout the year, they attempt to seize money, grain, bamboos, and trees [from the monasteries] as if these constituted their regular entitlement. They don't consider for a single day the sufferings they shall endure in hell to atone for this transgression. Literati and officials all assume that attitude, the unfortunates! They instruct their children accordingly and give moral lessons to their stewards. It is a slight profit for a great loss. Should they not be warned? Li I-chi [for having failed to restitute a loan made from the permanent assets of a monastery] became a monastery slave,[5] and that was an unusually light punishment. May it serve, now that worse faults are committed, to caution those who indulge in sins of this kind![6]

However, the monks themselves misappropriated consecrated property, despite the religious interdictions against profanations. In his *Pei-shan lu*,[7] the monk Shen-ch'ing (d. betw. 806–821) noted that the clergy in his time thought only of their advantage, forever eyeing the value of the permanent assets. Rich monks sought to obtain the management [of these assets] by corrupt means. Granaries emptied, fields fell fallow. Once installed, [the monks] maintained their positions, again by means of corruption. Should it befall them to be cited before the secular administration by their community, then the officials, whose complicity had been bought, returned the charges against the accusers. They lived in luxury, had fine harnesses, splendid carriages, and valets.[8]

In the course of the history of Buddhism, there undoubtedly always existed avaricious monks who busied themselves with trafficking. Commercial activities had been a vocation of Buddhism since its introduction into China. The sacred character of the common possessions of the saṃgha, however, seems to have normally protected them against appropriation by individuals. The facts reported by the *Pei-shan lu* speak to the development of new attitudes that were only to increase.

The underlying causes for the decadence of the disciplinary institutions, the corruption of the monastic community, and the ruin of the Buddhist patrimony must be sought in the internal contradictions within Buddhism itself and within the social milieus that were most supportive of Buddhism. Commercial activities were juxtaposed to religious activities in Chinese Buddhism. Loans and rents had to serve the same purpose as offerings. The functioning of these heterogeneous arrangements relied entirely on religious fervor. Furthermore, the secular promoters of the Buddhist movement, great families that were hostile to the Confucian tradition, imperial princesses and eunuchs, constituted a social group that had an interest in the acquisition of riches and commercial power. From the moment these milieus became aware of the private ends, political and economic, that their adherence to Buddhism enabled them to pursue—as soon as their detachment from the religion became more apparent—Buddhism began its decline in China. The degree of decay it reached rather quickly is known.

The power of the religious movement at its height was due to its expansion across the breadth of Chinese society and the multiplicity of the patronage system and religious groupings: disciples of eminent monks, peasants attached to monasteries and incorporated into the saṃgha, retainer-monks under the patronage of great families, communities sponsored by important personalities. This was the communion between disparate social classes that the great communal festivals and religious associations engendered, joining monks, influential families, and commoners. Economics, as we have seen, played a role in this complex web of relations, although the autonomous functioning and specific character associated with it in our modern societies was absent. However, a deep alteration of these structures took place under the T'ang, in the course of that eighth century which, in our view, marked the precise turning point in the history of Buddhism in China.[9] At that time, we also witness the formation of a social class of farmers and agricultural laborers. This historic process can be regarded as at one and the same time the signal and the cause of a new conception of social relations. Henceforth one was negotiating as between employers and employees. In the fiscal domain, a more exclusively monetary economy was in the making. The individual search for profit can legitimately be associated with an ever more accentuated isolation of the social classes. Buddhism developed its patronage system by adapting itself to ancient structures. The col-

lapse of these structures had a dissolving effect on a religious phenomenon that derived its strength from its universality. Other factors
must no doubt be taken into account, such as the closure of the routes
of communication with Central Asia, the nationalistic reaction that
followed the An Lu-shan rebellion, and the rise of the Neo-Confucian
movement. Yet as far as religion is concerned, the social realities are
always decisive.

CHRONOLOGICAL TABLE

Eastern Chin 317–420

NORTHERN AND SOUTHERN DYNASTIES

SOUTH	NORTH
Sung 420–479	Northern Wei 386–534
Ch'i 479–502	
Liang 502–557	Eastern Wei 535–550
	Western Wei 535–557
Ch'en 557–589	Northern Ch'i 550–577
	Northern Chou 557–581

Sui 581–618

T'ang 618–907

FIVE DYNASTIES

Later Liang 907–923
Later T'ang 923–936
Later Chin 936–946
Later Han 947–950
Later Chou 951–960
Northern Sung 960–1127

SOUTH	NORTH
Southern Sung 1127–1279	Liao 907–1125
	Chin 1115–1234

WEIGHTS AND MEASURES

Length	Chin Equivalent	T'ang Equivalent
1 *ts'un* (inch)	ca. 2.4 cm	ca. 3 cm
1 *ch'ih* (foot)	ca. 24 cm	ca. 30 cm
1 *chang* (10 *ch'ih*)	ca. 2.4 m	ca. 3 m
1 *li* (1,800 *ch'ih*)	ca. 432 m	ca. 450 m

Area	Chin Equivalent	T'ang Equivalent
1 *mu*	?	ca. 0.14 acre
1 *ch'ing* (100 *mu*)	?	ca. 14 acres

Capacity	Chin Equivalent	T'ang Equivalent
1 *ko*	ca. 0.02 l	ca. 60 ml
1 *sheng*	ca. 0.2 l	ca. 600 ml
1 *tou* (bushel)	ca. 2 l	ca. 6 l
1 *shih/hu* (10 *tou*)	ca. 20 l	ca. 60 l

Weight	Chin Equivalent	T'ang Equivalent
1 *liang* (tael)	ca. 14 grams	ca. 40 grams
1 *chin* (pound)	ca. 224 grams	ca. 640 grams

Standard Length of Cloth	Chin Equivalent	T'ang Equivalent
1 *p'i* (bolt)	?	ca. 1.8 x 40 *ch'ih* (silk)
		ca. 1.8 x 50 *ch'ih* (hemp)

Copper Currency Units
1000 *ch'ien* (cash) = 1 standard *kuan* (string of cash)

PRICES

Commodity	Mazār-tāgh (ca. 720)[1]	Tun-huang (745)[2]	Tun-huang (before 756?)[3]
A *tou* of wheat (*hsiao-mai*)	30 cash	32 or 37	49
Green wheat [oats] (*ch'ing-mai*)		30 or 35	33
Millet (*su*)	15	27 or 32	34
Another kind of millet (*mi*)		27 or 32	33
Peas (*wan-tou*)		29 or 34	35
A roll[4] of raw silk (*sheng-chüan*)		465	
Of Honan silk (*Honan fu shih*)		620	
Of unembellished red silk (*man-fei*)		550	
Of unembellished green silk (*man-lü*)		460	
A *t'un* (ca. 250 grams) of silk wadding (*ta-mien*)		150	
A roll of scoured silk (*ta-lien*)		460	
Of boiled silk from Shan-chün (*Shan-chün shu-shih*)		600	

Some Prices in Ninth and Tenth Century Tun-huang According to Sales and Loan Contracts[5]

Wheat [or sometimes barley] (*mai*) and millet (*su*) had
the same value;
Hemp (*huang-ma*) was worth twice the price of these cereals;
A *ch'ih* of cotton cloth (*pu*) was worth 1 *tou* (6 l) of these cereals;
A cow or an ox sold for ca. 15 *shih* (9 hectoliters) of cereals;[6]
A house cost between 30 and 70 *shih*.[7]

NOTES TO APPENDIX C

1. Chavannes, *Les documents chinois*, pp. 205–16.

2. P. 3348. Purchases made by the supply corps of the Tou-lu Army (see des Rotours, *Traité des fonctionnaires*, pp. 798–803). In the edition of this manuscript in the *Tun-huang to-so*, no. 66, pp. 261 ff., the reading *sheng* (the hundredth part of a *shih*) is certainly an error for *tou* (ca. 6 l).

3. P. 2826 v°.

4. At Tun-huang, the silk rolls were 60 cm wide on average. Their length varied between 23 and 26 *ch'ih* (ca. 7.5 m) or, more frequently, between 37 and 40 *ch'ih* (ca. 11 m). The prices indicated here must refer to the smaller rolls.

5. For further indications concerning measures and prices at Tun-huang, see Erik Trombert, *Le crédit en Chine d'aprés les contrats de Dunhuang*, Paris: Collège de France, forthcoming.

6. S. 5820 and 5826.

7. P. 3331. *Tun-huang shih-shih hsieh-ching t'i-chi yü Tun-huang tsa-lu* 2.132.

NOTES

Introduction

1. *Hsü kao-seng chuan* 25.651a.

2. I was fortunate to have direct access to the Chinese manuscripts from Tun-huang in the Pelliot Collection of the Bibliothèque Nationale in Paris. During the years 1951–1955, I completed the first volume of the catalogue of that collection (nos. 2001–2500), in collaboration with my friend Wu Chi-yü. The manuscript of that volume was awarded the Prix du Budget de l'Académie des Inscriptions et Belles-Lettres in 1957, and the Bibliothèque Nationale accepted its publication by the Singer-Polignac Foundation in 1970.

3. Maspero, *La religion chinoise*, p. 83: "Buddhism and Taoism spent their strength fighting one another; each was sufficiently powerful to prevent the triumph of the other but not to ensure its own."

4. Moreover, in the seventh and eighth centuries the same wealthy families constructed both Buddhist and Taoist temples, while the official cult called simultaneously on the services of the two communities.

5. See de Groot, *Sectarianism*.

1. The Immediate Facts

1. City situated to the west of modern Lin-chang hsien in Honan.

2. *Pien-cheng lun* 3.507b. See also *Fa-yüan chu-lin* 100.1025a. As the total number of establishments indicates, these figures must apply to the period around 534. See the table below.

3. *Pien-cheng lun* 3.503c.

4. On this question, see pp. 298–306.

5. Cf. the request made by Amoghavajra that the chapel (*fo-t'ang*) built by an association of the faithful in Hsi-ho be transformed into a monastery and bestowed an official name by the emperor. See p. 265 above. The bestowal of an official name (*ssu-o*) often occurred some time after the foundation. The monastery Pu-kuang in

Ch'ang-an, for example, was founded in the fifth year of Chen-kuan (631) by the heir apparent of the T'ang, and received the name of Ch'ung-hsing ssu in the first year of Shen-lung (705), after the creation of a Ch'ung-hsing monastery in each of the two capitals and in every prefecture had been decreed by the emperor.

6. On the subsequent regularization of the status of certain monks, see p. 10 above.

7. *Lo-yang ch'ieh-lan chi* 999a.

8. *Shih-chia fang-chih* B.973c.

9. *Nan shih* 70.11a–b, report by Kuo Tsu-chen.

10. *Pien-cheng lun* 3.503a–c, for the four southern dynasties, Sung, Ch'i, Liang, and Ch'en.

11. For the southern dynasties see *Shih-chia fang-chih* B.974a–c, in addition to *Pien-cheng lun* 3.

12. "Shih-Lao chih," *Wei shu* 114.3039.

13. Ibid.

14. "Shih-Lao chih," *Wei shu* 114.3042. De Groot, *Sectarianism* 1:33, understands 13,727 monks and nuns, but Ware's translation in "Wei Shou on Buddhism," p. 163, is more plausible. See also *Ts'e-fu yüan-kuei* 51.12a.

15. "Shih-Lao chih," *Wei shu* 114.3048: "After the Cheng-kuang era (520–525), there were altogether two million monks and nuns and the monasteries numbered more than thirty thousand." The *Fo-tsu t'ung-chi* 38.356b gives these figures for the year 542.

16. *Li-tai san-pao chi* 9.94b. Cf. *Fo-tsu t'ung-chi* 38.358c, year 574: two million returned to lay status in the territory of Chou, and ibid., year 576, where this figure rises to three millions after the conquest of the kingdom of Ch'i by the Chou. At that time, many monks sought refuge under the Ch'en in the South. We have to assume, then, that the figure of thirty-two thousand religious indicated for the Ch'en dynasty antedates the years 574–576.

17. *Pien-cheng lun* 3.509b–c.

18. *Fo-tsu t'ung-chi* 39.360a. Cf. *Hsü kao-seng chuan* 10.501c.

19. The *Shih-chia fang-chih* gives the figure of 236,200.

20. This should include the total number of monasteries founded, and the total number of religious ordained, under the Sui.

21. *Kuang-hung ming-chi* 7.134c: seventy thousand Buddhist and Taoist monks and nuns. At least fifty thousand of these can be assumed to have been Buddhists.

22. Estimate of Fu I. Cf. ibid. 134b. According to the same passage, there were at that time "84,000 monasteries and stūpa."

23. *Ta tz'u-en ssu San-tsang fa-shih chuan* 7.259a.

24. *Fa-yüan chu-lin* 100.1027c.

25. *T'ang hui-yao* 49.863; *T'ang liu-tien* 4.16a; *Chiu T'ang shu* 43.1831 (commentary): "The total number of *ssu* (monasteries) was 5,358 of which 3,235 were for monks and 2,122 were nunneries [sic]."

26. *Fo-tsu t'ung-chi* 42.385a: "In the fourth year of T'ai-ho, the Bureau of Sacrifices requested that all monks and nuns who were not regularly ordained should be permitted to register in order to receive, upon due examination, their official ordination certificates. Those who registered numbered seven hundred thousand." The *Ta Sung seng-shih lüeh* B.247c dates this measure 830.

27. *T'ang hui-yao* 49.864; *Fan-ch'uan wen-chi* 10.9a; *Chiu T'ang shu* 18A.604; *Tzu-chih t'ung-chien* 248.8015. The *Fo-tsu t'ung-chi* 42.386b gives the figure of 260,500 resident monks and nuns in the monasteries. The "Ho fei-hui zhu-ssu te-yin piao" (in *Li Wei-kung Hui-ch'ang i-p'in chi*, "Pieh-chi" 20.166) states: "We have today received the imperial order to destroy 46,000 monasteries and *araya* and to

return more than 410,000 monks, nuns, and slaves to the status of peasants liable to the Two Taxes [in grain and in cloth]. Several thousand *ch'ing* of high quality arable land have been confiscated." The figures given for the years 843–845 refer to laicized clergy; the size of the entire monastic community must have been larger.

28. *Wu-tai hui-yao* 16.5b. The sum of the numbers of monasteries destroyed (3,336) and surviving (2,694) equals 6,030.

29. *Fo-tsu t'ung-chi* 53.465c. Cf. ibid. 44.406c: "That year (1021), the number of Buddhist monks amounted to 397,615 and that of the nuns to 61,240 (i.e., a total of 458,855)."

30. Ibid. 48.435a.

31. "Shih-Lao chih," *Wei shu* 114.3045. Rules established by the *sha-men t'ung* Hui-shen and other ecclesiastical dignitaries.

32. According to *Kuang hung-ming chi* 7.134b, there were eighty-four thousand monasteries and stūpa around the year 624. It may be assumed that half of these sanctuaries (reliquaries in particular) were uninhabited. Nevertheless, some stūpa, storeyed towers containing relics, had a staff of monks attached for their maintenance, or "sweeping and watering." Cf. the petition of Amoghavajra in which he requests the official ordination of four unregistered monks (*wu-ming*), to be assigned to the maintenance of a stūpa in Lung-men, *Tai-tsung ch'ao tseng ssu-k'ung ta pien-cheng kuang-chih san-tsang ho-shang piao chih chi* 2.836a–b.

33. Probably at the beginning of the reign of Hsüan-tsung.

34. The figure of 6,030 religious houses in 955 corresponds to the 2,694 surviving monasteries that had received the imperial conferral of an official name (the most important, no doubt) and to the 3,336 private places of worship (*wu-ch'ih ssu yüan*) that had been destroyed. The consequences of the measures taken in 842–845 were still apparent a century later: the restitution of the Buddhist patrimony in buildings of the period before the destructions ordered by the T'ang emperor Wu-tsung had neither been possible nor considered desirable.

35. Here we have two concordant indicators, for the North and for the South, which are useful for delimiting the period of great fervor under the Nan-pei ch'ao: the first half of the sixth century marks one of the moments in which religious enthusiasm reached a peak in China, and perhaps also that in which China was most passionately Buddhist. See pp. 232–33.

36. By all indications it was particularly at the end of the seventh and during the very first years of the eighth centuries that building recommenced. Hsüan-tsung, at his accession, slowed, rather, the development of Buddhism; the available figures refer undoubtedly to the beginning of his reign. It should also be pointed out that, since the censuses have a bearing on official establishments only, variations in the number of the latter do not necessarily reflect significant variations in construction.

37. That is, the dean (*shang-tso*), the abbot (*ssu-chu*), and the overseer (*wei-na*). The sources show that the emperor did indeed appoint monks to these three posts for each official establishment.

38. It appears that, above all, the destruction affected the stūpa: "East and west of the passes and the mountains," reads *Li-tai fa-pao chi* 11.94b, "everything that had been constructed over the centuries in the way of Buddhist stūpa, whether officially or privately, was destroyed. The land was swept clear of them. The pious images were melted down. The sacred texts were burned. All the monasteries of the eight *chou*, numbering more than forty thousand, were given by the emperor to the princes and dukes to serve as mansions."

39. In 624, the stūpa and monasteries numbered to 84,000. See n. 32 above.

40. *Kuan-chung ch'uang-li chieh-t'an t'u ching* 813c.

41. *Hsü kao-seng chuan* 29.695a, biography of Chu-li.

42. *Nittō guhō junrei gyōki* ch. 1, K'ai-ch'eng 4 (839), nineteenth day of the inter-calary first month; Reischauer, *Record of a Pilgrimage*, p. 79. Other indications: thirty religious at the K'ai-yüan ssu in Yang-chou (modern Chiang-tu in Kiangsu), first day, eighth month, of the third year of K'ai-ch'eng (838); five religious at the Lu-shan ssu in Mou-p'ing hsien (in modern Shantung), namely the *san-kang* (dean, abbot, and overseer), the *tien-tso*, and the *chih-sui* (steward for the year), twenty-seventh day, second month, fifth year K'ai-ch'eng (840).

43. P. 2250, v°.

44. Another manuscript, P. 3947, gives the figure of 41.

45. A London manuscript, which dates from the Tibetan occupation of Sha-chou in 800, S. 2729, for reasons unknown gives considerably lower figures: Lung-hsing, twenty-eight monks; K'ai-yüan, thirteen; Ch'ien-yüan, nineteen; Yung-an, eleven; Chin-kuang ming, sixteen.

46. P. 5579.

47. P. 3167 v°, dated 895.

48. P. 3600.

49. Ibid. The number of nuns in one of the two monasteries which are not mentioned, the Sheng-kuang ssu and the Lung-hsiu ssu, is unknown.

50. P. 2368.

51. The figures indicate that the concentration of religious per monastery or chapel was higher in large towns than in the provinces (it appears also that they were higher in the South: nineteen, sixteen, twenty-nine, and twenty-six monks and nuns per establishment). At the end of the Northern Wei dynasty (389–534), Yang Hsüan-chih counted at Lo-yang 1,367 major and minor "monasteries" (*Lo-yang ch'ieh-lan chi* 1022a). More than a thousand of these were undoubtedly no more than small sanctuaries. Lo-yang was at that time a city of thirty-five wards (*li*) with more than 109,000 families and a population of probably close to half a million. Assuming that the average number of clergy per establishment remained around twenty, there would thus have been more than 27,000 Buddhist monks and nuns at Lo-yang, or 5–6 percent of the population of that great city.

52. *Hsü kao-seng chuan* 25.666c.

53. *Ts'e-fu yüan-kuei* 159.15b, decree of the second month, tenth year of K'ai-yüan (722).

54. The following constitutes evidence of the fact that the censuses at the beginning of the T'ang represented only regular monks in residence at official monasteries: In the twenty-second year of Chen-kuan (648) 17,000 religious were officially ordained at the request of Hsüan-tsang, who had returned from India three years earlier. Five were ordained in each monastery. There would thus have been 3,400 monasteries, a figure that accords approximately with that provided for the period (3,716 in 648). See *Ta tz'u-en ssu San-tsang fa-shih chuan* 7.259a.

55. A fragment of a census survives which was found at Tun-huang. This document (P. 2897), which must date from the ninth or tenth century, bears a seal that reads: "Seal of the director-general of Buddhist monks of Ho-hsi" (district founded in 711, with its government seat in Liang-chou, Kansu. See des Rotours, *Traité des fonctionnaires*, p. 803, n. 1). It is entitled: "Census of the monks and nuns of the seventeen monasteries [of Sha-chou] belonging to the territory under our administration." The list begins with the monastery Lung-hsing, but unfortunately only the names of the first two monks remain, together with their titles and functions in the community.

56. These may have been the ordinations requested by Hsüan-tsang in 648. See note above.

57. He was *wu-kuan*, i.e., unregistered. One also encounters the expression *wu-chi*, especially under the Wei.

58. *Hsü kao-seng chuan* 27.680c. Another example dates from the Chou period: in 567, the monk Fa-tsang enrolled in the official register on the occasion of the ordinations decreed by Emperor Ming. See ibid. 19.580c.

59. I.e., religious who were not enrolled in the official registers. See pp. 37–42 above.

60. Biography of Su Kuei, *Hsin T'ang shu* 125.4397–99.

61. *Kuang hung-ming chi* 7.134b.

62. For the global population figures, see Bielenstein, *The Census of China*.

63. On the increase of cultivated land under the Nan-pei ch'ao, see the indications provided by Wang Yi-t'ong, "Slaves," pp. 332–33 and note. On the improvement of agricultural tools, see Hsü Chung-shu, "On Some Agricultural Implements," p. 1159.

64. See p. 142.

65. In his "Yüan-tao," *Ch'üan T'ang wen* 558.7170; biography in *Chiu T'ang shu* 160.4195–204.

66. The myth of antiquity haunted the spirits of all those educated in the classical tradition. Their perception of antiquity was purely conventional, for social and economic conditions scarcely resembled those of the Han, much less of earlier times.

67. *Wen-hsien t'ung-k'ao* 23.17a.

68. *Fan-ch'uan wen-chi* 10.8b–9a. Yüan Chen (779–831) estimated that nine out of ten persons were unproductive (*yu-shih*). See *Yüan-shih Ch'ang-ch'ing chi* 28.4a.

69. We are dealing here with one of those forms of calculation that are entirely unmathematical but that the Chinese nevertheless seem to find persuasive, or to which they attribute at least some practical value. In the accounts of the monasteries at Tun-huang, produce of very different value are added together (oil and bran, for example). Here, the reference is to the number of nonagricultural classes, not to the relative size of each social group.

70. In practice, owing to the nature of the available sources, it is difficult to separate the general economic from the fiscal aspects.

71. *Kuang hung-ming chi* 6.127c.

72. See p. 104.

73. One did not not visit monasteries only to admire the beauty of certain structures and statues; in T'ang times, there were also amateurs of Buddhist statuettes. See p. 24.

74. Many of these undoubtedly devoted themselves to usury, commerce, or the exploitation of the magical arts (see pp. 197–200 above), but this does not affect the essential point, concerning the relationship between those engaged in working the land and the nonagricultural population.

75. *Kuang hung-ming chi* 6.127b.

76. "Shih-Lao chih," *Wei shu* 114.3043. Ware, "Wei Shou," translates as "days of labor," but it seems more probable that the figure refers to a sum of cash.

77. "Shih-Lao chih," *Wei shu* 114.3039.

78. Ibid. 3045. The rank of *sha-men t'ung* was the highest in the monastic hierarchy at the time.

79. *Lo-yang ch'ieh-lan chi* 1022a. It should be remembered, however, that after the massacre of the aristocracy of Lo-yang in 528, the survivors transformed their residences into monasteries in order to protect their properties.

80. Ibid. 1.1000a. Cf. Jenner, *Memories of Lo-yang*, pp. 148–49; Wang Yi-t'ung, *Buddhist Monasteries of Lo-yang*, pp. 15–16.

81. See p. 4 above.

82. *Lo-yang ch'ieh-lan chi* 2.1007a; Jenner, op. cit., p. 189.

83. "Shih-Lao chih," *Wei shu* 114.3038.
84. See Ware, "Wei Shou," pp. 150, 167–69, 174–78.
85. "Shih-Lao chih," *Wei shu* 114.3038.
86. See p. 234 below.
87. "Shih-Lao chih," *Wei shu* 114.3038. See also Ware, "Wei Shou," p. 149.
88. See pp. 19ff.
89. *Fa-yüan chu-lin* 100.1027c.
90. Annual tax revenues in money amounted to two million strings of cash in 748–755 (see Balazs, "Beiträge," 34:58). This constitutes a point of reference, even though taxes in cash still formed only a small fraction of public revenues at that time.
91. *Chiu T'ang shu* 88.2870, biography of Wei Ssu-li.
92. Ibid. 118.3418, biography of Wang Chin.
93. Pieces of metal that were fixed to projecting walls and resonated in the wind.
94. *Tai-tsung ch'ao tseng ssu-k'ung ta pien-cheng kuang-chih san-tsang ho-shang piao chih chi* 5.851b.
95. *Chiu T'ang shu* 101.3145, biography of Wei Ts'ou.
96. As Taoism organized itself into a great religion on the Buddhist model, it benefited in due course from the spending passion that was originally characteristic of the Buddhist movement.
97. *San-fu*: these prefectures corresponded roughly to the capital territory, see des Rotours, *Traité des fonctionnaires*, p. 553, note.
98. *Chiu T'ang shu* 183.4741–42, biography of Hsüeh Huai-i. On the gigantic construction works directed by Hsüeh, see also Forte, *Mingtang*.
99. *Fo-tsu t'ung-chi* 39.367a: "In the second year of Hsien-ch'ing, the emperor ordered the establishment of the Hsi-ming monastery. It had thirty large halls and four thousand storeyed pavilions and covered galleries."
100. "Chien Chung-tsung chih kung-chu fu-kuan shu," *Wen-yüan ying-hua* 698.4345–46.
101. See p. 172.
102. Chavannes, "Documents chinois," in Stein, *Ancient Khotan*, appendix A, pp. 205–16, no. 969–72. On the date of these manuscripts, see Maspero, *Documents chinois*, p. 187, note to no. 460.
103. See pp. 188–89.
104. See p. 168.
105. *Chiu T'ang shu* 48A.2103.
106. See p. 211.
107. See Balazs, "Traité économique," p. 232, n. 216; Yang Lien-sheng, *Money and Credit*, p. 2.
108. This was suggested by E. Balazs who considered that certain monasteries in the Yangtze valley, remote from the great arteries of communication, were ideal haunts for the illegal minting of cash ("Beiträge," vol. 35). That region was at any rate a traditional counterfeiting center.
109. *Chiu T'ang shu* 17A.517. In 829, copper casting of Buddhist statues was prohibited by decree, see *T'ang hui-yao* 49.861; *Hsin T'ang shu* 54.1390.
110. Balazs, "Beiträge," p. 237, n. 228.
111. See *Hsü kao-seng chuan* 19.581a; cf. *Pei shih* 53.1914.
112. *T'ang hui-yao* 49.861–62; *Chiu T'ang shu* 18A.605; *Fo-tsu t'ung-chi* 42.386a: "Gold and silver statues were to be made over to the Board of Finance, iron statues to be transformed into agricultural implements, and copper statues, bells, and chimes founded for coining money."
113. *T'ang hui-yao* 49.862.
114. *Fo-tsu t'ung-chi* 42.392b. To leave no doubt in the minds of his ministers,

the emperor explained that this did not in any way constitute a measure against Buddhism, "for how could these statues be the Buddha?" Rulers frequently affected the view that Buddhism was no more than a set of moral injunctions, an encouragement to charity. From that point of view, icons were useless and even harmful, for they distracted the mind from the essential.

115. *Wei shu* 19B.480, biography of Prince Ch'eng of Jen-ch'eng (467–519); a partial citation is included in "Shih-Lao chih," *Wei shu* 114.3044.

116. Under the Wei, a pound (*chin*) was only about a third of the unit's weight of 680 grams in the year 672 (on the latter, see Balazs, "Beiträge," 36:44).

117. "Shih-Lao chih," *Wei shu* 114.3037–38; *Kuang hung-ming chi* 2.104a.

118. "Shih-Lao chih," *Wei shu* 114.3036; *Fo-tsu t'ung-chi* 38.355a. The same imperial edict is mentioned in *Kuang hung-ming chi* 2.103c for the year 454. The Chung-hua ed. of the "Shih-Lao chih" cites the textual variant "25,000 pounds" for "250,000" (n. 18). The practice of casting Buddhist statues in the likeness of deceased emperors (*teng-shen fo*) had a tradition in Chinese history. Cf. *Fo-tsu t'ung-chi* 39.362a: In 618 three statues in the likeness of emperors were carved in sandalwood; *Chiu T'ang shu* 118.3418: Emperor Tai-tsung placed the thrones [and statues?] of the seven emperors after Kao-tsu [in the inner chapel].

119. *Kao-seng chuan* 13.412c.

120. *Fa-hua chuan-chi* 5.71a, biography of Seng-hung. Cf. *Kao-seng chuan* 13.410c.

121. Possibly the shortage of metals was felt earlier in the South than in the North, i.e., from the end of the Chin as the imperial edict of 416 suggests. In 435, under the Sung, Hsiao Mu-chih had similarly proposed that all projects for casting statues should first be reported to the imperial government. See p. 15.

122. Some statuettes were used for magical purposes, to which Fu I alludes incidentally in one of his memorials (ca. 624): "The monks and nuns made multicolored silk clothing with which they decked out clay statuettes to expel demons" (*Chiu T'ang shu* 79.2716, biography of Fu I). "Some," said Yao Ch'ung (ibid. 96.3028), "have statues made in the likeness of deceased persons and call this 'to secure blessings [for the dead]' (*chui-fu*)." The same practice is also found in the imperial cult. Furthermore, a rich folklore was associated with the statues in sanctuaries: statues that exuded, walked, nodded, emitted light, displaced themselves, could not be displaced, etc.

123. Literally, they do not worry about "the causes and fruits."

124. According to Buddhist theory, which affirms that in every act good and evil either cancel each other out or prevail one over the other.

125. *Kuang hung-ming chi* 28.329b.

126. *Hsiang-fa chüeh-i ching* 1337c. This work probably originated in the Sect of the Three Stages.

127. The character *lin* is no doubt a graphic error for *ts'un*.

128. *Ts'e-fu yüan-kuei* 159.12a. This decree, also mentioned in *Fo-tsu t'ung-chi* 40.373b, is reproduced with variants of detail in *T'ang hui-yao* 49.861: "If one must contemplate the venerable aspect of the Buddha," adds the *T'ang hui-yao* text, "nothing prevents him from going to do him homage in a monastery; and if one is in need of sacred texts for recitation, let him go and borrow them in a monastery. If the copies are rare, the monks will transcribe them for laymen."

129. *Hsü tzu-chih t'ung-chien* 7, "Sung chi" 4a.

2. The Secondary Facts

1. *San-kuo chih* 49.1185, biography of Liu Yao. See also p. 295.

2. *Po-chang ch'ing-kuei i-chi* 4.298a. The rules instituted by Master Huai-hai of Mount Po-chang for the benefit of Dhyāna communities were much reworked. We

possess the Yüan version as revised and corrected by the monk Te-hui, entitled *Ch'ih-hsiu Po-chang ch'ing-kuei*.

3. Huai-hai lived from 720 to 814; the first official *printing* of the Buddhist canon dates only from the end of the tenth century. See Demiéville, *Milindapañha*, pp. 181–84.

4. These were undoubtedly official deeds granting privileges to certain establishments or monks.

5. On minor offenses, the religious were to be judged by their peers. See the decree promulgated in 508 by Shih-tsung of the Northern Wei, in "Shih-Lao chih," *Wei shu* 114.3040; Ware, "Wei Shou," p. 158.

6. *Po-chang ch'ing-kuei i-chi*, ibid.

7. *Chin-shih ts'ui-pien* 118.1a.

8. One of the taxes to which monks were liable under the Sung bore precisely that name. See p. 34.

9. *Kuang hung-ming chi* 7.132b. For a reply by the "one-time monk" Wang Ming-kuang to the plan of Wei Yüan-sung, see ibid. 10.157a ff. It is dated the seventeenth day of the second month, first year of Ta-hsiang (579).

10. No doubt these corvées were military in nature. During the anti-Buddhist repression of 574–577, monks were rounded up to be enlisted as soldiers: "At that time," notes the biography of P'u-an, "severe [measures were carried out] for drafting recruits [for the army]. For every monk captured there was a reward of ten bales (*tuan*) of linen." See *Hsü kao-seng chuan* 27.681a.

11. *Fo-tsu t'ung-chi* 38.353a.

12. This had already ceased to be the case in the second half of the seventh century. See des Rotours, *Traité des fonctionnaires*, p. 773: "Since the reigns of Kao-tsung and the empress Wu, the empire had for a long time experienced no shortage of troops."

13. These figures are exaggerated, see above, p. 13.

14. The terms *lü* (battalion) here stands perhaps for *t'uan*, a unit of two hundred men. See des Rotours, *Traité des fonctionnaires*, p. 764, note.

15. *Kuang hung-ming chi* 7.134c.

16. *Fo-tsu t'ung-chi* 39.362c, eighth year of Wu-te.

17. *Kuang hung-ming chi* 7.134b. See also ibid., p. 134a: "The *I-ching* says, 'When male and female unite their seed, the ten thousand beings are born.' This is the great symbol of [the cooperation of] yin and yang, of [the succession of] father and son, and of [the union of] heaven and earth. It must not be thwarted. Now there are vigorous monks and pretty nuns who, lacking in propriety, do not marry. They practice voluntary abortion and thus reduce the number of families. Is this not wrong?" Knowing that his proposals would not be adopted, Fu I often had no other ambition than to infuriate the clergy and the faithful.

18. Balazs, "Beiträge," 36:16, nn. 27 and 29.

19. This constitutes an indirect admission of the diminishing fiscal revenues from the end of the eighth century onward. There had been more than five million taxable families on the eve of the An Lu-shan rebellion in 754 and 755. In the Ta-li reign period, there were no more than 1,800,000. See Balazs, "Beiträge," 34:15, 16. However, even counting only regular tax revenues from registered sedentary households (*pien-hu*), P'eng Yen's estimate seems exaggerated.

20. *Chiu T'ang shu* 127.3580-81, biography of P'eng Yen. See also *T'ang hui-yao* 47.837.

21. This tax was also paid by some of the laity.

22. See *Sung shih*, "Shih-huo chih," ch. 177, "I-fa"; "Seng-tao mien-ting ch'ien," *Chien-yen i-lai ch'ao-yeh tsa-chi*, "chia" 15.13a. *Fo-tsu t'ung-chi* 47.425c states that

the tax amounted to between one thousand and thirteen hundred cash. In the event of floods and other disasters, monks were required to pay a supplement which doubled the amount of the *mien-ting ch'ien* and was known as *k'uan-sheng ch'ien*. The case of an exemption of Buddhist and Taoist monasteries in Fukien mentioned in *Wen-hsien t'ung-k'ao* 26.260c.

23. Cloisters formed groups of buildings within a monastery. Monks belonging to these cloisters were often specialized in different disciplines.

24. *Pao-ch'ing Ssu-ming chih.* See Tsukamoto Zenryū, "Sō no zaiseinan to bukkyō," p. 584.

25. For details concerning this question, see Tsukamoto Zenryū, ibid., p. 583.

26. It may be noted that according to this table Dhyāna monks were considered the poorest among the Buddhist, and that the Taoist were at the bottom of the ladder.

27. Figures in strings of one thousand cash.

28. The stewards for the year (*chih-sui*) were selected among the monks who were best educated and who were good scribes. On the terminology of monastic offices in India, see Lévy and Chavannes, "Quelques termes énigmatiques," pp. 209–10. The Indian equivalent of the term *chih-sui* is not known.

29. On these great monasteries, see A. Forte, "Daiji," pp. 682–704.

30. See p. 10 above.

31. *Kuang hung-ming chi* 12.172a (refutation of the fifth point in Fu I's memorial).

32. Tun-huang manuscripts P. 3620 and 3608: A rebuttal of the report presented by Hsien-yü Shu-ming (i.e., Li Shu-ming, biography in *Chiu T'ang shu* 122.3506-7) and Ling-hu Huan (biography ibid. 149.4011-14) in which they requested that examinations for the clergy be made mandatory, and that monks should be barred from engaging in commerce. The text must date from the second half of the eighth century. Li Shu-ming's report is cited in *T'ang hui-yao* 47.837-88, where it is dated 778.

33. *Chiu T'ang shu* 127.3580, biography of P'eng Yen, council convened by emperor Te-tsung (r. 779-805). According to Twitchett, "The Monasteries and China's Economy," p. 542, P'eng Yen's memorial dates from "a period of high prices and inflation which began with the An Lu-shan rebellion, and which came to an end in 785-87." Besides, as Twitchett adds, P'eng's argument about five or six taxpayers supporting each monk, frequently encountered in this kind of writing, does seem to be a rhetorical figure. However, even if we assume P'eng Yen's claims to be greatly exaggerated, the essential fact remains that the existence of an overgrown monastic community meant a serious loss in tax revenues and labor services to the state.

34. In fact, 360,000 monks and nuns were laicized in 845, but more than 260,000 were clergy residing in monasteries, of whom the great majority were presumably maintained at state expense. It is to these, no doubt, that Sun Ch'iao is alluding.

35. *Fo-tsu t'ung-chi* 42.387b.

36. See p. 36 above.

37. *T'ang Lu Hsüan-kung tsou i* 4.34b ff., cited by Maspero, *Etudes historiques*, p. 177.

38. Report cited on p. 57 below. According to Yang Yen, the beginning of this widespread flight of the taxable peasantry went back to the year 750. The proportion of free peasants indicated allows us to calculate approximately their number: between 2,000,000 and 2,500,000, assuming a total population in China below fifty million at that time, and that the percentage figure is correct. Those numbers, however, are lower than the figures indicated in *Hsin T'ang shu* for the year 780 (see note above). In any case, there was a significant drop in the number of taxpayers during the second half of the eighth century. They numbered ca. eight million in 755; thus some

three to five million taxable persons seem to have eluded state control during the years that followed the An Lu-shan rebellion.

39. On the sale of ordination certificates, see pp. 48–57.

40. See p. 318, n. 26 above. At that time, 700,000 "clergy" presented themselves to have their diplomas examined.

41. "Shih-Lao chih," *Wei shu* 114.3039. Cf. Ware, "Wei Shou," p. 153: the expression *"enforced* registrations" is not in the text; this evidently concerns the beginning of the institution of the *seng-chi*.

42. "Shih-Lao chih," *Wei shu* 114.3040.

43. See pp. 114, 277. It may be noted that from the fifth century onward there existed a lower level of lay ordination that consisted of taking the so-called Bodhisattva Vows.

44. This term refers specifically to fiscal fraud. Cf. p. 328, n. 67 below.

45. "Shih-Lao chih," *Wei shu* 114.3048. It is quite possible that the Chinese themselves perceived little difference between peasant-monks and religious: neither the Buddhists nor the secular authorities found it necessary to make a distinction between these two classes of monks. The demarcation between them was in fact rather vague, since many monks led a lay life.

46. See p. 137.

47. See p. 186. Naba Toshisada, "Giransō," considers that the term *chi-chu seng,* "landlord monks," which figures in the list of the contracting parties at the end of certain deeds at Tun-huang, designated the *po-hsing seng.* They could, however, have been real monks since it was common at that time for monks to own land. The "lay monk" still existed in Ch'ing times. De Groot, *Sectarianism,* 1:122–27, points out that they were designated *ying-fu seng* at that period.

48. That period was characterized by a significant increase in fictitious ordinations. See p. 50–51.

49. *Hsin T'ang shu* 124.4384, biography of Yao Ch'ung. *Chiu T'ang shu* 96.3023 does not specify that they were peasant-monks.

50. Sanctuary dedicated to Liu Pei of the Shu Han.

51. *Hsin T'ang shu* 180.5332. Li Te-yü was in Szechwan during 830 and 831.

52. *Sung shih* 177.4296 ("Monograph on the Economy"). The integrity of the body, and especially hair, was extremely important for the Chinese. On their attitudes concerning hairstyle and dress, see Demiéville, *Le Concile de Lhasa,* pp. 207–12, and especially p. 211, on the tonsure.

53. *Fo-tsu t'ung-chi* 38.358c: "In the fifth month of the third year [of Chen-te] (574), the emperor of Chou decided to abolish Buddhism everywhere. . . . The sacred texts and the statues shall be entirely destroyed," read the proscription decree, "and the śramaṇa and the Taoist bonzes shall be returned to lay life. At that time there were more than two million religious who resumed their lay habit." On the history of that great repression see Tsukamoto Zenryū, "Hokushū no haibutsu ni tsuite."

54. "Shih-Lao chih," *Wei shu* 114.3036: "Those who have the vocation of the śramaṇa," read a decree of 453, "will be permitted to leave their families (*ch'u-chia*) regardless of age, provided that they are of good family (*liang,* as opposed to *chien,* used for the lowly classes, i.e., serfs, slaves, convicts, etc.), of good conduct, serious, of unblemished reputation, and well-regarded in their villages. As a general rule, fifty will be accepted [each year] in large prefectures, forty in small prefectures, and ten in commanderies and remote districts." Toward the end of the fifth century, these figures were doubled: "On the eighth day of the fourth month and the fifteenth day of the seventh month (major Buddhist festivals), it is permitted to ordain one hundred monks and nuns in large, fifty in medium-sized, and twenty in small prefectures" (ibid. 114.3039). Twenty-five years later, this regulation was still in force, as is indi-

cated by a decree of Empress Ling of 517: "For many years it has been the custom to carry out ordinations subject to certain restrictions. In the case of a large prefecture it is permitted to ordain one hundred religious" (ibid. 114.3042). On the principles applied to ordinations under the Northern Wei, see Abe Kuniharu, "Hokugi ni okeru do no kenkyū," p. 2.

55. See pp. 50, 56.

56. The *wei-na*, in particular, played an important role in the internal administration of the communities. According to the *Ch'ih-hsiu Po-chang ch'ing-kuei* 4, "Wei-na," "the *karmadāna* administers the monks and watches over discipline. If a monk [passing through] comes to hang his bowl and habit on the nail (*kua-ta*), [the *karmadāna*] examines the validity of his ordination certificate. When a dispute arises or negligence occurs, he reconciles the contending parties through arbitration. Whether it is the seniority of ordinations, the order of the disciples, or the calendars and accounts, there is nothing concerning the clergy inside and outside [the monastery] that does not fall under his responsibility. It is he who leads the alternating psalmodies. He is also obliged to take care of sick and deceased monks. . . . The *Chi-kuei chuan* [of I-ching] says: 'The first syllable of the word *wei-na* means to regulate, and *na* is the last syllable of *karmadāna*. It means "let the community rejoice." ' The *Shih-sung lü* says: 'Because in the monasteries no one knew when to strike the wooden board [to announce the hour], no one removed mud and dust, no one sprinkled the preaching hall and the refectory, no one established the arrangement of the beds, and because no one settled disputes among the monks, the Buddha instituted the *karmadāna*.' "

57. "Shih-Lao chih," *Wei shu* 114.3041. Cf. the same formula ibid. 3046–47: "If the number of monks is below fifty, they shall be resettled. The monks belonging to small monasteries (the term *ssu* refers here to any inhabited sanctuary, cf. p. 7 above) shall be moved to the larger ones in order that the contingent [of fifty] be filled."

58. *Chiu T'ang shu* 1.16–17, decree of the fifth month, ninth year of Wu-te. See also *Fo-tsu t'ung-chi* 39.363a, which mentions this decree and states that it was annulled in the sixth month as a result of an amnesty. It appears that similar provisions had been introduced in the fifth month of the fourth year of Wu-te (621), but without having been implemented either. See *Hsü kao-seng chuan* 24.633c (biography of Hui-ch'eng).

59. The derelict condition of a great number of Buddhist sanctuaries in China under the T'ang is confirmed by a passage in the *Hsiang-fa chüeh-i ching* cited above, p. 283. By the same token, the importance may be noted that the School of the Three Stages (*san-chieh chiao*) attached to the restoration of sanctuaries.

60. Act of grace promulgated by Wu-tsung on the occasion of the sacrifice in the southern suburb on the third day, first month of the fifth year of Hui-ch'ang. See *Wen-yüan ying-hua* 429.2174.

61. "Shih-Lao chih," *Wei shu* 114.3038. See also ibid. 3040–41, report of the controller of Buddhist clergy Hui-shen, winter of the second year of Yung-p'ing (509): "There are those who do not live in monasteries but travel and reside among the people. If the religion is disturbed and there is abuse, it is due to these people. Anyone found guilty of the offense [of vagrancy] shall be defrocked and returned to lay life."

62. Passes for monks were to remain in use. A specimen is extant in a Tun-huang document dating probably from the tenth century (P. 3975): "The present monk, named Pao-ying, is not to be hindered, wherever he may go, by the administrative authorities of prefectures, garrisons, or counties. These are ordered to let him pass. The twenty-eighth day, eighth month of the year *i-wei*." A seal is impressed upon the date, which reads, in seal characters: "New seal of the civil governor (*kuan-ch'a shih*)

of the prefectures of Kua-chou and Sha-chou." The same seal figures on the manu-script P. 3576, which is dated 989. The year *i-wei* here corresponds presumably to 959. The passes were known as *kuo-so, hsing-tieh,* or *ch'ang-tieh.* See des Rotours, "Les insignes en deux parties," p. 108, n. 1, and the passport issued to two Japanese monks on April 9, 855, a document published by Niida Noboru, *Tō Sō hōritsu,* pp. 844–45. The term *kuo-so* is also encountered in the biography of Wei Yüan-sung, the famous defrocked monk of Ch'eng-tu and advisor to Wu-ti of the Chou: "Since he did not have a pass, he dressed as a layman." See *Hsü kao-seng chuan* 25.657c. T'ang leg-islation provided special regulations concerning the movements of monks, see des Rotours, *Traité des fonctionnaires,* p. 383: "When [Taoist and Buddhist monks and nuns] were visiting families of the people, they were not allowed to stay for more than three nights. Those who stayed out for one night had to register. They could not register for more than seven consecutive days. If they had to travel a long distance, the prefectures and counties issued them passes *(ch'eng)."* The biography of Wang Chin in *Chiu T'ang shu* reports that this pro-Buddhist high official provided several dozens of monks from Mount Wu-t'ai with certificates *(fu-tieh)* issued by the imper-ial Secretariat so that they could be sent into the prefectures and counties to hold public sermons and make collections. The sums received were to be used for embell-ishments of the Chin-ko monastery at Mount Wu-t'ai, of which Wang Chin was a major benefactor.

63. *Wei shu* 4B.97.

64. *Ta T'ang nei-tien lu* 5.271b, "Chou chung-ching yao."

65. *Hsü kao-seng chuan* 24.633b, biography of Hui-ch'eng (555–630). Concerning the term *chia-seng,* see the following note. The fact that Hui-ch'eng was described as a *chia-seng* indicates that the monastery founded by the prince of Chin must have functioned as a family chapel. Sanctuaries founded by important personalities often served to ensure the perpetuation of the family cult. See above, p. 282.

66. *Ts'e-fu yüan-kuei* 159.11b. See also *T'ang hui-yao* 49.860. Emperors had pri-vate monks. Under Wu-ti of the Liang, these religious were called *chia-seng* ("family monks"). Several famous monks were *chia-seng* under Emperor Wu: Seng-ch'ieh-p'o-lo, *Hsü kao-seng chuan* 1.427a; Fa-ch'ung, ibid. 5.461b: "In the seventh year of T'ien-chien (508), Emperor Wu bade Fa-ch'ung (451–524) serve as a monk in his household and ordered that he be supplied with a chariot, oxen, servants, clothing, and food and drink, that he might lack none of these in any season"; Hui-ch'ao, ibid. 6.468b; and Seng-ch'ien (435–513), ibid. 6.476a. Under the T'ang, there was an "inner chapel" in the palace *(nei tao-ch'ang)* where the officiating monks were as numerous as those of a large monastery. On the *nei tao-ch'ang* under the reign of Tai-tsung (762–779), see *Chiu T'ang shu* 118.3417, biography of Wang Chin, and p. 292 above. Since the begin-ning of the eighth century, the privilege of maintaining a private chapel had been extended to imperial princesses: from 711 onward the latter were authorized to have "merit cloisters" *(kung-te yüan)* where they no doubt maintained religious of their choosing. See *Fo-tsu t'ung-chi* 40.373a, second year of Ching-yün. On the develop-ment of this institution and its extension under the Sung, see pp. 308–9.

67. The term *wei-lan* referred to various kinds of evasion of taxes and imperial requisitioning. See *Chiu T'ang shu* 105.3217, biography of Yü-wen Jung: "At the beginning of K'ai-yüan era (713–742) . . . people throughout the empire fled without leaving a trace in order to evade taxes and there was much 'fraud and abuse' *(wei-lan)."* The same text further on alludes to "families of retainers" having recently obtained patronage *(hsin-fu k'o-hu).* Private ordinations are only one aspect of this attempt to evade taxes and obtain private patronage.

68. The same phenomenon occurred in India: "Among the Śramaṇa, some became monks because they were in debt [the recovery of debts from a person who

had entered into religion was not permitted], others for dread of their ruler, others again because they were poor, and some because they truly desired to free themselves from the sufferings of present and future existences. See Demiéville, *Milindapañha*, p. 103.

69. *Kuang hung-ming chi* 12.85a, report by Huan Hsüan with a reply by the monk Hui-yüan.

70. See above, p. 115. "None of these," wrote Kuo Tsu-shen in his report, "are registered by the census."

71. Above, p. 10.

72. Above, p. 51. The official ordinations, which had been discontinued at the beginning of the reign of Hsüan-tsung, were only resumed around the year 741 at the instigation of the Ceylonese monk Amoghavajra. See *Fo-tsu t'ung-chi* 40.375b, twenty-ninth year of K'ai-yüan. The T'ang penal code provided a punishment of one hundred blows with a staff for anyone who entered into religion surreptitiously; the punishment could rise to penal servitude if the offender had his name crossed off the register of the taxable population (which seems to imply that entry into religion was not always accompanied by removal from the tax register). Officials and heads of monasteries were subject to the same punishment if they had connived in the offence by acquiescence. Officials who issued ordination certificates on their own authority were liable to one hundred blows with the staff for each monk privately ordained (*ssu-tu*), reaching the highest punishment, exile to a distance of three thousand *li*, for seventeen false ordination certificates. See *T'ang-lü shu-i* 12.223 (article 7).

73. See pp. 71ff above. The principle was not always respected by the monks themselves.

74. Above, pp. 245–47.

75. See above, pp. 112ff., 126ff.

76. According to a usage attested in later times, the official names were preceded by the characters *ch'ih-ssu*: "conferred by imperial order."

77. *Liang-ching hsin-chi*, "Shih-tzu chieh tung chih pei Chien-fa ni-ssu," p. 3. Another example: in 592, a private sanctuary received the name of Miao-sheng ssu. The emperor himself wrote this name on the panel which was to be placed at the entrance. Above, pp. 112–13.

78. *Chiu T'ang shu* 6.121; *Hsin T'ang shu* 4.90–91.

79. It was in the Lung-hsing ssu and Lung-hsing kuan that official ceremonies took place under the T'ang. See des Rotours, *Traité des fonctionnaires*, p. 88. Tunhuang had its Lung-hsing ssu.

80. Such acts of benevolence were often taken advantage of, with the result that there were sometimes several official monasteries of the same name in the same prefecture.

81. At the beginning of his reign, Hsüan-tsung promulgated a series of measures to curb the excessive increase in the number of constructions and monks that had been characteristic of the end of the seventh century and the first years of the eighth.

82. *Fo-tsu t'ung-chi* 40.373a. That same year the monk Hui-yün founded a monastery in the prefecture of Pien, which he named Chien-kuo ssu. As a result of an omen, the emperor conferred the name (*ssu-ming*) Ta-hsiang kuo ssu on this temple. This is a good example of the apparent inconsistency of imperial religious policy; in fact, the aim was always to protect the official cult and to curb the growth of private religion.

83. The term employed here is *kung-te*, "acts of piety." See above, p. 294.

84. *Fo-tsu t'ung-chi* 40.374a–b.

85. *Chiu T'ang shu* 127.3579, biography of P'eng Yen. See also p. 304.

86. *Fan-ch'uan wen-chi* 10.8b.

87. *Fo-tsu t'ung-chi* 42.392b.

88. See below, p. 294, concerning the probable meaning of the term *kung-te*.

89. Decree cited by de Groot, *Sectarianism*, 1:73.

90. *Fo-tsu t'ung-chi* 39.360c, sixteenth year of K'ai-huang (595).

91. The monastery where Pu-k'ung resided.

92. *Tai-tsung ch'ao tseng ssu-k'ung ta pien-cheng kuang-chih san-tsang ho-shang piao chih chi* 1.830b–31a.

93. On this term and its meaning, see pp. 66ff.

94. Above, p. 118.

95. We know from a passage in the economic monograph in *Sui shu* (cf. trans. in Balazs, "Traité économique," p. 165) that owners of personal retainers (*pu-ch'ü*) and slaves paid a tax for these to the government. According to a regulation of the year 769, private owners had to pay seven hundred strings of cash for one household serf and five hundred strings for a temporary agricultural laborer. See *T'ang hui-yao* 83.1534–5.

96. On the left bank of the river of Khotan.

97. It seems, says Chavannes, that the *hua-p'an* was an official responsible for collecting certain taxes within a specific ward. See *Les documents chinois*, pp. 210–11, document no. 969.

98. Chavannes, *Les documents chinois*, no. 969, ll. 9 and 12; no. 971, l. 13. The known dates of payment are the twenty-ninth day of the eleventh month and the twenty-second day of the first.

99. The act of grace promulgated by Shun-tsung on his accession in 805 gives a list of the properties in question: for the period from the first year of Hsing-yüan (784) to the thirteenth day of the tenth month, twelfth year of Chen-yüan (796), the commissioners for estates (*chuang-chai shih*) were ordered not to claim taxes due for shops (*tien-p'u*), chariot sheds (*ch'ü-fang*), mills on private properties (*yüan-wei*), and fallow lands (*ling-ti*), taxes to which ordinary persons (*po-hsing*) and people of all [other] categories (*chu-se jen*) would have been liable, and which amounted to the equivalent of more than 520,000 [strings of cash?] in grain, currency, silk, fodder, and other commodities. See *Ts'e-fu yüan-kuei* 491.5871b. The fiscal statutes governing real estate owned by the Buddhist Church in Yüan times showed the same diversity as those in the sixth century and under the T'ang. See Ratchnevsky, *Un code des Yuan*, introduction.

100. Above, p. 146.

101. On this principle of monastic discipline, see pp. 85ff.

102. *Fo-tsu t'ung-chi* 41.379b. See also ibid. 54.472b.

103. *Hsiang-fa chüeh-i ching* 1337b.

104. The text here uses the expression (*kua-ta*), literally "to hang [one's bowl and habit] on the nail," alluding to the right of visiting monks to be fed and lodged free of charge by the monasteries.

105. No doubt a reference to property exempted from taxation by special imperial favor.

106. On the mentality and conduct of these great monks, see p. 181.

107. The word *san* indicates that these were nominal titles without an appanage.

108. This seems to mean "with an inferior rank," for it would be illogical to receive a higher rank for the same payment.

109. *Wei shu* 110.2861.

110. This memorial by Hsin T'i-p'i, who served as comissioner of the Left (*tso shih-i*), is dated first year of Ching-lung (707) in *Wen-yüan ying-hua* 698.3603–4, "Chien Chung-tsung chih kung-chu fu-kuan shu," and second year of Ching-yün (711) in *T'ang hui-yao* 48.850–51. Clearly the first date is correct, since Chung-tsung

no longer reigned in 711. See also *Chiu T'ang shu* 101.3157–58, biography of Hsin T'i-p'i.

111. The *sha-mi* in *T'ang hui-yao* stands no doubt for *sha-men*, the reading in *Wen-yüan ying-hua*.

112. *Tzu-chih t'ung-chien* 209.6623.

113. In the same vein, Hsin T'i-p'i complains in his remonstrance with the emperor that thanks to the sale of titles, wealthy merchants had entered into "the class of persons wearing the sash and cap" (i.e., secular dignitaries of high rank), and that professional dancers and magicians had procured good positions for themselves.

114. According to the memorials of Hsin T'i-p'i and Yao Ch'ung, the three princesses T'ai-p'ing, An-lo, and Ch'ang-ning, the empress Wei, Wu San-ssu, and a certain Lady Chang were particularly notorious for peddling their influence with the emperor. See also *Chiu T'ang shu* 96.3026–29, biography of Yao Ch'ung, and ibid. 183.4734–36, biography of Wu San-ssu.

115. On monasteries having received an official title (*yu-ch'ih ssu* or *ssu-o ssu*), see pp. 43–48 above. The term *ch'ih* here might well apply to both the construction of monasteries and to ordinations.

116. *T'ang hui-yao* 47.836–7.

117. *Fo-tsu t'ung-chi* 40.373b.

118. *Ch'üan T'ang wen* 176.12a, "Kuei Wei Yüan-chung shu." See also *Hsin T'ang shu* 122.4346, biography of Wei Yüan-chung.

119. "They account for half [the travelers] on the highways," as another version has it. Monks constituted, along with merchants and officials, one of the most traveled groups in China, hence the evocative and oft-repeated image.

120. Those whose conduct made sport of their precepts (*wu-chieh hsing*).

121. *K'ung chi chung-pao chuan-fu ch'üan-men*. The word *fu* evokes an act of allegiance. Candidates for ordination attached themselves to a patron and became his clients (*men-t'u*). See above, p. 42. The meaning of the word *k'ung*, "in vain," becomes clear in the text that follows: in the case of nobles, officials, and persons of great merit (groups to which the religious normally belong), the rewards and exemptions from corvée duties and taxes have their justification; likewise, when the price for such favors is paid into the imperial treasury. Here, however, the expense is in vain because it does not benefit the empire.

122. They resumed probably at the end of his reign, which saw a revival of Buddhism. Ordinations multiplied from 741 onward, under the influence of the Ceylonese master Amoghavajra. See *Fo-tsu t'ung-chi* 40.375b (twenty-ninth year of K'ai-yüan).

123. *Ts'e-fu yüan-kuei* 159.17b, decree of the sixth month, nineteenth year of K'ai-yüan.

124. The institution of individual certificates for religious seems to fall well before that year. See p. 31 above: under the Chou (550–581), the monks of Wan-shou monastery in Ch'ang-an had received individual diplomas that exempted them their impositions. A decree of the year 714 (above, p. 284) alludes to certificates that a monk invited to celebrate a *chai* for a private individual was obliged to present to the secular administration. The innovation of 746 consisted no doubt of the requirement to carry these individual certificates, which were to be issued to newly ordained monks by the Bureau of Sacrifices. No specimens of *tu-tieh* have been preserved. There are, however, at least two provisional certificates extant among the Tun-huang manuscripts in Paris (see above, pp. 55–56). The *tu-tieh* indicated the secular place of residence, family name, religious name, and the names of the monastery and of the Buddhist master having conferred the ordination. They further bore the signatures and seals of the concerned authorities from the Board of Sacrifices (*ssu-pu*). All the

information necessary for making out a *tu-tieh* is provided in the petitions requesting the ordination of certain religious presented by Amoghavajra. See *Tai-tsung ch'ao tseng ssu-k'ung ta pien-cheng kuang-chih san-tsang ho-shang piao chih chi*, passim. A note in *Ta Sung seng-shih lüeh* B.246b mentions that the certificates of the Bureau of Sacrifices were made of fine silk or plain silk, with a roller and a metal case. See also *Fo-tsu t'ung-chi* 40.375c, sixth year of T'ien-pao (747).

125. *Hsin T'ang shu* 51.1347; *Chiu T'ang shu* 48.2087. The following translation is based on both versions. See also the complete text in *Ts'e-fu yüan-kuei* 509.15b.

126. In fact, the news reached Ch'ang-an only on December 22.

127. In modern Shansi. *Chiu T'ang shu* has "in Ho-tung," corresponding approximately to modern Shansi.

128. The *Chiu T'ang shu* does not specify the unit "strings of cash"; one million cash, however, would not be a sufficiently large sum to be mentioned as exceptional.

129. The succession of Su-tsung took place at this moment in the sequence of events. The *Hsin T'ang shu* states that when Su-tsung acceded to the throne, an appeal was launched to wealthy merchants to contribute a tax amounting to one fifth of their revenues.

130. The *Chiu T'ang shu* here refers also to the sale of official titles (*kuan-chieh*) to opulent families and rich merchants in the region between the Yangtze and the Huai river.

131. *Kuan-fu*: see des Rotours, *Traité des fonctionnaires*, p. 898, n. 5, according to which the name designated the superior prefecture comprising the capital territory, and by extension no doubt also the surrounding region.

132. *Chiu T'ang shu* 10.244.

133. P'eng-yüan was to the south of modern Ch'ing-yang fu in Kansu. The future Emperor Su-tsung arrived in that town toward the end of July 756. See des Rotours, *Traité des fonctionnaires*, p. 897, n. 3.

134. Ling-wu, in modern Kansu, was the seat of the *chieh-tu shih* of Shuo-fang (or Kuan-nei), near modern Ling-chou.

135. *Fo-tsu t'ung-chi* 40.375c. The term *hsiang-shui ch'ien* occurs in several sources. The scented water (Skr. *gandhavāri*) is no doubt that which served for the aspersions (Skr. *abhiṣeka*) of the occiput, according to a ritual made fashionable in Lo-yang by Amoghavajra around 740, and which had probably spread throughout China by the time of the An Lu-shan rebellion.

136. The first day of that year corresponded to January 25, 757.

137. These five mountains (in modern Honan, Shantung, Shensi, Hunan, and Hopeh) were both official sacred sites and Buddhist pilgrimage centers.

138. Another reading gives the figure of one hundred pages, but most sources read five hundred (viz. ca. two hundred thousand characters, accounting for versified passages and blanks).

139. *Fo-tsu t'ung-chi* 40.376a.

140. On the periodic transfer of the joint of the finger of Buddha Śākyamuni preserved in the Fa-men ssu, see p. 237 above.

141. *Fo-tsu li-tai t'ung-tsai* 13.598b. A passage in the biography of Tao-piao (740–823) in *Sung kao-seng chuan* 15.903c seems to confirm this date: "In the second year of Chih-te, as Su-tsung had authorized the ordination of lay persons able to recite seven hundred pages of sutra, Tao-piao was among the first in that examination."

142. *Sung kao-seng chuan* 8.756c–757a.

143. Des Rotours, *Traité des fonctionnaires*, p. 682.

144. *Sung kao-seng chuan* 757a.

145. See *Chiu T'ang shu* 106.3247, biography of Yang Kuo-chung.

146. P. 4072.

147. See des Rotours, *Traité des fonctionnaires*, references in the index.

148. This amounts to two strings and two hundred cash per religious for the cost of making out the certificates. The price of the certificates themselves is not included.

149. P. 3952.

150. Niida Noboru, *Tō Sō hōritsu*, p. 81.

151. The translation of this text, which teems with phrases peculiar to the administrative style and is moreover heavily mutilated, is presented with all reserves.

152. On this bureau, see des Rotours, *Traité des fonctionnaires*, pp. 50–59.

153. According to the "Monograph on Officials" in the *Hsin T'ang shu*, local recipients of honorary titles were periodically graded according to rank and reported to the Board of Finance in order that claims for tax exemption could be verified (see the translation in des Rotours, *Traité des fonctionnaires*, p. 59).

154. Given the competence of the body that issued the two documents examined above, it seems that the religious were assimilated with sinecure officials (*san-kuan*) and honorary title holders (*hsün-kuan*).

155. Cf. Twitchett, *Financial Administration*, pp. 81–82.

156. Above, p. 50.

157. See above, pp. 51–52, and p. 331, n. 122.

158. *Chiu T'ang shu* 118.3421, biography of Yang Yen. See also *Hsin T'ang shu* 145.4724.

159. See above, pp. 50–51.

160. *Ta Sung seng-shih lüeh* B.252b.

161. The author deliberately uses the old term *chu-hou*, evoking the feudal ages of the past.

162. See *Li Wei-kung Hui-ch'ang i-p'in chi*, "Pieh-chi" 5, p. 211. See also *Chiu T'ang shu* 174.4514 and *Hsin T'ang shu* 180.5329. Cf. Twitchett, "The Monasteries and China's Economy," pp. 546–47.

163. Modern Ssu-hsien, in Anhwei.

164. In fact, high officials addressed perfunctory petitions of this kind to the court but dispensed with any subsequent authorization by the emperor: This explains how Wang Chih-hsing could proceed with the installation of an ordination platform despite the fact that private ordinations were prohibited.

165. *Chiu-jih sha-mi*: recently ordained monks (*sha-mi* no doubt stands for *sha-men*.

166. The paragraph devoted to private ordinations in *Ta Sung seng-shih lüeh* B.252b, cited above, also refers to Wang Chih-hsing's ventures. The author explains that the sale of *tu-tieh* served no other purpose than to supply considerable revenues to the state in times of budget deficit. P'ei Mien is said to have been to first to conceive the idea [of an official sale of certificates] (this view is mistaken; as mentioned, Yang Kuo-chung had already envisaged the procedure in 756), which was implemented whenever wars demanded large sums of money. Thus Wang Chih-hsing of Hsü-chou memorialized the emperor to request the authorization to establish ordination platforms in the Buddhist monasteries of Lin-huai (the *Chiu T'ang shu*, which is surely more accurate, does not mention that there were several platforms). Upon payment of the required amount, one received the ordination. This went so far, that some, having made the payment, did not receive their ordination [certificates].

167. *Chiu T'ang shu* 17A.513, "Ching-tsung pen-chi."

168. On the site of modern Nan-ch'ang fu, Kiangsi.

169. See n. 164 above: at that time, the presentation of a petition to the court did not imply that the official awaited an authorization by the emperor.

170. *Chiu T'ang shu* 17A.519.

171. *Fang-teng chieh-t'an.* The origin of this institution is Mahāyānist (*fang-teng* is a translation of Skr. *vaipulya*): "All that is required [on these ordination platforms] is that [the postulant] has produced the spirit of *bodhi*. The meaning of *fang-teng* is *chou-pien* ('general', 'universal')." See *Ta Sung seng-shih lüeh* C, section 47. The extended ordination platforms seem to have originated in the middle of the eighth century. The *Ta Sung seng-shih lüeh*, ibid., states that on the twenty-eighth day of the third month, first year of Yung-t'ai (765), Tai-tsung decreed that the state would provide all that was necessary for the extended ordination platforms. In the fourth month, he ordered that ten reverends (*ta-te*) be appointed who would be chosen among the monks and nuns of the capital to be in charge of these platforms. The institution was to be perpetual. Probably recourse was taken to riddles in order to determine the postulants' capacities. A predilection for meditation themes (*kung-an*) was already very widespread in China at this time. Possibly institutions like the "extended ordination platforms" further developed a taste for subtleties that became extremely harmful to Chinese Buddhism from the end of the T'ang.

172. *Chiu T'ang shu* 17A.533.

173. P. 3774, l. 46.

174. See *Sung kao-seng chuan* 15.803c: The monk Tao-piao (740–823) had been able to accumulate a considerable capital in coin from the sale of ordination certificates with which he acquired a large tract of land for his community. See p. 120 below.

175. Private sales were no less known in Sung times than under the T'ang. According to *Hsü tzu-chih t'ung-chien ch'ang-pien* 18, second year of T'ai-p'ing hsing-kuo (977), "The vice-president of the Board of Public Works Hou She said: 'Ordination certificates for Buddhist monks and nuns are issued by the Bureau of Sacrifices. However, in the provinces (*tao*) one gives 100 cash to the responsible official [for a certificate]." Perhaps this should read "100 strings of cash" (a century later, the official price was 130 strings of cash), unless the figure refers to the fee for making out a *tu-tieh* or a downpayment on the total sum.

176. This insignia of honor had been especially created by Empress Wu of the T'ang to reward the translators of the *Mahāmeghasūtra*. See Demiéville, *Milinda-pañha*, p. 223.

177. Reference to the ordinations by special grace (*en-tu*), which under the T'ang were conferred at the same time as the ordinations by examination (*shih-ching tu-seng*).

178. See *Fo-tsu t'ung-chi* 45.414a.

179. Tsukamoto Zenryū, "Sō no zaiseinan to bukkyō."

180. *Yen-i i-mou lu*, p. 42.

181. Ibid.

3. The Indian Heritage

1. The commercial and financial practices mentioned in Indian treatises on discipline had been introduced into the saṃgha by great merchants converted to Buddhism. See pp. 74, 159, and 163 above on the role of the laity in the communities of the Lesser Vehicle and on the influence of merchants.

2. The *Pien-cheng lun* 3.503a gives the figures of 24,000 monks and nuns and 1,768 monasteries for the Eastern Chin. These probably apply to the end of the dynasty. See above, p. 6.

3. The Vinaya of the Mūlasarvāstivāda, translated at the beginning of the eighth century by I-ching, arrived too late to have had as much influence as its predecessors on the formation of monastic institutions.

4. *Liang-ch'u ch'ing-chung i,* "Pen," 840a.

5. The expression "within the passes" here designates the Northern Wei kingdom.

6. *Mo-ho seng-ch'i lü,* translated in extenso by Fa-hsien and Buddhabhadra in 416. In "Shih-Lao chih," *Wei shu* 114.3031, Wei Shou states that "Fa-hsien, deploring the incompleteness of the Vinaya, left Ch'ang-an to journey to India. He traveled through thirty countries, and wherever there were sutra and Vinaya he studied the writing and the language and translated them as he went along. He reached [China] in the second year of Shen-jui (415). . . . When he arrived in Chiang-nan, he discussed and corrected his translation with the Indian Dhyāna master Buddhabhadra. He entitled it *Seng-ch'i lü* because it was much more complete than its predecessors. This is what the śramaṇa receive today."

7. I.e., under the Sung, Ch'i, Liang, and Ch'en.

8. *Shih-sung lü,* translated by Pūnyatrata and Kumārajīva between 404 and 415.

9. The *Mi-sha-sai-pu ho-hsi wu-fen lü* translated by Buddhajīva in 424.

10. *Ssu-fen lü,* translated by Buddhayaśas in 408. This Vinaya was to be the subject of extended commentaries by Tao-hsüan in the seventh century (T. 1804, 1806, 1808).

11. One would think in particular of the development of the theory of *upāya,* i.e., that "the end justifies the means." It is probable that this development was also felt in the domain of the monastic economy. The importance attached in the Greater Vehicle to the cult of Buddhist icons and to charitable activities also changed the character of the monastic economy. See pp. 69, 169 above.

12. The secular authorities, especially under the Wei, also played an important role in the establishment of the monastic code and institutions.

13. See Lévy and Chavannes, "Quelques termes énigmatiques," pp. 194–95. At Tun-huang, some abbots (*ssu-chu*), probably those of smaller monasteries, were responsible for the accounts pertaining to the permanent assets. See P. 4012, administrative report of the abbot Shan-chu for a year *keng-tzu* (880?).

14. *Mi-sha-sai-pu ho-hsi wu-fen lü* 25.168c. The assets of the saṃgha are properties that cannot be divided (Pāli *avissajjiya*). The first four categories of *avissajjiya* were: *ārāmo ārāma-vatthu vihāra vihāra-vatthu.* See *Cullavagga* 4, 15, 2.

15. On the meaning of these two terms, see below.

16. *Shih-sung lü* 56.413c. It will be noted that the list is slightly different from that in the *Wu-fen lü.* Elsewhere, in the *Dharmaguptavinaya,* the goods of the saṃgha are divided into four lots: "These four parts [illicitly created by the six evil bhikṣu, viz. 1. *saṃghārāma* and goods of *saṃghārāma,* cells and goods of cells; 2. various receptacles and "heavy goods" of all kinds; 3. movable property; 4. plantations are the property of the saṃgha of the four directions. They must be neither divided nor appropriated nor traded. . . . Their appropriation, division, or trade are null and void and constitute a grave transgression (*thullaccaya*)." See *Ssu-fen lü* 50.943c.

17. *Ssu-fen lü shan-fan pu-ch'üeh hsing-shih ch'ao* B1.55c-56a. Despite the title, Tao-hsüan's invaluable work on the monastic rules and their Chinese interpretation is in fact a compilation concerning the four *Vinaya* translated into Chinese in the fifth century, rather than a commentary on the *Ssu-fen lü.*

18. *Ch'ang-chu ch'ang chu,* "the permanent among permanent assets," i.e., the estate. These are in fact the type of goods to which the term *ch'ang-chu* was originally applied. In modern China, the expression is a literary synonym for "Buddhist monastery."

19. This distinction is not explained. We know, however, that the goods in question comprised clothing, utensils, and medicines.

20. *Ssu-fen lü shan-fan pu-ch'üeh hsing-shih ch'ao,* ibid., and *Shih-shih yao-lan*

C.302c–303a. The latter source, which takes its inspiration from the commentary of Tao-hsüan, is much more explicit.

21. See below, pp. 85ff.

22. See below, pp. 224ff.

23. This distinction between *fo-wu* and *seng-wu* appears in the Vinaya of the Mahāsāmghika and in that of the Sarvāstivāda; it is absent from the other two treatises on discipline translated in the fifth century. The relatively archaic character of the latter has already been referred to.

24. See below on the question of precious metals. The Pāli Vinaya does not permit the samgha to own gold or silver. According to the *Mahāsāmghika*, however, which also mention gold statues, such possessions were permissible.

25. The Sanskrit term *kalpa* can have the meaning of "[conformity with] ritual," hence presumably its connotation of purity in a Buddhist monastic context. In fact, not all heavy goods were considered equally impure, nor their possession equally improper. In many cases, whether a given object was to be classified among heavy goods or light goods was a matter of interpretation. Tao-hsüan devoted the main part of his *Liang-ch'u ch'ing-chung i* (ca. 630) to the resolution of disputes arising from this issue.

26. This term, which occurs frequently in the Vinaya, corresponds to Pāli *kappyakāraka* (Skr. *kalpikāra*). Other expressions denoting these lay servants include "keeper of the gardens" (*shou-yüan jen, shou-yüan min* or *yüan-min* in the *Mo-ho seng-ch'i lü*) or "keeper of the flower gardens" (*shou hua-yüan*), terms that translate Sanskrit *udyānapāla* (cf. *Mahāvyutpatti* no. 3842). Again, they were known as "managers" (Chin. *chih-shih jen*, Skr. *vaiyāvṛtyaka*, Pāli *veyyāvaccaka*[*ra*]). Cf. Demiéville, "Concile de Vaiśālī," p. 272, n. 4. According to *Shih-shih yao-lan* C.303b, "Pure men (*ching-jen*) are keepers of the residential quarters of the samgha. Today, in the monasteries of the capital, they are called domestic servants (*chia-jen* [an expression also found in monastic accounts from Central Asia, see above, p. 47]). Bimbisāra made a gift of *ching-jen* to the gardens of the samgha to save the monks from committing sins. That is why they are called 'pure men.' " Tao-ch'eng added that the transcription of the Indian word was *ch'ih-li-to*. The Sanskrit term is *krita*, "purchased [man]."

27. It was equally possible to have recourse to the faithful (*upāsaka*), as attested by one of the account fragments from the monastery of Mazār-tāgh translated by Chavannes (see above, p. 20), documents that appear to date from the beginning of the eighth century. The following remark is found in no. 972: "Same day, paid 1,250 cash to buy 5 *shih* of millet; this millet was at once delivered to the house master (*chang-che*) Hui Tsao as provisions for the temple." It is thus possible that in Central Asian communities, which had remained more faithful to the disciplinary prescriptions than those in China, the activities of the steward for the year (*chih-sui*) were confined to scribal tasks and the supervision of receipts and expenses, and that he did not himself handle grain or money.

28. This tradition is undoubtedly of Mahāsāmghika origin. The importance and diffusion of the *Mo-ho seng-ch'i lü* under the Wei in northern China is known (cf. above, p. 66). A report of the controller of Buddhist clergy (*sha-men t'ung*) Hui-shen ("Shih-Lao chih," *Wei shu* 114.3040–1, cf. Ware, "Wei Shou," p. 158) recalls that those who have entered into religion must not accumulate the eight impure things. According to the Vinaya, states this report, carts, livestock, and servants (*ching-jen*) were impure goods which could not be kept by individual monks. An exception was made for the sick and for those above sixty years of age who were permitted to use a cart.

29. *Ta po-nieh-p'an ching shu* 10.98b.

30. *Fo-tsu t'ung-chi* 4.164a.

31. This is a consequence of the *virtue* of individuals. Analogously, objects of great value and talismans could not be held with impunity by commoners or risked turning into something worthless. They were therefore surrendered to the sovereign. This folkloric theme is well attested in East Asia.

32. Concerning the appropriation of monastic properties by great lay families under the Sung, see pp. 307ff. above; on the renting of cells in monasteries, see above p. 226.

33. *Fo-tsu t'ung-chi* 39.369a–b.

34. On the loan of permanent assets, see below pp. 169ff.

35. *Fo-tsu t'ung-chi* 39.369a.

36. *Fo-tsu t'ung-chi* 39.367b.

37. *Fo-ming ching* 21.272b–273a. This undoubtedly apocryphal passage mentions the theft of sacred texts, of statues, the property of stūpa, the permanent assets of the saṃgha, the recourse to violence and the abuse of authority, the investment of permanent assets for interest after their appropriation, mismanagement of possessions of the triratna, the personal use of various foodstuffs belonging to the community, encroachment on neighboring fields and buildings by displacement of boundary stones or markers, the seizure of lands and gardens by force, seizure of shops (*ti-tian*) for one's personal use under the pretext of serving the common good, the theft of free men and their sale as slaves, the falsification of measures used in commerce, resorting to the divinatory arts in order to extort the wealth of the people, etc.

38. The notions of religious *sin* and of *debt* overlap, or rather conflate into a single conception, an absurd idea for a modern. We shall return to this question on pp. 245ff. above.

39. See above, p. 166.

40. See above, pp. 210ff.

41. See *Shih-sung lü* 28.203a–b (*cīvara*): property not to be divided among the bhikṣu comprised lands, buildings, furniture, all types of carts, large objects and valuables made of iron, copper, stone, crystal, earthenware, cowrie, ivory, tooth, horn, leather, wood and bamboo, knives, tongs, cases, incense burners, etc. See *Mi-sha-sai-pu ho-hsi wu-fen lü* 20.139a–b and *Ssu-fen lü* 41.859b–c. The latter served as basis for Tao-ch'eng's commentaries in the first part of his *Liang-ch'u ch'ing-chung i*.

42. Lingat, "Vinaya et droit laïc," pp. 415–78.

43. At least in theory, for this rule was to some extent subject to secular law. See Lingat, "Vinaya et droit laïc."

44. This constitutes a sin requiring restitution and public repentance (*shih-to* or *ch'i-to*; Skr. *naiḥsargika prāyaścittika*).

45. *Mi-sha-sai-pu ho-hsi wu-fen lü* 5.30a–b (no. 14).

46. *Mo-ho seng-ch'i lü* 12.323c–324b (no. 30). See also *Ssu-fen lü* 10.633a–c (no. 30).

47. *Ken-pen shuo i-ch'ieh yu-pu p'i-nai-yeh* 24.757a–759b (no. 29). The Vinaya of the Sarvāstivāda corresponds to this version, see *Shih-sung lü* 8.59a–60c (no. 29).

48. Rāhula is described by the text as an old man; elderly and sick monks were entitled to a greater degree of comfort than the others.

49. *Nan-hai chi-kuei nei-fa chuan* 4.230a–c. Lingat, "Vinaya et droit laïc," drew attention to this important text.

50. Cf. *Liang-ch'u ch'ing-chung i*, "Pen," 230a–c: When the property of a monk is divided, one inquires first whether any of these possessions had been held in joint ownership (*kung-ts'ai*), then whether any heirs had been designated by the deceased, and finally whether there were any debts. See also *Ssu-fen lü shan-fan pu-ch'üeh hsing-shih ch'ao*, "Hsia," 1.116b, where debts and credits contracted by the Three Jewels and by individuals are mentioned. A distinction is made between the concepts of "communal estate" (*t'ung-huo*) and "joint ownership."

51. See the *Sa-p'o to-pu p'i-ni mo-te lo-ch'ieh* 4.588a, translated by Saṃghavar-man (ca. 433–442): a certain bhikṣu had taken up numerous loans on the market. When his creditors wanted to recover their funds, he refused to repay.

52. "In theory, the monk was to live only on the proceeds of his begging, to clothe himself only in rags gathered from refuse and patched together, to have no other shelter than a tree in the forest, and to make do with 'fetid cow's urine' for medicine." See Foucher, *La vie du Bouddha*, p. 262.

53. Foucher, *La vie du Bouddha*, pp. 239–40.

54. See above, p. 96. *Ken-pen sa-p'o to-pu lü she* 6.558b.

55. The *upāsaka* were not simple believers. They are usually thought of in their religious role rather than the legal function implied by the etymology of the word: in Siam, the *upaṭṭhāka* was the administrator of the secular property of a bhikṣu; his particular task was to procure whatever the monk needed by using the goods or income from the property in his trust. See Lingat, "Vinaya et droit laïc."

56. But also, according to the Vinaya, the ruling class: in the Indian and Indianized world, princes and chief ministers willingly dedicated themselves to commercial and financial operations. See above, p. 164, inscription pointed out by S. Lévy.

57. See above, p. 162.

58. See Maspero, *Etudes historiques*, pp. 195–208.

59. This distinction was maintained for a very long time. In the fifteenth century, Vietnamese law distinguished between "floating goods" (*fu-wu*)—articles in gold, silver, silks, grains, beds, mats, crockery, trays, etc.—and, on the other hand, dwellings (*chia-chai*) and lands. On this subject, see Deloustal, "La justice dans l'ancien Annam," pp. 38–39.

60. Antichresis is the pledge assigning the revenue of an immovable to a creditor until full payment of the debt.

61. This is what emerges from the loan contracts found at Tun-huang. See above, p. 185.

62. Under the T'ang, however, there existed a regulation that assigned an allotment of 30 *mu* (ca. 1.6 ha) to regular monks with minimal religious instruction, and 20 *mu* to nuns. See *T'ang liu-tien* 3, "Shang-shu hu-pu." These small plots of land, however, would not have been sufficient to provide for all the needs of the religious. See above, p. 133.

63. See Lingat, "Vinaya et droit laïc"; *Shih-sung lü* 28.202c.

64. The disciples were enjoined to nurse their master when he was ill. See *Ssu-fen lü shan-fan pu-ch'üeh hsing-shih ch'ao*, "Shang," 3.31a.

65. *Tai-tsung ch'ao tseng ssu-k'ung ta pien-cheng kuang-chih san-tsang ho-shang piao chih chi* 3.844a–845a. The collection of official documents pertaining to Pu-k'ung (Amoghavajra), and of memorials presented by him, was compiled ca. 778, some four years after his death, by the monk Yüan-chao.

66. The terms used is *ch'i-yin*, "contract seal." The use of a personal seal in private deeds was rare in T'ang times, and peculiar to Buddhist monks.

67. Probably one of Pu-k'ung's translations from the *Yogācārabhūmi*.

68. The term used is *i-shu*, "deed of bequest." The testament as a secret document to be made known only after the death of the *de cujus* (i.e., the person "from whom" another derived his claim) was unknown in China.

69. "She has no other *fang-tzu* (personal property kept in a cell)," an expression corresponding to the *chia-tzu* of the laity. Ling-hui's assertion is assuredly untrue. See below.

70. This text, the manuscript S. 2199, was translated by L. Giles in "Dated Chinese Manuscripts," *BSOS* 9 (1939): 1029–30.

71. Ch'ung-en was probably a member of the So family, a prominent family related by marriage to the Yen.

72. This is the manuscript P. 3410. Part of the beginning of the text is missing; the remainder is in very poor condition and the paper has considerably darkened so that the text is difficult and in places even impossible to read. The translation given here is therefore in many places conjectural. The text has been edited in *Tun-huang to-so* fasc. 3, no. 59, pp. 239–43.

73. I.e., the Prajñāpāramitāsūtra of Benevolent Kings *Jen-wang po-je po-lo-mi ching*, T. 8, no. 245, erroneously attributed to Kumārajīva (344–413).

74. According to *Shih-shih yao-lan* A.270c, the *wa* ("stockings") were originally "garments." The *Ssu-fen lü* is cited as saying: "In cold weather it is permitted to wear *wa*." A note adds that from the Three Dynasties to the Chin, *wa* in [the form of] horns were worn. They were attached to the belt and hung down to the ankles. Under the Wei, the meaning of the word changed to "stockings."

75. *Chien* ("mean"), as opposed to *liang*, a term applied to free men.

76. The following provision in Burmese law is analogous to the Chinese customary practice: "Upon the death of a religious, his parents and relatives are excluded from the succession to that part of his patrimony that derived from strangers. . . . As for possessions given to the deceased by his relatives, the latter alone are entitled to their inheritance, at the exclusion of the disciples of the deceased." Apart from possessions received from outsiders, then, all of a religious' acquests went to his or her lay families. Art. 18 of the *Manu Vaan*; see Lingat, "Vinaya et droit laïc."

77. With regard to Szechwan, see the "Monograph on Geography" of the *Sui shu* summarized in Balazs, "Traité économique," p. 312.

78. Cf. the deed of partition between brothers in P. 2685, edited in *Tun-huang to-so*, fasc. 3, no. 57, pp. 233–35. The acreages indicated are, in *mu* (1 *mu* = 5.4 acres): 11, 11, 14, 16, 5, 5, 6, 6, 9, 8, 5, 1, 4, 2, 1, 1, 1. The total acreage owned by the two brothers amounted to 106 *mu*, i.e., 5.7 ha.

79. P. 3774. This document appears to date from the period of the occupation of Tun-huang by the Tibetans (787–848).

80. This implies that the two brothers could have maintained a communal estate, regardless of Ch'i Chou's ordination.

81. On the purchase of ordinations see above, pp. 48–62.

82. It should be noted that the wealth of Ch'i Chou and his elder brother consisted mainly of herds. They had been among the rich stockbreeders of the region who had formerly owned 300 sheep, more than 30 calves and asses, and 10 plough-oxen. After a raid by pillagers, they recovered no more than 130 sheep, one ox, and 11 calves and asses.

83. On this point, actual practice stood in complete contradiction with the Vinaya. Cf. *Ssu-fen lü shan-fan pu-ch'üeh hsing-shih ch'ao*, "Hsia," 1.113a citing the *Shih-sung lü*: "When Upananda died, he left items of clothing behind worth four hundred thousand pounds of gold. The king, the nobles and his relatives all wanted their share of this heritage, but the Buddha declared that all these goods belonged to the saṃgha and that lay persons had no right to claim them.

84. "Parishes" were rather extensive and included several monasteries. That of Sha-chou had seventeen large and medium-sized establishments.

85. *Ssu-fen lü shan-fan pu-ch'üeh hsing-shih ch'ao*, "Hsia," 1.117a.

86. *Shih-shih yao-lan* C.309b–c explains that the division of the possessions of deceased monks was justified on religious grounds: "The *Vinayavibhāṣā* [of the Sarvāstivāda] says: 'How, it will be asked, may the clothing and the bowls of deceased bhiksu be shared out? This deceased monk, we answer, has in the past received the possessions of other monks in the same manner, and the possessions which he now

leaves after his death are in turn shared by others.' " The *Tseng-hui chi*—a work now lost but quoted several times in the *Shih-shih yao-lan*, cf. Yang Lien-sheng, "Buddhist Monasteries," p. 183, n. 33—states: "According to the rules established by the Buddha, the guiding thought behind the division of the clothes is to enable the living to witness and reflect upon the sharing out of the possessions of the deceased to the community: 'Such is what this person has come to, and such is what I shall come to myself!' In this way cupidity is thwarted among the religious."

87. *Ssu-fen lü shan-fan pu-ch'üeh hsing-shih ch'ao*, ibid.

88. It seems that this custom can be interpreted as follows: gifts made in the donor's lifetime enjoyed full legal validity. In order that this may also hold true after his death, they had to be validated by a deed of the community (a solemn declaration of acknowledgment proclaimed by herald, according to rules fixed by custom, and which had full legal force if the assembly had remained silent). It is not clear, meanwhile, why in the case of a bequest made by a novice this validation was not necessary. Perhaps because the possessions involved were of lesser value or, rather, because the property of a novice, whose status was not yet defined, was subject to secular law.

89. *Mi-sha-sai-pu ho-hsi wu-fen lü* 20.139a–b. Parallel text in *Ssu-fen lü* 41.859b–c.

90. See above, pp. 66ff.

91. It may be noted that the distribution of the property of deceased monks by drawing lots (by means of tablets, Skr. *alaka*, Chin. *ch'ou*) is also mentioned in the Vinaya of the Sarvāstivāda, *Shih-sung lü* 28.202a, where the expression "to drop tablets" (*to-ch'ou*) is used. The procedure reappeared later in China. See also n. 101 below.

92. *Ssu-fen lü shan-fan pu-ch'üeh hsing-shih ch'ao*, "Hsia," 1.116c. It also occurred, in the case of an insufficient number of garments, that they were made over in priority to the elderly. See *Shih-sung lü* 28.202a. The same practice is also indicated for Southeast Asia in Lingat, "Vinaya et droit laïc." If the goods could be divided in equal parts among all the religious, then the novices were entitled to only one-third of the share received by the monks and the nuns. See above, p. 90.

93. With the exception of the Vinaya of the Mahāsāṃghika.

94. *Shih-sung lü* 7.53a.

95. See also *Mo-ho seng-ch'i lü* 10.313a: "When selling goods within the community, it is permitted to raise the price [in the course of the sale]; there is no sin in obtaining such goods. If a preceptor (*upādhyāya*) or an instructor (*ācārya*) [i.e., a master, rather than a simple disciple] wishes to have them, he may not reduce the price (*ch'ao*)." Ordinary monks, by contrast, could show greater determination in their bargaining. The Vinaya of the Dharma-guptaka (*Ssu-fen lü* 8.651a) remains more austere: trading pure goods within the community is only permitted providing that it does not give rise to the kind of haggling that takes place in the markets. On commercial regulations pertaining to the clergy and the extent of their prominence in the Vinaya, see pp. 153–66.

96. *Mo-ho seng-ch'i lü* 31.479c.

97. The five qualities define an upright individual: absence of attachment, anger, fear, and fatuity, and knowledge of the appropriate.

98. *Shih-sung lü* 7.53a.

99. See *Sa-p'o to p'i-ni p'i-p'o sha* 5.536b.

100. *Shih-shih yao-lan* C.309b-c, art. "*ch'ang-i*" (auction sales of clothing).

101. *Ch'ih-hsiu Po-chang ch'ing-kuei* 6.1148c. Cf. ibid. 3.1129a. This work survives only in late recensions. One of these, by the monk Te-hui, published between 1336 and 1338, is included in the *Taishō* canon (no, 2025). The "Rules of Purity of the Master of Mount Po-chang [i.e., Huai-hai (749–814)]" were intended for the monks of the Dhyāna school. "Today," Te-hui adds, "the practice is to draw lots for articles, which prevents excessive shouting and disputes. In such cases, small pieces of paper

are used on which the Thousand Characters [of the *Ch'ien-tzu wen*] are inscribed. The writing is usually in seal script of the *kuan-fang* type. The size of the assembly is ascertained, and the person who presided over the funeral may gather a number of people to fold the tickets. In due course, he passes these on to the superiors of the two wings of the monastery who open the folds. The visitors' attendant distributes the tickets among the religious. . . . Each deposits one half of the ticket he has received in a circulating tray. A novice takes a half-ticket at random from the tray. The character on it is identified and announced. Each opens his half-ticket and if the half-character on it is the same, he responds. If he does not wish to buy the object in question, he does not respond. If after three calls there is no response, the superior casts the ticket into a basin filled with water. Another half-ticket is taken and the same procedure is resumed. Once all the tickets have been examined, purchases at fixed price [determined at the time of the calls] take place. Remaining articles, which after three days have not been purchased, are sold to the laity outside at the price previously determined" (3.1129b). On drawing lots for clothing in the Vinaya, see p. 340, n. 91 above.

102. Provisions were made for the sale of at least a part of these items. See the testament of Ch'ung-en above.

103. See below, p. 365, n. 23.

104. I.e., gifts received from officials.

105. On this title, which occurs frequently in Tun-huang manuscripts, see Demiéville, *Le Concile de Lhasa*, pp. 238–39, note.

106. *Lin-k'uang*: "approaching the tomb."

107. After the end of the T'ang, the titles of high court officials were commonly used to address local officials. Such titles must therefore not be taken to have precisely the same meaning as at Ch'ang-an.

108. There is an unexplained discrepancy: the total amounts in fact to 60,822 *ch'ih*.

109. Monastery serfs, designated here as *ssu-jen* ("people of the *ssu*"). On this particular class of dependents, see pp. 105–11 above.

110. Novices of both sexes here received one half of a share from donations. The Vinaya of the Sarvāstivāda only accords them one-third of the share of a bhikṣu. See *Shih-sung lü* 29.285c, on the distribution of gifts made by lay donors at the time of the fast (*upoṣadha*).

111. P. 2638. This manuscript was edited almost in extenso by Naba Toshisada, *Shina bukkyō shi gaku* 2.4, in one of the end notes. The monks and nuns received a total of ca. 15,492 m of cotton cloth, the novices ca. 2,106 m, together ca. 17,598 m. The proceeds of the sales were not distributed to the religious in entirety. A sizeable part was kept in reserve in the treasury of one of the monasteries. This latter part is designated in the *Po-chang ch'ing-kuei* by the technical term *ch'ou-fen*.

112. Rather, there is a deficit of 20 *ch'ih*. Likewise below.

113. The character *ch'en* is restored on the basis of other passages in this text.

114. Fifth of no. 96 in the series *ch'eng*. This document has been edited in the Bulletin of the Peking National Library, *Kuo-li Pei-p'ing t'u-shu kuan kuan-k'an* 5.6, November-December 1931, p. 79.

115. P. 2049, management report of the steward for the year Yüan-ta, at Ching-t'u monastery, dated second year Ch'ang-hsing (931).

116. A foot (*ch'ih*) of cotton cloth had the same value as a bushel (*tou*) of wheat or millet. Thus the equivalent of six or fifteen liters (*shih*) of cereals, respectively, was allotted to each monk. Fifteen *shih* represented approximately the price of an ox. See Appendix C, pp. 315–16.

117. This synthesis had already taken place under the Mahāsāṃghika. However,

that sect still resorted to the simple division of the clothing of deceased monks. See above, p. 88.

118. See above, pp. 129–35.

4. Lands and Dependents

1. The accounts of the Ching-t'u monastery contain several names of *chih-sui* (cf. above, p. 35) who seem to have succeeded one another with an interval of a few years.

2. Probable date.

3. P. 4081.

4. China did, however, have a tradition of Taoist hermits; and on this type of itinerant magicians was to be modeled an entire class of independent monks. See above, pp. 250, 252.

5. Cf. *Sacred Books of the East*, vol. 13, "Pātimokkha," p. 33; *Ssu-fen lü* 19.384c–385b; *Mo-ho seng-ch'i lü* 41.854a–b; *Shih-sung lü* 16.117a–b. This corresponded to a widespread taboo that was also not unknown in China but owed the benefit of a rational interpretation to Buddhism: one did not break the ground in order to avoid harming the insects that lived there.

6. *Mi-sha-sai-pu ho-hsi wu-fen lü* 6.41c–42a; *Ssu-fen lü* 11.641b; *Ken-pen shuo i-ch'ieh yu-pu p'i-nai-yeh* 27.775c–776a.

7. See above, p. 70.

8. This was especially the case in the Dhyāna school where labor served as a test of the firmness of a young recruit's vocation and where such trials formed part of the physical and moral discipline leading to illumination.

9. *Kao-seng chuan* 5.351c.

10. Ibid. 3.337b.

11. *Ken-pen sa-p'o to-pu lü she* 6.558b. Concerning the impurity of goods not acquired by begging or through pious donations, see p. 357, n. 28 below.

12. *Shih-sung lü* 53.430a.

13. Cf. above, p. 336, n. 26.

14. This conveys the idea of a semipastoral and semiagricultural production that did not have an equivalent in China.

15. *Mo-ho seng-ch'i lü* 16.353a. The offering of first-fruits to the saṃgha seems to have been a widespread custom; another example is found in *Shih-sung lü* 58.437b.

16. *Mo-ho seng-ch'i lü* 29.467b. For another narrative featuring Bimbisāra, in which he gives five hundred keepers of the gardens (*shou-yüan jen*) to the monks, see *Shih-sung lü* 58.433a.

17. Collections of Indian inscriptions confirm the reality of these practices.

18. *Kao-seng Fa-hsien chuan* 859b.

19. Cf. Balazs, "Beiträge," 34:45 ff.

20. Cf. Maspero, *Etudes historiques*, p. 163.

21. *Hsin T'ang shu* 51.1342. Such a provision, at any rate that concerning personal share lands, is only conceivable once the trading of large-scale farm lands had become customary. On this question, see pp. 129–30.

22. Cf. *Chou-li cheng-i*, "Ti-kuan ta ssu-t'u", 19.14a: "Each family receives one hundred *mu* of lands that are continuously cultivated (*pu-i*, i.e., without fallowing), two hundred *mu* of lands requiring one fallowing (*i-i*, i.e., one year out of two), and three hundred *mu* of lands requiring repeated fallowing (*tsai-i*, i.e., two years out of three)." "In restricted localities," says the *Hsin T'ang shu*, 51.1342, "the size of allotments is doubled in the case of lands requiring fallowing one year out of two (*i-i*); in broad localities, by contrast, in the case of lands requiring fallowing one year out of

three (san-i), the area is not doubled." It is certain that the term san-i designates triennial rotation with a one-year fallowing, for it would not make sense for the area of the allotments to be reduced when more frequent fallowings were necessary. Balazs, "Beiträge," 34:45, n. 123, interprets the term san-i to designate fallowing in three consecutive years, but also remarks that such a practice would have been scarcely conceivable in T'ang times.

23. T'ang-lü shu-i 30.228, art. 1, commentary.

24. Concerning the colonies of deported soldiers and peasants, see Balazs, "Beiträge," 34:73ff.

25. The use of the term Church is justified with respect to the Northern Wei. The "universal saṃgha" was then a reality, undoubtedly imposed by imperial policy in Northern China, and due to a marked desire at that time to conform to the monastic rules of India.

26. Wei shu 114, trans. Ware, "Wei Shou"; Hurvitz, "Wei Shou."

27. T'an-yao was appointed controller of Buddhist clergy (sha-men t'ung) at the beginning of the Ho-p'ing reign (460–465). The famous caves at Ta-t'ung in Shansi were due to his initiative. The office of sha-men t'ung held by T'an-yao constituted the highest rank of the monastic administration. It was a semisecular and semi-ecclesiastical appointment conferred by the emperor on eminent monks as counsellors to the sovereign in all Buddhist matters. The first tao-jen t'ung (controller of the religious, according to the old appellation) was Fa-kuo (cf. "Shih-Lao chih," Wei shu 114.3030), under T'ai-tsung. He died in 416–423. His successor was Shih-hsien (ibid. 3036), a member of the royal family of Cashmere. T'an-yao, who succeeded the latter, changed the title from tao-jen t'ung to sha-men t'ung. A biography of T'an-yao is found in Hsü kao-seng chuan 1.427c–428a.

28. The commandery of P'ing-ch'i was situated to the northwest of P'eng-ch'eng, at that time the capital city of the Wei near Ta-t'ung in Shansi.

29. Under the Wei, the administration of the saṃgha comprised a central office at the capital, which was originally named chien-fu ts'ao, Office for the Supervision of Meritorious Works, and renamed Office for the Illumination of Mysteries (chao-hsüan ts'ao) in 479. At the head of this office was the controller [general] of Buddhist clergy (sha-men [tu-]t'ung), later designated chao-hsüan t'ung. Under him served an overseer [of monks] ([tu-]wei-na, Skr. karmadāna). Subordinate to this central administration were the Offices of Buddhist clergy (seng-ts'ao) in the provinces and garrisons, which were similarly organized and in turn had provincial sha-men t'ung and wei-na.

30. Those guilty of a grave crime (chung-tsui) or of one of the Ten Abominations (shih-o), which ranged from conspiracy to incest.

31. The traditional formula designating the corvée duties that were levied by monasteries on their dependents.

32. For reasons explained below, I do not adopt Ware's interpretation, according to which the slaves were made to furnish a contribution of grain (Ware, "Wei Shou," p. 147).

33. "Shih-Lao chih," Wei shu 114.3037.

34. Fo-tsu t'ung-chi 38.355a.

35. Tsukamoto Zenryū, "Hokugi no sōgiko butsotoko."

36. See also Tzu-chih t'ung-chien 132.4148–9, which reproduces T'an-yao's petition under the entry mentioning the establishment of P'ing-ch'i commandery. The creation of the seng-ch'i hu thus took place immediately after the foundation of the commandery that comprised the two counties of Huai-ning and Kuei-an. See Wei shu 24.630, biography of Ts'ui Tao-ku.

37. There were apparently groups of families of military colonists with collective responsibilities, at the head of one of which was a certain Chao Kou-tzu.

38. "Shih-Lao chih," *Wei shu* 114.3042.

39. In the year 468, the Wei invaded part of the Sung territory north of the Huai. See *Wei shu* 50.1119, biography of Mu-jung Po-ao. Cf. Wang Yi-t'ong, "Slaves," n. 18.

40. For the T'ang period, cf. *T'ang hui-yao* 86.1569 ("Nu-pi"), which was inspired by the Wei code: "According to an ancient provision, those who are collectively implicated in the crime of rebellion have their patrimony confiscated and become official slaves (*kuan nu-pi*). With one degree of mitigation, they become "duty households" *fan-hu* (attached to officials: this was the case of those who were not installed at P'ing-ch'i); with two degrees, they become *tsa-hu* (households liable to miscellaneous [corvées]); and with three degrees, they revert to [the status] of freemen (*liang-jen*).

41. *Wei shu* 7A.139, third year of Yen-hsing.

42. "Shih-huo chih," *Wei shu* 110.2857.

43. See p. 108.

44. *T'ang liu-tien* 7.8a.

45. Millet was still the grain most commonly cultivated in the regions of colonization under the T'ang. See Balazs, "Beiträge," 34:74: "allgemein wurde Hirse angebaut."

46. The institution of the price-regulating granaries had a long history in China. Under the Han, granaries designated as *ch'ang-p'ing ts'ang* were instituted by Keng Shou-ch'ang under Hsüan-ti, during the Wu-feng reign period (57–54 B.C.). Cf. *Han shu* 24A.1141. The name was changed to *ch'ang-man ts'ang* under Ming-ti (r. A.D. 58–75). Under the T'ang, these granaries were subordinate to price-controlling offices (*ch'ang-p'ing shu*). Cf. des Rotours, *Traité des fonctionnaires*, pp. 441–42.

47. Famines occurred frequently during the He-p'ing (460–465), T'ien-an (466), Huang-hsing (467–470), and Yen-huang (471–475) reigns. See *Wei shu* 6, 7A, 7B, passim, and the decrees of the first year of T'ai-ho (477): "Let the humidity of the soil be examined and let every effort be made to extract the best benefit from the land"—"May no one be left with strength to spare and no lands incompletely exploited" (*Wei shu* 7A.143 and 144).

48. The biography of Ts'ui Tao-ku, the administrator of the P'ing-ch'i commandery from the time of its foundation, relates that he was unable to relieve the famine that prevailed in his district and that he died in the midst of a peasant uprising during the Yen-hsing era (471–475). See *Wei shu* 24.630.

49. It should be noted that only families able to provide sixty *hu* of millet annually were made *seng-ch'i hu*. Thus it appears that in principle they were given the freedom of choice.

50. There are several indications to that effect in the "Shih-Lao chih."

51. *Shih-sung lü* 56.413c.

52. The same term was used in the designation of the Buddha households (*fo-t'u hu*).

53. The *chien-fu ts'ao* was renamed *chao-hsüan ts'ao* in 479.

54. *Kuang hung-ming chi* 24.272c. Cf. *Fo-tsu t'ung-chi* 38.355b. Nor is it inconceivable, as was suggested by Ōmura Seigai (*Shina bijutsu chōsohen*, p. 176) that the saṃgha millet served to defray the cost for the famous Yun-kang Caves.

55. Decree of the year 511, see p. 104.

56. On the property held in perpetuity (*ch'ang-chu*) see above, pp. 66ff. Undoubtedly, the greatest effort to copy the Indian institutions and to conform to the prescriptions of the Vinaya was made under the Wei. Evidence of this can be seen in the terminology: certain terms which were current at the time (*sha-men, seng-ch'i, fo-*

t'u, ching-jen), but occur more rarely under the T'ang, were borrowed from the treatises on discipline translated at the beginning of the fifth century. In 424 an imperial decree ordered the monasteries to adopt the name *chao-t'i* (*caturdiśa: ssu-fang* [*ch'ang-chu*]). See *Fo-tsu t'ung-chi* 39.354a.

57. "Shih-Lao chih," *Wei shu* 114.3042.

58. "Shih-Lao chih," *Wei shu* 114.3041–2, decree of the fourth year of the Yung-p'ing reign. Cf. Hurvitz, *Wei Shou*, pp. 86–87.

59. In "Ryōko kō," *Shina bukkyō shigaku* 2.4 (1938): 35–36.

60. P. 2187, text no. 3.

61. Insignia to which officials above the third rank were entitled. See des Rotours, *Traité des fonctionnaires*, pp. 366–67. Thus there must have been halberds at the gates of certain official monasteries as well.

62. On the soothing effect of Buddhism on the Tibetans, see Demiéville, *Le Concile de Lhasa*, historical commentary, *passim*. The text implies that there were many barbarians among the dependents of the monasteries at Sha-chou.

63. The compliance of the secular administration with regard to the monks was an important element in the economic history of Chinese Buddhism. See above, p. 182.

64. See above, p. 43.

65. After the middle of the T'ang, it became customary in the prefectures to designate important officials with titles originally used only at court. Here the term *t'ai-pao* probably refers to the general Chang I-ch'ao, who reconquered Tun-huang and the northwestern marches in the middle of the ninth century and died in 872. See Demiéville, *Le Concile de Lhasa*, p. 37, note. The present text can therefore be dated to the end of the ninth or the beginning of the tenth century.

66. They always had been, but the author wishes to reaffirm their character as inalienable possessions.

67. A contract for the sale of a slave to a monastery peasant (? *ch'ang-chu po-hsing*) is extant. See the document edited in Niida Noboru, *Tō Sō hōritsu*, pp. 184–85.

68. P. 3490 v°.

69. P. 3859 r°.

70. Such an organization suggests a controlled and collective form of cultivation. It contrasts with the individualism prevalent among free peasants in the Tun-huang area and with the parceling of the land that was generally current in that region. It seems to have been the rule in the "colonies": in 1136, under the Southern Sung, "the government of Chiang and of Huai (the region of Anhwei) presented a memorial to the emperor requesting the transformation of the agricultural colonies into military colonies (*t'un-t'ien*). . . . Each area of 5 *ch'ing* (ca. 27 ha) would form an estate (*chuang*). The families of these estates (*k'o-hu*) were to be organized into groups of five families with collective responsibility and would be engaged in the cultivation of the lands [of that estate]. [Each group] would be supervised by a head of cultivation (*t'uan-t'ou*); the farmers of each estate would be supplied with five oxen, seed, and agricultural implements. Each family (*chia*) would receive individually a vegetable plot of 10 *mu* (0.54 ha). They would also be loaned a capital of seventy thousand cash, to be reimbursed, free of interest, within two years." See *Chien-yen i-lai ch'ao-yeh tsa-chi* 98, second month of the sixth year of Shao-hsing.

71. The hire for a unit of labor at Tun-huang was 1 *t'o* of wheat or millet or, according to some contracts, 8 *tou* and 7 *sheng*. Thus it would seems that a "load" represents .78 *shih* of cereals, or ca. 50 liters. According to the "Shih-huo chih" of the *Sui shu*, a good horse could carry 8 loads (*t'o*), or ca. 4 hectoliters of cereals, an ordinary horse 6 loads (ca. 3 hectoliters). See Balazs, "Traité économique," p. 172.

72. *Tun-huang shih-shih hsieh-ching t'i-chi yü Tun-huang tsa-lu* ch. "hsia," fasc. 2, p. 120.

73. The master of instruction was perhaps an overseer of farm work. Although the title appears elsewhere in Tun-huang manuscripts, however, it is impossible to confirm this hypothesis.

74. *Tun-huang shih-shih hsieh-ching t'i-chi yü Tun-huang tsa-lu*, ibid., p. 121.

75. Ibid., p. 122.

76. They were in fact simple advances. The term used is *pien* ("to place at the disposition") whereas loans with interest were designated as *tai* or *tai-pien*.

77. According to Naba Toshisada, *Shina bukky shi gaku* 2.4, all the petitions edited by Hsü Kuo-lin in *Tun-huang shih-shih hsieh-ching t'i-chi yü Tun-huang tsa-lu* and dated *hsin-ch'ou* or *ch'ou* date to the year 881.

78. *Tun-huang shih-shih hsieh-ching t'i-chi yü Tun-huang tsa-lu*, p. 119.

79. On agricultural loans, see pp. 174ff.

80. See p. 341 above, n. 105.

81. P. 2856, fol. 6 and 7 v°.

82. See also P. 3418 v°, which contains a list of payments in fodder made by private individuals (*po-hsing*) and in which also figure a number of monks who were apparently owners of fields.

83. See the tables at the end of Bielenstein, *The Census of China*.

84. These regulations cannot have extended to lands under cultivation so long as the conceptions opposed to the trading of peasant fields offered some resistance.

85. Shansi itself, with the loess deposits on its plateaux, was no exception to this rule: In the valleys, where large-scale cultivation ceased, one could expect to find private estates (*chuang*), gardens, thickets, and small enclaves of laid-out fields.

86. See above, p. 100.

87. The granting of appanages to eminent monks did occur, but such benefices were of a strictly personal character, and surely not transmissible. Among other famous examples, we may quote that of Chih-i: "It is appropriate to grant the master of Dhyāna Chih-i, the Buddhist hero whom today's Buddhist artisans follow as their patron, and who instructs both the clergy and laity, a part of Shih-feng county (modern T'ien-t'ai county, Chekiang) and to levy taxes for the needs of his community. Let two families be exempted from impositions so that he may employ them for firewood and water duty. May the authorities see to the implementation of this order" (imperial order of the Ch'en Emperor Hsüan-ti of 577), cited in *Kuo-ch'ing po-lu* 1. In 774, the master Pu-k'ung received the title duke of Hsiao principality, with tax revenue from three thousand families (*Fo-tsu t'ung-chi* 41.379a).

88. *Kao-seng chuan* 8.377b.

89. *Hsü kao-seng chuan* 17.568b.

90. *Shih wen-chi* 40.34a–38a.

91. On this mode of official recognition of privately founded places of worship, see pp. 43–44 above.

92. See Maspero, *Etudes historiques*, pp. 195–208, "Les termes désignant la propriété foncière en Chine."

93. See p. 129.

94. They were serfs who remained attached to their masters and their land. Once the concept of ownership had spread with the development of commerce, the monastery households could be reduced to slavery. That is what we find in the case of the "families under double imposition (*erh-shui hu*)" under the Liao (947–1122): "At the beginning of their reign, the Liao fawned even more on Buddhism. The emperor frequently made gifts of free peasants to the monasteries. Their imposition were divided into two parts, one of which went to the state, and the other to the monastery. Thus these families were called 'families subject to double imposition' " (*Chin-shih* 46.1033). In principle, these families should have remained under the con-

trol of the secular administration, but during the unrest that accompanied the succession of the Liao by the Chin they were all made slaves (nu-pi). See also the biography of Li Yen in Chin-shih 96.2127: "The emperor of the Liao had previously made a gift of people to the Lung-kung monastery in Chin-chou who were to pay taxes to the monastery. In time, however, they had all become slaves. Those who attempted to denounce the matter were killed in the island (?). Li Yen then submitted a detailed report to the court: 'Buddhist discipline prohibits the killing of animals, yet human beings are killed. The Liao transformed free peasants into families subject to double imposition: a profoundly iniquitous act!' Following this report, Shih-tsung (r. 1161–1189) ordered the emancipation of more than six hundred persons." Cf. the biography of Hsiang An, ibid., 94.2088: "As soon as he came to power, Chang-tsung (1190–1208) considered means to bring slavery in Buddhist and Taoist monasteries to an end. Grand Marshal K'o Ning stated in his report: 'This practice is now well entrenched. To attempt to put an end to it abruptly would create discontent. Since Your Majesty deplores the excessive number of these slaves, severe measures should be instituted to prevent a further increase. Thereby their numbers will be reduced by natural means.' Hsiang [a member of the imperial family] said: 'How can the clergy employ slaves? I request that irrespective of the manner in which they had originally been acquired, all be released and returned to the state of freemen. Even if it can be proven that these slaves have long been part of the monasteries' patrimony, they should be enfranchised.' The emperor acceded to Hsiang's recommendation in his edict, and most of the families under double imposition were subsequently returned to the state of freemen."

95. Shen-seng chuan 2.958b, biography of Fa-an.

96. See above, p. 37.

97. See above, p. 39.

98. Above all, for moral and economic tutelage: the monasteries had granaries (on agricultural loans, see pp. 174ff. above). Possibly, the monasteries also granted asylum to laymen in times of pillage or war. References to fortified monasteries, however, are rare. Following are two of them: at the beginning of the sixth century, Emperor Wu of the Liang supplied thirty soldiers to the A-yü-wang monastery (see below) to construct fortifications for it (stele edited in Chin-shih ts'ui-pien 108.8b). In 605, Emperor Yang of the Sui had a fourfold enclosure of earthwork constructed for a monastery of Yang-chou (Hsü kao-seng chuan 19.586a, biography of Chih-tsao).

99. Similar enfeoffments of the Church occurred in Europe to an even greater extent. See Bloch, La société féodale, p. 103: "The heads of the clergy thus had numerous lay dependents at their command, from military vassals, indispensable to the defense of such large possessions, down to the villeins and the dependents of lower station. These latter, in particular, thronged to the churches. Was it really that to live 'under the cross' rather than under the sword seemed a fate worth coveting? . . . Two things are certain. The durability that was peculiar to the ecclesiastic establishments, and the respect that surrounded them, made them particularly sought after by the humble as patrons. Second, he who gave himself to a saint not only contracted an insurance against the perils of the times; he also procured the no less valuable benefits of a pious work."

100. Cf. the indications concerning the sale of farmland in Balazs, "Traité économique," appendix 3, pp. 279–80.

101. China at that time still remained profoundly "feudal," and political conditions lent themselves to the formation of these new ties of dependence.

102. See above, p. 39.

103. The implication is that these laymen no longer provided taxes and labor services.

104. The color of garments worn by official slaves in antiquity.

105. Biography of Kuo Tsu-shen in *Nan shih* 70.1721–2.

106. The maps at the end of Bielenstein, *The Census of China*, illustrate well this general fact and its persistence through the course of history.

107. Cf. Gernet, "La vente en Chine."

108. The notion of property applied where it is least expected. The reverse obtained in the West, where uncultivated lands often became communal property.

109. Tomb lands were purchased from the gods in the first instance, or occasionally from private individuals (see the con tracts collected by Lo Chen-yü in *Ti-ch'üan cheng-ts'un*). For although fallow lands belonged to all, they belonged in the first place to the gods who had to guarantee their perpetual possession. In Han times, *ming-t'ien* were the only transmissible kind of landed property, whether by succession or purchase. Moreover, their price was relatively low (cf. Maspero, *Etudes historiques*, p. 154, to which I refer for this introduction, while also emphasizing aspects concerning techniques and topography which Maspero had left aside): two indications that these were uneven terrains with poor soils. The analogy between the *ming-t'ien* and tomb lands, sometimes even their identity, is beyond doubt (cf. Lo Chen-yü, op. cit., which features the purchase contract for a burial mound which is none other than a *ming-t'ien*). The Han minister Li Ts'ai was accused of having sold a lot of three hundred *mu* which was part of the tomb of Emperor Ching (cf. Maspero, ibid., p. 155).

110. See p. 119.

111. Biography of Fa-ning in *Hsü kao-seng chuan* 27.678a.

112. Mount A-yü-wang was situated near Ssu-ming (modern Ning-po, south of the bay of Hang-chou). For the information given here, see the steles of the A-yü-wang monastery reproduced in *Chin-shih ts'ui-pien* 108.8b and the stele of the Kuang-li ch'an-ssu of Ssu-ming in *Chih-yüan chi*, "Ch'ien-chi," 3.

113. Lit. "fields belonging to the property held in perpetuity."

114. The private properties *shu* and, especially under the T'ang, *chuang*, were constituted of high-lying terrain; like the monastic properties, they eventually incorporated low-lying lands. Cf. p. 129. The stūpa in question had been erected by Emperor An in 405.

115. These fiscal privileges were no doubt granted in the year 522, at the same time when Emperor Wu conferred its official name (o) on the monastery. On this practice, see p. 43 above.

116. Another anecdote which similarly illustrates the contiguity of monastic fields with pastures is found in *Hsü shih-shuo* 3.19b: Under the Later Chin (936–947), at the time when the imperial commissioner of Ho-tung, Liu Yüan-chih, was still only a commoner, he was grazing the horses of his adoptive father-in-law Li of Chi-yang when he intruded on some fields belonging to monks. The religious seized him and gave him a thrashing.

117. See p. 255.

118. *Kao-seng chuan* 3.342c.

119. The three payments mentioned here were from the principal bursar to the stewards for the year (*chih-sui*) of the estates (*chuang*). These managed all aspects of the development, frequently taking advantage of their distance from the monastery to enrich themselves by fraudulent means. On the estates of wealthy laymen, these bailiffs were known as *chuang-li*.

120. Chavannes, *Les documents chinois*, no. 969, l. 16. According to Maspero, *Les documents chinois*, p. 188, note to no. 460, the accounts of the monastery in question (in the Mazār-tāgh region) date to ca. 720–723.

121. See preceding note.

122. Chavannes, *Les documents chinois*, no. 970, ll. 3–4.

123. *Hsü kao-seng chuan* 25.654b.

124. On the sale of ordination certificates (*tu-tieh*), see p. 48ff. above.

125. Biography of Tao-piao (740–823) of the monastery of Mount Ling-yin in Hang-chou prefecture, *Sung kao-seng chuan* 15.803c.

126. *Fo-tsu t'ung-chi* 42.384c.

127. Biography of Wen-chü, *Sung kao-seng chuan* 16.808b.

128. "Shih-Lao chih," *Wei shu* 114.3046.

129. All of the official lands within the imperial territory were at that time administered by commissioners for estates ([*nei*] *chuang-chai shih*), an office normally held by eunuchs (see Katō Shigeshi, "Naishōtakushi kō"). It is known that the eunuchs maintained rather close relations with the monks, and the fact that the commissioners for estates were chosen among the eunuchs may have been partly responsible for the size of the monastic estates in the capital. On the political support extended to the monks by the court, see p. 283ff.

130. I.e., in this case, the officials authorized to carry out the sale on behalf of the state.

131. *Chin-shih ts'ui-pien* 114.1a.

132. "Shih-Lao chih," *Wei shu* 114.3044–5.

133. The decree is reproduced in *T'ang hui-yao* 50.878.

134. See also p. 331, n. 122 above.

135. *Chin-shih ts'ui-pien* 83.27a-b. This text was translated by Maspero in his *Etudes historiques*, p. 170.

136. Biography of the monk Yüan-kuan, *Sung kao-seng chuan* 20.839c.

137. *Fo-tsu t'ung-chi* 40.376c.

138. Biography of Yü Ch'ao-en, *Chiu T'ang shu* 184.4764.

139. Imprecations against despoilers seem to have been in general use in deeds of pious donation. Cf. the documents edited in Niida Noboru, *Tōsō hōritsu*, pp. 214 (col. 3 and 6), 217 (col. 5–6).

140. Inscription in *Chin-shih yüan* 2, edited in Niida Noboru, *Tōsō hōritsu*, pp. 215–16.

141. *Hsü kao-seng chuan* 29.697c.

142. At the time of the confiscation of the monastic properties in 845, the texts merely indicated the extent of their "good lands," whereas the total surface area of the land owned by Buddhist establishments was much larger. See p. 137: In the seventh century, tilled fields represented in some regions only a quarter to one half of the mountainous terrains in their possession.

143. *Sung kao-seng chuan* 19.832a.

144. The breeding centers were spread through Shensi and Kansu.

145. *Hsin T'ang shu* 50.1339, trans. in des Rotours, *Traité des fonctionnaires*, p. 901.

146. Maspero, *Les documents chinois*, no. 311, p. 148. This document shows that horses owned by Buddhist monasteries in Central Asia were registered by the secular administration. The monasteries at Tun-huang, by contrast, owned few horses. References such as "three *tou* of wheat delivered to the keeper of horses" (P. 3165 v°) are rare among the monastic accounts found at Tun-huang.

147. See p. 204.

148. P. 3234, fol. 21 v°.

149. See e.g. P. 2049, fol. 14 v°: 0.02 *shih* of koumiss (*su*) delivered by the shepherd.

150. P. 2049.

151. P. 2032.

152. P. 2040.

153. The term used in the Buddhist treatises on discipline; see p. 70 above.

154. The use of the numerary classifier for animals, *t'ou*, clearly indicates that they were not freemen.

155. Biography of Hui-chou (cf. above, pp. 123–24, *Hsü kao-seng chuan* 29.697c).

156. See above, p. 100. From its context, the expression *ying-t'ien* appears to refer specifically to the spring plowing. It is unlikely that slaves were made to pay taxes; contrary to Ware's translation ("Wei Shou," p. 147), the words *shu-su* probably mean simply "to bring in the harvest."

157. Ware's translation of *fo-t'u hu* as "stūpas' households" is unconvincing. Of the three dictionary meanings of the term *fo-t'u*—1. variant transcription of the name Buddha; 2. transcription of the word *stūpa*; 3. by extension, the monastery as a whole—the second is the least appropriate. The Three Jewels (*fo fa seng*) had in practice a concrete meaning, the Buddha being represented by sanctuaries with their statues. In principle, the *fo-t'u hu* were used precisely for the maintenance of the buildings. "Buddha households," as against "saṃgha households," is an entirely consistent expression. If further evidence were necessary, cf. the passage in the Vinaya of the Sarvāstivāda cited above, p. 102.

158. Mochizuki Shinkō, *Bukkyō daijiten*, vol. 5, pp. 4396b–4397c, devotes an article to the term *fu-t'ien* (*puṇyakṣetra*), "fields of merit." Several Buddhist texts are cited there which give different lists of these fields. The *Hua-yüan ching t'an-hsüan chi* 8 (cited on p. 4397b) enumerates the following terms: *en-t'ien, ching-t'ien, te-t'ien, pei-t'ien,* and *k'u-t'ien.* Normally three fields of merit are distinguished: the field of reverence (*ching-t'ien*), represented by the Buddha, the saints, and the saṃgha; the field of benevolence (*en-t'ien*), represented by the two kinds of Buddhist masters (preceptor, *upādhyāya,* and instructor, *ācārya*) and the father and mother; and finally, the field of compassion (*pei-t'ien*), constituted by the sick. Since in China the terms *ching-t'ien* and *pei-t'ien* were sometimes applied to fields the revenues of which were reserved for a special purpose (cf. above, p. 222), it could be surmised that the same was true of the term *en-t'ien.* In that case, the *en-tzu* would have been dependents assigned to work the fields reserved for the expenditures of the most eminent masters and monks of a monastery. But this is no more than an hypothesis, and it must be admitted that *en-tzu* is not a current term.

159. P. 2049, year 930.

160. P. 2032.

161. Stein, *Ancient Khotan,* appendix A, no. 16 (fragment from Dandān-Uiliq).

162. The current term used to designate slaves.

163. *Shih-sung lü* 34.250c–251a.

164. *Lo-yang ch'ieh-lan chi* 5.1018c.

165. *Wei shu* 7A.143.

166. Tsukamoto Zenryū, "Hokugi no sōgiko butsotoko." Another example of this practice under the Wei: "In the second month of the first year of T'ai-ho (477), the emperor visited the Yung-ning monastery where he celebrated a vegetarian feast (*chai*) and pardoned prisoners sentenced to the death penalty." See "Shih-Lao chih," *Wei shu* 114.3039.

167. This class of dependents appeared under the Three Kingdoms. The *pu-ch'ü,* who served as domestics and as private militiamen, were bestowed on high officials by the emperor. As private bondsmen, they enjoyed relative freedom, but they could not leave their masters and remained hereditarily attached to the same family. In *Liang-ch'u ch'ing-chung i,* "Pen," 845b, Tao-hsüan distinguishes three kinds of monastic dependents: 1. domestics (*shih-li kung-chi*); 2. *pu-ch'ü* and housekeepers; 3. slaves. "Although the [first] two categories are distinct," says Tao-hsüan, "since the former are free (*liang*) and the latter servile (*chien*), they are distinguished according

to whether they are with or without ties [to their master]." Thus there were two kinds of domestic servants, and the devolution of their wages depended on whether they were with or without ties to their master. The *pu-ch'ü* occupied an intermediate status between free servants and slaves.

168. Biography of Chang Hsiao-hsiu in *Liang shu* 51.752.

169. *Fan-ch'uan wen-chi* 10.8a.

170. "Shih-Lao chih," *Wei shu* 114.3043.

171. Surprisingly, Empress Ling did not adduce the fact that the ordination of slaves was prohibited by the Vinaya (cf. *Mahāvagga* I, 47, p. 199). The obstacle to a slave's entry into religion lay not in his lowly state as such; but since a slave was his master's property, his prior emancipation would have been prerequisite to an ordination. For analogous reasons, debtors could also not be ordained. See *Mo-ho seng-ch'i lü* 24.420a–b.

172. "Monograph on the Economy," *Hsin T'ang shu* 51.1345.

173. *Ts'e-fu yüan-kuei* 495.5927a.

174. Maspero, *Etudes historiques*, p. 177.

175. Biography of Yang Yen, *Chiu T'ang shu* 118.3421.

176. Maspero, *Etudes historiques*, pp. 177–78. Maspero emphasized that this reform tended to "recognize the new state of affairs." One can see much more in this, for the passage of a form of personal property law to a form of law pertaining to real estate is in itself a significant event.

177. *Ts'e-fu yüan-kuei* 495.5928b.

178. An administrative term. See also p. 131 above for another passage in which the term occurs unequivocally in this meaning. Maspero, *Etudes historiques*, p. 175 took the word in its literal sense of "point a finger."

179. P. 2032.

180. See below, pp. 145.

181. *Ch'üan T'ang wen* 19.3a–b.

182. *Hsü tzu-chih t'ung-chien ch'ang-pien* 262, eighth year of Hsi-ning. By implication, officials were, unlike peasants, at that time authorized to donate or sell their private properties to monasteries.

183. *Sung hui-yao kao* 121.31b, report of the twentieth day, seventh month of the first year Cheng-ho (1111). For the Yüan, cf. the report of Li Chieh, the prefect of Ch'u-chou (in modern Anhwei), cited in the introduction to Ratchnevsky, *Un code des Yuan*: "I have noted that the population in the Chiang and Huai region (Anhwei) emigrated during the war, abandoning their fields and dwellings. These either fell into the hands of strangers or were divided, according to convenience, among the neighbors, relatives, or friends of the same village. While the emigrants had not yet returned to their lands after the pacification, certain ill-intentioned and dishonest individuals claimed to be in possession of old sales contracts drawn up under the Sung, or of deeds of antichresis, or yet other documents." These illegitimate owners safeguarded themselves by donating the lands allegedly in their possession to monasteries.

184. This was already the case for the acquisition, by purchase or clearing, of elevated or uneven terrains. See p. 119 above.

185. P. 3947 v°; the part in question of this document is written in pale red ink and very difficult to read.

186. Cf. p. 50 above.

187. The square brackets here indicate characters that were added subsequently or in the form of notes.

188. The distinction is maintained between lands that were used to grow wheat or millet and all others (gardens, orchards, etc.).

189. I.e., a total of 13 1/2 ares. The fact that Kuang-yün had received a personal

share of land on the Chieh canal shows that this form of allotment persisted at Tunhuang at that time, but it should be noted that the size of the *k'ou-fen* was extremely reduced.

190. Other hire contracts for works in the Chinese Pelliot Collection from Tunhuang are: P. 2249 v°, P. 3964, P. 5008, and 5522, fol. 4 v°. The usual hire seems to have amounted to 8 *tou* and 7 *sheng* (ca. 50 liters) of cereals per month. Sometimes, as here, the amount is indicated as a "load" (*t'o*), which was probably the equivalent to about 87 *sheng*.

191. P. 3094 v°, document edited in Naba Toshisada, *Shina bukkyō shi gaku* 2.1.

192. The preceding no doubt concerned the personal lands held by the religious, since the dispositions that follow relates to the communities' lands. The phrase "in conformity with the law" refers to earlier provisions which are found in *Ta T'ang liu-tien* 3.10b. See also below.

193. In fact, the lands of large monasteries were always more extensive, amounting to between twenty and fifty ch'ing. Cf. above, p. 138.

194. *T'ang hui-yao* 59.1028, "Ssu-pu yüan-wai lang."

195. *T'ang liu-tien* 3, "Shang-shu hu-pu."

196. See *Po K'ung liu-t'ieh* 89.9a: "*Tao-shih* who had at least mastered the Book of Lao-tzu were provided with thirty *mu*; the same applied to Buddhist monks who had received full ordination." *Ta Sung seng-shih lüeh* B, "Seng-chu chih feng:" "*Tao-shih* who can understand the two chapters of the *Lao-tzu* are provided with thirty *mu*, and the same rule applies to monks who can understand the canonical texts."

197. By adding the *ch'ang-chu* lands to the lands that were held individually, an average of ca. fifty *mu* per religious is obtained.

198. The interest due at the end of the agricultural season always equalled half the amount of the loan.

199. P. 3150. Edited in Naba Toshisada, *Shina bukkyō shi gaku* 2.4.

200. Ikeda On, *Tun-huang and Turfan Documents* 3, no. 426, dates this contract to 943.

201. On the basis of the indications provided by this contract, it is possible to ascertain the productivity of land at Tun-huang at the time: The 3 *shih* borrowed should produce 1.5 *shih* of interest in one year, and 3 *shih* in two years. Yüan-chi could only be reimbursed by harvesting 6 *shih* from the 5 *mu* of land (not counting the value of seed and labor), i.e., a slightly more than .5 *shih* per *mu* per year. Cf. Balazs, "Beiträge," 34:52.

202. Levied on the produce of the land.

203. P. 3214 v°, edited in Naba Toshisada, "Girans."

204. Asakawa, "Monastic *shō* in medieval Japan," pp. 311–42.

205. An example of the justification of commercial operations on religious grounds.

206. This particular meaning of the term was known in China under the Northern Wei. See "Shih-Lao chih," *Wei shu* 114.3039. Concerning monk-peasants, see pp. 38 and 114 above.

207. See pp. 115ff. above.

208. Aoyama Sadao, "Sōgen shakai-keizai shiryō," pp. 119–33. It should be recalled that in modern times only 27 percent of the total surface area of China have been under cultivation.

209. *Chiu T'ang shu* 18A.606, fifth year of Hui-ch'ang; *Fan-ch'uan wen-chi* 10.9b; *Fo-tsu t'ung-chi* 42.387a, l. 17.

210. *T'ang hui-yao* 47.841.

211. *Wen-hsien t'ung-k'ao* 3.2b. 14 million ch'ing are the approximate equivalent of 75,600,000 ha. Before the middle of this century, China is said to have had 85 mil-

lion ha under cultivation. The surface area thus did not vary greatly. Yields, on the other hand, have much increased since T'ang times. An adult today cultivates only 4.5 ares, i.e., 8.5. T'ang *mu*, whereas for the eighth century one can assume an average of 30 *mu* per individual (for the total population of China ca. 750, see Bielenstein, *The Census of China*). According to Balazs, "Beiträge," 34:52, 15 *mu* were necessary to feed one person. Taking the fallow periods into account, however, and the fields planted with hemp, one might expect twice that amount of land per person.

212. See above, p. 133.

213. Maspero, *Etudes historiques*, p. 177.

214. P. 4021.

215. See above, p. 100 and, for a confirmation of this figure at Tun-huang, p. 352, n. 201.

216. The fact that the tax for this plot did not vary suggests that it was subject to a different form of taxation than the others.

217. P. 2049, 2032, 2040, and 3234.

218. See also the accounts of an unidentified monastery, in P. 4542: Revenues from the kitchen plot at Nan-sha, 17.55 *shih* of soya beans and 2.6 *shih* of wheat; revenues from the kitchen plot situated below the monastery, 13.05 *shih* of wheat. Total, 33.2 *shih*.

219. The *Chiu T'ang shu* and the *Fo-tsu t'ung-chi* give the same figure.

220. *Liang-jen chih-fu*: on the meaning of the expression *chih-fu*, see *Pei-wen yün-fu* (Commercial Press ed.), 4:2640b, where the examples cited are unequivocal. The present context also suggests this interpretation.

221. See above, p. 126.

222. This reading given by Tu Mu is more plausible than the ten *mu* indicated by other texts.

223. See above, pp. 11–12.

224. "Shih-Lao chih," *Wei shu* 114.3045.

225. *Tzu-chih t'ung-chien* 205.6498, first year T'ien-tse wan-sui.

226. Biography of Wang Chin, *Chiu T'ang shu* 118.3417.

227. See above, p. 40.

228. *Liao wen-ts'un* 4.21b, inscription of 1056.

229. Ibid., 5.21b. Cf. Wittfogel and Feng, *Liao (907–1125)*, pp. 295ff.

230. *Ch'ao-yeh tsa-chi*, section 1, 16.7b.

231. *K'o-p'ei*: a seasonal tax based on the extent of the land cultivated.

5. Industrial Installations

1. *San-kuo chih* 15.472.

2. The "Trog-Stössel" of the edition in Franke, *Keng Tschi T'u*.

3. *Chin shu* 33.1008, biography of Shih Ch'ung.

4. See Needham, "Mechanical Engineering," p. 195.

5. See his biography in *Pei shih* 44.1629–35; cf. *Wei shu* 66.1476–81.

6. Hulling or grinding, depending on the cereals, required different techniques and devices. On methods employed in Ming times, see *T'ien-kung k'ai-wu*, Yabuuchi ed., pp. 258–67. Cf. Twitchett, "Monasteries and China's Economy," pp. 534–35.

7. This seems to be implied by the terms used in a Tun-huang manuscript (P. 3207, note of the prioress T'i-yüan of An-kuo monastery, dated 884): "heaven-striking wood" (*ch'ung-t'ien mu*), a term that presumably designates the rocking arms, and "mortars" (*ts'ao*). See the illustration in Yabuuchi ed., *Tenkōkaibutsu no kenkyū*, p. 262, "*shui-t'ui*."

8. The large size is due to the absence of any kind of gear reduction.

9. See *Tenkō kaibutsu no kenkyū*, p. 264, for a sketch of an hydraulic *shui-mo*.

The various explanations concerning the terms *nien* and *wei* are contradictory. According to *T'ang-lü shu-i shih-wen* 4, *nien* designates the rotating stone and *wei* the fixed part of the same apparatus. The ordinary meaning of the word *nien* at least is clear: it designates a roller made of smooth stone. Cf. Twitchett, "The Monasteries and China's Economy," pp. 534–35.

10. The Cheng-ch'ü, which had been excavated during the Warring States period, passed through the modern counties of San-yüan, Fu-p'ing, and P'u-ch'eng before flowing into the Lo. See Chavannes, *Mémoires historiques*, 3:524. The three Po canals had been constructed by the Duke of Po under the reign of Emperor Han Wu-ti (140–87). See des Rotours, *Traité des fonctionnaires*, p. 496, no. 2.

11. *Hsü shih-shuo* 3.3a–b.

12. *Lo-yang ch'ieh-lan chi* 3.1010b.

13. Cf. Jenner, *Memories of Loyang*, appendix 3.

14. *Hsü kao-seng chuan* 17.568b, biography of T'an-ch'ung (515–594). According to ibid., 29.697c, additional mills had been acquired for the Ch'ing-ch'an ssu by the indefatigable efforts of the monk Hui-chou (559–627).

15. *Sui shu* 48.1292.

16. *Hsü kao-seng chuan* 29.696b.

17. *Chin-shih ts'ui-pien* 74.1a–2b. The Shao-lin monastery was situated on the northern slope of the Sung-shan in Teng-feng county, Honan.

18. *Nittō guhō junrei gyōki* 2, fifth year of K'ai-ch'eng (840), twelfth day of the seventh month. San-chiao was the name of a nearby post relay. Cf. Reischauer, *Record of a Pilgrimage*, p. 267.

19. See P. 2507 which contains a fragment of the Ordinances of the Department of Waterways. The *T'ang liu-tien* 7, "Shui-pu lang-chung," gives a different period of utilization: the gates were to be closed from the sixth to the second month. The regulation presumably varied according to the water management of different regions.

20. Cf. the reference to Li in *Hsü shih-shuo* cited above.

21. *Hsin T'ang shu* 126.4419 (biography of Li Yüan-hung). See also *T'ang hui-yao* 89.1622.

22. *T'ang hui-yao* 89.1622.

23. *Hsin T'ang shu* 83.3662–63, biography of the Chao-i princess.

24. *Chiu T'ang shu* 120.3449–67.

25. This reluctance on the part of officials to carry out orders curbing the privileges of important personalities offers a valuable element of interpretation for the historian. Their fear was well-founded for, in addition to the victim's reprisal, a reversal of the emperor's decision was always possible. The protection and immunity enjoyed by Buddhism in China can frequently be explained by that relative lack of authority on the part of the administration.

26. Kuo Tzu-i was not the only important official to have owned mills in the eight century. The *Chiu T'ang shu* 106.3238 reports that Li Lin-fu, at the height of his favor with Hsüan-tsung (between 734 and 752), owned trading houses, fields, gardens and water mills (*shui-wei*) that produced considerable revenues for him.

27. *T'ang hui-yao* 89.1622. The text is reproduced in the biography of Li Chi-fu in *Chiu T'ang shu* 148.3994.

28. P. 2049, management report of the "steward for the year" Yüan-ta. The rents received by the Ching-t'u monastery for its mills were moreover not paid in cereals but in flour.

29. P. 2032, account fragments of Ching-t'u monastery.

30. P. 2040, ditto.

31. Averages established from the accounts for some ten years that appear to be comprised between 924 and 945; manuscripts P. 2032, 2040, 2049, and 3234.

32. P. 2049, year 930, for example contains the indication of an expenditure in *ts'u-mien* for women who had been employed to sew canopies and to make a bonnet for the head of the bodhisattva.

33. Article in *Tōa keizai ronsō* 1.3 and 4 (1941) and 2.2 (1942). I have borrowed here from that study as well as the evidence from the Tun-huang manuscripts.

34. P. 2049, management report of Pao-hu.

35. P. 2032: the Ching-t'u monastery paid, at an unspecified time, 1.5 *shih*, 2 *shih*, then 1 *shih* of bran to millwrights (*wei po-shih*).

36. P. 3107, accounts of the abbess Sheng-ching for the year 886.

37. P. 2032.

38. P. 3005. These sieves were named *wei-san*. On the methods used for purifying flour, see *T'ien-kung k'ai-wu*, chap. 1, paragraph 4; Yabuuchi ed., p. 68.

39. P. 2032, accounts of the Ching-t'u monastery.

40. P. 2040.

41. P. 2049.

42. P. 2032.

43. P. 3424.

44. P. 3928 v°, edited by Naba Toshisada, in *Tōa keizai ronsō* 2.2 (1942): 175. Naba considers that in this document An Yü-lüeh was seeking to be employed as a miller. That, however, seems doubtful. The text in general is not clear; the only point that is certain is An Yü-lüeh's request to have his grain milled.

45. In "Ryōko kō," *Shina bukkyō shi gaku* 2.4 (1938): pp. 30–82.

46. See p. 151.

47. P. 2613.

48. P. 4542 v°.

49. P. 3787. See also P. 2974 and 3395 v°: 58.4 *shih* of wheat, 45.6 *shih* of millet, 5.2 *shih* of soya, and 2.8 *shih* of hemp collected in mill-rent for the year [*ping-*]*ch'en* (896). Accounts of Ch'ing-kuo, first month of the fourth year of Ch'ien-ning (897).

50. P. 5529, fragment 30.

51. P. 2049, management reports of Pao-hu and Yüan-ta.

52. P. 3167, accounts of the abbess Sheng-ching, dated second year of Kuang-ch'i (886). This text is preceded by the management report of the nun Ch'ang-pi, administrator of monastic property (*chao-t'i ssu*), dated third month of the second year Ch'ien-ning (895), and of the same provenance from the An-kuo ssu.

53. See p. 31 above.

54. According to the documents from Tun-huang, one liter of oil was worth 30 feet (*ch'ih*), or 9 m, of cloth. A *ch'ih* of cloth being worth 6 liters of cereals, the value of a liter of oil was equivalent to that of 180 liters of millet or wheat.

55. P. 3234 v°.

56. Ibid.

57. P. 2049.

58. P. 2032, 2040, 2049, 3234.

59. P. 3391 v°.

60. P. 2049.

61. Ibid.

62. P. 2032.

63. P. 2040.

64. P. 2049.

65. P. 2032.

66. P. 2040.

67. P. 2032.

68. P. 2040.

69. P. 3234.
70. P. 2049.
71. P. 2821.
72. P. 4542, accounts of an unidentified monastery.
73. P. 2567.
74. See pp. 189–90 below.

6. Commerce and Usury

1. We shall leave aside the Pāli Vinaya, for here we are only concerned with texts that were known in China. I have arranged the Vinaya in the order of their apparent complexity: Mahīśāsaka, Dharmagupta, Sarvāstivāda, Mahāsāṃghika, and Mūlasarvāstivāda.

2. *Mi-sha-sai-pu ho-hsi wu-fen lü* 5.37a–b (thirtieth *naiḥsargika prāyaścittika*).

3. A close intimate of members of the high society.

4. The expression designates "pure men" (*ching-jen*). See p. 336, n. 26 above.

5. *Ssu-fen lü* 8.618–19c (eighteenth *naiḥsargika prāyaścittika*).

6. *Shih-sung lü* 7.51a–b (eighteenth *naiḥsargika prāyaścittika*).

7. Saint Francis forbade his friars to carry money on their person (*Rule 2*, chap. 4: See *François d'Assise*, in *Sources Chrétiennes*, Paris: Cerf, 1981, p. 188). According to Erasmus and Margaret of Navarre, the rule was evaded by wearing gloves or wrapping the money. The taboo concerning precious metals is most explicitly stated by the Mahāsāṃghika. In that sect, the general prohibition governing commerce and the objects of commerce (precious metals and money) seems to have evolved towards a precise taboo that was more prone to evasion, by application of certain precautions, than was the original rule. Cf. Demiéville, "Concile de Vaiśālī," pp. 271–75.

8. An interesting remark with respect to the developments of icons among the Mahāsāṃghika.

9. *Mo-ho seng-ch'i lü* 10.310c–12c. Concerning the contact with gold and silver, especially with reference to the Mahāsāṃghika, see Demiéville, "Concile de Vaiśālī." Demiéville remarked that in the Pāli Vinaya the prohibition to touch gold, silver, or money extended to the saṃgha, who were not permitted to store precious metals. Cf. Horner, *Book of the Discipline*, 2:102: precious metals are made over to lay followers who exchange them on behalf of the monks, or a particularly *pure* monk deposits them in a place unknown to anyone else.

10. *Upāsaka*: lay believers having pronounced the vow of the triple refuge and received the first five precepts (*pañca śīlāni*): 1. not to kill living beings; 2. not to steal; 3. not to commit adultery; 4. not to lie; 5. not to inebriate oneself. Cf. Mochizuki Shinkō, *Bukkyō daijiten*, 2:1118–20.

11. *Ken-pen shuo i-ch'ieh yu-pu p'i-nai-yeh* 22.740c–41c (eighteenth *naiḥsargika prāyaścittika*). The pit dug by the Mahīśāsaka (see p. 158 above) to receive impure goods, the location of which was to remain concealed, has here become a regular depository for the valuables of the saṃgha.

12. *Mi-sha-sai-pu ho-hsi wu-fen lü* 5.36b–c (twenty-eighth *naiḥsargika prāyaścittika*).

13. *Ssu-fen lü* 8.620b–21b (twentieth *naiḥsargika prāyaścittika*).

14. The censure is extended to all possible objects of barter: bowls, garments, gold, silver, basins, medicinal cures, money, and grain among others.

15. *Shih-sung lü* 7.52a–53b (twentieth *naiḥsargika prāyaścittika*). Thus, for the Sarvāstivāda, the latter practice was not restricted to the disposal of the belongings of deceased monks. The same obtained for the Mahāsāṃghika (see below).

16. The six evil bhikṣu, whose violations of monastic discipline give rise to the

Buddha's enunciation of the prohibitions, are Nanda, Upananda, Punarvasu, Chanda, Aśvaka, and Udāyi. See Mochizuki Shinkō, *Bukkyō daijiten*, 5:5054–55.

17. *Mo-ho seng-ch'i lü* 10.312c–13c.

18. *Ken-pen shuo i-ch'ieh yu-pu p'i-nai-yeh* 22.741c–43a.

19. *Ken-pen shuo i-ch'ieh yu-pu p'i-nai-yeh* 22.743c–44c.

20. It appears that the Mahīśāsaka did not have the same notion of the impurity of precious metals as the Mahāsāṃghika or the Sarvāstivāda, since the former prohibited their use for the purchase of food (see p. 000 above) and the latter considered the consumption of food and the wearing of clothes purchased with precious metals as sinful acts of various degrees (p. 000 above).

21. *Mi-sha-sai-pu ho-hsi wu-fen lü* (twenty-eighth *naiḥsargika prāyaścittika*)

22. *Ssu-fen lü* 8.619c–20b (nineteenth *naiḥsargika prāyaścittika*).

23. This remark should be of interest to historians of India.

24. *Shih-sung lü* 7.51c–52a (nineteenth *naiḥsargika prāyaścittika*).

25. *Mo-ho seng-ch'i lü* 10.313c–14b.

26. Here are two phrases that presumably constitute a note: "These possessions of the Three Jewels must also be used to produce interest, and the goods obtained from interest earnings return to the Three Jewels in order to do them homage."

27. *Ken-pen shuo i-ch'ieh yu-pu p'i-nai-yeh* 22.743a–c (nineteenth *naihsargika prāyaścittika*). The first part of this section, reproducing the story of the exchange of garments by Upananda, figures in all the other Vinaya under the *naihsargika prāyaścittika* concerning buying and selling (*kraya-vikraya*). See p. 156 above. The last precaution corresponds to a clear distinction that was made between two domains of transactions between monks and laity: on the one hand, the exchange of gifts (worldly donations are repaid by the gift of the Law), and profane commercial operations on the other (business is business).

28. If a monk bought what he was supposed to beg it meant the end of the religion and the monastic way of life. To be sure, a bhikṣu who bought his own meal deprived the laity of a particularly favorable opportunity of acquiring a good karma. What is more, he created a dangerous precedent for the saṃgha as a whole. This thought is manifest in the story concerning the barter carried out by Upananda in the *Dharmaguptavinaya* (*Ssu-fen lü* 8.620b–c): "At that time the Bhagavat was in the garden of Anāthapiṇḍada, in the kingdom of Śrāvastī. Upananda, son of Śākya, was traveling on the paths of the kingdom of Kośala. He arrived in a village where there were no lodgings for [monks]. Having gone there, he exchanged some green ginger that he possessed for food and, having eaten, left again. Now Śāriputra was also traveling in that same kingdom of Kośala. When he came to the village where there were no lodgings, he had only his habit and his bowl to beg for food. One after the other, he stopped in front of each house where food had been sold [to Upananda]: "What do you want, reverend?" they asked him. "Something to eat," replied Śāriputra. "Then pay the price." "You must not speak thus; it would be improper for us [to buy our food]." "But Upananda," said the people, "traded his ginger for our food and, having eaten, departed.""

29. We have encountered this remarkable restriction above: barter is permitted within the community provided that it does not give rise to "the kind of haggling that goes on in the marketplace" (*Ssu-fen lü* 8.621a).

30. See pp. 158–59 above. It may justifiably be assumed that at the beginning gifts consisted only of the necessities of life, i.e., food, clothing, and shelter.

31. See the account above concerning the provision of inexhaustible property (*wu-chin wu*) by the *dānapati* for the restoration of monasteries (*saṃghārāma*), in *Ken-pen shuo i-ch'ieh yu-pu p'i-nai-yeh* 22.743b. See also the reference to a loan shop

established by a lay follower for the benefit of sick monks, in *Mi-sha-sai-pu ho-hsi wu-fen lü* 10.73a.

32. Especially those engaged in India's highly developed maritime commerce. In the fields of trade and banking, India was far in advance of China.

33. *Shih-sung lü* 56.415c ("*pi-ch'iu sung*"). Stūpa property here consists of the produce from the cereal-growing fields and the gardens on which the edifice stands that form part of the religious foundation.

34. In the region of modern Bombay.

35. It will be noted how low the interest rate was: 1 percent or less. Moreover, the nonrepayable assets constituted a foundation in perpetuity. It may be asked whether this is not at the origin of the expression "inexhaustible property" (*akṣaya*). On the differences with Chinese lending practices, see p. 175.

36. Lévi, *L'Inde civilisatrice*, p. 145.

37. Of these arrangements, the existence of which would seem highly likely even without the testimony of I-ching, I have found no mention either at Tun-huang or in China. It is known, however, that, in an analogous way, lands were specially designated for the expenses of incense and lamps (*hsiang-ti*). As for agricultural loans, they are amply attested for China.

38. *Nan-hai chi-kuei nei-fa chuan* 4.230c–31a. The final Mahāyānist note is indicative of the synthesis that had taken place between the tradition of the Vinaya and the notions associated with the Greater Vehicle.

39. They are the three Vinaya that we have already had occasion to characterize as "modernist": those of the Sarvāstivāda, the Mahāsāṃghika, and the Mūlasarvāstivāda.

40. *Mo-ho seng-ch'i lü* 10.311c.

41. See p. 163–64 above.

42. A bhikṣu was not permitted to adorn himself with flowers. For the bhikṣu, the garlands were therefore impure.

43. The saṃgha millet (see p. 104 above), for example, served both to defray the current expenses of the cult and for agricultural loans.

44. *Mo-ho seng-ch'i lü* 10.311c.

45. The rule governing the relinquishment of valuables remains obscure, for the monks either conformed to the prohibition against handling them, and thus had nothing to relinquish to the saṃgha, or deliberately violated the prohibition, in which case it is difficult to see why they should voluntarily give up their gains.

46. "The Sogdians excel in trade and love to make a profit. As soon as a man reaches twenty years of age he sets out to the neighboring kingdoms. Wherever there is a profit to be made, they have been." See Chavannes, *Documents sur les Tou-kiue*, p. 134. In the fifth and sixth centuries, there were many monks from Samarkand (surnamed K'ang, i.e., Sogdians) and from Persia (surnamed An, i.e., Parthians) among the foreign religious community in China.

47. See above, p. xi.

48. See p. 25 above.

49. Accounts of the Ching-t'u monastery, P. 2032.

50. Chavannes, *Les documents chinois*, no. 969, l. 7.

51. Ibid., no. 970, l. 17.

52. Ibid., no. 971, l. 9.

53. Ibid., no. 969, l. 11.

54. In modern times, monks from village sanctuaries have been organizers of fairs. Cf. Smith, *Village Life in China*, p. 149: "It appears to be a general truth that by far the larger part of these large fairs owe their existence to the managers of some temple. The end in view is the accumulation of a revenue for the use of the temple, which is accomplished by levying certain taxes upon the traffic and by collection of

a ground-rent." The system of economic control of the transactions by sponsors (monasteries or wealthy laymen) had been established by T'ang times.

55. Cf. p. 256.

56. *Nan shih* 29.772. Ts'ai Hsing-tsung was promoted prefect of Kuei-chi in modern Chekiang in 467, and the events reported here seem to have taken place shortly after that date.

57. To the term *ti-tien* may be joined that of *ti-ssu*. Michihata Ryōshū's study "Shina bukkyō ji-in no kin-yū jigyō" is devoted to these market shops. See also Balazs, "Traité économique," p. 240, n. 245, referring to the works of Katō Shigeru. The meaning of the word *ti* appears to have evolved since Han times, when it designated the inns where officials on their way to the capital were lodged, but where conceivably merchants met as well. The *ti-she* and *ti-tien* may thus at some time have begun functioning as warehouses and trading places. Goods, in particular cloth, were sold there on credit; see the biography of Prince Lun of Shao-ling in *Nan shih* 53.1323 where the managers of *ti-tien* are seen selling silk and cotton cloth on credit.

58. Also *k'o-yüan, k'o-fang, k'o-tien, k'o-ti*. On the innkeeping business operated by Buddhist communities, see pp. 224ff.

59. On the *chü-fang*, see Katō Shigeshi, "Shabō ni tsuite."

60. See above, p. 143.

61. *Shan-yu shih-k'o ts'ung-pien* 9.1b; *Shih-k'o shih-liao hsin-pien*, 15 109 supra, an inscription commemorating the installation of a hall by the master of the Law Ch'ang-yen of the Fu-t'ien monastery.

62. *Chin-shih ts'ui-pien* 130.48b, inscription on the occasion of the renovation of the Ta-hsiang monastery, "Ch'ung-hsiu Ta-hsiang ssu chi," *Shih-k'o shih-liao hsin-pien*, 2042 infra, dated fifth month, first year of the Hui-ch'ang reign period (841).

63. *Wen-yüan ying-hua* 429.2174. The produce from the lands of Buddhist hospitals must also have been placed at interest; see p. 222.

64. Or "inexhaustible property" (*wu-chin wu*).

65. See pp. 66ff. above.

66. A common theme of cautionary tales dealing with the alienation of permanent assets is the failure to restitute debts contracted out of *ch'ang-chu* property. Cf. ibid.

67. *Sung kao-seng chuan* 16.807c.

68. On the sale of ordination certificates after the An Lu-shan rebellion, see above, pp. 48ff.

69. Given the region, that of Hang-chou, this is likely to have been 10,000 *shih* of rice. According to the monograph on the economy in *Hsin T'ang shu* 54.1388, the average rice production was above 50 *shih* per *ch'ing* (i.e., 3,000 liters for an area of 5.4 ha). Thus the land provided in the present case would have amounted to some 200 *ch'ing*.

70. *Sung kao-seng chuan* 15.803c. The events in question apparently date to the Ta-li reign period (766–780).

71. See his biography in *Chiu T'ang shu* 187 B.4887–89. Li Ch'eng was an active participant in the campaign against An Lu-shan but fell into the hands of the rebels; it was then that he made a gift of his property to the Hui-lin monastery. All of his family were Buddhists and two of his sons became monks.

72. *Sung kao-seng chuan* 20.839c, biography of Yüan-kuang.

73. See Yang Lien-sheng, *Money and Credit*, p. 6: "The earliest known credit institution was the pawnshop, which first appeared in Buddhist monasteries in about the fifth century." This assertion is surely too categorical, for money loans had already long been known in China. On the other hand, it is true that there were no lending banks and that Buddhist communities must be credited with their creation.

The innovation was twofold: the appearance of credit shops and a new loan procedure.

74. *Ken-pen shuo i-ch'ieh yu-pu p'i-nai-yeh* 22.743a, providing a definition of the term *pledge*. See p. 159–60 above.

75. See ibid.

76. In time, the meaning of the two terms converged. Under the Sung, *tien* seems to be a virtual synonym for *chih*.

77. Yang Lien-sheng, "Buddhist Monasteries," p. 175. See *Lao-hsüeh an pi-chi* 6.52.

78. Magistrate of Chiang-ling county (Ching-chou prefecture, Hupeh) during the Yung-ch'u reign period (420–422).

79. *Nan shih* 70.1705. Assuming an average of thirty years per generation, this incident would have taken place in the last quarter of the fifth century.

80. *Nan Ch'i shu* 23.432. These objects had been deposited by Ch'u Yüan as pledges, presumably in the years before 482.

81. See pp. 175.

82. *T'ang liu-tien* as cited in Michihata Ryōshū, "Shina bukkyō ji-in no kin-yū jigyō," p. 128.

83. See above, p. 175. "For some time," reads a decree of the sixteenth day, second month, sixteenth year of K'ai-yüan (728), reproduced in *T'ang hui-yao* 88.1618, "The interest claimed on public and private loans has been excessive, to the great detriment of the poor. Henceforth an interest rate of no more than one quarter shall be applied to all [private] loans, and in the case of public loans [granted by the government], of one fifth." This decree also figures in *Ts'e-fu yüan-kuei* 159.16b.

84. Balazs, "Traité économique," p. 224, n. 172, is inclined toward that interpretation, supported by the vocabulary of loan contracts from Central Asia.

85. Chavannes trans., "Documents chinois," appendix 3 in Stein, *Ancient Khotan*, no. 9.

86. Ibid., no. 6.

87. Cf. Zürcher, *Buddhist Conquest*, p. 23.

88. *Kao-seng chuan* 4.347b, biography of Fa-ch'eng.

89. *Fo-tsu t'ung-chi* 39.369a, second year of the I-feng era (677). See the translation on p. 72 above.

90. *Sung kao-seng chuan* 5.736a, biography of Li-tsung.

91. Loans extended to members of the upper classes by the Inexhaustible Treasury of the Hua-tu monastery did not require a deed. See p. 210.

92. In T'ang times, pawn treasuries (*chih-k'u*) frequently figure among the possessions of wealthy private individuals. The T'ai-p'ing princess, known for her immense wealth, owned some. See *Chiu T'ang shu* 183.4740.

93. *Lao-hsüeh an pi-chi* 6.52.

94. *T'ai-chou chin-shih lu* 7.7a–b, stele entitled "Sung Pao-tsang yen ch'ang-ming pei"; *Shih-k'o shih-liao hsin-pien*, 11064 infra.

95. The purchase of these official diplomas became obligatory for religious in the middle of the eighth century. See p. 52 above.

96. *I-chien chih*, "Chih-kuei," 8.1280.

97. See above, p. 210.

98. See above, pp. 259ff. According to Yang Lien-sheng, "Buddhist monasteries," p. 175, the term *ch'ang-sheng k'u* (the complete expression seems to have been *ch'ang-sheng ch'ien k'u*, "treasury of long life money"; cf. the expression *ch'ang-sheng ch'ien* in *Shih-shih yao-lan* C.304b) is nothing but a current designation for the monastic treasuries. It does not appear before the Sung period, however, and the terms *ch'ang-sheng k'u* and *chih-k'u* (pawn treasuries) probably became synonymous

only at that time. The latter were not normally constituted on the basis of a sub-scription.

99. See above, p. 104.

100. On the reserves of the monasteries at Tun-huang, see pp. 187–91.

101. See pp. 109–10 above.

102. Before the secular administration? The formula employed here is *chiang tz'u-ch'i wei ling-liu*, probably meaning that the contract had executory power; *liu* is a homophonic substitute for an unknown character.

103. S. 1475, v° (9). Document edited in Naba Toshisada, "Ryōko kō," *Shina bukkyō shi gaku* 2.4 (1938), p. 41.

104. The use of personal seals in contracts is exceptional; the circular form seems to be of Tibetan origin.

105. P. 2686 v°. Edited by Naba Toshisada, ibid. See also Niida Noboru, *Tōsō hōritsu*, pp. 366–67. The provision that the amount owed will be doubled in default of repayment on the expiration date seems to be tacitly assumed in the two above contracts. The clause appears in the following deed, S. 1475 v°, fol. 11, edited by Naba, ibid.: "On the twelfth day of the fourth month of the year . . . the household So Man-nu, being out of cereals, addressed itself to the Ling-t'u monastery to supply it with two *shih* of wheat, measured in Chinese *tou*, from the provisions of its Bud-dhist account (*fo-chang*). [The household] requested that the [date for the] full resti-tution be fixed in the [eighth month] and that, should it exceed that date, [the amount owed] be doubled. [The creditor] shall be authorized to seize the [debtor's] movables and other effects in compensation for the price of the wheat."

106. At least in the case of commodities. Money loans are called *chü* or *ch'ü*.

107. See pp. 105 above.

108. These were probably constituted of net interest, for no loans are indicated among the section on expenditures in the accounts of the Ching-t'u monastery.

109. P. 2049 v°, management report of the monk Pao-hu.

110. If the same practice obtained for loans granted to the saṃgha households, this would explain the falsifications to which these operations gave rise. See p. 104 above. Contracts were normally written in duplicate, and each party retained a copy. The custom of recording loans on the registers of private individuals is analogous to the inscriptions on the *tabulae accepti et expensi* in ancient Rome.

111. P. 3234 v°, fol. 25 ff., accounts of the Ching-t'u monastery, concerning loans in hemp and soya made in 944 under the management of Kuang-chin at the East Gra-nary. A list of the same kind figures in P. 2953 v°. The rural districts (*hsiang*) where the borrowers lived are indicated: Yü-kuan, Shen-sha, Lung-lo, Tz'u-hui, Hsiao-ku, etc. In that incomplete list some fifty persons are mentioned. Among these are two religious and three households held in perpetuity (*ch'ang-chu po-hsing*), evidence that serfs did not always benefit from simple, interest-free advances of cereals.

112. It is difficult to give an exact figure because the respective values of the dif-ferent commodities are not known. Moreover, it is likely that the proportion of the different types of revenue varied from one establishment to another.

113. "Shih-Lao chih," *Wei shu* 114.3040; *Fo-tsu t'ung-chi* 40.375a–b, 29th year of K'ai-yüan (741); *Ch'ih-hsiu Po-chang ch'ing-kuei i-chi* 4.298a.

114. *Fo-tsu t'ung-chi* 39.361c, year 606.

115. Naba Toshisada considers that this year corresponds to 885 or 945.

116. The calligraphy and paper of the document suggest a date in the ninth or tenth centuries.

117. A *tou* of hemp was thus worth two *tou* of wheat or millet, and one *ch'ih* (thirty centimeters) of cloth one *tou* (six liters) of cereals.

118. P. 3631 v°.

119. See below.

120. *Sa-p'o to p'i-ni p'i-p'o sha* 5.532c.

121. *Shih-sung lü* 7.53a.

122. *Ken-pen shuo i-ch'ieh yu-pu p'i-nai-yeh* 22.744a.

123. See above, p. 161.

124. P. 4542.

125. "Shih-Lao chih," *Wei shu* 114.3041. The Wei court and the high clergy forming part of the close entourage of the emperor were upholders of an austere tradition that had long been overtaken by reality.

126. *Pei Ch'i shu* version.

127. *Pei shih* 86.2877. Parallel text in *Pei Ch'i shu* 46.643. Su Ch'iung died in 581.

128. See *T'ang-lü shu-i* 26.385, paragraph 10.

129. Another point worth raising, and one that is relevant to the psychology of the Chinese monks, is that those who understood best their role as monks did not disdain to devote themselves, on the edge of their religious activities, to operations of a purely worldly order. They had a sense of the border that separated the religious and the profane. Tao-yen was unable to deal with his material interests after having discussed the great mysteries of Buddhism. However, the incompatible could be reconciled provided that each type of activity took place at the proper time.

130. At Tun-huang, this circumstance may be due to the fact that the collections discovered in the Caves of the Thousand Buddhas derived from monastic libraries. But it is probable that the monks disposed of greater funds than laymen, and that there were more scribes among them.

131. Situated in northeastern Khotan, in the Taklamakā desert. The dates of the documents found at this site are spread between 768 and 790. At that time, eastern Turkestan was still under Chinese influence but no longer had any direct contacts with the central government.

132. See p. 127 above for another document from the same monastery.

133. For this manuscript, see Niida Noboru, *Tōsō hōritsu*, p. 253. See also Chavannes, "Documents chinois" (appendix A in Stein, *Ancient Khotan*), no. 5 (1.526–27). Chavannes missed the significance of the term *chü* with respect to money loans (cf. pp. 176–77 above). The manuscript is preserved in the Stein collection of Tun-huang manuscripts as S. 5867. See also the following note.

134. This contract antedates the preceding one. It must be assigned to the beginning of the year 782 (loans of cereals were made in the spring). At that time, the region continued to count the years according to a reign period that had already been superseded two years earlier. By contrast, in the preceding contract that dates from the second half of 782, the dating is correct.

135. Chavannes translated *chiu-yüeh nei* "within a period of nine months." But the expression means here "in the course of the ninth month." The formula is common, and the date corresponds to the general custom according to which loans of cereals were returned in the autumn.

136. This formula, referring to a money loan, appears to be a scribal error for *t'ung-pien jen.*

137. Chavannes, "Documents chinois" (appendix A in Stein, *Ancient Khotan*), no. 10, also in the Stein collection (S. 5871). Both documents are cited by Giles, *Six Centuries at Tun-huang.*

138. Cf. p. 180 above.

139. Cf. pp. 88ff. above.

140. Monastic dignitaries (*she-li* ["teacher"; Skr. *ācārya*], *shang-tso, ssu-chu,* etc.) were often identified by their lay family names. Dean Teng's personal name was

Shen-shan and he belonged to the Lung-hsing monastery. Two contracts survive concerning a loan of cloth he had made to an officer: One of them, P. 3004, records the advance of seven bolts of raw silk (sheng-chüan) made to the adjutant (ping-ma shih) Hsü Liu-t'ung. On the fifth day of the sixth month of the year i-ssu Hsü returns two and a half bolts. A date for the reimbursement of the remaining four and a half bolts is fixed in the fifth year. According to the second document, P. 3472, Adjutant Hsü Liu-t'ung left on a tour of duty to Hsi-chou (Kharakhja, 42 km east of Turfan) on the sixteenth day of the fourth month of the year wu-shen, and new dispositions were agreed upon between himself and the dean of the Lung-hsing monastery concerning the reimbursement of the outstanding bolts of raw silk.

141. Yü hsiang-yüan sheng-li. The formula occurs frequently in the contracts from Tun-huang. See note below.

142. P. 3124 r°. Edited in Naba Toshisada, "Giransō."

143. A vertical weaving loom.

144. The borrower signed with his personal name, Yen-ch'ang.

145. P. 3453. Edited in Naba Toshisada, "Giransō."

146. Chu hsiang-yüan chu-yüeh sheng-li. In other deeds, the short formula chu hsiang-yüan sheng-li is found (P. 3124, P. 4083). More rarely, a variant graph for hsiang-yüan is employed.

147. P. 3565. In some cases, monks made loans to fellow monks. See P. 3051, concerning the loan of a piece of raw silk measuring forty ch'ih . . . [two or three characters seem to be missing in the manuscript] nine ts'un made by the monk Fa-pao of the San-chieh monastery to another monk of the same monastery. Fa-pao departs to Hsi-chou where he will be in need of cloth (it is clear that Chinese cloth served as currency in Central Asia). The interest is one bolt of machine-made (li-chi) cloth [li-chi: vertical weaving loom]. The document dates probably from the year 956 (cf. the text dated 953 on the r°).

148. Niida Noboru, Tōsō hōritsu, pp. 259–60.

149. Cf. pp. 134–35 above.

150. The practice of antichresis can be traced to the end of the sixth century. It is mentioned in a text dated around 577; see Balazs, "Traité économique," p. 280.

151. On this category of religious, see p. 38 above. It may be noted that the borrower refers to himself by his secular family name, Ling-hu, followed by his name in religion, Fa-hsing.

152. Length of a warp of cloth at the loom.

153. The length of the lease is due to the small surface area of the land engaged. Its annual production should have amounted to some four shih of cereals.

154. The ti-tzu is the tax levied on the produce of the land, as opposed to the tax on the value of landed property that was incorporated in the hu-shui.

155. An amnesty freeing the debtor (Ling-hu Fa-shing) would render this agreement null and void. Hence this clause. It is also frequently encountered in sales contracts as a guarantee against eviction. In the event of an eviction by a third party, the seller is obliged to furnish the equivalent of the property sold. See Gernet, "La vente en Chine," p. 316.

156. P. 3155 v° 2. Edited in Niida Noboru, Tōsō hōritsu, pp. 351–53 and, with some inaccuracies, in Naba Toshisada, "Chūbantō jidai ni okeru giransō," pp. 161–63, and "Tō shōhon," 76–78. See also Twitchett, "The Monasteries and China's Economy," pp. 548–49.

157. P. 2049.

158. The custom of holding assemblies to examine the annual accounts at the beginning of the year is attested by the Japanese monk Ennin in Nittō guhō junrei gyōki: "Twenty-ninth day [twelfth month, 838–839]: In the evening, the religious and

laymen together burned [sacrificial] paper money. . . . After midnight they struck the bell of the monastery, and the congregation of monks gathered in the dining hall. . . . At that time the treasurer (k'u-ssu) and the bursar (tien-tso) were present in the assembly. They read out the management report for the year *shen* under its various headings for the information of the entire community" (Gyōki, chap. 1, Jōwa 5; Reischauer, *Record of a Pilgrimage*, pp. 65–66). The monastery in question was the K'ai-yüan ssu at Yang-chou (modern Chiang-tu, in Kiangsu). See also ibid., chap. 3, K'ai-ch'eng 5; Reischauer, p. 296 [Ennin was now at the Tzu-sheng monastery in the Ch'ung-jen ward at Ch'ang-an]: "Twenty-fifth day [twelfth month, 840–841]: As we were about to enter the New Year, the monks gathered in the great hall. . . . While the monks were eating their morning gruel, the management report prepared by the *karmadāna* overseer (wei-na), the bursar (tien-tso), and the steward for the year (chih-sui) was read to them in extenso. This report comprised all the expenditures in money and in commodities made in the course of the past year by the monastery and its estates (chuang), as well as its commercial transactions (chiao-i) and provisions for the reception of guests." In the monasteries at Tun-huang, the assemblies for the examination of the accounts usually took place in the North Cloister (pei-yüan).

159. It will be noted that revenues from agricultural land and gardens have different designations. Their management must have been separate and it does not appear that the two types of land were cultivated by the same work force. Cf. p. 126 above.

160. The most common sheet of paper measured about 28 x 45 cm.

161. Naba Toshisada considers that this year corresponds to 885 or 945.

162. P. 3352 v°. The total of the goods measurable in *shih* amounts to 385.73 *shih*. The remainder of 30.49 *shih* presumably represents the value of the cloth. Since 1 ch'ih of cotton cloth was worth 1 *tou* of cereals, the remaining 10.49 *shih* must represent the value of the 110 ch'ih of felt.

163. P. 2049.

164. P. 2032 and 2040.

165. P. 3763. On the basis of their names, the monks mentioned in this account appear to belong to the Ching-t'u monastery.

166. P. 3207. Accounts of the prioress Sheng-ching, dated fifteenth day of the twelfth month of the *ping-wu* year, second year of the Kuang-ch'i era, and covering the period from the first month of the year *ch'en* to the first month of the year *wu*.

167. P. 2821. Average over three years.

168. P. 3352 v°.

169. P. 2049, report of Yüan-ta, steward for the year 929.

170. Ibid., management report of Pao-hu, dated first month of the year 925.

171. See pp. 146ff. above.

172. The name of the monastery is unknown.

173. P. 2974 v° and P. 3395 v°.

7. The Circuit of Giving

1. "Shih-Lao chih," *Wei shu* 114.3036; Ware, "Wei Shou," p. 145.

2. Gernet, "Biographie du maître de *dhyâna* Chen-houei," p. 47.

3. See *Tai-tsung ch'ao tseng ssu-k'ung ta pien-cheng kuang-chih san-tsang ho-shang piao chih chi* 2.835a–b, request by Pu-k'ung that the artisan-monks occupied with ornamental work on the [Sheng] Chin-ko and [Sheng] Yü-hua monasteries at Mount Wu-t'ai be permitted to complete their task before being recalled to their monasteries. An example of a sculptor-monk was mentioned on p. 23 above.

4. *Chiu T'ang shu* 174.4519.

5. *Hung-ming chi* 6.35b. Criticism of the morals of the Buddhist clergy is already encountered at an earlier period, in the *Mou-tzu li huo lun*, the first treatise in the

Hung-ming chi (dated by some to the third century but according to Zürcher, *Buddhist Conquest*, p. 14, probably later).

6. Meaning that certain monks had farmers, slaves, or serfs under their orders.

7. *Chiu T'ang shu* 1.16.

8. *Ts'e-fu yüan-kuei* 159.17a.

9. *Hsiang-fa chüeh-i ching* 1337b–c.

10. *Pei-tu* means "cup crossing."

11. *Kao-seng chuan* 10.392a.

12. Ibid., 393c.

13. Certain popular sects recommended that their adepts beg for food, among them the early Sect of the Three Stages and the Pure Land sects. The monk Shao-k'ang (d. 805) begged for money in Hsin-ting commandery for one year in 795. Those who encountered him, old and young, persons of rank and commoners, all recited the name of Amitābha. See *Fo-tsu t'ung-chi* 41.380b.

14. Emending *li*, "grain" (and a classifier for relics), for *li*, "straw hat."

15. *Hsü kao-seng chuan* 25.659b.

16. *Hsü kao-seng chuan* 27.684b. P'u-yüan, at the end of the sixth century, is another example of a mendicant monk: "At times he begged for food and went his way among the villages." Ibid., 680b–c.

17. It may be noted in this regard that the biographies of the great monks included in *Chiu T'ang shu* 191 are classified among the "technicians" (*fang-chi*), together with physicians, astronomers, and alchemists.

18. P. 4081, accounts of the Ching-t'u monastery. On the word *ch'en*, see n. 23 below.

19. P. 2049, management reports of Pao-hu, steward for the year 924, and of Yüan-ta, steward for the year 930.

20. On these associations, see pp. 259ff.

21. Referring to the year 924. The term used, *sai* (an offering of thanksgiving), evokes Chinese peasant festivals marking the beginning and the end of the agricultural year.

22. The culminating moment of that festival of the second month was on the eighth day, the anniversary of the leap of Siddhartha, the future Buddha Śākyamuni, from the city walls.

23. *Ch'en* is an abbreviation for *ta-ch'en*, the transcription for Skr. *dakṣiṇā*, i.e., fees paid to the monks for rituals performed after the banquet (*chai*). They consisted of offerings of clothing, fabrics, or money. The term seems to refer specifically to offerings for mortuary services, and these were normally in the form of cloth.

24. These gifts were made in payment of official ceremonies performed in the major monasteries recognized by the court. These "state" establishments were primarily responsible for celebrating rites for the deceased emperors and their close relatives. On the official cult in these monasteries, see des Rotours, *Traité des fonctionnaires*, pp. 87–89, note.

25. The development of this festival of the dead and of filial piety in China is known. As P. Pelliot (*Bulletin de l'Ecole Française d'Extrême-Orient* (1901), 1:277–78; *T'oung Pao* 28(1031):428ff.) has shown, the word *p'en* is not a transcription of the last syllable of *ullambana*. The bowls (*p'en*), in fact, played an essential role in this festival. Maspero's remarks in *La religion chinoise*, p. 73, are suggestive of what the rite may have been as it was already practiced in tenth century Tun-huang: "At the ceremony for the salvation of deceased ancestors, a monk wearing a cap in the form of a lotus and holding the *kakkhara* in his hand, the "pewter staff" as the Chinese call it, with its sounding rings, represented Ti-tsang in a sort of dance as he journeyed through the hells, forcing demons to open the gates of the prisons where the

damned were held. To mark the opening of each gate, by a blow of his staff, he broke an earthenware bowl. The dead delivered by him crossed the infernal river in a boat, while some shavelings mimicked the movement of the oarsmen, seasoning their song with more or less licentious jokes."

26. A particularly heavy expenditure (amounting to more than 270 l. of flour). It would appear that hundreds of guests took part in this banquet.

27. There were other sutra recitations in town (ch'eng-shang chuan-ching) as well, e.g., in the sixth month (mentioned in the accounts of P. 2032) and on the eighteenth day of the third month (P. 2040), but the most important of these ceremonies was no doubt that in the twelfth month.

28. Recourse to these rites for warding off locusts was taken routinely. Cf. the biography of Yao Ch'ung in Chiu T'ang shu 96.3023–24: In the fourth year of K'ai-yüan (716), Shantung was invaded by locusts. The peasants burned incense, prostrated themselves, made offerings to the gods, and prayed for their benevolence. They watched the locusts devour their harvest before their eyes, but dared not interfere with them. Buddhism was in harmony with Chinese thinking on this subject, which opposed any rational attempt to resist the scourge: "To kill many insects," declared Lu Huai-shen, "damages the harmony of vital forces" (ibid., 3024–25).

29. P. 2032.

30. P. 2837.

31. For these dates, see Demiéville, Le Concile de Lhasa, pp. 176ff.

32. P. 2583 v°.

33. These goods were to be sold at auction during one of the great assemblies of all the clergy at Sha-chou. Afterward, the proceeds of the sale were distributed in equal parts among the monks and nuns on the one hand and the novices on the other. See pp. 88ff. above.

34. Ibid.

35. P. 2863, manuscript edited in Tun-huang to-so fasc. 4, no. 82.

36. See P. 2032; P. 2049; and P. 3234.

37. P. 2049, management report for the year 930.

38. P. 2032, accounts of the Ching-t'u monastery.

39. P. 3336 r° and v°.

40. Held in the thirteenth month after the burial. Other letters of invitation refer to the ta-hsiang, a service held in the twenty-fifth or twenty-seventh month.

41. P. 3367. The year chi-ssu corresponds no doubt to 969, for another letter of invitation dated 968 is addressed to the same monks. See Tun-huang shih-shih hsieh-ching t'i-chi yü Tun-huang tsa-lu B.105a.

42. P. 3367, dated most likely 968.

43. P. 2836 v°, dated 939.

44. P. 3152, dated 992.

45. Document cited in Tun-huang shih-shih hsieh-ching t'i-chi yü Tun-huang tsa-lu B.103a, dated 960. Peking manuscript jun-tzu 58.

46. Ibid., p. 104, dated 887. There are also two letters by unknown senders, ibid. p. 105, dated 968, and P. 3107, dated 858 or 918.

47. P. 3367; Tsa-lu, p. 105; P. 2836.

48. P. 3107; Tsa-lu, p. 104.

49. Tsa-lu, p. 103.

50. P. 3152.

51. The lei-ch'i [chai] or chai-ch'i. See Shih-shih yao-lan C.305b. This practice was based on the belief that the reincarnation of the soul took place within a period of 49 (7 x 7) days.

52. Chiu T'ang shu 96.3028–29.

53. See pp. 187–91 above.

54. *Lo-yang ch'ieh-lan chi* 2.1005a–b.

55. See the biography of Wang Chin in *Chiu T'ang shu* 118.2416–18 and ibid. 190C.5052 (biography of Wang Wei): "In the capital, [the brothers Wang] every day provided for more than ten eminent monks."

56. This sanctuary, founded by the monk T'an-ch'ung, received its official designation (o) as Ch'ing-ch'an monastery in response to a petition presented to the emperor by T'an-ch'ung.

57. *Hsü kao-seng chuan* 17.568b, biography of T'an-ch'ung. According to the figures given there, the monastery must have comprised fifty monks.

58. *Shih wen-chi* 40.35a.

59. *Hsü kao-seng chuan* 19.586a. The same passage mentions other gifts: one thousand bolts of cloth, five hundred bolts of silk, one piece of satin for each monk who took part in the vegetarian banquet: these were in payment for a religious service.

60. In contradiction to the disciplinary precepts set out by the Indian Vinaya treatises.

61. That is 360,000 cash per year, an enormous sum for the period.

62. *Kao-seng chuan* 7.374a.

63. "Shih-Lao chih," *Wei shu* 114.3039.

64. *Hsü kao-seng chuan* 19.580c.

65. See p. 233.

66. At the time this monastery was called Chen-chi ssu. It was situated east of the south gate of the I-ning ward in northwestern Ch'ang-an.

67. The *T'ai-p'ing kuang-chi* (cited below) attributes the foundation of the Inexhaustible Treasury to a disciple of Hsin-hsing, a certain Hsin-i whereas the earliest source, the *Liang-ching hsin-chi*, attributes it to the founder of the sect himself, Hsin-hsing. Yabuki Keiki, who devoted extensive studies to the history of the Sect of the Three Stages, was unwilling to pronounce himself on this issue, which, in any event, is secondary to the purposes of this study.

68. *Liang-ching hsin-chi* 3.27a–b. Cf. Ch'en, *Chinese Transformation of Buddhism*, p. 162.

69. I.e., those afflicted with disease. On the hospital services provided by Buddhism in China, see p. 222.

70. The expression *shih-nü* indicates—as do the offerings themselves—that the patrons were members of the upper classes, nobles and high officials.

71. The donor's haste is no doubt explained by the belief that the first to present his offerings was assured of having his wishes granted.

72. *T'ai-p'ing kuang-chi* 493.4047.

73. This second Inexhaustible Treasury had been created by the empress Wu Tse-t'ien. See *Liang-ching hsin-chi* 3.28: "The empress Wu had this treasury transferred to the Fu-hsien monastery (the former manor of the Lady Yang, the mother of the empress, transformed into a monastery in 675) in Lo-yang [Wu Tse-t'ien intended to make that city the principal capital]. Since however the riches of the empire ceased to flow into this new treasury, she decided to relocate it to its former place." Yet the indications are that from this time onward, there existed two treasuries, the older at Ch'ang-an and another at Lo-yang. See the stele of the master of Dhyāna Fa-tsang of the Ching-yü monastery in *Chin-shih ts'ui-pien* 71.1206a–b (*Shih-k'o shih-liao hsin-pien* ed., vol. 2): In the first year of the Ju-i reign (692), the sage empress having learned of the great purity of conduct of the master of Dhyāna [Fa-tsang], summoned him to oversee the Inexhaustible Treasury of the Fu-hsien monastery at Lo-yang. In the Ch'ang-an reign period (701–705), she issued a new order requesting [Fa-tsang] to oversee the Inexhaustible Treasury of the Hua-tu monastery."

74. The anniversary of the death of Hsin-hsing, the founder of the school.

75. Cf. des Rotours, *Traité des fonctionnaires*, pp. 281–314.

76. *Ch'üan T'ang wen* 28.11b–12a.

77. Decree of the sixth month, ninth year of K'ai-yüan (721), reproduced in *Ts'e-fu yüan-kuei* 159.15a.

78. *Shih-shih yao-lan* C.304b.

79. *Fen*: one tenth of a tael (*liang*).

80. S. 190, a manuscript held in the British Library and edited in Yabuki Keiki, *Sangaikyō*, annex, p. 155. The text is entitled "Summary explanation of the method of the Inexhaustible Treasury" (*Wu-chin tsang fa lüeh-shuo*).

81. S. 721; Yabuki Keiki, *Sangaikyō*, annex, p. 163.

82. Ibid.; Yabuki Keiki, *Sangaikyō*, p. 173.

83. *Hsü kao-seng chuan* 29.697a. This text uses the term *tsao-fu ch'u*, perhaps an equivalent of *kung-te ch'u*.

84. In 725, on the third day of the sixth month, the Sect of the Three Stages was prohibited by imperial decree: "The emperor ordered that the walls of separation of the cloisters of the Sect of the Three Stages be demolished so that these cloisters would communicate with the main courts [of the monasteries]. The monks of that sect were to live together [with the others]." See *K'ai-yüan shih-chiao lu* 18.679a.

85. See p. 169 above.

86. *Shih-shih yao-lan* C.304b.

87. See above, p. 210.

88. *Wu-chin tsang fa lüeh-shuo* (S. 190); Yabuki Keiki, *Sangaikyō*, Annex, pp. 157–58.

89. Cf. the texts of the sect recommending daily offerings, however small.

90. The four means of solicitation (*saṃgraha vastu*) at the disposal of the bodhisattva are: 1. liberality (*dāna*); 2. persuasiveness (*priyavāditā*); 3. altruism (*arthacaryā*); and 4. receptivity toward all beings (*samānārthatā*). See *Mahāvyutpatti* 35, pp. 71–72.

91. *Ta fang-kuang fo hua-yen ching* 7.437c.

92. *Wei-mo-chi so-shuo ching* B.550b.

93. S. 190; Yabuki Keiki, *Sangaikyō*, Annex, p. 155.

94. The three terms must be taken in a concrete sense; cf. p. 67 above.

95. A note specifies nonglutinous millet, glutinous millet, flour, oil, fat, unhulled millet, beans, soya, firewood, cooking stoves, salt, vinegar, honey, ginger, pepper, hemp, little milk (koumiss?), vegetables, and fruit.

96. Each receptacle is explicated according to ten subdivisions. The bodhisattva's ten kinds of liberality, the only receptacle of interest here, are according to Hui-yüan's (523–592) great work of exegesis, *Ta-ch'eng i-chang* 742c, 743a: 1. He gives his accumulated possessions to all beings; 2. He joyfully gives them all that is of personal use to him, in particular his body; 3. He gives them his transcendent body; 4. He gives them his royal power and riches exterior [to his person]; 5. He gives them at the same time of his body and of exterior riches; 6. He makes them a complete gift of all possible possessions, corporeal or material: kingdom, town, wife, children, head, eyes, limbs, joints, etc.; 7. He preaches to all beings the Law as formerly received, without attachment to it; 8. He preaches the future Law to all beings, without attachment to it; 9. He preaches the present Law to all beings, without attachment to it; 10. He annihilates himself entirely for the benefit of all beings without harboring the least thought of desire or regret.

97. See the commentaries to the Garland Sutra by Fa-tsang (643–712), T. 35, no. 1733, 6.232a–235c; and by Ch'eng-kuan (737–838), T. 35, no. 1735, 24.674a–683a.

98. This renowned commentator of major Mahāyāna scriptures and treatises was

born of a Parthian family at Nanking. He was invited by the future Emperor Yang-ti to reside at the Hui-jih monastery in Yang-chou (modern Kiangsu) where later a community of the Three Stages installed itself.

99. The same who ruined themselves through offerings to the Inexhaustible Treasury in the seventh and early eighth centuries. The aristocracy of Ch'ang-an seems to have played a considerable role in the history of Buddhism in China. These great families were also implicated in the scandal of the monks of Ch'ang-an in 446.

100. An allusion to the reciprocity of the gifts of the Law (fa, Skr. dharma) and of material goods (ts'ai, Skr. āmiṣa).

101. This was probably done by celebrating vegetarian feasts (chai) to ask for blessings.

102. The phrase might be punctuated after the word chin, as in the Taishō edition (reading tsang as the monk's name). But the expression shih wu-chin tsang is not unexpected, and the following phrase does not require a stated subject.

103. Hsü kao-seng chuan 11.514a.

104. S. 721; Yabuki Keiki, Sangaikyō, Annex, p. 163.

105. There exist certain analogies between the Wu-chin tsang and the associations of the faithful; see p. 276.

106. On Buddhist attitudes towards disease, see Demiéville, "Byō," pp. 224b–265a; on works of medical assistance, in particular, pp. 245a–249b.

107. Chavannes, Mission archéologique I.2, no. 1623.

108. Ibid., no. 1655.

109. Here follow some rather obscure details concerning the mode of payment.

110. Tun-huang shih-shih hsieh-ching t'i-chi yü Tun-huang tsa-lu B.125a. Peking manuscript, hsien-tzu 59.

111. Yu-p'o-sai chieh ching 1060c.

112. As material subsidies, alms made no difference to the condition of the deprived, the sick, and the poor: "If it is said," wrote Ming-kai in his refutation of Fu I's anti-Buddhist memorial, "that an end should be put to hoarding by monks and nuns so that the army and the people may be rich and at their ease, [I would reply that] one is rich or poor according to one's occupation, and of lowly or noble birth according to chance. The fool and the sage cannot swap their thoughts any more than the handsome and the ugly can exchange their bodies. 'Good and bad retribution,' says the sutra, 'are determined by karman.' And when the Shu[-ching] says that 'Good and evil fortune depend on Heaven' it means the same. Since the army and the people are poor, giving will do them no good; if they were intended to be rich, that is what they would be in any event" (Kuang hung-ming chi 12.172c).

113. Kao-seng chuan 9.387b.

114. Ibid. 12.406c.

115. Fo-tsu t'ung-chi 39.362a. The monastery was situated in the Kuang-te ward, adjacent to the West Market in Ch'ang-an.

116. Fo-tsu t'ung-chi 40.376a.

117. Sung kao-seng chuan 20.842b.

118. Hsü kao-seng chuan 29.694a.

119. Or "merit offices"? Cf. p. 368, n. 83 above.

120. Hsü kao-seng chuan 29.697a.

121. Nan-hai chi-kuei nei-fa chuan 4.230c–231a.

122. See Demiéville, "Byō," pp. 236a–b, referring to Mo-ho seng-ch'i lü 24.420c and Ssu-fen lü 41.861b–c.

123. T'ang hui-yao 49.863.

124. This was not, properly speaking, a charitable foundation but a cult foundation.

125. Takakusu Junjirō, "Le voyage de Kanshin," p. 3. See also Demiéville, "Byō," p. 248b.

126. Takakusu Junjirō, "Le voyage de Kanshin," pp. 471–72. See also Demiéville, "Byō."

127. Tzu-chih t'ung-chien 214.6809.

128. Hsü kao-seng chuan 20.602c.

129. Another example of the Chinese tendency to concretize Indian symbolic notions were, as we have seen, the Inexhaustible Treasuries: A rubric of Mahāyāna scholasticism in the Indian texts, under the Sect of the Three Stages the expression came to refer to veritable treasuries.

130. T'ang hui-yao 49.863. See also Demiéville, "Byō," p. 248a.

131. Mi-sha-sai-pu ho-hsi wu-fen lü 10.73a.

132. This layman also owned a dispensary (yao-tien). Such pharmacies are mentioned in the Mahāvagga IV, 33, 1:239–40, under the name of kappiyabhūmi, and in Nan-hai chi-kuei nei-fa chuan 4.230c where I-ching translates the term as ching-k'u (pure store) [ching = kappiya]. See Demiéville, "Byō," p. 245a.

133. The emperor Aśoka is believed to have instituted stores of medicines for the monks whose stocks were ensured each day by a provision of ten thousand coins of money taken from the daily earnings of twenty million coins from four thousand inns in the vicinity of the four gates of Pataliputra. Takakusu Junjirō, Record, p. 192. See Shan-chien lü p'i-p'o-sha 2.682a.

134. See Lo-yang ch'ieh-lan chi, passim.

135. Po Hsiang-shan chi 69.89, "Yu Feng-lo Chao-t'i Fo-kuang san ssu."

136. Chiu T'ang shu 187B.4889. This monastery had been installed in the former country estate of Li Ch'eng.

137. Liang-ching hsin-chi 3.28.

138. Wei Yüan-sung claimed that towards the end of the sixth century the monasteries were populated by soldiers. See Kuang hung-ming chi 7.132b.

139. This opinion was expressed in Eberhard, Das Toba-Reich, p. 238. But since the enthusiasm for Buddhism had spread throughout China, it may be unnecessary to assume such a calculated response. The military, on the other hand, were certainly aware of the diplomatic and commercial opportunities offered by Buddhism. See Wang Ming-kuang's refutation of Wei Yüan-sung's projects under the Chou: "In former times, we saw people leave their mountains and cross the seas, and the barbarian peoples of the East (?) and the North came to China with goodwill. But now that Buddhism is ruined, they have all been dispersed. . . . And yet it would hardly seem that the treasures and merchandise of foreign lands are of no use to us." See Kuang hung-ming chi 10.158b.

140. Yu-p'o-sai chieh ching 1061a.

141. Ibid.

142. Ch'ih-hsiu Po-chang ch'ing-kuei 4.1131b, "chih-k'o."

143. A major Buddhist center in northern Shansi, revered as the residence of the bodhisattva Mañjuśrī.

144. Certain well-visited p'u-t'ung yüan, like that at Chin-chou, provided no food.

145. Nittō guhō junrei gyōki chap. 2, K'ai-ch'eng 5; Reischauer, Record of a Pilgrimage, p. 211.

146. Monks were in principle entitled to food and lodging in all the monasteries they passed. See pp. 68–69 above. But this rule could not always be observed.

147. Cf. Gyōki, chap. 2, passim; Reischauer, pp. 211 ff.

148. Gyōki chap. 2, K'ai-ch'eng 5; Reischauer, pp. 258–59.

149. See Tsukamoto Zenryū, "Sekkeisan Unkyo-ji," p. 138. The word i was fre-

quently used to designate communal institutions and gratuitous services; cf. p. 378, n. 74 below.

150. A small sanctuary; cf. the term *ching-ch'a* used below.

151. Not identified.

152. *Sung kao-seng chuan* 17.815c.

153. *T'ang hui-yao* 76.1393, "K'o-chü." The Kuang-chai monastery was situated in the ward of the same name adjoining the imperial city to the east; the Pao-shou monastery in the neighboring I-shan ward, further east again. The latter had originally been a private mansion, transformed into a monastery in T'ien-pao 9 (750). The *Kuei-hsin tsa-chih*, paragraph 19, reports that at the time of the Jurchen invasion (shortly before 1127) the Sung emperor Kao-tsung, who was then in the Hang-chou area, issued an exceptional authorization to the officials and members of the nobility who had fled to the South to lodge in the monasteries.

154. The most striking is the case of the saṃgha millet, which degenerated into a business exploiting the misery of the peasantry.

155. *Ch'üan T'ang wen* 46.12b–13a, "Chin-tuan kung-ssu chieh ssu kuan chü-chih chao."

156. Ibid. 52.3a, "Hsiu-ch'i ssu kuan chao."

157. Ibid., 410.5b–6a, "Chin t'ien-hsia ssu kuan t'ing k'o chih." Cf. *Fo-tsu t'ung-chi* 42.387a, second year of Ta-chung; other texts include ibid. 51.452b and *T'ang ta chao-ling chi* 113.14a–15a.

158. *Nittō guhō junrei gyōki* chap. 2, K'ai-ch'eng 5 (second day of the third month, 840); Reischauer, *Record of a Pilgrimage*, p. 177.

159. *Fa-yüan chu-lin* 75.852b.

160. *Shang-shu ku-shih*, p. 14.

161. See p. 221 above.

162. Cf. the biographies of merchants of the Han period translated in Swann, *Food and Money in Ancient China*, pp. 413–64.

8. Economics and Religion

1. See above, p. 123.

2. According to Yang Hsüan-chih, "The Wei had been partial to Buddhism since Hsien-tsu (r. 466–471). But at the time of the empress Hu (516–528), their enthusiasm overflowed." See *Lo-yang ch'ieh-lan chi*, preface, 999b.

3. Chavannes, *Mission archéologique* 1.2:538.

4. The text reads "of their horses and their elephants," but the *Lo-yang ch'ieh-lan chi* has come down in a rather corrupt condition.

5. *Lo-yang ch'ieh-lan chi*, preface, 999a.

6. *T'ai-p'ing kuang-chi* 493.4047.

7. As mentioned above (p. 49), at the beginning of the eighth century certain members of that nobility to which the principal patrons of the Inexhaustible Treasuries belonged took to selling preferential ordinations. After a period of great fervor, corruption set in.

8. "Shih-Lao chih," *Wei shu* 114.3032.

9. *Kuang hung-ming chi* 6.127b.

10. "Shih-Lao chih," *Wei shu* 114.3038.

11. The official Taoist cult was only created at the beginning of the T'ang Dynasty, as a pure fabrication and in imitation of the Buddhist cult.

12. "Eighth month" should no doubt read "eighth day": the festival of the procession of the statues and their immersion in water took place on the eighth day of the fourth month.

13. Another description of a Chinese festival (see above, p. 239) shows what is to be understood by this term: masquerades, juggling tricks, magic, and games of all kinds.

14. *Lo-yang ch'ieh-lan chi* 3.1010b; cf. Jenner, *Memories of Loyang*, p. 208. The *Fo-tsu t'ung-chi* 38.354a mentions another festival of that kind under the Northern Wei in 424: "In the first year of Shih-kuang . . . on the eighth day of the fourth month, the statues of the monasteries were taken round the great streets of the town in carts. The emperor proceeded to a pavilion that topped one of the gates to view the spectacle closely and to scatter flowers as a sign of homage." A detail of style worth noting in Yang Hsüan-chih's description is the recourse to natural and cosmological comparisons: clouds, fog, forests, chants that deafen Heaven and shake the Earth, swamps covered with plants. This is a theme, of Chinese origin, that appears frequently in the context of festivals. Cf. above, p. 239, the description by Liu Yü: "The rolling of the drums shook the heavens and the torches illumined the earth." The religious festival was a means to act upon and regulate nature. To be sure, this intention remains in the background, but it is undeniably present.

15. *Hsin T'ang shu* 129.4482, biography of Yen T'ing-chih. There is no mention of this festival in the biography of Yen in *Chiu T'ang shu* 99, normally the more expansive source on matters concerning Buddhism.

16. *Fo-tsu t'ung-chi* 40.373a.

17. *Kuang hung-ming chi* 15.201c reports the same: The stūpa of the Fa-men monastery in the prefecture of Ch'i (Feng-hsiang) was opened once every thirty years, and on these occasions auspicious omens occurred. It was opened, in particular, in the fifth year of the Hsien-ch'ing period (660), and the relic was then taken to the imperial palace. See also *Fo-tsu t'ung-chi* 41.379c: "In the first month of the sixth year of Chen-yüan (790), the emperor ordered [the population] to go forth and welcome the bone of the Buddha Śākyamuni that was preserved at the Fa-men monastery at Feng-hsiang. The relic was taken into the palace and ceremonies were performed in its honor. Afterwards it was placed in each monastery [in turn] to receive homage. In the second month the bone was restored to its [original] monastery in great pomp."

18. *Chiu T'ang shu* 160.4198, biography of Han Yü.

19. Ibid. 4200.

20. It will be noted that here too the offerings were made at the beginning of the year.

21. The characters *chih* and *erh* that frame the last portion of the phrase leave no doubt as to the general meaning of this passage. De Groot, *Sectarianism* 1:53–54, gives it the opposite sense, which accords better with the theory he defends.

22. It is mainly these who are concerned, for the educated classes had more critical sense.

23. *Chiu T'ang shu* 160.4199–200.

24. Out of conformism, for fear of going against the current of the times, literati gave a greater place to Buddhism than is usually believed. Cf. the attitude of Yao Ch'ung with regard to Buddhist mortuary rituals, p. 207 above. But there was a limit that they would not cross.

25. Translation based on Granet, *Danses et légendes*, p. 321.

26. *Pei shih* 77.2624, biography of Liu Yü. Cf. *Sui shu* 62.1483–84.

27. See the suggestive indications given in Maspero, *Le taoïsme*, especially pp. 156–69.

28. See pp. 280ff.

29. Entitled "Wang-shen" in *Kao-seng chuan* 12, and "I-shen" in *Hsü kao-seng chuan* 27 and *Sung kao-seng chuan* 23.

30. On the autocremations, see Gernet, "Les suicides par le feu."

31. *Kao-seng chuan* 12.404c.

32. Ibid. 405b. These offerings were assuredly not destroyed, but consecrated to pious ends.

33. *Hsü kao-seng chuan* 27.679a–b. There are seven examples of suicide by fire in the *Kao-seng chuan*. They all date from the fifth century.

34. The case of T'an-ch'eng in the early Sung, see *Kao-seng chuan* 12.404a.

35. Fa-chin, in 436, ibid. 404b.

36. The case of Seng-tsang, under the T'ang. See *Hsü kao-seng chuan* 23.855b.

37. On the commercial exploitation of such activities, see p. 250 above; on the influence that they seem to have had upon the spread of Buddhism in China, p. 252.

38. *Kośa* 4:228.

39. *Miao-fa lien-hua ching* 6.53a–55a, "Yao-wang p'u-sa pen-shih p'in." This was the text recited by Hui-shao (loc. cit.), Hui-i (loc. cit.), and others, at the moment of their suicides.

40. *Fo-tsu t'ung-chi* 37.350b. See also ibid. 351b for his personal sacrifices of 545 and 547.

41. Wieger, *Textes historiques* 2:1419.

42. On the relationship between Buddhism and funerary practices, see pp. 281ff. above.

43. *Wei shu* 71.1571, biography of P'ei Chih. Cf. *Fo-tsu t'ung-chi* 38.355c, 4th year of Yen-ch'ang (515).

44. Giles, "Dated Chinese Manuscripts," *BSOS* 7, 1933–1935, p. 820 (S. 4528).

45. The custom of the gift and redemption of the faithful's person is also attested in the seventh century in the region of Bamiyan, west of Kabul. "Every king of Fan-yen-na (Bamiyan) holds an assembly of deliverance at this place. Beginning with the crown jewels and down to his wife and children, he gives everything to this monastery; next, having exhausted all the riches of his treasury, he gives himself. Then the ministers and magistrates flock to the monks and offer them rich gifts to redeem all the persons of the royal family." Julien, *Histoire*, p. 374.

46. There are frequent mentions of this practice, clearly Chinese in origin, in the lists of offerings received by the monasteries of Tun-huang. Cf. P. 3047 v°, f. 5.

47. *Kuang hung-ming chi* 28.323c.

48. Ibid. 324a.

49. *Fan-ch'uan wen-chi* 10.8b. The term "right contract" refers to the use of halved contracts as tallies (cf. des Rotours, "Les insignes en deux parties," pp. 10–15). The benefits of pious acts were accountable. Cf. *Chiu T'ang shu* 79.7515, report of Fu I dated seventh year of Wu-te: "By the spread of their ominous writings and the promulgation of their heresies, they opened, on false grounds, three roads (of transmigration into demons, pretas and animals), and laid out six other roads (of transition into asuras, men, and devas); thus they inspired the ignorant with dread and fear, and deceived the class of government officers, with the result that amongst the people, they who became acquainted with them believed such falsehoods thoughtlessly, without due inquiry after their toots and sources. And then they raked up the crimes committed by these people in times past, in order to gauge thereby their future happiness; they taught that the gift of one single coin would give them a chance of a thousandfold reward, and that one day's fasting might make them expect food for a hundred days. Thus they caused their ignorant victims of deception to try recklessly to do such good works [kung-te], so that, instead of fearing the laws and prohibitions, these people inconsiderately indulged in transgression of the precepts of the government" (trans. de Groot, *Sectarianism*, p. 37).

50. *Ta-ch'eng fa-chieh wu-chin tsang fa-shih* (S. 731), Yabuki Keiki ed., in *San-*

gaikyō no kenkyū, Annex, p. 163. The saying is cited from "Ti-yü chuan" (A Tradition concerning the hells).

51. Fo-ming ching 21.272b. Cf. p. 72 above.

52. Yabuki Keiki, Sangaikyō no kenkyū, ibid.

53. Conversely, pious deeds had the effect of creating a monetary capital in the beyond. In a tale in the fourteenth century novel Hsi-yu chi, the T'ang emperor T'ai-tsung raises a cash loan in hell from a certain Hsiang-liang of K'ai-feng. The latter and his wife live in poverty, spending everything they earn on alms to monks and on sacrificial money. By burning this, they have accumulated a sizeable capital in hell. Trans. in Wieger, Folklore chinois moderne, pp. 407, 417. Cf. also Hou Ching-lang, Monnaies d'offrandes.

54. Yabuki Keiki, Sangaikyō no kenkyū, ibid.

55. Tun-huang shih-shih hsieh-ching t'i-chi yü Tun-huang tsa-lu 1, f. 8b.

9. The Popular Social Environment

1. Fo-tsu t'ung-chi 39.363a.

2. Kuang hung-ming chi 24.279a.

3. Kuang hung-ming chi 12.172a (refutation of the fourth point in Fu I's memorial).

4. Sung kao-seng chuan 6.744b.

5. Certain Mahāyānist doctrines lent justification to this amoralism. A text from Tun-huang reveals clearly such conceptions of popular origin. Monks had an interest in investing these with doctrinal authority:

There are those who for all the world break their vows and who dissimulate immeasurable virtues.

They should be followed faithfully and respected in the highest degree.

Wisdom and folly, sanctity and profanity are unfathomable.

There are those who give themselves in everything an air of propriety,

others who demonstrate that they have not yet been able to renounce all their desires.

Those who judge by appearances consider these to be profane:

they fail to examine the interior which is holy.

It is like the four kinds of mango (āmra)

of which it is so difficult to determine whether or not they are ripe.

Such also are the disciples of the Tathāgata:

it is difficult indeed to determine whether or not they are faithful to the precepts.

Thus one should counsel others with zeal

and prevent them from committing the sin of blasphemy towards the Jewel of the saṃgha.

If one wishes to avoid being plunged into the sea of suffering,

he should constantly venerate this excellent field [of merit].

If one wishes to attain to happiness among the gods,

he should further pay homage to the saṃgha.

(Seng kung-te tsan, Peking Tun-huang manuscript "chou," no. 86; ed. in Tun-huang shih-shih hsieh-ching t'i-chi yü Tun-huang tsa-lu, vol. 1, "hsia," 70.

6. See, for example, the biography of Pei-tu, a monk who lived at the end of the fifth and beginning of the sixth centuries, in Kao-seng chuan 10.391b. Many elements of Taoist folklore found their way into the biographies of Buddhist monks.

7. Hsü kao-seng chuan 25.659b.

8. Fo-tsu li-tai t'ung-tsai 11.569.b–c.

9. The meaning is not clear. The decree appears to offer a choice to the clergy con-

cerned: they could either divest themselves of their possessions and lead a life in compliance with the precepts of their religion, or they could return to lay life.

10. The monasteries situated within the eastern and western halves of Ch'ang-an stood under the supervision of two commissioners of good works, positions normally held by eunuchs.

11. *Nittō guhō junrei gyōki* 3, same date. Cf. Reischauer, *Record of a Pilgrimage*, pp. 321–22. The text adds that 3,491 monks and nuns were defrocked in Ch'ang-an on that occasion.

12. Cited in de Groot, *Sectarianism*, p. 75.

13. The Buddhist equivalent of the expression *yao-tao*, "Taoist magician."

14. *Chiu T'ang shu* 174.4516, biography of Li Te-yü. All this recalls the holy water of the Yellow Turbans that was ingested after fasting and confession. At the level of popular religion, Buddhism and Taoism differ only in form, not in substance.

15. Cf. p. 237 above: the mutilations on the occasion of the festival of the transfer of the relic were the result of collective excitement and contagion.

16. *Hsü kao-seng chuan* 25.654b.

17. This concerned not only physical techniques: the "Shih-Lao chih," *Wei shu* 114.3032, reports about a Kashmiri monk named T'an-mo-ch'en who was skilled at fortune-telling and casting spells.

18. As mentioned in the previous section, Liu Yü's description of the New Year's festival also referred to the presence of monks among the crowd.

19. *Hsü kao-seng chuan* 25.657a–b.

20. There is an interlude in the narrative here: a young child clad in a sheepskin arrives on the scene to drink the alcohol dispensed at the festival, then begins to dance and turn so frenetically that the onlookers are dazed by the spectacle.

21. *Hsü kao-seng chuan* 27.682a.

22. It is unlikely that Buddhism multiplied the cult sites in China in an haphazard manner, for nothing is more persistent than sacred emplacements. Cf. Mus, *La lumière sur les six voies*, p. vii, who indicates that already in India Buddhist cults were superimposed upon local cults: "It suffices to recall that the map of the sacred sites of Buddhism, marked by a multitude of stūpa or architectural reliquaries, can be superimposed upon the map of local spirits; each stūpa passed under the protection of the local *yakṣa*."

23. See p. 114 above.

24. *Kao-seng chuan* 12.404a.

25. In particular those who died a violent death. In places where monks had sacrificed themselves, stūpa were erected.

26. On the numbers of these small sanctuaries under different periods, and the numbers of monks residing in them, see pp. 4ff. above.

27. The term used here is *ssu*, monastery, but as we have seen above (p. 7), the term was applied, until Sui times, to all inhabited places of worship regardless of size. Certain *ssu* housed no more than one or two monks.

28. "Shih-Lao chih," *Wei shu* 114.3045. See also the decree of 626 cited in *Chiu T'ang shu* 1.16–17 (cf. *Fo-tsu t'ung-chi* 39.363a, fifth month of the ninth year of Wu-te): "Since the preceding dynasties, monasteries were frequently founded without consideration of the tranquillity of the place. . . . Some adjoined market stalls and had butcheries and taverns as neighbors. Their halls were filled with dust, and a fetid odor of meat permeated the streets in which they stood."

29. Cf. Mochizuki Shinkō, *Bukkyō daijiten*, 4:3112–13.

30. *Hsiang-fa chüeh-i ching* 1337b.

31. Report of Ti Jen-chieh, in *T'ang hui-yao* 49.857.

32. *Ts'e-fu yüan-kuei* 159.17b. See also *T'ang hui-yao* 49.861, decree of the sixth month, nineteenth year of K'ai-yuan.

33. The terms most frequently employed to designate these small sanctuaries are *lan-jo* (*aranya*), and *fo-t'ang* (Buddhist chapel). Tu Mu's *Fan-ch'uan wen-chi* 10.9a also uses *shan-t'ai*, "mountain towers," and *yeh-i*, "country establishments" (?). *Ching-she* were simple huts inhabited by single monks. The term *chao-t'i*, after 424 the official designation for monasteries under the Wei (cf. *Fo-tsu t'ung-chi* 39.345a), became a name for small places of worship under the T'ang. The terms *ch'ieh-lan*, *fo-ch'a*, and *tao-ch'ang* could also refer to small sanctuaries.

34. Especially on the occasion of sacrifices to the soil god. See p. 261.

35. Cf. the biographies of master Hsiang and of P'u-an above. It will be noted, however, that the essential interdiction, that requiring abstinence from meat, was not always observed. The *Tun-huang tsa-lu* 23.2b reports that in the T'ai-ho era (827–836) there were monks in the South who enjoyed having wives and eating meat: "They permanently led a family life and were completely ignorant of their religion. The local peasants gave them their daughters and called them Master (*shih-lang*). When these peasants were ill, they made them round coins of paper and placed Buddhist statuettes beside them. Occasionally, they requested these monks to prepare some religious banquet (*chai*) for them. The following day they would slaughter sheep and pigs to feast, and this ceremony was called a 'fast of expulsion' (*ch'u-chai*)."

36. *Lo-yang ch'ieh-lan chi* 2.1009a.

37. *Hsü kao-seng chuan* 19.586a–b.

38. *Wei shu* 47.1048.

39. Taoist revolutionary movements: the first at the end of the Later Han (cf. Maspero, *Le taoïsme*, pp. 149ff.); the second, at the end of the Former Han. Another decree, dated 517, also referred to the potentially subversive nature of this kind of devotion and ordered the "complete prohibition of assemblies for [Buddhist] vegetarian feasts in the prefectures, garrisons, and the capital, and the suppression of their injurious conspiracies" (*Wei shu* 9.225, second year of Hsi-p'ing).

40. We shall return to this political aspect of Chinese Buddhism, see p. 286.

41. The groups of followers can be more or less engaged upon a path of contractual association. Cf. below, the contrast between the Buddhist associations of the sixth century in which the size of the contributions was left to the discretion of each member and those at Tun-huang, in the ninth and tenth centuries, where fixed dues were imposed by statute.

42. Ōmura Seigai, *Shina bijutsu chōsohen*, texts, p. 192–93, edits the text of an inscription dated seventh year of T'ai-ho (483) in which the names of two hundred members of an *i-hui* are listed. Another stele mentions the making of a Buddhist statue by an *i* comprising 78 lay and religious members; see ibid., pp. 187–88. Yamasaki Hiroshi, "Zui-Tō jidai ni okeru giyū oyobi hōsha ni tsuite" indicates a stele dated fourth year of Yung-hui (653) that is related to the erection of a statue by an association of that type. It is the latest extant example.

43. That is, in the beginning of February and the beginning of August.

44. *Shih-shih yao-lan* A.263a.

45. At the beginning of the eighth century, the associations of Samantabhadra in Tung-chou (modern Shensi) each had their statue of this divinity before which their assembly (*chai*) took place. See p. 264.

46. *Hsü kao-seng chuan* 27.682a.

47. The question of the relationship between Chinese and Buddhist places of worship may be raised here. According to the monk Ming-kai, writing ca. 625, the altars to the God of the Soil, indigenous cult places, and Buddhist sanctuaries in China all served identical functions: "I have witnessed the plantation of trees to mark the

emplacement of altars to the God of the Soil, the erection of stone slabs in honor of the emperor, the stamping of soil for the construction of terraces, the weaving of reeds for ornamentations, and when danger threatens one prays to the gods. One also prays to them to obtain rain or dry weather and gives them thanks when humidity and dryness arrive [in timely fashion]" (*Kuang hung-ming chi* 12.171a, refutation of the second point in Fu I's memorial). How much more, Ming-kai goes on to argue, do the great deities of Buddhism deserve not to be abolished.

48. See Naba Toshisada, "Tōdai no shayū ni tsuite" (2), p. 238. The earliest *she* comprised ten, twenty, twenty-five, and eventually up to one hundred families.

49. Cf. Maspero, *Le taoïsme*, p. 158: "According to the rules of the Three Chang, explains an author of the sixth century (*Erh-chiao lun*, written in 570, *Kuang hung-ming chi* 8.140c), at the time of the spring and autumn equinoxes, offerings were made to the stove god and sacrifices to the soil god. On the summer and winter solstices they made sacrifices to the dead, like the laity. Before [the sacrifice], healing charms and martial amulets were dispensed, as well as contracts with the soil god (*she-ch'i*)." Maspero thought that these were sales contracts for the purchase of the tombs (cf. the examples in Lo Chen-yü ed., *Ti-ch'üan cheng-ts'un*). However, the dates do not accord with those of the solstices. Perhaps the *she* represented a type of collective convention guaranteed by an oath in which the parties appealed to the soil god as witness?

50. *Fo-tsu t'ung-chi* 36.343a. See also *Shih-shih yao-lan* A.263a. The earliest texts say nothing about this *po-lien she* whereas later sources supply an increasing number of details on the subject.

51. In *Mission archéologique* and *Six monuments de la sculpture chinoise*.

52. A summary of the *Mahāprajñāpramitā* in 27 ch. by Kumārajīva (T. 8, no. 223).

53. *Hsü kao-seng chuan* 28.688a.

54. Ibid. 20.595b.

55. *Sung kao-seng chuan* 15.803a.

56. Ibid. 16.807b.

57. Ibid. 6.743c.

58. Emended for "every day" in the text.

59. *T'ai-p'ing kuang-chi* 115.800. Ennin reports another version of the same legend, translated in Reischauer, *Record of a Pilgrimage*, pp. 258–59.

60. For these two statesmen of the mid-eighth century, see p. 292 and passim. Cf. des Rotours, *Traité des fonctionnaires*, pp. 715–16, note.

61. *Tai-tsung ch'ao tseng ssu-k'ung ta pien-cheng kuang-chih san-tsang ho-shang piao chih chi* 3.840c–841a.

62. On the associations of the Liao period (907–1125), named *ch'ien-jen i* ("associations of a thousand"), see Tamura Jitsuzo, "Kittan bukkyō no shakaishiteki kōsatsu."

63. Among the Fonds Pelliot of Tun-huang manuscripts there is a fragment (P. 2086) of a copy of the *Shih-ti lun* (T. 26, no. 1522) that was produced by an association. The colophon, dated 594 and reproduced in Kanda Kiichirō, *Tonkō-hisekiryushinhen* fasc. 2, p. 50, mentions 27 association members (*i-jen*), among them a Buddhist monk.

64. P. 2189. The copy bears a colophon dated first day, fifth month of the third year of the Ta-t'ung period (537) under the Western Wei. Numerous texts of this genre (*fa-yüan wen*) are found among the collections of manuscripts from Tun-huang. *Kuang hung-ming chi* 28 also contains several examples of *yüan-wen*.

65. Cf. P. 4536 v°: "The sole aim of the members of our association is to take refuge in the Three Jewels. All their thoughts are attached to the other shore. Thus they are able to honor the principle of all associations (*i-i*). . . . They have tied together the bonds of pious affinity (*t'ung-chieh liang-yüan*). n

66. Dated by Chavannes to the seventh century; see *Mission archéologique*, no. 473, fig. 1683.

67. The members of certain *i* were thus designated by names that were used only within the society. Analogous ties of fraternity existed between the monks: those who were ordained on the same day received names with identical first characters. In a petition presented by Pu-k'ung concerning the ordination of seven monks (*Tai-tsung ch'ao tseng ssu-k'ung ta pien-cheng kuang-chih san-tsang ho-shang piao chih chi* 2.835c-836a), each of these was to receive a name in religion that would share the same first character. *She*-associations of monks are also known to have existed. The disciples of the monk Hsin-hsing, founder of the Sect of the Three Stages, had thus formed a fellowship of *bodhi* (*p'u-t'i chih yu*). Cf. Yabuki Keiki, *Sangaikyō no kenkyū*, p. 9.

68. Cf. P. 3707, which gives the name of *ch'in-ch'ing she*; P. 4987 [the former P. 5529 (11)] is entitled "Hsiung-ti chuan-t'ie." See also Giles, *Six Centuries at Tun-huang*, p. 37, which mentions a "Society of Brethren."

69. P. 3730 v°, *Mou-chia teng chin li she-t'iao*, edited in Naba Toshisada, "Tōdai no shayū ni tsuite" 4.125-26.

70. S. 1475 v°, f. 4; Naba Toshisada, "Tōdai no shayū ni tsuite" 3.82-83.

71. P. 3216 r°; Naba Toshisada, ibid. 3.76-77. See also P. 3266 v°; Naba Toshisada, ibid. 3.77-78: "Letter of candidature of Tung Yen-chin. The above-named Yen-chin, having lost his father and his mother, has uselessly spent all his life without belonging to any association (*she-i*). Presenting himself today before your honorable society, he wishes to join it in order to devote himself to the ritual activities of mutual help (*chui-hsiung chu-chi* or *chiu-chi*). He hopes that the three directors (*san-kuan*) will be good enough to enter his name in their registers. He undertakes to conform to the statutes . . . and will not presume to be negligent. He requests them to take a favorable decision. . . . Petition of the [prospective] member Tung Yen-chin who respectfully solicits his admission" (Naba, ibid.).

72. P. 3730 v°, Naba Toshisada, ibid.

73. Pelliot, "Une bibliothèque médiévale," p. 503.

74. It should be noted that the term *i*, "sense of duty," recurs frequently in the vocabulary designating the associations and their members from the fifth to the tenth centuries. It evokes free, though sometimes regulated, services that individuals bound by personal, family, or lineage ties owed one another. There is no doubt that the notion originally had a religious signification and that it was concretely related to the sacrifices to the gods of the soil: the sacrifice created an indissoluble bond between those vowing friendship.

75. The aim of certain *she* at Tun-huang was to ensure "loyalty in the empire and filial devotion in the families" (P. 3128). But those concerned did not seem to make a distinction between Chinese and Buddhist traditions: *she* that included Buddhist monks among their membership also aimed at fostering the classical manifestations of filial piety. It may be noted that the Taoist societies belonged to the same type of association as the *she* at Tun-huang. Cf. Maspero, *Le taoïsme*, p. 45: "The act of founding a community by converting the infidels created an indissoluble bond between the founder and his converts that extended down to the remotest of their respective descendants and that could be supplanted by no other relationship. Some of these families have traversed without hindrance two thousand years of Chinese history." The organization of the Taoist associations of the first centuries of the Christian era did not differ significantly from that of the *she* of the ninth and tenth centuries at Tun-huang. Their parish councils, consisting of officers wearing caps or crowns (*kuan-kuan*), libationers (*chi-chiu*), and masters of the registers (*lu-shih*), evoke the three directors (*san-kuan*) of the *she* at Tun-huang.

76. The gates of wards and houses were sacred boundaries, and the ceremonies performed by the *she* aimed at protecting both of these precincts against calamity.

77. *Tun-huang shih-shih hsieh-ching t'i-chi yü Tun-huang tsa-lu* 2.117.

78. P. 3145.

79. P. 2975 and 3286.

80. On the *chai* and the importance of the banquet in Chinese cults, see p. 257 above.

81. Above, p. 174. On financial mutual societies in Chinese Buddhism, see Yang Lien-sheng, "Buddhist Monasteries."

82. Cf. Smith, *Village Life in China*, pp. 153ff.

83. The remarks by R. Maunier, in *Coutumes algériennes* (Paris 1935), pp. 66–68, concerning the Kabyle festivals (*taoussa* and *maouna*) merit comparison with the Chinese case, not least because the peasant communities of Kabylia bear certain analogies with those of China: "The *taoussa* in Kabylia, especially, where it remains in vigor today, can be defined as follows: a subscription of money, in which all the guests participate, for the benefit of the host. Take for example the father of a family who finds himself under the obligation to offer a feast: for in the countries of Islam, Berber, or Muslim, feasts are obligatory, and they are also ostentatious; to give them is both an honor and a duty; he has to have his son circumcised or marry a daughter; yet he has no *douros* hidden away under a flagstone or in a jar; a feast has to be given; above all, sheep have to be killed. The only way for him to fulfil his duty is to appeal to the *taoussa*. The *taoussa*, then, has its rites and its effects. Its rites consist, in the first place, in the invitation or convening to the planned feast. Extending that invitation suffices to place each guest under an obligation of honor to contribute his share. Second, there is the contribution which takes place at the time of the feast. . . . The *taoussa*, therefore has not only a true legal effect, namely the obligation to contribute and the obligation to restitute; it also has the virtue of a *benediction*. For it is an act authorized by God. When a *taoussa* takes place, all those who have participated in the donation are invested with *baraka*, obtain the blessing. At the moment when the offerings are placed on the cloth, the herald pronounces these words: *El-kher*, "the good fortune or the blessing of God." Thus the *taoussa* is like the *maouna* (an institution of the same type but where the contribution consist of foodstuffs) a religious act with a mystical and symbolic value as well as an economic and juridical value." See further, for another civilization—the Greek *eranos*—L. Gernet, "Droit et prédroit en Grèce ancienne," *Année sociologique* (1951), pp. 40 ff. It may be noted that the culminating point in the ceremony is at the moment when the offerings are presented: this is when the divine blessing is expected to descend upon the participants. In the Buddhist banquets there also seems to have been a moment of that kind. See the text cited above, p. 269.

84. The Buddhist character of the *i-hui* of the sixth century left its traces in the vocabulary itself. Certain members bear titles that belong to the monastic hierarchy: *karmadāna* overseer (*wei-na* or *tu-wei na*), bursar (*tien-tso*), reciter (*pai-ni, bhaka*), attendant for incense and lamps (*hsiang-huo*).

85. Chavannes, *Mission archéologique*, 1, no. 1507. This inscription is dated 533.

86. Chavannes, *Six monuments de la sculpture chinoise*, no. 3.

87. Each member, in effect, had to place a mark or write the character *chih* ("perused") beside his name when the circular passed through his hands.

88. P. 3037, ed. by Naba Toshisada, "Tōdai no shayū ni tsuite" 2.45–46 and 3.68–69. The Ta-pei monastery makes its appearance only late in the chronology of the Tun-huang manuscripts. Thus the present piece might date from the period 930–990.

89. S. 1475, edited by Naba Toshisada, "Tōdai no shayū ni tsuite" 3.82–83.

90. The great spring assembly (ch'un-tso chü-hsi).

91. Giles, Six Centuries at Tun-huang, p. 38 (statutes of an association of women). It can be seen from this example that the traditional principles of the she, that required the members to be heads of families, were modified by Buddhism. Associations of women were not unknown. P. 3489 is another text that originated in such an association, founded by the housekeepers of a ward in Tun-huang: Statutes of the fourteenth day, first month of the year wu-ch'en. In the event of the decease of a relative of one of the members, each was to bring .1 shih of flour. Members arriving late to the rendezvous were fined one chiao of alcohol. The names of some of the members suggest that they were nuns.

92. These are the three directors (san-kuan) that figure in all the associations of Tun-huang. In addition to these three officers, there are occasional references to association elders (she-lao).

93. P. 3989.

94. Cf. the stele of 554 (Chavannes, Six monuments de la sculpture chinoise, no. 3): an association of ca. two hundred members that comprised two i-shih, the bhiksu Fa-kuo and Hai-ho.

95. P. 2708: eight clergy and ten laymen; P. 3707: sixteen laymen and three clergy; P. 5530 (18): thirty-eight laymen and two clergy; P. 3889: thirty-five laymen and one monk; P. 5529 (6): thirteen laymen and one monk; P. 5529 (1): fifteen laymen and one monk.

96. The following anecdote confirms this supposition. The principal wife of the king of Kao-ch'ang (in the region of Turfān) wished to establish a tie of fictive kinship with the master Hsüan-tsang during his enforced stay in that town so that he would aid her to obtain deliverance in her future existences. See Ta tz'u-en ssu San-tsang fa-shih chuan 1.225b.

97. P. 2032, accounts of the steward for the year (chih-sui) Hui-an.

98. These were the chai of the first, fifth, and ninth months. During these months, slaughtering and fishing were prohibited. Cf. T'ang-lü shu-i 30.10b. The T'ang hui-yao 41.732, decree of the fifteenth day, tenth month, twenty-second year of K'ai-yüan (734), however, gives the dates as the first, seventh, and tenth months.

99. P. 2049, f. 34, end of the scroll (expenditure in oil); f. 37 (flour). The assembly took place on the eighth day of the second month in the first year of Ch'ang-hsing (930).

100. Toshisada, "Tōdai no shayū ni tsuite" 3.

101. According to P. 3231, the fabrication of a hu-ping cake required five times as much flour as making a pu-t'ou, namely some five ko, corresponding to the ration for the midday meal of an adult.

102. Decree of the year 731, see p. 256 above.

103. See p. 264 above.

104. As mentioned above (pp. 210ff.), the Inexhaustible Treasuries were sustained by the lavish offerings of the great families of Ch'ang-an and by the fixed and modest levies paid in by commoners.

105. The same term is used in the circular letters of the associations at Tun-huang to designate the meetings of their members.

106. Hsiang-fa chüeh-i ching 1337b.

107. See pp. 213ff. above.

10. The Wealthy Laity

1. See p. 290.

2. Wei shu 83A.1819, biography of Feng Hsi. It is possible that these deaths were

considered necessary sacrifices, a theme that recurs frequently. The founding of places of worship was often connected with human sacrifice. Cf. the stūpa erected following the suicides of monks, p. 242 above.

3. Cf. *Pei Ch'i shu* 9.127.

4. *Pei Ch'i shu* 8.113; *Pei shih* 8.301; trans. in Balazs, "Traité économique," pp. 209–10.

5. Cf. Forte, *The Mingtang*, pp. 75–84.

6. Ibid., pp. 156–59.

7. See above, p. 20.

8. *Chiu T'ang shu* 82.2768, biography of Li I-fu.

9. *Chiu T'ang shu* 184.4758, biography of Kao Li-shih.

10. This presumably alludes to the preceding reign of Empress Wu, Chung-tsung, and Jui-tsung.

11. The word *chang* designated perhaps the tent that was erected for the funerary ceremonies. The pious foundations within the Buddhist communities probably served as models for this institution which recalls the Vietnamese *hu'ong-hoa* (Chin. *hsiang-huo*). Cf. Deloustal, "La justice dans l'ancien Annam," p. 48. On the development of these private chapels under the Sung, see p. 308.

12. *Chiu T'ang shu* 8.174.

13. *Chiu T'ang shu* 96.3028–29.

14. After the death of Emperor Hsien-tsu (r. 466–471) of the Northern Wei, a certain Wang Hsüan-wei, submitting to the great mourning of twenty-seven months (*chan-ts'ui*), constructed himself a hut of rush. Clad in unhemmed sackcloth and living on coarse gruel, he wailed and leapt unceasingly. On the hundredth day [after the emperor's death], he spent his family possessions to organize a Buddhist banquet for four hundred persons. On the day of the anniversary of the death of Hsien-tsu, he held another ceremony in which one hundred monks participated. On the last day of the year, Emperor Hsiao-wen ordered a white suit of silk trousers and a lined coat to be given to Hsüan-wei as Buddhist garments (?). See *Wei shu* 87.1891. The text reveals a curious synthesis between Chinese mourning rites and Buddhist practices.

15. It may be recalled here that the sites of tombs had much in common with the emplacements of monasteries. Both were situated in hilly terrain well removed from the domain of cultivated lands. See p. 118 above.

16. Li Yüan, of a fervent Buddhist family, retired to a cell in the Hui-lin monastery that stood on the former country estate of his father (see *Chiu T'ang shu* 187B.4889, biography of Li Ch'eng): one went to one's family monastery and not elsewhere.

17. *Hsiang-fa chüeh-i ching* 1336a.

18. See *Chiu T'ang shu* 2.31.

19. *Wei shu* 4B.97. The decree also mentions "gold and silversmiths," no doubt in reference to alchemists.

20. *Ts'e-fu yüan-kuei* 159.11b.

21. *Fo-tsu t'ung-chi* 38.355b.

22. Ibid. 355b–356a.

23. This cannot be attributed to coincidence. The political influence of certain monks and nuns, though occult and based on a network of complicities, was nevertheless considerable and at times decisive.

24. *Sung shu* 97.2386–87.

25. *Chiu T'ang shu* 79.2716, biography of Fu I.

26. See p. 238 above.

27. *Chiu T'ang shu* 160.4200, biography of Han Yü.

28. A nephew of Tou Te-ming, related to a distaff branch of the imperial family. Biography in *Chiu T'ang shu* 183.4724–25.

29. A protege of Wu San-ssu, a kinsman of the empress Wu Tse-t'ien. Biography in *Chiu T'ang shu* 92.2968–71.

30. *Chiu T'ang shu* 183.4739–40, appendix to the biography of Wu Ch'eng-ssu.

31. *Hsin T'ang shu* 83.3648, biography of the Ho-p'u Princess.

32. Ch'en Yin-k'o, "Wu Chao yü fo-chiao."

33. *Chiu T'ang shu* 105.3226–27, biography of Yang Shen-ch'in.

34. *Wei shu* 7A.150.

35. *Fo-tsu t'ung-chi* 38.356a, year 528. Cf. *Wei shu* 9.222, where this rebellion is dated 515. The text of the *Fo-tsu t'ung-chi* is inspired by a passage in the biography of Prince Yao in *Wei shu* 19.445–46.

36. See Ch'en Yin-k'o, op. cit.

37. Tsukamoto Zenryū, *Shina bukkyōshi kenkyū*, pp. 247–85.

38. See pp. 171–72 above.

39. *Fo-tsu t'ung-chi* 38.354b.

40. "Shih-Lao chih," *Wei shu* 114.3033–34. Cf. *Fo-tsu t'ung-chi* 38.354b.

41. Cf. pp. 118 and 143 above.

42. See p. 104 above.

43. See p. 181 above.

44. *Hsü shih-shuo* 3.10a–b.

45. *Wei shu* 48.1072, biography of Kao Yün.

46. On the Buddhist origin of this institution, see p. 170 above.

47. *Chiu T'ang shu* 183.4734.

48. I.e., 18,000 kg.

49. *Chiu T'ang shu* 184.4758, biography of Kao Li-shih.

50. Cf. Granet, *La féodalité chinoise*, p. 149: "The Chinese custom (especially but not exclusively in antiquity) . . . can by characterized as follows: Men were tied to the hereditary landed assets of their agnatic kin and the retainers enfeoffed to them. Women, by contrast, predestined by the rule of exogamy to be *exported*, represented essentially *exchange values* and were the *principlaes of all circulation of assets* that were not strictly hereditary and intransmissible from one feudal domain to another." Cf. ibid. on the relations of women with the great merchants.

51. *Chiu T'ang shu* 183.4734. These excessively luxurious constructions had political implications. The literati regularly compared them with the imperial palace, for they represented an incipient form of usurpation.

52. See Forte, *Political Propaganda*.

53. *Chiu T'ang shu* 118.3417, biography of Wang Chin. The mother of the brothers Wang was a devout Buddhist and no doubt she transmitted this religious faith to them. Certain families remained attached to Buddhism by tradition. Cf. the Hsiao and the Yang above, p. 287.

54. See *Tai-tsung ch'ao tseng ssu-k'ung ta pien-cheng kuang-chih san-tsang ho-shang piao chih chi*.

55. The *Jen-wang hu-kuo po-je po-lo-mi-to ching*, translated by Amoghavajra.

56. *Chiu T'ang shu* 118.3417–18, biography of Wang Chin. Cf. *Hsin T'ang shu* 145.4716–17.

57. The term *kung-te* translates Skr. *punya*: in China it was applied to all meritorious works including the casting of statues, constructions, copying of sacred texts, etc.

58. The existence at that time of private chapels called "merit cloisters" (*kung-te yüan*) supports this interpretation. Cf. p. 45 above.

59. See ibid.

60. *T'ang hui-yao* 48.854, decree of the first month, fifth year of Ta-chung.

61. *T'ang hui-yao* ibid.

62. "Wu shu" 4, *San-kuo chih* 49.1185. See also *Hou Han shu* 73.2368, biography of T'ao Ch'ien, and *Fo-tsu t'ung-chi* 35.331b. Cf. Zürcher, *Conquest*, p. 28.

63. *Tzu-chih t'ung-chien* 205.6498, first year of T'ien-ts'e wan-sui (695).

64. See pp. 263 and 271 above.

11. The Ruling Class

1. See p. 288 above.

2. Above, p. 326, n. 53.

3. Above, pp. 22 and 45.

4. Above, p. 22.

5. De Groot, *Sectarianism*.

6. *Lo-yang ch'ieh-lan chi* 2.1007a.

7. *Kuang hung-ming chi* 7.134c.

8. Cf. Weinstein, *Buddhism under the T'ang*, pp. 86–90.

9. See p. 285 above.

10. *Kuang hung-ming chi* 28.335a.

11. That is, one must not be attached to vain displays of splendor: a rationalist interpretation of an idealistic doctrine. See *T'ang hui-yao* 49.858. Empress Wu's project also gave rise to the celebrated criticisms by Ti Jen-chieh (ibid. 857) and Li Ch'iao (ibid. 857–58).

12. Memorial of 714. See *Chiu T'ang shu* 96.3028, biography of Yao Ch'ung.

13. Cf. above, p. 330, n. 110.

14. Reference to the contradiction between religious practice (constructions) and the principle of avoiding harm to all beings, a theme frequently taken up by the literati. Cf. the Song memorial cited in *Kuang hung-ming chi* 6.127c and pp. 14, 17 above.

15. *T'ang hui-yao* 48.850–51.

16. Cf. p. 254 above.

17. *Ch'üan T'ang wen* 39.17a.

18. "Shih-Lao chih," *Wei shu* 114.3030. Cf. *Kuang hung-ming chi* 2.102a.

19. "Shih-Lao chih," *Wei shu* 114.3036.

20. See p. 41 above.

21. *Ts'e-fu yüan-kuei* 159.17a.

22. Under the T'ang, the court simultaneously called upon Taoists and Buddhists. See des Rotours, *Traité des fonctionnaires*, p. 88, note: "For the days of state mourning, two of the great Buddhist and Taoist temples were designated in each of the two capitals for celebrations of the rites of simple abstinence." Analogous ceremonies took place in the prefectures. See *T'ang liu-tien* 4.14b–17a.

23. *Fo-tsu t'ung-chi* 37.358c.

24. *Chiu T'ang shu* 127.3579, biography of P'eng Yen.

25. *Fan-ch'uan wen-chi* 10.9a–b.

26. *Fo-tsu t'ung-chi* 42.385b.

27. See above, p. 100.

28. "Shih-Lao chih," *Wei shu* 114.3031. The emperor *was* the true Buddha. Therefore it was vain to pay homage to his simulacra. This idea was put forward by Wei Yüan-sung, one of the instigators of the repression of 574 under Emperor Wu of the Chou. See *Kuang hung-ming chi* 7.132a.

29. Cf. P. Demiéville, *Milindapañha*, pp. 218 ff (on the *Mahāmeghasūtra*). On the casting of statues in the image of the bodhisattva, see p. 23 above.

12. Internal Contradictions in the Buddhist Movement in China

1. The preceding Ta-li reign period (766–780), under Tai-tsung, had been marked by the greatest ascendancy of the Buddhist faction at court.

2. *Fo-tsu t'ung-chi* 46.419c, third year of Ta-kuan.

3. Ibid. 47.425b, seventh year of Shao-hsing.

4. The aim of these foundations was to obtain blessings for deceased parents, but the consequences of such sacrilege would affect the perpetrators themselves.

5. See p. 72 above.

6. *Fo-tsu t'ung-chi* 39.369a, commentary. On the history of the private chapels, see Michima Hajime, "Kizoku tai jiin keizaiteki kōshō." The stele of the Kuang-li ch'an-ssu (see p. 348, n. 112 above) informs us that in Sung times great families had appropriated the lands of the A-yü wang monastery. The phenomenon was widespread at that time.

7. *Pei-shan lu* 8.623c–624a.

8. See also, for a later period, *Yüan-tien chang* 33, "Shih tao," second year Huang-ch'ing (1313): "The rules of purity have fallen into abeyance. The incense and the lamps are extinguished. . . . Everywhere, the abbots and old monks have made off with the treasures of the permanent assets. They have left the monasteries to live in private dwellings. They have opened shops for loans against pledges. They drink alcohol and eat pungent vegetables (*hun*). They have wives and concubines. There is no difference between them and the laity. The harm they have done to the religion is immense." Modern popular sayings illustrate the amused scorn in which the clergy were held: "As a last resource, one becomes a monk"; "A glimpse of money makes the blind man see"; "When a monk sees money, he will sell his sutra"; "Nine out of ten nuns are prostitutes, the tenth is crazy." Cf. Plopper, *Chinese Religion*, pp. 199, 206, 207.

9. An indication revealing the appearance of a new state of mind among the wealthy laity in T'ang times is provided by a passage in the *Hsiang-fa chüeh-i ching* 1336a: "At that time, there shall be donors who shall institute Buddhist assemblies and invite the monks. But [at the same time] they will send keepers to guard the gates of the courts and the halls to prevent the bhiksu from entering these assemblies."

GLOSSARY

a-li-lo 荷藜勒
A-yü wang 阿育王
An-kuo ssu 安國寺
An-lo fo ssu 安樂佛寺

cha-ping 查餅
ch'a-p'i 茶毘
chai (mansion) 宅
chai (vegetarian feast) 齋
chai-ch'en 齋嚫
chai-ch'i 齋七
chai-chu 齋主
chan (appropriate) 占
chan-ts'ui 斬衰
chang (length) 丈
chang-che 長者
Chang Chi 張既
Chang-ching ssu 章敬寺
Chang Ch'iu 張求
Chang-ch'iu Tzu-t'o 章仇子他
Chang Hsiao-hsiu 張孝秀

Chang-hua 張花
Chang Ju-ying 張如瑩
chang-shih 長史
Chang T'ing-kuei 張廷珪
Chang Yüeh 張説
Ch'ang Ching 常景
ch'ang-chu 常住
ch'ang-chu chang-fu 常住丈夫
ch'ang-chu po-hsing 常住百姓
ch'ang-chu t'ien 常住田
ch'ang-ho 昌褐
ch'ang-hsüan 常選
ch'ang-i 唱衣
ch'ang-ming teng 長明燈
Ch'ang-ning 長寧
ch'ang-p'ing shu 常平署
ch'ang-sheng ch'ien k'u 長生錢庫
Ch'ang-sheng tien 長生殿
ch'ang-tieh 長牒
Ch'ang-yen 常儼
Chao Ch'ien 趙遷

chao-hsüan ts'ao 昭玄曹
chao-hsüan t'ung 昭玄統
Chao-i 昭懿
Chao Kou-tzu 趙苟子
chao-t'i 招提
chao-t'i chih yü 招提之宇
chao-t'i ssu 招提司
Chao-t'i ssu 招提寺
ch'ao (seize/measure) 抄
Ch'ao-hua ssu 超化寺
Chen Fa-ch'ung 甄法崇
Chen Pin 甄彬
Chen-chi ssu 真寂寺
ch'en (offering) 嚫/儭/襯
Ch'en Hsüan-yun 陳玄運
Ch'en Shao-ch'in 陳紹欽
ch'en-ssu 嚫司
Cheng Kuang-wen 鄭廣文
Cheng Shu-ch'ing 鄭叔清
ch'eng (pass/stage) 程
Ch'eng-kuan 澄觀
ch'eng-shang chuan-ching 城上轉經
ch'eng-t'ai 澄汰
chi-chiu 祭酒
Chi-chou 濟州
chi-fu chih wai 肌膚之外
Chi-t'ing shan 稽亭山
Chi-tsang 吉藏
chi tu-wei 騎都尉
ch'i (contract) 契
Ch'i-chou 齊州
Ch'i-fu ssu 啟福寺
ch'i-shih 七施
ch'i-to 棄墮
chia (family) 家
chia-chai 家宅

chia-jen 家人
chia-seng 家僧
chia-tsu 甲族
chia-tzu 家資
chia-tzu teng wu 家資等物
chia-yeh 家業
Chiang-ling 江陵
chiang-shuo 講説
Chiang-tu 江都
chiang tz'u-ch'i wei ling-liu 將此契為令六
chiao-i 交易
chiao-shou ho-shang 教授和尚
Ch'iao shan 焦山
chieh (parish) 界
chieh-chai 解齋
chieh-huo 解火
chieh-mo shou 羯磨受
chieh-t'an 結壇
chieh-tu shih 節度使
chieh-tu ya-ya 節度押衙
chieh-yu 結友
ch'ieh-lan 伽藍
chien (bay) 間
chien (mean) 賤
Chien-chen 鑑真
chien-fu 建福
chien-fu ts'ao 監福曹
Chien-ming ssu 建明寺
chien-shih 監使
chien tsao-ssu 監造寺
ch'ien (cash) 錢
ch'ien-chang hui-ts'an 前帳迴殘
ch'ien-ch'i 前妻
ch'ien-jen i 千人邑
Ch'ien Fu 錢輔
Ch'ien-tzu wen 千字文

Ch'ien-yüan ssu 乾元寺
chih (declare) 指
chih (administer) 知
chih (pledge) 質
chih-ch'ien 質錢
chih-chü 質舉
chih-chuang 置莊
chih ... erh 直 ... 耳
Chih-hsi 智禧
Chih-hsü 智勗
Chih-hsüan 知玄
chih-k'o 知客
chih-k'u 質庫
Chih-kuei 知瓌
chih-ming 知命
chih-shih 知事
chih-shih jen 執事人
chih-sui 直歲
chih-t'ien 置田
Chih-tsao 智璪
Chih-ts'ung 智聰
Chih-wen 智文
Chih-yen 智琰 (516–601)
Chih-yen 智嚴
ch'h (measure) 尺
ch'ih-li-to 吃栗多
ch'ih-pan 叱半
ch'ih-ssu 勅賜
Chin-chou 錦州
Chin-hsien kuan 金仙觀
Chin-hua 金華
chin-kang ch'u 金剛杵
Chin-ko ssu 金閣寺
Chin kuang-ming ssu 金光明寺
Chin kuang-ming tsui-sheng
    wang-ching 金光明最勝王經
chin-shih 進仕

ch'in-ch'ing she 親情社
Ching-ai ssu 敬愛寺
ching-ch'a 淨剎
Ching-chou 荊州
ching-fang 經坊
ching-jen 淨人
ching-k'u 淨庫
Ching-ming ssu 景明寺
ching-she 精舍
Ching-shui 淨水
ching-t'ien 敬田
ching-t'ien yüan 敬田院
Ching-t'u ssu 淨土寺
Ching-yü ssu 淨域寺
ch'ing (measure) 頃
Ch'ing-ch'an ssu 清禪寺
Ch'ing-ch'eng shan 青城山
ch'ing-chien 卿監
ch'ing-hsien ch'ien 清閑錢
Ch'ing-kuan 清觀
Ch'ing-liang 清涼
ch'ing-mai 青麥
ch'ing-shui 輕稅
ch'ing-wu 輕物
Ch'ing-yün 清蘊
chiu (stable) 廄
chiu-yüeh nei 九月內
ch'iu-tso chü-hsi 秋座局席
chou-yüan 咒願
ch'ou (tablets) 籌
ch'ou-fen 抽分
chu-chia nien-sung 諸家念誦
chu-ch'in 諸親
chu hsiang-yüan chu-yüeh
    sheng-li 著鄉元逐月生利
chu-i ch'ien 助役錢
chu-jen 主人

Ch'u Ch'eng 褚澄
ch'u-chai 除齋
ch'u-chia 出家
ch'u-hsiao 出孝
ch'u-na ch'iu li 出納求利
ch'u-shen wei-seng 出身為僧
ch'u-t'ien 廚田
ch'u-tai 出貸
Ch'u Yüan 褚淵
chü (loan) 舉
chü-chi 聚集
chü-fang 車坊
ch'ü (loan) 取
ch'ü-chi 取給
Ch'ü-chou 衢州
chuan (transfer) 轉
chuan-ching 轉經
chüan (tax exemption) 蠲
ch'üan-cheng 券證
ch'üan-ch'i 券契
ch'üan-ch'i chih wu 券契之物
chuang (estate) 莊
chuang (petition) 狀
chuang-chai shih 莊宅使
chuang-li 莊吏
chuang-t'ien 莊田
Chuang-yen ssu 莊嚴寺
chuang-yüan 莊園
Chüeh-shih 角詩
chui-fu 追福
chui-hsiung chu-chi/chiu-chi
  追凶逐吉／就吉
chun (equivalent) 准
ch'un-ch'iu fo-shih 春秋佛食
Ch'un-ming men 春明門
ch'un-tso chü-hsi 春座局席
chün-hu 軍戶

chün-tzu 君子
Chung Shih-ming 鍾世明
chung-tsui 重罪
chung-wu 重物
ch'ung (to pound) 舂
Ch'ung-en 崇恩
Ch'ung-jen fang 崇仁坊
ch'ung-shih 充使
ch'ung-t'ien mu 衝天木
Ch'ung-yün tien 重雲殿

en-t'ien 恩田
en-tu 恩度
en-tzu 恩子

fa (*dharma*) 法
fa (fine) 罰
Fa-an 法安
Fa-ch'eng 法乘
fa-ch'iao 法橋
Fa-chin 法進
Fa-ch'ing 法慶
Fa-hsiang 法向
Fa-hsien 法顯
Fa-hsiu 法秀
fa-hua 法化
fa-i hsiung-ti 法義兄弟
Fa-kuo 法果
fa-lü 法律
Fa-men ssu 法門寺
fa-shih 法事
Fa-tsang 法藏
fa-yüan wen 發願文
fan-ch'ang 梵場
fan chung-tsui 犯重罪
fan-hu 番戶

Fan-yang 范陽

fang-chang 方丈

fang-chi 方伎

fang chu-tsa ch'ai-k'o 放諸雜差科

fang-shou jen 防守人

fang-tzu 房資

fei-jen wu 非人物

fen (measure) 分

Fen-chou 汾州

fen-fen shou 分分受

fen-ssu 墳寺

feng (appanage) 封

Feng Hsi 馮熙

Feng Ssu 馮思

fo-ch'a 佛剎

fo-chang so 佛帳所

fo fa seng 佛法僧

fo-p'en 佛盆

fo-shih 佛事

fo-t'ang 佛堂

fo-tien 佛殿

fo-t'u 佛圖

fo-t'u hu 佛圖戶

fo-wu 佛物

fu (tax) 賦

fu seng-t'ung 副僧統

Fu I 傅奕

fu-hsiang 福祥

Fu-hsien ssu 福先寺

fu-hu 富戶

fu-jen 浮人

fu-ping 府兵

Fu-shang 富上

fu-t'ian 福田

Fu-t'ien ssu 福田寺

fu-tieh 符牒

fu-wu 浮物

han-shih 寒食

Han Yü 韓愈

hao-tsu kuei-yu 豪族貴遊

ho-pu 褐布

Ho-nan fu shih 河南府純

Ho-yang ch'ien 河陽錢

hou-tsang 厚葬

hsi (game) 戲

Hsi-chou 西州

hsi-fang fa-she 西方法社

hsi-lo 悉羅

Hsi-ming ssu 西明寺

Hsi-tung-sa 悉東薩

hsi-wan 戲頑

Hsi-yu chi 西遊記

hsia-chang 下帳

hsia-hsiang 狹鄉

hsiang (district) 鄉

hsiang (Skr. *nimitta*) 相

Hsiang (monk) 香

Hsiang An 襄唵

Hsiang-chou 相州

hsiang-huo 香火

hsiang-pao 相保

hsiang-ssu po-hsing 鄉司百姓

hsiang-ti 香地

Hsiao Chih-chung 蕭至忠

hsiao-hsiang 小祥

hsiao-mai 小麥

hsiao-shuo 小説

hsieh-k'ou 瀉口

hsien (horse pen) 閑

hsien-ch'ien ch'ang-chu 現前常住

hsien-pei 鮮卑

hsien-ti 閑地

hsien-tsai fu-seng shang ch'u-li 見在付僧上出利

Hsien-yü Shu-ming 鮮于叔明

hsin-fu k'o-hu 新附客戶

Hsin-hsing 信行

Hsin-i 信義

Hsin T'i-p'i 辛替否

Hsin-ting 新定

Hsin-yang 新陽

hsing (family name) 姓

hsing-che 行者

hsing-cheng 行政

Hsing-ch'eng 杏城

Hsing-ch'ing kung 興慶宮

hsing-hsiang 行像

Hsing-ning fang 興寧坊

hsing-tieh 行牒

hsiung-ti chuan-t'ie 兄弟轉帖

hsiu[?]-ju 秀(?)乳

Hsüan-ch'ang 玄暢

Hsüan-hsü 玄緒

Hsüan-yang men 宣陽門

Hsüeh Huai-i 薛懷義

Hsüeh Ts'un-ch'eng 薛存誠

hu (household) 戶

hu (measure) 斛

Hu Chao-i 胡昭儀

hu-fa 護法

hu-k'uo 戶口

Hu-kuo chen-shen 護國真身

Hu-kuo ssu 護國寺

hu-ping 胡餅

Hu San-hsing 胡三省

hu-shui 戶稅

hu-ts'ao 戶曹

Hua-feng kuan 華封觀

Hua-tu ssu 化度寺

Huai-hai 懷海

huang-ma 黃麻

hui (humanitarianism) 惠

hui (wisdom) 慧

Hui-an men 徽安門

Hui-ch'eng 惠澄

Hui-chou 慧冑

Hui-fan 慧範

Hui-hung 惠弘

Hui-i 慧益

Hui-jih ssu 慧日寺

Hui-lin ssu 慧林寺

Hui-shao 慧紹

Hui-shen 惠深

Hui-ta 慧達

hui-ts'an 會殘

Hui-yüan 慧遠

hun (pungent vegetables) 葷

i (association) 邑

i (sense of duty) 義

i-ch'ieh chai-hui 一切齋會

i-ch'ieh hui 一切會

I-ching 義淨

I-ching 易經

I-chou 益州

i-chun chiu-ko 一準舊格

i-fan t'ing 義飯廳

i-hao 邑號

i-hui 邑會

i-i 一易 (one fallowing)

i-i 義邑 (association)

i i-she 邑義社

i-jen 邑人

i-lao 邑老

i-lü 依律

I-ning fang 義寧坊

I-shan fang 翊善坊

i-she 邑社

i-shen 遺身

i-shih 邑師

i-shu 遺書

i-tzu 邑子

jan-teng 然燈

Jen-ch'eng 任城

jen-hu 人戶

jen-li 人理

jen shang tien-wu t'ung kuo-tzu 人上典物銅鍋子

jen-wu 人物

ju-tao 入道

k'ai (clear land) 開

K'ai-yüan ssu 開元寺

Kan-hua ssu 感化寺

k'an-ping jen 看病人

Kao Chao 高肇

Kao Li-shih 高力士

kao-shen 告身

kao-tieh 告牒

Kao Yün 高允

Keng-chih t'u 耕織圖

Keng Shou-ch'ang 耿壽昌

ko (measure) 合

Ko Wu 蓋吳

k'o (imposition/rental) 課

k'o (interest rate) 科

k'o-fang 客坊

k'o-hu 客戶

k'o-i 課役

k'o-she 客舍

k'o-ssu 客司

k'o-ti 客邸

k'o-tien 客店

k'o-tso ssu 客作肆

k'o-yüan 客院

k'ou-ch'eng jen 口承人

k'ou-fen t'ien 口分田

k'u (treasury) 庫

k'u-ssu 庫司

k'u-t'ien 苦田

k'u-tzu 庫子

kua (gourd) 瓜

kuan (string of cash) 貫

kuan-ch'a shih 觀察使

kuan-chia 官家

kuan-fang 關防

kuan-fu 官府

kuan-kuan (register) 官貫

kuan-kuan (officers) 冠官

kuan nu-pi 官奴婢

kuan-ti 官地

Kuan-ting 灌頂

k'uan-hsiang 寬鄉

k'uan-sheng ch'ien 寬剩錢

Kuang-chai fang 光宅坊

Kuang-chai ssu 光宅寺

Kuang-li ch'an-ssu 廣利禪寺

Kuang-te fang 光德坊

kung-te ch'u 功德處

kung-te fen-ssu 功德墳寺

kung-te shih 功德使

kung-te t'ung 功德銅

kung-te yüan 功德院

kung-ti 公地

kung-ts'ai 公財

kung-yang chü 供養具

k'ung chi chung-pao chuan-fu ch'üan-men 空竇重寶專附權門

K'ung Ning-tzu 孔寧子

k'ung-ming 空名

Kuo-ch'ing ssu 國清寺

Kuo-li Pei-p'ing t'u-shu kuan
　kuan-k'an 國立北平圖書館館刊
kuo-so 過所
Kuo Tsu-shen 郭祖深
Kuo Tzu-i 郭子儀
Kuo-yüan 果菀

Lai-t'ing fang 來庭坊
lan-jo 蘭若
lang-chün 郎君
lei-ch'i chai 累七齋
li (measure) 里
Li Ch'eng 李憕
li chi 立機
Li Chi-fu 李吉甫
li-ch'iu 立秋
li-ch'un 立春
Li Fu-kuo 李輔國
Li Hsü 李虛
Li Hsün 李訓
Li Huang 李晃
Li I-chi 李意及
Li I-fu 李義府
li-jen fang 癘人坊
li-jun 利潤
li-jun ju 利潤入
Li K'ai-fu 李開府
Li Kui-po 李歸伯
Li Lin-fu 李林甫
Li Piao 李彪
Li Shu-ming 李叔明
Li Te-yü 李德裕
Li Ts'ai 李蔡
Li-tsung 禮宗
li yao-shen 立妖神
Li Yüan 李源
Li Yüan-hung 李元紘

liang (freeman) 良
liang (ounce/tael) 兩
Liang fa t'uan ju-chai wen-shu
　梁法團入債文書
liang-hu 梁戶
liang-jen 良人
liang-jen chih-fu 良人枝附
liang-k'o 梁課
Liang-ling 兩嶺
liang-t'ien 良田
lien-chi shui-wei 連機水磑
lien-she 蓮社
lin (forest) 林
lin-k'uang 臨壙
Ling-hsiu ssu 靈修寺
Ling-hu Huan 令狐峘
Ling-hui 靈惠
ling-ti 零地
Ling-t'u ssu 靈圖寺
Ling-yen ssu 靈巖寺
Ling-yin shan 靈隱山
Liu-chung 柳中
liu-li ming teng 琉璃明燈
liu-po 六博
liu-wu 六物
Liu Yao 劉緐
Liu Yü 柳彧
lo (wheat) 羅
lo-chih 落脂
lou-chi ling 樓機綾
Lu Ch'ang-yüan 陸長源
Lu Chih 陸贄
Lu Hsüan 陸玄
Lu Huai-shen 盧懷慎
Lu Yu 陸游
lu-shih 錄事
Lung-hsing ssu 龍興寺

Lung-kung ssu 龍宮寺
Lung-men 龍門

ma-pu 馬步
mai (sell) 賣
mai (wheat) 麥
man-fei 縵緋
man-lü 縵綠
mao-i fen shou 貿易分受
Mao Tzu-yüan 毛子元
men-t'u 門徒
mi-she 米社
Mao-hsien ssu 妙顯寺
mien ch'ai-jen 免差人
mien-ting 免丁
ming-ching 明經
Ming-kai 明概
ming-t'ang 明堂
ming-t'ien 名田
mo-pao 墨寶
mou-chia teng chin li she-t'iao
　　某甲等謹立社條
mu (measure) 畝

Nan-shan 南山
Nao-ts'un 猱村
nei tao-ch'ang 內道場
ni sha-mi 尼沙彌
niao-wen 鳥文
nien (mill) 碾
nien-fo 念佛
nien-sung 念誦
nien-wei 碾(磑)磑
niu-ch'u 牛畜
nu-pi 奴婢
nung-kuan 農官

o (temple name tablet) 額
o-kuei 餓鬼

pai-ni 唄匿
p'an-kuan she-li 判官闍梨
p'ang-ch'ü 旁渠
Pao-ch'iung 寶瓊
pao-cheng 保證
Pao-en ssu 報恩寺
Pao-li ssu 寶曆寺
Pao-shou ssu 寶壽寺
Pao-ying ssu 寶應寺
pei-t'ien 悲田
pei-t'ien yüan 悲田院
Pei-tu 杯度
pei-yüan 北院
P'ei Chih 裴植
P'ei Mien 裴冕
P'ei Ts'an 裴粲
P'ei Tu 裴度
P'ei Yen 裴衍
P'ei Yu 裴瑜
P'eng Yen 彭偃
p'eng-tang 朋黨
p'i (measure) 疋
pieh-shu 別墅
pieh-wen 別文
pieh-yeh 別業
pien (loan) 便
Pien-i chih 辨疑志
pien hsiu 便休
pien-hu 編戶
pien-min 編民
pien-su jen 便粟人
ping-fang 病坊
ping-ma shih 兵馬使
P'ing-ch'i 平齊

po (to winnow) 簸
Po Chü-i 白居易
po-hsing 百姓
po-hsing seng 百姓僧
Po-hu t'ung 白虎通
Po-lien she 白蓮社
po-shih 博士
po-shih mien-ling 帛絁綿綾
po-t'u 白徒
p'o-p'en 破盆
P'o-t'o 婆陀
pu (cloth) 布
pu-ching 不淨
pu-ching yü 不淨語
pu-ch'ü 部曲
pu-hsiao 不肖
pu-i 不易
Pu-k'ung 不空
pu-lo 部落
pu-t'ou 倍愉
P'u-an 普安
P'u-chi ssu 普濟寺
P'u-chiu ssu 普救寺
P'u-chou 蒲州
P'u-hsien i-she 普賢邑社
P'u-kuang ssu 普光寺
p'u-p'en ch'ien 普盆錢
p'u-sa chieh 菩薩戒
p'u-t'i chih yu 菩提之友
p'u-t'i hsiang-huo she 菩提香火社
p'u-t'i so 菩提所
p'u-tien 鋪店
p'u-t'ung i-ch'ieh 普通一切
p'u-t'ung yüan 普通院
p'u-yeh 僕射
P'u-yüan 普圓

sai (offering) 賽
san (nominal title) 散
San-chiao shui-nien 三交水碾
San-chieh chiao 三界教
San-chieh ssu 三界寺
san-fu 三輔
san-i 三易
san-kang 三綱
san-kuan 三官
san-shih 散施
sang-tzu 桑梓
seng-ch'i hu 僧祇戶
seng-ch'i su 僧祇粟
seng-cheng 僧正
seng-cheng ho-shang 僧政和尚
Seng-hsien 僧遷
Seng-hui 僧慧
Seng-kung-te tsan 僧功德讚
seng-lu 僧錄
Seng-p'in 僧頻
seng shang tai-pien 僧上貸便
seng-shih 僧事
seng-shou 僧首
seng-ts'ao 僧曹
Seng-tsang 僧藏
seng-t'ung 僧統
seng-wu 僧物
Seng-yai 僧崖
Sha-chou 沙州
Sha-chou tu seng-t'ung
　　沙州都僧統
sha-men t'ung 沙門統
sha-mi 沙彌
sha-t'ai 沙汰
Shan-chün shu-shih 陝郡熟絁
Shan-ho fang 善和坊

shan-t'ai 山臺
shan-ti 山地
shang-shu 尚書
Shang-shu ssu-hsün kao-shen chih yin 尚書司勳告身之印
shang-tso 上座
Shao-k'ang 少康
Shao-lin ssu 少林寺
Shao-ling 邵陵
shao-p'ei 燒培
she (association) 社
she (lodging) 舍
she (soil god) 社
she-chang 社長
she-ch'i 社契
she-i 社邑
she-kuan 社官
she-lao 社老
she-li 闍梨
she-shih 捨施
she-ssu chuan-t'ieh 社司轉帖
Shen Chuan-shih 沈傳師
shen fo shih chi seng-liao 神佛食及僧料
Shen-hao 神皓
Shen-hui 神會
shen-jen 神人
Shen-ts'ou 神湊
shen tzu-fu 身資服
Shen-yung 神邕
sheng (measure) 升
sheng-chüan 生絹
Sheng-kuang ssu 勝光寺
Sheng-p'ing 升平
Sheng-shan ssu 聖善寺
shih (measure) 石

Shih Ching-chung 史敬忠
Shih Ch'ung 石崇
Shih-feng hsien 始豐縣
Shih-hsien 師賢
shih-lang 師郎
shih-li kung-chi 施力供給
shih-liao yüan 施療院
shih-nü 士女
shih-o 十惡
shih-to 拾墮
Shih-te 拾得
Shih-ti lun 十地論
Shih wu-chin tsang 十無盡藏
shih-yao yüan 施藥院
shih yü-shih 侍御史
shih-yung yeh 世永業
Shou-ch'ang 守昌
shou chih-ch'ien she-wu 收質錢舍屋
shou fo-i 受佛衣
shou hua-yüan 守華園
shou-p'en 受盆
shou-shih jen 授事人
shou ta-shih 首大師
shou-tao 受道
shou-yüan jen/min 守園人/民
shu (estate) 墅
shu-k'o 輸課
shu-su 輸粟
shui (rent) 稅
shui-mo 水磨
shui-nien 水碾
shui-tui 水碓
shui-wei 水磑
shui-wei chi nien 水磑及碾
ssu chia-jen 寺家人

ssu chia-nu 寺家奴

ssu-chi 寺籍

ssu-chu 寺主

ssu-fang 私房

ssu-hu 寺戶

ssu huang-t'ien fa 私荒田法

ssu-k'ung 司空

ssu-shou yin-yüan 四獸因緣

ssu so-kuan 寺所管

ssu-jen 寺人

Ssu-ming 司命

ssu-nung 司農

ssu-o 賜額

ssu-ts'ai 私財

ssu-tu 私度

su (koumiss) 蘇

su (millet) 粟

su-chiang 俗講

Su Ch'iung 蘇瓊

Su Kuei 蘇瓌

su-lao 宿老

suan-hui 算會

Suan-shan 蒜山

Sun Ch'iao 孫樵

sung huang-ch'ung 送蝗蟲

Sung Pao-tsang yen ch'ang-ming
teng pei 宋寶藏巖常明燈碑

ta-ch'en 達嚫

Ta-ch'eng fa-chieh wu-chin tsang
fa-shih 大乘法界無盡藏法釋

ta-hsiang 大祥

Ta-hsiang ssu 大像寺

ta-lien 大練

ta-mien 大綿

Ta-p'in ching 大品經

Ta-pei ssu 大悲寺

Ta-sheng tz'u ssu 大聖慈寺

ta-shih 大師

Ta-t'ung 大同

Ta tz'u-en ssu 大慈恩寺

Ta-tz'u ssu 大慈寺

ta-wang 大王

ta yao-tsang 大藥藏

Ta-yün ssu 大雲寺

t'a-shu 塔墅

tai (borrow) 貸

tai-pien 貸便

tai-wu jen 貸物人

T'ai-chi tien 太極殿

T'ai-shang kung 太上公

T'ai-p'ing ssu 太平寺

Tan Tao-k'ai 單道開

Tan-yang 丹陽

T'an-ch'eng 曇乘

T'an-chi 曇積

T'an-ch'ung 曇崇

T'an-hsien 曇獻

T'an-mo-ch'en 曇摩讖

T'an-piao 曇標

T'an-yao 曇曜

t'an-yüeh 檀越

tang (faction) 黨

Tao-an 道安

tao-ch'ang 道場

Tao-cheng li 道政里

tao-chü 道具

Tao-hsiu 道休

tao-jen t'ung 道人統

Tao-meng 道猛

Tao-ming 道明

tao-mu 搗木

Tao-piao 道標

tao-shih 道士

Tao-yen 道研
Tao-ying 道英
Te-mei 德美
te-t'ien 德田
t'e-chih 特旨
Teng-chou 登州
teng-shen fo 等身佛
teng yu ssu 燈油司
ti-chu seng 地主僧
Ti Jen-chieh 狄仁傑
ti-she 邸舍
ti-ssu 邸肆
ti-tien 邸店
Ti-tsang 地藏
ti-tzu 地子
Ti-yü chuan 地獄傳
t'i-o 題額
tiao (tax) 調
tieh (notification) 牒
tien (let, mortgage) 典
tien-chu 殿主
tien-p'u 店鋪
tien-tso 典座
t'ien (field) 田
t'ien-mu 田畝
t'ien-shou 田收
T'ien-tai 天台
t'ien-t'ang 天堂
t'ien-t'ou 田頭
t'ien-yüan 田園
Ting-chiao 定覺
to-ch'ou 墮籌
t'o (load) 馱
tou (bushel) 斗
Tou Huai-chen 竇懷貞
Tou-lu 豆盧
t'ou-hsia 頭下

tsa-hu 雜戶
tsai-chia 在家
tsai-i 再易
ts'ai (material goods) 財
ts'ai-chia 菜賈
Ts'ai Hsing-tsung 蔡興宗
ts'ai-shih 財施
Tsan-p'u 贊普
tsang (treasury) 藏
tsao-fu ch'u 造福處
ts'ao (mortar) 槽
ts'ao-tui 槽碓
ts'ao-yüan 草院
Tse Jung 笮融
Ts'en Hsi 岑羲
tso shih-i 左拾遺
tsu (rent) 租
ts'u-mien 粗麵 (?)
Ts'ui Ch'ün 崔群
Ts'ui Chung 崔眾
Ts'ui Hsiao-fen 崔孝芬
Ts'ui Liang 崔亮
Ts'ui Tao-ku 崔道固
ts'un (measure) 寸
ts'un (village) 村
ts'un fang fo-t'ang 村坊佛堂
tsung (measure) 綜
tsung tu-t'ou 從都頭
tu seng-cheng 都僧正
Tu Hung-chien 杜鴻漸
tu-liao 都料
Tu Mu 杜牧
tu-ssu 都司
tu-ssu p'an-kuan 都司判官
tu-ssu ts'ang 都司倉
tu-tieh 度牒
Tu Ying-ch'i 杜英奇

tu-t'ou 都頭
tu wei-na 都維那
tu ya-ya 都押衙
tu-yin 度印
Tu Yü 杜預
tu-yü hou 都虞侯
t'uan (cultivation group) 團
t'uan-t'ou 團頭
t'uan-min 屯民
t'uan-t'ien 屯田
Tung-lin ssu 東林寺
Tung-shan 東山
t'ung-chieh liang-yüan 同結良緣
T'ung-chin 童進
t'ung-ch'ü jen 同取人
T'ung-hua men 通化門
t'ung-huo 同活
t'ung-pien jen 同便人
T'ung-t'ai ssu 同泰寺
tzu kuan-nei 茲管內
tzu-i 紫衣 (p. 59)
tzu-ping 淬餅
Tzu-sheng ssu 資聖寺
tz'u-pei 慈悲
Tz'u-pei ssu 慈悲寺
tz'u-shih 刺史
tz'u shou-ming 賜收名

wa (stockings) 襪
wan-tou 碗豆
Wang Ch'i 王起
Wang Chih 王志
Wang Chih-hsing 王智興
Wang Chin 王縉
Wang-ch'uan 輞川
wang-hou i-fu 亡後衣服
Wang Hsüan-wei 王玄威

Wang Hung 王鉷
Wang Ming-kuang 王明廣
wang-shen 亡身
Wang Shou-t'ai 王守泰
Wang Tse 王則
Wang Wei 王維
wei (mill) 磑
wei-chia 磑家
wei-hu 磑戶
wei-k'o 磑課
wei-lan 猥/偽濫
wei-lan seng 偽濫僧
wei-na 維那
wei po-shih 磑博士
wei-san 磑傘
Wei Ssu-li 韋嗣立
Wei Ts'ou 韋湊
Wei Yüan-chung 魏元忠
Wei Yüan-sung 衛元嵩
wen-i 文移
wo-chiu 臥酒
wu-che ta-hui 無遮大會
wu-chi 無籍
wu-chi chih seng 無籍之僧
Wu Ch'i-yü 吳其昱
wu ch'ih-o 無敕額
wu-ch'ih ssu yüan 無敕寺院
wu-chin ts'ai 無盡財
wu-chin wu 無盡物
Wu-chin tsang 無盡藏
Wu-chin tsang fa lüeh-shuo 無盡藏法略説
Wu-chin tsang yüan 無盡藏院
Wu-chou 婺州
wu-kuan 無貫
Wu San-ssu 武三思
Wu-t'ai shan 五臺山

wu-wei 無為

ya-ya 押衙

yang (nourish) 養

Yang-chou 楊州

Yang Hsiu-ming 楊休明

Yang Jung 楊榮

Yang Kuo-chung 楊國忠

yang-nü 養女

Yang Shen-ch'in 楊慎矜

Yang-tu 楊都

Yang Yen 楊炎

Yao Ch'ung 姚崇

Yao-kuang ssu 姚光寺

yao-seng 妖僧

yao-tien 藥店

Yao-wang p'u-sa pen-shi p'in
   藥王菩薩本事品

yeh 業 (means of subsistance)

yeh-i 野邑

yen t'ieh shih 鹽鐵使

Yen T'ing-chih 嚴挺之

yin-tieh 印牒

Yin Yu 殷侑

yin-yüan chiang-shuo 因緣講説

ying-fu seng 應赴僧

Ying-fu ssu 影福寺

Ying-kan 英幹

ying-t'ien 營田

yu ch'ih-o 有敕額

Yu-chou 幽州

"Yu Feng-lo Chao-t'i Fo-kuang
   san ssu" 遊豐樂招提佛光三寺

yu-shih 遊食

yu-ts'ai 有才

Yü Ch'ao-en 魚朝恩

Yü-ch'ieh 瑜珈

Yü-ch'üan ssu 玉泉寺

Yü-chen (kuan) 玉真觀

yü-hsiang san-shih 浴像散施

yü hsiang-yüan sheng-li
   於鄉元生利

Yü-hua ssu 玉花寺

yü-lan p'en 盂蘭盆

yü-min 愚民

yü-shih ta-fu 御史大夫

yü-shih wei 御史尉

Yü-wang 育王

Yü-wen Jung 宇文融

Yü-wen T'ai 宇文泰

yüan (cloister) 院

yüan (garden) 園

yüan-chu 院主

Yüan-kuan 圓觀

yüan-min 園民

yüan-shui 園稅

Yüan-tao 原道

Yüan Tsai 元載

yüan-tzu 園子

yüan-wei 園磑

Yün-chü ssu 雲居寺

Yün-kang 雲崗

Yung-an ssu 永安寺

Yung-k'ang 永康

Yung-ning ssu 永寧寺

yung-tso jen 庸作人

yung-yeh 永業

BIBLIOGRAPHY

Abbreviations

P.: Chinese MSS. from Tun-huang, Pelliot Collection of the Bibliothèque
   Nationale.
S.: Chinese MSS. from Tun-huang, Stein Collection of the British Library
T.: *Taishō shinshū daizōkyō* 大正新修大蔵経. Tokyo, 1924–1935.

Primary Sources

Ch'ao-yeh tsa-chi. See *Chien-yen i-lai ch'ao-yeh tsa-chi*.
Chien-yen i-lai ch'ao-yeh tsa-chi 建炎以來朝野雜記 (1202/1216). By Li
   Hsin-chuan 李心傳. Facsimile of *Shih-yüan ts'ung-chu* 適園叢書 ed. in
   Sung-shih tzu-liao ts'ui-pien 宋史資料萃編 1, Taipei: Wen-hai, 1967.
Chih-yüan chi 芝園集. By Yüan-chao 元照 (1048–1116). In *Dainihon
   zokuzōkyō* 大日本続蔵経 1.
Ch'ih-hsiu Po-chang ch'ing-kuei 敕修百丈清規. Attrib. to Huai-hai 懷海
   (749–814). Recension (between 1336–1338) by Te-hui 德輝. T. 48,
   no. 2025.
Chin shih 金史. Attrib. to T'o-t'o 脱脱 (1313–1355). Peking: Chung-hua,
   1975.
Chin-shih ts'ui-pien 金石萃編 (1805). Comp. by Wang Ch'ang 王昶. Repr. in
   Shih-k'o shih-liao hsin-pien 石刻史料新編, Taipei: Hsin Wen Feng, 1977.
Chih-shih yüan 金石園 (preface 1848). Comp. by Liu Hsi-hai 劉喜海. Lai-
   fen t'ang ed.

Chin shu 晉書. Comp. by Fang Hsüan-ling 房玄齡 (578–648) et al. Peking: Chung-hua, 1974.

Chiu T'ang shu 舊唐書 (945). Comp. by Liu Hsü 劉昫 et al. Shanghai: Chung-hua, 1975.

Chou-li cheng-i 周禮正義 (1899). By Sun I-jang 孫詒讓. 1905.

Ch'üan T'ang wen 全唐文 (preface 1814). Comp. by Tung Kao 董誥 et al. Taipei: Ch'i-wen, 1961.

Cullavagga. Pāli Text Society ed. London: Luzac, 1964.

Dainihon zokuzōkyō 大日本続蔵経. Kyoto 1905–1912.

Fa-hua chuan-chi 法華傳記. By Seng-hsiang 僧詳 (fl. 667). T. 51, no. 2068.

Fa-yüan chu-lin 法苑珠林 (668). Comp. by Tao-shih 道世. T. 53, no. 2122.

Fan-ch'uan wen-chi 樊川文集. By Tu Mu 杜牧 (803–852). *Ssu-pu ts'ung-k'an* ed.

Fo-ming ching 佛名經. T. 14, no. 441.

Fo-tsu li-tai t'ung-tsai 佛祖歷代通載 (1341). By Nien-ch'ang 念常. T. 49, no. 2036.

Fo-tsu t'ung-chi 佛祖統記 (1269). By Chih-p'an 志磐. T. 49, no. 2035.

Han shu 漢書. Comp. by Pan Ku 班固 (32–92). Peking: Chung-hua, 1962.

Hou Han shu 後漢書. Comp. by Fan Yeh 范曄 (398–445). Peking: Chung-hua, 1965.

Hsiang-fa chüeh-i ching 像法決疑經 (T'ang). T. 85, no. 2870.

Hsin T'ang shu 新唐書 (1060). Shanghai: Chung-hua, 1975.

Hsü kao-seng chuan 續高僧傳. By Ta-hsüan 道宣 (596–667). T. 50, no. 2060.

Hsü shih-shuo 續世說 (1157). By K'ung P'ing-chung 孔平仲. In *Shou-shan ko ts'ung-shu*.

Hsü tzu-chih t'ung-chien 續資治通鑑. By Pi Yüan 畢沅 (1730–1797). In *Ssu-pu pei-yao*.

Hsü tzu-chih t'ung-chien ch'ang-pien 續資治通鑑長編 (1174). By Li T'ao 李濤. Peking: Chung-hua, 1979.

Hua-yen ching t'an-hsüan chi 華嚴經探玄記. By Fa-tsang 法藏 (643–712). T. 35, no. 1733.

Hung-ming chi 弘明集. By Seng-yu 僧祐 (435–518). T. 52, no. 2102.

I-chien chih 夷堅志. By Hung Mai 洪邁 (1123–1202). Peking: Chung-hua, 1981.

Jen-wang hu-kuo po-je po-lo-mi-to ching 仁王護國般若波羅蜜多經. Trans. by Amoghavajra (705–774). T. 8, no. 246.

Jen-wang po-je po-lo-mi ching 仁王般若波羅蜜經. Trans. by Kumārajīva (early 5th c.). T. 8, no. 245.

Ju T'ang ch'iu-fa hsün-li hsing-chi: see *Nittō guhō junrei gyōki.*

K'ai-yüan shih-chiao lu 開元釋教錄 (720). By Chih-sheng 智昇. T. 55, no. 2154.

Kao-seng chuan 高僧傳 (ca. 530). By Hui-chiao 慧皎. T. 50, no. 2059.

Kao-seng Fa-hsien chuan 高僧法顯傳 (416). By Fa-hsien 法顯. T. 51, no. 2085.

Ken-pen sa-p'o to-pu lü she 根本薩婆多部律攝. Trans. by I-ching 義淨 (635–713). T. 24, no. 1458.

Ken-pen shuo i-ch'ieh yu-pu p'i-nai-yeh 根本說一切有部毘奈耶 [*Mūla-sarvāstivādavinaya*]. Trans. by I-ching 義淨 (635–713). T. 23, no. 1442.

Kośa: The Abhidharmakośa of Vasubandhu. Trans. and annotated by Louis de la Vallée Poussin. Paris: Geuthner and Louvain: Istas, 1926.

Kuan-chung ch'uang-li chieh-t'an t'u ching 關中創立戒壇圖經. By Tao-hsüan 道宣 (596–667). T. 45, no. 1892.

Kuang hung-ming chi 廣弘明集 (664). Comp. by Tao-hsüan 道宣. T. 52, no. 2103.

Kuei-hsin tsa-chih 癸辛雜識 (ca. 1298). By Chou Mi 周密. In *Hsüeh-chin t'ao-yüan.*

Kuo-ch'ing po-lu 國清百錄. By Kuan-ting 灌頂 (561–632). T. 46, no. 1934.

Lao-hsüeh an pi-chi 老學庵筆記. By Lu Yu 陸游 (1125–1210). *Ts'ung-shu chi-ch'eng* ed.

Li Wei-kung Hui-ch'ang i-p'in chi 李衛公會昌一品集. By Li Te-yü 李德裕 (787–849). *Ts'ung-shu chi-ch'eng* ed.

Li-tai fa-pao chi 歷代法寶記 (8th c.). T. 51, no. 2075.

Li-tai san-pan chi 歷代三寶記. By Fei Ch'ang-fang 費長房 (ca. 561–597). T. 49, no. 2034.

Liang-ching hsin-chi 兩京新記 (8th c.). By Wei Shu 韋述. *Ts'ung-shu chi-ch'eng* ed.

Liang-ch'u ch'ing-chung i 量處輕重儀. By Tao-hsüan 道宣 (596–667). T. 45, no. 1895.

Liang shu 梁書. Comp. by Yao Ssu-lien 姚思廉 (d. 637). Peking: Chung-hua, 1973.

Liao wen-ts'un 遼文存. Transmitted by Miao Ch'üan-sun 繆荃孫 (1844–1919). 1896.

Lo-yang ch'ieh-lan chi 洛陽伽藍記 (547). By Yang Hsüan-chih 楊衒之.
T. 51, no. 2092.

Mahāvagga. H. Oldenberg ed., *Vinaya Piṭakam*.

Mahāvyutpatti. Sakaki Ryōzaburō 木神亮三郎 ed. Kyoto, 1916–25.

Mi-sha-sai-pu ho-hsi wu-fen lü 彌沙塞部和醯五分律 [*Mahīśāsakavinaya*].
Trans. by Buddhajīva (424). T. 22, no. 1421.

Miao-fa lien-hua ching 妙法蓮華經 [*Saddharmapuṇḍarīka*]. Trans. by
Kumārajīva (406) T. 9, no. 262.

Mūlasarvāstivādamātṛkā (cited from *Sa-p'o to p'i-ni p'i-p'o sha*, q.v.).

Mo-ho seng-ch'i lü 摩訶僧祇律 [*Mahāsāṃghikavinaya*]. Trans. by Buddhabhadra (416). T. 22, no. 1425.

Mou-tzu li huo lun 牟子理惑論. Anon. In *Hung-ming chi* 1.

Nan Ch'i shu 南齊書. Comp. by Hsiao Tzu-hsien 蕭子顯 (489–537).
Peking: Chung-hua, 1972.

Nan shih 南史 (.a. 629). Comp. by Li Yen-shou 李延壽. Peking: Chung-hua,
1975.

Nan-hai chi-kuei nei-fa chuan 南海寄歸內法傳. By I-ching 義淨 (635–713).
T. 54, no. 2125.

Nittō guhō junrei gyōki 入唐求法巡礼行記 [*Ju T'ang ch'iu-fa hsün-li
hsing-chi*]. By Ennin 圓仁 (793–864). Ono Katsutoshi 小野勝年 ed.,
Nittō guhō junrei gyōki no kenkyū の研究 (Tokyo: Suzuki gakujutsu
zaidan, 1964–1969).

Pao-ch'ing Sung Ssu-ming chih 寶慶宋四明志 (1227). By Lo Chün 羅濬 and
Fang Wan-li 方萬里. In *Sung Yüan Ssu-ming liu-chih* (1854).

Pei Ch'i shu 北齊書. Comp. by Li Pai-yao 李百藥 (565–648) et al. Peking:
Chung-hua, 1972.

Pei shih 北史 (ca. 629). Comp. by Li Yen-shou 李延壽. Peking: Chung-hua,
1974.

Pei-shan lu 北山錄. By Shen-ch'ing 神清 (d. 806–821). T. 552, no. 2113.

Pien-cheng lun 辯正論. By Fa-lin 法琳 (572–640). T. 52, no. 2110.

Po-chang ch'ing-kuei i-chi. See *Ch'ih-hsiu Po-chang ch'ing-kuei*.

Po Hsiang-shan chi 白香山集. Wan-yu wen-k'u ed., vol. 801.

Po K'ung liu-t'ieh 白孔六帖. Compiled by Po Chü-i 白居易 and K'ung
Ch'uan 孔傳. Taipei: Hsin-hsing shu-chü, 1969 repr. of Ming ed.

Sa-p'o to p'i-ni p'i-p'o sha 薩婆多毘尼毘婆沙 [*Sarvāstivādavinayavibhāṣā*].
T. 23, no. 1440.

Sa-p'o to-pu p'i-ni mo-te lo-ch'ieh 薩婆多部毘尼摩得勒伽 [*Sarvāstivādavi-
nayamātṛkā*]. T. 23, no. 1441.

San-kuo chih 三國志. Comp. by Ch'en Shou 陳壽 (233–297). Peking: Chung-hua, 1959.

Shan-chien lü p'i-p'o-sha 善見律毘婆沙 [*Samantapāsādikā*]. T. 24, no. 1462.

Shan-yu shih-k'o ts'ung-pien 山右石刻叢編 (1899). Comp. by Hu P'ing-chih 胡聘之. 1901.

Shang-shu ku-shih 尚書故實. By Li Ch'o 李卓 (T'ang). *Ts'ung-shu chi-ch'eng* ed.

Shen-seng chuan 神僧傳 (preface 1417). T. 50, no. 2064.

Shih-chia fang-chih 釋迦方志. By Tao-hsüan 道宣 (596–667). T. 51, no. 2088.

Shih-k'o shih-liao hsin-pien 石刻史料新編. Taipei: Hsin Wen Feng ed., 1978.

Shih po lun 釋駁論. By Tao-heng 道恆 (346–417). In *Hung-ming chi* 6.

Shih-shih yao-lan 釋氏要覽 (1019). By Tao-ch'eng 道誠. T. 54, no. 2127.

Shih-sung lü 十誦律 [*Sarvāstivādavinaya*]. Trans. by Punyatara, Kumā-rajīva et al. (early 5th c.). T. 23, no. 1435.

Shih wen-chi 釋文紀. By Mei Ting-tso 梅鼎祚 (1549–1618). *Ssu-k'u ch'üan-shu.*

Ssu-fen lü 四分律 [*Dharmaguptavinaya*]. Trans. by Buddhayaśas. T. 22, no. 1428.

Ssu-fen lü shan-fan pu-ch'üeh hsing-shih ch'ao 四分律刪繁補闕行事鈔. By Tao-hsüan 道宣 (596–667). T. 40, no. 1804.

Sui shu 隋書. Comp. by Wei Cheng 魏徵 (580–643) et al. Peking: Chung-hua, 1973.

Sung hui-yao kao 宋會要稿. Comp. by Hsü Sung 徐松 (1781–1848). Peking: Peiping National Library, 1936 facsimile ed.

Sung kao-seng chuan 宋高僧傳 (988). By Tsang-ning 贊寧. T. 50, no. 2061.

Sung shih 宋史. Attrib. to T'o-t'o 脫脫 (1313–1355). Shanghai: Chung-hua, 1977.

Sung shu 宋書. Comp. by Shen Yüeh 沈約 (441–513). Peking: Chung-hua, 1974.

Ta-ch'eng i-chang 大乘義章. By Hui-yüan 慧遠 (523–592). T. 4, no. 1851.

Ta fang-kuang fo hua-yen ching 大方廣佛華嚴經 [*Avatamsakasūtra*]. Trans. by Buddhabhadra (419). T. 9, no. 278.

Ta po-nieh-p'an ching shu 大般涅槃經疏 [*Mahāparinirvāna*]. T. 38, no. 1767.

Ta Sung seng-shih lüeh 大宋僧史略 (rev. ed. 999). By Tsan-ning 贊寧. T. 54, no. 2126.

Ta T'ang liu-tien 大唐六典 (736). Comp. by Li Lin-fu 李林甫 et al. Ed. of Konoe Iehiro 近衞家熙, 1724. Repr. Taipei: Wen-hai, 1962.

Ta T'ang nei-tien lu 大唐內典錄. By Tao-hsüan 道宣 (596–667). T. 55, no. 2149.

Ta T'ang Ta tz'u-en ssu San-tsang fa-shih chuan 大唐大慈恩寺三藏法師傳 (comp. 688). By Hui-li 慧立 and Yen-ts'ung 彥悰. T. 50, no. 2053.

Tai-tsung ch'ao tseng ssu-k'ung ta pien-cheng kuang-chih san-tsang ho-shang piao chih chi 代宗朝贈司空大辨正廣智三藏和尚表制集. By Yüan-chao 圓照 (ca. 778). T. 52, no. 2120.

T'ai-chou chin-shih lu 台州金石錄. Comp. by Huang Jui 黃瑞 (Ch'ing). Peking: Wen-wu, 1982.

T'ai-p'ing kuang-chi 太平廣記 (978). Peking: Chung-hua, 1961.

T'ang hui-yao 唐會要 (961). By Wang P'u 王溥. Peking: Chung-hua, 1955 ed.

T'ang liu-tien. See *Ta T'ang liu-tien.*

T'ang Lu Hsüan kung tsou i 唐陸宣公奏義. By Lu Chih 陸贄 (late 8th c.). In *Shih-wan chüan lou ts'ung-shu.*

T'ang-lü shu-i 唐律疏議 (653). Ed. *Tōritsu shogi* 唐律疏議. Kyoto: Chūbun shuppansha, 1974.

T'ang ta chao-ling chi 唐大詔令集 (1970). Comp. by Sung Min-ch'iu 宋敏求. *Ssu-k'u ch'üan-shu* ed.

T'ao-chai ts'ang-shih chi 陶齋藏石記 (1903). Comp. by Weng Ta-nien 翁大年. In *Shih-k'o shih-liao hsin-pien,* vol. 11.

T'ien-kung k'ai-wu 天工開物 (1637). By Sung Ying-hsing 宋應星. Yabuuchi Kiyoshi 藪內清 ed., *Tenkō kaibutsu no kenkyū* 天工開物の研究, Kyoto: Kōseisha, 1954.

T'ou-huang tsa-lu 投荒雜錄. By Fang Ch'ien-li 房千里 (T'ang). In *Ku-chin shuo-pu ts'ung-shu.*

Ts'e-fu yüan-kuei 冊府元龜 (1013). Comp. by Wang Ch'in-jo 王欽若 et al. Peking: Chung-hua, 1960.

Tzu-chih t'ung-chien 資治通鑑 (1085). By Ssu-ma Kuang 司馬光. Taipei: Hung-shih, 1974.

Wei-mo-chi so-shuo ching 維摩詰所說經 [*Vimalakīrtinirdeśa*]. Transl. by Kumārajīva (406). T. 14, no. 475.

Wei shu 魏書. Comp. by Wei Shou 魏收 (506–572). Peking: Chuang-hua, 1974.

Wen-hsien t'ung-k'ao 文獻通考 (before 1319). Comp. by Ma Tuan-lin 馬端臨. Wan-yu wen-k'u ed.

Wen-yüan ying-hua 文苑英華 (ca. 987). Facsimile of 1567 ed. Peking: Chung-hua, 1966.

Wu-tai hui-yao 五代會要 (961). By Wang P'u 王溥. In *Chü-chen pan ts'ung-shu.*

Yen-i i-mou lu 燕翼詒謀錄 (1227). By Wang Yung 王永. *Ts'ung-shu chi-ch'eng* ed.

Yu-p'o-sai chieh ching 優婆塞戒經 [*Upāsakaśila*]. T. 24, no. 1488.

Yüan-shih Ch'ang-ch'ing chi 元氏長慶集. By Yüan Chen 元稹 (779–831). *Ssu-pu ts'ung-k'an* ed.

Yüan tien-chang 元典章. By Wu Ch'eng 吳城. *Sung-fen shih ts'ung-k'an* ed.

Secondary Sources

Abe Kuniharu 安都国治. "Hokugi ni okeru do no kenkyū 北魏に於ける度の研究" Bukkyō ronsō 佛教論叢 (volume in honor of Tokiwa Daijō), pp. 1–22. Tokyo: Kōbundō, 1933.

Aoyama Sadao 青山定雄. "Sōgen no chinōshi ni mieru shakai-keizai shiryō 宋元の地方誌に見える社会経済史料." *Tōyō gakuhō* 東洋学報 25.2 (1938):119–135 (281–297).

Asakawa Kenji. "The Life of a Monastic *shō* in Medieval Japan." *Annual Report of the American Historical Association* 1.10 (1916).

Balazs, Etienne. "Beiträge zur Wirtschaftsgeschichte der T'ang-Zeit." *Mitteilungen des Seminars für Orientalische Sprachen zu Berlin* 34(1931):1–92; 35(1932):1–73; 36(1933):1–62.

———. "Le traité économique du Souei chou." *T'oung Pao* 42(1953):113–329.

Bielenstein, Hans. "The Census of China During the Period 2–742 A.D." *Bulletin of the Museum of Far East Antiquities* 19(1947):125–63.

Chavannes, Edouard. *Mission archéologique dans la Chine septentrionale.* Vol. 1, part 2. *La sculpture bouddhique.* Paris: Ecole Française d'Extrême-Orient, 1913.

———. *Les documents chinois découverts par Sir A. Stein.* Oxford: Oxford University Press, 1913.

———. "Documents chinois." In A. Stein, *Ancient Khotan,* App. A. Oxford: Oxford University Press, 1907.

———. *Six monuments de la sculpture chinoise* (*Ars Asiatica,* vol. 2). Brussels and Paris: G. van Oest, 1914.

Ch'en, Kenneth K. S. "On Some Factors Responsible for the Anti-Buddhist Persecution Under the Pei-ch'ao." *Harvard Journal of Asiatic Studies* 17(1954):261–73.

Ch'en Yin-k'e 陳寅恪. "Wu Chao yü fo-chiao 武曌與佛教." *Chung-yang yen-chiu-yüan li-shih yü-yen yen-chiu-so chi-k'an* 中央研究院歷史語言研究所集刊 5(1935):137–47.

Chü Ch'ing-yüan 鞠清遠. "Yüan-tai ti ssu-ch'an 元代的寺產." *Shih-huo* 食貨 1.6(1935):26–29.

Ch'üan Han-sheng 全漢昇. "Chung-ku fo-chiao ssu-yüan ti tz'u-shan shih-yeh 中古佛教寺院的慈善事業." *Shih-huo* 1.4(1935):1–7.

——. "Sung-tai ssu-yüan so ching-ying chih kung-shang yeh 宋代寺院所經營之工商業". *Kuo-li Pei-ching ta-hsüeh ssu-shih chou nien chi-nien lun-wen chi* 國立北京大學四十周年紀念論文集 "Anniversary Volume of the Foundation of the Peking National University," book 1, part 1, 1940, pp. 16–22.

Demiéville, Paul. "Les versions chinoises du Milindapañha." *Bulletin de l'Ecole Française d'Extrême-Orient* 24(1924):1–258.

——. "Byō." In *Hōbōgirin*, vol. 3 (Paris: Institut de France, 1937), pp. 224–65.

——. "A propos du Concile de Vaiśālī." *T'oung Pao* 40(1951):239–96.

——. *Le Concile de Lhasa.* Paris: Collège de France, 1952.

Dutt, Nalināksha. *Early Monastic Buddhism.* Calcutta: Calcutta Oriental Series 30, 1941–1945.

Eberhard, Wolfram. *Das Toba-Reich Nordchinas.* Leiden: Brill, 1949.

Franke, Otto. *Kêng Tschi T'u: Ackerbau und Seidengewinnung in China.* Hamburg: Friederichsen, 1913.

Giles, Lionel. "Dated Chinese Manuscripts in the Stein Collection." *Bulletin of the School of Oriental and African Studies* 7(1935):1–26, 809–36; 9(1939):1023–46; 10(1940):317–44.

——. *Six Centuries at Tun-huang.* London: China Society Sinological Series 2, 1944.

Groot J. J. M. de, *Le Code du Mahāyāna en Chine.* Amsterdam: Johannes Müller, 1893.

——. *Sectarianism and Religious Persecution in China.* Amsterdam: Johannes Müller, 1903.

Hänisch, Ernst. *Steuergerechtsame der Chinesichen Klöster unter Mongolenherrschaft.* Leipzig: Hivzel, 1940.

Ho Tzu-ch'üan 何茲全. "Chung-ku ta-tsu ssu-yüan ling-hu ti yen-chiu 中古大族寺院領戶的研究." *Shih-huo* 食貨 3.4(1936):2–41.

Horner, Isaline Blew. *Vinaya-pitaka: The Book of the Discipline*. London: Luzac (*Sacred Books of the East*), 1938–1966.

Hosokawa Kameichi 細川亀市. "Nihon chūsei jiin hō ni okeru sōzokuhō 日本中世寺院法に於ける相続法." *Shūkyō kenkyū* 宗教研究 n.s. 3.4(1936):75–97.

Hsü Kuo-lin 許國霖. *Tun-huang shih-shih hsieh-ch'ing t'i-chi yü Tun-huang tsa-lu* 敦煌石室寫經題記與敦煌雜錄, Shanghai: Shang-wu, 1937.

Katō Shigeshi 加藤繁. "Tō no shōen oyobi sono yurai ni tsuite 唐の荘園及びその由来に就いて." *Tōyō gakuhō* 東洋学報 7.3(1917):315–38.

——. "Naishōtakushi kō 内荘宅使考." *Tōyō gakuhō* 10.2(1920):221–43.

——. "Tōdai ni okeru fudōsanshitsu ni tsuite 唐代に於ける不動産質就いて." *Tōyō gakuhō* 12.1(1922):80–88.

——. "Tōsō kibō kō 唐宋櫃坊考." *Tōyō gakuhō* 12.4(1922):455–80.

——. "Shabō ni tsuite 車坊に就いて." *Tōyō gakuhō* 15.1(1925):105–9.

——. "Tōsō jidai no shōen no soshiki narabi ni sono shuraku to shite no hattatsu ni tsuite 唐宋時代の荘園の組織並に其の聚落としての飛達に就いて." In *Shinagaku ronsō* 支那学論叢 (volume in honor of Kanō Naoki), ed. by Suzuki Torao, pp. 853–81. Kyōto: Kōbundō shobō, 1928.

Lévi, Sylvain. *L'Inde civilisatrice*. Paris: Institut de Civilisation Indienne, 1938.

Lingat, Robert. "Vinaya et droit laïc." *Bulletin de l'Ecole Française d'Extrême-Orient* 37(1937):415–78.

Liu Fu 劉復 ed. *Tun-huang to-so* 敦煌掇瑣. 6 vols. Peking. *Chung-yang yen-chiu yüan li-shih yü-yen yen-chiu so chi-k'an* 中央研究院歷史語言研究所集刊 [Academia Sinica Institute of History and Philology special publications] no. 2, 1931–1932.

Makino Tatsumi 牧野巽. "Keigen jōhō jirui no dōshakumon 慶元条法事類の道釈門." *Shūkyō kenkyū* 宗教研究 9.2(1932):65–84.

Maspero, Henri. "Communauté et moines bouddhistes chinois aux IIe et IIIe siècles." *Bulletin de l'Ecole Française d'Extrême-Orient* 1(1910):1–11.

——. "Les origines de la communauté bouddhique de Lo-yáng." *Journal Asiatique*. 225(1934):87–107.

——. *Mélanges posthumes sur les religions et l'histoire de la Chine.* Vol. 1: *La religion chinoise dans son développement historique;* vol. 2: *Etudes historiques;* vol. 3: *Le taoïsme.* Paris: Musée Guimet (Bibliothèque de Diffusion, vol. 57–59), 1950.

——. *Les documents chinois de la troisième expédition A. Stein.* London: British Museum, 1953.

Michibata Ryōshū 道端良秀. "Shina bukkyō jiin no kinyūjigyō 支那佛教寺院の金融事業." *Ōtani gakuhō* 大谷学報 14.1(1933):91–129.

——. "Shina bukkyō shakai-keizai no kenkyū ni tsuite 支那佛教社会経済の研究について." *Shina bukkyō shigaku* 支那佛学史学 1.2(1937):111–25.

——. "Shukubō to shite no Tōdai jiin 宿房としての唐代寺院." *Shina bukkyō shigaku* 2.1(1938): 41–62.

——. "Tōdai no jiden to sōni no shiyū zaisan 唐代の寺田と僧尼の私有財産." *Eizan gakuhō* 叡山学報 17(1939):61–78.

Mishima Hajime 三島一. "Tōdai ni okeru dochō no mondai 唐代に於ける度牒の問題." *Shigaku zasshi* 史学雑誌 37.8(1926):780–83.

——. "Sōdai no baichō ni tsuite 宋代の売牒に就いて." *Shigaku zasshi* 40.12(1929):1513–14.

——. "Sōdai ni okeru jiin kazei ni kansuru ikkōsatsu 宋代に於ける寺院課税に関する一考察." *Shigaku zasshi* 44.7(1933):893.

——. "Tōsō jidai ni okeru kizoku tai jiin no keizaiteki kōshō ni kansuru ikkōsatsu 唐宋時代に於ける貴族対寺院の経済的交渉に関す一考察." In *Tōyōshi ronsō* 東洋史論叢 (volume in honour of Ichimura Sanjirō), pp. 1159–84. Tokyo: Fujisanbo, 1933).

Naba Toshisada 那波利貞. "Tō shōhon tōrei no ichi ibun 唐鈔本唐令の一遺文." *Shirin* 史林 21.4(1936):74–132.

——. "Ryōko kō 梁戸考." *Shina bukkyō shigaku* 支那佛教史学 2.1(1938): 1–39; 2.2(1938):27–68; 2.4(1938): 30–82 (collected in his *Tōdai shakai bunda-shi kenkyū* 唐代社会文化史研究. Tokyo: Sobunsha, 1974, pp. 269–394.

——. "Tōdai no shayū ni tsuite 唐代の社邑に就いて." *Shirin* 23(1983): 223–65; 495–534; 729–93 (collected op. cit., pp. 459–574).

——. "Bukkyō shinkō ni motozukite soshikiseraretaru chūbantō godaiji no shayū ni tsuite 佛教信仰基きて組織せられたる中晩唐五代時の社邑に就いて." *Shirin* 24(1939):491–652; 743–84 (collected op. cit., pp. 575–678).

——. "Chūbantō jidai ni okeru giransō ni kansuru hitotsu komponshiryō no kenkyū 中晩唐時代に於ける偽濫僧に関する一根本史料の研究." In *Ryūkoku daigaku bukkyō shigaku ronsō* 龍谷大学佛教史学論叢. Kyoto: Ryūkoku daigaku, 1939, pp. 129–241.

——. "Chūbantō jidai ni okeru Tonkō chihō bukkyō jiin no nengai keiei ni tsuite 中晩唐時代に於ける敦煌地方佛教寺院の碾岩経営に就いて." *Kyōto teikoku daigaku keizaigakubu, keizai kenkyūjo* 京都帝国大学経済学部—経済研究所—1(1941):23-51; 87-114; 2(1942):165-86.

Niida Noboru 仁井田陞. *Tōsō hōritsu bunsho no kenkyū* 唐宋法律文書の研究. Tokyo: Tōhō bunka gakuin, 1937.

Nogami Shunjō 野上俊静. "Ryōdai no yūkai ni tsuite 遼代の邑会に就いて." *Ōtani gakuhō* 大谷学報 20.1(1939):46-61.

Ogasawara Senshū 小笠原宣秀. "Tōdai sōryo to sono katsudō 唐代僧侶と其の活動." *Gendai bukkyō* 明代佛教 7.77 (October 1930): 29-54.

——. "Shina Nambokuchō bukkyō shakai kyōka 支那南北朝佛教と社会教化." *Ryūkoku shidan* 龍谷史壇 3.4(1932).

——. "Shina Nambokuchō jidai bukkyō kyōdan no tōsei 支那南北朝時代佛教教団の統制." *Ryūkoku shidan* 3.14(1934).

Ōmura Seigai 大村西崖. *Shina bijutsushi chōsohen* 支那美術史彫塑篇. Tokyo: Bussho Kankōkai zuzōbu 佛書刊行会図像部, 1915.

Ratchnevsky, Paul. *Un code des Yuan.* Paris: Collège de France, 1939; repr. 1985.

Reischauer, Edwin O. *Ennin's Travels in T'ang China.* New York: Ronald Press, 1955.

——. *Ennin's Diary: The Record of a Pilgrimage to China in Search of the Law.* New York: Ronald Press, 1955.

Rhys Davids, Thomas William, and Hermann Oldenberg, trans. and ed. *Vinaya Texts (Sacred Books of the East,* vols. 13, 17, and 20). Oxford: Clarendon Press, 1881-1885.

Rideout, J. K. "The Rise of Eunuchs during the T'ang Dynasty." *Asia Major,* n.s. 1(1949):53-72.

Rotours, Robert des. *Traité des fonctionnaires et traité de l'armée.* Leiden: Brill, 1948.

——. "Les insignes en deux parties (fou) sous la dynastie T'ang." *T'oung Pao* 41(1954):1-148.

Satō Mitsuo 佐藤密雄. "Hōgakuteki kenkai ni yoru ritsuzō to sōga ni tsuite 法学的見解による律蔵と僧伽に就いて." *Taishō daigaku gakuhō* 大正大学学報 8(1930):117-42.

Sogabe Shizuo 曽我部静雄. "Sōdai no dochō zakkō 宋代の度牒雑考." *Shigaku zasshi* 史学雑誌 41(1930):725-40.

Sudō Yoshiyuki 周藤吉之. "Tōmatsu Godai no shōensei 唐末五代の荘園制." *Tōyō bunka* 東洋文化 12(1953):1–41.

Takakusu Junjirō. "Le voyage de Kanshin en Orient (742–754)." *Bulletin de l'Ecole Française d'Extrême-Orient* 28(1928):1–41; 441–72.

Takakusu Junjirō, trans. *A Record of the Buddhist Religion as Practiced in India and the Malay Archipelago (A.D. 671–695), by I-ching* (1896). Repr. Taipei: Cheng Wen, 1970.

Takao Giken 高雄義堅. "Dochō kō 度牒考." *Rokujō gakuhō* 六条学報 226(1920).

——. "Hokugi ni okeru bukkyō kyōdan no hattatsu ni tsuite 北魏に於ける佛教教団の発達に就いて." *Ryūkoku daigaku ronsō* 龍谷大学論叢 297(1931).

——. "Shina bukkyō to kokka ishiki to no kōshō ni tsuite 支那佛教と国家意識との交渉に就いて." *Ryūkoku daigaku ronsō* 314(1936): 67–87.

Takeuchi Reizō 竹内理三. *Nihon Jōdai jiin keizaishi no kenkyō* 日本上代寺院経済史の研究. Tokyo: Okayama shoten, 1934.

Tamai Zehaku 玉井是博. "Tōdai no tochi mondai kanken 唐代の土地問題管見." *Shigaku zasshi* 文学雑誌 33(1920):597–633; 687–718; 758–90.

Tamura Jitsuzo 田村実造. "Kittan bukkyō no shakaishiteki kōsatsu 契丹佛教の社会史的考察." *Ōtani gakuhō* 大谷学報 18.1(1937):32–46.

T'ang Yung-t'ung 湯用彤. *Han Wei liang-Chin Nan-pei ch'ao fo-chiao shih* 漢魏兩晉南北朝佛教史. Shanghai: Shang-wu, 1938.

T'ao Hsi-sheng 陶希聖. "Yüan-tai fo-ssu t'ien-yüan chi shang-tien 元代佛寺田園及商店." *Shih-huo* 食貨 1.3(1935):32–38.

——. "T'ang-tai ssu-yüan ching-chi kai-shuo 唐代寺院經濟概説." *Shih-huo* 5.4(1937):33–38.

Tomomatsu Entei 友松圓諦. *Bukkyō keizai shisō kenkyū* 佛教経済思想研究. Tokyo: Tōhō Sho-in, 1932.

Tsukamoto Zenryū 塚本善隆. "Shinkō no sangaikyōdan to mujinzō ni tsuite 信行の三階教団と無尽蔵に就いて." *Shūkyō kenkyū* 宗教研究 3.4(1926):65–80.

——. "Sōchōtei no zaiseiken to bukkyō kyōdan 宋朝庭の財政権と佛教教団." *Shūkyō kenkyū*, 7.5(1930):1–30.

——. "Sō no zaiseinan to bukkyō 宋の財政難と佛教." *Tōyōshi ronsō* 東洋史論叢 (volume in honor of Kuwabara Jitsuzō), pp. 549–94. Tokyo: Kōbundō, 1931.

——. "Tō chūki irai no chōan kudokushi 唐中期以来の長安功徳使." *Tōhō gakuhō* 4(1933):368–406.

——. "Sekkeisan Unkyo-ji to sekkoku daizōkyō 石経山雲居寺と石刻大蔵経." *Tōhō gakuhō*, Supplement to 5(1935):1–245.

——. "Hokugi no sōgiko butsutoko 北魏の僧祇戸佛図戸." *Tōyōshi ken-kyū*, 2.3(1937):1–26.

——. "Hokushū no haibutsu ni tsuite 北周の廃佛に就いて." *Tōhō gakuhō* 16(1948):29–101.

——. *Shina bukkyōshi kenkyū: Hokugi-hen* 支那佛教史研究：北魏篇. Tokyo: Kōbundō, 1942.

Wang Yi-t'ung. "Slaves and Other Comparable Social Groups During the Northern Dynasties (386–618)." *Harvard Journal of Asiatic Studies* 16(1953):293–364.

Ware, James R. "Wei Shou on Buddhism." *T'oung Pao* 30(1933):100–81.

Wittfogel, Karl August, and Feng Chia-sheng. *History of Chinese Society: Liao (907–1125).* Philadelphia and New York: Macmillan, 1949.

Yabuki Keiki 矢吹慶輝. *Sangaikyō no kenkyū* 三階教の研究. Tokyo: Iwanami shoten, 1927 (repr. 1973).

Yamasaki Hiroshi 山崎宏. "Zui-tō jidai ni okeru giyū oyobi hōsha ni tsuite 隋唐時代に於ける義邑及び法社に就いて." *Shichō* 史潮 3.2(1933):122–65.

Yamasaki Hiroshi. "Tōdai ni okeru sōni shorei no mondai 唐代に於ける僧尼所隷の問題." *Shina bukkyō shigaku* 支那佛教史学 3.1(1939):1–27.

Yamasaki Hiroshi. *Shina chūsei bukkyō no tenkai* 支那中世佛教の展開. Tokyo: Shimizu shoten, 1942.

Yang Lien-sheng. "Buddhist Monasteries and Four Money-raising Institutions in Chinese History." *Harvard Journal of Asiatic Studies* 13(1950):174–91.

Yang Lien-sheng. *Money and Credit in China: A Short History.* Cambridge: Harvard University Press, 1952.

Additional Bibliography

Bareau, André. "Constellations et divinités protectrices des marchands dans le bouddhisme ancien." *Journal Asiatique* 247(1959):303–9.

Caswell, James O. *Written and Unwritten: A New History of the Buddhist Caves at Yungang.* Vancouver: University of British Columbia Press, 1988.

Chang Man-t'ao 張曼濤 ed. *Fo-chiao ching-chi yen-chiu lun-chi* 佛教經濟研究論集. Taipei: Ta-ch'eng wen-hua, 1977.

Ch'en, Kenneth K. S. "Anti-Buddhist Propaganda During the Nan-ch'ao." *Harvard Journal of Asiatic Studies* 15(1952):160–92.

——. "The Role of Buddhist Monasteries in T'ang Society." *History of Religions* 15(1976):209–30.

——. *The Chinese Transformation of Buddhism*. Princeton: Princeton University Press, 1973.

——. "The Economic Background of the Hui-ch'ang Suppression of Buddhism." *Harvard Journal of Asiatic Studies* 19(1956):67–105.

Ch'en Tso-lung 陳祚龍. Li T'ang ming-hsiang Yao Ch'ung yü fo-chiao 李唐名相姚崇與佛教." *Chung-hua fo-hsüeh hsüeh-pao* 中華佛學學報 2.10(1988):241–64.

Chiang Po-chin 姜伯勤. *T'ang Wu-tai Tun-huang ssu-hu chih-tu* 唐五代敦煌寺戶制度. Peking: Chung-hua, 1987.

Chikusa Masaaki 竺沙雅章. *Chūgoku bukkyō shakaishi kenkyū* 中国佛教社会史研究. Kyoto: Dōhōsha, 1982.

Chou Pen-chia 周本加. "Hsi-tsang min-tsu kai-ke ch'ien ti ssu-yüan ching-chi 西藏民主改革前的寺院經濟." *Hsi-tsang yen-chiu* 西藏研究 2(1985):39–47.

Dutt, Sukumar. *Buddhist Monks and Monasteries of India: Their History and Their Contribution to Indian Culture* (1962). Repr. Delhi: Motilal Banarsidass, 1988.

——. *Early Buddhist monachism, 600 B.C.–100 B.C.* (1924). 2d ed. New Delhi: Munshiram Manoharlal, 1984.

Forte, Antonino. *Political Propaganda and Ideology in China at the End of the Seventh Century*. Naples: Istituto Universitario Orientale, 1976.

——. "Daiji (Chine)." *Hōbōgirin*, vol. 6 (Paris: Institut de France, 1983), pp. 683–704.

——. *The Mingtang and Buddhist Utopias in the History of the Astronomical Clock: The Tower, Statue, and Armilliary Sphere Constructed by Empress Wu*. Paris and Rome: Ecole Française d'Extrême-Orient and Istituto Italiano per il Medio ed Estremo Oriente, 1988.

Fujieda Akira 藤枝晃. "Tonkō no sōni seki 敦煌の僧尼籍." *Tōhō gakuhō* 29(1959):285–338.

Fujii Kiyoshi 藤井清. "Tōdai jiryō ni tsuite 唐代寺領について." *Kanbungaku* 漢文学 2(1953):21–26.

Fujiyoshi Masumi 藤善真澄. "Zui Tō Bukkyō jidai kubun shiron 隋唐佛教時代区分試論." *Tōyō gakujutsu kenkyū* 東洋学術研究 14.3(1975): 17–44.

Gernet, Jacques. "La vente en Chine d'après les contrats de Touen-houang, IXe-Xe sièles." *T'oung Pao* 45(1957):295–391.

——. "Les suicides par le feu chez les bounddhistes chinois du Ve au Xe siècle." In *Mélanges publiés par l'Institut des Hautes Etudes Chinoises* 2 (Paris: Presses Universitaires de France, 1960), pp. 527–58.

Harata Kōdō 原田弘道. "Sōdai sōrin no seikaku 宋代叢林の性格." *Bukkyō keizai kenkyū* 佛教経済研究 13(1984):43–60.

Hasegawa Seiichi 長谷川誠一. "Keizai no shūkyō ni oyobi hoshita eikō 経済の宗教に及びほした影響." *Komazawa daigaku kenkyū kiyō* 16(1958):165–75.

——. "Keizaiteki shiten kara mita tōyō kodai shiso 経済的視点からみた東洋古代思想." *Bukkyō keizai kenkyū* 佛教経済研究 2(1969):85–109.

Hasegawa Shinichi 長谷川慎一. "Tōdai Tendai kyōdan no dōkō 唐代天台教団の動向." *Taishō daigaku sōgo bukkyō kenkyūjo nenpō* 大正大学綜合佛教研究所年報 3(1981):15–28.

Hattori Katsuhiko 服部克彦. "Hokugi Rakuyō ni okeru bukkyō jiin ni tsuite 北魏洛陽における佛教寺院について." *Ryūkoku shidan* 龍谷史壇 44(December 1958):182–92.

——. "Chūgoku ni okeru bukkyō jiin to tojō no kankei ni tsuite 中国における佛教寺院と都城の関係について." *Indogaku bukkyōgaku kenkyū* 印度学佛教学研究 9.1(1961):146–47.

——. "Hokugi Rakuyō ni okeru shaseki jiin no seikaku 北魏洛陽における捨宅寺院の性格." *Indogaku bukkyōgaku kenkyū* 12.1(1964):146–47.

——. "Hokugi Rakuyō ni okeru shaseki jiin no seikaku kattei 北魏洛陽における捨宅寺院の性格過程." *Bukkyō bunka kenkyūjo kiyō* 佛教文化研究所紀要 3(1964):35–45.

——. "Hokugi Rakuyō ni okeru kōzō kuyō 北魏洛陽における行像供養." *Ryūkoku shidan* 龍谷史壇 53(1964):20–33.

——. "Hokugi Rakuyō jidai ni okeru shomin to bukkyō 北魏洛陽時代における庶民と佛教." *Indogaku bukkyōgaku kenkyū* 印度学佛教学研究 17.1(1968):305–9.

Hayashima Kyōshō 早島鏡正. *Shoki bukkyō to shakai seikatsu* 初期佛教 と社会生活. Tokyo: Iwanami shoten, 1965.

Hirakawa Akira 平川彰. *Ritsuzō no kenkyū* 律蔵の研究. Tokyo: Sankibō busshorin 山喜房佛書林, 1960.

Ho Kuang-chung 賀光中. "Li-tai seng-kuan chih-tu k'ao 歷代僧官制度考." *Tung-fang hsüeh-pao* 東方學報 1(1957):239–87; (1958):187–236.

Horner, Isaline Blew trans. *The Book of the Discipline (Vinayapitaka)*. 6 vols. London: Luzac, 1949–1966.

Ho Tzu-ch'üan 何茲全. *Wu-shih nien lai Han T'ang fo-chiao ssu-yüan ching-chi yen-chiu* 五十年來漢唐佛教寺院經濟研究 (1934–1984). Peking: Pei-ching shih-fan ta-hsüeh, 1986.

Hosokawa Kameichi 細川亀市. "Sōhei to jiryō shōen" 僧兵と寺領荘園. *Shūkyō kenkyū* 宗教研究 n.s. 8.5(1921):127–40.

Hou Ching-lang. *Monnaies d'offrandes et la notion de trésorerie dans la religion chinoise*. Paris: Collège de France, 1975.

Hsiao P'ing-han 蕭平漢. "Heng-shan ssu-yüan ching-chi shih-t'an 衡山寺院 經濟試探." *Shih-chieh tsung-chiao yen-chiu* 世界宗教研究 2(1985):97–106.

Huang Min-chih 黃敏枝. *T'ang-tai ssu-yüan ching-chi ti yen-chiu* 唐代寺 院經濟的研究." Taipei: Kuo-li Taiwan ta-hsüeh wen-hsüeh yüan, 1970.

———. *Sung-tai fo-chiao she-hui ching-chi shih lun-chi* 宋代佛教社會經濟史 論集." Taipei: Hsüeh-sheng shu-chü, 1989.

Hurvitz, Leon. *Wei Shou, Treatise on Buddhism and Taoism* (An English Translation of the Original Chinese Text of *Wei-shu* 114 and the Japanese Annotation of Tsukamoto Zenryū). In Mizuno Seiichi 1956, vol. 16.

———. "Render Unto Caesar in Early Chinese Buddhism." In Liebenthal Festschrift, *Sino-Indian Studies* 5.3–4(1957):80–114.

Ikeda On 池田温. *Chūgoku kodai sekichō kenkyū: gaikan rokubun* 中国 古代籍帳研究：概観、録文. Tokyo: Tōyōbunka kenkyūjo, 1979.

Ikeda On, ed. *Kōza Tonkō (3): Tonkō no shakai* 講座敦煌III: 敦煌の社会. Tokyo: Taito shuppansha, 1975.

Ikeda On. *Tun-huang and Turfan Documents*. Tokyo: Tōyō bunka, 1987.

———. *Chūgoku kodai shahon shikigo shūroku* 中国古代写本識語集録. Tokyo: Okura shuppan, 1990.

Ishizu Terujū 石津照璽. "Bukkyōteki keiken no kihonteki tokushitsu to shūkyō no kihon kannen 佛教的経験の基本的特質と宗教の基本観念." *Indogaku bukkyōgaku kenkyū* 印度学佛教学研究 16.2(1968):1–9.

Jenner, William John Francis, trans. *Memories of Lo-yang: Yang Hsüan-chih and the lost capital (493–534)*. Oxford: Clarendon Press, 1981.

Kamata Shigeo 鎌田茂雄. "Chūgoku bukkyōdan no keisei 中国佛教団の形成." *Tōyō gakujutsu kenkyū* 東洋学術研究 14.3(1975):1–16.

Kanei Tokukō 金井徳幸. "Sōdai no sonsha to bukkyō 宋代の村社と佛教." *Bukkyō shigaku kenkyū* 佛教史学研究 18.2(1976):31–57.

Katō Shigeshi 加藤繁. *Shina keizaishi kōshō* 支那経済史考証, vol. 1. Tokyo: Tōyō bunka, 1952.

Katsumata Toshinori 勝又俊教. "Daichō bukkyōto to shakaiteki katsudō 大乗佛教徒の社会的活動." *Nihon bukkyō gakkai nenpō* 日本佛教学会年報 35(1970):17–32.

Kōji Eigaku 光地英学. "Jiin Keizai to sono shomondai" 寺院経済とその諸問題, *Bukkyō keizai kenkyū* 佛教経済研究 2(1969):3–40.

Kotō Ryōichi 近藤良一. "Tōdai zenshūteki keizai kiban 唐代禅宗的経済基盤." *Nihon bukkyō gakkai nenpō* 日本佛教学会年報 37(1972):137–51.

Kuwata Kōzō 桑田章三. "Tai no bukkyō to keizai タイの佛教と経済." *Hikone ronsō* 彦根論叢 167–68 (volume in Memory of Takeyasu Shigeji 竹安繁治), pp. 71–88. Hikone: Shiga daigaku keizaigakubu, 1974.

Lai Chien-ch'eng 頼建成. "Fo-chih yü T'ang-lü tui fo-chiao t'u ti yüeh-chih li: i hui-pang san-pao chi tao-hui san-pao wu wei-li 佛制與唐律對佛教徒的約制力：以毀謗三寶及盜毀三寶物為例." *Chung-kuo li-shih hsüeh hui shih-hsüeh chi-k'an* 中國歷史學會史學集刊 19.7(1987):135–46.

Michibata Ryōshū 道端良秀. *Tōdai bukkyōshi no kenkyū* 唐代佛教史の研究. Kyoto: Hōzōkan, 1957.

——. "Chūgoku bukkyō no keizai shisō 中国佛教の経済思想." In *Tōyō shisō ronshū* (volume in honor of Fukui Kōjun), pp. 645–65. Tokyo: Waseda daigaku, 1960.

——. "Chūgoku bukkyō to dorei no mondai 中国佛教と奴隷の問題." In *Bukkyō shigaku ronshū* 佛教史学論集 (volume in honor of Tsukamoto Zenryū), pp. 764–783. Kyoto: Tsukamoto hakushi shōju kinenkai, 1961.

——. "Chūgoku bukkyō ni okeru dorei shukke no mondai 中国佛教における奴隷出家の問題." *Indogaku bukkyōgaku kenkyū* 印度学佛教学研究 9.1(1961):28–33.

——. *Chūgoku bukkyō to shakai fukushi jigyō* 中国佛教と社会福祉事業. Kyoto: Hōzōkan, 1967.

——. "Chūgoku bukkyō keizai ni okeru seisan no mondai 中国佛教経済における生産の問題." *Indogaku bukkyōgaku kenkyū* 印度学佛教学研究 16.2(1968):64–67.

——. *Chūgoku bukkyō to shakai to sono kōshō* 中国佛教と社会とその交渉. Kyoto: Heirakuji shoten, 1975.

——. *Chūgoku bukkyō shakai keizaishi no kenkyū* 中国佛教社会経済史の研究. Kyoto: Heirakuji shoten, 1983.

Mishima Hajime 三島一. "Sōrin ni okeru koshi no shokushō ni kansuru hitotsu kōsatsu 叢林における庫司の職掌に関する一考察." In *Tōyōshi shūsetsu* 東洋史集説 (volume in honour of Katō Shigeshi), pp. 807–20. Tokyo: Fujisanbō, 1941.

——. "Tōdai jiko hokō 唐代寺庫補考." *Futamatsu gakusha daigaku sōritsu hachijū Shūnen kinen ronshū* 二松学舎大学創立八十周年紀念論集. Tokyo: Futamatsu gakusha daigaku, 1957, pp. 35–47.

——. "Tōdai jiin no jōjūsōbutsu riyō ni tsuite no hitotsu chiken 唐代寺院の常住僧物利用に就いての一知見." In *Tōyōshi ronsō* 東洋史論叢 (volume in honor of Wada Sei 和田清), pp. 937–48. Tokyo: Kodansha, 1961.

——. "Tonkō bunsho yori mita Tōdai jiin zaiseishi no hitotsu chiken 敦煌文書より見た唐代寺院財政史の一知見." *Futamatsu gakusha tōyōgaku kenkyūjo shūkan* 二松学舎東洋研究所集刊. Tokyo: Futamatsu gakusha daigaku, 1971, pp. 85–113.

Miyazaki Michisaburō 宮崎道三郎. "Shichiya no hanashi 質屋の話." In Nakada Kaoru 中田薫 ed. *Miyazaki sensei hōseishi ronshū* 宮崎先生法制史論集. Tokyo: Iwanami shoten, 1929, pp. 11–44.

Mizuno Kōgen 水野弘元. "Bukkyō ni okeru keizai shisō 佛教における経済思想." *Bukkyō keizai kenkyū* 1(1968):43–62.

——. "Bukkyō to keizai 佛教と経済." *Bukkyō keizai kenkyū* 6(1976):3–22; 7(1978):1–4; 9(1980):1–6.

Mizuno Seiichi 水野清一 and Nagahiro Toshio 長広敏雄 eds. *Yün-kang: The Buddhist cave-temples of the fifth century A.D. in North China/ Unkō sekkutsu: Seireki goseiki ni okeru Chūgoku hokubo Bukkyō Mitsuin no kōkogaku-teki chōsa hōkoku* 雲崗石窟―西暦五世紀における中国北部佛教密院の考古学の調査報告. 16 vols. Kyoto: Jimbunkagaku kenkyūsho, 1952–1956.

Moribe Hajime 森部一. "Shukke no haikei 出家の背景." *Akademia* アカデミア 37(March (1983):137–62.

Moroto Tatsuo 諸戸立雄. "Chūgoku ni okeru dochō shoju no nendai ni tsuite 中国に於ける度牒初授の年代について." *Bunka* 文化 15.4(1951): 376–92.

——. "Nanbokuchō Zui Tōsho no dōgyō to dochō no sei 南北朝隋唐初の童行と度牒の制." *Bukkyō shigaku* 15.2(1971):46–64.

——. "Hokugi no sōsei to Tō no dōsōkaku 北魏の僧制と唐の道僧格." *Akidai shigaku* 秋大史学 20(March 1973):1–17.

——. "Tōdai ni okeru dosōsei ni tsuite 唐代における度僧制について." *Tōhoku daigaku tōyōshi ronshū* 東北大学東洋史論集 1(1984):65–107.

Naba Toshisada 那波利貞. "Tonkō hakken bunsho ni yoru chūban Tōjidai no bukkyō jiin no senkoku fuhaku rui taifu eirijigyō unei no jitsukyō 敦煌発現文書に據る中晩唐時代の佛教寺院の銭穀布帛類附代営利事業運営の実況." *Shinagaku* 支那学 10.3(1941):433–510.

——. *Tōdai shakai bunkashi kenkyū* 唐代社会文化史研究. Tokyo: Sōbunsha, 1974.

Niida Noboru 仁井田陞. "Tōmatsu Godai no Tonkō jiin-dengo kankei bunsho 唐末五代の敦煌寺院佃戸関係文書." *Tonkō Torohan shakai keizai shiryō* I. Kyoto: Hōzōkan, 1959, pp. 69–90.

——. "Tō no sōdō jikan kankei no denryō no ibun 唐の僧道寺観関係の田令の遺文." *Bukkyō shigaku ronshū* (volume in honor of Tsukamoto Zenryū), pp. 567–72. Kyoto: Tsukamoto hakushi shōju kinenkai, 1961.

——. "Tōdai-hō no okeru dorei no shukke nyūdō to dorei kaihō 唐代法における奴隷の出家入道と奴隷解放." In *Bukkyō shisōshi ronshū* 佛教思想史論集 (Volume in honor of Yūki Reimon), pp. 451–64. (Tokyo: Daizō shuppansha, 1964).

Nishimura Genyū 西村元祐. *Chūgoku keizaishi kenkyū* 中国経済史研究. Kyoto: Nakanishi shuppansha, 1968.

Oda Yoshihisa 小田義久. "Saiiki ni okeru jiin keizai ni tsuite 西域における寺院経済について." *Ryūkoku daigaku bukkyō bunka kenkyūsho kiyō* 1(June 1962):140–47.

——. "Tō Seishū ni okeru sōden to jiden ni tsuite 唐西州における僧田と寺田について." In *Tōyōgaku ronshū* 東洋学論集 (volume in honor of Ono Katsutoshi), pp. 211–32. Kyoto: Ryūkoku daigakū tōyōshigaku kenkyūkai, 1982.

Ogasawara Senshū 小笠原宣秀. "Torohan shutsuto Tōdai keizai-bunsho no tokushoku 吐魯番出土唐代経済文書の特色." *Ryūkoku daigaku ronshū* 349(1955):1–15.

——. "Chūgoku chūsei ni okeru bukkyō seikatsu 中国中世における佛教
生活." *Indogaku bukkyōgaku kenkyū* 2.1(1953):67–71.

——. "Seiiki shutsuto no jirei bunsho sairon 西域出土の寺領文書再論."
Indogaku bukkyōgaku kenkyū 8.1(1960):105–9.

——. "Torohan bunsho ni araretaru giransō no mondai 吐魯番文書に現
れたる偽濫僧の問題." *Indogaku bukkyōgaku kenkyū* 9.2(1961):205–11.

——. "Tōdai seiiki no sōni shūdan 唐代西域の僧尼衆団." *Indogaku
bukkyōgaku kenkyū* 14.2(1966):79–84.

Saitō Haku 斉藤博. "Bukkyō keizai no genri kōsatsu 佛教経済の原理考察."
Bukkuyō keizai kenkyū 7(1978):141–64.

Sakurai Hideo 桜井秀雄. "Sōdōshū jiin no keizaiteki haikei 曹洞宗寺院の
経済的背景." *Bukkyōkeizai kenkyū* 4(1972):101–5.

Satō Tatsugen 佐藤達玄. *Chūgoku bukkyō ni okeru kairitsu no kenkyū*
中国佛教における戒律の研究. Tokyo: Mokujisha, 1986.

Seiiki bunka kenkyū 西域文化研究, vols. 2–3: *Tonkō Torohan shakai
keizai shiryō* 敦煌吐魯番社会経済資料. Kyoto: Hozokan, 1959, 1960.

Seiryō Shūni 青龍宗二, Saitō Haku 斉藤博, and Katō Tenhaku 加藤展博.
"Bukkyō shakai keizai ronri 佛教社会経済倫理." *Bukkyū keizai kenkyū* 5(1973):48–110.

Shigenoi Shizuka 滋野井恬. "Tōdai no jiden ni kansuru kōsatsu 唐代の寺
田に関する考察." *Horiku shigaku* 北陸史学 5(May 1956):33–48.

——. *Tōdai bukkyō shiron* 唐代佛教史論. Kyoto: Heirakuji shoten, 1973.

——. "Tōdai sōto no zeiyaku futan ni tsuite 唐代僧徒の税役負担につ
いて." *Ōtani gakuhō* 56.1(1976):21–32.

——. "Tōdai sōto no zeiyaku futan ni tsuite: Sōryo no kaeki menjo ni
kanrenshite 唐代僧徒の税役負担について：僧侶の課役免除に関連
して." In Bukkyōshi gakkai 佛教史学会 ed., *Bukkyō no rekishi to
bunka* 佛教と歴史と文化. Kyoto: Kōhōsha, 1980, pp. 198–215.

Sogabe Zhizuo 曽我部静雄. *Nitchū ritsuryō ron* 日中律令論. Tokyo:
Yoshikawa kōbunkan, 1963.

Sudō Yoshiyuki 周藤吉之. *Tō Sō shakai keizaishi kenkyū* 唐宋社会経済史
研究. Tokyo: Tokyo daigaku shuppankai, 1965.

Suzuki Chūsei 鈴本中正. "Sōdai bukkyō kessha no kenkyū 宋代佛教結社
の研究." *Shigaku zasshi* 史学雑誌 52(1941):65–68, 205–42, 303–33.

Takao Giken 高雄義堅. *Sōdai bukkyōshi no kenkyū* 宋代佛教史の研究.
Kyoto: Hyakkaen, 1975.

Takeuchi Reizō 竹内理三. *Narachō jidai ni okeru jiin keizai no kenkyū* 奈良朝時代における寺院経済の研究   Tokyo: Okayama shoten, 1932.

Tamai Zehaku 玉井是博. *Shina shakai keizai shi kenkyū* 支那社会経済史研究. Tokyo: Iwanami shoten, 1943.

T'ang Keng-ou 唐耕耦 and Lu Hung-chi 陸宏基, eds. *Tun-huang she-hui ching-chi wen-hsien chen-chi shih-lu* 敦煌社會經濟文獻真蹟釋錄. Peking: Shu-mu wen-hsien, 1986.

Tonami Mamoru 礪波護. "Tō chūki no bukkyō to kokka 唐中期の佛教と国家." In *Chūgoku chūsei no shūkyō to bunka* 中国中世の宗教と文化. Kyoto: Jinbun kagaku kenkyūjo, 1982, pp. 589–651.

Ts'ao Shih-pang 曹仕邦. "Chung-kuo seng-shih chang ti sha-men she-hui huo-tung tzu-liao 中國僧史上的沙門社會活動資料." *Ta-lu tsa-chih* 大陸雜誌 67.2(August 1983):47–49.

——. "Ts'ung tsung-chiao yü wen-hua pei-ching lun ssu-yüan ching-chi yü seng-ni ssu-yu ts'ai-ch'an tsai Hua fa-chan ti yüan-yin 從宗教與文化背景論寺院經濟與僧尼私有財產在華發展的原因." *Hua-kang fo-hsüeh hsüeh-pao* 華岡佛學學報 8(1985):159–191.

Tsukamoto Zenryū 塚本善隆. *Gisho shakurōshi no kenkyū* 魏書釈老志の研究 (1961). Repr. in *Tsukamoto Zenryū chosakushū* 塚本善隆著作集, vol. 1. Tokyo: Daito shuppansha, 1973.

——. *Hokuchō bukkyōshi kenkyū* 北朝佛教史研究. In *Tsukamoto chosakushū*, vol. 2. Tokyo: Daito shuppansha, 1974.

——. *Chūgoku chūsei bukkyōshi ronkō* 中国中世佛教史論攷. In *Tsukamoto chosakushū*, vol. 3. Tokyo: Daito shuppansha, 1975.

——. *Chūgoku kinsei bukkyōshi no shomondai* 中国近世佛教史の諸問題. In *Tsukamoto chosakushū*, vol. 5. Tokyo: Daito shuppansha, 1975.

Twitchett, Denis C. "Monastic Estates in T'ang China." *Asia Major* n.s. 5(1956):123–46.

——. "The Government of T'ang in the Early Eighth Century." *Bulletin of the School of Oriental and African Studies* 18.2(1956):322–30.

——. "The Monasteries and China's Economy in Medieval Times." *Bulletin of the School of Oriental and African Studies* 19.3(1957):526–49.

——. "The Fragment of the T'ang Ordinances of the Department of Waterways Discovered at Tun-huang." *Asia Major* n.s. 6(1957):23–79.

——. "Lands Under State Cultivation During the T'ang Dynasty." *Journal of Economic and Social History of the Orient* 2.2(1959):162–203.

——. "Some Remarks on Irrigation Under the T'ang." *T'oung Pao* 48(1961):175–94.

——. *Financial Administration Under the T'ang Dynasty.* Cambridge: Cambridge University Press, 1963.

——. "Chinese Social History from the Seventh to the Tenth Centuries: The Tunhuang Documents and Their Implications." *Past and Present* 35(1966):28–53.

——. "Merchant, Trade, and Government in Late T'ang." *Asia Major* n.s. 14(1968):63–95.

——. "The Composition of the T'ang Ruling Class: New Evidence from Tun-huang." In A. Wright et al., eds. *Perspectives on the T'ang*, pp. 47–85. New Haven: Yale University Press, 1973.

Weinstein, Stanley. *Buddhism Under the T'ang.* Cambridge, New York: Cambridge University Press, 1987.

Wright, Arthur F. "Fu I and the Rejection of Buddhism." *Journal of the History of Ideas* 12(1951):33–47.

Wright, Arthur F. and Denis Twitchett. *Perspectives on the T'ang.* New Haven: Yale University Press, 1973.

Wang Yi-t'ung, trans. Yang Hsüan-chih, *A Record of Buddhist Monasteries in Lo-Yang.* Princeton: Princeton University Press, 1984.

Yang Lien-sheng. *Les aspects économiques des travaux publics dans la Chine impériale* (Four lectures at the Collège de France), Paris 1964.

Yen Shang-wen 顏尚文. "Liang Wu-ti 'Huang-ti p'u-sa' ti li-nien chi cheng-ts'e chih hsing-ch'eng chi-ch'u 梁武帝「皇帝菩薩」的理念及政策之形成基礎." *Shih-ta li-shih hsüeh-pao* 師大歷史學報 7.6(1989):1–58.

——. "Liang Wu-ti shou p'u-sa chieh chi she-shen T'ung-t'ai ssu yü 'Huang-ti p'u-sa' ti-wei ti chien-li 梁武帝受菩薩戒及捨身同泰寺與「皇帝菩薩」地位的建立." *Tung-fang tsung-chiao yen-chiu* 東方宗教研究 1.10(1990):41–89.

Yoshimoto Tsutsuko 吉本慎子. "Chūban Tōjidai ni okeru bukkyō jiin no shakaiteki seiryoku (nisan no eiri jigyō ni tsuite) 中晚唐における佛教寺院の社会的勢力(二三の営利事業について)." *Shisō* 史窗 21 (December 1962): 124–30.

Yoshizawa Fumio 吉沢文男. "Bukkyō to keizaigaku no aida 佛教と経済学の間." *Bukkyō keizai kenkyū* 佛教経済研究 4(1972):67–90.

Zdun, Genowefa. *Metériaux pour l'étude de la culture chinoise du moyen âge: le Lo-yang k'ie-lan ki.* Warsaw: Editions scientifiques de Pologne, 1982.

Zürcher, Erik. *The Buddhist Conquest of China* (1959). Leiden: Brill, 1972.

——. "The sangha in China." In H. Bechert and R. Gombrich eds., *The World of Buddhism*, pp. 193–212. New York: Facts on File, 1984.

INDEX

178–86; *pien* (noninterest-bearing loans), 177; against pledges (*chih-chü*), 172–74, 228; *yü hsiang-yüan sheng-li*, 185

Buddhist religious, abbot (*ssu-chu*), 67, 182, 319*n*37, 335*n*13; attitude toward rules of discipline, 71, 250; in Chinese festivals, 254–56; *ch'u-chia* (to leave the family), 39, 197; common interests with wealthy laity, 289–90; and cultivation of land, 95–96; dean (*chang-tso*), 182, 319*n*37; disposition of personal goods, 85–92, 339*n*86, 340*nn*91, 101; family monks (*chia-seng*), 41–42, 328*n*66; fraudulent monks (*wei-lan seng*), 11, 37–40, 42; freedom to manage property, 92–93; gifts and offerings to, 200–10; government confiscation of property, 47–48; imperial donations to, 209–10; individually held lands, 132; inheritance rights, 78–85; irregular monks, 39, 41–42, 207, 250–53, 318*n*27, 327*n*61; itinerant monks, 41, 42, 199; kinds of, 4; *kuo-so* (passes), 327*n*2; laicization of, 35, 39, 40–41; lay monasticism, 37–38; magical powers, 253; and military service, 32–33, 324*n*10; monks of the people, 249–50; moral standards criticized, 197–200; number of, 4–12, 35–36, 318*n*15, 319*n*29; number of in monasteries, 8–11, 320*nn*42, 45, 51, 54; overseer (*wei-na*), 319*n*37, 327*n*56; peasant-monks (*po-hsing seng*), 39; pious works, 218; political influence, 284–85, 381*n*23; private ordinations (*ssu-tu*), 42–44, 329*n*72; specialization, 200; steward (*chih-sui*), 35, 325*n*28; supervisory monks (*san-kang*), 8, 43; tax exemptions, 30–35; tax obligations, 32, 324*n*22; tonsure, 39; usury, 178–86

Caves of the Thousand Buddhas, 362*n*130

Central Asian monastery, 47

Chai-chu (master of the banquet), 269–70

Chai (vegetarian feast), 257–58, 274–75, 369*n*101

Ch'ang-an (city), 3; aristocracy of, 369*n*99; milling installations, 143; monasteries of, 375*n*10

Ch'ang-an reign (701–705), 221

Chang-chi, 142

Chang-ch'iu Tzu-t'o, 285

Ch'ang-chu/ch'ang chu wu/seng wu (permanent assets of the samgha), 67–73, 92–93, 106, 335*n*14, 344*n*56; fiscal status of, 43, 46–48

Ch'ang-chu po-hsing (households held in perpetuity), 105–11, 149, 177

Ch'ang-chu t'ien (permanent lands), 118

Ch'ang-i (sale by auction), 88–92

Ch'ang-ning Princess, 50, 331*n*114

Chang-p'ing shu (price regulating granaries), 101, 344*n*46

Ch'ang-sheng k'u (Long Life Treasuries), 173–74, 360*n*98

Ch'ang-sheng (pawnshops), 171

Chang-tsung, Emperor (1190–1208), 346*n*94

Ch'ang-yen (monk), 21

Chang Yüeh, 33

Chang Y'ing-kuei, 301

Ch'ao-hua monastery, 141

Charity: in Buddhist communities, 221–23; in Japan, 222; in Mahāyāna Buddhism, 217–21, 227, 335*n*11; as means of propaganda and conversion, 219

Chavannes, Edouard, 232, 262, 267, 271, 362*n*133

Ch'eng, Prince of Northern Wei, 256

Cheng-ch'ü (canal), 143, 354*n*10

Cheng-shih monastery, 16

Ch'en Hsüan-yün (eunuch), 287

Chen-kuan (627–649), 232; official ordinations during, 11

Chen-yüan reign (785–805), 289

Chia-seng (family monks), 41–42, 328*n*66

Chia-tzu (movables), 151

Chien-fu (creation of blessings), 260

Chien-k'ang (Nanking), 3; monastery at, 14

Chien-ming monastery, 128

Chien-yen i-lai ch'ao-yeh tsa-chi, 34

Chih-chü (loans against pledges), 172–74

Chih-hsüan, 264

Chih-hsü (monk), 287

OTHER WORKS IN THE
COLUMBIA ASIAN STUDIES SERIES

Studies in Asian Culture

Translations from the Asian Classics

The Zen Master Hakuin: Selected Writings, tr. Philip B. Yampolsky   1971
Chinese Rhyme-Prose: Poems in the Fu Form from the Han and Six Dynasties Periods, tr. Burton Watson. Also in paperback ed.   1971
Kūkai: Major Works, tr. Yoshito S. Hakeda. Also in paperback ed.   1972
The Old Man Who Does as He Pleases: Selections from the Poetry and Prose of Lu Yu, tr. Burton Watson   1973
The Lion's Roar of Queen Śrīmālā, tr. Alex and Hideko Wayman   1974
Courtier and Commoner in Ancient China: Selections from the History of the Former Han by Pan Ku, tr. Burton Watson. Also in paperback ed.   1974
Japanese Literature in Chinese, vol. 1: Poetry and Prose in Chinese by Japanese Writers of the Early Period, tr. Burton Watson   1975
Japanese Literature in Chinese, vol. 2: Poetry and Prose in Chinese by Japanese Writers of the Later Period, tr. Burton Watson   1976
Scripture of the Lotus Blossom of the Fine Dharma, tr. Leon Hurvitz. Also in paperback ed.   1976
Love Song of the Dark Lord: Jayadeva's Gītagovinda, tr. Barbara Stoler Miller. Also in paperback ed. Cloth ed. includes critical text of the Sanskrit.   1977
Ryōkan: Zen Monk-Poet of Japan, tr. Burton Watson   1977
Calming the Mind and Discerning the Real: From the Lam rim chen mo of Tsoṇ-kha-pa, tr. Alex Wayman   1978
The Hermit and the Love-Thief: Sanskrit Poems of Bhartrihari and Bilhaṇ;aDa, tr. Barbara Stoler Miller   1978
The Lute: Kao Ming's P'i-p'a chi, tr. Jean Mulligan. Also in paperback ed.   1980
A Chronicle of Gods and Sovereigns: Jinnō Shōtōki of Kitabatake-Chikafusa, tr. H. Paul Varley.   1980
Among the Flowers: The Hua-chien chi, tr. Lois Fusek   1982
Grass Hill: Poems and Prose by the Japanese Monk Gensei, tr. Burton Watson   1983
Doctors, Diviners, and Magicians of Ancient China: Biographies of Fang-shih, tr. Kenneth J. DeWoskin. Also in paperback ed.   1983
Theater of Memory: The Plays of Kālidāsa, ed. Barbara Stoler Miller. Also in paperback ed.   1984
The Columbia Book of Chinese Poetry: From Early Times to the Thirteenth Century, ed. and tr. Burton Watson. Also in paperback ed.   1984
Poems of Love and War: From the Eight Anthologies and the Ten Long Poems of Classical Tamil, tr. A. K. Ramanujan. Also in paperback ed.   1985
The Bhagavad Gita: Krishna's Counsel in Time of War, tr. Barbara Stoler Miller   1986
The Columbia Book of Later Chinese Poetry, ed. and tr. Jonathan Chaves. Also in paperback ed.   1986
The Tso Chuan: Selections from China's Oldest Narrative History, tr. Burton Watson   1989
Waiting for the Wind: Thirty-six Poets of Japan's Late Medieval Age, tr. Steven Carter   1989
Selected Writings of Nichiren, ed. Philip B. Yampolsky   1990
Saigyō, Poems of a Mountain Home, tr. Burton Watson   1990
The Book of Lieh-Tzū: A Classic of the Tao, tr. A. C. Graham. Morningside ed.   1990
The Tale of an Anklet: An Epic of South India: The Cilappatikāram of Iḷankō Aṭikaḷ, tr. R. Parthasarathy   1993
Waiting for the Dawn: A Plan for the Prince, tr. and introduction by Wm. Theodore de Bary   1993

The Lotus Sutra, tr. Burton Watson. Also in paperback ed.   1993
The Classic of Changes: A New Translation of the I Ching as Interpreted by
    Wang Bi, tr. Richard John Lynn   1994
Beyond Spring: Poems of the Sung Dynasty, tr. Julie Landau   1994
The Columbia Anthology of Traditional Chinese Literature, ed. Victor H.
    Mair   1994
Scenes for Mandarins: The Elite Theater of the Ming, tr. Cyril Birch

Companions to Asian Studies

Approaches to the Oriental Classics, ed. Wm. Theodore de Bary   1959
Early Chinese Literature, by Burton Watson. Also in paperback ed.   1962
Approaches to Asian Civilizations, eds. Wm. Theodore de Bary and Ainslie T.
    Embree   1964
The Classic Chinese Novel: A Critical Introduction, by C. T. Hsia. Also in
    paperback ed.   1968
Chinese Lyricism: Shih Poetry from the Second to the Twelfth Century, tr.
    Burton Watson. Also in paperback ed.   1971
A Syllabus of Indian Civilization, by Leonard A. Gordon and Barbara Stoler
    Miller   1971
Twentieth-Century Chinese Stories, ed. C. T. Hsia and Joseph S. M. Lau. Also
    in paperback ed.   1971
A Syllabus of Chinese Civilization, by J. Mason Gentzler, 2d ed.   1972
A Syllabus of Japanese Civilization, by H. Paul Varley, 2d ed.   1972
An Introduction to Chinese Civilization, ed. John Meskill, with the assistance
    of J. Mason Gentzler   1973
An Introduction to Japanese Civilization, ed. Arthur E. Tiedemann   1974
Ukifune: Love in the Tale of Genji, ed. Andrew Pekarik   1982
The Pleasures of Japanese Literature, by Donald Keene   1988
A Guide to Oriental Classics, eds. Wm. Theodore de Bary and Ainslie T.
    Embree; 3d edition ed. Amy Vladeck Heinrich, 2 vols.   1989

Introduction to Asian Civilizations
Wm. Theodore de Bary, Editor

Sources of Japanese Tradition, 1958; paperback ed., 2 vols.   1964
Sources of Indian Tradition, 1958; paperback ed., 2 vols., 1964; 2d ed., 2 vols. 1988
Sources of Chinese Tradition, 1960; paperback ed., 2 vols.   1964

Neo-Confucian Studies

Instructions for Practical Living and Other Neo-Confucian Writings by Wang
    Yang-ming, tr. Wing-tsit Chan   1963
Reflections on Things at Hand: The Neo-Confucian Anthology, comp. Chu
    Hsi and Lü Tsu-ch'ien, tr. Wing-tsit Chan   1967
Self and Society in Ming Thought, by Wm. Theodore de Bary and the Confer-
    ence on Ming Thought. Also in paperback ed.   1970
The Unfolding of Neo-Confucianism, by Wm. Theodore de Bary and the Con-
    ference on Seventeenth-Century Chinese Thought. Also in paperback ed. 1975

Principle and Practicality: Essays in Neo-Confucianism and Practical Learning, eds. Wm. Theodore de Bary and Irene Bloom. Also in paperback ed.   1979
The Syncretic Religion of Lin Chao-en, by Judith A. Berling   1980
The Renewal of Buddhism in China: Chu-hung and the Late Ming Synthesis, by Chün-fang Yü   1981
Neo-Confucian Orthodoxy and the Learning of the Mind-and-Heart, by Wm. Theodore de Bary   1981
Yüan Thought: Chinese Thought and Religion Under the Mongols, eds. Hok-lam Chan and Wm. Theodore de Bary   1982
The Liberal Tradition in China, by Wm. Theodore de Bary   1983
The Development and Decline of Chinese Cosmology, by John B. Henderson   1984
The Rise of Neo-Confucianism in Korea, by Wm. Theodore de Bary and JaHyun Kim Haboush   1985
Chiao Hung and the Restructuring of Neo-Confucianism in Late Ming, by Edward T. Ch'ien   1985
Neo-Confucian Terms Explained: Pei-hsi tzu-i, by Ch'en Ch'un, ed. and trans. Wing-tsit Chan   1986
Knowledge Painfully Acquired: K'un-chih chi, by Lo Ch'in-shun, ed. and trans. Irene Bloom   1987
To Become a Sage: The Ten Diagrams on Sage Learning, by Yi T'oegye, ed. and trans. Michael C. Kalton   1988
The Message of the Mind in Neo-Confucian Thought, by Wm. Theodore de Bary   1989

Modern Asian Literature Series

Modern Japanese Drama: An Anthology, ed. and tr. Ted. Takaya. Also in paperback ed.   1979
Mask and Sword: Two Plays for the Contemporary Japanese Theater, by Yamazaki Masakazu, tr. J. Thomas Rimer   1980
Yokomitsu Riichi, Modernist, Dennis Keene   1980
Nepali Visions, Nepali Dreams: The Poetry of Laxmiprasad Devkota, tr. David Rubin   1980
Literature of the Hundred Flowers, vol. 1: *Criticism and Polemics*, ed. Hualing Nieh   1981
Literature of the Hundred Flowers, vol. 2: *Poetry and Fiction*, ed. Hualing Nieh   1981
Modern Chinese Stories and Novellas, 1919 1949, ed. Joseph S. M. Lau, C. T. Hsia, and Leo Ou-fan Lee. Also in paperback ed.   1984
A View by the Sea, by Yasuoka Shōtarō, tr. Kären Wigen Lewis   1984
Other Worlds; Arishima Takeo and the Bounds of Modern Japanese Fiction, by Paul Anderer   1984
Selected Poems of So Chongju, tr. with intro. by David R. McCann   1989
The Sting of Life: Four Contemporary Japanese Novelists, by Van C. Gessel   1989
Stories of Osaka Life, by Oda Sakunosuke, tr. Burton Watson   1990
The Bodhisattva, or Samantabhadra, by Ishikawa Jun, tr. with intro. by William Jefferson Tyler   1990
The Travels of Lao Ts'an, by Liu T'ich-yunao, tr. Harold Shadick. Morningside ed.   1990
The Columbia Anthology of Modern Asian Chinese Literature, ed. Joseph S. M. Lau and Howard Goldblatt   1995